European Union Politics

Edited by

Michelle Cini

OXFORD
UNIVERSITY PRESS

OXFORD

UNIVERSITY PRESS

Great Clarendon Street, Oxford OX2 6DP

Oxford University Press is a department of the University of Oxford.
It furthers the University's objective of excellence in research, scholarship,
and education by publishing worldwide in

Oxford New York

Auckland Bangkok Buenos Aires Cape Town Chennai
Dar es Salaam Delhi Hong Kong Istanbul Karachi Kolkata
Kuala Lumpur Madrid Melbourne Mexico City Mumbai Nairobi
São Paulo Shanghai Taipei Tokyo Toronto

Oxford is a registered trade mark of Oxford University Press
in the UK and in certain other countries

Published in the United States
by Oxford University Press Inc., New York

© Michelle Cini 2003

British Library Cataloguing in Publication Data

Data available

ISBN 0–19–924836–2

10 9 8 7 6 5 4 3 2 1

Typeset in ITC Stone Serif with ITC Stone Sans
by RefineCatch Limited, Bungay, Suffolk
Printed in Great Britain by
The Bath Press, Bath

Preface

The original idea behind this edited textbook on *European Union Politics* was to offer both teachers and students of EU politics an introductory text that would be both accessible to, and at the same time challenging for, undergraduates coming to the subject for the first time. In covering a large number of topics commonly taught on EU politics courses, in a 'whopping' 25-chapter book, it was hoped that the text would provide something for everyone. The assumption was, then, that tutors might use a sort of 'variable geometry' or 'pick and mix' approach to select those chapters most appropriate to the courses they are teaching. On that assumption, I would not necessarily expect the book to be read cover-to-cover, from beginning to end, even if in practice some prior knowledge of the institutions and the European policy process would certainly provide a useful background to those chapters in the fourth and fifth parts of the book.

This volume brings together a large number of academics, both established and relatively new members of the profession, all of whom are engaged in research on the topics about which they have written. The book itself is divided into five parts. After a short introduction, which introduces some of the basics (the institutions and decision-making procedures in particular), the book deals with the history of the European integration process, theories of European integration, the European institutions, and a select number of European policy areas (selected to emphasize the very different ways in which policy is made and implemented in the EU). The final part of the book, covering Chapters 21–25, raises issues of relevance to the study of EU politics that cut across the earlier chapters. This section highlights some (though inevitably not all) of the issues currently being debated by researchers and practitioners involved in European affairs. The content here is more research oriented (and in some cases will be more challenging for students) than some of the earlier chapters.

Even with 25 chapters, some very difficult decisions had to be taken as to what to omit from the book. I expect that a quick look at the contents page will lead all tutors (if not students) to prepare their suggestions for what ought to have been included. It is perhaps enough to state that my original list of potential chapters numbered 40!

Finally, and most importantly, thanks are owed to those who made this book possible. First, to Angela Griffin at OUP for suggesting this rather momentous project in the first place, and for getting it off the ground successfully in 2000–1; and next to Sue Dempsey, who stepped successfully into Angela's shoes at OUP so as to see the project through to the end. Thanks also to Bernardo Ivo Cruz, a graduate student and teaching assistant in the Department of Politics at the University of Bristol, for his efficient and thorough research assistance. As this is a book aimed at undergraduates, it also seems fitting to thank the many students who have taken my courses since the early 1990s, particularly those Bristol politics students who have taken my final year option. If you contributed in any way to my seminar, and handed your essays in on time, then this book is dedicated to you.

Michelle Cini

Bristol
October 2002

Contents

Part Three **Institutions and actors**

Part Four **Policies and policy making**

Part Five **Issues and debates**

Detailed contents

List of figures

List of boxes

List of tables

About the contributors

Anthony Arnull is Professor of European Law and Director of the Institute of European Law at the University of Birmingham, UK.

Angela K. Bourne is Lecturer in the Department of Politics at the University of Dundee, UK.

Michael Burgess is Professor of Politics, Director of the Centre for European Union Studies (CEUS), and Jean Monnet Professor of European Integration in the Department of Politics and International Studies at the University of Hull, UK.

Dimitris N. Chryssochoou is Reader in European Integration in the Department of Politics at the University of Exeter, UK.

Michelle Cini is Senior Lecturer in Politics and Jean Monnet Lecturer in European Community Studies in the Department of Politics at the University of Bristol, UK.

Michelle Egan is Assistant Professor in the School of International Service at the American University, Washington DC, USA.

Morten Egeberg is Professor of Political Science and Research Director at ARENA (Advanced Research on the Europeanization of the Nation State), the University of Oslo, Norway.

Rainer Eising is Lecturer in Political Science at the Fernuniversität Hagen, Germany.

Gerda Falkner is Research Professor at the Max-Planck Institute, Cologne, Germany and at the University of Vienna, Austria.

Eve Fouilleux is Chargée de Recherches, CNRS, at CRAP, Institut d'Etudes Politiques de Rennes, France.

John K. Glenn is Executive Director of the Council for European Studies, and a Visiting Scholar at New York University, USA.

Kerstin Junge is a graduate student in the Department of Political Science at the University of Birmingham, UK.

Jeffrey Lewis is Assistant Professor of Political Science in the Department of Political Science at Oklahoma State University, USA.

Johan P. Olsen is Professor and Research Director at ARENA, Norway.

David Phinnemore is Lecturer in European Integration in the Institute of European Studies, The Queen's University, Belfast, Northern Ireland.

Ben Rosamond is Reader in Politics and International Studies in the Department of Politics and International Studies at the University of Warwick, UK.

Roger Scully is Lecturer in European Politics in the Department of International Politics, University of Wales Aberystwyth, UK.

Karen E. Smith is Lecturer in International Relations at the London School of Economics, UK.

Carsten Strøby Jensen is Associate Professor at the Department of Sociology, University of Copenhagen, Denmark.

Emek M. Uçarer is Assistant Professor of International Relations at Bucknell University, USA.

Derek W. Urwin is Professor of Politics and International Relations at the University of Aberdeen, UK.

Amy Verdun is Associate Professor and Jean Monnet Chair in European Integration and Director of the European Studies Program in the Department of Political Science at the University of Victoria, Canada.

Antje Wiener is Reader and Jean Monnet Chair in European Integration in the Institute of European Studies, The Queen's University, Belfast, Northern Ireland.

Abbreviations

ACP	African, Caribbean, Pacific countries
AER	Assembly of European Regions
AFSJ	Area of Freedom, Security, and Justice
AIDS	Acquired Immune Deficiency Syndrome
AMCHAM	American Chamber of Commerce
AoA	Agreement on Agriculture
APEC	Asia Pacific Economic Co-operation
ARNE	Antiracist Network for Equality in Europe
ASEAN	Association of Southeast Asian Nations
BEUC	European Consumers' Bureau
BLEU	Belgium Luxembourg Economic Union
BSE	Bovine Spongiform Encephalopathy ('Mad Cow Disease')
BUAV	British Union for the Abolition of Vivisection
CAP	Common Agricultural Policy
CDU	Christian Democratic Union (Germany)
CEE	Central and Eastern Europe
CEEC	Central and Eastern European countries
CEEP	Centre Européen des Entreprises Publics (European Association for Public Sector Firms)
CEFIC	European Chemical Association
CEN	European Committee for Standardization
CENELEC	European Committee for Electro-technical Standardization
CIREA	Centre for Information, Discussion, and Exchange on Asylum
CIREFI	Centre for Information, Discussion, and Exchange on the Crossing of Frontiers and Immigration
CFI	Court of First Instance
CFSP	Common Foreign and Security Policy
CGS	Council General Secretariat
CM	Common Market
CMO	Common Market Organization
CNJA	Centre National des Jeunes Agriculteurs (French young farmers' association)
CNRS	Conseil National de Recherche Scientifique
CoE	Council of Europe
COPA	Comité des Organisations Professionelles Agricoles de la Communauté (European farmers association)
CoR	Committee of the Regions
COREPER	Committee of Permanent Representatives
CRAP	Centre de Recherches Administratives of Politiques
CSU	Christian Social Union (Germany)
CU	Customs Union
DG	Directorate-General
EAEC	European Atomic Energy Community
EAGGF	European Agricultural Guidance and Guarantee Fund
EC	European Community (or European Communities)
ECAS	European Citizen Action Service

ECB	European Central Bank
ECHR	European Convention on Human Rights
ECJ	European Court of Justice
Ecofin	Council of Economics and Finance Ministers
ECSC	European Coal and Steel Community
ECU	European Currency Unit
EDC	European Defence Community
EdF	Electricité de France
EDU	European Drug Unit
EEA	European Economic Area
EEB	European Environmental Bureau
EEC	European Economic Community
EFC	Economic and Finance Committee
EFTA	European Free Trade Association
EIB	European Investment Bank
EiOP	European Integration Online Papers
EJA	European Justice Area
EMS	European Monetary System
EMU	Economic and Monetary Union (or European Monetary Union)
EP	European Parliament
EPC	European Political Co-operation (or European Political Community)
EPP	European People's Party
ERASMUS	European Community Action Scheme for the Mobility of University Students
ERDF	European Regional Development Fund
ERPA	European Research Papers Archive
ERRF	European Rapid Reaction Force
ERM	Exchange Rate Mechanism
ERT	European Round Table (of Industrialists)
ESC	Economic and Social Committee
ESCB	European System of Central Banks
ESDP	European Security and Defence Policy
ESF	European Social Fund
ETSI	European Telecommunications Standards Institute
ETUC	European Trade Union Congress
EU	European Union
EURATOM	See EAEC
EURO-C	ETUC's consumer organization
EUROCHAMBRES	Association of European Chambers of Commerce and Industry
EURO-COOP	European Consumer Co-operatives Association
EURODAC	European Fingerprinting System
Europol	European Police Office
EWL	European Women's Lobby
FDP	Free Democratic Party (Germany)
FEU	Full Economic Union
FNSEA	Fédération Nationale des Syndicats d'Exploitant Agricoles (French agricultural association)
FPU	Full Political Union
FTA	Free Trade Area
FYROM	Federal Yugoslav Republic of Macedonia

GAC	General Affairs Council
GATT	General Agreement on Tariffs and Trade
GDP	Gross Domestic Product
GDR	German Democratic Republic
GMO	Genetically Modified Organism
GNP	Gross National Product
G8	Group of Eight Most Industrialized Countries
HLWG	High Level Working Group on Asylum and Immigration
IGC	Intergovernmental Conference
IPE	International Political Economy
IR	International Relations
ISPA	Instrument for Structural Policies for Pre-accession
JAC	Jeunesse Agricole Chrétienne
JHA	Justice and Home Affairs
LI	Liberal Intergovernmentalism
LMU	Latin Monetary Union
MEP	Member of the European Parliament
MLG	Multi-level Governance
MP	Member of Parliament
NAFTA	North Atlantic Free Trade Agreement
NATO	North Atlantic Treaty Organization
NGO	Non-Governmental Organization
NUTS	Nomenclature of Units for Territorial Statistics
NY	New York
OCA	Optimum Currency Area
OECD	Organization for Economic Co-operation and Development
OEEC	Organization for European Economic Co-operation
PES	Party of European Socialists
PESC	Politique Etrangère et de la Sécurité Commune
PHARE	Poland and Hungary Aid for Economic Reconstruction
PJCCM	Police and Judicial Co-operation in Criminal Matters
PLO	Palestine Liberation Organization
PNV	El Partido Nacionalist Vasco (Basque Nationalist Party)
PSC	Political and Security Committee
OSCE	Organization for Security and Co-operation in Europe
QMV	Qualified Majority Voting
SAA	Stability and Association Agreement
SAPARD	Special Accession Programme for Agriculture and Rural Development
SCA	Special Committee on Agriculture
SEA	Single European Act
SEM	Single European Market
SGP	Stability and Growth Pact
SLIM	Simpler Legislation for the Internal Market
SME	Small and Medium-sized Enterprises
SSC	Scientific Steering Committee
SSHRC	Social Sciences and Humanities Research Council (Canada)
TA	Treaty of Amsterdam
TACIS	Programme for Technical Assistance to the Independent States of the Former Soviet Union and Mongolia

TCN	Third-Country National
TEC	Treaty on the European Community
TEU	Treaty on European Union
UEAPME	European Association of Craft, Small, and Medium-sized Enterprises
UK	United Kingdom
UN	United Nations
UNICE	European Confederation of National Employers' Associations
US	United States
USA	United States of America
USSR	Union of Soviet Socialist Republics (the Soviet Union)
VAT	Value Added Tax
VOC	Volatile Organic Compounds
WEU	Western European Union
WTO	World Trade Organization
YES	Young Workers' Exchange Scheme

Introduction

Michelle Cini

Introducing the European Union

More than fifty years ago, at the end of a devastating war which destroyed much of Europe, a small group of politically influential figures put together a plan which was to culminate, in 1993, in the creation of the European Union (EU). Their plan involved the **delegation** of certain aspects of member state **sovereignty** to common, independent, and supranational institutions. These institutions were to represent a common or joint (European) interest, rather than the interest of any one European state. The Treaties agreed by the six founder member states, the 1951 Treaty of Paris and the 1957 Treaty of Rome, were important in framing the future direction of the European integration process. Yet no one in the 1950s could have predicted the precise form that the Union would eventually take. The incremental process by which the EU has been constructed has involved many different actors, not least those within the national governments of the member states—now numbering 15 (see Box 1.1), and those attached to the European institutions—the Commission, Parliament, Council, and the Courts (see Box 1.2). This is not to imply, however, that the EU is by any means a completed project: far from it. The European Union is still very much in the making, with discussions over EU enlargement, monetary union, European foreign policy and a Constitution for Europe much in the news as this book goes to press.

Despite the fact that it has been around for more than fifty years—albeit in a form that has been constantly changing (see Box 1.3)—the European integration process is not well understood. This is possibly because the EU does not fit with many of our preconceived notions of how politics is organized. It is often said that the EU is neither a conventional international organization nor a (national) state, even though many do now accept that the Union may be considered as a political system or **polity** in its own right. It is not surprising then that the EU is often defined as a unique or hybrid institution.

It is the EU's supranational characteristics that distinguish it most readily from other forms of international organization. But to call the EU supranational is to ignore the crucial role that states, and more specifically national governments, continue to play in European politics. The term 'supranational' (meaning 'above the national level') may be more appropriately applied not to the EU as a whole, but to specific EU institutions (the Commission, Parliament, and Court), or to European policies that have been 'communitarized', that is, policies in which the supranational institutions have a particularly important role, as in the cases of agriculture and competition policy. The *supranational* characteristics of the EU are thus contrasted against its *intergovernmental* aspects—those that suggest a greater role

Box 1.1 **The facts**

The EU's member states (and the candidate/applicant states)

The European Union has 15 member states.

Thirteen States are hoping to join the Union (though more would ultimately like to join). Ten of these are likely to join in May 2004.

Current members (as of 2003)

Austria
Belgium
Denmark
Finland
France
Germany
Greece
Ireland
Italy
Luxembourg
The Netherlands
Portugal

Spain
Sweden
United Kingdom (UK)

The candidate/applicant states

Bulgaria*
Cyprus
Czech Republic
Estonia
Hungary
Latvia
Lithuania
Malta
Poland
Romania*
Slovakia
Slovenia
Turkey*

* Asterisk denotes states that will not be joining in 2004.

Box 1.2 **The facts**

The European institutions

The term 'European institutions' usually refers to the four main EU organizations, but this very much depends on the context. These institutions are:

- The *European Commission* (or just 'the Commission'): the joint-executive and driving force of the Union.

- The *European Parliament* (or just 'the Parliament' or EP): representing the peoples of the Union.

- The *Council of the European Union* (the 'EU Council', 'the Council' or the 'Council of Ministers'): co-legislator and joint-executive, comprising the EU's member states/national governments.

- The *Court of Justice* (often called the 'European Court of Justice', the 'European Court' or the ECJ): ensuring compliance with and the consistency of European law.

See Chapters 9–12 for more detail on what these institutions do.

Other EU bodies include:

- The *Court of Auditors*: ensuring the lawful management of the European budget.

- The *Economic and Social Committee* (ESC or, sometimes, 'ECOSOC'): representing the opinions of organized civil society.

- The *Committee of the Regions* (CoR): representing the opinions of the regions and local authorities.

- The *European Ombudsman*: dealing with complaints of maladministration against the European institutions of their officials.

- The *European Central Bank* (ECB): taking responsibility for monetary policy and for foreign exchange.

- The *European Investment Bank* (EIB): financing public and private long-term investment.

There are a large number of small agencies and bodies attached to the European Union. See the europa website (**http://europa.eu.int**) for further information.

Source: **http://europa.eu.int/abc-en.htm.**

Box 1.3 **The facts**

Theoretical approaches to the study of the European Union

There are now many different theoretical approaches applied to the European Union. The best known are:

- **Neo-functionalism**

  and

- **Intergovernmentalism.**

However, some also see **Federalism** as a theoretical or conceptual approach to the EU.

More recent additions to the theoretical armoury of EU studies include:

- **Multi-level governance**

  and

- **Institutionalist theories** of the EU ('new institutionalism').

For more information on theories of European integration see Chapters 5–8.

---

for government-to-government co-operation, with much less of a role for the Commission, Parliament, and European Court.

Questions about how to define or explain the European Union are important as they draw our attention to the EU's distinctive features. But we should also remain aware that the EU shares many characteristics with national states and international organizations. In this respect we can learn a great deal by comparing the EU to other political systems and organizations (Sbragia 1992). In other words, even if we accept that the EU is indeed unique and distinctive, it may still prove enlightening to adopt a comparative approach when we study it.

This approach is reflected in some of the newer theories of European integration (see Chapter 8). While theorists have long sought to describe, explain, and even in some cases to predict the course of European integration (see Box 1.3), in more recent times, a growing number have shifted their attention to particular features of the EU system. In other words, instead of trying to explain the process of *integration*, they have preferred to research European Union *politics*, or 'how the EU works today' (Hix 1999: 1), asking the same questions that researchers might ask of the British, German, or American political systems. This relatively recent approach to the study of the EU is reflected in many of the chapters below.

Making policy in the European Union

By way of an introduction to the chapters that follow, this section reviews briefly the European Union's policy-making process (note, however, that policy implementation is dealt with in Chapter 22). Although the making of European policy—more specifically the decision-making or legislative process—is something integral to policy itself, and which is therefore dealt with in Part Four of this book, it may be helpful to spell out some of the more general characteristics of the European policy pro-

cess at this initial stage. This will provide the reader with a basic tool-kit for understanding references to (for example) pillars and procedures that may otherwise remain obscure.

There are various ways in which policy is made within the European Union. Indeed, variation across policy areas is now an important theme within the study of European Union politics, with this trend having been consolidated in the post-1985 treaty revisions (see Box 1.4). However, it is still

Box 1.4 **The facts**
The Treaty revisions

The Treaty of Paris setting up the European Coal and Steel Community (ECSC) was signed on 18 April 1951, and came into force in 1952. Its 50-year life ended in 2002.

The Treaty of Rome, setting up the European Economic Community (EEC) and the European Atomic Energy Community (EAEC or EURATOM), was signed on 25 March 1957 and came into force on 1 January 1958.

Since the 1950s, there have been a number of revisions to the treaties. The most important of these have taken place since the mid-1980s:

- The **Single European Act** (SEA, or just 'Single Act'): signed in 1986, came into force in July 1987.

- The **Maastricht Treaty** (creating a Treaty on European Union, or TEU): signed February 1992; came into force in November 1993.

- The **Amsterdam Treaty** (revising the Treaties): signed in 1997; came into force in 1999.

- The **Nice Treaty** (revising the Treaties): signed in 2000; came into force in 2003.

Box 1.5 **The facts**
The three pillars of the European Union

The Treaty on European Union (TEU), created at Maastricht in 1992 (and coming into effect in November 1993), created the 'European Union'.

The European Community (EC) remained in place after 1993, but became part of the wider European Union (EU).

The EU has three pillars:

- The first pillar (or 'Pillar 1') is a new improved version of the 'European Community', also called the 'Community pillar'. Most European policies (including EMU) come under this pillar.

- The second pillar (or 'Pillar 2') houses '**Common Foreign and Security Policy**' (CFSP).

- The third pillar (or 'Pillar 3') originally housed **Justice and Home Affairs**. However, after the Amsterdam Treaty came into force in 1999, the content of the pillar changed and it was renamed **Police and Judicial Co-operation in Criminal Matters** (PJCCM).

See Figures 4.1 and 4.2 in Chapter 4 for a depiction of what the EU's pillars looked like after Maastricht.

possible to make some general claims about the European policy process, even if we have to be careful not to make assumptions about specific policies and the procedures that apply to them. The biggest distinction to be made is across the three pillars of the European Union (see Box 1.5). The following paragraphs thus relate to Pillar 1, the European Community pillar, and not to Pillars 2 and 3 (common foreign and security policy, and police and judicial co-operation in criminal matters) as the latter are dealt with in Chapters 15 and 19.

In some of the earliest textbooks on the European Community, the adage that 'the Commission proposes, the Council disposes' was often repeated. As a general statement of how policy making operates today, this now presents a wholly inaccurate picture of how the EU operates. In the EC pillar, it is certainly true that the Commission still proposes legislation (though this is perhaps a less helpful summary of the Commission's role in Pillars 2 and 3). Indeed in Pillar 1, the Commission can draft legislation. But as we shall see below, the Parliament increasingly plays the role of *co*-legislator in the European legislative process.

In the EC pillar, it is fair to say that policy now emerges as a result of the interaction of a number of actors and institutions. First amongst these is what is sometimes referred to as the 'institutional triangle' of the European Commission, the European Parliament, and the Council of the European Union. However, many other European, national, and sub-national bodies, including interest groups, also play an important role in the making of European policy. The functions, responsibilities, and obligations of these actors and institutions depend on the particular rules that apply to the policy under consideration. While rather different rules apply to budgetary decisions, to international agreements, and for Economic and Monetary Union, much of the work of the EC pillar involves the making of legislation as described below.

Three legislative procedures shape how policy is made (see Box 1.6). These are the **co-decision** procedure, the **assent** procedure, and the **consultation** procedure. A fourth legislative procedure, the **co-operation** procedure, introduced in the mid-1980s, is now only rarely used. The procedure used is determined by the so-called **legal basis** underpinning the policy. This refers to a specific treaty provision. The legal basis is decided by the Commission, though the Commission's decision must be based on objective criteria so that it can be challenged through the courts if need be. Where there are grey areas, the choice of legal basis (and hence, legislative procedure) can be extremely contentious. This is because the different procedures allow different configurations of actors and institutions a say in the policy process. This is particularly important in determining the relative importance of the Council and the Parliament in the European policy process and is certain to influence the policy outcome.

The co-decision procedure (see Figure 1.1) was introduced in 1993, brought into effect by the Maastricht Treaty. Article 251 (EC Treaty) spells out how it should work. This provision was revised in the Amsterdam Treaty of 1997. Co-decision gives both the Parliament and the Council, as co-legislators, two successive readings of legislative proposals drafted by the Commission. If the two institutions are unable to agree at the end of this process, a 'conciliation committee' is set up. Conciliation involves

Box 1.6 **The facts**
Legislative procedures

Since the Amsterdam Treaty of 1997, there are three main legislative procedures in the EC pillar of the European Union:

- the consultation procedure
- the assent procedure
- the co-decision procedure.

selected members of the Council and Parliament (with the Commission also represented) who together try to hammer out an agreement. Once this is done, the agreement is passed back to the full Council and Parliament for consideration—a third reading. Co-decision is now the most widely applied legislative procedure in the EU's first pillar.

The assent procedure was introduced in the Single European Act of 1986. When this procedure is used, the Council must obtain the agreement (or 'assent') of the European Parliament before policy decisions are taken. Under this procedure the Parliament can say 'yes' or 'no' to a proposal, but does not have any right to propose amendments to it. Assent is used in only a relatively small number of policy areas, covering EU enlargement and international agreements, for example.

The consultation procedure, our third legislative procedure, was the original EC decision-making procedure, outlined in the Treaty of Rome. Consultation allows the European Parliament to give its opinion on Commission proposals, before the Council takes a decision. Once the Parliament's opinion is made known, the Commission can amend its proposal if it sees fit, before the Council examines it. The Council can then adopt or amend the proposal. If it wishes to reject it, it must do so unanimously (see Box 1.7). Under the majority of procedures within the EC pillar **qualified majority voting** now applies to votes taken in the EU Council. The use of **unanimity** is reserved for particularly sensitive political or constitutional issues. However, it is also in general use (with a few minor exceptions) in Pillars 2 and 3.

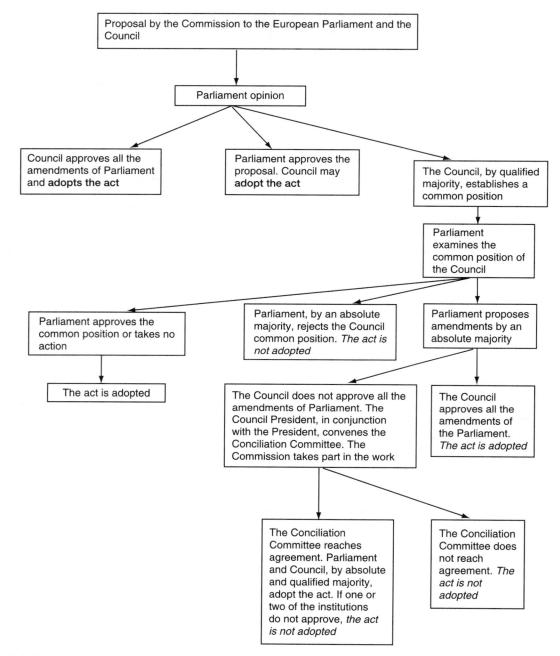

Fig. 1.1 Steps in the co-decision procedure

The decision-making procedures in the second and third pillars of the Union, those that deal with common foreign and security policy (CFSP) and police and judicial co-operation in criminal matters (PJCCM), are essentially intergovernmental, though the EC institutions do have some role to play if only at the margins. The policy process in these areas is dealt with in Chapters 15 and 19 respectively.

Box 1.7 The facts

The policy areas covered by simple consultation

- Police and judicial co-operation (Pillar 3)

- Revision of the Treaties

- Initiating enhanced co-operation

- Discrimination on the grounds of sex, race or ethnic origin, religion, political conviction, disability, age, or sexual orientation

- Implementation arrangements and new rights in the field of EU citizenship

- Agriculture

- Visas, asylum, immigration, and other policies associated with the free movement of persons

- Certain aspects of transport policy

- Competition rules

- Tax arrangements

- Economic policy

Source: **http://europa.eu.int/.**

The structure of the book

Even though this is a large book, containing 25 chapters, difficult decisions had to be taken at an early stage about what to include and what to leave out. This was especially challenging in Part Four of the book which deals with the European Union's policies. While this book is far from being the last word on EU politics, it was planned as a useful introduction to the subject, designed for those new or relatively new to EU affairs. Each chapter is written by an expert in their field, someone who has undertaken research on the topic about which they are writing. While there is no claim that the chapters that follow are comprehensive, each provides an excellent starting point for further study of the European Union.

This book is organized in the following way. It is divided into five Parts. *Part One* deals with the historical evolution of the European Community and Union. Chapter 2 covers the origins and early years of the integration process. Chapter 3 focuses more thematically on the single market, both as a historic 'event' and as a 'policy'. Chapter 4 then brings us up to date, covering the period from Maastricht in the early 1990s, to the Convention on the Future of Europe, which began in 2002.

Part Two covers theories of European integration, or perhaps more accurately, the various conceptual approaches used by academics to explain European integration and the politics of the European Union. Chapter 5 focuses on federalism and federation; Chapter 6 on neo-functionalism; and Chapter 7 on intergovernmentalism. All of these theories and approaches have long been associated with the European integration project. Once again, to bring us up to date, Chapter 8 considers a selection of theories and conceptual approaches that have more recently been applied to the study of the European Union and to the European integration process.

Part Three of the book then deals with the largest and most important of the European institutions: the European Commission; the Council of the European Union; the European Parliament; the Court of Justice; and the Community courts (Chapters 9–12). These chapters focus on the organization and functions of these institutions, and raise important questions about their future. Part Three also includes a chapter (Chapter 13) on the role of interest groups in the European Union.

Next, *Part Four* covers a number of European Union policies. Those included here are policies on enlargement, external relations/foreign policy, agriculture, social policy, regional policy, justice and home affairs, and economic and monetary union (Chapters 14–20). Although there are many omissions from this list, this sample was selected to provide a taste of the variation that exists in both policy content and the procedures governing decision making.

Finally, *Part Five* of the book comprises five chapters, each of which discusses an issue or theme that is not covered to any substantial degree elsewhere in the book. The five themes and issues that have been selected are Europeanization, Implementation, the Democratic Deficit, Differentiation, and Citizenship (Chapters 21–25). While this final Part may prove more of a challenge to students new to European integration, the topics covered here give an indication of where research on EU policies is heading. These concluding chapters may raise more questions than they answer, but they should provide readers with a good basic understanding of some of the issues currently of concern to European policy makers and those engaged in research in this field of European politics.

Part One

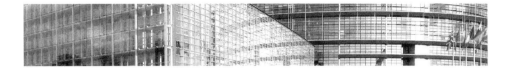

The historical context

Part One of *EU Politics* covers the historical evolution of the European integration process from the 1940s to 2002. In Chapter 2, Derek Urwin discusses how the European Community of the 1950s came to be set up. He charts the early years of the Community, and takes us up to the era of 'Eurosclerosis', the 1970s. Michelle Egan picks up the story from here in Chapter 3. This chapter adopts more of a thematic approach to the issue of the single market, so that the chapter not only explains the key events that occurred in the late 1980s, but also examines the context and implications of efforts to revitalize the European integration process at this point. In Chapter 4, David Phinnemore also adopts a thematic approach, focusing on the idea of 'European union'. In so doing he asks what European union now means for the EU. The chapter covers the period from the Maastricht European Council meeting of 1991 to the setting up of the Convention on the Future of Europe in 2002. In the process, this chapter examines the Treaty revisions introduced at both Amsterdam and Nice.

2 The European Community: From 1945 to 1985

Derek W. Urwin

READER'S GUIDE

This chapter reviews the principal developments in the process of European integration from the end of the Second World War through to the mid-1980s. While ideas and arguments in favour of European unity have a much longer history, the war and its aftermath contributed to providing a greater urgency and different context to the issue. In the mid-1980s the European Community took a series of decisions which launched it firmly on a trajectory towards intensive political, economic, and monetary integration. Between these two points, neither the support for integration nor the institutional and structural forms it took were preordained or without opposition. The rate and direction of integration depended upon a shifting constellation of forces: the nature of interactions between **federalist** ideas and their supporters, national governments and their assessments of national self-interest, and the broader international environment. Within these parameters, the chapter looks at the emergence of international organizations in Western Europe in the 1940s, the establishment of the Community idea from the **Schuman Plan** through to the **Treaty of Rome**, and the factors that contributed towards the seemingly erratic progress towards ever closer union made by the European Community after 1958.

Introduction

The institutional structure and operation of the European Union (EU) can trace a direct line of descent back to the establishment of the **European Coal and Steel Community** (ECSC). Indeed, while the intervening decades may have witnessed extensive embellishment and refinement, the broad outline and principle remain those of 1951. However, the idea and dream of a politically integrated Europe possess a much longer pedigree. Across the centuries, numerous intellectuals and political leaders have argued for and have attempted to bring order and unity to the fragmented political mosaic of the European continent. As part of this long-standing dream, an increased intellectual agitation for unity in Europe emerged in the nineteenth century, but almost exclusively by people who were, at best, at the fringes of political decision making. Their arguments and blueprints held little appeal or relevance for political leaders. However, there did emerge a more widespread recognition that some form of economic co-operation might well contain some potential political advantages for states. Those schemes that did become operative, however, were either short-lived or, like the **Zollverein** established among German states, highly region specific and protectionist in their external mien.

The peace process at the end of the First World War, by its emphasis upon national self-determination, made the continental political mosaic even more complex, so leading to a greater urgency for, and difficulty surrounding any process of, co-operation. After 1918, the hopes that had been invested in the **League of Nations**, as a world body dedicated to a co-operative peace, quickly foundered in a highly charged atmosphere of economic uncertainty and historic political antipathies. The Low Countries and the Nordic states did explore possibilities of economic co-operation, but with no significant outcome. A few politicians, most notably perhaps Aristide Briand, the French foreign minister, did raise the idea of political integration. But in concrete terms this did not advance beyond the 1930 Briand Memorandum, a generalized proposal advocating a kind of intergovernmental union with its own institutional infrastructures within the League of Nations. Outside political circles, a plethora of associations expounded schemes for co-operation and integration, but failed to achieve any positive results. By the 1930s economic depression and crisis, and the rise of fascism, had led countries to look to their own defences; the outbreak of war in 1939 simply confirmed the absence of any radical change to the European world of states. The history of European integration, therefore, as it is conventionally understood today, essentially begins in 1945. The chapter that follows charts that history, focusing on the period between 1945 and 1985.

The opening moves

The Second World War was a catalyst for a renewed interest in European unity. It contributed to arguments that nationalism and nationalist rivalries, by culminating in war, had discredited and bankrupted the independent state as the foundation of political organization and international order, and that a replacement for the state had to be found in a comprehensive continental community. These ideas were most forcefully expressed in the political vision of the Italian federalist, **Altiero Spinelli**, who produced a blueprint for a United States of Europe as the overriding priority for the post-war peace. His arguments found strong favour among the various national Resistance movements. However, the new European administrations seemed to give European unity a low priority, concentrating more upon issues of national economic reconstruction. But for several reasons the siren voices of **federalism** were heard by, and swayed, a larger audience than had been the case in the inter-war period, so enabling the possibility and dream of union to survive as an item on the European political agenda (see Box 2.1). Box 2.2 sets out the key dates in European integration during the period 1947 to 1957.

One important factor was the increasingly glacial international political climate. This division of Europe between East and West after 1945, and the subsequent Cold War between the world's two superpowers, the USA and the USSR, fuelled alarm in Western Europe about its own fragile defences in the light of what it feared were the territorial ambitions

of the USSR. This led to a deep involvement of the USA in European affairs in the late 1940s. The consequent ideological bipolarization in turn helped propel Western Europe towards defining itself as an entity with common interests. This changing mood was assisted by a general concern over the perilous state of the national economies, a concern that helped generate a widespread belief that economic recovery would require both external assistance from the USA and collaboration on development and trade across the West European states.

It was widely assumed across Western Europe that the lead in any moves towards closer collaboration, because of its wartime role, would be taken by the UK, and that, with Germany prostrate and militarily

Box 2.1 **Issues and debates**
The early years of European integration

Why European integration began, and the reasons why the subsequent plot developed the way it did, have been the subject of intense debate. There has been a tendency, especially among those strongly committed to a federal Europe, to see development moving, if not smoothly, then nevertheless inexorably along a single plane towards a predetermined goal. Yet the history of integration since the formation of the ECSC in 1951 has not been like that. The rate of integrative progress has been far from consistent, and all arguments and pressures for further advances have had to contend with equally powerful countervailing forces pulling in the opposite direction. Nor was there anything preordained about the structural route taken in 1950, or that future developments would revolve largely around a Franco-German axis. There might, both then and later, have been broad agreement about the desirability and principle of a united Europe; but there has rarely been consensus on anything else. As Robert Schuman, the French foreign minister, commented in May 1950 when he unveiled his plan for a pooling of coal and steel resources, 'Europe will not be made all at once, or according to a single plan'.

In reality, the story of integration is complex, with numerous sub-plots, varying strategies, and different ambitions. As advocated by the federalists, the role of ideas and beliefs has always been central to the progress of integration. Even so, there has been tension within the federalist camp as to the most appropriate strategy to adopt. Simplifying the complex strands of thought some-

what, there have been two competing strategic schools. On the one hand, there are those who have followed the arguments of people like Altiero Spinelli who, in the Ventotene Manifesto of 1940 and his subsequent writings and actions, urged a once and for all 'big bang' solution, an instantaneous and all-embracing transformation into a federal European state. On the other side was a more cautious and pragmatic strategy, encapsulated by the inputs of people like Jean Monnet and Robert Schuman, which envisaged a slower process of steady accretion through a series of limited actions and innovations. But while central and necessary, the force of ideas by itself has not been sufficient. The impact and rate of advance of the federalist impulse has been modified by the input and role of national governments—by their policies and by the degree to which integrative proposals have been seen as fitting with, or at the very least not seeming to threaten, what regimes perceive to be the national interests of their own states. The way in which processes of integration have developed over the past half-century, therefore, is the product of a complex interaction of centripetal and centrifugal pressures, of ideas, principles, and *realpolitik* scepticism. And all of this intricate dance has occurred within a broader and ever-shifting international political and economic environment which itself has affected, sometimes positively and sometimes negatively, the degree of enthusiasm for, commitment to, and rate of progress of integration.

Box 2.2 **Key dates**
European integration I: 1947–1957

1947	March	Announcement of Truman Doctrine by the USA. Signature of Treaty of Dunkirk by the UK and France
	June	Declaration of Marshall Plan by the USA
1948	January	Start of Benelux Customs Union
	March	Signature of Treaty of Brussels by the UK, France, and Benelux
	April	Establishment of Organization for European Economic Co-operation (OEEC) by 16 European states, the USA, and Canada.
	May	The federalist Congress of Europe meets at The Hague
1949	April	Signature of the Atlantic Pact and formation of the North Atlantic Treaty Organization (NATO) by 12 states
	May	Treaty of Westminster establishes the Council of Europe
1950	May	Schuman Plan proposes a pooling of coal and steel resources by France, the Federal Republic of Germany, and any other state wishing to join them
	October	Proposal for a European Defence Community (EDC)
1951	April	Treaty of Paris establishes the European Coal and Steel Community (ECSC)
1952	May	Signature of EDC Treaty
	July	ECSC comes into operation
1953	March	Draft Treaty of a European Political Community (EPC)
1954	August	French Parliament rejects EDC. The EDC and EPC plans collapse
	October	Treaty of Brussels is modified to establish West European Union (WEU)
1955	June	Foreign ministers of the ECSC states meet in Messina, Italy, to consider 'further European integration'
1957	March	Signature of Treaty of Rome establishes the European Economic Community (EEC) and the European Atomic Energy Community (EURATOM)

occupied, a British–French alliance would lie at the core of European organization. However, the initial moves towards enhanced collaboration by governments were limited in scope, with the wartime decision by the governments in exile of the Low Countries to establish a **Benelux** customs union an exception. While governments were more typically interested primarily in security arrangements, they did little more than consider mutual aid treaties of the traditional variety. The only formal agreements to emerge were the 1947 Treaty of Dunkirk between the UK and France, and its 1948 extension in the fifty-year Treaty of Brussels (formally the Treaty of Economic, Social, and Cultural Collaboration and

Collective Self-Defence), which incorporated the Low Countries as signatories, and which was later to serve as the basis of the **Western European Union** (WEU). While these treaties listed economic and cultural co-operation as objectives, they were first and foremost mutual security pacts with promises of reciprocal assistance, specifically to guard against possible future German aggression. While other countries and federalists alike looked to the UK to take a lead, the British attitude towards anything more than co-operation between independent states was consistently negative, at best deeply sceptical, and at worst totally hostile.

By 1948 the Cold War was in full swing. Heightened alarm over events in Central and Eastern Europe helped to consolidate the final marriage between Western Europe and the USA, with the formation of the North Atlantic Treaty Organization (NATO) in 1949. NATO was the conclusion of a programme of American support first outlined in the Truman Doctrine of March 1947, which pledged American assistance for 'free peoples who are resisting subjugation'. It provided a protective shield beneath which Western Europe was free to consider and develop its political and economic options without necessarily having to devote time and scarce resources to military defence. Equally, the USA, itself a federation, saw nothing inherently problematic about closer integration in Western Europe; indeed, also partly because of its own strategic interests, the USA lent its weight after 1947 to proposals for more intensive collaboration. The American commitment was strongly welcomed by the two leading states, the UK and France. But though they were expected to form the vanguard of the European future, neither saw this as leading to radical reconstruction. French European policy was dominated by the need to keep Germany weak and to control its future, a concern met by the military occupation of the country after

1945. The UK was suspicious of anything beyond close collaboration that might diminish its own **sovereignty** and freedom to act independently.

It was against this backdrop that the protagonists of a federal Europe nevertheless began to receive endorsement from a growing number of senior politicians from several countries (see Chapter 5). Soon, the dominant issue became not whether there should be integration, but rather what form it should take. Governments and political parties took positions on the question of whether this should only be intensive **intergovernmental** collaboration embedded in formalized treaties and arrangements, or something deeper that would embrace an element of **supranationalism** and the diminution of national sovereignty. This was the core of the debate at the Congress of Europe in 1948, which led to the establishment of the Council of Europe in 1949 (see Box 2.3).

Political developments were paralleled by activity on the economic front through the introduction of the European Recovery Programme, or Marshall Plan. The essence of the Plan was an American offer of economic aid to Europe. The aid, however, was contingent upon the administration of the relief

---

Box 2.3 **Case study**
The establishment of the Council of Europe

The Congress of Europe, a gathering of over 700 delegates or representatives of pro-integration or federalist organizations from 16 countries, along with observers from Canada and the USA, was held at The Hague (in the Netherlands) in May 1948. The Congress was too unwieldy to achieve any practical outcome, not least because it did not speak for governments. But in calling for a European federation or union, with its own institutions, a charter of human rights linked to a European court, a common market, and monetary union, it helped place integration more firmly and visibly on the agenda. It stimulated a process of discussion and debate that culminated in May 1949 in the establishment by ten states of the intergovernmental Council of Europe, the first post-1945 political organization on the continent. The Council, however, represented a victory for those, especially the UK, who wished only co-operation, not integration: decisions would

require the consent of all its members, and hence it could not enforce any view or policy upon reluctant member states. Federalists accepted the final outcome of the Council only reluctantly, accepting it as a start that would not preclude a search for something better. By contrast, for others it epitomized the totality of what was desirable or necessary. In seeking to accommodate two very contrasting positions, the product was very much a dead end. More importantly, however, the Council of Europe represented a watershed. It convinced the protagonists of a united Europe that they would have to narrow their horizons even further. It brought the curtain down on the willingness to compromise in order to keep reluctant states and governments on board. It was, therefore, the point at which the post-war belief that the UK should and would take the lead in radical political reorganization came to an end.

programme being collective in order to maximize its benefits. The USA further insisted that the European participants in the programme had to decide themselves how aid was to be distributed across the countries involved. These were the basic tasks of the Organization for European Economic Co-operation (OEEC), established in April 1948. The OEEC was primarily concerned with macro-economic co-operation and co-ordination. Like the Council of Europe, it was intergovernmental in nature, only able to operate with the full consent of all its members. Both organizations, however, had to have some permanent institutions to enable them to perform their allotted functions satisfactorily. While limited in scope and bound very much by the principle of voluntary co-operation, both nevertheless reflected a growing realization in Western Europe of the interdependency of states, and that these states, especially against the backdrop of the Cold War, would prosper or fail together. And both contributed significantly to a learning curve among the participants about how one should go about collaborating. Yet it remained the case that both organizations, in terms of the degree of integration and limitations on national sovereignty, operated on the basis of the lowest common denominator of intergovernmental co-operation. While this clearly met the needs of some states and governments, it was a situation that could not satisfy those who believed in the imperative of union (see Hogan 1987).

Key points

- The Second World War contributed to a new interest in European unity.

- The first post-1945 governments were more concerned with economic issues than with European integration.

- Federalists and supporters of integration expected the UK, because of its wartime role, to take the lead in reorganizing Europe.

- The Cold War heightened West European fears of insecurity and led to a massive American political and economic involvement in Europe.

- The European international organizations established in the late 1940s were all intergovernmental in nature.

The Community idea

If union were to become a political objective, a different path had to be sought, and federalists had to acknowledge that such a path would prove acceptable to only some countries. The radical redirection of effort was provided by the then French foreign minister, Robert Schuman, who in May 1950 cut through the tangled debate to propose a pooling of coal and steel resources. The Schuman Plan was the blueprint for the ECSC, formally established in April 1951 as Western Europe's first organization to involve the yielding of a degree of state sovereignty to a supranational authority (Diebold 1959).

That such a scheme could be proposed, drafted, and turned into reality was the outcome of a combination of shifting circumstances. It had an immediately identifiable and concrete goal, making it more attractive to senior politicians than an instantaneous federal transformation, no matter how strongly they might favour intensive integration. The drafter of the plan had been **Jean Monnet**, whose experiences as the supremo of national economic planning in France after 1945 had confirmed his long-held view that economic development and prosperity could best be achieved at a European rather than a national level, and that therefore the route to political integration was a long road that inevitably lay through economics. Equally importantly, Monnet had also consistently argued that peace and stability in Europe could only be achieved through a *rapprochement* between the historic rivals, France and Germany; for Monnet the two states had to form the core of any integrative venture. These were views to which Schuman also strongly subscribed. He was able to persuade his governmental colleagues in Paris of their virtues in part because of further changes in the international environment.

Relations between East and West had reached a nadir in 1948. One consequence was the decision by the USA, backed by the UK and a reluctant France, to form a German state out of the western military zones of occupation in the country. This decision and the establishment of an independent Federal Republic of Germany in 1949 destroyed at a stroke the foundation of France's post-1945 European policy. In addition, the compensatory decision to establish an International Ruhr Authority in April 1949 to supervise coal and steel production in West Germany's dominant industrial region failed to satisfy anyone. In 1950, with the Ruhr Authority increasingly ineffectual and on the point of being abandoned, Monnet's ideas offered France a way out of the dilemma, by indicating a strategy by which the new West Germany could be subject to external influence while it was still politically weak. Schuman's proposal proved equally attractive to the West German leader, **Konrad Adenauer**, who saw it as a potentially valuable element of his policy of tying the Federal Republic firmly to Western Europe politically, economically, and militarily. Submerging the country in European ventures, he hoped, would further reassure his neighbours that West Germany had abandoned the aggressive nationalism of the past. It is not insignificant that Schuman's announcement was for a structure enabling the pooling of French and West German coal and steel resources, which other countries were welcome to join if they wished. He further made it clear that a new structure would be created even if no other state wished to join: 'if necessary, we shall go ahead with only two [countries]'. Be that as it may, the Schuman Plan was overtly about more than just coal and steel: Schuman emphasized that it would set down 'common bases for economic development as a first step in the federation of Europe'.

Hence, the formation of the ECSC was the product of a combination of integrationist impulses and ideas, national self-interest, and international circumstances. Hailed by Jean Monnet as 'the first expression of the Europe that is being born', the ECSC set in motion a groundswell that some forty years later was to result in the European Union. While an invitation to join the new body was extended to all West European states, and especially the UK, only four other countries—Belgium, Italy, Luxembourg, and the Netherlands—felt able to accept the supranational principle of the ECSC. The institutional structure adopted by the ECSC—which included a supreme judicial authority—was to serve as a model for all future developments. The most innovative (and in the future a highly contentious) feature was the divided executive and decision-making structure: a High Authority vested with significant power to represent and uphold the supranational principle, and a Council of Ministers to represent and protect the interests of the governments of the member states (Poidevin and Spierenburg 1994).

But if the ECSC were to be merely the first step towards full union, more had to be done. Monnet himself saw the ECSC as the opening phase of a process of **sectoral integration**, where the ultimate goal of political union would be the long-term culmination of an accretion of integrative efforts, of trust and experience, in a sector-by-sector linkage of specific economic areas and activities that ultimately would result in a common economic market (see Chapter 6: 84–5). Discussions began more or less immediately on what—for example, transport or agriculture—would and should follow on from coal and steel as the next instances of sectoral economic integration.

The ECSC survived as a separate entity until 1967 when the merged European Communities (EC) was created. Its record of economic success, however, was rather mixed. Even though Jean Monnet had been appointed head of the High Authority, the latter failed to bring national coal and steel policies and practices fully under its control, and it had little or no control over or effect on other economic sectors. By themselves, these issues might in time have forced a re-evaluation of the strategy of sectoral integration. In the event, the direction taken by the latter was altogether surprising. The determining factor was a further transformation in the international climate, which had once again changed for the worse as armed conflict broke out in Korea during the ECSC negotiations. Concerned that the Asian war might be a prelude to war in Europe, the USA called for a strengthening of NATO, while simultaneously stressing that because of its global role and commitments, America itself could not provide the necessary additional resources. When the European members of NATO argued that their economies were too weak to bear substantial additional defence costs, the USA proposed a West German military contribution to NATO.

Only a few years after the overthrow of Nazism, the idea of a German army alarmed its neighbours. In France, the possibility of West German rearmament threatened once again to undermine the core of its European policy. Yet, prompted by Jean Monnet, who saw sectoral integration as a solution to the dilemma, the French government proposed a European Defence Community (EDC), modelled upon the ECSC, which would establish a Western European army that would include military units from all the member states, including West Germany. However, the exercise failed when the French National Assembly refused to take a decision to ratify the Treaty in 1954 (see Box 2.4).

Box 2.4 **Case study**
The European Defence Community

Under plans for a European Defence Community (EDC), German units would be part of a European army, all falling under an integrated European, and not an independent West German, command. The other member states would have only a proportion of their armed forces within the EDC framework. The EDC proposal was immediately seen by federalists and others as a significant second step towards integration. However, the question of the desirability or necessity of some form of political control over and direction of an EDC soon led to arguments for a European Political Community (EPC), something which would short-circuit **sectoral integration** by an immediate advance towards creating a comprehensive federation. The Dutch foreign minister, Johan Willem Beyen, took the argument one step further in 1952, suggesting a parallel drive to economic unity. Arguing that sectoral integration by itself was insufficient for economic development and unity, Beyen proposed that the EDC/EPC nexus be extended to embrace the construction of a **customs union** and **common market** (see Chapter 3).

Only the ECSC countries were willing to explore these possible new ventures. The UK declined a specific invitation to join the EDC, but because it wished NATO to be strengthened, it indicated support for a European army that would include a West German military contribution. The EPC idea remained at the draft stage, and Beyen's ideas were largely put on hold because it was clear, not least in the minds of supporters of further integration, that any advance down that road was dependent upon the success or failure of ratification of the EDC by the national parliaments of the proposed members. Ironically, the stumbling block was France, where the idea of a re-armed Germany, even within the EDC, remained deeply perturbing. France had originally wanted, and perhaps had

had expected, the UK to be part of the new organization as an extra guarantee against any possible resurgence of German militarism, the well-known British hostility to anything that smacked of supranationalism notwithstanding. In a sense, the French proposal for an EDC had been, for many of its politicians, a delaying tactic, perhaps even an idea so outrageous in its audacity that it would become mired in years of debate and argument. The extent to which the notion was embraced both within the ECSC states and beyond, and the speed at which the subsequent talks progressed, placed successive French governments, all short-lived, weak, and concerned more with mere survival than innovation, in a quandary. Confronted by strong political and popular opposition, all were unable or unwilling to make the effort to secure a parliamentary majority for EDC ratification (Aron and Lerner 1957).

After almost four years of stalemate France rejected the EDC in 1954 on a technicality (the vote was not on whether the treaty should be approved, but whether the parliament wished to discuss the treaty). With it fell the hopes for an EPC. The vote did not remove the issue of West German re-armament from the agenda. In a frantic search to salvage something from the wreckage, agreement was secured on a British proposal to revamp the 1948 Treaty of Brussels, bringing into it all the projected members of the EDC. A new body, **Western European Union** (WEU), was established, linking together the UK and the ECSC states in a defence arrangement within which West German re-armament would occur. In reality, WEU remained more or less moribund until the 1980s, and a rearmed West Germany entered NATO as a full and equal member. The outcome, therefore, was the one result that France had hoped to avoid by its advocacy of an EDC.

The consequences for integration of the EDC debacle seemed to be severe. It proved to be the high water mark of the sectoral approach to integration. Only the ECSC survived the damage to the integration cause, and there were fears that it too would collapse. A somewhat disillusioned Jean Monnet announced his attention not to seek reappointment as President of the ECSC High Authority in order to pursue the goal of integration as a private citizen. However, there remained across Western Europe a substantial degree of institutional co-operation built up over the previous decade: NATO, OEEC, the Council of Europe, and, of course, the ECSC. Within these networks there had survived in the little Europe of the 'ECSC Six' a strong commitment to further integration. At a meeting of their foreign ministers at Messina in Sicily in June 1955, the six members of the ECSC took a decisive step forward. Taking as their core text the 1952 Dutch proposal for abolition of quotas and tariffs within, and the introduction of a common external tariff for, the Community area, the foreign ministers agreed to launch 'a fresh advance towards the building of Europe'. This set in motion progress towards plans for a **customs union** and, ultimately, a **common market**, plans which culminated in March 1957 with the **Treaty of Rome** and the formation of the European Economic Community (EEC). Again, however, only the six members of the ECSC were willing to commit themselves to the leap of faith demanded by the Rome treaty.

Key points

- The Schuman Plan offered both a way in which France and the Federal Republic of Germany could become reconciled with each other, and a path towards integration that went beyond intergovernmental co-operation.

- The European Coal and Steel Community (ECSC) was the first step in an anticipated process of sectoral economic integration. It brought together six states that delegated some aspects of their sovereignty to a supranational authority.

- Hostility to, and the ultimate rejection of, plans for a European Defence Community (EDC) by France led to its abandonment. The failure of the EDC contributed towards a discrediting of the sectoral strategy and threatened to destroy the whole process of integration.

- In 1955 the ECSC states launched a rescue operation and committed themselves to further integration, signing the Treaty of Rome two years later.

Rome and the stalling of ambition

Because the new organization was to range over an extremely wide area of activity, the provisions of the Treaty of Rome were necessarily complex. Its preamble may have been less prescriptive than that of its ECSC predecessor, yet, in referring to the determination 'to lay the foundations of an ever closer union among the peoples of Europe', its implications were far-reaching. More specifically, the Treaty enjoined its signatories, among other things, to establish a **common market**, defined as the free movement of goods, persons, services, and capital, to approximate national economic policies, and to develop common policies, most specifically in agriculture. Although the objectives of the Treaty were expressed in economic terms, the Preamble implied that a political purpose lay behind them. In aiming ultimately to create something more than a common market, the Treaty emphasized the principle that the problems of one member state would be the problems of all. Box 2.5 sets out the key dates in European integration during the period 1958 to 1985.

The institutional structure was modelled on that of the ECSC, with the quasi-**executive** and **supranational** European Commission intended to be the motor force of integration; its authority was counterbalanced by the Council of Ministers representing the member states. Facing these executive bodies was

Box 2.5 Key dates
European integration II: 1958–1985

1958	January	Establishment of the EEC and Euratom
1959	January	First tariff cuts made by the EEC
1961	July	Fouchet Plan for a 'union of states' proposed
1961	July–August	The UK, Denmark, and Ireland apply for EEC membership
1962	January	EEC develops basic regulations for a Common Agricultural Policy (CAP)
	May	Norway applies for EEC membership
1963	January	President de Gaulle vetoes British membership. Signature of Franco-West German Treaty of Friendship and Reconciliation
1965	April	Treaty merging the executives of the three Communities signed in Brussels
	June	France walks out of the Council of Ministers and begins a boycott of EEC institutions
1966	January	The Luxembourg Compromise ends the French boycott
1967	July	The three Communities merged to form the European Community (EC)
	November	President de Gaulle vetoes British membership for the second time
1968	July	The EC establishes a customs union and agrees on a CAP
1969	December	The Hague summit agrees to consider EC enlargement and supports greater policy co-operation and economic and monetary union
1970	October	Werner Report on economic and monetary union. Davignon Report on foreign policy co-operation leads to establishment of European Political Co-operation (EPC)
1972	March	The currency 'snake' established, limiting margins of fluctuation between participating currencies
1973	January	Accession of the UK, Denmark, and Ireland
1974	December	Paris summit agrees to establish the European Council and accepts the principle of direct elections to the European Parliament (EP)
1976	January	Tindemans Report published, recommending reform of the EC institutions
1979	March	Establishment of the European Monetary System (EMS)
	June	First direct elections to the EP
1983	June	Signature of Solemn Declaration on European Union by the heads of state and government
1984	February	EP approves the Draft Treaty Regarding European Union
	June	Fontainebleau summit of the European Council agrees to take action on a number of outstanding issues hindering progress on integration
1985	March	European Council agrees to the establishment of a single market by the end of 1992
	June	European Council agrees on a reform of the Treaty of Rome

a much weaker Assembly with little in the way of significant decision-making powers. The Assembly, which quickly adopted for itself the title of European Parliament (EP), was soon engaged in a perpetual struggle to enlarge its own authority, including a demand for implementation of the Treaty provision on direct elections. The final major EEC institution was the European Court of Justice (ECJ) which rapidly, not least by its ruling that EEC law took precedence over national law, asserted itself as a major bonding force. The new EEC shared its assembly and court with the ECSC and the less significant European Atomic Energy Community (Euratom), also set up in 1957 by a second Treaty of Rome to promote collaboration on the development of nuclear energy for peaceful economic purposes. The three Communities retained separate executive structures until 1967 when they were merged to form the European Community (EC).

The Treaty of Rome set a target for its objectives. Within specified time limits the implementation and completion of a **customs union**, and then a common market, was to be achieved through a three-stage process. The auguries were initially bright. Under the leadership of a proactive Commission, early progress towards the goals of Rome was satisfactory. By 1961 EEC internal tariff barriers had been substantially reduced and quota restrictions on industrial products largely eliminated. Towards the end of the decade the EEC could proudly claim that the customs union had been implemented ahead of schedule. Internal EEC trade flourished, rates of economic growth were impressive, and work had begun on establishing a common agricultural policy. These positive advances raised hopes among those committed to the establishment of a political union that that goal might also be expedited. Indeed, Walter Hallstein, the forceful West German statesman and economist who served as President of the Commission from 1958 to 1967, could inform journalists that perhaps he should be regarded as a kind of Western European prime minister. The optimism, however, proved to be premature. Broadly speaking, the transformation of the EEC into a common market was scheduled to be spread over a period of 12–15 years. By the early 1970s, however, the EEC seemed to be no nearer that goal than it had been a decade earlier. A series of circumstances had led to its derailment.

The issues that the EEC was obliged to confront in the 1960s were issues that have remained central ever since. In simple terms, they related to the **deepening** and **widening** of the Community: the extent to which, and the rate at which, more intensive integration should be pursued, and how these aspects of integration should relate to the **enlargement** of the EEC. The specific context in which these issues emerged in the 1960s had a focal point in the French president, **Charles de Gaulle**. While he was generally supportive of the EEC as a means of retaining French influence in Western Europe, forging in particular a close relationship with Konrad Adenauer and the German economic giant across the Rhine in 1963, de Gaulle was suspicious of anything that might affect that influence and undermine French sovereignty. In 1961 he had tried to push the EEC down a somewhat different route, floating the idea of a 'Union of States' that would entail the incorporation of the EEC into a new intergovernmental organization for the co-ordination of foreign and defence policy. His proposal was given detailed institutional flesh in the subsequent **Fouchet Plan**. But the idea received at best little support outside West Germany, and was rejected in 1962 after a series of acrimonious meetings. While the smaller EEC members were concerned about being presented with some kind of Franco–German fait accompli, the episode merely added extra substance to de Gaulle's long-standing suspicions that the EEC, or anything like it, might well act as a brake on his ambitions for France.

Two further episodes heightened the mood of crisis. First, the immediate economic success of the EEC as a trading bloc after 1958 had persuaded other Western European states that had previously rejected involvement to revise their opinion and seek membership. The most important candidate was the UK, which applied for membership in 1961. In 1963, and again in 1967, de Gaulle, against the wishes of his five partners, vetoed the British application on the grounds that the country, because of its Commonwealth links and close relationship with the USA, was not sufficiently committed either politically or economically to Europe or to EEC objectives. Although not subject to a veto, the other applicant states declined to proceed without the UK. Second, according to the schedule set by the Treaty of Rome, the EEC was expected to take some decisive decisions in 1966, including a move to an extension of **qualified majority voting** (QMV) in the Council of Ministers. At the same time the EEC was faced with approving financial arrangements for the Common Agricultural Policy (CAP) and a Commission proposal for enhancing supranational authority by giving more powers to itself and the EP. The latter proposal clearly involved a diminution of national sovereignty, as would any extension of qualified majority voting which would reduce the number of areas where **unanimity** across the member states was necessary. Instead, for many decisions a two-thirds majority would suffice, with the result that a state could be outvoted but could not block the decision by exercising a veto. While the Treaty of Rome had envisaged a steady diminution of the right of a member state to exercise a veto, de Gaulle was not prepared to accept the increased risk of France being outvoted in key decisions. In 1965 he provoked a crisis by withdrawing all French participation in Council of Ministers business except for that dealing with low-level and routine technicalities. The EEC almost ground to a halt. The crisis was resolved only by the Luxembourg Compromise of 1966 (see Box 2.6).

Overall, the results of de Gaulle's actions seemed to indicate that political integration, as advocated by federalists, was off the agenda, and that the future development of the EC would be more as an inter-governmental grouping of independent states. This shift of emphasis and mood seemed to be symbolized by the resignation in 1967 of Hallstein as Commission President. To some extent, the early rapid progress after 1958 had been possible not only because of favourable internal and external economic conditions, but also because, apart from the furore over the Fouchet Plan, national leaders had remained relatively uninvolved in EEC business, being content to allow the Commission to push things forward. If, however, future progress was to be governed by the Luxembourg Compromise, a more positive national governmental input would be required. But even that might be insufficient as long as Charles de Gaulle remained in power. Hence, any way forward had to await the French president's retirement in 1969.

Key points

- The Treaty of Rome (1957) set out a plan and schedule for a customs union and a common market as a prelude to some form of political union.

- In the 1960s the European Economic Community (EEC) was faced by issues of deepening and widening the Community structure, with a division of opinion emerging between France and its five partners.

- In 1965 a serious dispute between France and the other member states over institutional change crippled the EEC. It was resolved by the Luxembourg Compromise.

Box 2.6 **The facts**
The Luxembourg Compromise

The Luxembourg Compromise (or Luxembourg Agreement) is the name often given to the agreement among the then six member states of the European Community, concluding the 'empty chair crisis' of 1965. The agreement stated that in cases of the vital national interest of one of the member states the Council would aim to find a consensus solution, thus creating a de facto veto right.

The Compromise had practical effects for both the Council and the Commission. In the case of the Council, member states were more willing to accept an extension of majority voting, knowing that in the final instance they could invoke the Luxembourg Compromise and veto unwanted legislation. In the case of the Commission, it meant that this institution had to make more of an effort to ensure that its proposals would not impact upon the vital interests of any member state. In so doing, it made the Commission much more cautious in its policy proposals. These effects were felt despite the fact that the Luxembourg Compromise was never recognized by the European Court of Justice as legally binding.

The emergence of summits

In 1969, at a summit meeting in The Hague in the Netherlands intended to discuss the options open to the EC, the six heads of government attempted to restore some momentum to the stalled organization. The summit in The Hague opened the way for the enlargement of the EC, especially for the British. It agreed to extend the budgetary competence of the European Parliament (EP), and argued for more common policy. It also called for a move towards Economic and Monetary Union (EMU), initially through an exchange rate system for the EC, as an important step towards the ultimate goal of political union (see Chapter 20). In practice, the meeting in The Hague inaugurated summitry as a new style of EC decision making, recognizing that integration could only develop further if it was able to reconcile itself with national concerns. Summitry, that is, the use of European summits to set the political agenda of the Community, was to be formalized and placed on a regular footing with the establishment of the European Council in 1974 as a meeting place for the leaders of national governments (see Chapter 10).

Achievement of the objectives declaimed at The Hague was only partially successful. The first enlargement of the EC duly occurred in 1973 with the accession of the UK, Denmark, and Ireland (Nicholson and East 1987). The other candidate for membership of the 1960s, Norway, had already withdrawn from the final negotiations as a result of a referendum in 1972 which, against government advice, had rejected EC membership (see Chapter 14). Equally, the EC began to be able to assert a more positive and united presence in international affairs. Represented by the Commission, it spoke with one voice in international trade negotiations, and after the **Davignon Report** on policy co-operation in 1970, the member states, through **European Political Co-operation** (EPC), developed an impressive and, on balance, quite successful structure and pattern of collaboration on, and co-ordination of, foreign policy (see Chapter 15). After the mid-1970s, two structural funds, the European Regional Development Fund (ERDF) and the European Social Fund (ESF), began to play an important role in providing aid for economic and employment restructuring (see Chapters 17 and 18). The CAP had also come fully on stream in 1972, though in its final form it developed as a protectionist device that shielded European farmers from the full impact of market forces and from the necessity of taking markets and demand into account when planning production (see Chapter 16).

However, while the balance sheet around the end of the 1970s did feature many positive aspects, there was also a debit side. The achievements gained could not disguise the fact that on the broader front of the ambitions of the Treaty of Rome the EC still seemed to be marking time. A common market seemed to be as far away as ever, with the prospect of political union even more remote. The major integrative impetus propounded at the summit in The Hague had been Economic and Monetary Union (EMU). The leaders had set up a committee under the Luxembourg premier, Pierre Werner, to put some flesh on the proposal. The Werner Report of 1970 outlined a three-stage process for the full implementation of EMU by 1980 (see Chapter 20).

The decade, however, had not progressed very far before this rekindling of ambition was thwarted. In 1972 the EC did attempt to establish a European zone of stability by imposing limits on how far EC currencies would be permitted to float against each other (the so-called '**snake**'), but this barely got off the ground. Undermined not least by the quadrupling of oil prices in 1973—the consequence of war in the Middle East—the 'snake' structure was already dead when it was abandoned in 1976. In addition, the EC experienced both rapidly growing unemployment and inflation in the 1970s. The consequent political and electoral pressures forced governments to turn more to national issues and national defence. Some stabilization was eventually achieved after 1979 with the relaunch—sponsored by the European Council—of a monetary policy. The European Monetary System (EMS) did, through an Exchange Rate Mechanism (ERM), have currency stabilization as an objective. However, by itself the EMS could not achieve monetary union. It was a more modest design and could only be a first step on the road back to EMU. In the 1980s the EMS was deemed, perhaps because of its modesty, to have had some success in curbing currency fluctuations, inflation, and unemployment, thereby contributing to the return of EMU to the central EC agenda in 1989 (see Chapter 20).

On the broader integrative front, the initiative had passed firmly to the European Council. Its formation in 1974 confirmed the central role that had to be adopted by the heads of government in determining the future path of the EC. More specifically, it brought to an apogee the **Franco-German axis** that lay at the core of the EC that had been, two decades earlier, an essential sub-theme for people like Monnet and Schuman. Formalized in a Treaty of Friendship and Reconciliation in 1963, the relationship and its significance for the EC was to become far more overt in the 1970s. While the two states might not always be able to impose their will upon their partners, their active consent was vital for any progress to be made. Although the leaders of the two states, Valéry Giscard d'Estaing and Helmut Schmidt, accepted the need to utilize and develop the EC as an instrument of pragmatic integration, both tended to evaluate ideas in terms of national interest and seemed reluctant to pursue an advanced federalist route. That Franco-German drive had to await the arrival in power of François Mitterrand and Helmut Kohl in 1981 and 1982 respectively (Simonian 1985). With the Commission seemingly downgraded and kept firmly on a short leash, the real achievements that were gained could not conceal the fact that the EC was not progressing, or at least was doing so only minimally, towards the aims of the Treaty of Rome.

Nevertheless, the EC, and the European Council in particular, continued to pay lip-service to the ideal of full economic and political union. From its commissioning of the 1976 Tindemans Report, which recommended strengthening the EC institutions and the adoption of more common policies, through to its 1983 Solemn Declaration on European Union, the European Council sponsored studies on how to advance the cause of union or rhetorically reasserted its faith in the ultimate goal. In 1974, the Council of Ministers had eventually agreed to implement the Rome requirement that the European Parliament (EP) should be elected directly by the national electorates. The first direct elections were held in 1979. They gave the EP a sense of greater legitimacy, a feeling that it now had a mandate to review existing structures and to urge the EC to progress to a more cohesive and genuine union. With its moves co-ordinated by the veteran federalist, Altiero Spinelli, who had been elected to the Parliament, the EP produced a Draft Treaty Establishing the European Union. While the European Council took no immediate action on the EP proposals, the Treaty nevertheless provided a working basis for and contributed towards the developments that within a decade led to the establishment of the European Union (EU).

At the end of the day, however, initiative and commitment had to come from the European Council. To do so, it needed to take on board a growing number of issues that it had earlier sought to shelve or avoid: the EC's budget and how national contributions to it were determined; the burgeoning costs, problems, and distorting consequences of the CAP; the need to consider and develop further common policies; future enlargements; and a more detailed and positive response to how the EC should fit into a rapidly changing international world. Indeed, adapting to the international environment seemed to increase in urgency in the 1980s. European leaders began to worry that in a new economic era of high technology, which required massive investment, Western Europe was already lagging far behind the market leaders, the USA and Japan. Increasingly, the argument was heard that European survival and competitiveness in this brave new world could be achieved only through co-operation and a common front.

Moreover, the EC states had become alarmed in the late 1970s by an increasingly bellicose Soviet foreign policy that it feared might destabilize the West European status quo. After 1980 they became equally alarmed at the aggressive American response, fearing that they might be dragged into conflict by an American policy over which they had no influence. After 1985 and the arrival of Mikhail Gorbachev as leader of the USSR, the two superpowers began to talk to each other about means of reducing tension and accommodating each other's interests. Almost predictably, the EC states began to express concerns that the two superpowers might reach an agreement that would not take their interests into account.

This international background provided, as it often had done in previous decades, a necessary stimulus for more visible activity on the domestic West European front. Partly by choice and partly by necessity, European Council sessions turned to internal matters. At the core of this new activity was President Mitterrand of France. After the failure of his initial attempts to reflate the French economy after 1981, Mitterrand concluded that recuperation could more readily be achieved by means of European integration, especially when working in close harness with West Germany. With the encouragement of Mitterrand and others, there emerged, in short, a new sense of direction and purpose. In 1984 the Fontainebleau summit meeting of the European Council reached agreement on tackling a backlog of issues that had hitherto stalled the integration progress. With these agreements behind them, members of the European Council were able to take a series of decisions intended to advance the cause of union. They agreed to the establishment of a single internal market by the end of 1992 and to a major revision of the Treaty of Rome. In so doing, they pushed the EC decisively towards a more intense economic integration, the Treaty on European Union, and the establishment of the EU (see Chapter 3).

Key points

- The summit of 1969 in The Hague opened the way for the admission of new members to the EC and agreed to seek new initiatives in policy co-operation, especially economic and monetary union.

- The practice of summitry was institutionalized by the establishment of the European Council in 1974.

- In 1984 the European Council reached agreement on several important outstanding issues. This permitted it the following year to consider future developments. It committed the EC to a single internal market and a major overhaul of the Treaty of Rome. These initiatives were helped by concerns that Western Europe's international status, both political and economic, had declined.

Conclusion

The story of the events that led to the Treaty of Rome, and then to its reform in the 1980s, do not portray an inevitable and steady progression towards European union. Behind the rhetoric of inexorable progress towards the goal of 'an ever closer union', there lies a rather more complex reality. Thus, it might be more appropriate to liken the story of integration to a roller coaster ride, where the uphill and downhill gradients that determined the speed of the ride were the product of a multitude of factors.

The history of the formative decades of European integration was the product of an array of complex interactions. The world of ideas and the agitation of committed federalists had to contend with and were counterbalanced by the roles played by national leaders and governments and their assessment of how developments and proposals might impinge upon national self-interest. No matter how intricate the consequent dance, the steps and routines were influenced by and contained within parameters set by the broader flows of the international political and economic environment. And at the heart of this complex product lay the health of the relationship between France and West Germany. When all, or perhaps only most, of these factors were in positive conjunction with each other, progress could be rapid, significant, and impressive. When they were not, the process of integration was more likely merely to mark time.

QUESTIONS

1 Why did it prove difficult to establish a momentum for integration in the years immediately following the end of the Second World War?

2 How important was the development of international European organizations between 1945 and 1950 as a necessary condition for European integration?

3 What lessons for the future could be adduced from the strategy of sectoral integration in the 1950s?

4 To what extent does the failure of the European Defence Community (EDC) suggest that there are some areas of policy that are not amenable to integration?

5 How important were the crises of the 1960s in shaping the future development of the European Community (EC)?

6 How important was the establishment of the European Council as a mechanism for promoting further integration in the European Community (EC)?

7 To what extent was a collaboration between France and the Federal Republic of Germany necessary for a process of integration to begin?

8 To what extent has the international political and economic environment stimulated or hindered processes of integration?

GUIDE TO FURTHER READING

Arter, D., *The Politics of European Integration in the Twentieth Century* (Aldershot: Dartmouth, 1993). A broad historical survey which also considers developments in Eastern Europe.

Burgess, M., *Federalism and European Union: The Building of Europe, 1945–2000* (London: Routledge, 2000). A detailed revisionist history of the development of integration which highlights the central role of federalist ideas and influences.

Duignan, P., and Gann, L. H., *The United States and the New Europe 1945–1993* (Oxford: Blackwell, 1994). A general survey which examines European developments from an American strategic and policy perspective.

Fursdon, E., *The European Defence Community* (Basingstoke: Macmillan, 1980). A rigorous and detailed analysis of the EDC proposals, especially from a military perspective.

Milward, A. S., *The Reconstruction of Western Europe 1945–1951* (London: Methuen, 1984); and Milward, A. S. *The European Rescue of the Nation-State* (London: Routledge, 1992). Two controversial revisionist analyses of the first post-war decades which argue for the pivotal role of national governments and national self-interest as the driving force of integration.

Pryce, R. (ed.), *The Dynamics of European Union* (London: Croom Helm, 1987). A collection of useful analyses of specific episodes in the history of the EC when political union was on the agenda.

Stirk, P. M. and Willis, D. (eds), *Shaping Postwar Europe* (London: Pinter, 1991). A collection of useful chapters surveying the various arguments and different kinds of integration sought from 1945 up to the formation of the EC.

Urwin, D. W., *The Community of Europe* (London: Longman, 1995). A broad introductory survey of the post-1945 history of European co-operation and integration.

——, *A Political History of Western Europe since 1945* (London: Longman, 1997). A broad historical survey in which EC developments are reviewed in parallel with international issues and national politics.

WEB LINKS

www.let.leidenuniv.nl/history/rtg/res1/ Leiden University's History Department has an interesting site on the history of European integration.

http://europa.eu.int/abc/history/index-en.htm The EU's own website includes a good chronology of events in the history of the European integration process.

www.iue.it/LIB/SISSCO/UL/hist-eur-integration/Index.html The European University Institute in Florence has a European integration history project which includes some helpful links.

www.lib.berkeley.edu/GSSI/eu.html The University of California at Berkeley runs this general EU gateway, which includes links to historical documents and research papers on the history of the EC.

3 The single market

Michelle Egan

READER'S GUIDE

This chapter charts the evolution of the single market project, from its original conception in the 1950s to its realization in the 1990s. Although much works remains to be done in the forging of a single market in Europe, large steps were taken in this direction after 1985. This required new principles and approaches to economic or market integration at the time, without which the single market ambition would have remained little more than an ideal. The chapter begins within the Treaty of Rome, and focuses first on the association between a common (single) market and the harmonization of national laws at European level. It explores the role of the European Court in the development of new principles (or the 'new approach') and the importance of the spread of neo-liberal ideas to the success of plans in the 1980s for market integration. The chapter charts the rise of 'mutual recognition' as a supplement to harmonization, and to the single market programme. The chapter concludes with a brief look at how theories of European integration have explained the advent of the single market.

Introduction

This chapter discusses the creation of the single European market after 1985, and pays particular attention to the integration of national economies and the removal of **barriers to trade** that impede cross-border transactions. Charting the integration process from its beginnings in the 1950s, the chapter looks at the different strategies used to foster **market integration**, at the role of the European Court of Justice in tackling trade barriers, and at how private firms participated in these developments. A further section looks at the origins and content of the '1992' single market programme, and at the efforts to make the single market work effectively. The final section draws on traditional international relations theories of European integration (intergovernmentalism and neo-functionalism), as well as on more recent theories of regulation and governance in order to explain the dynamics of market integration.

Market integration in historical perspective

In the space of one year, from the Messina Conference in June 1955 to the Venice Conference in May 1956, the idea of economic unification among six West European states had taken root. Detailed objectives and timetables were hammered out throughout months of lengthy discussion. In what became known as the Spaak Report, after its principal author, the idea of an entirely new kind of inter-state economic relationship was taken as the basis for treaty negotiations (Bertrand 1956: 569).[1] The Spaak Report provided a blueprint for a single market in Western Europe, with three main elements: (a) the establishment of normal standards of competition through the elimination of protective barriers; (b) the curtailing of state intervention and monopolistic conditions; and (c) measures to prevent distortions of competition, including the possible harmonization of legislation at European level. The economic intent of such proposals dovetailed with the **federalist** agenda (Laurent 1970; see also Chapter 5). Yet turning the single market idea into a political reality has been extremely contentious and protracted.

The Treaty of Rome (1957) follows the Spaak Report in many respects. Its immediate objectives were to establish a **common market** by promoting and co-ordinating economic activities, ensuring stability and economic development, and raising standards of living. At the core of the proposed European common market was the creation of a **customs union** (see Box 3.1). This meant that member states would not only abolish all their customs duties on mutual trade, but also apply a uniform tariff on trade with non-EC countries. The other measures proposed to promote internal trade liberalization, including free movement of labour,

Box 3.1 **The facts**

Stages in economic integration

- *Free Trade Area*—reduces tariffs to zero between members.
- *Customs Union*—reduces tariffs to zero between members and establishes a common external tariff.
- *Single Market*—establishes a free flow of factors of production (labour and capital, as well as goods and services).
- *Economic Union*—involves an agreement to harmonize economic policies.

services, and capital, and a limited number of sectoral policies (agriculture, transport, and competition), were to be regulated and managed at the European level.

The transformation of the Community into a common market was to take place over a period of 12 to 15 years. It began with efforts to create a single market by addressing traditional tariffs, starting with the elimination of customs duties and quantitative restrictions in 1958, and by introducing a **common external tariff** in 1968. Internal tariff reductions were also frequently extended to third countries (that is, non-member states). This limited the discriminatory effects of the customs union to non-members, which was politically important in the formative period of the EC (Egan 2001: 41).

Membership of the European Community meant more than simply a customs union, however. There was also a commitment to 'free movement'. The treaty established the 'four freedoms'—the free movement of goods, services, capital, and labour, as central features of the single market. However, the requirements for each freedom varied according to the political exigencies at the time the treaty was drafted. The removal of trade barriers for *goods* focused on the removal of tariffs and quantitative restrictions, and then on the removal of **non-tariff barriers**. This meant dismantling quotas, subsidies, and voluntary export restraints, and measures such as national product regulations and standards, public purchasing, and licensing practices which sometimes reflected legitimate public policy concerns, but were often a thinly disguised form of protectionism designed to suppress foreign competition (Egan 2001: 42). For the free movement of *capital*, the goal was freedom of investment to enable capital to go where it would be most productive. Yet vivid memories of currency speculation in the interwar period meant that liberalization was subject to particular conditions or 'safeguard clauses', frequently used during recessions. With regard to free movement of *services*, it meant the freedom of establishment for industrial and commercial activity, that is, the right to set up in business anywhere in the Community. However, the treaty provisions on services contained virtually no detail on what should be liberalized (Pelkmans 1997). For *labour*, the

provisions for free movement meant the abolition of restrictions on labour mobility, allowing workers to get jobs anywhere in the EC.

National governments were receptive to early efforts to eliminate trade barriers and create a customs union because they were able to use social policies to compensate for the increased competition stemming from market integration. Favourable starting conditions for the European trade liberalization effort were thus due to the fact that it occurred against the backdrop of the mixed economy and welfare state, which were central components of the post-war settlement (Tsoukalis 1997). Yet even with these national policies, it was still felt politically necessary to provide some sort of financial aid at the European level to ease the effects of competition through basic investment in underdeveloped regions, suppression of large-scale unemployment, and the co-ordination of economic policies (see Spaak 1956; Bertrand 1956).

But while the Community experienced substantial economic growth and increased trade among member states, the transition to a common market did not remove all obstacles to the expansion of trade. The prevalence of domestic barriers to trade and the pervasive role of nation states as regulators of economic activity across all four freedoms signalled the enormity of the task (Tsoukalis 1997: 78). A major characteristic of Western Europe has been its historical and national variation in areas such as industrial relations, social welfare, and financial systems (Zysman 1994; Berger and Dore 1996; Rhodes and van Apeldoorn 1998). There are systematic differences in how national economies are organized, and member states have chosen ways of regulating production, investment, and exchange that constitute different varieties of capitalism (Hall and Soskice 2001: 15). Thus, efforts to create a single market in Europe have sought to unify disparate interests and market ideologies, and the process of market integration has often been deeply contested. The clash between **laissez-faire** and **interventionist** ideologies began in the earliest years of the European Community. The implied commitment to a free market economy, stressing the virtues of competition and greater efficiencies through specialization and economies of scale, was balanced by a

Box 3.2 **Core ideas**
The characteristics of capitalism

Neo-liberalism

- Market liberalization: reducing red tape; reducing government rules; freer markets; removing restrictions to trade; providing a regulatory climate attractive to capital.

- A laissez-faire approach: a hands-off approach by government.

- Regulatory competition among member states: competition among different national regulatory policies rather than the harmonization of policies.

- The rejection of greater regulatory powers for democratic institutions at European level; the insulation of the market from political interference; the retention of political authority at national level.

- Supporters include multinational companies, industry associations, financial institutions, free market think-tanks, and pro-business groups within German CDU-CSU and FDP, the British Conservative Party, and other conservative parties across Europe.

Regulated capitalism

- Market intervention: government intervention in market.

- Social market economy/social solidarity: welfare state; distributive politics, emphasis on equity.

- Social dialogue and social partnership between producers and labour

- Increased capacity at the European level to regulate the market by upgrading the European Parliament, promoting the mobilization of particular social groups, and reforming institutions to make legislation easier to agree through the use of qualified majority voting.

- Supporters include Jacques Delors, Social Democrat-Christian Democrat parties, especially German, Austrian, Italian, and Spanish Social Democrats.

Source: Adapted from Hooghe and Marks (1997).

---

widespread acceptance of *dirigisme* and intervention by state agencies and nationalized monopolies. More recently, this tension has been further refined as a distinction between 'regulated capitalism' and 'neo-liberalism' (Hooghe and Marks 1997; see Box 3.2). Different and sometimes competing strategies contributed to the fragmentation of the European market, preventing new firms from entering the market and taking advantage of new commercial opportunities. How, then, did the Community tackle such deep-seated differences in rules, standards, and practices as it sought to create a single European market?

Key points

- The objective of creating a single European market can be traced to the Spaak Report of 1956 and the Treaty of Rome, which was agreed the following year.

- The aim of the Treaty was to liberalize trade by dismantling barriers to trade among the six members of the Community.

- Difficulties arose as a consequence of the variety of economic interests and ideologies across Western Europe.

Harmonization: The politics of intervention

In order to tackle those domestic regulations that thwarted the creation of a common or single market, the European Community promoted a policy of harmonization (or standardization) that was to provide a lightning rod for criticisms of the integration process (see Box 3.3). The harmonization of policies was a means of reconciling differences in national regulatory practices and creating common rules (Cosgrove Twitchett 1981). It covered areas such as food standards, industrial property rights, public procurement, technical or administrative barriers to trade, industrial safety and heath regulations, and rules governing unfair competition (von der Groeben 1985). Though the Commission outlined a General Programme for the elimination of technical barriers to trade in 1969, and established an ambitious timetable, progress was minimal. Moreover, revisions to the General Programme in 1973 to take account of the concerns of the three new states joining the Community at that time (Denmark, Ireland, the UK) led to the missing of many deadlines.

This complex and highly technical harmonization programme also had limited political appeal. Public opposition mounted over efforts to regulate what many felt were long-standing national customs, traditions, and practices (Dashwood 1983; see Box 3.3). After years of fruitless arguments about harmonizing noise limits on lawnmowers, the composition of bread and beer, and tractor rear-view mirrors, nothing much had been achieved. Although the Commission repeatedly drew attention to the benefits of harmonization in creating a large 'barrier-free' single market, this was met with criticisms from member states that it was over-zealous, and 'pursuing of harmonization for harmonization's sake.' As a result, only 270 directives or laws were harmonized between 1969 and 1985 (Schreiber 1991).

However, the reasons for such limited results stem from a number of factors. First and foremost, the decision rule of **unanimity** on single market issues made it extremely difficult to get agreement amongst member states, and allowed individual governments to exercise their veto on specific legislative proposals. Second, harmonization was a complex technical process, and efforts to address non-tariff barriers were hampered by rapid changes in production and technology that often made agreements obsolete by the time they were adopted. The relative lack of political interest in the process of harmonization was understandable, as there was little to be gained by explaining the importance of technical issues to the wider public (Puchala 1971). Moreover, the

Box 3.3 **Case study**
The politics of harmonization

The Dutch spread jam on their bread for breakfast. They like it smooth and sugary. Most French people would not touch smooth jam with a barge pole, much less a butter knife. They commonly eat jam straight from the jar with a spoon. Negotiations meant getting the Dutch who wanted more sugar in their jam and the French who wanted more fruit to compromise. Just as that happened Britain, the largest jam consumer, joined the EC, and a further problem emerged: marmalade. It seems that the low-quality jam in much of Europe was called marmalade,

a confusion Britons refused to tolerate. In the end, after further negotiations, the terminology changed and low-grade jam simply became jam. After two decades of haggling, the European Commission unveiled a jam standard in 1979 only to find the French still unwilling to accept the resulting compromise. By 1984, everyone was on board, and yet it did not escape the attention of European officials that it had taken 25 years to decide on jam, and it could take seemingly endless years of negotiations for the many thousands of other products involved in cross-border trade in Europe.

Source: Adapted from Egan (2001).

harmonization approach reflected an interventionist mode of market integration that was increasingly viewed as outmoded, given changes in economic production in favour of greater flexibility. The inappropriateness of harmonization in addressing barriers to trade reflected a *regulatory mismatch* where the instruments chosen were ill-suited to the problem (Breyer 1982). A more appropriate solution was needed to realize the single market.

Thus from 1973, the Commission began to introduce a more flexible regulatory strategy, using what was called a 'reference to standards' approach as an alternative to harmonization. This was to prove an important step in finding new ways to address the proliferation of non-tariff barriers created by divergent national standards and regulations. This new strategy provided an opportunity for the European Commission to set out broad regulatory guidelines, leaving the private sector or non-governmental bodies to provide the necessary standards. This was a substantial change from the more detailed and government-driven process of harmonization. Choosing the European standards bodies, two relatively obscure private entities known as CEN and CENELEC, as the principal recognized entities to draft the necessary rules for

market access, the European Commission shifted more responsibility and delegated more tasks to the private sector. While CEN and CENELEC brought together firms and trade associations, along with a limited number of consumer groups and trade unions, this strategy met with political opposition.

Key points

- Harmonization was the main strategy used to integrate national markets in the 1960s and 1970s. This meant agreeing upon a common set of European rules and standards.

- Harmonization achieved limited success due to a number of factors, including: unanimous decision making; rising protectionism; the sheer number of non-tariff barriers; and a lack of political will.

- Pressures for regulatory reform to replace harmonization resulted in a 'reference to standards' approach in which the European Commission used the private sector to supply rules and standards for market access.

The free trade umpire: The European Court of Justice and judicial activism

The problems associated with addressing trade restrictions through harmonization did not go unnoticed by the European Court of Justice (ECJ), which has often used its judicial power for the purposes of fostering an integrated economy (see Chapter 12). Indeed, a large measure of the credit for creating a single market belongs to the judicial activism of the ECJ. Confronted by restrictions on their ability to operate across national borders, firms began to seek redress through the Community legal system. The Court was asked to determine whether the restrictions on imports imposed by member states were legitimate under the treaty. Examples of member states' restrictions included Italy's pro-

hibition on the sale of pasta not made with durum wheat, Germany's 'beer purity' regulations prohibiting the sale of any product as 'beer' that was not brewed with specific ingredients, and Belgian regulations that required margarine only to be sold in cube shaped containers to prevent confusion with butter which was sold in round shaped containers. As many of its decisions illustrate, the Court had the task of reconciling the demands of market integration with the pursuit of legitimate regulatory objectives and policy goals advanced by member states.

Several landmark cases limited the scope and applicability of national legislation. One of the most important in this regard came in the *Dassonville* case in 1974. Dassonville imported whisky into Belgium purchased from a French supplier. They were prosecuted by Belgian authorities for violating national customs rules that prohibited importation from a third country without the correct documentation. Dassonville argued that the whisky had entered the French market legally, that it must therefore be allowed to circulate freely, and that restrictions on imports within the EC were illegal. In a sweeping judgment, the Court argued that 'all trading rules that hinder trade, whether directly or indirectly, actually or potentially, were inadmissible'. National measures that negatively impact upon trade were therefore prohibited (Stone Sweet and Caporaso 1998: 118). This was softened by the recognition that reasonable regulations made by member states for legitimate public interests such as health, safety, and environment policies were acceptable if there were no European rules in place. The judgment was predicated on the belief that the European Commission should adopt harmonized standards to allow free movement across markets, while at the same time giving the ECJ the opportunity to monitor member states' behaviour and scrutinize permissible exceptions.

In what is probably its best known case, *Cassis de Dijon*, the Court, in 1979, ruled on a German ban on the sale of a French blackcurrant liqueur because it did not conform to German standards in terms of alcoholic content (see Egan 2001: 95). The Court rejected German arguments that Cassis, with its lower alcoholic content, posed health risks, but noted that the protection of the consumer could be aided by the labelling of alcoholic content. Most importantly, it clearly defined what national measures were deemed permissible. The most cited part of the ruling suggested that 'there was no valid reason why products produced and marketed in one member state could not be introduced into another member state'. The notion of equivalence of national regulations, which this ruling introduced,

opened up the possibility that harmonization would not always be necessary for the construction of a single market. This was the crucial step in launching a new regulatory strategy, **mutual recognition**, which would make for an easier circulation of trade and commerce in the Community.

Mutual recognition implies that it is only in areas that are not mutually equivalent that member states can invoke national restrictions, practices, and traditions, and restrict free trade in the Community. The Court argued that derogations from (or exceptions to) the free trade rule for the purposes of public health, fair competition, and consumer protection were possible, but that they had to be based upon reasonable grounds. Governments, whether national, local, or subnational, must demonstrate that any measure restricting trade was not simply disguised protectionism.

Anxious to safeguard the Community-wide market, the Court has continued to determine on a case-by-case basis whether specific laws are valid under the Treaty. However, faced with a growing number of cases, the Court in the *Keck* case (1993) reduced the scope of judicial scrutiny where cases applied to all traders operating in specific national territory, under certain conditions. Thus, the Court would not examine issues such as Sunday trading, mandatory closing hours, or other issues that had a limited effect on cross-border trade and that reflected national moral, social, and cultural norms.

Key points

- Legal rulings by the ECJ in cases such as *Dassonville* and *Cassis de Dijon* have played a key role in reinvigorating the single market idea.

- Mutual recognition is now a key concept in trade liberalization. Where there is a prior degree of regulatory convergence across member states, policies no longer have to be harmonized.

Market making: The politics of neo-liberalism

Throughout the 1970s and early 1980s, member states' efforts to maintain import restrictions and discriminatory trade practices thwarted efforts to create a single market. Growing recognition of a competitiveness gap *vis-à-vis* the United States and Japan, on the one hand, and newly industrializing countries, on the other, led to strenuous efforts to maintain overall levels of market activity and provide conditions for viable markets (Pelkmans and Winters 1988: 6). However, while past economic policies had succeeded in promoting national economic growth, the tools of national politics were no longer able to cope with changes in the international economy. **Neo-corporatist** class compromises and consensual incomes policies, which underpinned **Keynesian** economic policy, were under immense pressure.[2] As trade deficits soared, attention focused on the strengthening of European strategies in areas such as research and development, public purchasing, and technical standards, as a way to improve the environment in which companies operated.

Assessments were so bleak that, on the twenty-fifth anniversary of the Treaty of Rome, *The Economist* put a tombstone on its cover to proclaim the EC as good as dead and buried. These assessments contributed to a growing consensus among business and political leaders that a collective strategy was needed to stop an 'escalating trade war' (*Financial Times*, 25 July 1980). Business interests were promoted through the establishment of a European Roundtable of Industrialists to provide momentum and pressure for a single market. Through the European Roundtable, heads of European companies put forward numerous proposals to improve European competitiveness. Their influence on the European agenda was accomplished largely through a campaign of proactive lobbying, ambitious proposals, and visible engagement in the policy process (*Financial Times*, 20 March 2001). Further pressure came from the American Chamber of Commerce (AMCHAM), which gathered widespread complaints from American companies about industry standards, border formalities, and export licences, identifying France and Italy as the worst offenders. The European Confederation of National Employers' Associations (UNICE) also articulated the concerns of many trade associations about the effects of non-tariff barriers.

This lobbying was welcomed by the European Commission, which throughout the early 1980s continued to put pressure on member states with a stream of studies, resolutions, and declarations about making the single market a reality. Renewed interest was reflected in mammoth sessions of the Council of Ministers in February and March 1983 devoted to the single market, and in the creation of a new Internal Market Council. Responding to this groundswell, European Commissioner Narjes, then responsible for the internal market portfolio, forwarded a list of the most problematic barriers existing in the member states. More than 300 national measures were viewed as causing significant problems in preventing cross-border trade (*Financial Times*, 23 September 1980; *The Economist*, 22 October 1983).

Governments, well aware that their efforts to create national champions, protect labour markets, and maintain public spending were not stemming rising trade imbalances and deficits, sought new solutions. Efforts to contain import competition and stabilize industries had failed. Disenchantment with Keynesian tax-and-spend policies led to a shift towards market liberalization. This did not mean a common consensus around **neo-liberalism**, however, since different conceptions of the operation of the market economy and the agenda for European integration continued. The British and French positions at the time show the scope of this debate. While the British government advocated a genuine common market in goods and services, and promoted a radically neo-liberal agenda, the French government argued for the creation of a common industrial space in which trade barriers could be reduced internally, provided that external trade *protection* would compensate for increased internal competition (Pearce and Sutton 1983).

Though some political opposition to the single

market continued, major steps taken at the European Council meeting in Fontainebleau in 1984 broke the immobility that had stifled progress. Key was the agreement of long-running disputes over Britain's contribution to the Community budget and the pending Iberian enlargement. The meeting also established the Dooge Committee to focus on the reform of the institutional and decision-making structure of the Community. Further agreement at the 1985 **intergovernmental conference** in Milan to 'study the institutional conditions under which the internal market could be achieved within a time limit' proved critical for the market integration process. This built on several earlier developments. In 1983, the Spinelli Report had drawn attention to the need to link national regulations and institutional reform. And in 1984 the European Parliament's draft Treaty on European Union also focused on the need for institutional reform, and more particularly on increased parliamentary powers and the greater use of qualified majority voting in the Council. On the basis of these and other ideas presented at the intergovernmental conference, the proposed treaty reforms were brought together under what was to become the Single European Act (SEA) (see Box 3.4).

Historically significant as the first substantial treaty reform undertaken by member states, the SEA endorsed the single market and altered the decision-making rules for single market measures (with exceptions such as taxation and rights of workers) from **unanimity** to **qualified majority voting** (QMV). This linked institutional reforms to substantive goals, and made it more difficult for recalcitrant member states to simply veto legislative action, as had been the case under harmonization. The SEA also strengthened the powers of the European Parliament with respect to single market measures by allowing for the rejection or amendment of proposals under the **co-operation procedure**.

Key points

- The tools of domestic policy no longer seemed able to solve the problems of international competitiveness for the EC's member states.

- Business supported the need to enhance European competitiveness by improving market access, reducing border restrictions, and attracting investment, and engaged in extensive lobbying for single market.

Box 3.4 **The facts**
The Single European Act

The Single European Act of 1986 was the first real revision to the Treaty of Rome of 1957. It served largely as a vehicle for the single market programme, but was also important in setting the scene for the institutional and policy reforms of the 1990s. The SEA confirmed the use of qualified majority voting in areas related to the single market, in order to allow for the speeding up of decision making (and to prevent a small number of states from vetoing the programme). It introduced a new decision-making procedure—co-operation—which would give the European Parliament a second reading of draft European legislation (and more influence over the legislative process as a consequence). It introduced EC action into new policy areas, and extended the Community's role in others.

Policies covered included environment policy, science and technology policy, and economic and social cohesion. It also laid the groundwork for Economic and Monetary Union (EMU) and for the Common Foreign and Security Policy (CFSP) (that would be agreed at a later stage at Maastricht), and stated that its goal was ultimately that of European union.

The SEA was signed in early 1986 (after an intergovernmental conference starting in September 1985). Ratification of the Treaty in national parliaments took longer than expected, with problems for the Danes and the Irish in particular. However, the SEA could finally come into effect on 1 July 1987, after an Irish referendum on 26 May voted in its favour.

The 1992 Programme: A blueprint for action

By early 1985 the stage was set for an ambitious initiative. The newly appointed Commission president, Jacques Delors, and his Commissioner responsible for the Internal Market, Lord Cockfield, a British neo-liberal jurist and former Secretary of State for Industry, put together a package of proposals that aimed to achieve completion of the single market by 1992. The 300 proposals became a Commission White Paper entitled 'Completing the Internal Market'. These were subsequently amended, with some measures discreetly withdrawn when they failed to win support and others overtaken by new or amended proposals. The final 282 legislative proposals became known as the '1992 Programme'.

The White Paper contained a comprehensive assessment of the remaining obstacles to trade, grouped together in three major categories: physical, technical, and fiscal barriers (see Box 3.5). Lord Cockfield used this very simple and deceptive categorization to introduce a series of measures across goods, services, capital, and labour markets to improve market access, prevent distortions to competition and restrictive business practices, and co-ordinate policies to prevent market failure. The European Commission bolstered support for its initiative by commissioning a series of economic evaluations on the 'costs of non-Europe', popularly known as the Cecchini Report (1988) after its lead author. Although much of this report is now

---

Box 3.5 **The facts**
The single market programme

The single market programme involved the removal of three kinds of trade barriers: physical barriers to trade; technical barriers to trade; fiscal barriers to trade.

Physical barriers: the removal of internal barriers and frontiers for goods and people. This involved:

- The simplification of border controls (including the creation of a single administrative document for border entry).

Technical barriers: it was here that the bulk of proposals fell. It involved:

- Co-ordinating product standards, testing, and certification (under the 'new approach').

- The liberalization of public procurement (with open tender and cross-border bids).

- The free movement of capital (by reducing capital exchange controls).

- The free movement of services (including the opening up of financial services, such as banking and insurance, to operate under home country control or supervision).

- The liberalization of the transport sector (rail, road, and air; establishing rights of 'cabotage' which allows free movement between any two cities within a Community member state; the liberalization of markets and removal of monopolies, state subsidies, and quotas or market-sharing arrangements).

- The free movement of labour and the mutual recognition of professional qualifications (including non-discrimination in employment)

- The Europeanization of company law, intellectual property, and company taxation (including the freedom of establishment for enterprises; the agreement of a European Company Statute; new rules of trade marks, copyright, and legal protection).

Fiscal barriers: the harmonization of divergent tax regimes. This includes:

- Harmonization of value added or sales tax; the agreement of standard rates and special exemptions from sales tax or VAT; it also covers other forms of indirect taxes with the aim of reducing restrictions on cross-border sales (especially 'duty free').

considered excessively optimistic, the estimated trade and welfare gains from removing barriers to trade were compelling. Not only would there be lower trade costs and greater economies of scale, as firms exploited increased opportunities, but it was expected that there would also be greater production efficiency achieved through market enlargement, intensified competition, and industrial restructuring.

At the core of the single market project was the concept of mutual recognition, the consequence of which would be increased competition not only among firms within the EU, but also among different national regulatory systems (see Sun and Pelkmans 1995). Governments sponsoring regulations that restricted market access would be under pressure since firms from other EU member states would not be required to abide by them, putting their own local firms at a disadvantage. Given the diversity of national regulatory standards, however, the European Commission would continue to promote harmonization where mutual recognition was not applicable, and in areas where substantial progress on harmonization had already been made, such as pharmaceuticals, cars, and food standards.

The European Commission sought to apply this innovative strategy to the service sector as well. The concept of 'home country control' was to allow banks, insurance companies, and dealers in securities to offer the same services elsewhere in the Community that they offered at home. A single licence would operate, so that these sectors would be licensed, regulated, and supervised for the most part by their home country.

A policy framework for action on the legislative proposals contained in the White Paper was also required. Building on the legal decisions outlining the doctrine of mutual recognition as a broad free trade principle, and reference to standards as a more flexible regulatory strategy, the Commission drafted a proposal on harmonization and standards in 1985 (Pelkmans 1987). This 'new approach', as it was called, received overwhelming support from member states and reflected a critical effort to address barriers to trade by sharing regulatory functions between the public and private sector. Where possible, there was to be mutual recognition of regulations and standards. In other cases,

Community-level regulation was to be restricted to essential health and safety requirements, mandatory for all member states. The means to comply with these requirements were to be established by the European standards bodies, CEN, CENELEC, and the newly created European Telecommunications Standards Institute (ETSI) (Egan 2001). The increased use of private sector resources has however been criticized by consumer groups who felt that the scales of consultation were tipped too heavily against them, in favour of industry.

Despite being a rather dry bureaucratic document, the White Paper gained widespread political support by providing a target date for the completion of the single market. Though the single market 'is not something you can fall in love with', as Jacques Delors once stated, the White Paper constitutes a radical break with Europe's interventionist tradition, emphasizing the merits of economic liberalism. Tapping into these sentiments, the White Paper included a diversity of measures across the four freedoms, such as the abolition of frontier controls, mutual recognition of goods and services, rights of establishment for professional workers, and the abolition of capital-exchange controls. While the bulk of the measures outlined in the White Paper focused on market access or **negative integration** measures, such as removing technical barriers to trade, dismantling quotas, and withdrawing licensing restrictions for cross-border banking and insurance services, they were complemented by a series of market-correcting or **positive integration** measures such as health and safety standards, rules for trade marks and deposit insurance, and solvency ratios for banks and insurance.

While most attention focused on the political deadline of 1992, the overall 'single market scorecard' revealed several problematic areas. Continued obstacles to cross-border movements in food, veterinary, and phytosanitary standards were indications of the complexities involved. The resistance to tax harmonization was more predictable, since the issue of distortions created by differential tax regimes has been problematic since the early days of the common market. The White Paper also conspicuously avoided a number of issues including a strong social dimension, as well as other politically sensitive areas such as textiles, clothing, and taxation of savings and investment income, despite the evident distortions and restrictions in these areas.

Completion of the single market meant tackling politically difficult dossiers and ensuring that the legislation was put into effect in all member states; otherwise the confidence of consumers and producers in realizing economic benefits would be undermined. Nationally important sectors such as utilities (gas and postal services, for example) were given special exemptions in the single market on the basis of social and economic arguments that 'universal services' must be provided, resulting in natural monopolies and limited competition. With rapid liberalization and technological pressures that enabled new entrants to bypass public networks, however, the traditional economic rationale for such

dirigiste policies was being undermined. Pressure to open up telecommunications, electricity, and gas markets resulted in the Commission forcing liberalization of these basic services through its competition powers. Initial resistance in France, Germany, and Austria can be attributed to concerns about the effects of greater competition on employment in these heavily protected sectors.

Key points

- The 1992 Programme provided a clear outline for a legislative agenda laid down in the White Paper on the internal market.

- The project was sold as a package of measures to liberalize trade and generated widespread interest among interest groups and national politicians.

Maintaining and correcting the market

The single market programme turned out to be about much more than free movement and the removal of trade barriers among the Community's member states. As we shall see, it also involved a number of interventionist policy measures, and institutional steps to ensure the implementation and effectiveness of the new legislation.

Market correcting: The politics of regulated capitalism

The renewed emphasis on market integration through the '1992 Programme' also brought pressures for ancillary policies along social democratic lines (Scharpf 1999). Dealing with the pressures from increased competition led to policy proposals reflecting the ideological cleavages that had always underpinned the Community project. Fearful that excessive competition would increase social conflict, proponents of a regulated capitalism approach (see Box 3.2) proposed a variety of inclusive mechanisms to generate broad-based support for the single market. These included structural policy for poorer regions to promote economic and social cohesion,

consumer and environmental protection, and rural development (see Chapters 16 and 18). Labour representatives and some employers also sought to address the impact of market integration through the creation of an ongoing social dialogue (see Chapter 17). These initiatives were narrower than the traditional social market philosophy and distinct from *dirigiste* policies of state ownership and control, but they complemented efforts to shift regulation to the European level. The effort to promote a European social dimension also acknowledged that the domestic political pressures on national welfare states meant that they could no longer compensate for the effects of integration as they had done in the past (Scharpf 1999).

The goal of regulating markets, redistributing resources, and shaping partnership among public and private actors led advocates of regulated capitalism to propose provisions for transport and communications infrastructure, information networks, workforce skills, and research and development (Hooghe and Marks 1997). The progressive expansion of activities at the European level brought into focus two long-standing opposing views about the economic role of governments. Despite the neo-liberal rhetoric, some have argued that the single market has progressively increased the level of statism or interventionism in Western Europe (Messerlin 2001). The economic consensus in favour of market forces and neo-liberalism under the single market programme in the 1980s has been offset by increased intervention or regulated capitalism in labour markets (on issues such as the minimum wage and working time), and new provisions for culture (broadcast quotas), industry (shipbuilding, textiles, and clothing), and technology (conservation and new energy resources, biotechnology, and broad-band networks) in the 1990s. The market-orientated policies underpinning the single market, such as the elimination of trade barriers, the establishment of the four freedoms, and the rules governing competition policy, have been balanced by a number of market-interventionist measures.

Market maintenance: The politics of efficiency and effectiveness

The credibility of the single market process is dependent on its living up to the spirit, as well as the letter, of a 'barrier free' market (*The Economist*, 26 September 1992). Although the single market was conceptualized as an economic project, its institutional and political framework has become increasingly important. Facing the challenges of constructing a single market, the EU was forced to tackle not only the design and passage of legislation but also its implementation and evaluation (Radaelli 1998). Since the Community level of governance does not derive its authority and legitimacy from direct electoral support, the effectiveness and credibility of the single market depends on a variety of factors including: (a) support from within member states; (b) internal management and co-ordination within the Community institutions; and (c) industrial strategy and behaviour (Wallace and Young 2000). This has meant that market management issues are increasingly salient, and efforts to make the single market work in practice have risen on the political agenda (Metcalfe 1996).

The rather anticlimactic arrival of the single market

on 1 January 1993 did not signal an end to the single market project, however. The poor performance of member states in terms of implementation has been considered a particularly crucial shortcoming. As the adoption of legislation requires implementation at the national level, the success of the single market project depends on the transposition of directives into national law (see Chapter 22). In some instances, poor preparation and lack of commitment by national administrations and legislators have accounted for some of these problems. In other cases badly drafted rules that did not anticipate implementing difficulties were also to blame (Radaelli 1998). To tackle such problems, and to ensure that implementation problems did not cause further trade barriers, the European Commission produced the 1992 Sutherland Report on the internal market, which emphasized the need for administrative partnerships between the Commission and public administrations at the national level (European Commission 1992*a*).

Problems with the functioning of the single market led member states to back the Action Plan for the Single Market in June 1996. Under the guidance of the Internal Market Commissioner, Mario Monti, the Action Plan has sought to make rules more effective, has dealt with market distortions (in the fields of taxation and competition), has aimed to remove certain barriers and obstacles to market integration (as in the utilities sectors), and has tried to ensure an internal market that benefits all citizens of the Union (one based on consultation, dialogue, and representation). Emphasis has also been placed on the policing of the single market to ensure that common rules for industrial and consumer products were respected, and that the application of mutual recognition was correctly applied. Having established a clear deadline of January 1999 for implementing outstanding directives, the Action Plan also introduced a 'scoreboard', hoping to generate adverse publicity for those member states that were lagging behind (European Report, 28 November 1997).

The aim of improving the functioning of the single market has also resulted in an internal review and evaluation of the European Commission's own organizational structure and effectiveness (see Chapter 9). Responding to business criticisms about regulatory over-production has resulted in legislative codification and simplification of Community legislation through such measures as the SLIM programme (Simpler Legislation for the Internal Market). Other measures have included an annual business survey, questionnaires, and dialogues with business and citizens. These measures have also improved the visibility of the single market project, which became overshadowed by the negotiations on EMU. To further improve compliance, the Commission has actively pursued infringement proceedings (under Article 169 of the Treaty) whereby they formally notify member states of their legal obligations, and then proceed to take legal action if non-compliance continues to thwart the operation of the single market. Member states have also established compliance units and telephone 'hotlines' to assist business and consumers in overcoming any persistent difficulties they face.

As we have seen, the functioning of the single market also depends on the effective participation of the private sector. In many cases the negotiations within CEN, CENELEC, and ETSI have taken longer than anticipated, as they have struggled to produce the thousands of European standards needed to meet the regulatory requirements of the single market. The Commission has pressured the standards bodies to rectify what it perceives to be the lack of efficiency, accountability, and transparency in the standardization process. During the 1990s, internal reforms have increased their output and they have been warned that their work is under increased scrutiny in an environment of renewed political commitment to the single market. The understanding is that industry, if it wants harmonized standards, must provide sufficient resources to complete the task.

Although business was expected to benefit from greater market access, few assessments have focused on the impact of changing economic conditions upon industrial behaviour and strategy. While the growth of European mergers and acquisitions, joint ventures, and strategic alliances is testimony to strategic positioning among firms, companies, when polled, still believe they face serious obstacles that prevent them from realizing the full benefits of the single market. Divergent standards and tax issues topped their list, with the constant output of new national regulations also seen as a considerable constraint on the full implementation a Europe-wide strategy (European Commission 1997). The need to improve the functioning of both capital and product markets is also important, given the export to Central and Eastern Europe (CEE) of the single market as a model of liberalization, following the publication of a further White Paper in 1995 that formed the basis for CEE countries to align their policies and regulations with the single European market.

The perceived effectiveness and credibility of the market integration project has become an increasingly important issue. Even where there are well-defined legal and judicial mechanisms, attention must focus on mechanisms of enforcement and compliance or 'post decisional politics' (Puchala 1971). That being the case, this chapter has demonstrated that market building is an ongoing process, and work must continue after legislation has been signed into law to make sure single market policies operate successfully in practice.

Key points

- The market-orientated policies of the 1980s were balanced by a number of market-interventionist measures in the 1990s.

- The operation of the single market is under tremendous political scrutiny. Concerns have been expressed about the implementation of legislation by member states, lack of standards to meet regulatory requirements, and internal co-ordination and management within the institutions.

- Various initiatives have been introduced to police and enforce the single market in order to enhance its credibility.

Theorizing the single market

Though the single market process has had a long gestation, many studies focus primarily on the 1980s to explain the causes, consequences, and content of the single market programme. Some scholars highlight the economic factors driving the 1992 project, whereas others emphasize the political origins of the Single European Act to explain this resurgence of activity. These studies fall squarely within the major theoretical debates in the field of integration studies (see Chapters 5–8), and draw on different factors to explain the *relance européen* (the relaunch of the European project).

Intergovernmentalists (see Chapter 7) claim that the institutional dynamics that underpin the single market project were the result of a convergence of policy preferences in the early 1980s (Moravcsik 1991). Parties that advocated neo-liberal market reforms came to power in a number of states such as Britain, Denmark, and Belgium. Coupled with developments in France, where failed efforts to pursue a Keynesian fiscal policy to counter economic recession forced the post-1981 Socialist government to reverse its policies in 1983, the resulting Single European Act represented a familiar pattern of bargaining and negotiation between the UK, Germany, and France to reach a common solution. For intergovernmentalists, national interests and policies are thus expected to continue to constrain integrationist impulses. Garrett (1992) adds an important nuance to the intergovernmentalist position, arguing that in important areas of legal activity, the Court was constrained by member states' governments. According to Garrett, the Court anticipates reactions from member states, and serves their interests (especially the most powerful member states) in rendering its judgments.

By comparison, the neo-functionalist account stresses the importance of supranational actors in shaping the single market agenda. Sandholtz and Zysman (1989) stress the importance of the Commission as an innovative policy entrepreneur in shaping the European agenda, supported by big business interests seeking to reap the benefits of an enlarged market. Burley and Mattli (1993) add

to the neo-functionalist argument by claiming that Court rulings have resulted in interactions between national and European courts, creating a distinctive legal regime that shapes rules and procedures governing markets. When political attempts to create a common market stalled, the Court advanced its supranational authority over national courts, expanding its jurisdictional authority in order to make a pivotal contribution to the promotion of free trade (see Egan 2001; Shapiro 1992). Cameron (1992) seeks to blend these different theoretical perspectives by arguing that the 1992 initiative was the result of the complex interaction of different actors and institutions, simultaneously accelerating economic integration and supranational institution building, while also representing intergovernmental bargaining among states.

The lively debate on the politics of the single market has predominantly been tied to the mast of international relations. While international relations theories have focused on the impact of market integration on the member state's capacity to act, and the degree to which the emerging European political system has strengthened or weakened the state, or embedded it in a system of multi-level governance, an emphasis on state resources, power, and bargaining to understand the driving factors of economic integration remains the dominant approach. More recently, the single market process has been examined through the lens of comparative policy analysis. Empirical studies have shown that European policies are a patchwork of different policy styles, instruments, and institutional arrangements (Héritier 1996). One crucial element of this debate is the argument that the EU as a political system specializes in regulation (Majone 1996). With limited fiscal resources at its control, the EU has sought to expand its influence through the supply of regulations where the costs are borne by the firms and states responsible for complying with them. Demand for European regulations is the result of pressure from firms that prefer the certainty of a single European rule rather than 15 different national rules. Thus, the single market is an effort to reduce transaction costs and resolve problems of heterogeneity through collective action and co-ordination. Majone (1995) argues that such market preservation is best achieved by non-majoritarian institutions (such as courts or regulatory agencies) due to their insulation from political pressure. Given their technocratic approach, they can better achieve a credible commitment towards maintaining a single market than traditional political interests such as parties, legislatures, and interest groups.

Focusing on issues of governance, other scholars have stressed the impact of the single market on regions, sectors, and classes by looking at the relationship between economic development and democratic conditions, seeking to demonstrate that the single market may not be entirely benign in its consequences (Scharpf 1999; Hirst and Thompson 1996; Amin and Tomaney 1995). Across Europe, the uneven pattern of economic development, the different models of capitalism, and the effect of business and consumer behaviour and preferences serves to remind us that market integration has differential effects and outcomes on both political systems and policies.

Key points

- Two main approaches, intergovernmentalism and neo-functionalism, have been used to account for the resurgence of European integration in the mid-1980s.

- Other approaches have focused on the implications of the single market programme. Majone's regulatory approach focuses on the supply and demand factors driving economic integration, and the growth of non-majoritarian institutions that depoliticize decision making, reduce transaction costs, and promote efficient outcomes.

- Scharpf stresses the impact of shifting economic policies to the European level upon democratic legitimacy, and the limited role of national welfare and distributive policies to compensate for increased competition due to the retrenchment and pressure upon welfare states.

Conclusion

Though it is not yet complete, the single European market has achieved an impressive amount in a remarkably compressed period of time. Ranging across a number of policy areas, European efforts to remove obstacles and distortions in goods, services, capital, and labour have transformed the European economic landscape. Over the past four decades, the process of integrating divergent national markets, based on different models of capitalism, has meant balancing different ideological and economic perspectives. The pressures for neo-liberal market reforms, with their emphasis on liberalization and competition, have been offset by new demands for regulated capitalism, with their emphasis on social solidarity and economic intervention. The process has been shaped by a mix of regulatory styles, instruments, and philosophies that reflect the policy styles and traditions of different member states. Thus, various strategies and policies have been tried and tested to see how best to synthesize 15 different sets of rules, regulations, and practices into a workable functioning internal market. Each strategy seems to reflect the dominant mode of governance at the time. Efforts at harmonization in the 1950s and 1960s reflect the corresponding practices of *dirigisme* and interventionism, whereas later efforts at mutual recognition and standardization reflect the changing emphasis in the 1980s and 1990s towards the dynamics of regulatory competition and private sector governance.

The single market is one of the most noteworthy accomplishments of the European integration project. Yet we need to recognize that there is more to the functioning of the single market than the passage of legislation. The politics of bargaining and negotiation need to be balanced by the politics of rule enforcement and compliance (see Chapter 22). Understanding the single market requires more than just an analysis of its origins; it is also important to look at matters of implementation and effectiveness. This also requires us to link economic performance and political development to an understanding of how political processes and institutions evolve to support the growth of a single market and its ancillary policies. While no region in the world today comes as close as the European Union to a 'single market' within its territory, it is important to remember that those originally involved in the project believed that 'it is not just a movement for free trade between separate economies. It is a movement to fuse markets and economies into one'.[3]

QUESTIONS

1 What are the main barriers to trade in the EU?

2 What type of policy instruments has the EU used to integrate national markets?

3 How successful has the EU been in establishing a single market free of restrictions to trade and commerce?

4 What were the driving forces behind the 'relaunch' of the single market project in 1980s?

5 How have different theories and approaches been used to explain the single market programme?

6 What role has the ECJ played in addressing barriers to trade?

7 Explain the different types of regulatory strategy used to tackle barriers to trade in Europe. What accounts for their success or failure?

8 What are the main challenges faced by the EU in making the single market operate efficiently and effectively?

GUIDE TO FURTHER READING

Armstrong, K., and Bulmer, S., *The Governance of the Single European Market* (Manchester: Manchester University Press, 1997). A good, thorough analysis of the way in which the single market is governed in different sectors.

Camps, M., *The European Common Market and American Policy* (Princeton, NJ: Center for International Studies, 1956). A short and informative discussion of early developments in the common market. A useful appendix.

Egan, M., *Constructing a European Market. Standards, Regulation and Governance* (Oxford: Oxford University Press, 2001). This book provides an in-depth understanding of the regulatory strategies used to address barriers to trade and the role of the private sector in shaping those markets.

Moravcsik, A., *The Choice for Europe: Social Purpose and State Power from Messina to Maastricht* (Ithaca, NY: Cornell University Press, 1998). An important focus on the treaty changes from an intergovernmentalist perspective.

Pelkmans, J., and Winters, A., *Europe's Domestic Market* (Royal Institute for International Affairs: Chatham House, 1988). This study provides an early overview of the single market project, and remains a valuable reference tool.

Scharpf, F., *Governing in Europe* (Oxford: Oxford University Press, 1999). This book focuses on the governance of the single market drawing on rational choice and political economy. It is primarily concerned with the trade-off between democratic legitimacy and increased economic integration focusing on efficiency and competition.

Tsoukalis, L., *The New European Economy* (Oxford: Oxford University Press, 1997, 2nd edn). A nicely written assessment of the politics and economics of integration that links topics thematically rather than by sector/issue area.

WEB LINKS

www.eurunion.org/infores/standard.htm The official website of the European Union. Information and sources on standards, including details on the 'new approach'.

http://europa.eu.int/comm/internal_market/en/index_ob.htm The official website of the European Union on the single market. It includes an update on the single market and information on a variety of policy areas.

www.newapproach.org European standards activities under the 'new approach' directives representing the standardization organizations: CEN, CENELEC, and ETSI.

ENDNOTES

1. Paul-Henri Spaak, the Belgian foreign minister, is acknowledged in some European circles as the real father of the common market. He advocated a shift from preoccupation with political-military issues to novel interstate economic linkages within a joint market based along the lines of the American single market.

2. Corporatism is a pattern of political activity that allows government and interest groups (business and labour) to negotiate specific policies usually related to working conditions and employment as a means of diluting social tensions and satisfying the demands of interest groups. The early post-war years in Europe were characterized by acceptance of Keynesian ideas on the role of governments in managing the economy through manipulating both tax and expenditure (borrow and spend) to secure full employment.

3. Walter Hallstein, Speech at Harvard University, 22 May 1961.

4 Towards European union

David Phinnemore

READER'S GUIDE

The focus of this chapter is the emergence and development of the European Union (EU). Key issues include the significance for the idea of 'union' of the Treaty on European Union (1992), often known as the Maastricht Treaty, and of Economic and Monetary Union (EMU). The chapter underlines the extent to which the EU continues to be characterized as much by its differences as by uniformity. The chapter also examines the origins and impact of the Treaty of Amsterdam (1997) and the Treaty of Nice (2000), presenting their key reforms and assessing the extent to which they contribute to the idea of the EU as a 'union'. The chapter concludes by introducing the 'Future of Europe' debate launched in 2001, which should lead to a further reform of the EU.

Introduction

The underlying theme of this chapter is that the European Union (EU) is less than its title implies. This is obviously the case when one considers the use of the term 'European'. There are many different definitions of what 'European' means, not least in the geographical sense. And no matter which definition one adopts, there can be little doubt that the EU in 2003, with only 15 members, does not cover all European states. This is something that has been recognized, most obviously in the provisions of Article 49 of the Treaty on European Union (TEU),

which allows any 'European' state to seek membership of the EU.

This chapter is not, however, concerned with the question of the EU's membership and geographical coverage (for which see Chapter 14). Its focus is more on the extent to which the EU is a 'union', a question also raised in Chapter 5. For although it has long been the goal of the member states to create a European 'union', the extent to which they have achieved this is open to question. Indeed, whereas 'union' might conjure up ideas of coherence and

Box 4.1 **The facts**
From intergovernmental conference to treaty

The EU and the European Community (EC) were both established by treaties concluded between their original member states. If the member states wish to reform either the EU or the EC they need to amend its founding treaties. This is done via an intergovernmental conference (IGC) where the member states negotiate the amendments. Agreed amendments are then brought together in a treaty (for example, the Treaty of Amsterdam) which all member states must then sign and ratify. Ratification normally involves each member state's parliament approving the treaty by vote. In some member states, treaties are also submitted to the people for approval via a referendum.

uniformity, the EU today is characterized as much by variation and diversity. This is recognized not just by academics and other commentators, but also by the EU's institutions and its member states. Hence, voices are often heard calling for change. It is in part the desire to ensure that the EU behaves and acts as a 'union' that is behind the ongoing process of reform which has so dominated the EU's agenda since the mid-1980s. Indeed, since the TEU was agreed in December 1991, two intergovernmental conferences (IGCs) have been convened to reform the Union (see Box 4.1), with a third scheduled to begin its work in 2004.

What this chapter does, then, is discuss the structure of the EU and how this has been affected by certain key developments over the last decade. The chapter examines not only the origins of the EU, but also the background to and content of the Treaty of Amsterdam (1997) and the Treaty of Nice (2000). In between discussing how these treaties have changed the EU and impacted on the idea of 'union', consideration is given to the significance of the launch of economic and monetary union (EMU), a process which simultaneously promotes closer union and **differentiated integration** within the EU, thus suggesting that member states may pursue integration in different ways or at different speeds in the future (see Chapter 24). The chapter concludes by introducing the issues that the EU and its member states are addressing as part of the 'Future of Europe' debate launched by the Laeken European Council in December 2001. Before then, however, the EU as a 'union' and the Treaty on European Union (TEU) need to be considered.

The European Union as a European union

The idea of creating a European union has long been a goal of those European states committed to European integration. This was made clear in the 1950s when the six original members of the European Economic Community (EEC) expressed their determination in the first recital of the preamble to the Treaty of Rome 'to lay the foundations of an ever closer union among the peoples'. They reaffirmed this in 1972 when they expressed their intention to convert 'their entire relationship into a European Union before the end of the decade'. In joining them as members of the European Community (EC), new members from 1973 (Denmark, Ireland, and the United Kingdom), 1981 (Greece), and 1986 (Portugal and Spain) also signed up to this goal. And reaffirmation of the commitment was central to the Solemn Declaration on European Union proclaimed at the Stuttgart European Council in June 1983 and, in part, inspired the Single European Act (SEA) of 1986 (see Chapter 3: Box 3.5). This, as its preamble noted, was adopted in response to the member states' desire 'to transform' their relations into 'a European Union', to 'implement' this European Union, and invest it 'with the necessary means of action'. However, at this point no European Union was created (see Box 4.2).

The establishment of the EU was not, however, far off. With the EC having entered a period of renewed dynamism following the launch of the Single Market Programme and the entry into force of the SEA in the second half of the 1980s (see Chapter 3: 36), further steps towards European union were being urged by senior European leaders such as the French president, François Mitterrand, and the German chancellor, Helmut Kohl, as well as by the Commission president, Jacques Delors. All this, plus the collapse of communist regimes in Central and Eastern Europe in 1989 and the end of the Cold War, led in 1990 to the launch of two intergovernmental conferences (IGCs), one on economic and monetary union and a second on political union. Out of these emerged the Treaty on European Union (TEU).

Agreed at Maastricht in December 1991 and entering into force on 1 November 1993, the Treaty on European Union (TEU)—often referred to as the 'Maastricht Treaty'—was designed to expand the scope of European integration, reform the EC's institutions and decision-making procedures, and bring about economic and monetary union (EMU) (see Box 4.3). Moreover, the goal of ever closer union was to be furthered by bringing together the EC, the European Coal and Steel Community (ECSC), and the European Atomic Energy Community (EURATOM or EAEC) as part of an entirely new entity, to be called the European Union. This European Union was to be more than simply the existing supranational Communities. Established in 1993, the EU was to comprise not just the **supranational** activities of the Communities, but also **intergovernmental co-operation** in the areas of, on the one hand, foreign and security policy, and on the other hand, police and judicial co-operation in criminal matters. Box 4.4 sets outs the key events in the period from 1986 to 2004.

This mix of supranational integration and intergovernmental co-operation meant that in many respects the new EU fell short of what might normally be considered a 'union'. Such a political and legal entity might be expected to have a coherent and uniform structure. In the case of the EU, and reflecting the fact that it was very much the product of bargaining between its member states, uniformity

Box 4.2 **Core ideas**

European Union to European union

Note the use of the word 'union' in these two treaty clauses:

> DETERMINED to lay the foundations of an ever closer union among the peoples of Europe (*Preamble, Treaty of Rome*, 1957).

> By this Treaty, the HIGH CONTRACTING PARTIES establish among themselves a EUROPEAN UNION, hereinafter called 'the Union' (*Article 1, Treaty on European Union*, 1992).

is essentially lacking. In an early assessment of the nature of the EU, Curtin (1993) referred to its constitutional structure as a 'Europe of bits and pieces'. Depending, for example, on the policy area, the roles of the relevant institutions involved in decision making differ. In the early years of the EC, there was essentially one approach, the so-called **Community method**. This is no longer the case. Hence, commentators today regard the EU conceptually in terms of 'polycentricity' (Peterson and Bomberg 2000: 20), that is, as having many different centres of gravity.

That the EU lacks uniformity in terms of its structures and policy-making procedures is evident from the terminology widely used to describe it. To many, whether they are practitioners, academics, or others, the EU is thought of as a being akin to a Greek temple consisting of three 'pillars'. The first of these pillars comprises the original three Communities (the EC, EURATOM/EAEC, and, prior to mid-2002, the ECSC—see Box 4.5), while the second and third pillars consist of essentially intergovernmental co-operation in the areas of the Common Foreign and Security Policy (CFSP) and justice and home affairs (JHA). Changes in the relationship between the pillars since 1993 have meant that the boundaries between them have become blurred. Hence, de Witte (1998) prefers to think of the EU as a French-style gothic cathedral with the EC as its central nave and the CFSP and what is now the renamed third pillar, Police and Judicial Co-operation in Criminal Matters (PJCCM), making up

Box 4.3 **The facts**
The Treaty on European Union

The impact of the Treaty on European Union on the process of achieving 'ever closer union' was considerable. Most significantly it formally established the European Union. In addition it promoted European integration in a whole variety of ways, whether through the promotion of co-operation in the two new intergovernmental pillars on foreign and security policy and justice and home affairs, or through the expansion of EC activities. Indeed, thanks to the TEU, the EC was formally given new competences in the fields of education, culture, public health, consumer protection, trans-European networks, industry, and development co-operation. Citizenship of the Union was also established. And, of course, the TEU set out the timetable for EMU by 1999. As for existing competences, some were expanded, notably in the areas of social policy, the environment, and economic and social cohesion, although in an attempt to assuage concerns of over-centralization of power, the principle of subsidiarity was introduced. Moreover, the TEU saw the establishment of new institutions and bodies including the European Central Bank, the Committee of the Regions, and the Ombudsman. As for existing institutions, the powers of the EP were increased, not least through the introduction of the new co-decision procedure, the greater use of qualified majority voting in the Council was agreed, the Court of Auditors was upgraded to an institution, and the Court of Justice gained the power to fine member states.

Box 4.4 **Key dates**
1986–2004

1986   Single European Act signed (17 and 28 February)
1987   Single European Act enters into force (1 July)
1991   Maastricht European Council agrees Treaty on European Union (9–10 December)
1992   Treaty on European Union signed (7 February)
1993   European Union established (1 November)
1996   1996 IGC launched (29 March)
1997   Amsterdam European Council agrees Treaty of Amsterdam (16–17 June)
        Agenda 2000 published (15 July)
        Treaty of Amsterdam signed (2 October)
1999   Stage III of EMU launched (1 January)
        Treaty of Amsterdam enters into force (1 May)
2000   2000 IGC launched (14 February)
        Nice European Council agrees Treaty of Nice (7–11 December)
2001   Treaty of Nice signed (26 February)
        Irish people reject Treaty of Nice in a referendum (7 June)
        Laeken European Council adopts Declaration on the Future of the Union (14–15 December)
2002   Introduction of the euro (1 January)
        Launch of the Convention (28 March)
        Irish people approve the Treaty of Nice in a second referendum (19 September)*
2004   New IGC to be launched*

* At the time of writing whether enlargement negotiations are to be completed by the end of 2002 is unknown. The date of the first enlargement to include Central and Eastern European countries has been set as 1 May 2004.

Box 4.5 **The facts**

The European Communities: From three to two

Originally there were three European Communities: the European Coal and Steel Community (ECSC), the European Economic Community (EEC), and the European Atomic Energy Community (EAEC). The EEC was formally renamed the European Community (EC) in 1993 thanks to the TEU (though the name was often used informally as shorthand for the EEC before that date). Since then, the ECSC has been disbanded, its founding treaty having expired after 50 years, as envisaged, in July 2002.

the 'somewhat darker side aisles'. This may or may not be a more attractive analogy. The point is, however, that the pillar idea has stuck (see Figure 4.1).

To supporters of supranational integration, the establishment of the EU in 1993 on the basis of three 'pillars' represented a clear setback. This was because the introduction of the intergovernmental pillars threatened to undermine the supremacy of the 'Community method', the use of the supranational Community institutions and decision-making procedures to develop, adopt, and police policy among the member states. On the other hand, adopting a mix of supranational and intergovernmental pillars merely formalized existing practice. Even prior to Maastricht, the EC's member states were pursuing intergovernmental co-operation outside the framework of the EC. The most obvious example was in the area of foreign policy co-operation (see Chapter 15: 229), which had been taking place since the early 1970s. All the same, the mix of supranationalism and intergovernmentalism, particularly given that the Community institutions, with the exception of the Council, were at best marginal players in Pillars 2 and 3, meant that the EU when established was less of a union than many either hoped or feared it would be.

The idea of the new EU as a union was also undermined by certain features of the Maastricht Treaty (TEU). First, plans for economic and monetary union (EMU)—the most important new area of EC activity

The European Union		
Pillar 2	**Pillar 1**	**Pillar 3**
Common	The	Justice
Foreign and	European	and
Security	Communities:	Home
Policy	EC	Affairs
(CFSP)	ECSC	(JHA)
	EURATOM/	
	EAEC	

Fig. 4.1 The pillar structure after Maastricht

agreed at Maastricht—were set to create a three-tier EU with the member states divided up between those which would become full participants, those that would fail to get in (that is, not meet the **convergence criteria**), and those—the UK and Denmark—that either had availed or could avail themselves of opt-out clauses from the process. It seemed that a permanent **differentiation** between member states in a major policy area was being enshrined in the EU's treaty base. Second, it was agreed that closer integration in the area of social policy would only be pursued by 11 of the then 12 member states. Resolute opposition to increased European social policy competences meant that new legislation resulting from the so-called 'Social Chapter' of the Treaty would not apply to the UK. Third, Denmark was later granted a de facto opt-out from involvement in the elaboration and implementation of foreign policy decisions and actions having defence implications. All this created the image of a partially fragmented EU.

That the Maastricht provisions did not all apply to the same extent to all member states was significant as such differentiation had never been enshrined in the EU's treaty base before. This is not to say that differentiation between member states had never existed (see Chapter 24: 384). But it had been temporary, with new member states given strict time limits for fulfilling the requirements and obliga-tions of membership. Hence, there were fears that the Maastricht opt-outs, as they would come to be known, would set a precedent leading, at worst, to an **à la carte** EU with member states picking and choosing the areas in which they were willing to pursue closer integration. Such fears were initially assuaged when, at the time of the 1995 enlargement, the EU refused to consider any exemptions or opt-outs from the existing *acquis*. The new member states—Austria, Finland, and Sweden—had to and indeed did accept all the obligations of membership, including those concerning social policy, EMU, and the CFSP (foreign policy), the latter being significant because each of the three countries was still technically neutral.

Key points

- Despite 'ever closer union' being a long-established goal of the EC member states, the EU was not created until 1993.

- The EU lacks a uniform structure, consisting as it does of one supranational and two inter-governmental pillars.

- The Treaty on European Union (TEU) introduced permanent opt-outs from certain policy areas for some member states.

Reviewing the Union: The 1996 IGC and the Treaty of Amsterdam

The fact that the EU when it was created was less than its title implied was recognized not only by those studying the EU but also by those working in its institutions and representing its member states. Indeed, even those who drafted the TEU acknowledged that what they were creating was not the final product but part of an ongoing process. In the very first Article of the Treaty, the member states proclaimed that the establishment of the EU 'marks *a new stage* in the process of creating an ever closer union among the peoples of Europe' (emphasis added). They then proceeded to facilitate the process by scheduling an intergovernmental conference (IGC) for 1996 at which the Treaty would be revised in line with its objectives. Among these was (and indeed remains) the idea of 'ever closer union'.

Views on the purpose of the 1996 IGC differed. For the less integrationist member states, notably the UK, the IGC would provide an opportunity to review the functioning of the new Union and fine-tune its structures. Nothing radical would have to be done since the EU was essentially new. For others, a more substantial overhaul was not ruled out. The IGC would provide an opportunity to push ahead with the goal of creating an 'ever closer union'; something which the EP was particularly keen to see, as its draft constitution of February 1994 had demonstrated. Ever closer union, it was argued, was necessary if the EU wished to rectify the shortcomings of the structures created at Maastricht and prepare itself to admit an increasingly large number of applicant countries, mainly from Central and Eastern Europe. Moreover, several member states were growing increasingly impatient with the reluctance of the less integrationist member states to countenance closer integration. And there was also the need to bring the EU closer to its citizens. Popular reaction to Maastricht had shown that more needed to be done to convince the people of the value of 'union'. Not only had the Danish people initially rejected the Maastricht Treaty in June 1992, but also the French people only narrowly approved it in a referendum in September 1992.

The shortcomings of the structures created at Maastricht were highlighted in reports produced by the institutions in 1995. The Council, Commission, and European Parliament (EP) all agreed that the pillar structure was not functioning well and that the intergovernmental nature of decision making in Pillar 3 on justice and home affairs was a significant constraint on the development of policy. As for Pillar 2 on the CFSP (foreign policy), its inherent weaknesses had been highlighted by the EU's response to the disintegration of Yugoslavia. Such shortcomings needed to be addressed, all the more so since enlargement was now firmly on the agenda, with the European Council at Copenhagen in June 1993 having committed the EU to admitting Central and East European countries once they had met the accession criteria (see Chapter 14: 218). Enlargement was going to be a permanent item on the agenda of the EU. Preparations would have to be made, notably where the size and composition of the institutions were concerned. In addition, there was the matter of **qualified majority voting**. Its extension to replace **unanimity** would be necessary if the EU were going to survive enlargement and avoid decision-making

paralysis. Also needed within an enlarged EU, at least in the eyes of supporters of closer integration, were mechanisms that would allow those member states keen on closer integration to proceed without the need for the unanimous agreement of the others. There was consequently much discussion of ideas concerning a **'core Europe'**, **variable geometry**, and a **multi-speed** EU (see Chapter 24).

It was against this background that preparations for reforming the EU took place. These began in earnest in 1995 with the formation of a 'Reflection Group' headed by Carlos Westendorp of Spain and consisting of a representative of each head of government and two nominees of the European Parliament. The Group proved to be less successful in identifying reform options than many had hoped. Its reports tended to contain little more than a record of often highly divergent national positions. It nevertheless suggested three key aims of the 1996 IGC: bringing the EU closer to its citizens; improving its functioning in preparation for enlargement; and providing it with greater external capacity. In doing so, the Reflection Group promoted the idea of 'flexibility'—of introducing mechanisms to facilitate 'closer co-operation' among groups of willing member states. It was therefore advocating the opportunity for undefined differentiated integration within the EU.

The IGC necessary to reform the EU was launched in March 1996, with the early stages of the negotiations confirming expectations that any agreement on reform would not be easily reached. Progress under the Irish presidency did, however, lead to a draft Treaty being produced for the European Council meeting held in Dublin in December 1996. This, though, left many issues unresolved. And with a general election due in the UK in May 1997, it was clear that finalizing agreement on many of these matters would have to wait until after that had taken place. Certainly the Labour victory did make the job of drawing the IGC to a close easier for the Dutch presidency. On the other hand, however, differences between other member states now came into the open. Added to this, attention was being distracted away from the unresolved issues on the IGC's agenda by a new French government intent on seeing the EU commit itself to greater action on economic growth and employment.

The Treaty of Amsterdam

What eventually emerged from the 1996 IGC was the Treaty of Amsterdam, signed on 2 October 1997, a treaty which attracted far less popular attention than the Maastricht Treaty in 1992–3. This does not mean that it was an insignificant treaty, however. It certainly caught the attention of lawyers and practitioners, re-numbering as it did all but four Articles in the Treaty of Rome and TEU. Moreover, in terms of substantive changes to the EU, it added to the EU's objectives the establishment of 'an area of freedom, security and justice' and—in what is often referred to as communitarization—shifted much of justice and home affairs activity from Pillar 3 (justice and home affairs) into the EC pillar (Pillar 1) of the Union. As a result, the thrust of co-operation in Pillar 3 was re-focused on police and judicial co-operation in criminal matters, and the pillar was renamed accordingly. At the same time, provision was made for **Schengen** co-operation to be incorporated into the EU. Schengen co-operation had been initiated in the mid–1980s and was aimed at the removal of border controls between participating states. On the one hand these developments meant greater coher-

ence in EU activity. Much of justice and home affairs was now being subjected to the Community method and Schengen was being brought within the framework of the EU. On the other hand, the changes were accompanied by increased **differentiation** within the EU. The UK, Ireland, and Denmark gained various kinds of 'opt-out' from both the new 'area of freedom, security and justice' and Schengen co-operation. Figure 4.2 depicts the pillar structure after the Treaty of Amsterdam (and still in place in 2003).

The potential for differentiation in and the fragmentation of the Union was also increased by the introduction of mechanisms for 'closer co-operation'. Under these, member states that wished to could use the EC framework to seek enhanced co-operation among themselves. They could do so with a number of provisos: the mechanisms were only to be used as a last resort, a majority of member states had to be participating, and the co-operation had to be open to all other member states. Moreover, closer co-operation could not detract either from the principles of the Union and the *acquis* or from the rights of member states. Nor could it be applied under Pillar 2 on the CFSP. Such restrictions, as well as constraints imposed by the de

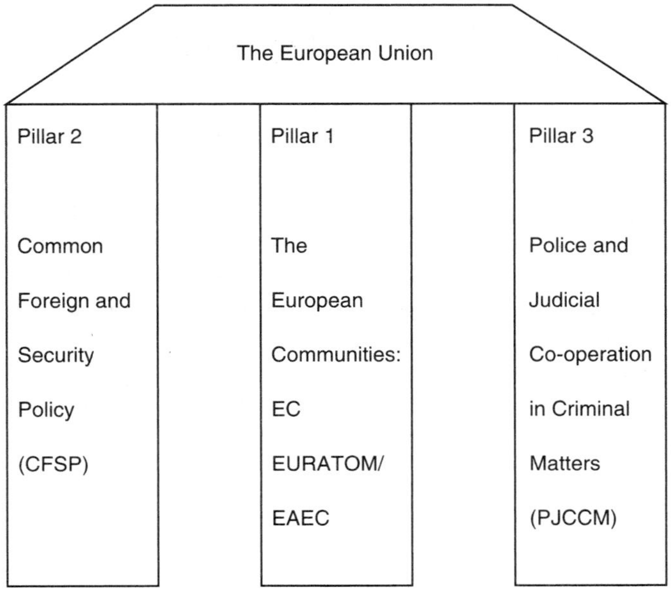

The European Union		
Pillar 2	Pillar 1	Pillar 3
Common Foreign and Security Policy (CFSP)	The European Communities: EC EURATOM/ EAEC	Police and Judicial Co-operation in Criminal Matters (PJCCM)

Fig. 4.2 The pillar structure in 2003

facto veto which each member state had over their use, meant that the provisions would be difficult to use. In fact none of the provisions on closer co-operation had been used by 2003. All the same, the possibility of using differentiation within the EU was being established.

The Treaty of Amsterdam lessened differentiation within the EU in its repeal of the UK's opt-out from social policy agreed at Maastricht and the bolstering of the EC's social policy competences (see Chapter 17: 268). Moreover, an employment policy chapter was added to the Treaty of Rome, in part as an attempt to assuage popular concerns that the EU did not have its citizens' interests at heart. The need to make the EU more citizen friendly was also behind other new emphases, not least in enhanced EC competences concerning consumer and environmental protection, a new emphasis on **transparency** and **subsidiarity**, and a reassertion that EU citizenship does not undermine national citizenship.

In terms of addressing the shortcomings of Pillar 2, the member states at Amsterdam resisted calls for a communitarization of the Common Foreign and Security Policy (CFSP), preferring to maintain the existing intergovernmental arrangements and therefore the pillar structure of the EU. Reforms were, however, introduced in an attempt to improve the consistency of action at the EU level by involving the European Council more, creating the post of High Representative (or 'Monsieur/Madam PESC' as, using the French acronym for CFSP, the post became known), establishing a policy planning and early warning unit, seeking to develop long-term strategies, clarifying the nature of the different instruments available, defining more precisely the EU's concept of security (the so-called 'Petersberg tasks' of humanitarian and rescue tasks, peace-keeping, and crisis management, including peace-making), and allowing for 'constructive abstention' so that states abstaining could not block CFSP initiatives (see Chapter 15: 237). The desire to deepen integration further was asserted in the renewed commitment to a common defence policy and even a common defence.

Finally, the Treaty of Amsterdam was supposed to prepare the EU institutionally for enlargement. Here, it failed. Rather than agreeing reforms, it simply deferred the resolution of key questions, such as the size of the Commission, the redistribution of member states' votes in the Council, and the nature of majority voting, to a later date. **Unanimity** was replaced by **qualified majority voting** (QMV) in some 19 instances, but even here, thanks to German insistence, progress was far less than was either anticipated or desired by many member states. This was underlined in a declaration issued by Belgium, France, and Italy to the effect that further reform should be a precondition for the signing of the first accession treaties with applicant countries. This is not to say that the Treaty of Amsterdam failed totally to introduce institutional reform. The size of the European Parliament (EP) was capped at 700 members, and the **assent** and **co-decision** procedures were extended to some new and to some old treaty provisions thus enhancing the legislative role of the EP. The EP's hand in the appointment of the Commission was also enhanced, as was its right to set its own rules for its elected members (or MEPs).

Key points

- Early experiences of the EU raised concerns about the functioning of the pillar structure.

- The desire not to be held back by more recalcitrant member states led to mechanisms for closer co-operation between interested and willing member states.

- Despite the acknowledged need to introduce institutional reforms in preparation for enlargement, the Treaty of Amsterdam failed to prepare the EU sufficiently to admit more than a handful of new members.

Preparing the Union for enlargement: The 2000 IGC and the Treaty of Nice

For the EU, enlargement raises challenges to the idea of 'union'. Admitting ten countries, most of which have been undergoing processes of wholesale economic transformation from command economies to fully functioning market economies, is something that the EU has never done before. The challenge for the EU therefore consists, at least in part, of accommodating and integrating the new members. At the same time, it has to ensure that its *acquis*, the integration achieved so far, and the notion of 'union' are neither impaired nor undermined, and that its institutions can continue to function as decision-making and decision-shaping bodies. Moreover, confronted with the prospect of what amounts to almost a doubling of its membership, the EU is faced with the challenge of ensuring that the commitment towards 'ever closer union' can and will be maintained. In the past this has led to a widening versus deepening debate. At present, however, the commitment to widening is firm. Nevertheless, preparations for enlargement need to be made.

Preparing the EU institutionally for enlargement was originally a key objective of the 1996 IGC. As noted, the resulting Treaty of Amsterdam failed, however, to deliver. Instead, it was decided to postpone reform. To this end, a Protocol was adopted in which it was agreed that at the time of the next enlargement, the Commission would consist of one national per member state provided that by that date the weighting of votes within the Council had been modified either via a reweighting or through the adoption of a dual majority system of voting (see Chapter 10). Any reweighting would have to compensate the larger member states for giving up the existing possibility to nominate a second Commissioner. The Protocol also provided for an IGC to carry out a 'comprehensive review of . . . the composition and functioning of the institutions' at least one year before the membership of the EU exceeds 20 member states.

In reality the provisions of the Protocol were mainly ignored. For even before the Treaty of Amsterdam entered into force on 1 May 1999, the European Council at its gatherings in Cardiff and Vienna in 1998 had identified institutional reform as an issue of primary concern for the EU. Then, at Cologne in June 1999, it agreed to hold an IGC in 2000 to address the key institutional questions left unresolved at Amsterdam. The issues—the size and composition of the Commission, the weighting of votes in the Council, and the possible extension of qualified majority voting in the Council—became known as the 'Amsterdam leftovers'.

What pushed the European Council into calling an IGC for 2000 were changes in the EU's handling of the enlargement process. In July 1997, a matter of weeks after the Amsterdam European Council, the Commission had published Agenda 2000, its blueprint for enlargement. Following its recommendations, the Luxembourg European Council of December 1997 agreed to launch an inclusive accession process with all applicant states (excluding Turkey) but open accession negotiations proper with only six of the applicants. It was felt at the time that six new members could be squeezed into the EU without necessarily holding an IGC. Within 18 months, however, attitudes towards enlargement were changing and, in the aftermath of the Kosovo conflict of 1999, the decision was taken to open accession negotiations with six more applicant countries and recognize all applicants including Turkey as 'candidate countries'. Opening up the possibility of large-scale enlargement made the need to address the 'Amsterdam leftovers' more urgent. Hence an IGC was called.

The 2000 IGC opened in February 2000 under the Portuguese presidency of the Council with only a limited agenda. This reflected the preferences of most member states for a focused IGC, which would deal almost exclusively with the 'Amsterdam leftovers'. This was not to say that others, including the Commission and the EP, did not favour a broader agenda. A Commission-inspired Wise Men's Report, published in October 1999, also voiced strong support for a reorganization of the treaties and integrating the Western European Union (WEU) into the EU as a step towards a common defence policy. The Commission's report of January 2000 also reminded the member states that it was incumbent on them to ensure that the IGC reformed the EU in such a way that it would remain flexible enough 'to allow continued progress towards our goal of European integration. What the Conference decides will set the framework for the political Europe of tomorrow'. The EU, it warned, 'will be profoundly changed by enlargement, but must not be weakened by it'. As for the EP, it came out strongly in favour of a wider agenda, dismissing the 'excessively narrow agenda' adopted by the European Council meeting in

Helsinki in December 1999 as one which 'might well jeopardise the process of integration'.

The IGC initially overlooked the calls of the Wise Men, the Commission, and the EP. It focused very much on the 'Amsterdam leftovers' although 'closer co-operation' was added to its agenda by the meeting of the European Council in Feira in June 2000. By this time, however, certain member states were beginning to think more openly about the future of the EU. Hence, the IGC negotiations were soon taking place against a backdrop of speeches from the German foreign minister, Joschka Fischer, advocating in a personal capacity 'a European Federation' (see Box 4.6), and the French president, Jacques Chirac, championing proposals for a European constitution.

Box 4.6 **Issues and debates**

From confederacy to federation: Thoughts on the future of European integration

Speech by Joschka Fischer at the Humboldt University in Berlin, 12 May 2000 (excerpts)

Quo vadis Europa? is the question posed once again by the history of our continent. And for many reasons the answer Europeans will have to give, if they want to do well by themselves and their children, can only be this: onwards to the completion of European integration. A step backwards, even just standstill or contentment with what has been achieved, would demand a fatal price of all EU member states and of all those who want to become members; it would demand a fatal price above all of our people. . . . The task ahead of us will be anything but easy and will require all our strength; in the coming decade we will have to enlarge the EU to the east and south-east, and this will in the end mean a doubling in the number of members. And at the same time, if we are to be able to meet this historic challenge and integrate the new member states without substantially denting the EU's capacity for action, we must put into place the last brick in the building of European integration, namely political integration. . . . Permit me therefore to remove my Foreign Minister's hat altogether in order to suggest a few ideas both on the nature of this so-called finality of Europe and on how we can approach and eventually achieve this goal. . . . Enlargement will render imperative a fundamental reform of the European institutions. Just what would a

European Council with thirty heads of state and government be like? Thirty presidencies? . . . How long will Council meetings actually last? Days, maybe even weeks? How, with the system of institutions that exists today, are thirty states supposed to balance interests, take decisions and then actually act? How can one prevent the EU from becoming utterly intransparent, compromises from becoming stranger and more incomprehensible, and the citizens' acceptance of the EU from eventually hitting rock bottom? Question upon question, but there is a very simple answer: the transition from a union of states to full parliamentarization as a European Federation, something Robert Schuman demanded 50 years ago. And that means nothing less than a European Parliament and a European government which really do exercise legislative and executive power within the Federation. This Federation will have to be based on a constituent treaty. I am well aware of the procedural and substantive problems that will have to be resolved before this goal can be attained. For me, however, it is entirely clear that Europe will only be able to play its due role in global economic and political competition if we move forward courageously. The problems of the 21st century cannot be solved with the fears and formulae of the 19th and 20th centuries.

Source: **www.auswaertiges-amt.de/www/en/infoservice/presse/.**

Other proposals on the future shape of the EU from, among others, the UK prime minister, Tony Blair, and his Spanish counterpart, José-Maria Aznar, soon followed.

Many of the proposals were ambitious and could not be addressed within the IGC, where progress on the key issues was already proving to be slower than had been hoped. This was due, not least, to major differences between the member states on how best to deal with them. As much was evident from the harsh words exchanged at the Biarritz European Council in October 2000. And the situation was not helped by the heavy-handed manner in which France, now holding the Council presidency, was managing the IGC. Accusations abounded that the French were abusing their position as chair by promoting what was essentially a French agenda rather than seeking to broker compromises between the member states. At no point were the accusations louder than at the Nice European Council which, after more than four days, eventually agreed a treaty. Once tidied up, this was signed on 26 February 2001.

The Treaty of Nice

What the member states agreed at Nice attracted much criticism. Although it was rightly heralded as paving the way for enlargement, for many it produced sub-optimal solutions to the institutional challenges raised by the prospect of an enlarged membership. All the same, Nice better equips the EU to accept new members, thereby avoiding institutional paralysis. For example, QMV has been extended to nearly 40 more treaty provisions, albeit in many instances ones concerned with the nomination of officials rather than policy making, although some ten policy areas have seen increased use of QMV. Reaching a decision using QMV will not, however, become any easier. Despite a reweighting of votes—each member state will see its number of votes increase with the larger member states enjoying roughly a trebling and the smaller member states roughly a doubling of their votes—the proportion of votes required to obtain a qualified majority, that is, to get a decision accepted, remains at almost the same level as before and is actually

set to increase. Moreover, a new hurdle has been introduced. On top of the other requirements, any decision can, at the behest of any member state, be required to have the support of member states representing 62 per cent of the EU's total population.

Further with regard to the 'Amsterdam leftovers', Nice provides for a staged reduction in the size of the Commission. From 2005, each member state will have one commissioner. Then, once the EU reaches 27 members, the Commission will be reduced to no more than 26 members. There is, however, a proviso: an equitable rotation system has to be agreed. Staying with the institutions, Nice revised the cap on the size of the EP upwards to 732 while maximum sizes for the Committee of the Regions and the Economic and Social Committee (see Chapter 1: 2) were also agreed. Reforms were also introduced to the competences and organization of the Court of Justice and the Court of First Instance (see Chapter 12: 190).

The imminence of enlargement coupled with an awareness of existing institutional difficulties also accounts for Nice's enhanced stress on democracy and rights within the treaties. This is particularly evident in the inclusion of a 'yellow card' procedure for member states that risk breaching the principles on which the EU is founded. Thanks to Amsterdam, the voting and other rights of such member states may be suspended. Moreover, Nice revises the mechanisms for what was 'closer co-operation' but is now renamed 'enhanced co-operation'. These become easier to use mainly because the number of states needed to start a project and the opportunities open to single states to block projects are reduced. The mechanisms for enhanced co-operation were also extended to non-military aspects of the CFSP.

As noted earlier, the availability of such mechanisms raises the prospect of the EU becoming a less uniform union, particularly since some of the hurdles to their use have now been reduced. At the same time, the Treaty of Nice arguably strengthens the Union. In the area of CFSP, and following the development of the European Rapid Reaction Force (ERRF), the Treaty effectively makes the EU responsible for implementing the defence-related aspects of policy. The EU therefore takes on many of the roles of the now essentially redundant Western European Union. Finally, Nice increases the focus on Brussels as the de facto capital of the EU. Once membership of the EU reaches 18, all European Council meetings are set to be held in Brussels. Until then, each presidency will now host one of its European Council meetings in the Belgian capital.

A preliminary assessment of Nice would therefore suggest that it will both strengthen and potentially weaken the EU. On the other hand, it has increased the chances of a more 'European' EU. It may not have contained any commitment to 'ever closer union', but it does seek to prepare the EU for enlargement.

This desire to facilitate enlargement may appear to have eclipsed the past purpose of treaty reform, in essence the furthering of the goal of 'ever closer union'. Certainly there are voices in the EP expressing concern over Nice's impact. Its weak points are deemed to be indicative of a drift towards intergovernmental methods and the consequent weakening of the Community method (Leinen and Méndez de Vigo 2001: F). On the other hand, Nice sets in motion a process that draws on the speeches made by the likes of Fischer and Chirac in 2000 to promote a debate on the future of the EU. To some,

the Commission especially, this debate provides an opportunity to create a stronger, more integrated EU with a less fragmented structure. Others, however, envisage greater flexibility, a clear delimitation of competences, and a weakening of commitments to 'ever closer union'.

Key points

- Changes in the approach the EU was adopting towards enlargement in 1999 gave greater urgency to the need to address the 'Amsterdam leftovers' and agree institutional reform.

- The Treaty of Nice may have paved the way for enlargement, but to many it provided sub-optimal solutions to the institutional challenges posed by a significantly larger EU.

- While criticized for potentially weakening the EU, Nice has initiated a process designed to respond to calls for a European Federation and a European Constitution.

Conclusion: Beyond Nice and the future of the Union

The process that Nice has initiated was outlined in a *Declaration on the Future of the Union* in which the member states called for 'a deeper and wider debate about the future of the European Union'. According to the Declaration, this debate was to focus, *inter alia*, on four issues: how to establish and monitor a more precise delimitation of powers between the EU and its member states; the status of the Charter of Fundamental Rights proclaimed at the Nice European Council; a simplification of the Treaties with a view to making them clearer and better understood; and the role of national parliaments in the European architecture. In addition, the 'post-Nice' process was to find ways of improving and monitoring the democratic **legitimacy** and **transparency** of the EU and its institutions in order to bring them closer to the citizens. Solutions to all the

issues covered by the process would then be dealt with in a further IGC scheduled for 2004.

At the time, the agenda for the 'future of Europe' debate appeared quite limited. However, by the time the debate was formally launched by the European Council meeting in Laeken in December 2001, the use of the term '*inter alia*' had been seized on and a whole raft of often wide-ranging questions was tabled for discussion. In all, the so-called 'Laeken Declaration' contained more than 50 questions dealing with matters ranging from the democratic legitimacy of the EU to the future of the pillar structure and co-operation in the area of social exclusion. Moreover, the discussions were not to be pursued within the traditional framework of an IGC, at least not initially. Instead a Convention comprising representatives of member state governments, members of parliaments, MEPs, and Commission representatives, as well as government representatives and MPs from the 13 candidate countries, was established. Presided over by a former French president, Valéry Giscard d'Estaing, the Convention began work at the end of February 2002. Within just over a year it was expected to report on options for the future of the EU. See Box 4.7.

Box 4.7 **Case study**

The Laeken declaration on the future of the European Union, December 2001 (excerpts)

[T]he Union stands at a crossroads, a defining moment in its existence. The unification of Europe is near. The Union is about to expand to bring in more that ten new Member States .. At long last, Europe is on its way to becoming one big family, without bloodshed, a real transformation clearly calling for a different approach from fifty years ago, when six countries first took the lead. . . . The European Union needs to become more democratic, more transparent and more efficient. It has to resolve three basic challenges: how to bring citizens, and primarily the young, closer to the European design and the European institutions, how to organize politics and the European political area in an enlarged Union and how to develop the Union as a stabilizing factor and a model in the new multipolar world. . . . Citizens often hold expectations of the European Union that are not always fulfilled . . . Thus the important thing is to clarify, simplify and adjust the division of competences between the Union and the Member States in the light of the new challenges facing the Union. . . A first series of questions that needs to be put concerns how the division of competence can be made more transparent. Can we thus make a clearer distinction between three types of competence: the exclusive competence of the Union, the competence of the Member States and the shared competence of the Union and the Member States? At what level is competence exercised in the most efficient way? How is the principle of subsidiarity to be applied here? And should we not make it clear that any powers not assigned by the Treaties to the Union fall within the exclusive sphere of competence of the Member States? And what would be the consequences of this? The next series of questions should aim, within this new framework and while respecting the 'acquis communautaire', to determine whether there needs to be any reorganisation of competence. How can citizens' expectations be taken as a guide here? What missions would this produce for the Union? And, vice versa, what tasks could better be left to the Member States? What amendments should be made to the Treaty on the various policies? How, for example, should a more coherent common foreign policy and defence policy be developed? Should the Petersberg tasks be updated? Do we want to adopt a more integrated approach to police and criminal law cooperation? How can economic-policy coordination be stepped up? How can we intensify cooperation in the field of social inclusion, the environment, health and food safety? But then, should not the day-to-day administration and implementation of the Union's policy be left more emphatically to the Member States and, where their constitutions so provide, to the regions? Should they not be provided with guarantees that their spheres of competence will not be affected? Lastly, there is the question of how to ensure that a redefined division of competence does not lead to a creeping expansion of the competence of the Union or to encroachment upon the exclusive areas of competence of the Member States and, where there is provision for this, regions. How are we to ensure at the same time that the European dynamic does not come to a halt? In the future as well the Union must continue to be able to react to fresh challenges and developments and must be able to explore new policy areas. Should Articles 95 and 308 of the Treaty be reviewed for this purpose in the light of the 'acquis jurisprudentiel'? . . . Who does what is not the only important question; the nature of the Union's action and what instruments it should use are equally important. Successive amendments to the Treaty have on each occasion resulted in a proliferation of instruments, and directives have gradually evolved towards more and more detailed legislation. The key question is therefore whether the Union's various instruments should not be better defined and whether their number should not be reduced. In other words, should a distinction be introduced between legislative instruments be reduced: directly applicable rules, framework legislation and non-enforceable instruments (opinions, recommendations, open coordination)? Is it or is it not desirable to have more frequent recourse to framework legislation, which affords the Member States more room for

Box 4.7—*continued*

manoeuvre in achieving policy objectives? For which areas of competence are open coordination and mutual recognition the most appropriate instruments? Is the principle of proportionality to remain the point of departure? . . . [H]ow can we increase the democratic legitimacy and transparency of the present institutions . . .? How can the authority and efficiency of the European Commission be enhanced? How should the President of the Commission be appointed: by the European Council, by the European Parliament or should he be directly elected by the citizens? Should the role of the European Parliament be strengthened? Should we extend the right of co-decision or not? Should the way in which we elect the members of the European Parliament be reviewed? Should a European electoral constituency be created, or should constituencies continue to be determined nationally? Can the two systems be combined? Should the role of the Council be strengthened? Should the Council act in the same manner in its legislative and its executive capacities? With a view to greater transparency, should the meetings of the Council, at least in its legislative capacity, be public? Should citizens have more access to Council documents? How, finally, should the balance and reciprocal control between the institutions be ensured? A second question, which also relates to democratic legitimacy, involves the role of national parliaments. Should they be represented in a new institution, alongside the Council and the European Parliament? Should they have a role in areas of European action in which the European Parliament has no competence? Should they focus on the divisionof competence between Union and Member States, for example through preliminary checking of compliance with the principle of subsidiarity? [A] third question concerns how we can improve the efficiency of decision making and the workings of the institutions in a Union of some thirty Member States. How could the Union set its objectives and priorities more effectively and ensure better implementation? Is there a need for more decisions by a qualified majority? How is the co-decision procedure between the Council and the European Parliament to be simplified and speeded up? What of the six-monthly rotation of the Presidency of the Union? What is the future role of the European Parliament? What of the future role and structure of the various Council formations? How should the coherence of European foreign policy be enhanced? How is synergy between the High Representative and the competent Commissioner to be reinforced? Should the external representation of the Union in international fora be extended further? . . . [A further question] concerns simplifying the existing Treaties without changing their content. Should the distinction between the Union and the Communities be reviewed? What of the division into three pillars? Questions then arise as to the possible reorganisation of the Treaties. Should a distinction be made between a basic treaty and the other treaty provisions? Should this distinction involve separating the texts? Could this lead to a distinction between the amendment and ratification procedures for the basic treaty and for the other treaty provisions? . . . The question ultimately arises as to whether this simplification and reorganization might not lead in the long run to the adoption of a constitutional text in the Union. What might the basic features of such a constitution be? The values which the Union cherishes, the fundamental rights and obligations of its citizens, the relationship between Member States in the Union?

Source: European Council, 'Laeken Declaration on the Future of Europe', 15 December 2001. At **http://europa.eu.int/futurum/documents/offrep/doc/51201_en.htm**.

For supporters of integration disappointed by the outcomes of Amsterdam and Nice, this 'post-Nice' process was welcomed as providing a further opportunity to promote the idea of 'ever closer union'. Developments they had in mind included the adoption of a European constitution, something that the EP in particular had long been championing and the French and German governments had publicly endorsed. The EP was also keen to see the communitarization of a strengthened foreign policy and remaining third pillar matters, formal recognition of the EU's legal personality, election of the Commission president, simplification of decision-making procedures, and an extension of its own powers (Leinen and Méndez de Vigo 2001). Many of these ideas were shared by the Commission, which also proposed removing existing opt-outs (European Commission 2002*a*). Pursuing such an agenda would enhance the idea of the EU being a union.

What form the EU will have as a consequence of the post-Nice process remains to be seen. In all likelihood the aspirations of those keen to see a uniform entity develop will not be fully met. Further integration can, however, be expected. There has, in the history of the EU and its predecessors, rarely been a point when ideas for increased integration were not being aired. As Mazey (2001: 47) notes, the future is unlikely to see pressures for integration cease— indeed they may even increase. Yet, further integration may not necessarily lead to a more uniform union. With opt-outs now enshrined in its treaty base, the EU is divided between those inside and those outside the eurozone. This suggests that enhanced co-operation between groups of member states, particularly with an enlarged membership, seems likely to become a permanent characteristic of the EU. This may disappoint some, but to most it will be the pragmatic if not logical consequence of a larger and more diverse Union.

QUESTIONS

1 Is it appropriate to describe the EU in terms of 'pillars'?

2 What is meant by 'ever closer union'?

3 Do opt-outs and mechanisms for enhanced co-operation undermine the EU as a union?

4 What impact did the Treaty of Amsterdam have on the pillar structure of the EU?

5 Why did the 1996 IGC fail to adopt the institutional reforms necessary to prepare the EU for enlargement?

6 Has the Treaty of Nice prepared the EU for enlargement?

7 What impact will enlargement have on the prospects for further integration in the EU?

8 Why was the agenda for the Future of Europe debate expanded between Nice and Laeken?

GUIDE TO FURTHER READING

Baun, M. J., *An Imperfect Union: The Maastricht Treaty and the New Politics of European Integration* (Boulder, Colo.: Westview, 1996). An introductory account of the establishment of the EU in 1993 and its early development.

Church, C., and Phinnemore, D., *The Penguin Guide to the European Treaties: From Rome to Maastricht, Amsterdam, Nice and Beyond* (London: Penguin, 1996). A comprehensive guide to the treaty base of the EU, which reproduces the provisions of the Treaties in their current form.

Galloway, D., *The Treaty of Nice and Beyond* (Sheffield: Sheffield Academic Press, 2001). A detailed analysis of key reforms introduced by the Treaty of Nice.

Laffan, B., O'Donnell, R., and Smith, M., *Europe's Experimental Union: Rethinking Integration* (London: Routledge, 2000). A challenging and thought-provoking analysis of what the EU is.

Lynch, P., Neuwahl, N., and Rees, W. (eds), *Reforming the European Union from Maastricht to Amsterdam* (London: Longman, 2000). A volume assessing developments in the EU during the 1990s paying particular attention to the reforms introduced by the Treaty of Amsterdam.

Monar, J., and Wessels, W. (eds), *The European Union after the Treaty of Amsterdam* (London: Continuum, 2001). An informative collection of studies explaining the significance for the EU of the institutional and policy reforms introduced by the Treaty of Amsterdam.

WEB LINKS

http://europa.eu.int/comm/nice_treaty/index_en.htm Treaty of Nice website.

http://europa.eu.int/comm/archives/igc2000/index_en.htm Archives of the 2000 IGC.

http://europa.eu.int/en/agenda/igc-home/ Archives of the 1996 IGC.

http://europa.eu.int/futurum/index_en.htm Commission website of the debate on the 'Future of Europe'.

www.europarl.eu.int/europe2004/index_en.htm EP website of the debate on the 'Future of Europe'.

http://europa.eu.int/comm/justice_home/unit/charte/index_en.html Website of the Charter of Fundamental Rights.

http://europa.eu.int/comm/governance/index_en.htm Commission website on European Governance.

http://europa.eu.int/abc/treaties_en.htm The European Treaties.

Part Two

Theories and conceptual approaches

Part Two of *EU Politics* addresses the various theories and conceptual approaches that have been applied to the European integration process and to the politics of the European Union. It begins, perhaps unconventionally, by looking at the themes of federalism and federation, in Chapter 5. Michael Burgess reviews the uses and abuses of the 'f-word' by unpacking what federalism really means in the case of the European Union. In Chapter 6, Carsten Strøby Jensen introduces the first attempt at constructing a comprehensive theory of European integration: neo-functionalism. In Chapter 7, Michelle Cini considers how intergovernmentalist theory challenged the dominance of neo-functionalism to become by the 1980s the main reference point for theorizing European integration. Challenges from the 1980s on are assessed in Chapter 8. Here, Ben Rosamond looks at recent theories and conceptual approaches to the study of the EU that have emerged from the sub-disciplines of Comparative Politics and International Relations.

Federalism and federation

Michael Burgess

READER'S GUIDE

When studying theories of European integration, it has been customary for both students and academics either to downgrade or completely overlook the significance of federalism. Even when federal ideas have grudgingly been recognized, they have tended to be subsumed within other theoretical or conceptual categories, such as **neo-functionalism**, so that until fairly recently federalism has been almost invisible in the study of EU politics (at least in the English language). In the introductory section, this chapter begins by confronting the problems involved in studying the idea of a 'federal Europe'. Section two adds definitional clarity to our subject, while the third section provides a short survey of federal models, with the aim of locating the European Union in a comparative federal framework. Section four involves a detailed investigation of the contribution of Jean Monnet to the goal of a federal Europe, and this is followed by an assessment of the meaning of a federal Europe. The conclusion brings together various strands of conceptual and empirical analysis in order to underline the extent to which the European project has moved 'from quantity to quality'.

Introduction

In contemporary discourse it is common to refer to the phrase 'a federal Europe' when alluding to the *finalité politique* (end-State) of the European integration process. The assumption here is that a federal Europe is the ultimate destination or terminal end-point of the European integration process. However, some commentators and observers of the EU believe that this end-point has already arrived. This is particularly important since reference to federalism in certain eurosceptic member states, such as Denmark,

Sweden, and especially the UK, is often couched in gloomy language, intended to convey a strong sense of threat to the autonomy and integrity of the nation state.

Broadly speaking, the phrase a 'federal Europe' refers to a conception of the EU that is constantly changing, but which has at its core a set of basic principles or assumptions that indicate a voluntary union of states and citizens committed to the shared goals of welfare, security, and prosperity, and which is structured in a manner specifically designed to preserve nation states' identities, cultures, and interests, where these are consistent with the overall well-being of the union. In practical terms this means that the union is based upon a combination of centralist and decentralist imperatives that facilitate 'common solutions to common problems'. In some policy areas the EU acts on behalf of its constituent members as a whole, while in others it leaves action to the individual member states. This broad conception of a federal Europe, as we shall see, is based upon a simple axiom: 'unity in diversity'. Where and when unity is required by common consent, the EU will act accordingly, while diversity will prevail in cases where and when the member states have agreed to act alone. The EU, it should be remembered, is a voluntary union based upon political consent and legal agreement.

Unfortunately the word 'federal' sometimes serves to muddy the waters. It has different connotations in some countries than in others. To the British, it commonly refers to centralizing tendencies that have the effect of strengthening the European level at the expense of national interests, while in Germany, Belgium, Spain, and Italy it is understood to refer to a decentralized polity where power is dispersed among the constituent member states. Consequently, a federal Europe means different things to different people at different times and in different political systems. Political elites and mass publics in the EU entertain a variety of preconceptions about different phraseology. For some, to speak about 'European unity', for example, is to suggest something different from 'European Union'; it is to support **co-operation** rather than **integration**. If we follow this distinction, there is a sense, then, in which it is possible to advocate greater unity, but not union. It is therefore important to note that the elite use of language, terminology, and definition plays a crucial role in creating images capable of mobilizing EU publics both in support of and against the goal of 'an ever closer union among the peoples of Europe', one of the primary goals of the EU.[1]

This chapter explores the conceptual relationship between **federalism**, **federation**, and European integration in order to explain what is meant by the phrase a 'federal Europe'. This, after all, was the ultimate goal of **Jean Monnet**, the architect and builder of European integration, whose impact on the European Union even today remains indelible. Its purpose, then, is to clarify what is meant by a federal Europe, so that careful analysis and measured reflection can take the place of unthinking knee-jerk reflex reactions to a phrase that operates at different levels of public discourse. In a nutshell, this chapter sets the record straight. We begin with a short survey of the basic conceptual relationship between federalism, federation, and European integration, and then look briefly at a variety of federal models, before exploring the constitutional and political implications of Monnet's Europe.

Federalism, federation, and European integration

In the mainstream political science literature, the terms 'federalism' and 'federation' have usually been used interchangeably. They refer to a particular kind of union among states and citizens. However, the word 'federal' has become a term that embraces a wide variety of different relationships tending toward unity, union, league, and association that ranges from the domestic arena of trade unions, sports clubs, and parent-teacher associations to the organization of the state, the political system, and governments at the international level. Deriving from the Latin term *foedus*, meaning covenant, the term 'federal' has evolved slowly to refer to different forms of human association. These imply a voluntary agreement or bargain among individuals, groups, and collectivities, in order to maintain their interests, identities, and integrity in pursuit of commonly shared interests and goals. Probably the best shorthand definition of this peculiar set of relationships is Daniel Elazar's allusion to 'self-rule plus shared rule' (Elazar 1987: 12). See also Box 5.1.

It is less important to arrive at a precise definition of the word 'federal' than it is to underline the core principles that lie at its root. *Foedus* (covenant) and its cognate *fides* (faith and trust) suggest what has been referred to as a 'vital bonding device of civilization' (Davis 1978: 3). And the words which best serve to convey its meaning include the following: mutual respect, recognition, and toleration; equality of partnership; reciprocity; compromise; conciliation; and consent. In this sense, the notion of a federal union is founded upon a set of values and beliefs that are rooted in what is intrinsically a moral imperative drawing its intellectual basis from the

German term *Bundestreue* ('federal comity' or a federal arrangement made for mutual benefit) (de Villiers 1995: 1–36). This imperative is *moral* in the extent to which it corresponds to a fundamental conviction about the need to work for the interests and benefits of the common weal or welfare. In turn, the political implications of this conviction suggest that the constituent units of such a union or association must always act in the best interests of the whole union. The commitment is therefore a moral commitment that hinges upon the reconciliation of the interests of each individual component part with those of others and of the totality of the union or state.

If we return to the terms 'federalism' and 'federation', we can now appreciate more fully the nature of the union that is inherent in the appellation 'federal'. It is a particular kind of union whose legitimacy rests firmly upon its capacity to sustain the sort of federal values identified above. This statement enables us to focus upon what we mean by federalism and federation. Let us first consider federation. Here it is appropriate for us to take a modestly revised version of Preston King's definition

---

Box 5.1 **Core ideas**
What is federalism?

Federalism can be defined in a number of different ways. Here are some examples:

'a system of government which unites separate states while allowing each to have a substantial degree of autonomy. A federal style of government usually has a written constitution (e.g. the US) and tends to stress the importance of decentralized power and, in its democratic form, direct lines of communication between the government and its citizens' (Oxford English Reference Dictionary, 2nd edn, 2001).

'The basic idea behind federalism can be simply stated. It is that relations between states should be conducted under the rule of law. Conflict and disagreement should be resolved through peaceful means rather than through coercion or war' (R. Laming: **www.federalunion.uklinux.net/about/federalism.htm**).

'. . . suggests that everybody can be satisfied (or nobody permanently disadvantaged) by nicely combining national and regional/territorial interests within a complex web of checks and balances between a general, national, or federal government on the one hand and a multiplicity of regional governments on the other' (McLean 1996: 179).

'Federalism is present when 'the principle of the division of powers between centre and regions is established constitutionally and citizens hold an identity at both levels. At the minimum the component states should have the right to territorial integrity, to some representation in the institutions of the central or federal government, and to be protected by the federal government from external aggression' (McKay 1996: 15).

of federation as a basis for our survey. Federation is said to be:

an institutional arrangement, taking the form of a sovereign state, and distinguished from other such states solely by the fact that its central government incorporates [constituent territorial units into its decision-making procedure] on some constitutionally entrenched basis (King 1982: 77).

This definition is both precise and comprehensive, and it lucidly expresses the hallmark of all federal states, namely, the notion of 'constitutional entrenchment', that is, the formalization of the division between the centre and the component parts within a constitution. Accordingly, it is not in itself the division of competences that is of pivotal significance, but both the principle and the fact that there is a constitution. Federations vary enormously in how they are structured and in their distribution of powers and competences, but what lies at the core of every federal state is the inviolable right of each constituent unit—whether state, canton, province, or *Land*—to its own constitutional integrity. A federation or federal state, then, is conventionally understood to be a particular kind of state wherein **sovereignty** is divided and shared between a central (federal) government and the constituent (member state) governments, and rooted in a written constitutional guarantee that can only be amended by special procedures that reinforce legitimacy by maximizing political consent.

The term 'federalism' is much more difficult to conceptualize because it is homonymous, expressing more than one distinct meaning. Federalism is the driving force or dynamic that informs federation and can be construed in three separate ways: (i) as ideology, (ii) as philosophy, or (iii) as empirical fact. It can be *ideological* in the sense that it is a body of ideas that actively promotes federation. It can be a *philosophy* of federal ideas and principles that prescribes federation as the good life, or as the best way to organize human relations. Indeed, there exists a rich and well-established European philosophical tradition of federalism that includes such prominent Western political philosophers as Johannes Althusius, Immanuel Kant, Jean-Jacques Rousseau, and Pierre-Joseph Proudhon, as well as more recent contributors such as Alexandre Marc and Denis de Rougemont (see, for example, Carney 1964; Hueglin

1999; Riley 1973, 1976, and 1979; Elazar 1989; and Burgess 2000).

There is, however, a third meaning that can be attributed to federalism, namely, as an *empirical* fact. This pays homage to the complexity of human beings. The reasoning runs in the following way. Since we are each unique human beings that comprise bundles of different identities institutionalized in various forms of *voluntary* human association, it follows that the *formal* organization of human relations must be founded upon 'diversity' as its cardinal principle. Consequently, we require unity but not uniformity. In other words, we require a form of association which recognizes and can accommodate this complexity so that we have the relative autonomy to determine ourselves as individuals, groups, and collective identities within the union while simultaneously promoting the wider interests of the commonwealth. Transferred to the EU, this line of reasoning suggests that the 'ever closer union among the peoples of Europe' should be based upon the federal principle of 'unity in diversity'. Accordingly, the EU must be rooted in Elazar's notion, identified above, of 'self-rule plus shared rule'. The primary building blocks of the EU have already been formally reaffirmed in Article F(1), Title I, 'Common Provisions' of the Treaty on European Union (TEU), ratified in 1993, which committed the Union to respect the national identities of its member states.[2] Clearly the principal focus of 'diversity' in the EU is the 15 member states and the 15 national governments that represent them. In this rather narrow sense, then, the member states constitute one dimension of 'federalism' in the EU. They are, in addition, the constituent units of an emergent federal union (see Box 5.2).

However, if we were to focus solely upon the EU Council and the European Council (see Chapter 10) to the exclusion of other actors and institutions in the EU, this would approximate not to a 'federal', but rather to a 'confederal' conception of Europe. What then is the difference between the two? The conceptual distinction between federation and **confederation** is that the latter is a much looser form of union that is much less binding and regulated than the former, and which does not operate directly upon the citizens of the union in the way

Box 5.2 **Core ideas**
Federalism and subsidiarity

Depending on the definitions one uses, federalism and subsidiarity may be related concepts. For some subsidiarity is a guiding principle of federalism; whereas for others subsidiarity seems to imply the antithesis of federalism. Although discussed before, subsidiarity was introduced to the EC through the Single European Act of 1987. However, at this point it only applied to the treaty's environmental provisions. It was in the Treaty on European Union, agreed at Maastricht, that the subsidiarity principle became a general principle of Community law. Article 3b of the Treaty reads as follows:

> the Community shall act within the limits of the powers conferred upon it by this Treaty and of the objectives assigned to it therein. In areas which do not fall within its exclusive competence, the Community shall take action, in accordance with the principle of subsidiarity, only if and in so far as the objectives of the proposed action cannot be sufficiently achieved by the Member States and can therefore, by reason of the scale or effects of the proposed action, be better achieved by the Community. Any action by the Community shall

not go beyond what is necessary to achieve the objectives of the Treaty.

In the Preamble of the Treaty, there was also the suggestion that subsidiarity was related to decentralization. Article A implies that decision should be taken as closely as possible to the citizen.

However, these provisions leave much room for debate about the implications of subsidiarity. Some see it as little more than a 'rhetorical device' that no one can really disagree with or, more specifically, stress that it is not really about the allocation of competences between national and European levels of governance, but is about how they ought to be exercised (Dinan 2000: 440). Some even feel it should lead to the wholesale repatriation of European law to either the national or regional/local levels of governance.

After the Maastricht Treaty attempts were made to set out rules to operationalize the principle of subsidiarity (for example, by ensuring the Commission exercises self-restraint when drafting new legislation)—at the European Council meeting in Edinburgh in December 1992, most notably. The draft agreed in Edinburgh was incorporated into the Amsterdam Treaty in 1997.

Source: Dinan 2000: 439–41.

---

that federation does. Confederation is, in short, a form of union where the constituent units rather than the central authority remain the decisive force, and institutionalized diplomacy takes the place of federal government (Forsyth 1981).

Nevertheless, this confederal dimension to the EU is also subject to a wide variety of federalist forces and influences at both the EU and member-state levels, pressures that emanate from within both the Commission and the European Parliament (EP) at the EU level and from a host of interest groups, public organizations, and civil associations at the member-state level (Burgess 1989). The underlying commitment to building Europe that is evident in this multiplicity of forces—both state and non-state—has as one of its common goals the desire to institutionalize the concrete achievements of integration. Accordingly, this example of 'federalism without federation' impels us to focus

upon the peculiar relationship between federalism, federation, and European integration. It is important to look a little more closely at this relationship here before we examine it in more detail in the next section.

The evolution from a 'Community' to a 'Union' (see Chapter 4) corresponds to both a *quantitative* and a *qualitative* change in European integration. If we take the term 'integration' broadly to mean the coming together of previously separate or independent parts to form a new whole, we can see that it is a multidimensional process in that the shift from community to union has led to changes in the legal, economic, social, and political aspects of integration. Indeed, the EU is currently taking great strides in political integration, with the building of a constitutional and political Europe in the wake of the Single European Market (SEM) established by the Single European Act (SEA) and ratified in 1987. As

Jean Monnet, the principal architect of the Community, predicted, quantity (economic integration) appears to have led to an increasing emphasis upon quality (political integration). In other words, the objective is not just building an economic union whose sole purpose is, say, capital accumulation. Rather, European integration involves the construction of a viable, working political union founded upon peace, order, security, and welfare. In short, the EU as a federal union is supposed to represent a new moral force for good in European and world affairs.

Political elites in the member states and in the central institutions of the EU are now fully engaged in qualitative change, namely institutional reappraisal and constitution building. Consequently, today's EU comprises an institutionalized form of interstate relations, but also represents a radically new departure in the building of a union—a union of states *and* peoples. The EU, we are reminded, acts simultaneously upon *both* states and citizens in what remains Monnet's construction of Europe. We will explore the nature of the relationship between federalism, federation, and European integration a little later when we focus upon Monnet's conception of Europe and its political implications. The next section looks at the variety of federal models, in order to view the EU from a comparative federal perspective.

Key points

- Federalism is about 'self-rule plus shared rule' and 'unity in diversity'.

- There is an important moral dimension to federalism, as it is all about toleration, mutual respect, and equality of partnership, amongst other principles.

- Federalism also implies an institutional dimension, involving the sharing of powers between the centre and the regions or states, within the framework of an overarching constitution.

The variety of federal models

It is important to understand at the outset that, as Ronald Watts (1999: 1) has emphasized, there is no single, pure model of federation that is applicable everywhere. Historically, federal states have emerged at different times to suit different circumstances. In some cases they have been the result of long and complicated processes of aggregation, whereby previously separate parts have come together or have been created to form a new state, such as the United States of America (1789) or Switzerland (1848); while in others they have been the product of different kinds of devolution or decentralization, such as Canada (1867), Australia (1901), or India (1950).

The historical origins of federations vary with each different case and the motives for union are not always very clear. Generally speaking, however, two fundamental factors are invariably evident in some form at the creation of most, if not all, such voluntary unions. These are, first, the perception of an external threat that precipitates some form of union—as with the early evolution of Switzerland—chiefly for the purpose of security and sometimes called a *Kriegsverein* (military union); second, the drive to secure economic welfare—as with the early Dutch and German cases—often guides political and economic elites in their search for markets and trade. This is often called a *Zollverein* (customs union). Sometimes both of these motives are evident simultaneously, as with the examples of Canada, Australia, the United States, and, arguably, the EU (see McKay 2001).

Most mainstream studies of federations acknowledge the variation that exists in their internal structures. They recognize that there are broadly three types of federations: (i) the Westminster model; (ii) the republican-presidential model; and (iii) a hybrid type. Examples of the Westminster model, which is based upon representative and responsible government, are found in Canada, India, and Australia as former parts of the British Empire and then the Commonwealth. The republican-presidential model, by contrast, is most closely associated with the United States. Some might consider Belgium, with its constitutional monarchy and cabinet government responsible to the lower house, the Chamber of Deputies, to be closer to the Westminster model than to the republican-presidential type. Hybrid examples that combine elements of these two models are Germany, Austria, and Switzerland. However, while these groups of comparisons work well from the standpoint of internal structures, we must also consider how they would change if we adopted a different perspective, one which focused on the distribution of powers in federations. This viewpoint alters the comparison in significant ways. Watts (1999: ch. 9) has emphasized that the basic design of all federal models expresses the hallmark of self-rule and shared rule through the constitutional distribution of powers between those assigned to the federal government for common purposes and those assigned to the constituent states for the purposes of local autonomy and the preservation of distinct identities and specific interests.

According to the definition used earlier in this chapter, the EU is clearly not yet a fully fledged federation. Indeed, it is not yet a state and it may never become a state in the sense that we understand conventional federations. It does, however, already possess many state-like characteristics, such as a common currency (the euro), an independent central bank, an embryonic fiscal base, a single market, two distinct levels of government, dual citizen identities, and an evolving Common Foreign and Security Policy (CFSP), together with a yet incipient Common Defence Policy. And while many important policy sectors remain in the hands of the member governments, the EU also has ultimate authority in commercial transactions, transport, fisheries, and agricultural policies, as well as significant influence in environmental, regional development, and industry sectors. Consequently, the EU is already very close to being a new kind of state, or at least a 'federal-type' union, to the extent that it has increasingly adopted the institutional and policy features that are characteristic of established federations. The conventional strands of government as we know them—the legislative, executive, and judicial branches—are not organized along the same lines as the purported '**separation of powers**' in the United States, but they were origin-

ally arranged in the Treaty of Rome (1957) in such a manner as to balance the interests of individual constituent member states with those of the union as a whole, leaving plenty of scope for the later evolution of an 'ever closer union'. The increasingly complex decision-making procedures, involving **co-operation** and **co-decision** procedures, between the intergovernmental EU Council (the Ministers) and the European Council (heads of government), and the supranational Commission and European Parliament, are similar in many respects to those of a working federation. These, then, are just a few examples of how and why observers and commentators often perceive the EU as approximating to a federal Europe. Clearly there is plenty of evidence to substantiate this public perception.

Before leaving this short survey of the variety of federal models, we turn to their significance for the EU. What does the federal experience tell us about the EU? This is a question that resonates differently in different member states. Far from having little knowledge and experience of federations, the British have historically been involved in the application of the federal idea to a number of countries. Various federal models were used by the former Colonial Office to resolve an assortment of questions dealing with state building and national integration in the Empire and Commonwealth, including India, Australia, Canada, Central Africa, and the West Indies. To the British, then, federations have been practical proposals for export. But they were constructions for others, not for the British themselves. Thus, the federal idea has become associated with the creation of a constitutional and political force whose principal purpose was state and nation building. In short, for the British, the federal idea embodies, rightly or wrongly, connotations of centralization (Burgess 1995; but see Box 5.3).

Given this historical background, it is easy to understand British hostility to the building of a federal Europe. This perspective on federalism in the EU context inevitably pushes public debate and discourse down a road that leads many citizens in Denmark and Sweden, as well as in the UK, to the nightmare scenario of a 'superstate'. But this dystopia is not shared by the citizens of the majority of member states in the EU. Quite the reverse. In most of Europe the perception of the word 'federal' is

Box 5.3 **Case study**
Federalism 'between the wars'

The federalist movement in Europe emerged in the period between the First and Second World Wars. In the aftermath of the horror of the First World War, Count Richard Coudenhove-Kalergi, an Austrian count, argued the case for a European Union (a pan-Europa) as a way of countering the growing power of the USA and of Russia. His plans were picked up by Aristide Briand in the 1920s, who as French foreign minister proposed union as a way of maintaining the peace between France and Germany in 1929. Other proposals for federal union came from the UK, from writers such as Lord Lothian, Lionel Robbins, and William Beveridge, who predicted that Europe would make the same mistakes in the 1930s as it had done before the 'Great War' of 1914–18. Lord Lothian was

amongst those who gave their support to the establishment of the Federal Union, which was set up in 1938. By 1940 the Federal Union had recruited 10,000 members in 200 branches (Dedman 1996: 19). Once the Second World War had begun British federalist writings began to have a strong influence on thinking within the European resistance movements, particularly in Italy, and even before the war was over, there were plans for a new world order. Amongst those influenced was Altiero Spinelli, whose Ventotene Manifesto became a reference point for post-war federalists (Dinan 2000: 231). While imprisoned on the island of Ventotene, Spinelli also translated many of the Federal Union's tracts into Italian.

decentralist rather than centralist and a federal union is a political organization that both divides and shares power rather than concentrating it (as does a unitary state) in one centre.

There are, then, various federal models which furnish us with important lessons for the building of a federal Europe. The context, though, is of pivotal significance. The post-war experiment in European integration and co-operation is based on the territorial dispersion of power and is not designed to replicate, must less to replace, the constituent national and multinational states that comprise the EU. Nonetheless, the EU is greater than the sum of its parts. The genius of the federal idea lies in its simplicity: it seeks to bind the parts together in a way that benefits the whole. Let us now turn to look at Monnet's conception of Europe and its political

implications in order to understand precisely how and why the idea of a federal Europe has become a practical proposition.

Key points

- There are at least three different models of federalism: the republican-presidential model, the Westminster model, and a third hybrid version.

- The EU is not yet a fully fledged federal state. It does, however, have certain federal characteristics.

- British hostility to the federal model owes much to the fact that federalism has been associated with nation building and centralization.

Monnet's conception of Europe and its political implications

Jean Monnet was born in Cognac, France in 1888 and is considered one of the founders of the European Community. Monnet's conception of Europe

was rooted in his desire to remove for ever the causes of war—what he regarded as civil war—that periodically served to tear Europe apart. He sought, in an elemental sense, to identify the forces that drove Europeans to fight each other and, in contrast, to understand those forces that instilled in them a fundamental desire to co-operate with each other. In short, he wanted to persuade Europeans to channel their conflicts into a form of co-operation that would enable them to achieve their goals by seeking out and distilling their common interests. He believed that in every set of circumstances that might conceivably generate conflict there lurked a latent common interest that merely needed to be uncovered. This meant that states, governments, and citizens could be persuaded to transform their rivalries and animosities by changing the context in which these conflicts occurred. It was what he called 'the ECSC [European Coal and Steel Community] method' of establishing 'the greatest solidarity among peoples' so that 'gradually' other tasks and other people would become subject to the same common rules and institutions—or perhaps to new institutions—and this experience would 'gradually spread by osmosis'. No time limits were imposed on what was clearly deemed to be a long, slow, almost organic, process of economic and political integration:

We believed in starting with limited achievements, establishing *de facto* solidarity, from which a federation would gradually emerge. I have never believed that one fine day Europe would be created by some great political mutation, and I thought it wrong to consult the peoples of Europe about the structure of a Community of which they had no practical experience. It was another matter, however, to ensure that in their limited field the new institutions were thoroughly democratic; and in this direction there was still progress to be made ... the pragmatic method we had adopted would ... lead to a federation validated by the people's vote; but that federation would be the culmination of an existing economic and political reality, already put to the test ... it was bringing together men and practical matters (Monnet 1978: 367).

This extract from Monnet's *Memoirs* throws the relationship between federalism, federation, and European integration into sharp relief. It underlines the interaction between politics and economics as the driving force behind integration. In explaining how Europe could be built by piecemeal, incremental steps—concrete achievements that were tried and tested—Monnet both confronted and

confounded his contemporaries with the innovative idea of creating a federation via a hitherto unprecedented route (see also Chapter 6).

Changing the context of international relations in favour of the 'common interest' between states ensured that their energies were diverted from the competitive power politics that led to war, into new areas of unity and co-operation that transcended the state. In consequence, the EU has introduced a rule of law into relations between European countries which, as Duchêne (1994: 405) remarked, has 'cut off a whole dimension of destructive expectations in the minds of policy makers'. It has in practice domesticated the balance of power so that the power politics of the so-called 'realist' school of international relations has been replaced by 'aspirations that come nearer to the "rights" and responsibilities which reign in domestic politics'. In other words, Monnet's approach to the building of a federal Europe meant gradually internalizing what were previously the externalities of the state. This, it hardly needs emphasizing, was a major breakthrough in conventional interstate relations. Nonetheless, in seeking to build a federal Europe principally by means of a series of economic steps, Monnet was attempting something which had no historical precedent. Indeed, the EC and, since 1993, the EU has evolved in a very different way to other federations. To the extent that it has developed by the gradual 'aggregation' of previously separate political units, it is admittedly similar to the process by which the United States of America was consolidated during the years 1787–89. Here, however, the analogy ends. Past federations have been constructed as a result of treaty-like political negotiations which created a new federal constitution and government. There is no historical precedent for the creation of a multinational, multicultural, and multilingual federation or federal union composed of 15 or more national states, with mature social, economic, political, and legal systems. In this regard the EU is a colossal and original enterprise.

What, then, are the political implications of Monnet's Europe? How did he seek to transform his Europe by incremental economic steps into a federal Europe? And what sort of timescale did he envisage for this grand metamorphosis? The answers to these questions require us to return to some of the assumptions, already identified above, upon which his conception of Europe was originally based. If we recall Monnet's fervent belief in the significance of context and how it was possible to change the nature of problems by changing the context in which they were located, it was his own practical logic that compelled him to give that context a solid form. And it was institutional innovation that answered the call for new habits of thought and action.

The key to understanding the relationship between federalism, federation, and European integration lies in the belief that the forging of functional links between states in a way that does not directly challenge national sovereignty in a formal sense, will gradually open the door to federation. These so-called 'functional' links were primarily economic activities and they were perfectly expressed in the ECSC initiative of the early 1950s (see Chapter 2). This innovative form of supranational organization was to be the foundation of a European federation that would evolve only slowly to engage national elites in a process of mutual economic interest. These concrete benefits would gradually form that crucial solidarity—the common interest—which Monnet believed indispensable for the removal of physical and mental barriers (see also Chapter 6).

Institutional innovation, then, was vital to the success of European integration. Europeans were limited only by their imagination. If they could develop the vision to look beyond the national state to solve what were actually common problems, they could forge new co-operative links and foster new habits of working together in novel institutional circumstances. And novel institutions also implied novel decision-making processes and procedures to keep the wheels of integration turning. Nothing succeeds like success and as long as the 'Community experiment' yielded results that furnished tangible benefits for its participants, their commitment, based upon their perceptions of the national interest, was assured.

The political implications of Monnet's conception of Europe were and remain far-reaching principally because his particular approach to European integration was the one that succeeded. But Monnet was not without serious competitors in this quest and it is helpful for us to consider his approach from the standpoint of a much more conventional mainstream federalist perspective. Let us put Monnet, as it were, face to face with his main federalist rival, namely, Altiero Spinelli. Spinelli, an Italian, made the goal of a federal Europe his lifelong personal crusade. For our purposes, it is Spinelli's critique of what he called 'Monnet's method' that is of primary concern and we will use his critique to explore what he considered its political implications to be (see Burgess 2000; Pinder 1998).

The essence of the **Monnet Method**—his political strategy—for European integration was something that eventually came to constitute a major theoretical controversy about federalism, federation, and European integration. It was also the crux of Spinelli's opposition. This was that Monnet's own method of piecemeal, cumulative integration whereby 'political' Europe would be the 'culminating point of a gradual process' contained the huge assumption that at some future undefined point a qualitative change would occur in the constitutional and political relations between states and peoples. But he believed that this would happen only when 'the force of necessity' made it 'seem natural in the eyes of Europeans' (Monnet 1978: 394–5). In short, Monnet's approach to federation rendered constitutionalism—a political Europe—contingent upon the cumulative effect of functional achievements.

It was precisely at this juncture—in the interaction between politics and economics—that Spinelli entered the theoretical debate. Spinelli argued that the weakness of the 'Monnet Method' lay in its failure to deal with the organization of political power at the European level (Burgess 2000: 58). This meant that the political centre would remain weak and impotent, lacking the capacity to go much beyond what already existed. Spinelli's verdict on Monnet's conception of Europe can be succinctly summarized in the following way: it failed according to its own terms of reference. It simply did not possess that inherent sustaining dynamic which Monnet believed, at least initially, would evolve inexorably toward a union of peoples. The predicted shift from *quantity* to *quality* did not occur precisely because of Monnet's excessive reliance upon a functionalist or incrementalist logic. His confidence in such a logic was misplaced because he failed to confront the realities of organized political power. Only strong independent central political institutions could provide European solutions to European problems. Without these institutions, national responses would prevail. Spinelli acknowledged that Monnet had made the first steps easier to achieve, but he had done so by making the later steps more difficult. The building of a 'political' Europe based upon economic performance criteria would not necessarily follow, according to Monnet's logic, and as a consequence Spinelli argued that Europe might very well remain little more than a 'Common Market' (see Box 5.4).

In retrospect, Spinelli's criticisms of Monnet seem in one sense to have been vindicated. The EC/EU's central political institutions have certainly grown in political influence, but their powers and competences remain weak in certain important respects. The European Parliament (EP), for example, still has only very limited powers of accountability over the Council, while its control over the budget remains only partial and the application of **co-decision** is not yet extensive. These inter-institutional defects and deficiencies, however, are observations that rest on a conventional understanding of what federalism is. Not everybody wishes to see the EP's powers, functions, and role continue to grow exponentially. Indeed, some critics of the EP insist that its place in the institutional scheme of things remains ambiguous (see Chapter 11). Moreover, it could be argued that Spinelli underestimated the political will of the member states, invested in the European Council. In recent years this has taken several crucial steps forward in strengthening the EP and in buttressing **qualified majority voting** (QMV) in the Council. A series of intergovernmental conferences dating back at least to 1985 have produced the Single European Act (SEA), the Treaty on European Union (TEU), the Treaty of Amsterdam (TA), and more recently the Treaty of Nice, each of which has contributed to the building of a political Europe. Consequently, there remain certain grounds for optimism concerning Monnet's shift from *quantity* to *quality*. There is some evidence that we have witnessed *both* an expansion of quantity as well as a shift toward quality. In this respect, then, the political implications of Monnet's conception of Europe remain unclear.

If we move away from the institutional focus for a moment and turn our attention instead to policy matters, the profile of European integration becomes much more substantive and sophisticated. Here *quantity* has shifted unequivocally to *quality*. More and more policy matters that were formerly the exclusive domestic affairs of the member states have gradually been transferred to the EC and then the EU, so that Monnet's Europe has become a de facto polity with conspicuous policy outputs. The combination of an expanding policy arena increasingly subject to majority voting, and that is treaty-based, has therefore corresponded to the transformation of a 'Community' into a 'Union' in which salient supranational, federal, and intergovernmental features coexist, admittedly often uncomfortably, in permanent interplay and reciprocity.

Box 5.4 **Issues and debates**
Pragmatists v radicals

According to Harrison (1974) an important distinction to be made is that between radical federalists and moderates or pragmatists who accept a more incremental approach to unification, but are proud to carry the federalist flag. The radical federalists wanted a 'big bang' approach, creating a federal Europe by creating from the outset federal-type institutions. The more moderate federalists have much in common with neo-functionalists (see Chapter 6), and foresaw a federal outcome from an incremental or gradualist process of functional integration. Using this distinction, Altiero Spinelli was associated with radical federalist ideas, whereas Jean Monnet was a moderate federalist.

The political implications of Monnet's conception of Europe, then, harbour grounds for both optimism and pessimism. Much depends upon political leadership and the fortunes of the latest highly controversial enterprise, namely, the introduction of the euro in January 2002. The drive toward Economic and Monetary Union (EMU) is unquestionably a political imperative and constitutes yet another incremental step on the road towards a federal Europe. Accordingly, we will turn now to look more closely at what is meant by this ambiguous phrase.

Key points

- Jean Monnet was one of the founders of the European integration process.

- His federalism vision was an incremental one, constructed upon a functionalist logic.

- The so-called Monnet Method, a piecemeal approach to the construction of a federal Europe, contrasted with Spinelli's vision, which involved an immediate shift of political power at the European level.

The meaning of a federal Europe

In certain EU member states, students who are interested in European integration and its current institutional manifestation, namely the EU, are often confronted with the phrase 'a federal Europe' as if it were synonymous with eternal infamy. As we noted in the Introduction to this chapter, a conspicuous odium surrounds the word 'federal' and an acute anxiety is often attendant upon references to 'a federal Europe'. The phobia of federalism that is evident in some circles of opinion in the member states must be addressed, because it reflects genuine fears that deserve to be taken seriously. Mindful of such fears and anxieties, let us enter the conceptual world of a federal Europe to try to address the concerns of those who remain firm opponents of the idea, for whatever reason.

We have already explained and defined the meaning of federalism, federation, and European integration and we have briefly explored the relationship between these terms. One conclusion that we drew was that in the specific context of European integration, federalism is a particular form of political integration. It is based upon a conception of Europe that implies 'self-rule plus shared rule'. In other words, it refers to a particular way that we might prefer to organize Europe. And this particular conception of Europe has both organizational and institutional implications for the building and design of Europe—a voluntary union, we are reminded, that is to be founded upon liberal democratic principles which recognize, respect, and tolerate difference and diversity. What, then, will this 'federal Europe' look like? How will it be organized and constructed?

Spinelli always claimed that we must begin with what has already been implemented. We cannot go back to the drawing board. Consequently we have to accept Monnet's legacy. We have to build upon the *acquis communautaire*—the Community patrimony—and try to transfer as many intergovernmental functions and responsibilities into the *acquis* as changing political circumstances will allow. The EU remains, after all, at the mercy of intergovernmental whims and vagaries. But a federal Europe implies a much more binding and regulated union, where there is a much more equitable working relationship between the EU's central institutions than a purely intergovernmental perspective would allow.

From a federalist perspective, there is currently no institutional *balance* as such, but instead an institutional *imbalance*. The proverbial dice are still loaded in favour of the constituent member states' interests rather than those of the union as a whole. There is therefore a need to review and reappraise the existing institutional framework and its interinstitutional relations, powers, and competences.

The *organization* of the EU is predicated upon

the existence of a voluntary union with a central authority (in Brussels) that is a creature of its member states. And it is here that federalism and federation, properly understood, constitute the antidote to public misgivings. It is precisely a federal Europe that guards against the feared usurpation of power either by the constituent members of the union or by the new central authority itself. Indeed, one of the purposes of a federal union or federation (as opposed to a unitary, legislative union) is precisely to place formal limits upon the growth of the central authority. But this is not to suggest that there should be no central authority or that it must be prevented from growing at all. There is no such thing as a union characterized by non-centralization. It is rather to accept and acknowledge that the EU must be based upon limited centralization. The organization of the EU based upon federal principles furnishes a guarantee that its increasing strength and capacity to mobilize resources will be limited, controlled, justified, and made persistently accountable.

The construction of Europe is, then, a question of organization. According to federal principles that imply a contractually binding, but limited, form of union in which power is divided and shared between the component states that created it, on the one hand, and the overarching central authority of the union, on the other, there are potentially an infinite number of institutional variations and jurisdictional permutations available. Monnet's approach meant that the architects of Europe had no need to start with a constitution and never had to concern themselves very much with the contentious question of national sovereignty. A federal Europe was to be the culmination, not the beginning, of a long process of economic integration. In view of these circumstances, it is hardly surprising that Monnet should have placed greater emphasis upon the unprecedented institutional innovation of the supranational High Authority rather than the familiar European Assembly when he created the ECSC in 1951.

The institutional framework of the European federal project has always been lopsided, with the dice heavily loaded in favour of the member states represented in the Council, and later the European Council, so that **intergovernmentalism** has co-existed with **supranationalism** from the outset. But as the policy commitment of the Community has expanded from the late 1950s, the growing influence and powers of both the EP and the European Court of Justice (ECJ)—in conjunction with an intermittently assertive European Commission—have strengthened the federal elements that sit alongside the confederal European Council of heads of state and government. And it is important that we do not forget that the EU Council (composed of national ministers) and the European Council, in representing the member state governments, are also both *central institutions* of the EU. From our standpoint in this chapter, they are essentially confederal and also constitute an intrinsic part of the EU's constantly evolving institutional composition.

This brings us to the future of institutional reform. Historically it has to be admitted that the EC/EU has merely tinkered with the system so that it has been modified rather than fully reformed. Consequently the central institutions of the EU today that service a union of 15 member states are remarkably similar to those that were established for the six founding members of the EEC in the Treaty of Rome in 1957. From the standpoint of the new millennium, it has to be acknowledged that thus far there seems to be very little millennial thinking about this colossal problem. One significant development, however, has come in the form of evidence of a shift in elite governmental thinking in favour of constitutionalizing the EU. By identifying what each EU institution should do, this would draw firm lines to divide and share powers and competences among the EU's federal and confederal institutions so that both transparency and accountability could be effectively transmitted to both EU elites and mass publics. Accordingly, at the Laeken meeting (see Chapter 4: 58–61) in December 2001, the member governments took the step, albeit tentatively, towards a new constitution for the EU at the next intergovernmental conference in 2004. A review of the treaties and the working methods of the EU has already begun, but much remains to be done. Nonetheless, it is beginning to look as if the constitutional and political chickens of Monnet's Europe are finally coming home to roost.

Paradoxically, the meaning of a federal Europe is

both simple and complex. At its most elementary level it means 'common solutions to common problems' based upon 'self-rule plus shared rule'. A more sophisticated interpretation compels us to look very closely at the basis of the EU's emerging constitution: its principles, objectives, institutional powers and relationships, and its policy-making and implementation structures. This combination of the simple and the complex means a federal Europe that would constitute a new kind of union of states and citizens. This would rely on both integration and co-operation in an increasingly competitive world of globalized relationships where the familiar 'nation state' competes with rival non-state international actors. In short, the introduction of an EU constitution would simply represent the latest European adaptation to international developments.

Key points

- To address the extent to which the EU is already federal involves looking at the organization of the Union.
- The EU remains more confederal or intergovernmental than federal.
- The EU is involved in a process of institutional reform, which could lead to the drafting of a European constitution and further moves in a federal direction.

Conclusion: From quantity to quality

This chapter has explained the meaning of a federal Europe by exploring the conceptual interrelationships between federalism, federation, and European integration and by examining the political implications of Monnet's conception of Europe. It has demonstrated that a federal Europe will not be either a United States or Switzerland writ large. It will not replicate the conventional processes of traditional state building and national integration that we associate with the contemporary nation state. Nor will it approximate to the sort of international organizations with which we customarily identify, such as the United Nations. Instead an emerging federal Europe would constitute a new kind of political union in world affairs standing in a long line of voluntary historical unions stretching back several centuries. This new form of union can be described as either 'neo-federal' or neo-confederal', but there is no doubt that it represents a new era in the history of interstate relations in Europe (Burgess 2000: ch. 8). In this sense, quantity is about to transform into quality.

QUESTIONS

1 What is the relationship between federation, federalism, and European integration?

2 What was Jean Monnet's contribution to federal union in Europe after the Second World War?

3 Why did Altiero Spinelli criticize the so-called 'Monnet Method' of European integration?

4 Why do the British have a particularly hostile attitude to European federalism?

5 What are the key characteristics of a federal union?

6 Which model of federalism does the EU most resemble?

7 In what sense is there a moral dimension to federalism?

8 How might a confederal union differ from a federal union?

GUIDE TO FURTHER READING

Burgess, M., *Federalism and the European Union: The Building of Europe 1950–2000* (London: Routledge, 2000). A historical account of the integration of Europe, focusing on the role played by federalist ideas.

—— and Gagnon, A.-G. (eds), *Comparative Federalism and Federation* (Hemel Hempstead: Harvester Wheatsheaf, 1983). An edited book looking at the concepts of federalism and federation, and including a range of country case studies which identify different traditions of federalism and federation.

Elazar, D. J., *Exploring Federalism* (Tuscaloosa, Ala.: University of Alabama Press, 1987). An excellent study of what federalism means from an authority on the subject.

Forsyth, M., *Union of States* (Leicester: Leicester University Press, 1981). A seminal study of confederation. While its focus is on European integration, this book draws on many example of confederation and federation to explore the process by which states transform themselves.

Jeffrey, C., and Sturm, R. (eds), *Federalism, Unification and European Integration* (London: Frank Cass, 1993). An edited book which looks at federalism in the new unified Germany, in a European context, from a variety of different perspectives.

Pinder, J., *European Community: Building of a Union* (Oxford: Oxford University Press, 1995). A useful general text on the European integration process, written from a federalist perspective, and the historical process from EC to EU.

WEB LINKS

www.federalunion.uklinex.net Website of the UK's Federal Union, an organization set up in 1938 to campaign for federalism in the UK, in Europe, and in the world. Lots of useful 'pro-federalist' material.

http://europa.eu.int/comm/public-opinion/archives/eb/eb44/eb44_en.htm Eurobarometer. Some public opinion data on 'The regions and a federal structure for Europe'.

www.sussex.ac.uk/Units/SEI/oern/index.html Opposing Europe Research Network: academic website, including a number of papers on the phenomenon of euroscepticism in Europe.

ENDNOTES

1. Preamble to the Treaty establishing the European Economic Community (EEC), Text of the Treaty, *Treaties Establishing The European Communities* (Abridged Edition) (Luxembourg: Office for Official Publications of the EC, 1987): 119.

2. Title I, Common Provisions, Article F(1), *Treaty on European Union* (Luxembourg: Office for Official Publications of the EC, 1992): 9.

6 Neo-functionalism

Carsten Strøby Jensen

READER'S GUIDE

This chapter reviews a theoretical position, neo-functionalism, which was developed in the mid-1950s by scholars based in the United States. The fundamental argument of the theory is that states are not the only important actors on the international scene. As a consequence, neo-functionalists focus their attention on the role of supranational institutions and non-state actors, such as interest groups and political parties who, they argue, are the real driving force behind regional integration efforts. The chapter that follows provides an introduction to the main features of neo-functionalist theory, and to its historical development since the 1950s. It focuses, more specifically, on three theses advanced by neo-functionalists: the spillover thesis; the elite socialization thesis; and the supranational interest group thesis. The chapter also considers the main critiques of the theory to explain why it went out of fashion in the 1970s. The final section scrutinizes the revival of interest in neo-functionalism in the late 1980s and 1990s, as well as providing some examples of how today's neo-functionalists differ from those of the 1950s.

Introduction

Neo-functionalism is often the first theory of European integration studied by students of the European Union. This is largely for historical reasons, as neo-functionalism was the first attempt at theorizing the new form of regional co-operation that emerged at the end of the Second World War. Although few researchers of European integration would now accept all neo-functionalist arguments, the theory remains important because its concepts and assumptions have become part of the so-called **Monnet Method** of European integration (see Chapter 5: 72–6). Indeed, at times it has been difficult to separate the theory of integration from the reality of the EC/EU. This has been something of a curse for neo-functionalism, as it has meant that its success as a theory became inextricably tied to the success of the European integration project. But it does mean that it is possible to chart the history of the EC/EU through the lens of neo-functionalism, as we shall see below.

The chapter begins by asking 'what is neo-functionalism?' The purpose of this first section is to outline the general characteristics of the theory. The second section then summarizes the rise and fall from grace of neo-functionalism between the 1950s and the 1970s. The third section examines three theses which form the core of neo-functionalist thinking. These are: (a) the spillover thesis; (b) the elite socialization thesis; and (c) the supranational interest group thesis. These three arguments help to expose neo-functionalist beliefs about the dynamics of the European integration process. The fourth section reviews the main criticisms of the neo-functionalist school, while the final section turns to more recent adaptations of neo-functionalist ideas, accounting for the renewal of interest in this approach to the study of regional integration at the end of the 1980s. The chapter concludes by stressing that although some researchers have rediscovered neo-functionalism long after the mid-1950s, its application is very different today. Despite a revival of interest in some of its key concepts, for most students of European integration, neo-functionalism remains as much outside the mainstream of theorizing in the field as it was back in the 1970s.

What is neo-functionalism?

The story of neo-functionalism began in 1958 with the publication by Ernst B. Haas of *The Uniting of Europe: Political, Social and Economic Forces 1950–1957*. In this seminal book, Haas explained how six West European countries came to initiate a new form of supranational co-operation after the Second World War. Originally, Haas's main aim in formulating a theoretical account of the European Coal and Steel Community (ECSC) was to provide a scientific and objective explanation of regional co-operation, a grand theory that would explain similar processes elsewhere in the world (in Latin America, for example). However, neo-functionalism soon became very closely associated with the EC case and with, moreover, a particular path of European integration. Moreover, some argued that despite the scientific language, neo-functionalism was imbued from the outset with pro-integration assumptions that were not made explicit in the theory.

Three characteristics of neo-functionalist theory help to address the question: what is neo-functionalism? First, neo-functionalism's core concept is that of spillover. This is covered in more detail later in the chapter. It is important to note at this point, however, that neo-functionalism was mainly concerned with the *process* of integration (and had little to say about end-goals, that is, how an integrated Europe would look). As a consequence, the theory sought to explain the dynamics of change to which states were subject when they co-operated. Haas's theory, then, was based on the assumption that co-operation in one policy area would create pressures in a neighbouring policy area, placing it on the political agenda, and ultimately leading to further integration. Thus, spillover refers to a situation where co-operation in one field necessitates co-operation in another. This might suggest that the process is automatic, that is, beyond the control of political leaders. However, when we look at the various forms of spillover identified by Haas, we will see how this 'automatic' process might be guided or manipulated by actors and institutions whose motives are unequivocally political.

Box 6.1 **Core ideas**
Key features of neo-functionalism

- Neo-functionalism is a theory of regional integration which seeks to explain the *process* of (European) integration.

- The theory was particularly influential in the 1950s and 1960s.

- The main focus of the theory is on the 'factors' that drive integration: interest group activity; political party activity; the role of governments and supranational institutions.

- The driving force of integration is deemed to be the self-interest of groups and institutions. They may well have different goals in mind, but the actions they choose, in order to achieve those goals, drives forward the integration process.

- The theory is said to be elitist in the sense that it relies on the 'permissive consensus' of the peoples of Europe. In other words, regional integration is seen as an elite-driven process.

- The concept of spillover is also known as the 'expansive logic of integration'. The 'spilling over' of integration can occur across sectors, but may also involve a shift to a new centre of popular loyalty (at a supranational level).

A second, albeit related, point which helps to explain neo-functionalism concerns the role of societal groups in the process of integration. Haas argued that interest groups and political parties would be key actors in driving integration forward. While governments might be reluctant to engage in integration, groups would see it as being in their interest to push for further integration. This is because groups would see integration as a way of resolving problems they faced. Although groups would invariably have different problems and, indeed, different ideological positions, they would, according to neo-functionalists, all see regional integration as a means to their desired ends. Thus, one might see integration as a process driven by the *self-interest* of groups, rather than by any ideological vision of a united Europe or shared sense of identity.

Finally, neo-functionalism is often characterized as a rather elitist approach to European integration. Although it sees a role for groups in the integration process, integration tends to be driven by functional and technocratic needs. Though not apolitical, it sees little role for democratic and accountable governance at the level of the region. Rather, the 'benign elitism' of neo-functionalists tends to assume the tacit support of the European peoples—a 'permissive consensus'—upon which experts and executives rely when pushing for further European integration. See Box 6.1 for a summary of the key features of neo-functionalism.

Key points

- Neo-functionalism is a theory of regional integration, popular in the 1950s and 1960s.

- The theory deals with the dynamics of the integration *process*, particularly with regard to the European case. The core concept of neo-functionalism is spillover.

- The theory assumes that integration relies on the self-interest of societal groups. It is also often considered a rather elitist theory.

A brief history of neo-functionalism

Neo-functionalism is very much connected to the case of European integration. Indeed, most neo-functionalist writers have focused their attention on Europe (Lindberg 1963; Lindberg and Scheingold 1970, 1971). This was not their original intention, however. Rather, an early objective was to formulate a general or **grand theory** of international relations, based on observations of regional integration processes. Political and economic co-operation in Latin America was one of the cases investigated to that end (Haas and Schmitter 1964). It was in Europe, however, that political and economic integration was best developed and most suited to theoretical and empirical study. Therefore Europe and European integration became the major focus of neo-functionalists during the 1960s and 1970s.

With the benefit of hindsight the success of neo-functionalism is understandable, as it seemed that the theory explained well the reality of the European integration process at that time. Until the 1970s, neo-functionalism had wide support in academic circles, though after that it lost much of its appeal among researchers. Indeed, it almost disappeared as a theoretical and empirical position in the study of European integration. One reason for this was that neo-functionalism lacked a theoretically solid base for its observations. Another reason was that the kind of incremental political integration that neo-functionalism predicted did not take place. From the mid-1970s, political co-operation seemed less compelling and researchers became more interested in other kinds of theories, especially those that stressed the importance of the nation state. Even Haas was among those who recognized the limitations of neo-functionalism. On this point he wrote that 'the prognoses often do not match the diagnostic sophistication, and patients die when they should recover, while others recover even though all the vital signs look bad' (Haas 1975: 5).

In the late 1980s and during the 1990s neo-functionalism underwent a sort of revival. The new dynamism of the EC/EU, a consequence of the single market programme (see Chapter 3), made theories focusing on processes of political integration relevant once again (Tranholm-Mikkelsen 1991). And even traditional critics of neo-functionalism, such as Paul Taylor, accepted the need to examine this approach more closely. On this point, Taylor (1993: 77) wrote that:

The student of the European Community . . . needs to return to the writings of . . .—the neo-functionalists—whose writings for many years have been unfashionable. They provide the essential context of theory in which to place the practice of diplomacy and even the speeches of Prime Ministers so that they might be better understood.

Since this revival of interest in neo-functionalism, a number of scholars have sought to adapt the theory to their own research agendas—whether on the European integration process writ large, on specific policy areas, or on the role of the supranational institutions. These new approaches will be reviewed towards the end of this chapter.

Key points

- Neo-functionalism was fashionable amongst elites and academics until the 1970s.

- From the 1970s, other theoretical and conceptual approaches seemed to fit the reality of European integration much better than neo-functionalism, and the theory became absolete.

- In the 1980s, with the revival of the integration process, there came also a renewed interest in neo-functionalism. This led to a wave of further research, which used certain elements of the neo-functionalists' conceptual tool-kit.

Supranationalism and spillover

The key question asked by neo-functionalists is whether and how economic integration leads to political integration. And if it does so, what kind of political unity will result? In this respect neo-functionalism differs from other traditional approaches to international relations theory. Traditionally more **realist** positions have stressed the power games that occur between states. Among neo-functionalists it was believed that economic integration would strengthen all the states involved, and that this would lead to further political integration. The fundamental idea was that international relations should not be seen as a zero-sum game, and that everybody wins when countries become involved in processes of economic and political integration.

Another important aspect of neo-functionalist theory is related to the development of supranational institutions and organizations. Supranational institutions are likely to have their own political agendas. Over time, neo-functionalists predict, the supranational agenda will tend to triumph over interests formulated by member states. As an example one might look at how the European Parliament (EP) operates. Members of the EP are directly elected within the member states. One would therefore expect it to be an institution influenced very much by national interests. In the Parliament, however, Members of the European Parliament (MEPs) are not divided into groups relating to their national origin. They are organized along party political and ideological lines. In other words, social democrats from Germany work together with Labour members from the UK, and liberals from Spain work with liberals from Denmark. According to neo-functionalist theory MEPs tend to become more European in their outlook, as a consequence of these working practices, though in practice this may be disputed empirically. This is often referred to as 'elite socialization'. The fact that MEPs work together across borders makes it difficult for them to focus solely on national interests. This also makes the EP a natural ally for the European Commission in its discussions with the EU Council, even if the

institutions do not always agree wholeheartedly on matters of policy.

Political integration is therefore a key concept for neo-functionalists, though it is possible to identify a number of different understandings of political integration in their writings. Lindberg (1971: 59), for example, stressed that political integration involves governments doing together what they used to do individually. It is about setting up supranational and collective decision-making processes. By contrast, Haas tended to see political integration in terms of shifts in attitudes and loyalties among political actors. In 1958 he famously wrote:

Political integration is the process whereby political actors in several distinct national settings are persuaded to shift their loyalties, expectation and political activities toward a new centre, whose institutions possess or demand jurisdiction over the pre-existing national states. The end result of a process of political integration is a new political community, superimposed over the pre-existing ones (Haas 1958: 16).

Neo-functionalist writers developed at least three different arguments about the dynamics of the integration processes: (a) the spillover thesis; (b) the elite socialization thesis; and (c) the thesis on supranational interest groups. The following subsections set out the content of these theses and the following section presents critiques of these arguments.

Spillover

Spillover is neo-functionalism's best known concept, one which has been widely used both by social scientists and by practitioners. According to Lindberg (1963: 10), the concept of spillover refers to a process where political co-operation conducted with a specific goal in mind leads to the formulation of new goals in order to assure the achievement of the original goals. What this means is that political co-operation, once initiated, is extended over time in a way that was not necessarily intended at the outset.

In order to fulfil certain goals, states co-operate on a specific issue. For example, the original aim may be the free movement of workers across EU borders. But it may soon become obvious that different national rules concerning certification prevent workers from gaining employment in other EU states. For example, nurses educated in one member state may not be allowed to work in another because of differences in national educational systems. As a consequence, new political goals in the field of education policy may be formulated so as to over-come this obstacle to the free movement of labour. This process of generating new political goals is the very essence of the neo-functionalist concept of spillover.

Spillover refers . . . to the process whereby members of an integration scheme—agreed on some collective goals for a variety of motives but unequally satisfied with their attainment of these goals—attempt to resolve their dissatis-faction by resorting to collaboration in another, related sector (expanding the scope of mutual commitment) or by intensifying their commitment to the original sector (increas-ing the level of mutual commitment), or both (Schmitter 1969: 162).

A distinction is often drawn between three types of spillover: functional (or technical) spillover, political spillover, and cultivated spillover (Nye 1971; Tranholm-Mikkelsen 1991: see also Box 6.2).

An example of *functional spillover* may be seen in the case of the single European market (see Chapter 3). The single market was functionally related to common rules governing the working environment. For example, some of the trade barriers to be removed under the single market programme took the form of national regulations on health and safety matters, as different health and safety regulations across the Community prevented free movement. The functional consequence of establishing a single market was, then, that the member states ended up accepting the regulation of the certain aspects of the working environment at European level (Jensen 2000).

Political spillover refers to situations where policy areas are deliberately linked together, not because they are functionally or technologically related, but for political or ideological reasons (Nye 1971: 202). Special interests are often promoted via so-called **'package deals'**, where steps are taken to treat a number of apparently discrete issues as a single (composite) item, enabling all (or the majority

of) actors to safeguard their interests (Lindberg and Scheingold 1970: 116).

For example, if one member state has an interest in a certain policy area, for example to prevent cuts in agricultural spending, while another member state has interests in industrial policy, these member states may agree, formally or informally, to support each other in negotiations. As a result the two policy areas become linked with in the bargaining process. Package dealing can often be observed during treaty revisions (see Box 6.3).

Cultivated spillover may be observed in situations where supranational actors like the Commission try to push forward a supranational or transnational agenda, even where member states are reluctant to accept further integration. In the EU, the Commis-sion often acts as a mediator of national interests in Council negotiations, with the aim of establishing compromises among member states. But when neo-functionalists talk about cultivated spillover they are referring to situations where actors like the Commission act not only as mediators, but also more directly as agents of political integration or as **'policy entrepreneurs'**.

Thus, spillover processes may be seen partly as the result of unintended consequences. Member states might deliberately accept political integration and the delegation of authority to supranational institu-tions on a particular issue. However as a result of that decision, they may suddenly find themselves in a position where there is a further need for even more delegation. As a result, Lindberg and Scheingold are right to stress that political integration need not be the declared end-goal for member states engaging in this process. The latter have their own respective goals, which are likely to have more to do with policy issues than with integration per se. As Lindberg and Scheingold write:

We do not assume that actors will be primarily or even at all interested in increasing the scope and capacities of the system per se. Some will be, but by and large most are concerned with achieving concrete economic and welfare goals and will view integration only as a means to these ends (Lindberg and Scheingold 1970: 117).

In this sense the establishment of supranational institutions such as the EU may be seen as the result of unintended consequences of actions among the actors involved in decision making.

Box 6.2 **Core ideas**
Types of spillover

- **Functional spillover** takes place when co-operation in one sector/issue area creates pressures for co-operation in another related area.

- **Political spillover** refers to situations characterized by a more deliberate political process, as when actors

make package deals in order to establish common agreement in a range of policy areas.

- **Cultivated spillover** occurs in situations where supranational actors like the European Commission establish an agenda which involves the deepening of political integration at the supranational level.

Box 6.3 **Case study**
Establishing a European social dimension

During the 1990s critics of the EU often said that it dealt mainly with matters relating to big business. The Union, it was said, was not concerned with the problems of ordinary Europeans. Some trade union officials argued that the single market would lead to social dumping (that is, the lowering of social standards in order to enhance competitiveness), if the Community did not establish some kind of cross-national social and labour market policy. In the Commission this criticism was widely accepted during the 1990s, and in order to react to this point the Commission

launched the idea of a 'social dimension' for the European Community. The idea was that economic liberalization would be balanced by a social policy, ensuring a safety net for European workers. From a neo-functionalist perspective this can be seen as an example of political and cultivated spillover. The Commission tried to establish a political connection between the single market and the establishment of a social dimension in Europe, although these areas are not functionally related (Jensen 2000).

Elite socialization

The second aspect of neo-functionalist theory concerns the development of supranational loyalties by participants such as officials and politicians in the decision-making process. The thesis here is that, over time, people involved on a regular basis in the supranational policy process will tend to develop European loyalties and preferences (Pentland 1973). For example, Commission officials are expected to hold a European perspective on problem solving so that their loyalty may no longer be to any one national polity, but rather to the supranational level of governance.

We can well imagine how participants engaged in an intensive ongoing decision-making process, which may extend over several years and bring them into frequent and close personal contact, and which engages them in a joint problem-solving and policy-generating exercise, might develop a special orientation to that process and to those interactions,

especially if they are rewarding. They may come to value the system and their roles within it, either for itself or for the concrete rewards and benefits it has produced or that it promises (Lindberg and Scheingold 1970: 119).

Thus neo-functionalists predicted that the European integration process would lead to the establishment of elite groups loyal to the supranational institutions and holding pan-European norms and ideas. This elite will try to convince national elites of the advantages of supranational co-operation. At the same time neo-functionalists also predicted that international negotiations would become less politicized. The institutionalization of the interactions between national actors, and the continued negotiations between different member states, would make it more and more difficult for states to adhere to their political arguments, *and* retain their credibility (Haas 1958: 291). As a result, it was expected that the agenda would tend to shift towards more technical problems upon which it was possible to forge agreement.

The formation of supranational interest groups

According to neo-functionalist theory, civil servants are not the only groups that develop a supranational orientation. Organized interest groups are also expected to become more European, as corporations and business groups formulate their own interests with an eye to the supranational institutions (see Chapter 13). As economic and political integration in a given region develops, interest groups will try to match this development through a process of reorganization, to form their own supranational organizations. For example, national industrial and employers organizations established a common European organization, UNICE, in 1958, at much the same time as the European Community was established. In so doing, their intention was to influence future Community policy. Early neo-functionalists also saw a similar role for political parties.

Furthermore, neo-functionalists believed that interest groups would put pressure on governments to force them to speed up the integration process. These groups were expected to develop their own supranational interest in political and economic integration, which would ally them to supranational institutions, such as the European Commission. Thus, 'in the process of reformulating expectations and demands, the interest groups in question approach one another supranationally while their erstwhile ties with national friends undergo deterioration' (Haas 1958: 313).

Before we examine criticisms of the neo-functionalist approach, it is important to stress the following point. Neo-functionalism is often compared to or is seen as connected with federalism (see Chapter 5). Federalists argue that the EU should establish strong federal institutions leading in the end to the creation of a federation with some similarities to the USA. Sometimes neo-functionalism is seen as a theoretical approach that supports a federalist agenda. Neo-functionalists, like federalists, talk about processes of political integration, and about the advantages of this process. (See Box 6.4

Box 6.4 **Core ideas**

Neo-functionalist expectations about the European institutions

Neo-functionalists have formulated theories which they have used to predict the behaviour of the European institutions.

- **The European Commission** is expected to act as a 'political entrepreneur', as well as a mediator. The Commission will, according to neo-functionalist theory, try to push for greater co-operation between the member states in a direction that leads to more and more supranational decision making.

- **The European Court** is expected not only to rule on the basis of legal arguments, but also to favour political integration. In this way, the Court will seek to expand the logic of Community law to new areas.

- **The European Parliament** is expected to be a supranationally orientated institution and to be a natural ally of the European Commission. Although MEPs are elected by the nationals of their home country, they are divided politically and ideologically in their daily work. Neo-functionalists expect MEPs to

 develop loyalties towards the EU and the 'European idea', so that they would often (though not always) defend European interests against national interests.

- **The Council of Ministers** is expected to be the institution where national interests are defended. However neo-functionalists would expect member states from time to time to be influenced by the logic of spillover, which will lead them to argue for more and more economic and political integration, despite their national interests. The member states are also expected to be influenced by the fact that they are involved in ongoing negotiations in a supranational context. This makes it difficult for a member state to resist proposals which lead to further political integration.

for neo-functionalists' expectations about European institutions.) However neo-functionalists like Haas (Haas 1971: 20–1) stressed that neo-functionalism and federalism are very different in several respects. Most important of these, according to Haas, is that federalism is a political position, while he claimed that neo-functionalism is both theoretical and scientific. Federalists are interested in how things ought to be, while neo-functionalists analyse the processes of integration and disintegration from a scientific point of view. However, critics of neo-functionalism might dispute the claim that neo-functionalism is devoid of a political agenda.

Key points

- Neo-functionalists believe that there are three types of spillover—functional, political, and cultivated. Each accounts for a different dynamic of the integration process.

- 'Elite socialization' implies that over time people involved in European affairs shift their loyalties to the European institutions and away from their nation state.

- Neo-functionalists believe that interest groups also become more European, placing demands on their national governments for more integration.

Critiques of neo-functionalism

We now review briefly the main criticisms of neo-functionalism made by observers such as Haas (1975, 1976), Moravcsik (1993, 1998), Taylor (1990, 1993), Keohane and Nye (1975), and Keohane and Hoffman (1991).

Neo-functionalism has been criticized on both empirical and theoretical grounds. At an empirical level the criticism, for obvious reasons, focused on the absence (or slow pace) of political integration in Western Europe during the 1970s and up to the mid-1980s. Neo-functionalism had predicted a pattern of development characterized by a gradual intensification of political integration, a development that by the 1970s had clearly not taken place. The French boycott of the European institutions in the mid-1950s had led to a more cautious phase in the evolution of the Community, and a recognition of the importance of political leaders as constraints on the process of integration. Indeed, with the European Community having suffered numerous crises, it could even be argued that the integration process had reversed. Moravcsik writes that:

Despite the richness of its insights, neo-functionalism is today widely regarded as having offered an unsatisfactory account of European integration. . . . The most widely-cited reason is empirical: neo-functionalism appears to mispredict both the trajectory and the process of EC evolution. Insofar as neo-functionalism advances a clear precondition about the trajectory in the EC over time, it was that the technocratic imperative would lead to a 'gradual', 'automatic' and 'incremental' progression toward deeper integration and greater supranational influence (Moravcsik 1993: 476).

Even Haas talked about the possibility that there might be a disintegrative equivalent to spillover, which might be labelled 'spillback'!

However, alongside these empirical critiques lie theoretical objections, which cover a broader spectrum. Here we shall focus on three main types of criticism. The first set of objections was aimed at the theses advanced by neo-functionalists. An example of this is Taylor's challenges to the elite socialization thesis, and to the idea that supranational loyalties would emerge in institutions such as the Commission. Taylor (1990) pointed out that, rather than integration making officials more European, it was the interests of the member states in having 'national' civil servants in the Commission that increased as political integration intensified. Member states became increasingly aware of the need to ensure that they reached 'their' quota of European civil servants (Taylor 1990: 180) and that their interests were represented. Moreover, it was surmised that European civil servants would become more nationally orientated when vital political issues were on the agenda (see also Hooghe 2002).

The second set of objections was based on criticism of the theories formulated by Haas himself. By the late 1960s Haas had accepted that the prediction that regional organizations such as the EU would develop incrementally, propelled forward by various dynamics such as spillover, failed to encapsulate the reality of European co-operation (Haas 1975, 1976). He recommended a different approach to regional integration, based on theories of interdependence which were being developed in the mid-1970s by Keohane and Nye (1975, 1976), amongst others. This approach argues that institutions such as the EC/EU should be analysed against the background of the growth in international interdependence, rather than as regional political organizations (Haas 1976: 208). Referring to European integration, Haas wrote that 'What once appeared to be a distinctive "supranational" style now looks more like a huge regional bureaucratic appendage to an intergovernmental conference in permanent session' (Haas 1975: 6). In so arguing, Haas himself abandoned the theory he had been so instrumental in developing.

Haas had argued that one of the factors reducing the level of predictability or inevitability of integration was the replacement of traditional forms of functional policy links (that is, functional spillover) by what he referred to as 'deliberated linkage'. In essence, what Haas was saying was that political and cultivated forms of spillover were replacing the original functional logic. This meant that over time the political linkage of package deals became more and more central and more and more complex, increasing the uncertainty surrounding the integration process both for the researcher and for the participant (Haas 1976: 209). Haas emphasized another, and possibly more important deficiency— that the theory of regional integration had focused too narrowly on the region as an isolated entity, ignoring the impact of external factors.

In the third group of objections to the theory, it was argued that neo-functionalism had placed undue emphasis on the supranational component in regional integration. Critics suggested that greater importance should be attached to the nation state, and that regional forms of co-operation should be analysed as intergovernmental organizations. This line of attack was adopted by Moravcsik (1993, 1998) amongst others, under the rubric of **liberal intergovernmentalism** (see Chapter 7): 'Whereas neo-functionalism stresses the autonomy of supranational officials, liberal intergovernmentalism stresses the autonomy of national leaders' (Moravcsik 1993: 491). This can be read as a claim that the nation state remains the core element in any understanding of international relations, including interpretations of the development of co-operation within the EU framework. If we accept this thesis, it obviously imposes limits on opportunities for political integration. The assumption appears to be that political integration is based exclusively on the aggregate interests of the single nation state and on its determination to survive. Nation states are thus prepared to cede formal competence to supranational institutions only if by so doing can they ensure, or possibly regain, control of specific areas of policy.

Finally, there is also a different type of criticism, which relates to what we might call the elitist nature of neo-functionalism. This criticism attacks the prescriptive implications of the approach, rather than the theory itself and so is of a different nature from the critiques already outlined. The argument here is that neo-functionalism not merely is a scientific and objective theory of regional integration, but has also become an essential part of a model of European integration. It is this model, which some call the 'Monnet Method' or the 'Community Method', that is subject to the criticism that it does not involve European citizens in this momentous process of change, and that it is therefore undemocratic. Neo-functionalism sees integration primarily as a process of functional or technocratic change, with experts largely running the show. This has led to accusations that neo-functionalist integration implies 'integration by stealth'. Not only is this not an appropriate model for European integration in the early twenty-first century, it is also no longer an accurate depiction of the process itself, though as we shall see in Chapter 23 on the democratic deficit, not everyone would agree that things have changed very much from the early days of the Community.

As the above suggests, the original neo-functionalist project has been subjected—from many different angles—to critical reappraisal at both the theoretical and empirical levels. Yet this did not mean that neo-functionalism died as a theoretical project. As we shall see in the next section, neo-functionalist theory experienced a sort of renaissance in the late 1980s and 1990s, as neo-functionalist concepts such as 'spillover' were once again used to explain contemporary developments in European integration.

Key points

- Neo-functionalism is criticized on both empirical and theoretical grounds.

- On empirical grounds it was argued that neo-functionalism no longer fitted with the reality of the EC in the 1970s.

- On theoretical grounds, critics denied the importance of elite socialization, stressed the importance of the international dimension of integration, and sought to reposition the nation state at the heart of the study of the EC.

The revival of neo-functionalism

After years of obsolescence, neo-functionalism experienced a revival in interest in the late 1980s and early 1990s. There are a number of reasons for its renewed popularity. The first has to do with general developments in the European Community. The Single European Act (See Chapter 3: Box 3.4) and the creation of the goal of a single market (Chapter 3) marked a new phase of economic and political co-operation in Western Europe in the mid-1980s. And the processes of integration associated with these developments seemed very much in line with the sort of spillover predicted by neo-functionalist theory (Tranholm-Mikkelsen 1991).

However, this renewed interest in neo-functionalism involved much more than just a step back to the 1960s. Rather than simply adopting the traditional or classical model, many of those who sought to re-use neo-functionalist theory accepted it as a partial theory, that is, as a theory which would explain some but not all of the European integration process. This contrasts with the earlier ambition of the neo-functionalists—to create a **grand theory** of European integration.

An important contribution to this new approach was made by Stone Sweet and Sandholtz (1998; see also Stone Sweet and Brunell 1998). Although not neo-functionalists in any traditional sense, Stone Sweet and Sandholtz do claim that their theoretical considerations have 'important affinities with neo-

functionalism' (Stone Sweet and Sandholtz 1998: 5). They argue that the traditional distinction made in the theoretical study of European integration—that it is either supranational or intergovernmental—is no longer sufficient. While both tendencies are represented in the real world of European politics, they appear differently in different policy areas within the Union, so that some are characterized by more intergovernmentalism, others by more supranationalism (Stone Sweet and Sandholtz 1998: 9). However, Stone Sweet and Sandholtz do not use the spillover concept when they seek to explain processes of political integration and the formation of supranational institutions. Instead they develop what they call a 'transaction-based' theory of integration. This draws attention to the increasing levels of transactions (such as in the fields of trade, communications, travel) across EU borders, which in turn increase demands for European-level regulation (Stone Sweet and Sandholtz 1998: 11). In time, these demands generate a process of institutionalization leading to the establishment of what the authors call 'supranational governance'.

One of the supranational institutions analysed using this approach was the European Court of Justice (Stone Sweet and Caporaso 1998; see also Chapter 12). Stone Sweet and Caporaso observe how the Court interprets the Treaty expansively within its rulings. In doing so, they confirm their theses about the autonomy of the EU's supranational institutions and about supranational governance. Others have also used the European Court to provide evidence of the existence of neo-functionalist dynamics in the EC. Burley and Mattli (1993) argue that the European Court has been a very important institution in the building of a supranational community as it has played an active role in the creation of Community authority in legal matters. They stress that the founding member states of the Community had no intention of giving the court supremacy over national legal systems. However the European Court was able to develop its doctrine over the course of the 1960s and 1970s. According to Burley and Mattli, the Court has also been able to advance political integration by using technical and apolitical arguments in the legal arena, a process which is close to the type of integration mechanisms proposed by neo-functionalist theory.

Along similar lines, references to neo-functionalist theory have increased dramatically since the late 1980s. And in policy areas such as defence (Guay 1996), social policy (Jensen 2000), and telecommunications (Sandholtz 1998), and on the question of attitudes among European civil servants (Hooghe 2001), authors have discussed neo-functionalism as a possible frame for explaining specific forms of integration—even if they have refrained from 'buying into' all aspects of the 'classical' theory of the 1950s and 1960s.

Conclusion

Since the first writings of E. B. Haas in the 1950s, theories of regional integration, or neo-functionalism as it is more popularly called, have had their ups and downs. As a means of explaining co-operation between states in the 1960s, neo-functionalism became very popular. The new types of co-operation that developed after the Second World War, especially in Europe, demanded new research perspectives. Neo-functionalism was able to describe and explain these developments in a way that was novel and of its time. In the period after the war, the fashion was for grand theorizing, the construction of scientific theories that would explain the 'big picture'. Nowadays, theorists (and particularly those working on the EU) are content to devote their energies to the generation of less ambitious, middle-range theories (see Chapter 8: 112), that explain only part of the process.

Focusing on the supranational aspects of the new international organizations, neo-functionalism explained co-operation using concepts like spillover and loyalty transfer. States were expected to co-operate on economic matters in order to realize the economic advantages that come with increased levels of trade. This would lead to demands for political co-ordination across state borders, and in some cases to the establishment of supranational institutions. Co-operation in one policy area would involve co-operation in new areas, thereby initiating an incremental process of political integration. Over time, the supranational institutions would become more and more independent and able to formulate their own agendas, forcing the national states to delegate further competences to the supranational level.

Yet by the mid-1970s neo-functionalism was no longer a credible position to hold. Even traditional proponents of the theory, like Haas, argued that it could not fully explain European developments in regional co-operation. Indeed, he accepted that the European Community did not develop in the way that neo-functionalists had predicted. States remained key actors and it became hard to distinguish supranational institutions from more traditional international organizations.

Supranationalism did experience a revival in the late 1980s and 1990s, however. The establishment of the Single European Market and the creation of the EU at Maastricht opened the door to new interest in supranational developments and institutions. The EU suddenly began to look much more like the kind of institution that Haas and others predicted would emerge as a result of regional economic and political integration. But although there was some interest in neo-functionalism at this time, most of the 'new' neo-functionalists felt free to pick and choose from those elements of the theory that best suited their research agendas. Finally, despite the renaissance of the theory in the 1980s and 1990s, neo-functionalism is still rarely considered to be at the forefront of research on European integration and EU politics. It seems that the mainstream now belongs much more to intergovernmentalism and other newer competing theories of the EU (see Chapters 7 and 8).

QUESTIONS

1 What do neo-functionalists mean by political integration?

2 How helpful is the spillover concept in explaining the development of European integration since the 1950s?

3 How can private interest groups influence the processes of political integration?

4 How convincing is Moravcsik's critique of neo-functionalism?

5 According to neo-functionalist theory, what role do the supranational institutions play in the European integration process?

6 What evidence is there that 'loyalty-transfer' among the civil servants in the supranational institutions actually occurs?

7 What are the similarities and the differences between traditional neo-functionalism and the theory of supranational governance?

8 Does the conduct of the European Court support the neo-functionalist thesis?

GUIDE TO FURTHER READING

Moravcsik, A., *The Choice for Europe: Social Purpose & State Power from Messina to Maastricht* (London: University College London Press, 1998). The seminal text on liberal intergovernmentalism by its key proponent. It: includes a very useful critique of neo-functionalism.

Pentland, C., *International Theory and European Integration* (New York, The Free Press, 1973). A classic study of European integration theory, which though dated still provides a helpful introduction to neo-functionalism.

Sandholtz, W., and Stone Sweet, A. (eds), *European Integration and Supranational Governance* (Oxford: Oxford University Press, 1998). An edited volume which develops the notion of supranational governance, drawing on aspects of neo-functionalist theory.

Sweeney, J. P., *The First European Elections: Neo-functionalism and the European Parliament* (Boulder, Colo.: Westview Press, 1984). An interesting study of the first EP elections from a neo-functionalist perspective.

Tranholm-Mikkelsen, J., 'Neo-functionalism: Obstinate or Obsolete? A Reappraisal in the Light of the New Dynamism of the EC', *Millennium: Journal of International Studies*, vol. 20 (1991): 1–22. The key reference for examining the application of neo-functionalism to the post-1985 period.

Intergovernmentalism

Michelle Cini

READER'S GUIDE

This chapter provides an overview of intergovernmentalist theory, focusing particularly on the works of Stanley Hoffmann and Andrew Moravcsik. It first introduces the basic premises and assumptions of intergovernmentalism, identifying its realist underpinnings and the state-centrism which provides the core of the approach, before examining in more detail the specific characteristics of Hoffmann's work. The next section examines some of the ways in which intergovernmentalist thinking has either spawned or has become attached to new avenues for research on European integration. The topics covered in this section are confederalism; the domestic politics approach; and analyses that point to the 'locked-in' nature of nation states within the integration process. The chapter concludes by focusing on Moravcsik's liberal intergovernmentalism, which since the mid-1990s has become the main focal point for intergovernmentalists.

Introduction

From the mid-1960s to the present day, intergovernmentalism–in one form or another–has been situated at the heart of European integration theory. For decades, students of European integration learnt about the two competing approaches which served to explain (and in some cases to predict) the course of European integration: neo-functionalism (covered in Chapter 6) and intergovernmentalism. Although this dichotomy has been replaced by a new division, responding to the 'governance turn' addressed in Chapter 8, intergovernmentalism, or at least a modern variant of it, continues to dominate much of the academic discourse on European integration. It is in this sense that one might see it as the dominant paradigm for explaining European integration at the start of the twenty-first century.

This chapter provides a general introduction to the arguments and critiques of intergovernmentalist theory. It does so by focusing on the works of Stanley Hoffmann (particularly in the 1960s), and Andrew Moravcsik (from the early 1990s). It also considers some of the premises and assumptions underpinning intergovernmentalist thinking. The chapter begins by addressing the question 'what is intergovernmentalism?' In this section, the general characteristics of the approach are outlined. The section that follows summarizes Hoffmann's writings in the 1960s, and identifies criticisms of his particular brand of intergovernmentalism. Hoffmann's ground-breaking insights into the phenomenon of European integration, together with critiques of his work, led to new developments in theories of

European integration from the 1970s on. Although these might not always be termed 'intergovernmentalist' in a narrow sense, they are premised upon a 'state-centrism' which owes much to Hoffmann's work. Important examples of these 'variants' of intergovernmentalism are dealt with in the remainder of the chapter. The first highlights the confederal characteristics of the European Union (EU). The second draws attention to the importance of domestic politics; while the third brings together examples of research that considers how states, still central actors, become 'locked into' the European integration process. The final section looks at the work of Andrew Moravcsik and more specifically at his 'liberal intergovernmentalist' (LI) theory of European integration. Although this is an extremely rich and influential theory, LI is subject to many criticisms. These are addressed at the end of the chapter.

What is intergovernmentalism?

Intergovernmentalism is a theory of European integration, or perhaps more accurately a conceptual approach that explains the European integration process (see Box 7.1). It is characterized by its **state-centrism**. In other words, intergovernmentalism privileges the role of (national) states within the European integration process. It sees integration as a **zero-sum game**, claims that it is limited to policy areas that do not touch on fundamental issues of national sovereignty, and argues that 'European

integration is driven by the interests and actions of nation states' (Hix 1999: 15).

Intergovernmentalism is drawn, whether explicitly or implicitly, from classical theories of International Relations, and, most notably, from realist or neo-realist analyses of interstate bargaining. **Realism** incorporates the claim that international politics is about the interaction of self-interested states in an anarchic environment, where no global authority is capable of securing order

Box 7.1 **Core ideas**
Intergovernmentalism as theory and method

In this chapter, intergovernmentalism is defined as a theory of European integration. This implies that intergovernmentalism is an approach that explains what European integration (or European co-operation) is about. But intergovernmentalism may also serve as a model of European integration. This is something rather different. This sort of intergovernmentalism is prescriptive

in the sense that it advocates reducing the role of the supranational institutions (Commission, Parliament, and courts) in favour of a greater role for the European Council and EU Council. It might also imply a desire to reinstate the unanimity voting rule in the Council and to repatriate European policies to the national level.

(Morgenthau 1985). From this perspective, states are seen as rational, unitary actors that define their interests based on an evaluation of their position in the system of states (Rosamond 2000: 131). State interest is, therefore, primarily about survival, with other concerns, such as economic growth, of secondary importance. Thus, the theory 'is centred on the view that nation states are the key actors in international affairs and the key political relations between states are channelled primarily via national governments' (Nugent 1999: 509).

Neo-realism (Waltz 1979), like realism, assumes states to be self-regarding actors coexisting in an anarchical system. However, it also understands that there is some potential for order, on the basis of international co-operation (see Axelrod 1984; Keohane 1988), if only as a rational means to state survival. According to neo-realists, **'regimes'** are arenas for the negotiation of zero-sum agreements, with the outcomes of those negotiations shaped by the distribution of state power within the regime. Yet, despite the promise of international co-operation, neo-realism is underpinned by the assumption that states have their own distinctive problems and concerns, and that they face very different internal circumstances. This means that their policy preferences (or interests) will often fail to converge. As a consequence, any attempt to build a community *beyond the state* will be fraught with difficulties, and may even intensify the sense of difference felt across state borders. Neo-realists accept that international institutions of all kinds are established to reduce the level of anarchy within the states system, and see the EU as just another of these institutions, albeit within a highly institutionalized setting. While neo-realists have not been particularly interested in any explicit way in European integration (but see Grieco 1995, 1996), their influence on intergovernmentalism is clear for all to see (Rosamond 2000: 132). The point should be stressed however, that intergovernmentalism and (neo-)realism are certainly not synonymous (Church 1996: 25).

The term 'intergovernmentalism' is not only associated with EU politics, however. It also refers to a type of decision making that occurs within all international organizations. International organizations are intergovernmental bodies in that they are forums in which states can meet to discuss common issues, share ideas, and negotiate agreements. They are usually based on international treaties, and membership is voluntary. They tend not to have powers of taxation, and rely therefore on member states' contributions for their operation. Generally, they do not have independent powers, and usually they find it difficult to enforce decisions where individual members are recalcitrant (McCormick 2002: 4). While some international organizations stray from this model, intergovernmentalists (in the EU sense) apply this kind of framework to their understanding of the EU.

According to intergovernmentalists, there are costs and benefits attached to involvement in European integration. (Note, however, that intergovernmentalists may prefer to talk of European *co-operation*, rather than of integration.) Participation in co-operation of this kind will rest on a weighing up of the pros and cons of membership and on the extent to which European integration improves the efficiency of bargains struck among its member states. The main aim in engaging in this qualitative cost–benefit analysis is to protect national interests.

Co-operation within the EU, then, is essentially conservative and pragmatic. It rests on the premise that common solutions are often needed to resolve common problems. To put it another way, co-operation has nothing to do with ideology or idealism, but is founded on the rational conduct of governments as they seek to deal with the policy issues that confront them in the modern world. For intergovernmentalists, European integration is normal or even 'mundane' behaviour on the part of state actors (O'Neill 1996: 57). There is nothing particularly special about it, other than that it has taken a highly institutionalized form in Western Europe since the 1950s. As international co-operation always occurs simultaneously on a variety of levels, taking many different forms, co-operation within the EU is deemed to be only one example of a more general phenomenon. This is why intergovernmentalists are reluctant to admit that there is a European integration *process*, as such. Rather, they see co-operation occurring in fits and starts, and not as a trend heading inexorably in one direction, towards some sort of European political community or federal state.

As an institutionalized form of interstate co-operation, the argument goes, European integration facilitated the survival of the West European state in the bi-polar context of the post-1945 period (see Box 7.2). It was perhaps not so surprising to hear arguments in the early 1990s that European integration would probably not survive the end of the Cold War (Mearsheimer 1990). Yet even if this prediction has proved inaccurate, (and some might say that it is still too early to tell), there is no disputing the fact that the nation state has survived (O'Neill 1996: 54), despite the post-1945 sentiment that nationalism ought to be constrained.

At the heart of the intergovernmental thesis lies a particular conception of the **sovereignty** of national states. Sovereignty remains a very emotive word, particularly when raised in the context of EU politics. It has various meanings, holding associations with 'notions of power, authority, independence, and the exercise of will' (Nugent 1999: 502). One useful definition states that sovereignty implies 'the legal capacity of national decision-makers to take decisions without being subject to external restraints' (Nugent 1999: 502); another claims that sovereignty is 'the right to hold and exercise authority' (McCormick 2002: 10). However, many use the word sovereignty as little more than a synonym for 'independence', particularly in public discourse (for example, in the media).

According to intergovernmentalists, not only are the member states deemed to be the most important actors by far, they also manage to involve themselves in European integration without ceding sovereignty. This implies that states remain very much in control of the process. According to intergovernmentalists, European co-operation implies at most a pooling or sharing of sovereignty, rather than any *transfer* of sovereignty from national to **supranational** level (Keohane and Hoffmann 1991: 277).

European co-operation might also involve some **delegation** of sovereignty. Indeed, intergovernmentalists accept that European integration involves the delegation of functions from state executives and, to a lesser extent, parliaments of the member states, to the European institutions—the Commission and the Court of Justice in particular. The argument is that national governments find it in their interest to hand over certain regulatory functions in order to make co-operation work more effectively (to make commitments more credible) (see p. 104 below). This emphasis on delegation colours how intergovernmentalists understand the role of the EU's supranational institutions. Rather than assuming that the institutions are capable of playing an independent or autonomous role within the European integration process, intergovernmentalists stress that the supranational actors

Box 7.2 **Core ideas**

The European rescue of the nation state

In his book, *The European Rescue of the Nation-State* (1992), the economic historian Alan Milward analysed European integration in the 1940s and 1950s. He argued that the European integration process in the post-1945 period 'saved' rather than undermined the nation state. Governments at this time had a number of difficult problems to resolve, caused by increasing interdependence and increased disaffection from social actors. The successful delivery of policy programmes was a matter of survival for the states of Western Europe (Rosamond 2000: 138). European integration thus became a means to this end. As Rosamond (2000: 139) notes, 'The idea of

integration as a progressive transfer of power away from the state managed by emerging supranational elites is given little credence by this hypothesis'. Rather, the key actors are governmental elites.

However, read in a particular way, Milward's work can be seen as challenging the standard polarization of intergovernmentalism and supranationalism. Integration does not necessarily entail the drift toward supranational statehood and states can be seen as controlling agents with an interest in the promotion of degrees of integration (Rosamond 2000: 139).

are little more than the servants of the member states. While the supranational institutions are permitted more of a role in less controversial policy areas, the functions they perform in sensitive policy domains is bound to be severely curtailed. The European institutions that really matter, then, are the EU Council (of national ministers) and the European Council (of heads of state and government), while the role of the other European institutions is considered somewhat marginal.

Key points

- Intergovernmentalism has been influenced by realist assumptions. It privileges the role of the state within European integration.

- Intergovernmentalists believe that sovereignty rests with the EU's member states, although it may be in states' interests to share/pool sovereignty and to delegate it to European institutions.

Hoffmann and his critics

Intergovernmentalism, as a theory of European integration, emerged in the mid-1960s, out of a critique of neo-functionalist theory (see Chapter 6) and as a reaction to federalist assumptions (see Chapter 5) that the European Community (EC) would eventually transform itself into a fully fledged state. By the end of the 1960s it had become the dominant paradigm used to explain European integration, replacing the earlier neo-functionalist orthodoxy and reflecting more accurately, it seemed, the practice of European integration by that time. After the 'boycott' of the European institutions in mid-1965 by the French president, General de Gaulle, his 'empty chair policy', and the signing of the accord which came to be known as the Luxembourg Compromise in early 1966, a tide seemed to have turned in the history of European integration. The persistence of the national veto post-1966, instability in the global political economy, and institutional changes which privileged the Council of Ministers and institutionalized the European Council as key decision makers within the Community (O'Neill 1996: 57–9) all pointed to the limits of supranationalism and to the continued primacy of state actors in European politics. That the Commission began to play a more cautious role post-1966 than it had done in the early years of the EC was also an important factor supporting the intergovernmental thesis.

It was Stanley Hoffmann who laid the foundations of the intergovernmentalist approach to European integration upon which most of the state-centric variants from the 1970s on drew. His intergovernmentalism rejected neo-functionalist theory, claiming that while concentrating on the *process* of European integration, neo-functionalists had forgotten the *context* within which it takes place (Rosamond 2000: 76). More specifically, Hoffmann rejected neo-functionalist claims that European integration was driven by a sort of snowball effect known as **spillover** (see Chapter 6: 84–6), arguing that this was more an 'act of faith' than a proven fact. He stressed that international politics remained characterized by a perpetual conflict over interests (O'Neill 1996: 61).

According to Hoffmann, there was nothing inevitable about the path of European integration (Cram 2001: 60) and neither was there evidence of any political will to create a federal state in Europe (O'Neill 1996: 63). If anything, the federalist rhetoric simply highlighted the enduring qualities of the national state—in that it sought to replicate it on a European scale. As for neo-functionalism, not only did it ignore the global context within which European integration took place, he argued, it also missed the cultural differences that were continuing to influence how states perceived their interests. Thus Hoffmann contrasted the idea of 'the logic of integration' against his own preferred 'logic of diversity', reiterating the point by stating that European integration involved a dialectic of fragmentation and unity. This diversity was a consequence of the unique context of internal domestic politics, and of global factors (that is, the situation of the state in the international system), both of which contributed to inexorable centrifugal forces that placed limits on European integration (Rosamond 2000: 76).

Hoffmann's intergovernmentalism offered a 'systematic contextualization' (Rosamond 2000: 75) of the events of the mid-1960s, drawing on empirical studies of French presidential politics under President Charles de Gaulle. In this sense it was much more than just an application of realist theory to the EC case. Indeed, Hoffmann's view was that in the post-1945 period, nation states were dealing with regional issues in very different ways than had earlier been the case. While he accepted that traditional, exclusive notions of sovereignty were now obsolete, and that there was a blurring of the boundaries between the national state and international organizations (Hoffmann 1966: 908), this did not mean that nation states and national governments had lost their significance. National sovereignty and the nation state were being tamed and altered, he argued, but they were not being superseded (Hoffmann 1966: 910–11), and while the national dimension may well have seemed less important in the immediate post-1945 period, it had not taken long for states to reassert themselves (Hoffmann 1996: 867–9). Indeed, national states had proven extremely resilient actors in international politics (O'Neill 1996: 60). 'The nation-state is still here, and the new Jerusalem has been postponed because the nations in Western Europe have not been able to stop time and to fragment space' (Hoffmann 1966: 863). Thus, from the title of one of his best known articles, he claimed the nation state to be 'obstinate not obsolete' (Hoffmann 1966). Despite the fact that societal changes posed real challenges for the nation state, state governments remained powerful for two reasons—first, because they held legal sovereignty over their own territory; and second, because they possessed political legitimacy, as they were democratically elected (George and Bache 2001: 13).

Although he recognized the successes of European co-operation, its distinctive characteristics, and the possibility that it may well produce more than zero-sum outcomes (Hoffmann 1995: 4), Hoffmann argued that the events of the 1960s highlighted the differences between member states as much as it pointed to common interests. This was an important point, since 'preference convergence' was deemed a prerequisite for European integration. Thus where states met with uncertainty, and as supranational institutions began to develop agendas of their own, national governments would respond by going their own way (Rosamond 2000: 78).

Hoffmann's starting point was the political rather than the technocratic (Rosamond 2000: 78). Crucial in this account was the distinction that he made between high and low politics. Whereas high politics (and the political sphere) was said to touch on national sovereignty and issues of national identity, low politics (the economic sphere) tended to be more technocratic, and much less controversial. According to Hoffmann, there were clear boundaries between less dramatic economic integration possible in areas of low politics, and the 'impermeable' and very 'political' domain of high politics (O'Neill 1996: 61) where integration would not occur. While functional spillover might occur in the former, there could be no assumption that states would allow it to be transferred to the latter.

Although Hoffmann's analysis was based very generally upon realist assumptions, he differed from realists in his approach to the concept of the state. Indeed we might say that 'Hoffmann's intergovernmental position was more sophisticated than that of realists . . . and his political awareness was also greater than that of the neo-functionalist writers who tended to adopt a rather simplified pluralist view of political processes' (George and Bache 2001: 13). To Hoffmann, states were more than just 'black boxes'. They represented communities of identity and belonging: '[T]hey are constructs in which ideas and ideals, precedents and political experiences and domestic forces and rulers all play a role' (Hoffmann 1995: 5). Hoffmann was particularly critical of earlier theorists of European integration who had tended to adopt a simplistic and unrealistic view of how governments defined their interests. He argued that these interests were not reducible to power and place alone (Hoffmann 1995: 5), but were calculated on the basis of various historical, cultural, and indeed political concerns.

Hoffmann's intergovernmentalism has been subject to a number of critiques. Many of these reject his rigid demarcation of high and low politics (O'Neill 1996: 65). Even in the 1970s, there were claims that the existence of European Political Co-operation (EPC), the forerunner to today's European foreign policy and an area of 'high politics', seemed to disprove this particular aspect of his theory. This seems be have been borne out by recent events, most notably since the establishment of the single currency and the common foreign and security policy. Indeed, since the 1960s, Hoffmann has softened his line on this issue.

Hoffmann was also criticized for playing down the constraints imposed on states as a consequence of their increasing **'interdependence'** (O'Neill 1996: 65; see Box 7.3). Moreover, it was argued that he failed to take into consideration the novelty and the complexity of the European integration project. The EC, it was claimed, was about more than just the creation of a regional regime, and the bargains struck at European level could not simply be reduced to a set of national interests (Rosamond 2000: 79).

While Hoffmann's intergovernmentalism was not a theory in any systematic sense (Church 1996: 26), and was, rather, part of an approach that dealt with the wider phenomenon of regional co-operation, it was extremely influential. It set the agenda for future research undertaken in the field of integration theory from the 1970s on. Thus, accepting the limits of Hoffmann's approach as it was constructed in the 1960s did not mean opting for a supranational theory of integration. Rather, it allowed a door to be opened to new approaches to the study of European integration, three of which are dealt with in the next section.

Key points

- Stanley Hoffmann was the key proponent of intergovernmentalism in the mid-1960s. His work on French, European, and international politics led him to critique the work of the neo-functionalists.

- Hoffmann distinguished between high and low politics, arguing that while functional integration might be possible in less controversial areas (the economic sphere), states would resist any incursions into areas of high politics (the political sphere).

- Critics have questioned Hoffmann's use of the high/low politics distinction, based on empirical evidence (such as recent moves towards foreign policy integration). However, his approach has been extremely influential.

Box 7.3 **Core ideas**
Interdependence and intergovernmentalism

Interdependence theory emerged in the 1970s, its key proponents being Robert Keohane and Joseph Nye (1975). Its main influence on intergovernmentalism was to set it in a broader context than had earlier been the case. It was argued that 'Many of the factors that have influenced . . . [the] development [of the EC] have applied to it alone, but many have not' (Nugent 1999: 511). In other words, in many instances what we might consider to be the effects of European integration are really effects of a much wider phenomenon. Changes to the international political economy—international modernization in particular—has led to greater and greater levels of interdependence, and these have changed the way in which states and other non-state actors relate to each other in the international sphere (Nugent 1999: 511).

While interdependence theory cannot really be considered a discrete theory of European integration, it does add to our understanding of its background conditions, and helps to make the point that the EC might not be quite as unique as some (such as the neo-functionalists) claim. While it highlights the fact that states may not always be able to act unconstrained within the international system, it is best viewed as a response to a rather specific weakness in intergovernmentalism, rectified by an increasing emphasis on the global dimension.

Beyond intergovernmentalism

This section presents some examples of how Hoffmann's intergovernmentalism has been supplemented and adapted since the 1960s. While setting aside for the moment the most important example (liberal intergovernmentalism), this section first deals with confederalism; second, with the 'domestic politics approach' to European integration; and finally with a number of analyses that have sought to explain how states become locked into the European integration process.

Confederalism

As a model or framework for European integration the idea of confederation (Forsyth 1981) seems closely allied to intergovernmentalism. Confederation may be viewed as a particular type of intergovernmental arrangement, in which national sovereignty remains intact despite the establishment of a common institutional framework (O'Neill 1996: 71). O'Neill calls it the antithesis of federalism, a concert of sovereign states. Wallace stresses that there must be no assumption that confederation will lead ultimately to unity. Rather, it implies that the 'Community is stuck, between sovereignty and integration' (Wallace 1982: 65).

Confederal approaches draw attention to the institutionalized nature of the European integration process, recognizing (unlike intergovernmentalism) its distinctiveness. Along similar lines, Paul Taylor (1975) has argued that confederation (or confederalism) is a helpful supplement to intergovernmentalism, allowing us to move beyond its inherent constraints, while retaining its state-centric core. In this respect, Wallace points to the importance of supranational/international law in distinguishing confederalism from intergovernmentalism. Taylor puts it rather differently. He suggests that 'The salient feature of confederal Europe is that the scope of integration is extensive . . . but the level of integration is low' (Taylor 1975: 343). Moreover, 'The Europe of this Confederal phase of integration is . . .

decentralized but highly interdependent, potentially autarchic but in practice united by intense practices of consultation' (Taylor 1975: 343). It is also characterized, he claims, by the defensive posture of national governments against the further extension of the powers of supranational actors, by an interpenetration of European politics into the domestic sphere, and by an oscillation between advanced proposals for integration and retreats into national independence. While much of this argument is state-centric, with Taylor arguing that the nation state is likely to be strengthened through confederation, it adds to intergovernmentalist understandings of European integration, by emphasizing the framework within which co-operation and integration take place.

The domestic politics approach

In the 1970s and 1980s, an approach that focused on domestic politics and policy making became fashionable in the field of European integration studies. Although not a hard theory of European integration, the approach was critical of intergovernmentalism's failure to capture the transnational nature of the EC policy process (Church 1996: 26) and sought, as a consequence, to focus attention on the impact of domestic politics on EC policy making (Bulmer 1983). In this, we can identify the origins of what today might be seen as part of the 'Europeanization' literature (see Chapter 21). We might also see this approach as one that links Hoffmann's intergovernmentalism to later state-centric research projects—and particularly to liberal intergovernmentalism (below at p. 103) (Rosamond 2000: 76).

The idea behind the domestic politics approach was that it was said to be impossible to understand the EC without taking domestic politics into consideration (Bulmer 1983). To that end Bulmer, a key proponent of this approach, sought to identify the domestic determinants of preference formation

(Rosamond 2000: 80). He claimed that one way of doing this was to engage in in-depth case studies of the European policy process, to allow for variations in patterns of policy making to be identified, and for emphasis to be placed on the linkages between the national and supranational dimensions of European politics. Bulmer was particularly interested in two dimensions of domestic politics: policy-making structures and attitudes towards the EC (Bulmer 1983).

There are a number of elements involved in this approach, which when taken together provide a framework for analysing the behaviour of member states. First, the national polity was considered the basic unit of the EC. Second, each national polity was assumed to be different, in terms of its unique socio-economic characteristics, with these differences shaping national interests. Third, European policy was said to be only one facet of national political activity. Fourth, the national polity was depicted as lying at the juncture of national and European politics. And finally, an important lens through which one might understand these elements is that of the 'policy style' concept (Bulmer 1983: 360).

The importance of the domestic politics approach is that it demonstrated how intergovernmentalists had failed to look in any coherent way within the member states when analysing the European integration process (Bulmer 1983). Although it was stated earlier in this chapter that intergovernmentalism is closely related to (neo-)realism in International Relations, newer variants of intergovernmentalism have also been greatly influenced by neo-liberal ideas. **Neo-liberalism**, as an approach to the study of International Relations, is concerned with the *formation* of state preferences (Rosamond 2000: 135) or 'national interests'. Whereas neo-realism is focused exclusively on politics between nations, neo-liberalism draws attention to the content of the 'black box' of domestic politics and tries to address from where national interests originate. It therefore places the national **polity**, rather than just national executives, or governments, at the heart of the European integration project. Although the influence of neo-liberal ideas in the domestic politics approach may not be explicit, many of its concerns are similar. This is a point which will be

picked up on again when we come to look at the work of Moravcsik.

The 'locking-in' of states

As a more recent example of how intergovernmentalism has evolved, a number of analyses try to explain how states have become *locked into* the European integration process. These draw heavily on a particularly Germanic approach to the study of federalism, whereby 'interlocking politics' (*Politikverflectung*) characterizes interactions between different levels of government (Risse-Kappen 1996: 60–1). While these approaches rest on state-centric premises, they move quite far beyond classical intergovernmentalism to show how European integration is about much more than interstate bargains. In the process, they emphasize the importance of institutional factors (see Box 8.1) and show how intergovernmentalist ideas may provide a starting point from which new arguments about and analyses of the European integration process develop.

Wolfgang Wessels (1997) has advanced an argument about European integration which rests soundly on state-centric premises in that it sees national interests as the primary driving force of integration. It also, however, links 'integration processes to the evolution of the state' (Wessels 1997: 274–5). He called this his 'fusion thesis'. In this approach, Wessels argues that after 1945, West European states became increasingly responsible for the welfare of their citizens, enhancing their legitimacy as a consequence. But for the welfare state to persist, national economies needed to be strong. In order to maintain economic growth to this end, states recognized the need to open up their markets, which led governments to rely more and more on the joint management of shared policy problems. This is what Wessels means when he talks of the 'fusion' of the West European states (1997: 273)— in essence a 'merger of public resources located at several state levels whereby steering instruments are increasingly used in concert' (Wessels 1997: 274). This amounts to much more than a pooling of sovereignties. As states have become more interdependent, they have lost the ability to act autonomously, blurring the lines of accountability and responsibility that connect citizens to the state. He claims that it is increasingly difficult to reverse these trends without drastic action being undertaken.

Also grounded in state-centrism, Fritz Scharpf (1988) drew an analogy between German federalism and the EC. He did this to explain how European integration has become almost irreversible, because of the intense institutionalization to which it has been subject. Like Wessels, Scharpf focuses on how EC decision making has offered states the ability to solve problems jointly. He argues, however, that the outcomes of these decisions are likely to be sub-optimal, in that they do not emerge from any assessment of the best available solutions, but are reached through a process of bargaining which inevitably leads to compromises being struck. In other words, as national interests determine policy positions, creative (and rational) problem solving is not possible (Scharpf 1988: 255). No member state is therefore likely to be entirely satisfied by what the process of integration has to offer. This is something that will contribute over time to the slowing down of European integration. Yet the institutionalization of the decision-making process means that retreating from integration is not an option. This means that states are trapped in a Community from which they cannot escape, in a paradox characterized by Scharpf as 'frustration without disintegration and resilience without progress' (Scharpf 1988: 256).

More recently, historical institutionalists have sought to explain how states become locked into the European integration process through a process of **path dependence**. The argument, advocated by Paul Pierson (1998) amongst others, is that the more states integrate, the more future options become constrained (see Chapter 8: 116). While this does not imply an inevitability about the 'process' of integration, it does mean that the only way of escaping from further integration is by provoking a dramatic break with past practice, a so-called 'critical juncture'.

Key points

- Confederalism complements intergovernmentalism, by acknowledging the institutionalized character of the EC.

- The domestic politics approach claimed that it is impossible to study European integration without looking at policy making within the member states.

- Wessels' fusion thesis, Scharpf's joint decision trap, and Pierson's path dependence explain how states have, over time, become locked into the European integration process.

Liberal intergovernmentalism and its critics

In 1988, Robert Putnam published an influential article in which he explored the dynamics of domestic and international politics using the metaphor of 'two level games' (Putnam 1988). 'Two level games' are played by states. The first game refers to how states define their policy preferences (or national interest) within the domestic environment. The second game is played on the international stage and involves the striking of interstate bargains.

Putnam's core point is that national executives play games in two arenas more or less simultaneously. At the domestic level, power-seeking/enhancing office holders aim to build coalitions of support among domestic groups. At the international level, the same actors seek to bargain in ways that enhance their positions domestically by meeting the demands of key domestic constituents (Rosamond 2000: 136).

Putnam's main aim was to provide a framework for analysing the myriad entanglements involved in domestic-international interactions (Putnam 1988: 433). This image of the two-level game is helpful as it provides a starting point for understanding Moravcsik's theory of liberal intergovernmentalism.

Moravcsik's liberal intergovernmentalism

Since the early 1990s, Andrew Moravcsik's theory of liberal intergovernmentalism (LI) has become one of the most influential accounts—if not the pre-eminent one—of the European integration process. It has become a touchstone against which all integration theory is now judged, 'a model of **parsimony** and clarity' (Risse-Kappen 1996: 63), even for those who do not agree with its assumptions or its conclusions. Drawing on and developing earlier intergovernmentalist insights, it offers a theoretical approach which is much more rigorous than its antecedents (George and Bache 2001: 13), incorporating within it both realist and neo-liberal elements (Rosamond 2000: 136) and dealing explicitly with the interface between domestic and international politics. It was 'initially presented as a framework for synthesizing theories into a coherent account of large EU decisions taken under unanimity, though it can be applied to other types of decisions as well' (Dinan 2000: 280).

LI identifies the EU as a successful intergovernmental regime designed to manage economic interdependence through negotiated policy co-ordination. The theory is based on assumptions drawn from the 'rational actor model', in that it assumes that states behave rationally, 'which means that the actions of states are assumed to be based on utilizing what are judged to be the most appropriate means of achieving their goals' (Nugent 1999: 509).

In true intergovernmentalist fashion, LI emphasizes the importance of the *preferences* and *power* of states. While national politicians embody state interests that reflect domestic policy preferences, all decisions made by the EU are ultimately the result of bargaining amongst states. Agreements are (usually) reached on a lowest common denominator basis, with clear limits placed on the transfer of sovereignty to supranational agents. Thus, according to Moravcsik, 'The broad lines of European integration since 1955 reflect three factors: patterns of commercial advantage, the relative bargaining power of important governments, and the incentives to enhance the credibility of inter-state commitment' (Moravcsik 1998: 3). When economic or commercial concerns converge, integration takes place.

There are two separate dimensions to LI: the supply and the demand side (see Figure 7.1). The argument is that both the *demand* for co-operation which derives from the national polity, and the *supply* of integration, arising out of interstate negotiations, are important in understanding European integration outcomes. To explain the link between the demand and supply sides, the theory is divided into three steps, each of which is explained by a different set of factors (and drawing on different theories): economic interest; relative power; and credible commitments (Moravcsik 1998: 4).

First, drawing on liberal theories of *national preference formation*, and applying a domestic politics approach, Moravcsik shows how 'state goals can be shaped by domestic pressures and interactions

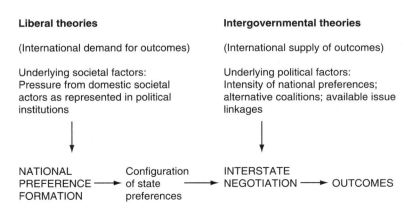

Fig. 7.1 The liberal intergovernmentalist framework of analysis

which in turn are often conditioned by the constraints and opportunities that derive from economic interdependence' (Nugent 1999: 509). Thus he identifies underlying societal factors that provoke an international demand for co-operation. National political institutions are subject to myriad pressures from nationally based interests, provoking a process of preference formation. State preferences are formed, and these feed into interstate negotiations, as groups compete with each other for the attention of government elites. To put it another way, policy preferences at national level are constrained by the interests of dominant, usually economic, groups within society. Resting on a very pluralistic understanding of state-society relations, the theory sees national governments as representing these interests in international forums. Thus Moravcsik believes national interests to be derived from the domestic politics of the member states and not the 'sovereign state's perception of its relative position in the states system' (Rosamond 2000: 137), that is, from geopolitical concerns. As Moravcsik has stated: 'the vital interest behind General de Gaulle's opposition to British membership in the EC . . . was not the pursuit of French *grandeur* but the price of French wheat' (Moravcsik 1998: 7).

The second and supply-side strand of LI is based on *intergovernmentalist theories of interstate relations*, with European integration supplied by intergovernmental bargains (such as treaty reforms) (Moravcsik 1998: 7). This part of LI 'draws on general theories of bargaining and negotiation to argue that relative power among states is shaped above all by asymmetrical interdependence, which dictates the relative value of agreement to different governments' (Moravcsik 1998: 7). Thus, this second element in the theory emphasizes the centrality of strategic bargaining among states and the importance of governmental elites in shaping interstate relations. At this point, states are considered as unitary actors, and supranational institutions are deemed to have a very limited impact on outcomes. In other words, the theory focuses mainly on the European and EU Councils. This generally involves a two-stage process of negotiation. First, governments must resolve the policy problems that confront them, taking decisions to that effect; and only second do they try to reach agreement on institutional mechanisms

which would allow them to implement those decisions. Important is the process by which states engage in interstate bargaining. Various strategies and techniques, such as 'coalitional alternatives to agreement', the linking of issues, and threats of exclusion and inclusion, shape outcomes. A bargaining space (a sort of window of opportunity) is formed out of the amalgamation of national interests, with the final agreement determining the distribution of gains and losses. This points to the restrictive range of possible integration outcomes. Yet Moravcsik accepts that interstate bargains can lead on occasion to **positive-sum outcomes** (Hix 1999: 15). As a consequence, governments will bargain hard to gain the upper hand. Not surprisingly, the **power** of individual states is very important in determining whose interests matter. And consequently, Moravcsik focuses his attention largely on the preferences of the largest EU states: UK, France, and Germany. In stressing the point that integration *benefits* states, that states face few constraints in the Council, and that interstate negotiations enhance their domestic autonomy, this part of the theory addresses the issues of why governments engage in European integration when it might otherwise seem an irrational thing to do (Rosamond 2000: 138).

The third element within LI is *institutional delegation*. The argument here is that international (European) institutions are set up to improve the efficiency of interstate bargaining. 'To secure the substantive bargains they had made . . . governments delegated and pooled sovereignty in international institutions for the express purpose of committing one another to cooperate' (Moravcsik 1998: 3–4). Thus, the European institutions create linkages and compromises across issues, where decisions have been made under conditions of uncertainty, and where non-compliance would be a temptation. In other words, institutional delegation reflects the desire for 'credible commitments'.

In this respect Moravcsik's work has been influenced by the liberal institutionalism of Robert Keohane (1989). Keohane views institutions as ways of facilitating positive-sum bargaining ('upgrading the common interest') among states, but claims that there is no evidence that supranational institutions bias the outcomes of decisions away from the longer-term self-interest of the member states (Rosamond 2000: 143). In line with this sort of thinking, according to Moravcsik, 'The entrepreneurship of supranational officials . . . tends to be futile and redundant, even sometimes counterproductive' (Moravcsik 1998: 8) (see Box 7.4).

Together, these three elements result in integration outcomes (treaty change, for example). Applying the theory to actual cases in the history of European integration, Moravcsik came to the following conclusions. First, he concluded that the major choices made in favour of European integration are a reflection of the preferences of national governments and not of supranational organizations. Second, he stressed that these national preferences reflect a balance of domestic economic interests, rather than any political bias of politicians or national strategic security concerns. Finally, he concluded that the outcomes of the negotiations reflect the relative bargaining power of the states, and that the delegation of decision-making authority to supranational institutions reflect the wishes of governments to ensure that commitments made were adhered to (George and Bache 2001: 14). In short, 'European integration can best be explained as a series of rational choices made by national leaders' (Moravcsik 1998: 18).

Critiques of LI

Although Moravcsik's LI theory has been subject to a great deal of criticism it remains an extremely useful instrument for organizing data and constructing empirical studies. At the same time, it presents a serious challenge for competing models that seek to explain the European integration process (Rosamond 2000: 145). This is largely because LI has been said to offer an 'almost uncompromising framework' (Nugent 1999: 510), which can be hard, if not impossible, to reconcile with alternative interpretations of European integration and EU politics.

Perhaps the most often repeated criticism of LI is that it simply does not fit the facts. This tends to be argued on the basis of empirical analyses and specific case studies of EU politics. This is, however, part of a related criticism, which is that Moravcsik's work has too narrow a focus to be called a theory of European integration, as he is 'too selective with his empirical references when seeking to demonstrate the validity of . . . [the] framework in the EU context' (Nugent 1999: 510). In other words, thus far LI has been applied only to those cases that will (almost inevitably) result in proving that the theory is correct. It has been claimed, by Scharpf (1999: 165), for example, that applying the theory to cases of *intergovernmental negotiation*, where economic integration is the main concern and where decisions are taken on the basis of unanimous voting in the Council, will invariably lead to the conclusions that Moravcsik reaches. 'Given this focus for his attention, it is hardly surprising that Moravcsik comes to the view that the EC is primarily motivated by the aggregation and conciliation of national interests' (Wincott 1995: 602). However, in 'harder'

Box 7.4 **The facts**
Moravcsik's five case studies

In *The Choice for Europe* (1998), Andrew Moravcsik applies his LI theory to five cases in the history of the European integration process. These are:

1   The negotiation of the Treaty of Rome (1955–8).

2   The consolidation of the common market and the Common Agricultural Policy (CAP) (1958–83).

3   Monetary co-operation and the setting up of the European Monetary System (EMS) (1969–83).

4   The negotiation of the Single European Act (SEA) (1984–5).

5   The negotiation of the Treaty on European Union (TEU) (1988–91).

cases, where international negotiations are not the primary form of decision taking, and where majority voting applies, LI may not produce such clear-cut results.

The critique is often set out in the following way: that Moravcsik's theory may well apply for the majority of 'history-making' decisions (Peterson 1995) which deal with the future of European integration, that is, those high-profile policy steps of major constitutional significance, which often involve treaty change and occur through interstate negotiation (Wincott 1995: 602). LI is much less able to explain the way in which the EU works in matters of day-to-day politics, however.

The second criticism that is often raised with regard to Moravcsik's work is that his conception of the state is a rather narrow one. LI pays little attention to the way in which the 'state' may be broken down into its component parts. Critics argue that in order to understand fully how governmental positions (or preferences) are determined (Nugent 1999: 510), a more subtle analysis of domestic politics is required. Indeed, as George and Bache (2001: 14) claim: 'in some ways it [LI] was less sophisticated in its account of domestic politics than was that suggested by Hoffmann'. In Moravcsik's pluralist or liberal view, the primary determinant of government preferences is the balance between *economic* interests (George and Bache 2001: 14). But in practice, there is a huge range of diverse influences that are likely to impinge on national preference formation. Risse-Kappen (1996: 63) points, for example, to the potential importance of domestic structures. On this basis, Moravcsik's account is too simplistic when it focuses solely on economic and (to a lesser extent) on geopolitical concerns (Wincott 1995: 600–1). Moreover, it is argued that the two-level game metaphor does not depict the reality of EU politics today—and that the EU is now much more of a multi-level than a two-level polity (see Chapter 8).

Third, and highly important as a critique of LI, is that the theory understates the constraints faced by key policy makers. The case of the single market programme is often used to back up this argument. There are, however, a number of dimensions to this general critique. First, it is frequently argued that Moravcsik plays down to too great an extent the role

of supranational actors within the European integration process. In other words, he does not provide a full enough account of the supply side of his model, when privileging interstate negotiations. As the roles of the European Commission and the European Court of Justice (ECJ) are judged to be relatively unimportant, if not entirely irrelevant, in terms of policy outcomes, their interests and strategies do not figure particularly strongly in Moravcsik's work. Many academics have contested the underestimation of the supranational institutions' potential influence over integration outcomes (even at times in history-making decisions).

Moravcsik's portrayal of the Commission as exercising a role of little more than a facilitator in respect of significant decision-making has attracted particular criticism, with numerous empirically-based studies claiming to show that the Commission does exercise an independent and influential decision-making role, be it as . . . an *animateur*, a policy entrepreneur, or a motor force (Nugent 1999: 510–11).

Cram (1993), for example, has provided empirical evidence of how the Commission has been able to influence policy outcomes, by means of its policy entrepreneurship. Wincott (1994) and Burley and Mattli (1993) have highlighted the European Court's impact on European integration, through its innovative legal rulings in human rights cases, for example. Pollack's analysis (1997) has shown how, despite the fact that supranational institutions tend to operate within the boundaries set by member-state preferences, they are able to exploit the differences between these preferences in order to promote their own independent agendas. As Rosamond (2000: 143) points out, this adds a layer of institutionalism to intergovernmentalism, while retaining many of its core characteristics.

A similar point also applies to non-state 'transnational' actors, such as European firms and European interest groups. Cowles (1995) has demonstrated, for example, how important business groups were in influencing the single market project in the 1980s. While she accepts that business groups were not the sole cause of the '1992' programme,

intergovernmental theory cannot explain the activities of the key non-state actors in the 1992 process. The single market programme was not merely the result of conventional statecraft. Nor were Member States' actions predicated solely on the basis of domestically defined interest group activity, as suggested by a recent version of intergovernmentalism [LI] . . . Indeed, the story of the ERT [European Round Table of Industrialists] points to the fact that non-state actors—and in particular, multinational enterprises—also play two-level games in EC policy-making (Cowles 1995: 521–2).

This point is not just about which actors and institutions matter in the process of European decision making. It also reflects Moravcsik's emphasis on the more formal aspects of that process, at the expense of the informal, 'behind-the-scenes' dimension. If informal politics matter in shaping policy outcomes, this may mean that actors who appear on the surface to be responsible for decision taking may not really be in control of the process. As Wincott has stated—again of the single market case—'the basic, innovative policy techniques required for the internal market programme had been fashioned in the daily work of the supranational institutions long before the Member States considered these issues' (1995: 606). In this way, the substance of interstate negotiations had already been framed well before intergovernmental conferences and European summits met to take their formal decisions.

Finally, Wincott has criticized LI for not being a theory, at least in his understanding of the term. He makes this claim as he believes that a rigorous theory ought to spell out the conditions under which the theory might be refuted or disproved.

Wincott argues that LI does not do this, but engages in an act of closure on certain types of argument about European integration. He claims that LI should therefore be considered an 'approach' rather than a theory—one that brings together three existing theories (preference formation, intergovernmental bargaining, and institutional delegation) to provide a 'pre-theory' or 'analytical framework (Forster 1998: 365) that can be applied to the European integration process.

Key points

- LI provides a tripartite explanation of integrative outcomes: as national preference formation; as interstate bargaining; and as institutional delegation.

- The theory supplements a rich account of bargaining inside the Council, with a concern for how national interests (or preferences) are formed. Moravcsik argues that it is mainly powerful domestic economic interests that determine national interest.

- Moravcsik is criticized for focusing only on 'history-making decisions' (treaty change, in particular) and for ignoring day-to-day politics and the multi-level character of the EU.

Conclusion: The future of intergovernmentalism

This chapter has reviewed the general approach to European integration known as 'intergovernmentalism', which is associated—in its classical form—with the work of Stanley Hoffmann. The chapter has shown how intergovernmentalist premises (and more specifically, state-centrism) have provided the foundations for a range of theories and models, which have sought to specify the structure of the EC, the nature of decision making, and the 'locking-in' of states within the European integration process. Andrew Moravcsik's work now provides the core intergovernmentalist thesis. Even if one is not convinced by all of his arguments, his LI provides a theoretically rigorous and rich point of departure for critiques.

But what future might we imagine for intergovernmentalism(s)? While it continues to provide inspiration for scholars of European integration, new developments within the study of the EU have tested the resilience of intergovernmentalist arguments. Yet, intergovernmentalism has been flexible enough to adapt to new conditions and new theories which appear to resonate with today's European integration process, and to cope with the empirical evidence provided by recent treaty change, as well as by less high-profile policy developments. As we shall see in the next chapter, there are many who contest the (liberal) intergovernmentalist account of Euro-

pean integration. But for all of us researching and studying the EU, it makes an important contribution to our understanding of what European integration is or might be.

QUESTIONS

1   How plausible are intergovernmentalist accounts of European integration?

2   Why do you think Andrew Moravcsik's theory of liberal intergovernmentalism (LI) has been so influential?

3   What are the main critiques of LI?

4   How useful a model for explaining the EU is confederalism?

5   What are the main elements of Stanley Hoffmann's intergovernmentalism?

6   How central is the nation state within the process of European integration?

7   In what sense and to what extent is European integration a 'mundane' affair?

8   How might Moravcsik respond to recent critiques of his LI?

GUIDE TO FURTHER READING

Hoffmann, S., *The European Sisyphus. Essays on Europe 1964–1994* (Oxford: Westview Press, 1995). An excellent collection of Stanley Hoffmann's work, showing how his ideas have changed (or not) over the years. Includes seminal articles published in the 1960s which set the scene for future intergovernmentalist writings.

Moravcsik, A., *The Choice for Europe. Social Purpose and State Power from Messina to Maastricht* (London: University College London Press, 1998). The seminal LI book. Chapter 1, 'Theorizing European Integration', provides a critique of neo-functionalism and sets out the characteristics of LI in some detail.

O'Neill, M., *The Politics of European Integration. A Reader* (London: Routledge, 1996), ch. 4. Ostensibly a 'reader', this book also includes a useful chapter on state-centric approaches to European integration.

Rosamond, B., *Theories of European Integration* (Basingstoke: Macmillan, 2000), ch. 6. The most recent, overarching text on European integration theory, with numerous references to intergovernmentalism, and one chapter devoted to 'Intergovernmental Europe'.

WEB LINKS

www.people.fas.harvard.edu/~moravcs Andrew Moravcsik's home page. Includes access to published and forthcoming papers.

8 New theories of European integration

Ben Rosamond

READER'S GUIDE

This chapter deals with recent theoretical work on the EU. It concentrates upon approaches, which, in various ways, seek to depart from the established theoretical positions established by neo-functionalism (see Chapter 6) and -intergovernmentalism (see Chapter 7). This chapter commences with a discussion of how 'newer' approaches identify the limitations of the 'classical' debate. Much of this discussion hinges on how analysts characterize the EU. For many the EU is best conceived of as a political system, which suggests that the theoretical tools of conventional political science and policy analysis might have greater explanatory power than approaches from the discipline of International Relations. To explore the plausibility of this proposition, this chapter discusses in turn the contribution to EU studies of new institutionalist political science, approaches from policy analysis, the idea of **multi-level governance**, and **constructivism**. The chapter also explores how International Relations theories might be brought back in to EU studies. The purpose of the chapter, aside from introducing the contemporary theoretical repertoire in EU studies, is to show how the EU raises significant questions about the nature of **authority**, **statehood**, and the organization of the international system in the present period.

Introduction

Much of the academic work on the EU remains under the spell of the 'classical' debate between neo-functionalism and intergovernmentalism (see Chapters 6 and 7). There is a rationale for continuing to explore the opposition between these two schools. Thinking in this way forces us to address key issues of continuity versus change in European politics. Does the growth of the EU imply the transcendence of the European nation-state system? If so, does this bring to the fore a new group of activist supranational institutions and confirm the rise to prominence of powerful **non-state actors**?

Alternatively, are the member states the key actors in this process and are the EU's key dynamics intergovernmental? These rival academic discourses have their equivalents in the policy world. The strategy of the founding fathers of integration (such as Jean Monnet and Robert Schuman) has often been thought of as 'neo-functionalist', while politicians still tend to use a vocabulary that is underwritten by statist and intergovernmentalist assumptions.

However, recent years have witnessed concerted attempts to 'think otherwise' about the EU. This chapter deals with these 'new' theoretical prospectuses. It is worth pausing to consider what 'new' might mean in this context. The term implies, after all, that some theories are 'old' or perhaps redundant. In particular, many academics who offer new theoretical prospectuses tend to begin with the proposition that the 'classical' terms of debate— as represented by the rivalry between neo-functionalism and intergovernmentalism—fail to capture adequately what is going on in the contemporary EU. This chapter is attentive to this premise and begins with a deeper discussion of its soundness as a proposition for theoretical departure.

This discussion alerts us to the importance of thinking carefully about theoretical work. Theory is not simply a self-indulgent exercise. Nor can it be sidestepped by any serious student of the EU. Rather, being conscious about the theoretical propositions chosen by authors is vital because alternative 'readings' of the EU and European integration follow from alternative theoretical premises. That said, writers rarely (these days at least) attempt to construct 'grand theories' of integration. Instead, since the 1970s, they have tended to build theories to aid understanding and explanation of *elements* of (a) the integration process, and (b) EU governance. Even the direct descendants of neo-functionalism and intergovernmentalism (discussed in the previous two chapters) have limited ambitions. For example, Sandholtz and Stone Sweet's theory (1998) of **supranational governance** explicitly 'brackets' the origins of the EU, because the theory has no way of explaining this. Moreover, Moravcsik (2001) has recently emphasized that his **liberal intergovernmentalism** (LI) is not intended to be a comprehensive theory of European integration, but rather a theory of intergovernmental bargaining only (see also Chapter 7).

These caveats still do not bypass the objection that the old debate between neo-functionalism and intergovernmentalism fails to capture highly significant attributes of the present EU. The principal objection, explored in the first substantive section of this chapter, is that 'old' theories are rooted in an outdated conception of what the EU is. However, we need to be aware that the study of the EU is not something that simply ebbs and flows with the development of European integration and the evolution of the EU. It is also—and perhaps more predominantly—bound up with the developments in social scientific fashion. Many think about this in terms of theoretical 'progress'—that is, as social science in general and political science in particular improves its techniques, so we can expect objects of study such as the EU to be treated 'better' than hitherto.

The limits of the classical debate

As the previous two chapters have indicated, the legacies of neo-functionalism and intergovernmentalsm remain intact in much current writing about integration and the EU. Moreover, even when analysts of the EU attempt to offer an alternative point of theoretical departure, they invariably set their co-ordinates with reference to the established neo-functionalist and intergovernmentalist positions. There is always a danger that the histories and trajectories of neo-functionalism and intergovernmentalism can end up being caricatured in such accounts. It is not the job of this chapter to offer a revisionist reading of the 'classical' theoretical literature, suffice to say that the early texts of integration theory repay careful reading by present-day students. This is not just because of the obviously useful legacies of ideas such as **'spillover'**. It is also true to say that the ways in which these 'old' theories are criticized is open to contest. Indeed the idea that there is a convenient and rigid division between 'new' and 'old' theories is open to considerable critical scrutiny (see Haas 2001).

The 'old' debate has been criticized on at least three interrelated counts: its alleged inability to capture the reality of integration and the EU; its supposed entrapment in the disciplinary wilderness of International Relations; and its so-called 'scientific' limitations.

On the first of these, neo-functionalists—in particular—were heavily criticized for the lack of correspondence between their theory of integration and the unfolding reality of European integration. The assertion of intergovernmental politics from the mid-1960s, the obstinacy of nationalist sentiment within the member states, and the peculiarity and non-replicability of the European experience all provided serious body blows to neo-functionalist discourse by the mid-1970s (see Chapter 6). Similarly, intergovernmentalism is open to the charge that it offers only a partial representation of both integration and EU governance. The focus on politics between member state executives and the claim that substantive change in European integration is traceable only to intergovernmental

bargains stands at variance with much of the empirical evidence gathered by those at the 'coalface' of EU studies (see Chapter 7). However, while much of what goes on within the EU—in terms of day-to-day legislative and regulatory activity—is bound up with the actions of 'non-state actors', this does not mean that neo-functionalism is necessarily best placed to make a comeback.

To take an example, one of the big debates to emerge in the literature of the late 1980s and early 1990s concerned the origins of the single market programme as codified in the Single European Act (SEA) (1987) (see also Chapter 3). Intergovernmentalists honed in on the SEA as an obvious case of treaty reform initiated by an intergovernmental bargain. It was argued that change became possible because of the convergent interests of the three most powerful member states (France, Germany, and the UK). Moreover, these national preferences emerged out of processes of domestic political exchange in all three countries (Moravcsik 1991). Against this it was claimed that the SEA represented the formal consolidation of practices that had emerged in recent years. This in turn reflected acts of institutional creativity by the Commission, the jurisprudence of the Court of Justice, and processes of institutional interaction (Wincott 1995). At the same time, neo-functionalists found some evidence of spillover as initiatives to create the single market prompted calls for incursions into the realms of social policy and monetary union (Tranholm-Mikkelsen 1991). But while the evidence for this spillover was impressive, it was also true that there was much more taking place in the Communities besides progression to the single market and beyond. In any case, other (newer) theoretical perspectives had developed strong explanations of how and why the single market and subsequent progress to monetary union came about.

The next criticism of 'old' theories builds on the allegation that they emerge from the disciplinary homeland of International Relations (IR). From this vantage point, IR is claimed to be a discipline preoccupied with two core themes: questions of war and peace and relations between *states*. European integration was originally of interest to IR scholars because European states seemed to be embarking on a project that sought to undermine and eliminate the recurrent causes of war on the continent. This led IR-derived theories into two ways of thinking. Neo-functionalists became concerned with the progressive mechanics of the integration process, while intergovernmentalists developed an interest in the ways in which diplomacy between national governments either survived or became institutionalized in the context of European integration.

This in turn sparks two types of complaint. The first is that the EU is about much more than the 'integration question'. Simon Hix (1994, 1999) makes the point that the question of whether there should be more or less *integration* does not motivate the behaviour of most of the actors involved in the business of the EU. Rather, he argues, these are individuals and groups pursuing their interests within a complex political system. As analysts of the EU, we are in fact confronted with the evergreen political science question of 'who gets what, when, how?' to use Harold Lasswell's classic formulation (Lasswell 1950). If we think that the 'integration question' is all that the EU is about, then we fall into the same trap as those politicians who conceptualize the EU in terms of the simple zero-sum opposition between 'nation state' and federal 'superstate'. This leads to the second type of complaint. This maintains that we need to break out of the 'state fixation' that characterizes so much of the routine academic and political discourse about the EU. For one thing, many—perhaps most—students of the EU would want to argue that the EU has evolved into a peculiar form of polity or political system that does not really fit into any established template for understanding the state. On the other hand, the EU is a system that delivers coherent and binding policy outputs. The allegation is that IR perspectives fail to deal with these criticisms.

The third criticism of the classical debate brings together a number of concerns about the type of theory involved. Neo-functionalism in particular has been criticized as a '**grand theory**'—an attempt to develop a set of general 'laws' about the dynamics of regional integration across the world. Such attempts at overarching theory came under intense scrutiny in the early 1970s and it is no coincidence that this was the period in which neo-functionalism was abandoned by its foremost practitioners (Moravcsik 1998: 11; Rosamond 2000: 190). In place of grand, universal theories, social scientists became more interested in developing '**middle range theories**'. As the name suggests, middle range theories do not have totalizing ambitions; they seek to explain aspects of a phenomenon rather than its whole. As we will see below, most current theoretical work is concerned with explaining aspects of the policy process and regulatory fabric of the EU. Theories of European integration are by and large obsolescent.

Of course, this criticism often merges with the critique of IR to suggest that the problem of IR is that it continues to trade in the currency of grand theory. Another way of thinking about this problem is to identify 'old' theory as concentrating on the *form* that integration will take. For many contemporary scholars of the EU, this is simply an irrelevant question. What merits attention and explanation is the processes through which the EU delivers authoritative outputs and not the 'big picture' question of what the EU is becoming.

It would be a mistake to think that these criticisms have been completely decisive and have ushered EU studies into a new theoretical age. Each is contested, and even where scholars agree that there is some substance in the above, many argue that the theoretical landscape is more nuanced and complex than many of the critics of classical theory suggest. Some of these points will be elaborated more fully in the conclusion to this chapter. For now it is worth recognizing that not all critiques would take the failures of neo-functionalism and intergovernmentalism to match 'reality' as a legitimate starting point. Theorists working in what is sometime called the '**constitutive**' **tradition** regard the relationship between theory and reality as intimate and problematic and would choose altogether different criteria for evaluating theories than their ability to correspond to and/or predict the 'real' world.

Moreover, the dismissal of IR as a parent discipline has been taken to task by those who suggest that what goes on within IR departments and journals bears little resemblance to the grand theorizing and state-fixated area of study depicted by the critics

(Rosamond 2000). In any case, it is a bold claim that overstates the extent to which the study of European integration was ever cordoned off as a subfield of IR. The likes of Ernst Haas, Karl Deutsch, Leon Lindberg, and Philippe Schmitter studied the early communities as self-conscious (and often pioneering) exponents of the latest political science (Haas 2001). Integration theory's most obvious connection to IR was its contribution to the emergence of International Political Economy (IPE), a sub-area that explicitly emphasizes the fuzziness of the boundaries between domestic politics and international relations (Katzenstein, Keohane, and Krasner 1998). Others suggest that IR theories retain a valuable place in EU studies because they act as valuable tools for understanding the global environment within which the EU operates (Hurrell and Menon 1996; and Peterson and Bomberg 1999).

The third point—the type of theorizing involved in the 'old' debate—is less a criticism than an observation about how the study of a phenomenon (in our case the EU) is bound up with the ebbs and flows of social science, as much as it is related to the context supplied by that phenomenon.

Another way of thinking about this shift from the 'old' to the 'new' is supplied by Markus Jachtenfuchs (2001). He draws a distinction between a classical phase of integration theory where the 'Euro-polity' was the **dependent variable** and the current 'governance' phase in which the 'Euro-polity' becomes the **independent variable**. In other words, the EU has shifted from being a phenomenon that analysts seek to explain to becoming a factor that contributes to the explanation of other phenomena. This amounts to moving from asking 'why does integration occur?' to posing the question 'what effect does integration have?' While the evolution of the EU may explain why the nature of EU studies (and the theoretical work that informs it) has shifted in this way, it is clearly not the only reason. It is important to remember that the preoccupations and fashions of the political sciences also change over time. Theoretical development (or, for some, progress) in a particular field is about assimilating the currently predominant conceptual tool-kit and the preoccupations of social science. Some would say that this delivers progress in a field in the form of better explanations of the reality of the object of enquiry (in our case the EU) and more rigorous forms of social science. Others would argue that our knowledge of the social world is governed by prevailing conceptions of what counts as valid knowledge, thereby skewing the game in favour of some forms of theory over others.

Key points

- Recent years have seen renewed interest in theorizing the EU. Most scholars accept that there has been a significant shift towards newer styles of theoretical work.

- Critics of the classical debate regard neo-functionalism and intergovernmentalism as theories that ask the wrong sorts of question about the EU.

- Discussion about the obsolescence of 'old' theories raises some interesting questions about the nature and purpose of theory.

Institutionalism and the EU

By the standards of regional integration schemes worldwide, the EU is heavily institutionalized. It possesses a distinctive set of supranational institutions such as the Commission, the Parliament, and the Court of Justice (see Chapters 9–12). In addition, the EU features a number of intergovernmental bodies, not to mention several smaller bodies, such as the Economic and Social Committee (see Chapter 1: 2), that wield less in the way of formal power yet form distinct cogs in the European policy-making machinery. The treaties define the roles of these various institutions as well as the ways in which they are supposed to interact.

Three points are worthy of note. First, the founders of the European Communities sought to capture their desired balance between national and supranational forces through careful institutional design. Most accept that the balance has altered over time (Wallace 1996), but the formal institutional structure of European integration has remained remarkably resilient for half a century. Second, close observers of the EU often note the growth of distinct cultures within the various institutions. It is not just that there is a particular modus operandi within the Commission, but that individual Directorates-General (DGs) of the Commission possess distinct institutional cultures. The same is true of different Councils. Third, scholarship has revealed the existence of various informalities within the formal institutional shape of the EU. This work suggests that much that is decisive within the policy process is the consequence of regularized practices that do not have formal status within the treaties. In spite of that, these established routines are frequently thought of as institutions.

So much of the corpus of EU studies involves the analysis of formal and informal institutions and the impact that institutionalized practices have upon policy outcomes. At the same time, as studies of the EU have multiplied in recent years, so the wider world of political science has become infused with the so-called '**new institutionalism**' (Hall and Taylor 1996). See Box 8.1.

It would be a mistake to regard the new institutionalism as a single theoretical perspective. Institutionalists agree, more or less, that institutions matter. As Schneider and Aspinwall note:

Institutions contain the bias individual agents have built into their society over time, which in turn leads to important distributional consequences. They structure political actions and outcomes rather than simply mirroring social activity and rational competition among disaggregated units (Schneider and Aspinwall 2001: 2).

Importantly, institutionalists of different hues have alternative accounts of just how much institutions matter. Schneider and Aspinwall think about institutional political science as a spectrum. At one end of this spectrum sits an economistic-**rationalist** position which sees institutions as the consequence

Box 8.1 **Core ideas**

Institutions and the new institutionalism

For most students of politics, 'institution' brings to mind phenomena such as the legislative, executive, and judicial branches of government—what we might think of as ongoing or embedded sets of formalities, often underwritten or codified by constitutional prescription. Early political science dealt with the study of this sort of institution. Scholars explored how such bodies operated, how they interacted, and how they supplied sets of rules that helped to account for the ways in which political systems operated. Often such studies concluded that institutional patterns reflected the character of a country's politics. This 'old' institutionalism was criticized—especially by behaviouralists—for an over-emphasis on the formal, codified aspects of politics at the expense of looking at the nitty-gritty of politics: the interaction of groups in pursuit of their interest and the basis, form, and consequences of individual and collective political behaviour. However, classical institutional studies did bequeath a concern

with the impact of rules upon the behaviour of actors and thus upon political outcomes more generally. 'New' institutionalism proceeds from the axiom that 'institutions matter' as shapers of and influences upon the behaviour of actors (rather than as mere expressions of political culture). This is combined with a broader definition of 'institution' to embrace not only formal rules, but also forms of ongoing social interaction that form the 'compliance procedures and standard operating practices' in the political economy, to borrow Peter Hall's well-established definition (Hall 1986: 19). Thus, from the new institutionalist vantage point, we may be talking about anything from written constitutional rules through to norms or even collectively recognized symbols when we speak of institutions. With this in mind, it is hardly surprising that the EU has become a favoured venue for the practice of new institutionalist political science.

of long-run patterns of behaviour by self-seeking agents. Institutions, in this account, are both modifiers of the pursuit of self-interest and a medium through which actors may conduct their transactions with greater efficiency. At the opposite end of the spectrum is a sociological position where actors' interests are actually constructed through processes of institutional interaction. Hall and Taylor's landmark discussion (Hall and Taylor 1996) identifies three subspecies of institutionalism: rational choice, historical, and sociological. Each of these has a presence in EU studies (see Table 8.1).

Rational choice institutionalism is the most obvious—and, for some, the most successful—way in which rational choice approaches to politics have infiltrated EU studies (Dowding 2000). Rational choice theory—perhaps the dominant (though much criticized) strand in contemporary American political science—is based on the idea that human beings are self-seeking and behave rationally and strategically. The goals of political actors are organized hierarchically. They form their preferences on the basis of their interests. Institutions are important because they act as **intervening variables**. This means that institutions do not alter preference functions, but will have an impact upon the ways in which actors pursue those preferences. Consequently, changes in the institutional rules of the game, such as the introduction of the co-decision procedure (which, following the Maastricht and Amsterdam treaties, gave the Council and the European Parliament co-legislative power in certain areas) or alterations to the voting rules within the Council (say from unanimity to qualified majority), will induce actors to recalculate the ways in which they need to behave in order to realize their preferences.

By and large, rational choice institutionalists have been interested in how their theory develops

propositions about the changing relative power of institutional actors in the policy process. As Crombez (2001) shows, scholars of this persuasion assume that institutional actors seek policy outcomes that correspond as closely as possible to their preferences. The construction of formal models, often deploying the type of reasoning found in formal economic analysis, allows for the empirical research on specific cases to be mapped against the formal decision rules that apply. Thus EU studies has developed lively debate about matters such as the agenda-setting power of the various institutions.

For their proponents (such as Dowding 2000), such rational choice perspectives offer rigorous foundations for the development and testing of falsifiable hypotheses. This improves knowledge in a progressive way. Scholars work from a set of (admittedly stylized) assumptions to produce progressively better understandings of how the EU works. For their opponents, rational choice institutionalists miss the point. Their focus on formal rules leads them to ignore the various informal processes that grow up around the codified practices. It is these informalities that better explain policy outcomes. Moreover, rational choice accounts of actor preferences tend to leave these fixed rather than recognizing the ways in which processes of socialization can mould interests and identities (Hooghe 2002). See Box 8.2.

Historical institutionalists are interested in how institutional choices have long-term effects. Institutions are designed for particular purposes in particular sets of circumstances. They are assigned tasks and in this process acquire interests and ongoing agendas. If institutions interact with one another in a decision-making process then patterns that are constitutionally prescribed or evolve in the early lifetime of the institutions concerned may 'lock in' and also become ongoing. This 'lock in'

Table 8.1 The 'new institutionalisms'

	Type of institutionalism		
	Rational choice institutionalism	Historical institutionalism	Sociological institutionalism
Research objective	The changing relative power of institutions	The long-term effects of institutions	The role of culture OR persuasion and communicative action

Source: Adapted from Hall and Taylor 1996.

Box 8.2 Issues and debates
Rational choice and the science of EU studies

Supporters of rational choice institutionalism believe that this approach to the EU is able to build knowledge in a systematic way. Scholars working under the auspices of rational choice subscribe to particular methods of theory building. This usually involves the development of models capable of generating hypotheses, which can then be subjected to confirmation or disconfirmation through exposure to hard empirical evidence. Such work relies on the deployment of (often quite stylized) assumptions and the use of game theory as tool of analysis. The substantial work of Geoffrey Garrett and George Tsebelis (for example Tsebelis 1994; Garrett and Tsebelis 1996) yields the counterintuitive claim that the co-decision procedure has strengthened the Council at the expense of the Commission and the European Parliament. The analysis is sophisticated, but relies on the assumption that institutions' preferences are arranged along a continuum according to the amount of integration that they favour. For critics, this type of work may produce intriguing results, but it relies too much on unrealistic assumptions and describes games that bear no relation to the complex interactions that take place between EU institutions on a day-to-day basis. Another dimension to this debate is that rational choice institutionalists often advance the view that theirs is a more rigorous form of political science than that offered by either EU studies 'traditionalists' or those of a more constructivist persuasion.

means that a 'path-dependent' logic may set in. The ongoing nature of institutional interests (their continuing agendas and their preference for self-preservation) means that institutions become robust and may well outlive their creators. This also means that institutions may have an impact that their creators could not have foreseen, not least because they survive to confront new circumstances and new challenges. But these new challenges are met through the prism provided by pre-existing institutions. Thus the range of possible action and policy choice is constrained. Policy entrepreneurs may attempt to redesign institutions to meet current needs, but they do so in the face of institutional agendas that are locked in and which are, therefore, potentially difficult to reform.

Like the other two variants of institutionalism, historical institutionalism is not exclusive to EU studies. But its applications are obvious. That said, scholars use this basic template in various ways. Paul Pierson's well-known discussion of path dependency (Pierson 1998) looks at the problem of unintended consequences. He argues that the immediate concerns of the architects of the European Communities (EC) led them into acts of institutional design that ultimately helped to erode the capacity of national governments to control the governance of their economies. So while the intention of West European governments of the 1950s may have been to rescue the nation state (Milward 1999), Pierson's work suggests that the long-term consequence of their deliberations may have been to engineer precisely the obverse. The implications for research from this theoretical insight are quite interesting. It pushes students of the EU to think about policy pathways— how particular EU-level competences emerge over time as a result of specific decisions. We are asked to think about how rational acts at one point in time influence rational action in the future.

Less wedded to rational actor assumptions is historical institutionalist work, such as that of Kenneth Armstrong and Simon Bulmer (1998) in their study of the single market. Armstrong and Bulmer are more interested in the way that institutions can become carriers of certain ideas, values, and norms over time. Once again we are directed towards thinking about how such normative and ideational 'matter' is loaded into institutions at their inception. But students of the EU are also invited to explore how institutional cultures (say of the Commission generally or of specific DGs) impact upon all stages of the policy process, influence action and policy choice, and (perhaps) assist in the conditioning of the interests of actors.

This last comment provides a link to sociological institutionalism, a strand of literature that is closely bound up with the constructivist 'turn' in international and European studies. This is discussed later in the chapter, so the exposition in this section will be relatively brief. It is important to remember that sociological institutionalists tend to reject the other institutionalisms because of their inherent 'rationalism'. The meaning of this term is again discussed below, but for now it is important to remember that sociological institutionalists/constructivists operate with a quite distinct **ontology** (an underlying conception of the world). This boils down to a very particular take on the nature of actors' interests. While rational choice and (most) historical institutionalists see interests as exogenous (external to) interaction, so sociological institutionalists see them as endogenous (internal). That is to say that interests are not pre-set, but rather the product of interaction between actors.

This leads sociological institutionalists towards a concern with two broad issues: the 'culture' of institutions and the role of persuasion and communicative action within institutional settings (Börzel and Risse 2000). By 'culture' is meant the emergence of common frames of reference, norms governing behaviour, and 'cognitive filters'. As Hall and Taylor note, in this account 'institutions do not simply affect the strategic calculations of individuals, as rational choice institutionalists contend, but also their most basic preferences and very identity' (Hall and Taylor 1996: 948). With this in mind, sociological institutionalist analysis of the EU looks at the ways in which ongoing patterns of interaction and 'normal' forms of behaviour emerge within institutional settings. As one writer puts it, 'institutions have theories about themselves' (Jachtenfuchs 1997: 47). Thus institutions contribute to actors' understandings of who they are, what their context is, and what might be the motivations of other actors. This sort of work aims to add substance to often heard claims such as the idea that different DGs of the European Commission function in quite distinct ways. Another area in which the application of this sort of thinking seems appropriate is the investigation of whether formally intergovernmental processes such as those associated with the Common Foreign and Security Policy (CFSP) conform to established patterns of interstate interaction, or whether they bring about

new norms of exchange between the envoys of member states.

The roles of communication, argument, and persuasion are seen as particularly important in these contexts. These deliberative processes are likely to occur in settings where norms have been established, but they also contribute to the establishment of common understandings. Thus, sociological institutionalists often embark upon empirical quests for so-called 'norm entrepreneurs'— 'well placed individual actors . . . [who] . . . can often turn their individual beliefs into broader, shared understandings' (Checkel 2001d: 31). Sociological institutionalism is not simply interested in the EU level of analysis. Much work is being done on the interaction of national and European-level norms and in particular on the ways in which 'European' norms filter into the existing political cultures of the member states (Börzel 2002).

Key points

- The EU has become a major venue for the application of 'new institutionalist' political science and for debates between its main strands.

- In this wide-ranging literature, institutions tend to be defined broadly as ongoing practices rather than simply as formal, constitutionally created bodies.

- Rational choice institutionalists are interested in how the relative power of actors shifts in accordance with changes in institutional rules.

- Historical institutionalists focus on the long-term implications of institutional choices made at specific points in time.

- Sociological institutionalists pay attention to the 'culture' of institutions and the ways in which patterns of communication and persuasion operate in institutional settings.

- Much contemporary work on the EU follows from these basic premises. However, there is much dividing the practitioners of the different institutionalisms, leading to considerable debate about the extent to which the three approaches can combine to form a distinct research programme.

Theories of policy making and the EU

One of the major features of EU studies in recent years has been the growth of work that draws on theories of public policy making. This is barely surprising. The EU is a major source of authoritative policy outputs in Europe. Moreover, most observers agree that there has been a substantial 'drift' of policy-making competence from member states to the European level since the initiation of the Communities in the 1950s. Consequently, there is an obvious and increasing need to make sense of how policy is made in this context. This confirms the idea, discussed above, that the EU is about rather more than 'integration'. If we think of the EU as a policy system, then it follows that scholarship needs to explore the ways in which policy agendas are set, policies are formulated, decisions are made, and legislation is implemented.

This also constitutes a move away from the idea that the key EU outputs are 'big' history-making decisions such as treaty revisions. Much of what the EU does is in the area of technical regulation and the finer points of economic governance. Others—such as those scholars associated with the multi-level governance school discussed below—note that different patterns of policy making occur in different areas of EU activity. Thus, the politics of agricultural regulation might be quite dissimilar to the politics of merger control. This suggests that detailed empirical scholarship is needed on a sector-by-sector basis if we are properly to comprehend the complexity of EU governance. However, this does not mean that theory is irrelevant or marginal to this enterprise. All political science—however empirical—is informed by theory.

The EU has always been a port of call for theoretical work constructed elsewhere in the social sciences and the concern with the minutiae of policy making suggests an important role for theories of policy analysis. In their discussion of EU decision making, John Peterson and Elizabeth Bomberg (1999) suggest that different levels of action in the EU require different sorts of theory. They identify three levels of action: super-systemic, systemic, and meso (sectoral). At each level analysts are interested

in different variables—respectively, changes in the wider environment of the EU, institutional change, and resource dependencies. Thus, each level requires different theoretical tools. IR theories work well at the super-systemic level, while new institutionalist theories suit the systemic level of analysis.

At the sectoral level, where regulatory complexity prevails and where 'stakeholders' in the policy process exchange information and resources, Peterson and Bomberg recommend the deployment of policy network analysis. The concept of policy networks provides a way of thinking about complex decision-making situations characterized by ongoing relations between multiple 'stakeholding' actors. They are situations where ideology is largely secondary and expertise is at a premium. This is not to say that politics is absent. On the contrary, policy network analysis deals with the politics of influence and mutual dependency in situations where power is dispersed. The actors involved in policy networks have, by definition, an interest in policy outcomes. In national contexts—where the policy network approach was first developed—emphasis was placed upon the relationships between government departments, pressure groups, and various agencies and organizations. The main insight of such work was that networks often involved the ongoing exchange of resources between their component members. The impact of such work is that it guides us away from thinking about policy making in terms of rule-bound interactions between (constitutionally defined) institutions. It emphasizes the need to understand the specific relations of mutual dependency that obtain in different sectors.

Opinion is divided as to whether policy network analysis has a place in the study of the EU. Kassim (1994), for example, criticizes policy network approaches for neglecting the interaction of institutions that is so central to a proper understanding of the EU policy process. Peterson (1995a), on the other hand, points to the regulatory, uneven, fluid, and multi-actor character of the EU policy game as ample justification for the application of the policy network template to the EU. Also, as Richardson (2001) reminds us, the concept of policy networks (as opposed to the rather more rigid idea of 'policy communities') is fluid and adaptable and thus well suited to the fact that EU policy making is segmented, complex, and populated by multiple stakeholders.

The take-up of this approach by students of the EU begs the interesting question of whether the tools used to study national governance and policy making can be applied straightforwardly to the European level. This takes us back to some of the fundamental issues discussed at the beginning of this chapter. But policy network analysis is not alone in making this assumption.

Another good example emerges from the work of Giandomenico Majone (1994) who has been a central figure in the development of ideas regarding the 'regulatory state'. The regulatory state literature offers of view of how the management of advanced capitalist economies has shifted in recent times in the face of challenges posed by changes in the global economy. In Majone's terms, the EU has many of the key features of a regulatory state, the paradigm example of which is the United States. Regulatory states are distinct from positive interventionist states. Whereas the latter involve government intervention to engineer the redistribution of resources (usually through the mechanism of the welfare state), so the former busy themselves only with the rectification of market failure. Much of what the EU does is bound up with the regulation of the single market. It—pretty much—lacks the welfare function associated most with the post-war (West) European state. The EU's relatively modest resources are best targeted at regulatory forms of policy making. But Majone's point is that regulation is a form of governance that is becoming widespread across the western world. It is not a development unique to the EU. However, the EU can be thought of as a set of regulatory institutions created by the member states to solve problems of market imperfection. In this respect Majone's analysis shares a great deal with an approach called principal-agent analysis that is found in some forms of rational choice institutionalism (Pollack 1997a) and in Moravcsik's developed form of liberal intergovernmentalism (Moravcsik 1998).

Not everyone would agree that the EU is solely a regulatory state, but the model of negative market integration/regulation is increasingly seen as one important dimension of the way in which governance in Europe is delivered (Jørgensen and Rosamond 2002). Indeed, one thing that would appear to unite political scientists working on the EU with, on the one hand, scholars of international political economy and, on the other, analysts of national and subnational policy making is an interest in *governance* (Pierre 2001). The term is usually defined in terms of the range of actions and institutions that supply order. What we conventionally understand as *government* is one way in which order is delivered, but the literature on governance suggests that the traditional methods of public regulation, intervention, and legislation are being displaced and that authority is becoming dispersed amongst a variety of actors. The state retains a key role in governance, but its role is being reformulated and, arguably, residualized. The EU is thought of as a very interesting and pertinent laboratory for the exploration of these trends, a point taken up by the literature on multi-level governance.

Key points

- The status of the EU as a polity that is responsible for the delivery of coherent and meaningful policy outputs challenges us to think about it in terms other than the classical theoretical discourse of integration.

- With this in mind many have sought to treat the EU as a policy system. This requires the application of the tools of policy analysis. Many of these approaches, such as policy network analysis, originally emerged in the study of national political systems.

- A slightly different take on this question is to think about the EU in terms of trends that are shaping the ways in which governance is delivered in modern complex societies.

Multi-level governance

Much of the work introduced in the previous section builds on the claim that policy making within both nation states and the EU is a complex affair that cannot be captured by static models of the decision-making process focusing on formal legislative institutions. Analysts who adopt the theoretical language of policy networks and the regulatory state force us to question whether there is any meaningful distinction between policy making at different levels of governance. Perhaps the crucial changes are taking place in terms of policy-making styles rather than policy-making levels. We can take this a little further to say that the character of governance in Europe has changed significantly over the past 50 years. If we adopt this position, then we might suggest that the boundaries between national policy making and European policy making have been blurred to the point of insignificance. The EU policy process is not something that simply happens at the European level. It penetrates into national political and legal systems in complex ways. So while there has been an undoubted 'drift' of authority in various policy areas to the European level (Hooghe and Marks 2001; Schmitter 1996), we need to move away from the image of there being two distinct domains of politics in Europe—the national and the supra-national/European level.

This claim represents a direct challenge to theories such as Moravscik's liberal intergovernmentalism (LI) (see Chapter 7: 103). LI relies on the idea of a two-level game to describe how governments' preferences emerge in the context of domestic politics and are then the foundations for inter-governmental bargaining within European-level institutions. Such a picture is directly challenged by the idea of multi-level governance.

The term 'multi-level governance' (MLG) has become commonplace in EU studies in recent years and the term is usually used to capture the peculiar qualities of the EU's political system. The two leading proponents of the idea define MLG as 'the dispersion of authoritative decision-making across multiple territorial levels' (Hooghe and Marks 2001: xi). Rather than thinking about the extent to which Europe has become 'integrated', it is helpful to explore how *loci* of authority have shifted over the past half-century. Hooghe and Marks find that authority has become more dispersed since the late 1950s. So while there has been a drift of authority from the national to the European level, there has also been a general devolution of decision-making competence in most West European countries. At the same time, however, national governments remain important sites of authority.

So we have a picture of the EU policy process consisting a several tiers of authority (the European, the national, and the subnational). But the idea of MLG goes beyond this. It also emphasizes fluidity between these tiers, so that policy actors may move between different levels of action. Moreover, dispersion of authority is uneven across policy areas.

At present MLG remains more of an organizing metaphor than a theory. It is within this metaphor that particular approaches—such as policy network analysis—can sit comfortably. But it does rest on some fundamental theoretical preconceptions that differentiate it squarely from LI (Marks, Hooghe, and Blank 1996). We have already noted the departure from the conceptions of political space offered by two-level game theorists. It is also worth saying that MLG proceeds from a more pluralistic and organizational conception of the state than the likes of LI. This means that analysts beginning with an MLG frame of reference dispute quite fundamentally the intergovernmentalist account of what the EU is. The MLG version of the EU is a 'set of overarching, multi-level policy networks [where] . . . [t]he structure of political control is variable, not constant across policy space' (Marks Hooghe, and Blank 1996: 41). In many ways MLG represents an attempt to capture the complexity of the EU, but it also represents a clear denial of the idea that there can be a single all-encompassing theory of the EU.

Key points

- The literature on multi-level governance (MLG) encourages us to think about the EU as a political system across multiple levels including national and subnational arenas of action as well the institutional environment of Brussels.

- MLG is premised on the idea that authority has

gradually moved away from national governments over the past half-century. But authority has not simply shifted upwards to state-like European institutions; it has become dispersed among a variety of private and public agents.

- This yields a picture of complex, variable, and uneven patterns of policy making in contemporary Europe.

Social constructivist approaches to the EU

Constructivism has been the big news in IR theory over the past few years. The work of constructivist scholars like Alexander Wendt (1999) has come to pose a serious challenge to the established schools of IR theory. Until recently, the main debate in mainstream IR was between forms of realism and liberalism. While realists offer a state-centric view of the world that emphasizes the primacy of self-help and power, liberals contemplate the ways in which international co-operation, commerce, and institutionalization are able to temper tendencies towards war in the international system. Constructivists note that both of these approaches emerge from similar foundations. They are both *rationalist* theories. Defining rationalism takes us into the complex realm of metatheory, and we cannot do justice to it here (see S. Smith 2001 for a deeper discussion). They tend to operate with a view of the world (an ontology) that sees interests as materially given. They also adhere to a postivistic conception of how knowledge should be gathered. This involves a commitment to 'scientific' method, the neutrality of facts and the existence of observable realities (S. Smith 2001: 227). While such sentiments characterize much social science, they are not shared universally. Ranged against rationalism is a range of *reflectivist* approaches—such as postmodernism, forms of feminism, and varieties of critical theory—that begin from wholly different premises (Keohane 1988 discusses this distinction).

The appeal of constructivism—or at least the type

of constructivism that has entered the IR mainstream in the last decade—is that it claims to offer a middle way between rationalism and reflectivism. Constructivists such as Wendt see interests as socially constructed rather than pre-given, which means that regularities in the international system are the consequence of collective (or 'intersubjective') meanings. So the challenge to rationalism is primarily ontological. Constructivists, as we have seen with the discussion of sociological institutionalism earlier in this chapter, are interested in how collective understandings emerge and how institutions constitute the interests and identities of actors. However, writers like Wendt and Jeffrey Checkel (2001c), who has written extensively about Europe, insist that constructivism can and should share the rationalist commitment to developing knowledge through clear research programmes, refutable hypotheses, and the specification of causal mechanisms that produce regularities.

This is undoubtedly what most IR constructivists aspire to. However, not all of those working within a broadly constructivist tradition accept that a constructivist ontology is compatible with a rationalist **epistemology** (i.e. the way in which knowledge is acquired). There is no need to pursue this debate here beyond acknowledging its existence, and pointing out that it raises some fundamental questions about what amounts to 'proper' or 'good' social science. This has obvious implications for a subdiscipline such as EU studies because contests over these questions will affect what is published in academic journals and books about European integration and, by extension will influence how the subject is taught in universities.

The editors of the first collection of constructivist essays on the EU accept that the various authors occupy different positions along the continuum between rationalism and reflectivism (Christiansen, Jørgensen, and Wiener 2001*a*). Moreover the commitment to 'break bread' with rationalist theories such as liberal intergovernmentalism varies from author to author. That said, constructivists argue that they are best placed to study integration as a *process*. While intergovernmentalists recommend that the EU be studied as an instance of interstate bargaining and comparativists think about the EU as a political system, constructivists purport to investigate the character of the move from a bargaining regime to a polity (Christiansen, Jørgensen, and Wiener 2001*a*: 11). Thus if we think about European integration as a process bound up with change, then it makes sense to draw on a metatheoretical position that treats reality as contested and problematic. This means that constructivist-inspired work should focus on 'social ontologies and social institutions, directing research at the origin and reconstruction of identities, the impact of rules and norms, the role of language and political discourse' (Christiansen, Jørgensen, and Wiener 2001*a*: 12).

Perhaps the best way to unravel constructivism in EU studies is to mention a few examples of what constructivists actually work on. Many are interested in how European identities emerge. So the idea of a 'European economy', a 'European security community', or 'European citizenship' should not be read as a consequence of actors' interests changing rationally in response to external material changes such as the onset of globalization or the end of the Cold War. Rather, constructivists insist that we need to investigate the ways in which these identities

are constructed through the use of language, the deployment of ideas, and the establishment of norms. We also need to pay attention to the ways in which these norms and ideas are communicated and to the processes of learning or socialization that take place among actors. 'Norms' are particularly important in the constructivist vocabulary. These are defined as 'collective expectations for the proper behaviour of actors with a given identity' (Katzenstein 1996: 5). It is through the internalization of norms that actors acquire their identities and establish what their interests are. This is what constructivists mean when they talk about the 'constitutive effects' of norms.

The emerging constructivist research agenda in EU studies (which has much in common with that of sociological institutionalism outlined earlier in this chapter) also pays attention to the ways in which European-level norms, ideas, and discourses penetrate into the various national polities that make up the EU (Börzel 2002).

Key points

- Constructivism is a recent import to EU studies, having taken on a particular character in debates in international theory.

- Constructivism is not a theory of integration, but a position on the nature of social reality (an ontology). It follows that there are many constructivist approaches and significant disagreement about the compatibility of constructivism with rationalist theories.

- Constructivists are interested in European integration as a process. They focus in particular on questions of identity and the ways in which European norms are established and play out within the EU institutions and the member states.

International Relations and International Political Economy revisited

We saw earlier in this chapter that the discipline of International Relations (IR) has been thought of by some as an inappropriate disciplinary homeland for students of the EU. If the EU is about much more than 'integration', runs the argument, then we need to break away from a discipline that is really only capable of asking questions about whether there is more or less integration and which actors influence the integration process. One counter-argument, as we have seen, is to challenge this image of what IR is all about. For example, there are plenty of scholars working in IR departments, attending IR conferences, and writing in IR journals who see the discipline as being at the forefront of thinking about emergent transnational economic and social spaces and the forms of governance that arise in such circumstances. Another is to question the notion of a hard boundary between 'political science' and IR and to point out that integration theory was founded by figures—like Karl Deutsch and Ernst Haas—who were engaged in the explicit application of the newest political science ideas to the study of a very interesting new phenomenon (regional integration in Europe) (Haas 2001).

This is a debate worth having, but in recent years there have emerged other reasons for 'bringing IR back in'. Two, in particular, stand out: (a) the possibility that the EU can be studied as an instance of the so-called 'new regionalism' that has emerged in recent years across the world as (perhaps) a response to globalization, and (b) the growing significance of the EU as an actor on the world stage.

The EU and the 'new' regionalism

Regional integration—especially in the form of free trade areas and customs unions—is not a new phenomenon. However, the period since the mid-1980s has been characterized by the growth of many regional economic blocs in the global political economy. Among the most conspicuous are the North American Free Trade Agreement (NAFTA), Asia Pacific Economic Co-operation (APEC), and Mercusor in South America. Not surprisingly, these cases of 'regionalism' have generated considerable scholarly interest and analysts have been keen to explore the possibility that their more or less simultaneous emergence has something to do with exposure to common stimuli.

The most obvious explanation for the revival of regional integration is the development of **globalization**. Globalization is a deeply contentious topic, but is usually thought of as a combination of things like heightened capital mobility, intensified cross-border transactions, the multinationalization of production, and the spread of neo-liberal economic policy norms—in short, the growth of market authority at the expense of formal political authority. This debate is very complex, but one line of argument is that regionalism (as represented by NAFTA, Mercusor, and so on) is the primary way in which states have responded to globalization. The move to regionalism suggests that states have seen fit to pool resources in order to recapture some of the authority that globalization has taken away.

Debate exists over the extent to which states actually and effectively lead the creation of regional integration schemes. This is where a distinction between regionalism and regionalization is important in the literature. While regionalism describes state-led projects of institution building among groups of countries, regionalization is a term used to capture the emergence of a de facto regional economy, propelled by the cross-border activities of economic actors, particularly firms. The question here is whether the formal institutions of regional integration are created to deal with and regulate this emergent transnational economic space, or whether the growth of cross-border activity is stimulated by the decisions of governments. These are empirical questions at one level, but the two positions in this particular debate emerge from two different theoretical accounts of the world—one largely state-centric and one not.

There is also a debate in international economics about the impact of regional agreements on the global economy. All of the instances mentioned above are actual or aspirant free trade areas. The question is whether the creation of regional free trade zones creates or diverts trade on a global scale. Put another way, it asks whether we are heading for a regionalized world (of competing regional blocs) or a globalized world. Again, such matters can be measured empirically, but theoretical intervention is needed if we are fully to understand the meaning of a term like 'globalization'. Notice, also, how much of the foregoing implies a particular type of relationship between globalization and statehood and, it should be said, between structure and agency. Alternative accounts place differential emphasis upon the structural qualities of globalization—its ability to set imperatives and shape the behaviour of actors.

The theoretical relevance of the questions raised in the preceding paragraphs becomes especially apparent when we think about their application to the EU. Thinking theoretically, as James Rosenau and Mary Durfee (1995) point out, involves asking the 'of what is this an instance?' question. The 'new regionalism' literature forces us to ask whether the EU is a comparable case to, say, NAFTA. If the answer is yes, then the study of comparative regional *integration* is brought back in with the EU as one of the primary cases.

Of course, the EU is at best a deviant case of regionalism. Its longevity rules out any claim that the EU was *created* as a response to global economic upheavals in the late 1970s and early 1980s. Moreover, compared to other cases of regionalism the EU is considerably more institutionalized and much more deeply integrated. Yet at the same time the acceleration of economic integration through the single market programme and progress towards monetary union has coincided with the growth of regional projects elsewhere.

The problem is not a new one for theoreticians of European integration. In many ways, the problem defined the project of the first generation of integration theorists. For neo-functionalists (as we have seen in Chapter 6), comparison was a 'must' because only then might a generalizable theory of regional

integration emerge from the case study supplied by the EC. Integration theorists and their critics have long grappled with the so-called $n = 1$ problem, that is, the uncomfortable possibility that the EU may be nothing other than an instance of itself.

The EU as an actor

The external policy of the EU is discussed at length elsewhere in this book (see Chapter 15). The task here is to concentrate on what this might mean for the ways in which we might conceptualize and theorize the EU's role in the global political economy.

The question that first emerges is whether we can conceptualize the EU as an *actor*. That is to say, is the EU a discernible entity with its own capacity to act on the basis of its own interests? To be sure, the EU possesses certain formal roles in world politics and in the management of the global economy. It speaks with a common voice in international trade negotiations and has the makings of an embryonic foreign and security policy (M. Smith 2001). On the other hand it consists of 15 member states, all of which operate as actors within the current international system (note how the very phrase 'international system' connotes an order founded on the interaction of authoritative national states).

That the EU is not a state (at least in the conventional modern sense of the term) is not really in dispute. But is it becoming one? If this is the case, then we might want to argue that the EU is an embryonic state writ large, formed through the gradual merger of its component member states. This might then allow us to slot the EU—as a constituent unit of the international system—into long-established theories of IR, such as realism. This would construe the EU as an entity seeking to advance its own interests and, particularly, to render itself secure from external threat.

However, we might be reluctant to arrive at this conclusion. The EU might appear to be a rather unique entity, lacking those decisive authoritative attributes normally associated with modern (supposedly sovereign) nation states. If we think about the image of the EU that is described by the literature on multi-level governance (discussed earlier in this chapter) and project this outwards, then students of integration are confronted with something that seems to fit very badly with conventional theories of IR (Ruggie 1998: 173–4). Indeed, rather than trying to fit the EU into IR theory, perhaps IR theorists need to look carefully at their established theoretical tool-kits if they are properly to comprehend the EU. Theories such as neo-realism and neo-liberal institutionalism (which dominate theoretical discourse in IR, especially in the United States) are built around the idea of states as the dominant units of analysis in the world system. The EU might be a freak occurrence, specific to the peculiarities of Western Europe, but the ways in which the boundaries between domestic and international politics have become blurred, along with the styles of governance that have evolved, may well have much wider application.

One rider to this is that the EU's external action takes place, whether in terms of foreign policy or commercial (trade) policy, in conditions that still respond to the rules of state-centred international politics. Thus, for the EU to acquire legitimacy and recognition as a valid actor in the system, we might hypothesize that it has to conform to the rules of that system. This in turn would create pressures for

the EU to become state-like. Therefore, the paradox is that while the EU may appear to transcend the international system, it is still in meaningful ways constituted (as constructivists would put it) by the norms of that very system. See Box 8.3.

Key points

- The dismissal of International Relations (IR) as a suitable (co-)parent discipline for EU studies may be somewhat premature.

- Much recent conceptual thinking in IR has been directed towards the analysis of the growth of regionalism in the global political economy, of which the EU may be a (peculiar) instance.

- Also important is recent thinking that challenges the state-centric vision of the world that has characterized much mainstream IR theory. The particular character of the EU as a presence in the global system confronts this traditional imagery by pointing to a number of ways in which structures of authority and patterns of politics may be changing.

Box 8.3 **Core ideas**
The EU and statehood

Much of the routine political discourse surrounding European integration bothers itself with the question of whether the EU is becoming a 'federal superstate', which, by definition, is supplanting the powers of its constituent member states. While such debates will seem simplistic to close students of the EU, they open up interesting avenues for theorists. Without doubt, the EU lacks some of the classical indices of 'statehood' as it has come to be understood (not least in Europe) over the past three and a half centuries. For example, the EU lacks fixed territorial boundaries and it does not possess monopolistic control over the legitimate means of violence. It does not engage in extensive programmes of redistribution, yet it does exercise meaningful and emphatic authority over the governance of its constituent economies, and by extension over the lives of hundreds of millions of Europeans. Moreover, the

presumption of many current theorists is that the EU is sufficiently similar to national political systems to allow the deployment of the tools of normal political science and policy analysis. But statehood also has external dimensions. Thus world politics has developed into a game played between states with the notion of 'sovereignty' as the ultimate rule. Much contemporary IR literature debates the extent to which processes such as globalization have begun to transform this system. Yet the language of statehood, international politics, sovereignty, and diplomacy remains central to world politics. We might argue that the condition for admission to the world polity remains the achievement of statehood. So the question becomes whether the EU is being constituted and shaped by the existing world system or whether it is contributing to a radical reshaping of world politics.

Conclusion

The revival of interest in theory in EU studies has occurred within the context of some serious thinking about the role of theory in political science. Some of the 'new' theories discussed in this chapter have emerged from a concern to render theoretical work more rigorously 'scientific'. Other newer approaches have emerged from positions that explicitly challenge the rationalist mainstream in social science. Others still—notably certain constructivists—try to occupy a middle position between rationalism and reflectivism. These debates have begun to intrude into EU studies (Christiansen, Jørgensen, and Wiener 2001b) and have been played out more extensively in the broader IR literature (Baylis and Smith 2001). To the newcomer, this might seem like complex academic navel gazing and thus divorced from the real business of studying the EU.

But theoretical reflection and debate simply brings out into the open assumptions that reside in any empirical discussion of the EU. Alternative theories have different accounts of social reality and sometimes lead to quite different strategies for acquiring valid knowledge about that world. This translates eventually into a set of disagreements about matters fundamental to this book: what sort of entity is the EU and how should it be studied?

Much of the 'new' theoretical work introduced above represents a self-conscious departure from thinking about the EU in terms of 'integration'. Its status as a supplier of authoritative policy outputs suggests that the tool-kit of political science and policy analysis might be useful. At the same time, however, the fact that the EU is not a state as conventionally understood poses all sorts of challenges to those seeking to understand not only European integration, but also the nature of world order in the early twenty-first century. The EU may offer a clear indication of what a 'denationalized' world order might look like (Kohler-Koch and Eising 1999). It sits between nation states and the international system and arguably transforms both through its very existence.

The facts that the EU is multidimensional, that integration is uneven, and that EU governance is composed of multiple, co-existing policy modes all force us to think carefully about how the nature of authority is changing. The trick—as employers of the 'multi-level governance' metaphor remind us—is to think about the EU as an integral part of this changing pattern of governance. To treat the EU as a political system 'above' national political systems ignores the complex interpenetration of the domestic and the supranational in contemporary Europe. The task of theories—whether drawn from the formal disciplinary domains of 'International Relations' or 'political science'—is to offer ways of organizing our thoughts about what is going on in this context. We might continue to be confused about the complexity of the EU, but the present vibrant theoretical culture in EU studies at least gives us a chance of being confused in a reasonably sophisticated way.

QUESTIONS

1 Is it fair to say that Comparative Politics provides a better disciplinary homeland for EU studies than International Relations?

2 Is there a single institutionalist research agenda in EU studies?

3 How helpful is the idea of 'multi-level governance' for organizing the way we think about the EU?

4 How might one study the EU from a policy networks perspective?

5 What added value do social constructivists bring to the study of the EU?

6   How might we go about theorizing the EU's role in the world?

7   To what extent is it possible to compare the EU with other instances of 'regionalism' in the global political economy?

8   Why is it important to theorize European integration and the European Union?

GUIDE TO FURTHER READING

Breslin, S., Hughes, C., Phillips, N., and Rosamond, B. (eds), *New Regionalisms in the Global Political Economy: Theories and Cases* (London: Routledge, 2002). State of the art collection on the new regionalism. The introduction plus the essays by Hettne and Söderbaum, Wallace, and Lee offer useful supplementary material to this chapter.

Christiansen, T., Jørgensen, K. E., and Wiener, A. (eds), *The Social Construction of Europe* (London: Sage, 2001). A collection of constructivist-inspired readings of aspects of European integration. Contains critical responses and a notable new essay by Ernst Haas, the founder of neo-functionalism.

Hix, S., *The Political System of the European Union* (Basingstoke: Macmillan, 1999). A landmark text on the EU that begins from the claim that the EU is best studied through the lens of comparative politics.

Hooghe, L., and Marks, G., *Multi-level Governance and European Integration* (Boulder, Colo.: Rowman and Littlefield, 2001). The first book-length discussion of the theory and practice of multi-level governance.

Rosamond, B., *Theories of European Integration* (Basingstoke: Palgrave, 2000). A critical discussion of past and present theories of integration.

Schneider, G., and Aspinwall, M. (eds), *The Rules of Integration: Institutionalist Approaches to the Study of Europe* (Manchester: Manchester University Press, 2001). A rigorous set of essays exploring the contributions made by the various forms of institutional analysis to the study of the EU.

WEB LINK

http://eiop.or.at/erpa/erpaframe.html European Research Papers Archive. A collection of online working papers relating to EU studies, where much innovative theoretical work is showcased for the first time.

Part Three

Institutions and actors

Part Three of *EU Politics* introduces the European institutions. In Chapter 9, Morten Egeberg shows us how important organizational factors are for understanding the European Commission. In Chapter 10, Jeffrey Lewis unpacks the many, often confusing component parts of the Council of the European Union. In Chapter 11, Roger Scully explains the organization and functioning of the European Parliament and how this has altered since the early years of the European Community; while in Chapter 12, Anthony Arnull accounts for the changing role of the European Courts within the European Union. As a contrast to Chapters 9–12, Chapter 13 by Rainer Eising focuses attention on a different set of actors, namely interest organizations, to consider how interests have become increasingly involved and affected by the European integration process, particularly since the mid-1980s.

9 The European Commission

Morten Egeberg

READER'S GUIDE

This chapter provides a general introduction to the organizational characteristics of the European Commission. It argues that it is more productive to compare the Commission to national executives or to a government than to a secretariat of a traditional international organization. It begins with a summary of the Commission's functions within the EU's policy process. It then considers the question of Commission influence and autonomy, before moving on to look at the structure and demography of the organization, that is, at the role of the President of the Commission and the Commissioners, at the Commissioners' personal staffs, at the Commission administration, and at the committee system that pervades the internal life of the Commission. The chapter concludes by emphasizing that the Commission is moving away from its intergovernmentalist roots towards becoming much more of a European(ized) institution than in has been since its inception.

Introduction

To many observers, the Commission is a unique institution. It is much more than an international secretariat, but not quite a government, though it has many governmental characteristics, as we shall see. Embracing both political and administrative responsibilities and a wide range of formal and informal functions within the EU's policy process, the Commission has, not surprisingly, been labelled a 'hybrid' body. This is not least because the Commission encompasses elements of both intergovernmentalism (a national dimension) and supranationalism (a European dimension). It is the opposing pull of these two elements that forms the focal point of this chapter. By exploring the national and supranational features of the Commission's organization, the chapter reopens the question: what sort of organization is the European Commission?

The chapter begins with a brief review of the Commission's main functions, which revolve around its role in the EU policy process. These involve the Commission in agenda setting, and more specifically in the drafting of legislation, in the implementation of policies (albeit at arm's length) and the management of programmes, and in the formulation and negotiation of certain aspects of the EU's external relations. Moreover the Commission also has a role to play in mediating between the Parliament and Council and amongst national government and other non-state actors involved in

European policy making, and—somewhat paradoxically—in presenting its own, or a European, perspective on issues and events. The second section focuses on the question of Commission influence and autonomy, viewing this matter through the lens of integration theorists. In the sections that follow, attention turns to organizational matters, with the focus first on the Commission President and College of Commissioners, second, on the Commissioners' cabinets (their personal staffs), third on the Commission Administration, and finally on the role of committees within the Commission. In perusing these sections, however, readers should be aware that at the time of writing (2002) the Commission is in the throes of an organizational reform, which may well alter some of Commission's structure and processes. However, the conclusions to the chapter are likely to hold true all the same—that the Commission is becoming a more European institution than it ever was in the past.

The functions of the Commission

The European Commission is composed of a political executive wing (the Commissioners and their staffs) and an administrative wing (the 'services'). It has a wide range of functions within the EU system—policy initiation, the monitoring of policy implementation, the management of European programmes, an important external relations role, and other functions which involve it as a mediator amongst the 15 member states and between the EU Council and the European Parliament (EP), as well as asserting its own European identity as, effectively, a sixteenth member state. The Commission is clearly involved in the EU's policy process from start to finish. But contrary to popular belief, the Commission is not an EU legislator. It does not make European law—that is the function of the EU's Council and the EP (usually acting together). But this is not to say that the Commission is unimportant, far from it. This is primarily because, in much the same way as are national **executives**, the Commission is responsible for the initiation and formulation of policies, usually in the form of legislative,

budgetary, or programme proposals. To put it bluntly, the Commission drafts the legislation. It is in this sense that in the majority of policy areas—that is, in those policies falling under the first or EC pillar of the EU, such as the **single market** (see Chapter 4)—the Commission performs an exclusive **agenda-setting** role. Other actors, such as the European Council (the heads of state/government), the EP, national officials, and interest groups, may also take initiatives and advance policy proposals. But it is generally up to the Commission to decide whether these ideas will be picked up and subsequently passed on to the legislature in the form of a formal legislative proposal, even if in practice, these sorts of policy initiative quite often originate from outside the Commission. By contrast, under the two intergovernmental pillars—the Common Foreign and Security Policy (CFSP) or second pillar or the third pillar covering Police and Judicial Co-operation (formerly Justice and Home Affairs)—the Commission does not have an exclusive agenda-setting role, although it may still be active in developing policy programmes. And even here there are challenges to the Commission role, even though this can be relatively marginal. Under the EU's foreign and security policy, for example, the Secretary-General of the Council has also been appointed as the High Representative for the Union's CFSP. The strengthening of the Council's General Secretariat in this respect presents a direct challenge to the Commission's executive role, and illustrates the considerable tension between **intergovernmentalism** and **supranationalism** in this particular policy arena.

Also very much in line with the functions performed by national executives, the Commission has an important role to play in the implementation of European policies (see Chapter 22). What this means in an EU context is that the Commission is responsible for the *monitoring* of implementation within the EU's member states. In much the same way as occurs, say, in Germany, the execution or putting in to effect of policy remains largely the responsibility of the state (that is, the regional or *Land*) governments. However, before implementation can occur at the national or subnational level it may be necessary for secondary (or administrative) legislation to be agreed. This is because laws made by the Council, usually together with the EP, tend to take the form of broad policy guidelines or frameworks, rather than detailed steering instruments. Thus it is up to the Commission, in close co-operation with the member states, to detail and fill in EP/Council legislation by agreeing more specific rules, often in the form of *Commission* directives or regulations, in what is called **delegated legislation**. Only in very few policy areas, such as competition policy, is the Commission responsible for implementation in the sense of handling individual cases (see also Chapter 22). However, the Commission is also responsible for ensuring that member states and other actors implement European policy, where they have a legal obligation to do so. This function has led some to talk of the Commission as the 'guardian of the treaties'.

Much of the Commission's time is spent on its much less glamorous function of policy management or administration. While this has never really been a priority for the Commission, it has had to turn its attention in recent years to improving the way it handles existing policies and programmes, as this is where the Commission has been subject to a great deal of criticism (including accusations that the way it operates encourages fraud within the system). Since the mid–1990s, then, the Commission leadership has sought to restrict the number of proposals being initiated, and to focus much more attention on, as former president, Jacques Santer, put it, 'doing less, but better'. This is clearly also one of the primary objective of the 2000–5 Commission's reform agenda. See Box 9.1.

Finally, the Commission's external representation role has become increasingly important, particularly since the early 1990s. Just like national governments, the Commission staffs and runs delegations (in effect, EU embassies) around the world. There are no fewer than 130 offices in non-member countries. Also under the rubric of external representation the Commission acts as the main negotiator for the Union in trade and co-operation negotiations and within international bodies such as the World Trade Organization (WTO) (see Chapter 15).

The Commission also performs other less tangible and more diffuse functions within the EU. Important amongst these is its role as a mediator amongst the EU's 15 member states, and between the EP and the Council. Thus, the Commission does its best, once it has produced a proposal, to ensure that agreement is reached within the Union's legislative bodies. After having agreed a policy proposal internally (see below for more on the internal functioning of the Commission), the officials who drafted the proposal may attend meetings of the relevant EP committee and plenary sessions (see Chapter 11), the relevant Council working party, the Council Committee of Permanent Representatives (COREPER), and the relevant Council ministerial meeting (see Chapter 10) in order to defend their line, and, if necessary, to mediate between conflicting parties. The Commission also presents policy documents to heads of state/government at European Council (summit) meetings and at **Intergovernmental Conferences** (IGCs). Somewhat paradoxically, the Commission not only is helping in the process of achieving a final agreement, but also has its own institutional position to advance, one which may involve the presentation of a more European picture of events than emerges from national quarters (or even the EP).

Box 9.1 Case study
Reforming the European Commission

Although Romano Prodi did not become president of the Commission until September 1999, the reform process began as soon as he was nominated in June of that year. Even though there was a good deal of continuity, as Prodi—and then Neil Kinnock—picked up where Jacques Santer had left off, the pressure was on the Commission to act, and to be seen to be acting, to resolve the shortcomings identified in the reports of the Committee of Independent Experts of 1999 and elsewhere. The reforms, as they were initiated, were very much presented as a clean sweep, a new phase in the Comision's history. The old discredited regime had gone, and a new, more open, and responsive phase in the Commission's history was about to begin. While preparations were made to draft a Consultative, and then a White Paper on Reform to be lauched early in 2000, the Reform Task Force began churning out documents which appeared for all to see on the Commission's website.

It is the White Paper that most clearly spells out the approach the Commission is taking as it operationalizes its reform ambitions. The Paper was released in March 2000, and now forms the framework within which more detailed proposals are being decided and negotiated. It begins by establishing the premises on which the reform agenda has been set. Thus:

A strong, independent and effective Commission is essential to the functioning of the European Union as a whole and its standing in the world. Fulfilling the tasks established by the Treaties requires substantial improvement in structures and in systems. Working practices, conventions and obligations that have accumulated over decades now inhibit the Commission's effectiveness. Administrative reform will help the Commission to fulfil its institutional role as motor of European integration. It is thus a political project of central importance for the European Union (European Commission 2000*b*: 5).

It also sets out the key themes that will structure the reform process. It states that 'The Commission . . . needs to be independent, accountable, efficient and transparent, and guided by the highest standards of responsibility' (European Commission 2000*b*: 5). It is only by working towards the application of these principles that 'a culture based on service' (p. 7) can be introduced to the Commission. It is by focusing on these themes and principles that a window is opened to the thinking of the Commission as regards the cultural change it would like to see taking hold.

Independence is the first theme. The White Paper takes this to refer to the independence of the Commission from national, sectoral, and other influences. 'For the Commissioners and individual officers, it means that they shall neither seek nor take instructions from any government or from any other body', and neither should those bodies seek to influence the Commission (p. 7). The second theme is Responsibility. Here a distinction is made between political responsibility, which 'lies with each Commissioner and, collectively, with the College', and an administrative responsibility, which the White Paper calls 'day-to-day management responsibilities' and which rests with the Directors-General. It emphasizes the importance of having a clear definition of tasks for both departments and individuals (p. 7). The third theme is Accountability, which the White Paper admits 'goes hand in hand with the exercise of responsibility'. This is not only about the reporting of the Commission to the Parliament and Council, but also about 'exercising good stewardship of the variety of resources available to the Commission [which] means ensuring that they are used efficiently and effectively' (p. 8). Efficiency is the fourth theme. In this context, efficiency refers to 'the challenge of ensuring maximum results with limited resources', what economists would identify as productive efficiency. Emphasized here is the need to improve and simplify procedures. Decentralization also gets a special mention as it 'too can increase efficiency and, linked to a clear allocation of responsibility, will empower officials to exercise their own initiative (p. 8). The final theme is that of Transparency within the Commission, deemed a 'prerequisite for the greater openness towards the outside world required in the Treaty'. 'This means transparency internally in terms of communicating effectively at all levels, showing receptiveness to new ideas and taking a positive attitude to criticism; and externally as an organization fully open to public scrutiny.'

At the centre of the reform programme is the focus on the prioritization of 'core functions'. These are taken to include 'policy conception, political initiative and enforcing Community law'. With more than half of Commission officials engaged in managing programmes and projects, something deemed an inefficient use of limited resources, there is a need to concentrate more on 'core policy objectives'. Non-priority areas need to be identified and resources reallocated where necessary. A judgement needs to be made as to whether the Commission's resources are 'commensurate with its tasks'. If they are not, the Commission will need to discontinue tasks. This

Box 9.1—*continued*

forms the first strand of the Commission reform. It takes the shape of the introduction of new 'policy-driven decision-taking mechanisms' involving the evaluation of results (p. 6).

The second and third strands are concerned with the creation of 'optimal structures and systems for the deployment of its resources'; in other words, the management of human and financial resources. Changes in human resources policy are intended to 'place a pre-mium on performance, continuous training and quality of management, as well as improving recruitment and career development', amongst other things (p. 6). As for financial management, an overhaul of the existing system is planned in order to introduce an effective internal control system which defines clearly 'the responsibilities of each actor' and which involves 'regular checks by the new Internal Audit Service on the quality and reliability of each internal control system' (p. 7).

Key points

- The European Commission has a variety of functions to perform in the EU system, including policy initiation, implementation, management, external relations.

- The Commission is involved in almost all aspects of the European policy process.

- The Commission plays a much reduced role in Pillars 2 and 3 of the EU (those dealing with foreign policy, and police/judicial co-operation).

Commission influence

It is all very well to state that the Commission is involved at almost all stages of the EU policy process (at least in Pillar 1/EC affairs), but to what extent does the Commission have any real influence? In studies of the European Commission, there is a great deal of dispute over whether Commission initiatives make a significant difference or not to EU outcomes.

On the one hand, intergovernmentalists believe national governments are the real driving forces in the European project. In the *liberal* intergovernmentalist version of this theoretical stance (see Chapter 7), it is accepted that the Commission has an important role to play in first pillar policies (such as the internal market and agricultural policy). However, they claim that the authority it exercises as an agenda setter and overseer of implementation at the national level is merely a derived and delegated authority (Moravcsik 1998). According to this view, the Commission may facilitate intergovernmental co-operation, but it has no real power basis of its own, as the Commission's powers are decided upon and framed by the member states within treaty negotiations.

Intergovernmentalist thinking on the role of the Commission is countered by those whose approach might be labelled as 'supranationalist' or 'institutionalist'. Most of these institutionalists would argue that there is ample evidence that the Commission has displayed strong leadership and has even had a profound effect on the outcomes of 'history-shaping' and frame-setting IGCs and European Council meetings on a number of occasions. For example, Armstrong and Bulmer (1998) assign a highly significant role to the Commission (and indeed to other EU institutions) in the process that led to the creation of the **single market**. The single market programme is one of the important frameworks within which the Commission operates under the first (EC) pillar (see Chapter 3 and 4). Institutionalists argue that treaty-based frameworks, which are the main focus of intergovernmentalists, are quite often vague and ambiguous constructions that need to be translated into practical politics through day-to-day policy making. And when it comes to this sort of crucial follow-up work the Commission is one of the key actors.

Another, but related, scholarly dispute questions the extent to which the Commission is able to affect decisions even within its own organizational boundaries. Not surprisingly perhaps, to intergovernmentalists the Commission appears very much as an arena permeated by national interests. From this perspective, Commissioners, their personal staffs (cabinets), as well as officials in the Commission's departments (services), are primarily pursuing the interests of their respective national governments. By contrast institutionalists tend to emphasize that the Commission, like other institutions, furnishes individual actors with particular interests and beliefs, and that it may even be able to resocialize people so that they gradually come to assume supranational identities. From an organizational perspective, both approaches may be partly correct in their assumptions (Egeberg 1996).

Key points

- Intergovernmentalists see the Commission as relatively insignificant.
- By contrast, institutionalists (supranationalists) view the Commission as having an independent impact on policy outcomes.

The President and the College of Commissioners

The European Commission has both a political and an administrative dimension. While there is no doubt that the actions of the administrative branch also have political significance, there is still a useful distinction to be made between the Commission's political leaders—the 'College of Commissioners'—and the officials who sit in the Commission's services (or departments). Because the Commission has both a political and an administrative wing, it has often been portrayed as a hybrid and unique kind of institution. This may be understandable if we compare the Commission to a secretariat of a traditional international organization, since secretariats tend to comprise only an administrative component. However, if we conceive of the Commission as a kind of government, its basic structure suddenly looks much more familiar. From this perspective Commissioners are roughly equivalent to government ministers and the administrative departments have a structure, which is similar to that of a national bureaucracy or civil service.

The 'College' consists of 20 Commissioners, including the President of the Commission. Within the Commission's internal decision-making process contentious issues that have not been resolved at the lower echelons of the Commission are lifted to this highest political level in the last instance. The College strives to achieve consensus through arguing and bargaining. If this does not result in a consensus, voting may take place, although this seems to be relatively rare. When it does happen, all Commissioners, including the President, carry the same weight—one vote each and an absolute majority is necessary for a final decision to be reached. Since the College operates on the basis of the principle of **collegiality**, in other words since all Commissioners are collectively responsible for all decisions taken, it would be reasonable to assume that a relatively large proportion of all decisions are referred to the College. Although a minister in a national government is usually granted greater room for manoeuvre than a Commissioner, the principle of collegiality may also be found at the national level, as it is in the Swedish Council of Ministers.

The President of the Commission, who chairs the meetings of the College, used to be thought of as *primus inter pares* (first among equals) as he (there has so far been no female President) had no more powers than any other member of the College. Since the early 1990s, however, the role of the President has become more important, so that it is now accepted that the work of the College is subject to the President's political leadership (see below). And like a national prime minister, the President also has at his disposal a permanent secretariat, the Secretariat-General (or General Secretariat as it is sometimes called).

Commissioners have policy responsibilities (portfolios) which involve oversight of one or more Commission department. These departments are known as Directorates-General or simply as DGs. As DGs tend to be organized sectorally (according to purpose) or functionally (according to process), one might expect this to provide a source of conflict among Commissioners. This expectation is explained in Box 9.2. This tendency may have been exacerbated by the decision taken in 1999 by the Commission President, Romano Prodi, to house individual Commissioners in the same building as their departments rather than in a separate

building just for Commissioners and their staff. Physical proximity might be expected to foster some common perceptions among the political leaders and their officials, but it might also reinforce sectoral and functional cleavages within the Commission.

Although Commissioners are not supposed to take instruction from outside the Commission, and do not represent their national governments in any formal sense, they are, nevertheless, nominated by them. As of 2002, each of the five larger countries—Germany, France, the UK, Italy, and Spain—has two Commissioners, while the other member states have to make do with one each. The future enlargement of the Union could increase the size of the College significantly, thereby threatening its decision-making capacity. A possible solution is to let all member states, both large and small, nominate only one Commissioner each.

Before appointing Commissioners, however, the national governments must first agree on a candidate for the Commission Presidency. This is necessary if the new President is to be given an opportunity to influence the composition of the College. Over time the President's role in selecting his/her colleagues has grown. In the revisions to the Treaty, agreed at Amsterdam in 1997, the President is able, for the first time, to reject candidates nominated

---

Box 9.2 **Case study**

Politics in the Commission

How politics within the Commission may reflect the sectoral and functional specialization of its organizational structure and related interest groups

The weekly newspaper, *European Voice* (31 May–6 June 2001) reported that the Transport Commissioner Loyola de Palacio was set for a clash with the Environment Commissioner Margot Wallström over the future direction of EU transport policy. 'Officials from Wallström's services have only just begun studying de Palacio's White Paper on transport after it was released for consultation between Union executive departments. But already they say there are "things missing" from the 120–page document that are likely to prompt criticism from Wallström.' The news-

paper reported that Wallström was likely to intervene with some concerns raised by environmental interest groups over the policy proposal, which seeks to freeze road traffic at its current 44 per cent share of all transport, but makes no attempt to reduce its overall growth. 'Green groups say the White Paper fails to live up to the Amsterdam Treaty obligation to bring environmental objectives into all policy areas. . . . Environmentalists insist the proposal will make it harder for the EU to comply with its Kyoto obligations to reduce greenhouse gas emissions.'

by member governments. The President will also have the final say in how portfolios are allocated and will even have the right to reshuffle the team during the Commission's five-year term of office by redistributing dossiers (files).

National governments have increasingly seen their role in the make-up of the College of Commissioners diminish. By contrast, the European Parliament (EP) has gradually gained more of a stake in the process in a number of different ways. First, the term of office of the Commissioners has been extended from four to five years, so as to bring it into close alignment with the term of the EP. This means that the appointment of a new College takes place after the EP elections to allow MEPs to have a say on the matter. Not only is the EP consulted on the choice of President, but it also has the right to approve their appointment. Moreover, steps have also been taken to render the Commission more directly accountable to the Parliament, as illustrated by the fact that the EP committees now scrutinize nominated Commissioners, and are even able to dismiss the entire College by taking a vote of no confidence. Further initiatives in a similar vein have been launched by the EP, which, if realized, would bring the EU closer than it is at present to a parliamentary system.

What kind of College demography does this inspire? First, it means that the political leadership of the Commission always has a fixed mix of nationals. Second, it tends to bring people into the College who have the same political party background as the national government nominating them. The norm seems to be that one of the two Commissioners selected by the larger countries will come from the biggest opposition party, or main coalition partner, though this does not always hold true. Over time, nominations to Commission posts have included people with impressive political experience, and it is not unusual to see prominent national ministers in the list of nominees. Such a recruitment pattern obviously furnishes the College with political capital, though probably not in a strict party political sense. A coherent party platform for the College is almost unthinkable under the current appointment procedure. Instead, Commissioners' nationality is likely to be a more crucial background factor to take into account in explaining their conduct. This is so since national governments, lobbyists, and the like tend to contact 'their' Commissioner(s) as a first port of call, when they want to obtain information or have a say at the very highest level of the Commission structure. And Commissioners may also become involved in social networks with their compatriots—for example, in gatherings at their respective Permanent Representations (their national embassies) in Brussels.

It should not be concluded from this, however, that Commissioners act primarily as agents of the national government that nominated them. In fact, it is the Commissioner's portfolio which is more likely to explain their behaviour with regard to a particular decision. However, like national ministers, Commissioners see multiple and often conflicting role expectations imposed upon them: at one and the same time they are supposed to feel some allegiance, albeit informal, to the geographical area from which they originate, to champion Commission interests, and to advance their own portfolio. Balancing these diverse pressures is not always an easy task.

It would seem, then, that the organizational characteristics that may lead Commissioners to act in line with national interests are the nomination and appointment procedures, and the fact that the temporary nature of their posts might create incentives for behaving in a manner that could help them to be nominated for a second term. Yet, there are also organizational features that are more in line with the institutionalist perspective (as outlined above). The new prerogatives of the Commission President over the composition of the College and the distribution of portfolios, which previously could have 'national flags' attached to them, are, together with the enhanced accountability to the EP, obvious examples. The sectoral and functional specialization of the services that tend to force Commissioners to be defenders of particular portfolio interests rather than national interests are also illustrating, however (see Box 9.2). And last but not least, the effect of formal rules banning Commissioners from taking instruction from national governments should not be underestimated. Over time, these formal norms also seem to have become increasingly underpinned by cultural norms that deem the blatant promotion of national interests as inappropriate conduct for a Commissioner.

Key points

- The European Commission is composed of a political leadership in the form of the College of Commissioners.
- Commissioners are appointed by national governments, but they are expected to act independently.
- The Commission President has gained more powers since the 1980s, so that the current President is no longer simply 'first among equals'.

Commissioners' cabinets

Like many national ministers in Europe, Commissioners have their own political secretariat or private office. The Commissioner's 'cabinet' (note that the French pronunciation is often used), as it is called, is organizationally separate from the administrative services of the Commission. It is composed of people trusted by the Commissioner in question, and who may be hired and fired at their discretion. Consequently, their tenure can last only as long as their Commissioner's. The creation of cabinets gives more weight to the College, making it more likely that the Administration will adhere to political guidelines. These personal offices of the Commissioners are modelled on and named after the French *cabinets*. Each one consists of five to seven advisers, plus a number of clerical staff. Their role is to help push Commissioners' ideas down to the services, on the one hand, and on the other, to edit and filter policy proposals coming up from the DGs before they are referred to the Commissioner and the College. As an integral part of this 'editorial work' a Commissioner's cabinet frequently interacts with other cabinets in order to register disagreements and pre-empt objections that might be raised at the level of the College. Due to the principle of collegiality, in essence a form of mutual responsibility, each of the 20 cabinets covers all Commission portfolios. Thus, a Commissioner's cabinet is vital as a source of information about issues beyond their own remit. Ahead of the weekly meeting of the College, the *chefs de cabinet* (cabinet heads) convene to ensure that the Commission acts as coherently and cohesively as possible. At these inter-cabinet gatherings the head of the President's cabinet, as chair, naturally assumes the role as mediator and broker, as necessary.

In addition to the role played by cabinets in co-ordinating, both vertically and horizontally, the flow of information within the Commission, they also have important functions at the interface between the Commission and the outside world. Cabinets are crucial points of access for governments, lobbyists, and other actors and institutions keen to influence the Commission. Their role is to assist Commissioners in this respect, with cabinet members responsible, amongst other things, for writing Commissioners' speeches, standing in for them, and representing them at conferences and meetings. Cabinets have also acted as a kind of liaison office between the Commissioners and 'their' respective governments, particularly via 'their' Permanent Representations. Thus, they are able to inform the national governments about forthcoming Commission proposals that might become politically interesting from a national point of view, whilst at the same time acting as a conduit for information about national positions on policy initiatives under consideration in the Commission.

Cabinets have often been portrayed as national enclaves. This description was appropriate given that (in the past) the nationality of cabinet personnel directly reflected the nationality of the lead Commissioner. More specifically, the norm in the past was that only one member of a cabinet should be of a nationality different from that of the Commissioner. For example, in the Brittan cabinet of 1989–92, when Sir Leon Brittan dealt with competition matters, his cabinet included an Irish national, Catherine Day. The Prodi Commission changed this pattern. Since it came into office in 1999, cabinets have been staffed multinationally, with a cap placed on the number of advisers permitted. More specifically, at least three different nationalities should now be represented in each cabinet, and the head or the deputy head of the cabinet should be of a different nationality from that of the Commissioner. Moreover, at least half of cabinet members should now be recruited from within the Commission services. This may also have interesting implications for the role of nationality in the cabinets since those coming from the Commission administration may have weaker ties to any particular national constituency. One reason why this recruitment provision was introduced was that cabinets had traditionally been stepping stones for rapid advancement to senior posts in the Commission's services. This had been criticized by staff unions for causing some demoralization down the ranks. So, relying more on internal recruits to staff the cabinets could reduce the extent to which outsiders are brought over the heads of existing civil servants into senior posts, in a process known generally as **parachutage**. Those who have come to the cabinets from outside the Commission have for the most part served in national administrations, but some have also come from other kinds of organizations, for example from the political party to which the Commissioner belongs.

Before the Prodi Commission's reforms of the cabinet system one would probably have concluded that the structure as well as the demography of these internal bodies would tend to foster highly intergovernmental patterns of behaviour by the Commission. However, the structure and demography of the cabinets have changed. Thus, multinational staffing and an increased emphasis on internal recruitment seems to fit better with institutionalist explanations. As a consequence of these reforms, it would seem very likely that the role of cabinets as the interface between national governments and the Commission will be profoundly redefined.

Key points

- Each Commissioner is supported by a personal staff, known as a 'cabinet'.

- The cabinet, traditionally a 'national enclave' within the Commission, has become more multinational in recent years.

The Commission services

As is the case in national executives, the political leadership of the Commission is served by an administrative staff. In the Commission this administration is often referred to as the Commission 'services' (see Box 9.3). Its main components of the Commission's administration are the 23 Directorates-General (DGs) that are roughly equivalent to the administrative components of national government departments, and which now cover almost all possible policy fields. The basic principles of organizational specialization are also quite similar to those of national ministries. While DG Agriculture and DG Justice and Home Affairs reflect a sectoral organization, DG Budget and DG Personnel and Administration are organized around the functions they perform. Precisely because they are functionally orientated, DG Budget and DG Personnel and Administration are also said to be the Commission's horizontal services, that is, the administrative units that are assigned co-ordination tasks or that deal with issues cutting across sectoral departments. The Secretariat-General is the most important of these horizontal services. As the permanent office of the Commission President it plays an important role in shaping a coherent policy profile for the Commission as a whole, and also has a crucial part to play in managing relationships between the Commission and other key institutions inside and outside the Union. The role of Secretary-General, the head of the secretariat, very much parallels that of a permanent secretary within national prime ministers' offices. In other words, he or she may be identified as the first

Box 9.3 The facts
Commission services

General services
- European Anti-Fraud Office
- Eurostat
- Press and Communication
- Publications Office
- Secretariat-General

Policies
- Agriculture
- Competition
- Economic and Financial Affairs
- Education and Culture
- Employment and Social Affairs
- Energy and Transport
- Enterprise
- Environment
- Fisheries
- Health and Consumer Protection
- Information Society
- Internal Market
- Joint Research Centre

- Justice and Home Affairs
- Regional Policy
- Research
- Taxation and Customs Union

External relations
- Development
- Enlargement
- EuropeAid—Co-operation Office
- External Relations
- Humanitarian Aid Office (ECHO)
- Trade

Internal services
- Budget
- Financial Control
- Group of Policy Advisers
- Internal Audit Service
- Joint Interpretation and Conference Service
- Legal Service
- Personnel and Administration
- Translation Service

among equals, of the administration. Examples of other horizontal services are the Press and Communication Service, the Statistical Office (Eurostat), the Translation Service, and the Legal Service. The Legal Service provides much of the Commission's legal expertise, though lawyers are also found in large numbers in other parts of the Commission. Thus, the Legal Service primarily serves as an expert body which other departments consult. It makes sure that legislative proposals drafted within the DGs comply with the technical and linguistic standards that are deemed appropriate for EU legislation, thereby pre-empting future challenges to European legislation in the European or domestic Courts (see Chapter 12).

Headed by a Director-General, DGs usually consists of several Directorates, with each of these headed by a Director. Each Directorate is further split into Units. Obviously, some tasks and new policy initiatives do not fit well into this strictly specialized hierarchical structure. To meet such needs, special task forces or interdepartmental

working groups are created. Sometimes these temporary or *ad hoc* bodies become institutionalized and end up as new DGs or departments. This was the case with Merger Task Force, which eventually became Directorate B of DG Competition. The DGs usually have a total permanent and full-time staff of about 300–600 each, but their size varies considerably. The largest DG, DG Personnel and Administration, has around 3,000 employees, while another big player, DG Agriculture, has 1,000. DG Financial Control, by contrast, has only 200 staff. Together the DGs and the horizontal services employ approximately 22,000 people. Of these about 1,000 are temporary posts. All posts are grouped into five grades, and these are further divided into several points. The most prestigious grade, the so-called A-grade, consists of around 7,000 officials engaged in policy making and policy management. When we think of Commission 'officials' we are usually only referring to staff in this category (rather than those in the executive, clerical and manual grades). Within the A-grade we find eight points, ranging from

A1—Director General—at the top to A8—assistant administrator—at the bottom. The so-called LA-grade comprises translators and interpreters, B- and C-grade officials undertake more routine and technical administrative tasks, and, finally, D-grade employees take care of service and manual jobs.

In addition to staff paid by the Commission, the services also include between 700 and 800 Category A officials seconded from the member governments. These seconded officials, or 'detached national experts', have their salaries paid by their national employer. In the early days of the High Authority of the European Coal and Steel Community, the forerunner of the Commission (see Chapter 2), most officials were appointed on temporary contracts or seconded from the member states. Over time this has changed. As we have seen, an overwhelming majority of the posts are now permanent, while temporary jobs are used for hiring personnel who might provide additional expertise on particular policy issues that are under consideration in the services.

Recruitment of new A-grade candidates for a career in the Commission services is based largely on the meritocratic principle. What this means is that appointments should be made on what a person has achieved in his or her educational and professional career so far, rather than on any other criteria, such as a candidate's social or geographical background, their gender, or the extent to which an applicant has 'good contacts'. This principle is inherently linked to an understanding of what a modern and well-functioning bureaucracy should look like if it is to avoid nepotism, favouritism, and corruption. Thus, in accordance with this principle, those who want to embark on a Commission career are normally required to hold a university degree. Subsequently, they have to pass a competitive exam called the *concours*. The *concours* is modelled on the French standard entry route into the higher civil service which means in practice that all applicants have to pass written as well as oral tests. These tests are arranged in the member states on a regular basis and may involve as many as 50,000 applicants. However, no more than 150–250 reach what is called the 'reserve list', and even these lucky few are still not guaranteed a job; rather they have to wait for a vacancy and hope that they will be contacted about

it. At this stage visibility is likely to be crucial, so that those with good networking skills are likely to be at an advantage.

A quota system regulates the intake of new recruits on a geographical basis. As a result, those hired should be drawn proportionately from all member states, so that larger countries provide more candidates than smaller ones. On first sight this sort of quota arrangement seems to be completely at odds with the meritocratic principle outlined above. But it does ensure that the Commission—or rather, the A-grade—is not over-populated by a cohort of staff from only a few of the EU's member states. See Box 9.4.

Once in post, seniority matters for promotion at the lower levels of the A-grade. In addition to an official's immediate superior, the staff unions also play a significant role in decisions about promotion at this level. For appointments as Head of Unit and above (A4 to A1), achievements in earlier positions matter more than seniority as a criterion for promotion. The role of staff unions is also considerably reduced at these senior levels. Instead, nationality reappears as a crucial factor, and increasingly so the more senior the level of the appointment. Obviously, the narrower the pyramid, the more complicated it becomes to manage the national quota system in a fair manner, while at the same time paying heed to merit as the basic norm for promotion. In these cases, national governments are often keen to look after 'their share' of jobs, and it has conventionally been up to Commissioners and their cabinets to intervene if the 'balance' is deemed to be threatened. In addition to concerns about proportionality, a top official's immediate subordinate and superior should be of a different nationality. The argument goes that a multinational chain of command will prevent policy proposals from reflecting only narrow national concerns.

As noted above, the term *parachutage* refers to the practice whereby people from outside the Commission are slotted into the higher echelons of the apparatus, without being subject to the normal appointments process. However, rather than interpreting this phenomenon as a way of safeguarding national interests, it has been observed that it is most commonly used to cope with the strains of enlargements and also with the quota system (Page 1997).

Box 9.4 **Case study**
Personnel policies

How personnel policies in the Commission are increasingly 'normalized' or 'domesticated'

The weekly *European Voice* (21–27 February 2002) published a small notice that neatly illustrates how personnel management in the Commission has become more multifaceted than we expect to find it in international organizations. While balancing meritocracy and a proper national balance has been the dominant concern, gender equality has also become an issue in the Commission. In the notice, the European Ombudsman, Jacob Söderman, calls for urgent action over *ethnic* imbalance. He says the European Commission does not take possible racism in recruitment seriously enough. 'When I look around the various institutions—the Commission, Parliament and Council—the only staff I see from ethnic groups are security guards and cleaners. Given that an estimated 30 million people of ethnic minority origin live in the EU, I wonder why so few appear to be in more senior posts.'

New member states have a right to a share of posts at all levels of the hierarchy, and this has meant that highly experienced national officials have had to be brought into the senior ranks of the Commission. While this sort of system is frustrating for well-qualified internal candidates looking for promotion, it is difficult to see how these problems might be overcome under the current conditions. If we put enlargement aside, though, both the Santer and the Prodi Commissions have claimed that more weight should be assigned to merit and internal recruitment and less to nationality and parachuting. This is something being addressed in the Prodi/Kinnock reform exercise within the Commission, and the policy has obtained increasing support in rulings of the European Court of Justice (ECJ) and from the Commission's staff unions. It would seem that while the services should continue to maintain a broad geographical balance, nationality will no longer be allowed to be the determining factor in appointing a new person to a particular post. The aim is clearly to abolish the convention of attaching national flags to senior positions.

In accounting for the behaviour of Commission officials, how important is their national background? Given the enduring interest that national governments have shown towards recruitment and appointments we are led to think that nationality matters very much indeed (see Box 9.4). However, the attention devoted to the issue does not necessarily correspond to the impact that national origins might have. There is no doubt that officials bring to the Commission administrative styles and general attitudes that can be linked to their country of origin. For example, officials stemming from federal states like Germany or Belgium seem to view the prospect of a federal Europe more favourably than do those from unitary states, probably because the former are already familiar with that kind of a system. However, the extent to which experience of national administration affects the Commission must depend on the career patterns of the officials involved. In the early years of the Commission, when many officials were on temporary contracts or secondments from their national governments, more Commission officials were imbued with national styles and attitudes. Under the current staffing regime, though, relatively few officials have in fact had the opportunity to acquire much administrative experiences back home. Thus, they are arriving at the Commission without much 'baggage' in this respect. An exception to this rule, however, is likely to be when national officials are 'parachuted' into senior posts (see also Hooghe 2002).

Although an increasing number of Commission officials are without administrative experience in their home country, they may still make interesting interlocutors for their compatriots. A common language and nationality facilitate interaction so that Commission officials become points of access for those keen to know what is going on in the Commission. Moreover, officials of the same nationality often socialize together in Brussels and this may be enough to sustain a sense of national belonging. However, there is no evidence of a direct link between an official's administrative style, personal attitudes or informal contact patterns, and his or her behaviour in the Commission, as organizational roles, decision-making procedures, and the eyes and ears of colleagues and bosses tend to diminish this sort of variation in conduct. In fact, the attachment of officials to their DGs seems far more important than their national background as an explanation for the preferences and for the choices they make in their daily work.

Certain organizational characteristics suggest that the conduct of Commission officials is intergovernmentally driven in the sense that it reflects national interests and influence. These include the national quota and the temporary contracts systems. Quotas might serve to legitimate national identities and, consequently, national policy orientations, while those on temporary contracts may have an incentive to pursue the interests of their current employer back home—usually their national government. However, there are also a number of organizational features that suggest that the institutionalist perspective is more accurate. Examples include the fact that specialization in the Commission occurs according to sector or function rather than geography; that there is a clear majority of permanent posts; that

recruitment is on merit; that the Commission comprises multinational units and chains of command; and that there are life-long career patterns, which facilitate the resocialization of personnel. Over time these institutional factors have gained in importance: the proportion of officials on temporary contracts or secondments has been constantly declining; and recruitment on merit and internal promotion to senior levels in the Commission has gained ever increasing support, particularly from the European Courts, the staff unions, and, indeed, the College of Commissioners. However, the current practice of allowing new member states to have a share of the senior jobs in the Commission immediately after accession probably represents the most serious challenge to further development in this direction.

Key points

- The Commission's administrative services comprise sectoral and functional (horizontal) departments, called Directorates-General (DGs).

- Officials within the services are recruited on a merit basis with a view to an appropriate geographical balance among member countries.

The committee system

In order to assist the Commission in its preparatory work on new legislation and in other forms of policy making, between 300 and 400 temporary expert committees and about 150 standing advisory groups have been established. The practical work on a policy initiative often starts in such a committee, which usually is composed of national officials and other experts. Committees of this sort are supposed to provide additional expertise on a particular subject and thus complement the work of the Commission's permanent staff. They may also serve as an arena for floating policy ideas and anticipating future reactions to them. Involving interest organizations that might ultimately be affected by a new proposal

might make political support and legitimacy more likely. The Commission particularly welcomes European interest groups (see Chapter 13). Where these sorts of interest organizations have been lacking, the Commission has actively tried to encourage their formation. This is understandable since it is far more convenient to communicate with one group than with 15 or more, all representing different national, sectional interests. Encouraging the establishment of transnational interest groups may serve other purposes as well, though. Like the Commission itself, interest group systems structure themselves primarily along functional and sectoral lines, rather than territorially. Thus, the Commission may see transnational interest groups as future partners in an evolving EU polity.

Commission officials chair expert committees and advisory groups, calling officials from member governments to participate. The Commission covers their travel expenses, and they are expected to behave like independent experts and not as government representatives. However, Commission officials will normally use the opportunity of their presence to collect information about national policy positions. In practice, most national officials do not completely put their role as government representatives to one side when they come to Brussels (Egeberg 1999).

When committee work comes to an end, the policy proposal is processed in the administrative and political ranks of the Commission before it is submitted to the Council and the EP. When a final decision has been reached in the Council, the issue is again handed over to the Commission for implementation (see Chapter 22). As mentioned earlier, some Council directives may need to be supplemented by rules of a more technical nature. This kind of legislative work is delegated to the Commission in the same way as national legislatures may let governments hammer out specific regulations. In order to monitor the Commission's legislative activity, however, the Council has set up so-called **comitology** committees (also sometimes known as 'implementation committees'). The membership of these committees are national government representatives, though it is the Commission which calls and chairs the meetings, sets the agenda, submits the proposals requiring discussion, and writes the protocols. Some comitology committees are only entitled to advise the Commission (advisory committees). Others have competence to overrule the Commission's proposals under certain conditions (management committees and regulatory committees). In practice, however, the Commission usually get its own way, though this is not to say that national representatives have no influence. It is, of course, also quite possible that the Commission deliberately chooses proposals that national governments are likely to endorse (see Schaefer et al. 2000).

It might seem self-evident that national officials act more in the national than in the European interest. This is not least because committees represent rather secondary attachments for officials, thus imposing far fewer demands and incentives on officials than their jobs back home; and because officials, in the comitology setting, are formally expected to behave as government representatives. However, most national officials attending expert and comitology committee meetings have highly specialized jobs back home, and are therefore more used to framing issues in sectoral and functional terms rather than in terms of national interest. Arguably, the specialized EU committee system only serves to sustain the sectoral identities that national officials already have.

Key points

- Committees have an important role to play in the work of the Commission.
- Comitology committees monitor the Commission when it is issuing delegated legislation.

Conclusion

The Commission has often been portrayed as a hybrid and unique organization because of its mix of political and administrative functions. This is understandable if the Commission is compared to the secretariat of a traditional international organization, since such secretariats are not expected to have a political will of their own. However, the Commission is probably better compared to a national executive. Like governments, the Commission is headed by executive politicians who are responsible for various administrative services. In a fashion similar to national executives the

Commission is authorized to initiate and formulate policy proposals, and to monitor the implementation of policies. The Commission has not, however, achieved full control of all executive tasks at the EU level, sharing its executive function with the EU Council. Most importantly, perhaps, the Union's Common Foreign and Security Policy (CFSP) is largely the executive responsibility of a strengthened Council (General) Secretariat.

This chapter has focused on how the various parts of the Commission are organized and staffed, and how these structural and demographic features might be related to the way decision makers actually behave. Do these factors reflect an intergovernmental perspective on the Commission, or do they instead evoke behavioural patterns that are more in line with what institutionalists would predict? At all levels—the College, the cabinets, the services, and the committees, there are components that are certainly more in line with intergovernmental decision processes than with other kinds of processes. However, those organizational components that work in the opposite direction are becoming more and more important. These components tend to focus attention on sectoral, functional, or institutional cleavages, that is, on lines of conflict and co-operation that cut *across* national boundaries, and that evoke non-territorial feelings of belonging among Commissioners and their officials. If these trends persist, the Commission is set to become much more of a European institution that in the past, though one which will inevitably continue to exhibit a mix (albeit a different mix) of both intergovernmental and supranational characteristics.

QUESTIONS

1   To what extent is the Commission comparable to a national government/executive?

2   How influential is the Commission within the EU policy process?

3   How important is the national background of Commissioners in shaping the way in which they take decisions?

4   What is the role of the Commissioners' cabinets?

5   How are the Commission services organized, and what are the possible implications for patterns of conflict within the Commission?

6   To what extent are the structural and demographic characteristics of the Commission related?

7   How might nationality affect decision making within the services?

8   What is comitology?

GUIDE TO FURTHER READING

Cini, M., *The European Commission: Leadership, Organization and Culture in the EU Administration* (Manchester: Manchester University Press, 1996). This is a broad introductory text that covers most aspects, including the historical roots of the Commission.

Coombes, D., *Politics and Bureaucracy in the European Community. A Portrait of the Commission of the E.E.C.* (London: George Allen & Unwin, 1970). The 'classic' academic text on the Commission in its early period. It is empirically rich and firmly anchored in administrative and political theory.

Edwards, G., and Spence, D. (eds), *The European Commission*, 2nd edn (London: Cartermill, 1997). This anthology also covers most topics, and is particularly detailed and informative on the structure and personnel of the Commission.

Hooghe, L., *The European Commission and the Integration of Europe. Images of Governance* (Cambridge: Cambridge University Press, 2001). The author maps officials' attitudes on topics like intergovernmentalism and supranationalism, regulated capitalism and liberalism, and tries to explain them by using survey and interview techniques.

Nugent, N., *The European Commission* (Basingstoke: Palgrave, 2000). This is probably the most empirically rich and up-to-date book on the Commission.

Page, E. C., *People Who Run Europe* (Oxford: Clarendon Press, 1997). The author presents the Commission with a view to administrative traditions and practices in national bureaucracies.

Stevens, A., with Stevens, H., *Brussels Bureaucrats? The Administration of the European Union* (Basingstoke: Palgrave, 2001). The book contains much detailed information on administrative life and practices in Brussels.

WEB LINKS

http://europa.eu.int/comm This is the official website of the European Commission. It has links to its work programme, documents, calendar, the Commissioners, the services, and the delegations.

www.eurunion.org The European Union in the United States. The website of the EU delegation of the European Commission, based in the USA.

www.cec.org.uk The European Commission Representation in the UK.

10 The Council of the European Union

Jeffrey Lewis

READER'S GUIDE

This chapter looks at the heart of decision making in the EU, the Council of the European Union (or EU Council). The Council is the EU institution which unabashedly represents national interests in the European integration process, and, as such, it is a site of intense negotiation, compromise building, and at times acrimonious disagreement between the member states. From the heads of state and government to the ministers, and all the way down the ladder to the expert-level *fonctionnaires* (bureaucrats), the Council embeds governments of the EU into a complex, collective decision-making system which penetrates deeply into the national capitals and domestic politics of the member states. The result, as this chapter explains, is the most advanced and intensive forum of international co-operation between sovereign nation states in the modern world. This chapter looks at the organization and functioning of the Council, at its component parts (the European Council, the EU Council, the Committee of Permanent Representatives—Coreper, Working Groups, the Secretariat), and at how it has evolved and continues to evolve as an institution over time.

Introduction

The focus of this chapter is the Council of the European Union, also known as the EU Council and the more outdated 'Council of Ministers'. The Council is very much at the centre of EU decision making and plays a pivotal role in the making of European policy. Although ostensibly representing the interests of the EU's 15 member states, the Council is also a European institution; and though formally one of the EU's legislative bodies, it is also an important arena for interstate diplomacy and negotiation.

To explore these at times paradoxical characteristics of the EU Council, this chapter begins by outlining the way in which the institution is structured. The first section also emphasizes the difference between the EU Council and the European Council (the latter involving heads of state and government, rather than just national ministers). In the second section, the operation of the Council comes under scrutiny. Here, the focus is on the presidency, which rotates from member state to member state, as well as on the relationship between the Council, the Commission, and the Parliament. In the third section, the layers of Council decision making are peeled away, and we focus, from the top down, on European Council summits, on Council meetings themselves, on the work of Coreper (involving senior national civil servants), and that of the more technical working groups. This section also considers the increasingly important role of the Council's own officials in the Council General Secretariat. Finally, the chapter turns to consider some of the challenges facing the Council—the institutional challenges, the democratic deficit, and the wider implications of enlargement.

The heart of EU decision making

The Council of the European Union is the institutional heart of decision making in the EU. It is the institution designed to represent the member states and, as the creation of sovereign nation states, it was unsurprisingly endowed with extensive legislative and executive functions. The central legislative function is that all EU proposals (originating from the Commission) must be approved by the Council before becoming EU law. Despite newer decision-making procedures granting the European Parliament (EP) a more co-equal status (called **co-decision**), the Council remains at the core of the EU's legislative process. The Council has a central **executive** function as well: to provide leadership and steer the pace and direction of European integration, seen especially in areas of diplomacy and foreign affairs.

Legally speaking, there is only one Council, but this is misleading since in reality there are 16 different formations organized by policy specialization.[1] Each formation of the Council was created to manage a specialized policy sector, and the participants authorized to adopt legislative acts are the national ministers from each of the member states who hold responsibility for that sector. Hence, the 15 EU ministers of agriculture preside over the Agricultural Council, the environmental ministers over the Environment Council and so on. See Box 10.1.

Historically, the 'senior' Council formation with general institutional responsibilities and charged with overall EU policy co-ordination has been the foreign affairs ministers who meet as the General Affairs Council (GAC). More recently, the finance and economics ministers have increased in stature through their work on the Economic and Financial Affairs Council, otherwise known as Ecofin. The newest Council additions include the interior (home

Box 10.1 **The facts**
Formations of the Council

General Affairs (GAC)	Justice, Home Affairs and Civil Protection
Agriculture	Internal Market, Consumer Affairs and Tourism
Economic and Financial Affairs (Ecofin)	Research
Environment	Budget
Transport and Telecommunications	Culture
Employment and Social Policy	Development
Fisheries	Education and Youth Affairs
Industry and Energy	Health

Source: Annex, Council's Rules of Procedure (2000/396/EC, ECSC, Euratom).

affairs) ministers who meet in the Justice and Home Affairs Council, and the defence ministers who meet in a 'jumbo' Council format with the foreign ministers to discuss European Security and Defence Policy (ESDP).

The policy segmentation of the Council's work into distinct, separate formations is a hallmark of how the EU works. Each formation has its own pace and legislative agenda, with some meeting monthly (GAC, Ecofin, Agriculture) and others meeting only twice per year (Culture, Education). Each Council also has its own identity and culture of co-operation, often including a set of informal (unwritten) rules and even distinctive working habits. Whereas the Budget Council has a habit of stopping negotiations as soon as a sufficient qualified majority is found, the GAC goes to great lengths to search for consensus and to 'accommodate even the most awkward of positions' (Westlake 1995: 170). Taken together, 'the Council' is a multifaceted decision-making structure across a wide range of policy domains, with negotiations going on concurrently. In one guise or another, the Council is almost continually in session.

But the ministers are only the tip of the iceberg. If it were only the ministers meeting for at most a few days per month in Brussels, the EU would be an incoherent and chaotic system of decision making. The work of the Council involves a much larger contingent of national officials. First, there are the EU permanent representatives who staff the Committee of Permanent Representatives

(Coreper). Coreper is responsible for preparing forthcoming Council meetings and these preparations often involve intensive discussions to pave the way for agreement by the ministers. The EU permanent representatives (two per member state: each appoints their own EU ambassador and a deputy) live in Brussels, meet weekly, and literally 'eat, drink, and breathe EU issues seven days a week' (Barber 1995). Each member state also maintains a Permanent Representation in Brussels run by the EU ambassador and deputy and staffed by policy specialists from different national ministries. But that is still not all. The bulk of day-to-day Council activity takes place at the expert working group level. At any point in time, the Council has between 150 and over 250 working groups in existence. Working groups examine proposals in the early stages of negotiation and serve as a clearing house for non-controversial and technical issues to be settled and as an early warning system for complications or political issues that will need to be addressed at the level of Coreper or the ministers. In total, the Council involves thousands of national officials meeting in dozens of working group, Coreper, or ministerial settings each week to negotiate and decide on EU proposals. If you add up all of the national civil servants and policy specialists involved, estimates place the total number who work on EU affairs at around 25,000 (Wessels and Rometsch 1996: 331).

Of all the EU institutions, how the Council operates in practice is perhaps the least documented.

Part of this stems from inaccessibility, but more important is the Council's enigmatic appearance. It is the 'chameleon' of EU institutions (Wallace and Hayes-Renshaw 1995: 563) because it blurs **intergovernmental** and **supranational** organizational traits and behaviour. The standard, glossary image of the Council is one of a stronghold of individualistically orientated national actors who focus more or less exclusively on their own self-interests rather than on the welfare of others or the group as a whole. This interpretation of the Council also forms a basic theoretical foundation for intergovernmentalist approaches. But the Council is a more complex and variegated institutional construct. The Council, as an institution, equals more than the sum of its parts (the member states). National actors in the Council also act collectively, and many develop a shared sense of responsibility that the work of the Council should move forward and the legislative output of the Council (even if in only one specialized policy area) should be a success. As a chamber of continuous negotiation across a wide range of issues, national actors often develop long-term relations of trust, mutual understanding, and obligations to try and help out colleagues with domestic political difficulties or requests for special consideration. Council participants can also develop collective interests in the process of joint decision making itself. This can become a kind of 'global, permanent interest' in addition to the specific national interest on a given subject or proposal. In short, the member states who participate in the system also become socialized into a collective decision-making system (see Chapter 6). As one leading scholar on the Council has summarized the enigma, 'The Council of the EU is both an institution with collective EU functions and the creature of member governments' (Wallace 2000b: 16).

The Council and the European Council: Not the same thing

No portrait of the Council would be complete without inclusion of the role of the European Council. The European Council is the pre-eminent political authority for the EU because it brings together the 15 heads of state and government (and the President of the European Commission). Overall strategic guidance for the EU is supplied by the European Council, and in recent years, the prime ministers, chancellors, and presidents meeting in the high-profile summits have assumed extensive responsibility for such key subjects as institutional reform, the budget, enlargement, and foreign, security, and defence policy. Issues such as future national budgetary contributions, relative voting weights, or how to finance new foreign policy missions have proven too politically charged for the ministers to settle and they have relied on the European Council to break deadlocks, overcome interministerial discord (especially between finance and foreign affairs), and broker the big, interlocking package deals for which the history-making 'constitutional' turning-points in the EU are famous. The European Council meets at least twice a year (in June and December), and often twice more at 'informal' gatherings organized around a specific topic or theme (such as the 2000 Lisbon summit on economic and social affairs). European Council summits attract intense public scrutiny, are covered by roughly 1,200 journalists, and increasingly are accompanied by large turn-outs of protestors (ranging from farmers to anti-globalization groups) and this has recently led to violent clashes with police (as during the 2001 summit in Gothenburg, Sweden).

The European Council was an innovation of the early 1970s, and by 1974 was informally institutionalized. Many EU scholars credit the European Council with holding the Union together during the nearly two decades of **Eurosclerosis**. For the first dozen years or so, the European Council was not a legally recognized part of the Community's institutional system, and was not acknowledged in the Treaties until the Single European Act of 1986. Thus, the European Council was considered an extra-legal institution of the EU. Though it receives mention in the 'common provisions' section of the Treaty on European Union, it is still separate from the original European Community institutions. It remains so, in order not to appear to be becoming too closely controlled by the member states, and to avoid upsetting the delicate institutional balance between intergovernmentalism and supranationalism. While the European Council rarely makes a decision on a specific proposal (though there is nothing legally preventing them from doing so), the summits supply the EU with critical navigation and the usual output for a meeting is a 20 to 30-page *communiqué* (known as the 'presidency conclusions') which summarizes positions on issues and sets priorities for future EU policy making.

Key points

- The Council was designed to represent the member states, and has both executive and

legislative functions in the EU system of governance.

- The European Council is a distinct component of the Council, which brings the heads of state and government together in multi-annual summits to discuss pressing business and provide strategic guidance.

- As an institution, the Council is enigmatic: it is both defender of the national interest and a collective system of decision making, blurring the theoretical distinctions between intergovernmentalism and supranationalism.

How does the Council work?

The most common way to portray the Council is as a hierarchy of levels. The European Council forms the top level, and below this the ministerial level, with the GAC (foreign ministers) and Ecofin (finance ministers) as *primus inter pares*. Below them is the Coreper level which serves as a process manager between the ministers and the working groups that form the base of the hierarchy. This portrayal is not wrong, but it is distorted. The reality is a more labyrinthine and nuanced decision-making system, with significant variation by issue area. In some policy areas and with issues that are of a highly technical nature, the specialists in the working group may forge substantive agreement on important issues. In other cases, the permanent representatives who meet in Coreper conduct detailed negotiations over substance, perhaps because of their legal expertise in applying Treaty articles, or institutional memory in a specific policy area, or sometimes to 'keep the lid' on a controversial subject that risks becoming hamstrung by the ministers. Sometimes in a kind of role reversal, the ministers prepare discussions for Coreper and send a file back down the hierarchy for a decision to be made. It is also not uncommon, particularly when a presidency is not run efficiently (see below), for a ministerial meeting or even a European Council summit to have the detailed, technical minutiae of a proposal on their agenda for discus-

sion. In organizational imagery, the actual operation of the Council is perhaps closer to a network relationship of inter-organizational authority than a corporate hierarchy which is the typical portrayal.

The role of the rotating presidency

The Council presidency rotates between member states every six months. The presidency is responsible for planning, scheduling, and chairing meetings of the Council and European Council. The same goes for all meetings of Coreper and the working groups. The presidency also represents the EU internationally by acting as a spokesperson in EU external affairs. The true genius of the rotating presidency is that it acts as a great equalizer between big and small states, giving tiny Luxembourg the same chance to run things as, say, Germany, France, or Britain. The order of rotation was originally alphabetical, but is now set to give some variation between big and small, newer and older member states. The order also alternates so that no member state becomes permanently fixed in either the January–June or July–December slot, since that would entail always handling the same fixed aspects of the legislative agenda (such as setting annual fisheries quotas in the autumn or agricultural prices in the spring).

Holding the chair carries formidable logistical duties, as the Council's work is organized into a six-month calendar. Planning for the presidency usually begins 18 months prior to the start date. Despite the workload, the presidency is highly coveted by member states as a chance to run things, since that member state not only organizes meetings but has a close involvement in setting the agenda—what issues are covered and in what order, and in finding solutions—brokering deals, suggesting compromises, drafting conclusions. The EU presidency involves much quiet diplomacy, behind the scenes, and often in bilateral conversations at the margins of meetings (known as 'confessionals'), in order to make progress on new proposals as well as deal with the inevitable unexpected developments and crises as they arise. Running the presidency is a real art form, requiring the ability, for example, skilfully to detect when an issue is ready to be sent from the working group to Coreper or from Coreper to the ministers. It also involves subtle diplomatic skills such as knowing in what order to call on member states during discussions to ensure the best chances of success (or failure), when to call for coffee breaks, and how to time the right moment for suggesting a 'presidency compromise'. The presidency can be an important source of leadership in the EU, and member states see their turn at the helm as a chance to leave their imprint on the integration process. As the visibility of EU politics has increased across Europe, the pressures on the EU presidency to deliver a successful set of accomplishments at the end of a six-month rotation have grown quite intense.

The presidency is a great example of the Council's enigmatic identity, since the country holding this position must simultaneously work to advance collective European solutions and be on the lookout for a particular set of national interests. This can be a delicate balancing act to maintain, especially in policy areas where there are highly mobilized domestic constituencies and costly economic issues at stake. Member states that perform well during their presidency rotation and handle this balancing act with a deft touch can accumulate a great deal of political capital and respect. The Finnish presidency of 1999 helped earn that country a reputation for being very communitarian and skilful at compromise building despite being relative newcomers to the EU game. Likewise, it is possible for a country to be seen as using the presidency to pursue a more narrow national agenda or to push through new policies without widespread support, as the French found out during their rotation in 2000, when smaller states accused them of trying to force through new voting weights which advantaged the big states.

Relations with other EU institutions

From the earliest days of the Union, interactions between the Council and the Commission have constituted the main pulse and dynamic of European integration. But as the two institutions were created with a certain degree of inbuilt tension, with the Council representing individual member states and the Commission representing the 'European' interest, relations have at times been quite strained. The worst crisis in the history of the Union, the empty chair crisis of 1965, was prompted when the French president, Charles de Gaulle, felt the Commission had overstepped their authority in seeking to obtain their own sources of revenue (see Chapter 2). During other periods, relations between the Council and the Commission have been smoother, such as the period in the late 1980s when the Council adopted the bulk of legislation to create the single market in a steady stream. More recently, signs of strains have shown up again in areas of foreign policy, between the External Affairs Commissioner and the Council's Secretary-General and High Representative of CFSP (foreign policy), over who should represent the EU internationally.

In contrast to the Council's relations with the Commission, its relations with the European Parliament (EP) for most of the Union's history were fairly much at arm's length and mostly one-sided. Prior to the **Maastricht** Treaty, the Council merely had to consult the EP before adopting legislation, and amendments proposed by the EP were not binding. This all changed when the co-decision procedure was introduced to selected issue areas, the essential feature of this procedure being that the EP is a co-equal legislator with the Council, since it is now much more difficult for the Council to ignore or overrule EP amendments. Since the 1990s, with each new Treaty (Maastricht, Amsterdam, Nice), co-decision has been introduced or extended to more issue areas. Under co-decision rules, where the Council disagrees with EP amendments there is a procedure known as 'conciliation' where the two sides meet to reach compromise on a final text. Conciliation meetings have dramatically intensified relations between the Council and the Parliament over the last decade. The growth of co-decision (and conciliation) represents a new dynamic of inter-institutional networking in the EU.

Key points

- The Council has a clear hierarchical structure from the heads of state and government down to the experts, but in practice the lines of authority and decision making are more akin to a complex network relationship.

- Leadership of the Council is supplied by a rotating presidency which alternates every six months.

- Relations with the Commission are an integral part of the EU's federal-like system of overlapping powers, and the Commission's right of initiative gives it the sixteenth seat at the table.

- Relations with the European Parliament have become more intense as the co-decision procedure has grown and the EP is treated more like a co-legislator in key areas of EU policy making.

The layers of Council decision making

From the top down, the following section looks at the Council hierarchy, moving from the European Council to the Council of the EU, then to Coreper and the Council's working groups. The section also considers the changing role performed by the Council's General Secretariat.

European Council summitry

Over the last thirty years, the European Council has been at the heart of the major 'history-making' moments of European integration. This includes the creation of the European Monetary System in the late 1970s, the resolution of major budgetary disputes in the early 1980s, launching new inter-governmental conferences that would lead to new Treaty agreements (SEA, TEU, Amsterdam, Nice), and so on. As the grouping that brings together the heads of government and state (in the case of France and Finland), no other EU body can match the political authority of the European Council. As a result, the summit conclusions pack tremendous legitimation for daily decision making at the ministerial, Coreper, and working group levels. For instance, following the European Council's special meeting in October

1999 in Tampere, Finland to discuss the creation of a 'common area of freedom, security, and justice', the policy area of Justice and Home Affairs (JHA) received a great burst of activism, including a new influx of Commission proposals and the adoption of several new directives by the JHA Council in areas covering immigration, asylum policy, and cross-border crime (see Chapter 19).

The Ministers' Council(s)

In terms of formal decision-making authority, the ministers are the national representatives empowered to vote and commit member states to new EU legislation.[2] As we shall see, much informal decision making takes place in Coreper and the working groups, but it is important to understand the distinction between formal (juridical) and informal (de facto) decision-making authority since the ministers are the elected officials who are accountable to their domestic constituencies for the policies adopted in Brussels.

Three Council formations have more work and meet more frequently than the others: the General Affairs Council or GAC, dealing mainly with foreign affairs, the Economics and Finance Council (Ecofin), and Agriculture. These three meet each month, usually for one or two days. The workload is particularly intense during certain periods, such as the end of a presidency when there is a final push to complete a legislative calendar. For most of the EU's history, the GAC was the senior formation of the Council, with responsibility for the overall co-ordination of EU policies and the 'horizontal' (cross-cutting, intersectoral) nature of agendas. The premier position of the GAC also reflected the fact that many of the foreign ministers were responsible for interministerial co-ordination of EU policy in the national capitals. Today, the GAC still covers horizontal and institutional issues, but because of the growth of EU external relations (trade, aid, foreign policy) which commands so much time and attention, the work of the GAC has lost some of its focus especially as an overall co-ordinator of Council business (Gomez and Peterson 2001). The GAC's senior status has also been checked by the increased authority of Ecofin. This reweighting in the Council's balance of power reflects the new importance of EU macroeconomic and monetary policy making with the introduction of the Single Currency as well as a parallel development in many of the national capitals, where the ministry of foreign affairs has lost some of its co-ordinating power in the domestic interministerial balance. There are even signs of some rivalry and discord between the foreign affairs and finance ministers, such as the case in 2000 where the foreign ministers endorsed a new multi-annual financial assistance package for Montenegro as part of the EU's stability plan in the Balkans, while the finance ministers in Ecofin baulked and rejected any such package on grounds such as cost and risk. After going back and forth between the GAC and Ecofin ('like a ping pong game' as one EU official recalled), the issue was resolved by the heads of state and government at the European Council level (who overruled the opposition arguments coming from Ecofin).

The types of legislative acts adopted by the ministers vary by policy area. In traditional 'Community pillar' (first pillar) affairs, legislation is typically in the form of directives, regulations, or decisions (see Figures 4.1 and 4.2 for the three pillars).[3] For Justice and Home Affairs (third pillar) and Common Foreign and Security Policy (second pillar), most legislative acts are made in the form of a joint action or a common position. Depending on the issue area, there are a number of different decision-making procedures which generally dictate what type of legislative act will be used. The number of decision-making procedures is extensive (determining the level of involvement by the EP under **consultation, co-operation, co-decision, assent**, and so on); depending on how you count them, there are close to 30 in all! See Box 10.2 for definitions.

Box 10.2 **The facts**
Types of Council acts

Regulation: is binding in its entirety and directly applicable in all member states.

Directive: is binding as to the result to be achieved, but leaves to the national authorities the choice of form and methods.

Decision: is binding in its entirety upon those (and only those) to whom it is addressed.

Recommendations and opinions: have no binding force.

Joint action: addresses specific situations where operational action by the EU is deemed to be required; covers objectives, scope, the means to be made available to the EU, if necessary their duration, and the conditions for their implemetation.

Common position: defines the approach of the EU to a particular matter of a geopolitical or thematic nature; member states shall ensure that their national policies conform.

Source: Adapted from the Treaty on European Union, Articles 14, 15, and 249.

There are also rules for voting. Voting rules divide into two main categories: **unanimity** and **qualified majority voting** (QMV), though some procedural issues are passed by a simple majority vote (8 out of 15). The key to understanding how the Council reaches decisions is to understand the different dynamics between unanimity and QMV. Under the unanimity decision rule, any member state can block a proposal with a 'no' vote. If a delegation wants to signal disagreement with some aspect of a proposal, but not block adoption by the others, they can abstain. Abstentions do not count as 'no' votes. Since the 1986 Single European Act (SEA), many areas of policy are no longer subject to unanimity, though key areas which still are include CFSP, JHA, taxation, and institutional reform.

QMV now applies to most areas under the first ('Community') pillar and its inclusion of the SEA was considered a crucial precondition for establishing a Single Market and adopting the roughly 260 specific legislative acts by the 1992 deadline (see Chapter 3). Under QMV rules, each member state has a 'weighted' vote based crudely on size: Germany, France, Britain, and Italy have ten votes each; Spain has eight; the Netherlands, Belgium, Greece, and Portugal have five; Austria and Sweden have four; Denmark, Ireland, and Finland have three; and Luxembourg has two votes. Out of the total 87 votes, 67 votes are required for a qualified majority and 26 votes against a proposal constitute a 'blocking minority'. In anticipation of future enlargement(s) to Central and Eastern Europe, the voting weights were reconfigured during the Treaty of Nice negotiations and are subject to change in 2005 (see Table 10.1).

But even where QMV applies, voting is an uncommon occurrence. Very rarely is there ever a 'show of hands'; typically, the presidency summarizes discussion and announces that a sufficient majority has been reached, or asks if anyone remains opposed, and, if not, notes the matter is closed. Voting is also unpopular in the EU because there is a highly ingrained culture of consensus, and it is simply considered inappropriate to 'push for a vote' where there is one or more delegation with remaining-objections or difficulties. But the potential recourse to the vote (the so-called 'shadow of the vote') is a powerful reminder to delegations to

Table 10.1 Voting weights in an EU of 27 member states

	Weighted votes
Germany	29
United Kingdom	29
France	29
Italy	29
Spain	27
Poland*	27
Romania*	14
Netherlands	13
Greece	12
Czech Republic*	12
Belgium	12
Hungary*	12
Portugal	12
Sweden	10
Bulgaria*	10
Austria	10
Slovakia*	7
Denmark	7
Finland	7
Ireland	7
Lithuania*	7
Latvia*	4
Slovenia*	4
Estonia*	4
Cyprus*	4
Luxembourg	4
Malta*	3
Total	**345**

*EU applicant countries.
Source: Treaty of Nice.

avoid becoming isolated by simply saying 'no' and being unopen to compromise. For this reason, Council participants claim that the fastest way to reach consensus is with the QMV decision rule.

A feature common to all formations of the Council is how the agenda is structured at Council meetings. The agenda has two parts: Part A contains issues that need no further discussion and are approved in a single block by the ministers at the beginning of each meeting. This can be quite a long list of 20–30 items, known as 'A points', and not necessarily in the ministers' areas of expertise. Part B is the portion of the agenda which does require discussion by the ministers. These issues, known as 'B points', are the focus of the ministers' discussions. Because of time constraints and the size of the EU—a single *tour de table* where each of the 15 delegations (and the Commission and presidency) states their position or notes problems can take well over an hour—the number of substantive B points that can be covered in any detail is limited.

The meetings themselves take place in Brussels (except during April, June, and October when they are held in Luxembourg as part of an agreement from the 1960s over how to divide where the EC institutions would be located). The official residence of the Council is the Justus Lipsius building, inaugurated in 1995 and named after a sixteenth-century philosopher. The meetings take place in large rooms equipped with rectangular tables and surrounded by interpreters' booths to provide simultaneous translation into the official EU languages. The meetings are far from intimate; typically, each delegation (and the Commission) will have three seats at the table (minister, permanent representative, assistant) and up to another half-dozen who are waiting in the margins for a specific agenda point to be discussed. Normally, there are more than 100 people in the room at any one time, with many bilateral conversations, much note passing, and strategizing going on at the same time as the individual who has the floor is speaking. The presidency sits at one end of the table alongside officials from the Council's Secretariat (CGS), with the Commission delegation at the opposite end and the member state delegations along both sides. The member state holding the presidency purposely retains a separate national delegation around the table to look out for and represent national positions so as to not interfere with the task of chairing the meeting.

Coreper

Coreper is the preparatory body of the Council, making it one of the most intense sites of negotiation in the EU. Whereas the ministers meet at most once per month, Coreper meets weekly. Officially, Coreper is charged with 'preparing the work of the Council', a description that reveals remarkably little

about how important the committee has become in making the Council run smoothly. Whereas any particular ministerial Council will be focused on a particular sectoral issue or set of policies, the members of Coreper negotiate across the entire gamut of EU affairs and thus hold the unique responsibility for maintaining the performance of the Council as a whole.[4] In short, Coreper acts as a process manager in the Council system between the ministers and the experts in the working groups. As an institution, Coreper has a unique vantage point because it is vertically placed between the experts and the ministers and horizontally situated with cross-sectoral and interpillar policy responsibilities. This also gives the permanent representatives a unique policy-making role. Relative to the experts meeting in the working groups, they are political heavyweights; but compared to the ministers, they are both policy generalists and experts in the substantive questions of a file.

Because of the heavy workload in preparing forthcoming Councils, since 1962 Coreper has split into two groups: I and II (see Box 10.3). Coreper I is made up of the deputy permanent representatives and they are responsible for preparing the so-called 'technical' Councils (Internal Market, Environment, Transport, etc.). The ambassadors (who hold the title of 'EU permanent representative') preside over Coreper II and primarily work to prepare the monthly General Affairs Council (GAC) as well as issues with horizontal, institutional, or financial implications.

Coreper I and II are functionally independent bodies (responsible for different formations of the Council) though the EU ambassadors and Coreper II have a more senior status in Brussels and the national capitals. The permanent representatives (ambassadors and deputies) live in Brussels and hold their positions for several years; some stay for a decade or longer, often outliving their political masters (ministers, prime ministers) and providing crucial continuity in the representation of national interests. The selection of an EU ambassador and deputy is considered a top appointment by member states, and some argue this may be the single most important posting that a member state will make.

The most critical feature of Coreper is nowhere discernible in the Treaties, namely the intensity

Box 10.3 The facts
Division of labour between Coreper I and Coreper II

Coreper I

Single European Market (Internal Market, Consumer Affairs, and Tourism Council)
Conciliation in areas of co-decision
Environment Council
Employment and Social Policy Council
Transport and Telecommunications Council
Industry and Energy Council
Fisheries Council
Research Council
Culture Council
Education and Youth Affairs Council
Health Council
Agricultural Council (veterinary and plant health questions)

Coreper II

General Affairs Council
Justice, Home Affairs and Civil Protection Council
Development Council
Budget Council
Multiannual budget negotiations
Structural and cohesion funds
Institutional and horizontal questions
Association agreements
Accession
IGC personal representatives (varies by member state and IGC)

of the negotiations that take place to prepare the ministers' meetings. Aside from the weekly meetings, Coreper also holds restricted lunch sessions (not even translators are allowed in the room) to sort out the most sensitive and tricky problems. The permanent representatives also sit beside the minister at Council meetings, and attend European Council summits. But putting a finger on the precise added value of Coreper is tricky since the permanent representatives have no formal decision-making authority. It is clear however that Coreper is an important de facto decision-making body, seen by the steady stream of 'A points' which are sent to the ministers for formal adoption. Over the years, Coreper has functioned under a fairly heavy cloak of confidentiality and insulation from domestic politics and domestic constituent pressures. This insulation enables a level of frankness in Coreper discussions essential to reaching compromise across so many different subject areas.

Because of the intensity of negotiations and the long periods of tenure, Coreper officials often develop close personal relations with one another, based on mutual trust and a willingness to try and help each other. In this kind of normative environment and under the pressures to keep the Council moving forward, the permanent representatives

are always on the lookout for ways to reach compromise. At times, the search for collective solutions can border on collusion, and the permanent representatives will at times 'go out on a limb' to sell the results of an agreement back home to the relevant authorities. The permanent representatives also exemplify the enigmatic identity of the Council—in order to succeed, they must at the same time represent a national set of interests and share a responsibility for finding collective solutions. Coreper illustrates how the Council does more than just defend national interests, it is also a collective decision-making body embedded in social relations and informal norms of mutual responsiveness, empathy, and self-restraint.

Working groups

The expert group is the workhorse of the Council. Currently numbering over 250, the working group level is a vast network of national officials who specialize in specific areas (such as food safety, the Middle East, olive oil, financial services) and form the initial starting point for negotiations on any new proposal or issue. The working group is also used in the later stages of negotiation for contemplating specific points of disagreement, and can serve as a convenient location for placing a proposal in 'cold storage' until the political climate is more favourable for an agreement. Some working groups are permanent, while others are ad hoc and disappear after tackling a specific question or issue. The working groups are staffed by officials who travel from home capitals or from the Brussels-based Permanent Representations, depending on the issue area involved. The purpose of the working group is to 'pre-solve' as much technical and fine detail as possible, leaving areas where there is disagreement or the need for political consideration to the permanent representatives or the ministers who have neither the time nor, in many cases, the substantive knowledge to hold such finely grained discussions.

It is easy to assume that the working group level is well catalogued, orderly, and coherent, but the reality is much the opposite. The working group level suffers from bureaucratic sprawl in the Council system, and because it covers such a wide range of issues and policy sectors, it is very difficult to monitor. For example, at the beginning of 2001, there were over 50 groups linked to the General Affairs Council (GAC) alone: 16 groups covering horizontal questions (for example enlargement and legislative codification) and 41 groups dealing with external relations (for example Africa, international aspects of terrorism, the Middle East peace process).[5] Because of the variable pace and workload of the Council, some working groups are more active during specific legislative calendars than others. Coreper officials claim that a given presidency will closely follow the work of a dozen or more working groups because of the 'ripeness' of certain files for a decision or because the priorities of a presidency place the spotlight on certain legislative fields.

The working group 'expert', though a vital part of the Council's performance, is not always appreciated at other levels of the Council. The permanent representatives meeting in Coreper, for example, can view their own national experts with some disdain for what one described as their 'bloody single-mindedness' over technical merits without an appreciation of political realities or the broader picture. Likewise, an expert will sometimes feel undermined when a permanent representative or a minister concedes a point that they spent five months defending as absolutely essential at the working group level.

Although there is substantial variation by issue area, we do have rough estimates of how the division of labour in the Council breaks down. Approximately 70 per cent of all issues are resolved at the level of the working groups; another 10–15 per cent is settled in Coreper; and the remaining 10–15 per cent is discussed and resolved at the level of the ministers (Hayes-Renshaw 2001: 13). Though these figures can easily be misleading, since the 30 per cent handled in Coreper and the Council involve the really serious political minefields, the overall picture clearly shows the importance of the working group level in processing and packaging the lion's share of EU negotiations.

Council General Secretariat

The Council employs a permanent secretariat of approximately 2,500 officials known as the Council General Secretariat (CGS), or just the 'Council Secretariat'. Jobs are carefully allotted to all 15 member states, with the majority being linguistic and clerical positions. The top jobs are the 'A-grade' (policy-making) positions which number about 300 in total. At the very top are the highly prestigious Secretary-General and Deputy Secretary-General positions which are only filled after an agreement is made by the heads of state and government. The CGS is the administrative backbone and institutional memory of the Council. Organizationally, it is divided into the Private Offices of the Secretary-General and the Deputy Secretary-General, a Legal Service, a Press Office, and ten Directorates-General for different policy areas (see Box 10.4).

The Council Secretariat (CGS) is officially charged with keeping records of all meetings, including note taking (and producing the minutes of the meeting), and translating all documents into the EU's 11 official languages. It is also an important asset and ally of the presidency, by providing logistical assistance, offering advice, and even helping to find ways of reaching constructive solutions (the famous 'presidency compromise'). Over the years, the CGS has earned a reputation of being a dedicated, highly

---

Box 10.4 **The facts**

Organization of the Council General Secretariat

Private Office of the Secretary-General and High Representative of CFSP

Private Office of the Deputy Secretary-General

Legal Service

Directorate-General A: Administration, Protocol

Directorate-General B: Agriculture, Fisheries

Directorate-General C: Internal Market, Customs Union, Industrial Policy, Telecommunications, Information Society, Research, Energy, Transport

Directorate-General E: External Economic Relations, Common Foreign and Security Policy

Directorate-General F: Relations with the European Parliament, the Economic and Social Committee and the Committee of the Regions; Institutional affairs, Budget and staff regulations, Information policy, Transparency, Public Relations

Directorate-General G: Economic and financial affairs, EMU

Directorate-General H: Justice and Home Affairs,

Directorate-General I: Protection of the environment and of consumers, Civil protection, Health, Foodstuffs legislation, Drug addiction, AIDS

Directorate-General J: Employment and Social policy, Regional policy and economic and social cohesion, Education and youth, Culture, Audiovisual media

Source: Council website.

---

professional team. The commitment of the CGS personnel to the Council's work has also earned them the reputation of being 'honest brokers' and helping the presidency find solutions acceptable to all (see Box 10.5).

Perhaps the key factor in the ascendance of the CGS in EU politics is the office of the Council Secretary-General. In the history of the EU, the position has only changed hands five times. There is no official rule about how long a Secretary-General serves for, but the long tenure of the position gives the Council an important element of continuity and leadership. Under Niels Ersbøll, the long-serving Secretary-General (1980–94) from Denmark, the CGS was transformed from relative obscurity to a central position in Council negotiations, albeit a behind-the-scenes role that is not often credited in public (Hayes-Renshaw and Wallace 1997: 108–9). The position of Secretary-General has been granted new authority following the decision by the heads of state and government at the 1999 Cologne summit to upgrade the office to include the title of High Representative of Common Foreign and Security Policy (unofficially dubbed 'Mr CFSP') and to appoint the then Secretary-General of NATO, Javier Solana, to the position. The Deputy Secretary-General is now entrusted with the task of overseeing the day-to-day operations of the Council, and participates in the weekly Coreper II meetings.

Key points

- European Council summits are the source of most of the EU's 'history-making' decisions.

- The ministerial Councils are divided by policy sector, and three (the GAC, Ecofin, Agriculture) stand out for the level of work and frequency of meetings.

- Coreper is the official preparatory body for the Council which gives the EU ambassadors and deputies the primary responsibility of pre-negotiating and discussing the agendas of every forthcoming Council session.

- The working groups are the biggest single dimension of the Council's work, involving thousands of national experts and handling the technical and finely grained detail of specific proposals.

- The Council has a permanent secretariat, the CGS, which helps facilitate meetings, takes notes, translates documents, and serves as an adviser to the presidency.

Box 10.5 Core ideas
The Council General Secretariat as honest broker

The CGS has earned a reputation for finding creative EU solutions to deadlocked negotiations and helping defuse potential political crises. In particular, the CGS legal staff, who are well versed in the intricacies of the Treaties, are a team of committed Europeanists and an important source of supranational entrepreneurship in the EU. The head of the Council's Legal Service is Director-General Jean-Claude Piris, and he is legendary for his ability to devise innovative legal solutions to seemingly intractable problems. The most famous is his work on devising a Danish 'opt-out' to the Maastricht provisions on joining the Single Currency and foreign policy co-operation with defence implications (following Denmark's 'no' vote). The opt-outs were a creative way to make the refoms palatable to Danish voters yet avoided renegotiating the entire Treaty. Although some point out that the Danish opt-outs also had the unintended consequence of creating a precedent for other member states to use in the future when they disagreed with new EU policies, creating new momentum for an **à la carte** (pick-and-choose) EU.

Another example, again involving Denmark, was the 1998 EU blocking regulation of the US law (known as the Helms–Burton Act) extending the embargo on Cuba to include the right to sue overseas companies that had invested in expropriated property (the EU argued that this amounted to an extraterritorial U.S. law regulating EU companies). The legal basis for the proposed EU blocking regulation included Article 308 (formerly Article 235) which is the so-called 'implied powers' provision enabling EU actions in new areas when deemed necessary to attain Treaty objectives. But the use of Article 308 had become extremely politicized in Denmark where a pending court case involved a citizens group which argued that Article 308 resulted in an unconstitutional surrender of national sovereignty. This was a proposal which all EU member states supported as a strong and co-ordinated 'antidote' to the US law, but it was impossible for Denmark to accept the legal formulation because of domestic political opposition. Once again, the crack legal staff of the CGS, under the direction of Jean-Claude Piris, were able to come up with a novel solution: they drew a legal reference to an obscure 1968 Brussels Convention on judicial co-operation and argued that under these circumstances the EU blocking regulation did not create any *new* EU competencies, and hence, there was no need for the Article 308 formulation. Described by participants at the time as a 'creative legal gimmick', this allowed the EU foreign ministers to adopt the new EU law without appearing to create any new EU competencies.

Finally, the CGS has become such a skilful adviser to the presidency that some member states have started to ask the CGS for help with domestic co-ordination meetings on EU policy. During the 1998 Austrian presidency, members of the GCS were asked to travel to Vienna and brief the cabinet ministers on the state of the Agenda 2000 negotiations, which covered reform of EU spending policies and the 2000–6 budget. As one adviser in the Secretary-General's office recalls, the trip to Vienna was designed so that the CGS would 'orchestrate an internal co-ordination meeting' among the Austrian ministries to help produce a set of presidency conclusions (Interview, Brussels, May 2000). This case nicely illustrates how the CGS is viewed and trusted as an 'honest broker'.

Institutional evolution over time

Of all the accolades that one can find written about the Council's ability to forge compromise among sovereign states with divergent interests, few claim that the Council is an efficient decision-making system. It takes about 18 months on average for a new proposal to pass through all stages of negotiation in the Council and EP, though there are some cases that take much longer. A few notorious examples include the directive on lawnmower noise (84/538/EEC) that took about a dozen years to harmonize a maximum decibel level, or agreement on the chocolate directive (2000/36/EC) establishing an EU definition for chocolate products which took 26 years! In short, EU decision making is a 'gas-guzzling' form of governance (Hayes-Renshaw and Wallace 1997: 284).

The ministers' meetings in particular show signs of strain. Never known for their punctuality and often the brunt of jokes for their lack of preparedness, ministers do not always hold highly productive meetings. One former British minister, Alan Clark (1993: 139), recalls his fondness of Council meetings in his memoirs: 'The ministers arrive on the scene at the last minute, hot, tired, ill or drunk (sometimes all of these together), read out their piece and depart'. This has become more problematic as the competencies of the EU have evolved and agendas have grown more extensive, and even overloaded. For example, GAC agendas grew from an average of 8.4 agenda items per meeting in 1990 to 36.2 in 2000 (Gomez and Peterson 2001: 7–8). One implication is that as agendas continue to swell, discussions over substance are really taking place at the level of Coreper, seen by the growth of 'A points', and are merely rubber-stamped by the ministers. In 1995, the number of items on the GAC agenda that were passed without debate was 34 per cent of the total; in 2000, that figure had increased to 54 per cent (Gomez and Peterson 2001: 9). Another implication of this overload is that overall co-ordination increasingly is left to the European Council. But there are real limits to this, as Peterson and Bomberg (1999: 259) have questioned, 'How can impossibly busy political leaders, meeting for the equivalent of less than a week in any given year, be a source of control and innovation?' In light of these dysfunctions and in anticipation of adding new members from Central and Eastern Europe, the EU Constitutional **Convention** has been charged with devising innovative institutional solutions.

Since the 1990s, the issue of the **'democratic deficit'** has been at the top of the EU's agenda (see Chapter 23). Yet the inner workings of the Council have so far avoided scrutiny. Reducing the 'democratic deficit' has centred on reforming the EU's decision-making procedures, increasing involvement by the European Parliament, and introducing the subsidiarity principle to keep decisional authority as close to the citizens as possible. But addressing the democratic deficit inside the Council remains controversial. Every member government pays lip-service to the need for the

Union to be more transparent, more accessible, and more connected to EU citizens but there is less agreement among them on how best to accomplish this task in Council deliberations. One innovation was to hold 'public debates' by broadcasting select Council meetings on television, but this has the perverse effect of stifling real dialogue, since the ministers simply began reading from set speeches. Instead of increasing the transparency of the Council's work, public debates merely promote the reading of '16 successive monologues' (by the 15 ministers and the Commission representative) (Galloway 1999). According to the Council's Rules of Procedure, every six months the GAC and the Ecofin should hold a public debate on the work programme of the current presidency as well as at least one public debate on important new legislative proposals (Article 8).

While the EU doggedly remains hard to predict, there are two areas that show signs of posing future challenges with potentially unsettling implications. The first issue is enlargement (see Chapter 14). Can the Council continue to operate in the same way in an EU of 27 or more member states? Some believe that the Council will become such an unwieldy and heterogeneous body that it will become little more than a 'talking shop' of ministers. An EU of 27 will place new strains on the Council's decision-making structures—originally built for six members—and is likely to slow down the pace and output of new legislation even further. Enlargement is also likely to increase the workload of Coreper and the expert groups which will hold greater responsibilities for discussing substantive issues and finding agreements at their levels. Finally, how easily the Council's decision-making system can consolidate its new members will depend on how quickly and extensively they become socialized to the EU's normative environment. If, for example, the new members are slow to absorb the established norms of compromise and accommodation, the Council may develop a more rigid 'veto culture' or even divide into different voting blocks along geographic or GDP lines.

The second issue is **differentiation** or **variable geometry** (see Chapter 24). How will the Council change as the EU becomes more polycentric and differentiated? 'Enhanced' forms of co-operation, which were for the first time incorporated into the

Treaties at Nice, pose certain risks in altering the very finely tuned mechanisms of exchange and consensus seeking which have become a reflexive habit among Council participants. While many view differentiation as a method of promoting diversity and preventing the blockage of integration by reluctant or recalcitrant members, others see it as setting a dangerous precedent for different 'classes' of membership which challenge the principle of equality.

Key points

- The Council has grown in membership and scope to the point where decision-making structures are under strain, ministerial discussions are limited to a few substantive issues, and agendas are overcrowded. Many believe the Council needs serious institutional reform, but there is little agreement on what to change.

- Efforts to 'democratize' Council negotiations, by holding public debates on television, has resulted largely in staged performances for the cameras while the substantive discussions have taken place elsewhere (restricted sessions, Coreper, working groups).

- Enlargement to 27 or more members will result in new voting weights in the Council and presents certain challenges to prevent negotiations from becoming too unwieldy, depersonalized, and unreceptive to compromise building.

Conclusion: National, supranational, or both?

The Council is the main decision-making body of the EU. It is the premier EU institution for representing national interests and power. But it is also a collective system of governance which locks member states into permanent negotiations with one another. National officials who participate in this system have developed their own 'rules of the game' which include a culture of behaving consensually through compromise and mutual accommodation. Thus, strictly speaking, the Council is both an institution that represents national interests and a body at the supranational level that makes collective decisions. Researchers making a close study of the Council often find evidence that it blurs the traditional distinctions between the national and European levels, between intergovernmentalism and supranationalism. As a leading study of the Council concludes, national officials who participate in this system face a 'continuous tension between the home affiliation and the pull of the collective forum' (Hayes-Renshaw and Wallace 1997: 279). It is this feature more than any other that really distinguishes the Council of the European Union from other international institutions and forums of interstate co-operation.

But whether the Council can continue to operate as it has for the last 50 years remains an open question. There are signs of strain on decision makers, as agendas continue to balloon and the lines of co-ordination and coherence between Councils continue to atrophy. Enlargement of the EU to 27 or more members risks stretching the system, already considered by many as over capacity at 15, to the point of paralysis. There are also serious questions of democratic accountability which remain unanswered, as Council deliberations continue to be obscure and mysterious to EU citizens. At a minimum, there appear to be sharp trade-offs between greater transparency which is ineffective (public debates leading to set speeches) and more effective decision making which takes place behind closed doors and out of the public spotlight (lunches, restricted sessions). Finally, the new focus on differentiated integration could also have perverse effects on Council decision making as some member states may find themselves excluded from certain discussions altogether, as we already see in areas of eurozone policy making (see Chapter 20). This would have the unprecedented effect of creating different tiers or classes of membership. But over the years the EU has shown a remarkable capacity to cope with crises and come up with innovative governance solutions. The issue of 'institutional reform' is thus likely to be unresolved for some time, and may even become an endemic feature of the EU's agenda.

QUESTIONS

1 In what manner does the Council perform both legislative and executive functions in the European Union?

2 What kind of institution is the Council? Is it intergovernmental or supranational?

3 How do the member states co-ordinate the representation of national interests in Council negotiations?

4 What role does the rotating presidency play in EU governance?

5 How does the Council General Secretariat act as a 'neutral umpire' and facilitator of meetings?

6 How and why have European Council summits increased in importance over time?

7 How might future enlargement(s) to Central and Eastern Europe affect the operations of the Council?

8 Is the Council democratic? How could the Council improve upon its public image of being inaccessible, remote, and secretive?

GUIDE TO FURTHER READING

de Bassompierre, G., *Changing the Guard in Brussels: An Insider's View of the EC Presidency* (New York: Praeger, 1988). A candid, highly readable account of the role of the presidency in running the Council.

Bulmer, S., and Wessels, W., *The Council: Decision Making in the European Community* (London: Macmillan, 1987). A detailed analytical and historical overview of EU Council summitry.

Hayes-Renshaw, F., and Wallace, H., *The Council of Ministers* (New York: St. Martin's Press, 1997). The definitive study of the Council as a decision-making institution.

Noël, E., 'The Committee of Permanent Representatives', *Journal of Common Market Studies*, vol. 5, no. 3 (1967): 219–51. The best early examination of Coreper—a classic.

Peterson, J., and Bomberg, E., *Decision Making in the European Union* (Basingstoke: Macmillan, 1999). An impressive research design that uses extensive interview data and case study analysis to provide an overview of the dynamics of Council decision making.

Sherrington, P., *The Council of Ministers: Political Authority in the European Union* (London: Pinter, 2000). A more recent survey of the Council utilizing interview data and detailed case studies of the Ecofin, Environment, Labour and Social Affairs, and Education Councils.

Westlake, M., *The Council of the European Union* (London: Cartermill, 1995). A comprehensive survey of the Council, including a useful comparison of the working methods of different formations of the Council.

WEB LINKS

http://ue.eu.int/en/summ.htm The Council's official home page. The website includes links to specific policy areas such as Common Foreign and Security Policy, Justice and Home Affairs, Economic and Monetary Union, etc. There is also a link to the EU presidency which offers basic information about meetings such as dates and agendas as well as the 'presidency conclusions' of recent European Council summits. Access to documentation (including the minutes of Council meetings since 1999) continues to improve, and it is quite easy to locate recent Council acts, though the archives remain spartan.

http:/ue.eu.int/en/info/eurocouncil/index The website of the European Council.

ENDNOTES

1. Prior to the 1999 Helsinki agreement by the heads of state and government to shrink the number of Council formations to 15 (which proved impossible to pin down), the Council had swelled to as many as 23 different groupings.

2. Article 203 (formerly Article 146) holds: 'The Council shall consist of a representative of each Member State at ministerial level, authorized to commit the government of that Member State'.

3. The Council also issues opinions and recommendations which are not legally binding acts but they do carry political weight. Some argue that their increased use reflects the Council putting pressure on the Commission for certain proposals and limiting their autonomous rights of initiative.

4. There are a few areas Coreper does not cover. Due to the highly technical nature of administering the Common Agricultural Policy (CAP), the Agricultural Council has its own preparatory body, the Special Committee on Agriculture (SCA). Another is eurozone macroeconomic and monetary policy, which is prepared by the Economic and Finance Committee (EFC) for the Ecofin Council.

5. Council of the European Union, 5 February 2001, 5916/01.

11 The European Parliament

Roger Scully

READER'S GUIDE

This chapter is concerned with understanding the role of the European Parliament (EP) within the institutional system of the European Union. Unlike the bodies covered in the previous two chapters, the Commission and the Council, the EP has only recently assumed prominence in the EU's governing structures. The first section of the chapter outlines the origins of the Parliament as an essentially marginal institution within the developing structures of European co-operation. The following section then reviews in detail the significant increases in powers experienced by the EP in recent times, and discusses how these have transformed the relative status of the Chamber. After that, the chapter goes on to examine the complex world of the internal politics of the EP—the membership, organization, and working practices of the Parliament. Finally, the last section considers the 'electoral connection': the links between the EP and the European public. The chapter concludes that the European Parliament has been strikingly successful in gaining more powers in recent years, but far less successful as a 'democratic link' between the EU and the public.

Introduction

Compared to many national and even subnational parliaments (or assemblies, or congresses), the EP enjoys a relatively low public profile. Scholars of the European Union, too, have not traditionally devoted substantial attention to the EP, judging it less important than other governing institutions of the Union. However, since the mid–1980s, the EP has experienced probably more significant changes than any other major EU body. Moreover, the cumulative effect of many of these changes has been to enhance greatly the importance of the Parliament within the Union's governing structures. For much of its life, the EP could have justly been labelled a 'multilingual talking shop'. This is no longer the case.

This chapter examines the development of the EP and its contribution to the political system of the EU. As with parliamentary institutions in other political contexts, there are at least three major topics that need to be addressed in order to understand the role of the EP adequately. These are:

- The EP's work in developing and shaping policies and laws.

- The internal politics of the Parliament, and the Chamber's role as an arena for competition between different political parties and ideologies.

- The role of the Parliament as 'voice of the people': a chamber composed of elected representatives, which collectively links the political system to the public.

As we shall see, while the EP has developed considerably as an institution, it still faces significant challenges with regard to the issue of **representation**— challenges that matter not just for the EP, but potentially for the EU as a whole. Before we examine all this, however, a brief overview of the origins and development of the EP is necessary.

The origins and development of the European Parliament

In 2002, the European Parliament celebrated its fiftieth birthday. For much of those 50 years, however, the institution was largely marginal to the development of European integration. To understand that, and to appreciate how far the EP has come since the mid–1980s in particular, we have to be aware of the Parliament's rather humble beginnings.

What is now the EP began life as the Common Assembly of the nascent European Coal and Steel Community (ECSC) in 1952. This new assembly was not central to the plans of the 'founding fathers' of integration. 'In **Jean Monnet**'s vision, it was, together with the European Court of Justice . . . an institution of control and scrutiny, not of decision-making' (Neunreither 2000: 133). Thus, the new chamber was given limited and specific powers. It could only give (non-binding) opinions on new policies and laws. It could, in principle, dismiss the High Authority, the forerunner to today's European Commission, for gross mismanagement. But other than that, it was restricted to discussion and scrutiny. Furthermore, the assembly's membership was not to be elected by voters; rather, the

membership was drawn from among the members of member states' national parliaments. Though this provided a direct link between the ECSC and national political systems, it also ensured that the Common Assembly, as well as having restricted powers, could only ever be a part-time institution, as members still had national parliamentary responsibilities to fulfil.

The assembly met, originally, in Strasbourg. Among the many reasons for this was the symbolism of a parliamentary chamber meeting to discuss European co-operation in a city long part of disputed territory between France and Germany. Support staff for the assembly were originally based in Luxembourg, alongside the ECSC High Authority. Later, as what became the EU increasingly centred its operations in Brussels, the EP has come to conduct more of its operations and base more staff in the Belgian and EU capital. However, rather than centre all of the EP's activities there, national governments have continued to insist (against the wishes of most EP members) that the EP still hold plenary sessions in Strasbourg, and maintain some staff in Luxembourg. This situation has hampered the work

Table 11.1 The expansion of the European Parliament

Year	No. of MEPs	No. of member states	Status of MEPs	Title of chamber
1952	78	6	Nominated	ECSC Common Assembly
1958	142	6	Nominated	EC Common Assembly
1973	198	9[a]	Nominated	European Parliament
1979	410	9	Elected	European Parliament
1981	434	10[b]	Elected	European Parliament
1986	518	12[c]	Elected	European Parliament
1994	567	12[d]	Elected	European Parliament
1995	626	15[e]	Elected	European Parliament

[a] Enlargement to Denmark, Ireland, and the UK.
[b] Enlargement to Greece.
[c] Enlargement to Spain and Portugal.
[d] German enlargement and seat redistribution.
[e] Enlargement to Austria, Finland, and Sweden.

of the EP, meant the costly duplication of buildings and other facilities, and understandably generated some ridicule.

The original Common Assembly, of nominated national parliamentarians, consisted of 78 members from the then six ECSC member states. By its fiftieth birthday, the European Parliament (EP) (as it had renamed itself in 1962) comprised 626 elected representatives from 15 EU members (see Table 11.1). The Treaty of Rome in the late 1950s had called for the Chamber to become an elected one. In fact, the first EP elections did not take place until 1979. A central reason for this delay was that governments and parties hostile to the development of stronger European-level institutions foresaw that an elected EP would be in a powerful position to argue for greater powers: after all, the EP would be (as, indeed, it remains), the only directly elected European institution, and it could use this democratic legitimacy to argue for enhanced prerogatives for itself. Such fears proved well founded, and whatever wider concerns remain regarding EP elections, the elected parliament has proven to be a strong advocate both of closer European integration generally, and of more powers for itself in particular (Corbett 1998, 1999). By the mid-1990s, the EP was no longer a marginal institution, essentially shouting from the sidelines; rather, it was a central, 'mainstream' part of the Union's governing system.

Key points

- The European Parliament originated as an unelected, part-time institution with limited powers.

- The EP's powers were originally restricted to supervision and scrutiny of other institutions, apart from the ability to remove the High Authority/Commission in exceptional circumstances.

- Over time, the Chamber has changed its name (to the European Parliament), grown substantially in size, and become an elected institution.

The powers and influence of the Chamber

Since the 1970s, treaty amendments and institutional agreements have granted the EP considerably greater formal powers (see Table 11.2). The first major advance for the Parliament came in the realm of the Community budget. Two treaties in the 1970s granted the Parliament the right to propose modifications to planned 'compulsory' spending (mainly on agriculture), to insist on amendments to 'non-compulsory' spending, and the right (if supported by an absolute majority of all MEPs, and two-thirds of those voting) to reject the budget outright. This power has been exercised twice—in 1979 and 1984. In the event of a rejection of the budget, the treaties allow the Community, however, to continue to exist for each month of the following year on the basis of 'twelfths', that is, spending continues at a level equivalent to one-twelfth of appropriations for the previous financial year. The Parliament's budgetary role was further enhanced from the late 1980s on by a series of 'Inter-Institutional Agreements' between

Table 11.2 The development of the European
Parliament's powers

Year	Event	Impact on EP powers
1970	Treaty changes on budget	Greater budgetary powers for EP
1975	Treaty changes on budget	More budgetary powers for EP; EP given considerable influence over non-CAP spending
1980	Isoglucose judgment of ECJ	Right of consultation for EP reinforced
1987	Entry into force of Single European Act	Co-operation procedure introduced for some legislation, giving EP greater scope for delay, amendment, and blocking laws; assent powers to EP on some matters
1993	Maastricht Treaty enters into force	Co-decision procedure introduced for some legislation; EP given approval power over nominated Commission
1999	Amsterdam Treaty enters into force	Co-decision procedure altered in EP's favour, and extended in scope; EP given formal right to veto Commission's for President nominee

the Council, Commission, and Parliament, which agreed that parliamentary approval would henceforth be needed for increases in compulsory spending; these agreements ran parallel to multi-year budgetary deals that, by fixing for several years ahead broad spending priorities, allowed the Parliament to give greater attention to monitoring EU expenditure.

The Parliament has made more limited progress in terms of 'executive oversight', if only because the EU lacks a clear 'executive branch' to oversee. An increasing number of executive functions—particularly in foreign affairs—are wielded by national governments or their representatives, who are reluctant to yield to EP scrutiny. Nonetheless, the Parliament can still dismiss the Commission, and in March 1999, would have used the power in response to evidence of mismanagement in the Commission had it not been pre-empted by the resignation of all 20 Commissioners (see Box 11.1). And the EP's role was enhanced by the Maastricht Treaty (1992), which gave the Chamber approval power over the new Commission nominated by national

---

Box 11.1 **Case study**

The ins and outs of the Santer Commission

The fate of the 1995–9 European Commission, led by President Jacques Santer, illustrates some of the powers of oversight and control that the EP now possesses. The Santer team was nominated by national governments in the summer of 1994, to replace the outgoing Commission of President Jacques Delors. In July 1994, only shortly after they had themselves been elected, MEPs held a debate and vote on Santer as the nominated Commission President; after he had been endorsed, a second vote was held the following January on Santer's team of Commissioners. The latter vote followed a set of 'confirmation hearings', when EP committees subjected prospective Commissioners in their area of responsibility to questioning. The Maastricht Treaty required the nominated Commission to receive the endorsement of the EP. The vote on Santer had no official standing (other than that Santer had stated that he would not take office without EP support); the Amsterdam Treaty gave the EP powers to hold a separate vote on the President. In February 1999, after a number

of allegations of waste and financial mismanagement in the Commission, and with the EP having refused to endorse budgetary accounts, the Santer Commission resigned to pre-empt the EP, for the first ever time, using its longest-standing and ultimate power: to dismiss a Commission. (Santer in fact resigned after being told by Pauline Green, an MEP from the British Labour Party and then leader of the Socialist group in the EP, that the Socialists—then the largest party group in the chamber—would no longer oppose a censure motion forthcoming in Parliament. With the Commission's censure supported by most other MEPs, this made defeat for Santer and his colleagues inevitable.) The replacement Commission team, headed by the former Italian prime minister, Romano Prodi, was subjected not only to more intense confirmation hearings; Prodi was also forced to concede that he would require the resignation of any Commissioner subject to the passage of a censure motion in the EP.

governments. This provision was interpreted in 1994/95 as allowing Parliament both to vote on the Commission President-designate and on the Commission as a whole; the Amsterdam Treaty formally approved Parliament's veto over the President-designate (Westlake 1998). Furthermore, EP committees increasingly pursue day-to-day scrutiny of the Commission.

The greatest and most recent advances by the EP are in the area of EU lawmaking. Prior to the Single European Act, the EP's role here was very limited. EU laws (other than Commission legislation) were processed via '**consultation**'. The Parliament could offer an opinion, but could not force the Commission or Council to respond to this opinion. Aside from using delaying tactics (by failing to present its opinion), the EP had no formal mechanism of influencing legislation. (But see Box 11.2.)

A fierce lobby for greater parliamentary powers bore some fruit in the Single European Act. Consultation was retained for most laws. However, for most legislation related to the Single Market, the '**co-operation**' procedure was introduced. This permitted the EP to propose amendments (which, if supported by the Commission, could be overturned only by a unanimous Council but accepted by a qualified majority of states), or issue a veto that could only be overturned by a unanimous Council of Ministers. This was undoubtedly a significant advance for the EP. The Single European Act also gave the EP '**assent**' power (i.e. a simple yes/no vote) over matters like association agreements with non-EU states, and the accession of new members to the Union.

The Maastricht Treaty (TEU) produced a further significant change; after Maastricht, around one-quarter of laws were processed under another new procedure, '**co-decision**'. Co-decision laws were designated as joint Acts of the Parliament and Council (rather than Acts of the Council alone), and the procedure added an irrevocable parliamentary veto to previous arrangements. Most observers saw this as a considerable step forward. Indeed, 'Maastricht marks the point in the Community's development at which the Parliament became the first chamber of a real legislature. . . . The co-decision procedure means that it has now come of age as a law-making body' (Duff 1994: 31). It should be noted that the way in which **Maastricht** originally shaped the co-decision procedure did cause concern among many MEPs, because it appeared to allow for the Council, at the end of the procedure, to reject a compromise with Parliament and impose a 'take-it-or-leave-it' choice on MEPs. This possibility not only prompted the academic debate referred to in the main text; it also led MEPs to revise their Rules of Procedure so as to make it as unlikely as possible that governments would try to back MEPs into a corner (see Hix 2002*a*).

The 1997 Amsterdam Treaty revised co-decision in a manner somewhat beneficial to the Parliament, and also extended it to further areas of EU law. The procedure is now used for around half of EU laws, with the vast majority of the rest operating under consultation.

The precise degree to which the various changes have boosted the EP's role within the institutional structures of the EU, and why, has been a matter of some debate by scholars. Of course, any formal power granted an institution only becomes relevant if there is a willingness to use that power. In the complex world of European lawmaking, where the

---

Box 11.2 **Core ideas**
The Isoglucose ruling

The 1980 *Isoglucose* ruling of the Court of Justice (ECJ) did require that the EP be properly consulted over draft laws, generally interpreted to mean that the EP could delay matters by failing to offer its opinion, possibly indefinitely. Corbett, Jacobs, and Shackleton (1995) document the Commission changing a proposal (on the issue of economic and monetary union) in the face of a threatened parliamentary delay (1995: 193). However, a recent judgement of the ECJ has stated that indefinite delay is not a legitimate parliamentary tactic on legislation designated as 'urgent' by the Council (Corbett 1996: 39–40).

EP has to interact with the Council and the Commission, some scholars argued that the veto power granted the EP under assent and co-decision would be of little benefit to the Parliament, as it would leave the EP with some uncomfortable 'take-it-or-leave-it' choices. A strong 'revisionist' perspective suggested that the co-operation procedure had actually given the EP greater scope to set the legislative agenda (see Garrett and Tsebelis 1996; Tsebelis and Garrett 1997). However, this argument, developed through abstract theoretical models of legislative bargaining, has been subject to theoretical criticism (Scully 1997a, 1997b; Moser 1997; Rittberger 2000) and appears to be disproved by the empirical evidence of the Parliament's success in advancing legislative amendments increasing significantly under co-decision compared to the co-operation procedure (Kreppel 1999; Shackleton 2000; Tsebelis et al. 2001).

How important, then, is the EP as a policy-shaping chamber compared to other parliaments, like those in the EU member states? Such comparisons are difficult to make with any degree of precision. Two things, however, do seem fairly clear. The first is that, in terms of formal prerogatives, and even after the expansion of co-decision, the EP is still in a more restricted position than many national parliaments. But the second, and arguably more important, point is that the EP evinces substantially more willingness to exploit its powers than do most national legislatures. Indeed, the EP has often sought to maximize the use of the formal powers granted it (Corbett 1998). The principal reason for this is that in most national chambers, parliamentarians are bound by strong ties of party loyalty to support or oppose a government. In the EP, there is no clear government to either support or oppose, while party loyalties are also more diffuse. It is thus less surprising than it may initially appear that those who have attempted to compare the EP's policy-shaping influence with that of national chambers conclude that the EP ranks higher in this regard than many, if not most, of its national counterparts (Scully 2000; Bergman and Raunio 2001).

Key points

- The EP gained significant powers over the European budget in the 1970s.

- In the 1990s, the Parliament gained an enhanced role in the appointment and supervision of the Commission.

- The EP gained significant powers over EU legislation in the 1980s and 1990s through new legislative procedures introduced in several treaties.

- The EP's willingness to use the powers granted it has made it far more important in the EU, and probably more influential over policy, than many national parliaments in Europe.

The internal politics of the European Parliament

Life inside the EP is complex. This complexity arises not only from the very detailed and technical matters of EU policy that the Parliament spends much of its time dealing with; complexity is virtually inherent in the multinational, multilanguage, and multiparty political environment that the EP constitutes. This section of the chapter highlights some of the major features of politics within the Parliament.

MEPs in the 1999–2004 Parliament represent over 100 separate national parties or similar organizations from the 15 member states. The Parliament thus has within it a very considerable diversity of political viewpoints, as well as previous political experiences. To an increasing extent, MEPs are professional politicians for whom being in the EP is a full-time job. Although turnover at each election tends to be high (about 50 per cent of members at the beginning of each parliament were not MEPs in the previous one), there are also a substantial number of members who have built long-term political careers at the European level. And although some parties have been known to use the EP as a sort of 'political retirement home'—the current EP contains several former national prime ministers among its membership—most members work hard. The EP was once known for very high levels of absenteeism amongst members compared to national parliaments; this is no longer the case. The EP also used to be known as a bastion of pro-integrationist opinion. In part this was because those less interested in the EU were more reluctant to offer themselves as candidates for the EP. However, the current Parliament includes the largest number of eurosceptic and anti-EU figures in the Chamber's history. However, it has often been suggested that MEPs' pro-integrationist views could also be explained by an intensive process of **socialization** operating on many members: that the experience of serving in the EP helped make them substantially more 'pro-European'. However, a recent detailed study shows that there is little or no evidence to support such a viewpoint (see Scully 2003).

Individual national party delegations to the EP join together in multinational party groups, based broadly around political ideology. Being members of both national party and European party groups, nationally elected yet working in a European institution, makes the task of the individual MEP as a representative potentially quite complicated. As Table 11.3, which draws on a survey of MEPs conducted in 2000, demonstrates, most MEPs recognize the importance of representing multiple different 'constituencies'. The party groups themselves seek to bring together likeminded members from different states, yet they must always remain aware of differing national traditions and interests. Recent research on the party groups has shown that in votes held in the EP the groups are—given the diversity of the membership of the larger ones in particular— quite remarkable for their high degree of unity: much higher than that of the two parties in the US Congress, for instance (Raunio 1997; Hix and Lord 1997). Yet this unity must often be built on the basis of substantial 'give and take' between national delegations within the group, and often agreement on the basis of the lowest common denominator; even so, dissent from party group positions most often occurs when large numbers of MEPs from one or more national delegations refuse to support a group line (Kreppel and Tsebelis 1999; Hix 2002b).

Table 11.3 Perceived importance among MEPs of different groups represented (per cent)

Group	Of little importance		Of great importance		
	1	2	3	4	5
All people in Europe	13.7	8.9	18.9	26.3	32.1
All in own county	3.7	6.9	19.1	34.0	36.2
Voters for own party	4.3	9.6	24.5	33.0	28.7
Voters in own constituency	6.1	7.3	16.2	33.0	37.4
National party	4.9	11.4	24.3	33.5	25.9
EP party group	7.0	11.4	28.6	38.4	14.6

Source: The MEP2000 Survey, conducted by the European Parliament Research Group.

Although the party groups are ideologically based, intergroup relations in the Parliament have traditionally been based on co-operation rather than confrontation. The largest groups in the Chamber have always been from the centre right (the European People's Party (EPP) group of Christian Democrats and some Conservatives) and the centre left (the Party of European Socialists (PES) group representing moderate social democrats and socialists). For many years, these two blocs co-operated in sharing out most of the senior posts in the EP, as well as seeking consensus in most other matters before the Parliament. The 1999–2004 Chamber has seen increasing conflict between the major groups, however, and growing levels of voting division along left–right lines in the Chamber (Hix 2002b). A prime example has been the election of the Parliament's president: for some years, the two leading groups had shared this job (which is held by each incumbent for two and a half years, half of a five-year EP term) between them and supported each other's candidates when the other group's 'turn' came. In both July 1999 and January 2002, however, a PES candidate sought (unsuccessfully) the presidency in opposition to candidates endorsed by the EPP. In 1999, the socialists unsuccessfully challenged the EPP presidential candidate, the Frenchwoman, Nicole Fontaine. In 2002, in return for the Liberal group having supported Fontaine, the EPP backed the Liberal leader, the Irishman Pat Cox, who narrowly won the presidency from the British Labour MEP David Martin.

Party interests play an important part in the organization of business in the EP. The parliamentary hierarchy is headed by the Conference of Presidents, comprising the President (Speaker) of the EP, a number of Vice-Presidents, and the Presidents of the party groups. This body handles much of the scheduling of parliamentary business, and the allocation of things like committee chairships. The business of the Parliament itself is organized very tightly. The parliamentary timetable defines specific weeks as set aside for plenary sessions (usually one four-day session per month in Strasbourg, with a few additional 'mini-sessions' of two days in Brussels), other weeks being for committee work (usually two weeks in a month), with the balance of time reserved for 'party group weeks' and 'constituency weeks'. This 'hyper-organization' of the parliamentary timetable extends also into the conduct of plenary sessions. Largely because of the need for the provision of translation facilities, time for debates and individual contributions is organized very closely— literally more or less down to the second!

The EP has a now well-established system of permanent committees (17 in the 1999–2004 Parliament—see Box 11.3). These committees cover most areas of EU policy, and individual committees undertake both legislative work (scrutinizing draft legislation and drawing up amendments) and oversight activity (looking into the conduct of policy) in their area of responsibility. This is unlike, for instance, the British House of Commons, where legislative committees (Standing Committees) are separate from oversight committees (Select Committees). Some committees have also taken on a broader role: the Institutional Affairs Committee in previous parliaments (now the Constitutional Affairs Committee) sought to develop visionary proposals for deepening integration; the Women's Rights and Equal Opportunities Committee has often sought to broaden the degree to which gender-related considerations are incorporated into the EU; and the Foreign Affairs Committee has rarely felt itself restricted to discussing matters linked to the Union's Common Foreign and Security Policy. Many committees contain considerable expertise on their subject matter within their membership, and the committee system as a whole is widely regarded as the place where the bulk of the serious work of the Parliament is done. That work can sometimes be shaped by the influence of strong committee chairs. But, at least as often, committee work is led by the 'group co-ordinators' appointed by the major party groups to each committee (Whitaker 2001). And, on particular matters of policy, there is considerable scope for individual MEPs to have an impact, particularly if they are appointed *rapporteur*: the person delegated by a committee to prepare its report on a specific topic.

Plenary sessions include the great set-piece occasions of the EP's business. MEPs are frequently addressed by prime ministers and foreign ministers of member states, and sometimes of third countries. And on occasion, as with the debates held in July 1994 and 1999 over the nominations of Jacques

---

Box 11.3 **The facts**

Standing committees in the European Parliament

Foreign Affairs, Human Rights, Common Security and
   Defence Policy
Budgets
Budgetary Control
Citizens' Freedoms and Rights, Justice and Home Affairs
Economic and Monetary Affairs
Legal Affairs and the Internal Market
Industry, External Trade, Research and Energy
Employment and Social Affairs

Environment, Public Health and Consumer Policy
Agriculture and Rural Development
Fisheries
Regional Policy, Transport and Tourism
Culture, Youth, Education, the Media and Sport
Development and Co-operation
Constitutional Affairs
Women's Rights and Equal Opportunities
Petition

Box 11.4 **Case study**

The problems of multilingual parliamentary plenary sessions

The 15 member states of the EU produce, collectively, 11 official languages for the Union (to say nothing of other 'minority' languages like Catalan and Welsh). MEPs are permitted—indeed, expected—to make plenary speeches in their 'native' language. Even with excellent translation facilities, the resulting 'Tower of Babel' effect can often hamper the cut and thrust of debate when the EP is in plenary session. At a minimum, debate becomes more cumbersome. When speakers are using some of the less common languages (say Portuguese or Finnish) their words are translated into certain 'core' languages (usually English and French) before being retranslated into other tongues (like Danish and Italian). Even when translation is

entirely successful this can produce bizarre consequences: a joke can potentially produce three waves of laughter! Often the effect of translation is to lose subtleties of meaning, the passion of speeches, and even to produce total misunderstandings. The classic case occurred in the late 1990s. A French MEP was lamenting that discussion of an issue was not employing the common sense of the country people of Normandy, from where he hailed. Those hearing the English translation, however, were told 'to solve this problem, we need Norman Wisdom'. Needless to say, to a large section of his audience, the serious point this MEP was seeking to make was entirely lost.

Santer and Romano Prodi respectively as Commission president, debates can be genuinely dramatic events. Far more commonly, plenary sessions are tedious in the extreme: speeches tend to be more than anything about putting certain views 'on the record' rather than trying to persuade people, while voting time witnesses large numbers of votes, often on unrelated topics, being held one after the other. The problems of a multilingual institution also hamper plenary debates, making it often boring at best, confusing and even farcical at worst (see Box 11.4).

Where does power ultimately lie in the EP? Compared to the executive-dominated parliaments of many countries in Europe, power in the EP is much more widely diffused. The complex multiparty environment of the EP, and the fact that the use of some of the EP's major powers requires the mobilization of 'super-majorities', makes compromise the order of the day, and places a premium on negotiating skills. (Notably, the passage of amendments or the rejection of the position of the Council of Ministers in second and third readings of bills under the co-operation and co-decision procedures requires the support of an absolute majority of *all* MEPs, not simply among those participating in a vote.) The importance of committees also helps to diffuse power. This diffusion of power, and lack of a controlling, 'governing' power in the Chamber,

undoubtedly makes the politics of the EP complex. But it also permits an individual parliamentarian, through political skill, to achieve probably more in the EP than in many other parliamentary institutions.

Key points

- The membership of the EP comes from many different national political parties, is increasingly dominated by full-time MEPs, and now includes a significant number of 'eurosceptics' as well as integration enthusiasts.

- Party groups draw together individual national party delegations into broadly ideological collectives. These groups often have to compromise between different national viewpoints. The groups organize much of the work of the EP.

- Committees are where much of the detailed work of the EP is done. They provide opportunities for individual MEPs to make an impact on policy.

- EP plenary sessions are hampered by translation problems, and, with rare exceptions, tend to be dull and undramatic.

Elections and the public

Even in many non-democratic political systems, parliamentary-type institutions have been established, and are regarded as crucial representative institutions. In democracies, the election of representatives to debate and give assent to major items of public policy has often been regarded as crucial to the functioning of the entire political system: public authority is legitimated by receiving the endorsement of the people's representatives, and popular support for the system is maintained by the democratic process giving people a voice in the institutions of power (Packenham 1970). But how effectively does the EP act as the 'voice of the people' in the EU?

The starting point for analysing this is, of course, the EP elections. Table 11.4 summarizes the representation elected from each member state. Even in a fairly large institution of 626 members, representation is inevitably spread fairly thinly across 15 member states. This problem is exacerbated in larger states because the allocation of MEPs over-represents (in relation to their share of total EU population) the smaller countries. Added to the distance of the institution from the public, and the complexities of the EU policy process, this makes it difficult for the public to have any sense of connection to the EP.

The elections themselves have witnessed levels of turnout generally lower than those obtaining in national parliamentary elections; moreover, as shown in Figure 11.1, and despite the growing powers of the Chamber, aggregate turnout has fallen in each of the last four EP polls, and in 1999 it fell below 50 per cent of eligible voters. Research on EP elections has suggested that in addition to declining voter participation, they have several other salient characteristics. Voters tend to perceive them as of less importance than national elections, a perception encouraged by the fact that the campaigns in each

Table 11.4 Representation in the European Parliament

Country	No. of MEPs	People per MEP	Constituency type	People per constituency (average)
Austria	21	385,000	National	8,085,000
Denmark	16	332,000	National	5,312,000
Finland	16	323,000	National	5,168,000
France	87	678,000	National	58,986,000
Greece	25	422,000	National	10,550,000
Luxembourg	6	72,000	National	432,000
Netherlands	31	508,000	National	15,748,000
Portugal	25	399,000	National	9,975,000
Spain	64	616,000	National	39,424,000
Sweden	22	402,000	National	8,844,000
Germany	99	829,000	Nat./Reg.	82,071,000*
Belgium	25	409,000	Regional	2,556,250
Ireland	15	249,000	Regional	933,750
Italy	87	663,000	Regional	11,536,200
UK	87	681,000	Regional	4,937,250

* MEPs listed by 16 *Länder* on German EP Information Office Site (average inhabitants per constituency when calculated by *Länder* is 5,129,438).

Source: Based on 1999 figures.

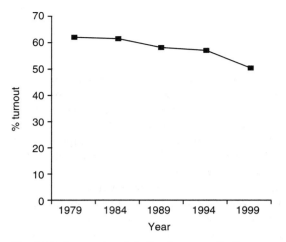

Fig. 11.1 Turnout levels in five European Parliament elections

Table 11.5 The European Parliament after the 1999 elections

Party group	Political orientation	No. of MEPs (% of total)
European People's Party	Centre Right (Christian Democrats & Conservatives)	233 (37.2%)
Party of European Socialists	Centre Left	180 (28.7%)
Liberal, Democratic and Reformist	Liberal	51 (8.2%)
Green and Radical Alliance	Environmentalist & some Regionalists	48 (7.5%)
European United Left	Left wing (includes some ex-Communists)	42 (6.7%)
Europe of Nations	Eurosceptic and generally right wing	30 (4.8%)
Europe of Democracies and Diversities	Eurosceptic/anti-EU	16 (2.6%)
Non-attached	Various, but includes some right wing	26 (4.2%)

member state tend to be dominated by national parties, fighting for the most part on national—rather than European—issues. In general, governing parties tend to do quite poorly, as many voters indulge in a 'protest vote' against government parties. In sum, EP elections tend to be treated by both parties and the people as 'second order national elections', rather than as contests in which alternative visions of 'Europe' are debated about and decided upon by voters (van der Eijk and Franklin 1996). Thus, it was not very surprising that fewer people than ever bothered to participate in 1999, or that the election result showed a setback for the parties of the centre left (by now dominant in most member states' governments) in favour of centre-right parties. These elections also produced the highest support levels yet for explicitly eurosceptic or anti-EU parties, who now have significant representation in the EP (see Table 11.5). Franklin (2001) shows, however, that much of the decline since 1979 in EP election turnout can be accounted for by the fact that no new members joining after that date employ compulsory voting laws (unlike Belgium, Greece, Luxembourg, and, until 1993, Italy).

The perception that many have drawn from EP elections, that the Parliament is failing to establish any sense of public involvement in the EU political system, is, if anything, further heightened when one examines the evidence of studies of public opinion.

General measures of public support for European integration showed steady decline in the 1990s. Detailed analyses of attitudes towards the EP are rare (though see Niedermayer and Sinnott 1995), but the evidence we do have indicates that public knowledge of the Parliament is too low, and support for the Chamber far too shallow, for the EP to have any wider legitimating impact on the EU as a whole. Surveys conducted in 2000 suggested that while over 90 per cent of European citizens have at least heard of the EP, regular awareness through the media is much lower (around 50 per cent on average). When asked whether they wanted the EP to become more important, 43 per cent of EU citizens in 2000 responded positively, a decline from 62 per cent in 1991. Yet this response reflects, in all probability, not the rational reaction of voters to the increase in powers experienced by the Parliament over the intervening period, but rather a high degree of what public opinion specialists term 'non-attitudes': that voters may be able to articulate answers to a question on the EP, but that this draws on little other than a general attitude towards the EU as a whole. Overall, it is difficult to dissent from the view that the Parliament suffers from a 'failure to even begin to penetrate the consciousness of so many of its electors' (Blondel, Sinnott, and Svensson 1998: 242).

Thus, while it may be increasingly important as a policy-shaping chamber, the EP continues to fall short in many respects as a representative one. The EP has done little to generate the wider public sense of legitimacy for the EU as a whole in the manner that elected parliaments elsewhere are believed to. In the long run, this situation may bring damaging consequences for the Parliament: as one sympathetic observer has suggested, 'it risks . . . [an] insidious withering away of its basis of legitimacy because of voter disinterest' (Neunreither 2000: 135; see also Scully 2000).

Key points

- The EP is an elected chamber, but representation is spread quite 'thinly' across the EU.

- EP elections tend to operate as 'second-order national elections', with low (and falling) turnout levels, and little debate about Europe featuring in the campaigns.

- Public knowledge of the EP is very limited, and what support exists for the Chamber is based on very limited understanding of its role.

- This lack of public awareness and interest may bring the role of an elected EP into question in the future.

Conclusion

The EP has developed substantially as an institution in recent times. Once a marginal participant in the EU's political system, it is, as we have seen, now a far more substantial player. Many scholars, for some time, claimed the existence of a 'democratic deficit' in the Union's governing structures (see Chapter 23). Insofar as this deficit is conceived narrowly as an absence of powers for the elected institution in the EU, that deficit has largely now been bridged. However, while it has been strikingly successful in accruing greater powers, we have also seen that the Parliament has been far less adept at connecting the European public to politics in the EU. Addressing this task, rather than gaining more powers, is surely now the principal challenge facing Europe's elected parliament.

QUESTIONS

1   How might the EU have developed differently if the EP had been a powerful institution right from the beginning?

2   Why do you think national governments increased the powers of the EP during the 1980s and 1990s?

3   Are there further powers that the EP ought to seek, in addition to those it now has?

4   Some people have suggested that the European Commission be elected from among the membership of the EP, rather than separate from the Parliament and nominated by national governments. How might this innovation alter the internal politics of the EP if it were ever implemented?

5   Are MEPs European politicians, national ones, both, or neither?

6   Are EP elections a waste of time?

7 What practical steps could the EP take to build awareness and support of the institution among the European public?

8 'The EP is no longer a marginal player in the European policy process.' Discuss.

GUIDE TO FURTHER READING

Bergman, T., and Raunio, T., 'Parliaments and Policy-making in the European Union', in J. Richardson (ed.), *European Union: Power and policy-making*, 2nd edn (London: Routledge, 2001). An excellent chapter that considers the development of the EP and assesses national parliaments' role in the EU.

Corbett, R., *The European Parliament's Role in Closer EU Integration* (London: Macmillan, 1998). A detailed historical study of the EP's efforts to promote European integration and enhance its own role, written by someone heavily involved in the process.

Jacobs, F., Corbett, R., and Shackleton, M., *The European Parliament*, 4th edn (London: John Harper, 2000). A superb introduction to the ins and outs of the EP, written by two current officials of the Parliament's staff, and one former official, now an MEP.

Kreppel, A., *The European Parliament and the Supranantional Party System: A Study in Institutional Development* (Cambridge: Cambridge University Press, 2002). A highly important recent study of the development of the EP and the party group system.

Shackleton, M., 'The European Parliament', in J. Peterson and M. Shackleton (eds), *The Institutions of the European Union* (Oxford: Oxford University Press, 2002). A clear, concise, and informative overview of the history, structures, and powers of the EP.

Steunenberg, B., and Thomassen, J. (eds), *The European Parliament on the Move: Towards Parliamentary Democracy in Europe?* (London: Rowman and Littlefield, 2002). A collection of interesting articles about various aspects of the politics of the EP.

van der Eijk, C., and Franklin, M. (eds), *Choosing Europe? The European Electorate and National Politics in the Face of Union* (Ann Arbor, Mich.: University of Michigan Press, 1996). The classic—though pessimistic—study of European Parliament elections and all their faults.

WEB LINKS

www.europarl.eu.int/home/default_en.htm The home page for the EP's own multilingual website, with considerable information on the members and activities of the Parliament, and links to official documents.

www.lse.ac.uk/Depts/eprg The home page for the European Parliament Research Group, a multinational team of researchers who study the EP. The page includes contact details of leading scholars, details of published work and ongoing research, and a series of working papers.

www.electionworld.org/election/europeanunion.htm Contains detailed election results for EP elections, analysed by party group and by member state.

12 The Community Courts

Anthony Arnull

READER'S GUIDE

This chapter deals principally with the organization, jurisdiction, and role of the Court of Justice of the European Communities. It considers some of the main powers conferred on the Court to enable it to discharge its task of ensuring that the law is observed in the interpretation and application of the Treaties. The chapter also looks at the Court of First Instance of the European Communities (CFI), which is responsible, subject to oversight by the Court of Justice, for dealing with some cases at first instance. The way in which the Court has exercised its powers, and the criticism it has sometimes attracted, is also considered. Both Community Courts are experiencing increasing difficulty in coping with their workloads and some of the changes to the judicial architecture of the Union which may be anticipated, particularly as a result of the Treaty of Nice, in order to tackle this problem are briefly outlined.

Introduction

According to Article 6(1) of the Treaty on European Union (TEU), one of the principles on which the Union is founded is the rule of law. This means essentially that the Union is governed by objective rules laid down in advance which are enforced by an independent judiciary (see Arnull forthcoming 2002: 329–55). Responsibility for ensuring that the rules laid down under the Union Treaties are observed is shared between the national courts of the member states and the so-called Community Courts, comprising the Court of Justice of the European Communities and the Court of First Instance of the European Communities (CFI). The CFI was set up in 1988 to reduce the workload of the Court of Justice and improve judicial scrutiny of factual matters. Its decisions on questions of law are subject to appeal to the Court, but its decisions on questions of fact are final.

The Court of Justice is sometimes referred to as the European Court of Justice or the European Court. Although there is nothing wrong with these terms in themselves, they tend to cause confusion with two other courts which are nothing to do with the European Union. The first is the European Court of Human Rights, which was established under the European Convention on Human Rights and sits in Strasbourg (France). The other is the International Court of Justice, which is the principal judicial organ of the United Nations and sits in The Hague (Netherlands).

The Community Courts are located in Luxembourg, where they share the same infrastructure. Until recently the Treaties described the CFI as 'attached' to the Court of Justice. This meant that the CFI was not strictly a separate body and could for some purposes be regarded as included in the term 'Court of Justice'. In this chapter, however, that term is confined to the Court of Justice itself and is not used to mean both the Court of Justice *and* the CFI. As a result of the Treaty amendments agreed at Nice, the CFI is no longer referred to as 'attached' to the Court of Justice and may in due course be elevated to the status of an institution in its own right.

The Court has sometimes used the powers conferred on it by the Treaties in a bold and creative way to fill in gaps in the legal framework they lay down. Some of its decisions have helped ensure the achievement of the Treaties' objectives notwithstanding legislative inertia on the part of the Council. In the 1970s, for example, the Court interpreted the EC Treaty rules on the right of establishment, the freedom to provide services, and equal pay for men and women as conferring rights directly on individuals without the need for legislative implementation. In its case law on the free movement of goods, the broad scope given by the Court to the Treaty provisions had the effect of reducing the burden on the Community legislature and redirecting its activities. The Court has also played an important role in preserving the balance envisaged by the Treaties amongst the other institutions and between the institutions and the member states. This is due mainly to the growth in the number of legislative procedures and increased use of qualified majority voting (QMV) since the 1980s. The procedure applicable, including the voting method, and the type of act that may be used (see Box 12.1) are laid down in the Treaty provision on which proposed acts are based, the so-called **legal basis**. The question whether the correct legal basis has been chosen often nowadays leads to dispute. An example of a case when this occurred is *Germany* v *European Parliament and Council* (2000), where the Court quashed a directive prohibiting the advertising and sponsorship of tobacco products. Its judgment clarified the Community's powers to adopt measures to improve

Box 12.1 **The facts**
The main types of binding act

The EC Treaty provides for three main types of binding act to be adopted. **Regulations** take effect on their own terms and are directly applicable, which means that they do not normally require implementation by member states. **Directives** are addressed to all or some of the member states. In theory, directives specify an objective which must be achieved by a certain date and leave it to the member states to decide how best to do so. In practice, directives have become increasingly detailed so that the margin of discretion left to the member states has been substantially reduced. A **decision** is directed to specific addressees and is binding on them. Other types of act

may be adopted under Title V (on the Union's common foreign and security policy) and Title VI (on police and judicial co-operation in criminal matters) of the Treaty on European Union. Particularly worthy of note are **framework decisions** adopted under Title VI. These resemble EC directives, but the Treaty expressly provides that they shall not produce direct effect. This means that they do not confer on individuals rights which the national courts must protect. After the events of 11 September 2001, framework decisions were adopted on a European arrest warrant and on combating terrorism.

the establishment and functioning of the internal market and to protect public health.

The creation at **Maastricht** of a European Union with new 'pillars' possessing stronger intergovernmental features than the original Communities (see Chapter 1) led to the imposition of express limits on the powers of the Court. It was made clear that the powers enjoyed by the Court under the Community Treaties (the Court, the now-defunct ECSC, and the Euratom Treaty) did not extend to Title V or (except in limited circumstances) to Title VI of the Treaty on European Union. At **Amsterdam**, the scope of Title VI was extended and the Court was given important new powers to rule on disputes concerning its application. Nonetheless, those powers remain more limited than those it enjoys under the Community Treaties. This chapter will concentrate on the Court's powers under the EC Treaty since these are of the greatest practical importance.

Key points

- The Community Courts comprise the Court of Justice and the Court of First Instance (CFI) of the European Communities. Together with the national courts of the member states, the Community Courts are responsible for enforcing the rules laid down under the EU Treaties, especially the EC Treaty.

- The case law of the Court has had a major impact on the achievement of the objectives of the Treaties. It has also helped to define more clearly the powers and responsibilities of the other institutions.

- The Court's powers under Title VI of the Treaty on European union are more limited than those it enjoys under the Community Treaties. It has no jurisdiction over Title V of the Treaty on European Union.

Background and organization

The Court of Justice consists of 15 judges (one from each member state) and is assisted by eight advocates general. The judges and advocates general, who have the same status, are sometimes referred to collectively as the members of the Court. They are appointed by the member states acting together for renewable terms of six years. To be eligible for appointment, candidates must be 'persons whose independence is beyond doubt and who possess the qualifications required for appointment to the highest judicial offices in their respective countries or who are jurisconsults of recognized competence'. In practice, the members of the Court have come from a variety of backgrounds, including the national judiciary, legal practice, the civil service, and universities. Their approach to a case may be affected as much by their professional background as by their nationality.

Among the eight advocates general, there is always one from France, Germany, Italy, Spain, and the United Kingdom. The remaining posts rotate among the other member states. One advocate general is assigned to each case. His or her function is normally to present to the Court an independent and impartial opinion on the case with a recommendation as to how it should be decided. The opinion is delivered after the parties have made their submissions but before the judges begin their deliberations, from which the advocate general is excluded. In most (but by no means all) cases the Court follows the advocate general's opinion and advocates general have made an important contribution to the coherence and comprehensibility of the case law. Nonetheless, in straightforward cases the opinion of an advocate general is an unnecessary luxury. At Nice the member states accordingly agreed to permit the Court to decide cases without an advocate general's opinion, where they do not raise any new points of law.

The Court sits either as the full Court or in smaller divisions known as 'chambers'. Once the advocate general's opinion has been delivered, the Court begins its deliberations. These take place in secret, with only the judges present. The final decision is, if necessary, taken by majority vote, but all the judges taking part in the case are required to sign the judgment. There are no dissenting judgments, that is, opinions from judges in the minority explaining why they disagree with the outcome. The collegiate character of the Court's judgments helps to protect it from outside pressure, but contributes to their dry and impersonal style. Attempts to achieve a consensus or to accommodate the views of the minority can also sometimes result in a loss of coherence, a problem which is exacerbated by the Court's heavy workload. The difficulty of preserving the effectiveness of the full Court as a decision-making forum and maintaining consistency between the chambers has become more acute as the Court has grown in size.

The CFI consists of one judge from each member state. They must be of undoubted independence and 'possess the ability required for appointment to high judicial office'. There are no permanent advocates general in the CFI, but a judge may be asked to perform the function of an advocate general in important or difficult cases. In practice, this is hardly ever done. The CFI has the right to sit in plenary session but rarely does so, normally sitting in chambers of three or five judges. The Court of Justice helps to maintain consistency between the chambers of the CFI through the appeals process. Like the Court of Justice, the CFI delivers a single collegiate judgment. Again, there are no dissenting judgments. Certain simple cases assigned to a three-judge chamber may be delegated to a single judge for decision.

Key points

- The Court of Justice consists of 15 judges and eight advocates general. One advocate general is assigned to each case, with responsibility for giving an independent and impartial opinion to the Court as to how it should be decided.

- The CFI consists of 15 judges. It does not have any permanent advocates general.

- Both the Court of Justice and the CFI deliver single collegiate judgments. There are no dissenting judgments.

Jurisdiction

The proceedings which may be brought before the Community Courts fall, broadly speaking, into two categories: references for **preliminary rulings** and **direct actions**.

References for preliminary rulings

Much of the responsibility for applying the rules laid down in the EC Treaty and the acts of the Community legislature belongs to the national courts of the member states, but this state of affairs gives rise to a potential problem. If the internal market (or 'single market') is to work properly, the relevant rules must have the same effect in all the member states. However, the nature of the judicial process and varying legal traditions mean that, left to their own devices, it would be highly unlikely that courts in, say, Edinburgh would always apply Community law in the same way as courts in, say, Athens. To help safeguard the uniform application of Community law, Article 234 (formerly Article 177) of the EC Treaty therefore lays down a procedure which enables national courts to refer to the Court of Justice questions of Community law that they must decide before giving judgment. A 'reference' therefore represents an interlude in proceedings which began, and will finish, in a national court. Courts can obviously only decide issues raised by cases brought before them. The reference procedure has brought before the Court a host of issues which it might not otherwise have had a chance to consider and has enabled it to influence directly the application of Community law in the member states. References from national courts now often represent the largest category of cases brought before the Court in

Box 12.2 **Case study**
A new legal order

Van Gend en Loos v Nederlandse Administratie der Belastingen (1963)

A trader imported into the Netherlands from Germany a quantity of ureaformaldehyde. The Dutch authorities sought to apply an *ad valorem* import duty of 8 per cent, but the trader objected. He said that, on the date when the EEC Treaty entered into force, imports of ureaformaldehyde were charged with an import duty of only 3 per cent and that, by increasing the duty, the Netherlands had infringed what was then Article 12 of the Treaty. The dispute reached a Dutch court, which referred two questions to the Court. One of them asked whether a trader could rely on the Treaty in circumstances like these, an issue on which it was silent. In one of the most momentous declarations it has ever made, the Court observed:

the Community constitutes a new legal order of international law for the benefit of which the states have limited their sovereign rights, albeit within limited fields, and the subjects of which comprise not only Member States but also their nationals. Independently of the legislation of Member States, Community law therefore not only imposes obligations on individuals but is also intended to confer upon them rights which become part of their legal heritage. These rights arise not only where they are expressly granted by the Treaty, but also by reason of obligations which the Treaty imposes in a clearly defined way upon individuals as well as upon the Member States and upon the institutions of the Community.

The Court concluded that 'Article 12 must be interpreted as producing direct effects and creating individual rights which national courts must protect'.

a single year (see Box 12.2 for an example). At present, the CFI has no jurisdiction to give preliminary rulings, but the Treaty of Nice enables the Council to confer such jurisdiction on it.

Various types of question may be the subject of a reference to the Court for a preliminary ruling. The Court may be asked what the Treaty, or an act of one of the institutions, means. It may also be asked whether such an act is valid or not. References may in addition be made on whether a provision of Community law produces direct effect, that is, whether it confers rights on private parties (such as individuals and companies) which national courts must protect. This was made clear in a famous case decided in 1963 called *Van Gend en Loos* (see Box 12.2). Here a reference from a Dutch court led to a ruling that established that provisions of the EC Treaty were capable of producing direct effect. It was implicit in that conclusion that directly effective provisions of Community law would take precedence over inconsistent provisions of national law, an implication that the Court duly spelled out the following year in *Costa* v *ENEL*, a reference from an Italian court. Subsequent case law made it clear that all provisions of the Treaty that were unconditional and sufficiently clear to be suitable for

judicial application would have direct effect and that they might be enforceable not only against member states (so-called *vertical direct effect*) but also against private parties (so-called *horizontal direct effect*). The same is true of provisions contained in regulations. The provisions of directives are also capable of producing direct effect, but only in proceedings brought against public bodies. Because the Treaty says only that directives are binding on member states, the Court has concluded in a series of references that they cannot be enforced in the national courts against private parties. See Box 12.3.

If the Court in *Van Gend en Loos* had come to the opposite conclusion, that the effect of the Treaty in the national systems depended on the law of the country concerned, the Treaty would have had direct effect in some member states but not in others. The effect of such an outcome would have been to undermine the common (and later 'single') market, perhaps fatally. Although the Treaty was (and remains) silent on the question whether it produces direct effect, the importance of this should not be exaggerated. The Treaty was the product not of a legislative process but of diplomatic negotiations. It contains language on which the national delegations were able to reach agreement, but that is all. It

Box 12.3 **Core ideas**
The direct effect of directives

Faccini Dori v Recreb (1994)

Ms Faccini Dori concluded a contract at Milan Central Railway Station for an English language correspondence course. Some days later, she thought better of it and tried to cancel the contract. She relied on an EC directive on the protection of the consumer in respect of contracts concluded away from the seller's business premises. The directive would have given her a right of cancellation, but Italy had not transposed it into national law by the due date. The seller sued Ms Faccini Dori for the price of the course and the national court asked the Court whether individuals could rely on a directive in circumstances like these. The Court said they could not. The Treaty only made directives binding on the member states to which they were addressed. Only by way of regulation could the Community enact obligations for individuals, such as the seller, with immediate effect. The Court added, however, that any relevant national legislation should be interpreted in the light of the wording and purpose of the directive. Where that did not help, member states might sometimes be required to compensate individuals for loss suffered through failure to transpose a directive.

cannot be inferred that the delegations were all in agreement on the precise scope of each provision nor that the Treaty excluded issues that were not expressly mentioned. The principles of direct effect and precedence, which the preliminary rulings procedure gave the Court the opportunity to lay down, enabled the Community to break free from the traditional model of public international law in which treaty obligations only took effect between states. The preliminary ruling procedure forged a partnership between the Court of Justice and the national courts which juridified the process of implementing the EC Treaty and removed it from the realm of diplomatic negotiation.

A reference may be made by 'any court or tribunal of a Member State'. Whether a national body satisfies that description is a question of Community law for the Court of Justice itself to determine. The Court has traditionally taken a relatively broad view on the matter and has not regarded the body's status under national law as decisive. The relationship between the national court and the Court of Justice in reference proceedings is co-operative rather than hierarchical in nature. Both courts have distinct but complementary roles to play in finding a solution to the case which is consistent with Community law. It is for the national court to decide questions of national law and questions of fact and to apply the ruling to the dispute between the parties. This means that it is the national court, which in the last resort

decides whether national law satisfies the requirements of Community law. This is important because democratic states which respect the rule of law do not disregard judgments of their own courts. The role of the Court in the procedure is limited to answering the questions of Community law raised by the case which need to be decided before the national court can give judgment. (It is for this reason that the Court's ruling is described as 'preliminary'.) The answers given by the Court are couched in abstract terms, although in practice they sometimes leave the national court with little room for manoeuvre. The success of the procedure depends on the willingness of the national courts to apply loyally the rulings of the Court. The courts of some member states have sometimes proved reluctant to embrace wholeheartedly the case law of the Court. In France, for example, it was not until 1989 that the administrative courts accepted that Community law took precedence over inconsistent provisions of national law. In Germany, the Federal Constitutional Court has reserved the right, notably in its notorious *Maastricht* decision of 12 October 1993, to ensure that the Community institutions observe the limits of their powers and do not infringe the fundamental rights protected by the German Constitution. In practice, however, the Federal Constitutional Court appears to accept the precedence of Community law. By and large most national courts have played their part in the preliminary rulings procedure remarkably conscientiously (Alter 2001; Slaughter, Stone, and Weiler 1998).

The Treaty draws a distinction between courts whose decisions are subject to appeal in the national system and top courts whose decisions are final (either generally or in the specific case). Except where the validity of a Community act is at issue (see Box 12.4), lower courts have a discretion when there is a point of Community law that needs to be decided. They can either ask for a preliminary ruling or decide the point for themselves. Top courts have no discretion: they must refer such points to the Court of Justice. In principle, a lower national court is the sole judge of whether a reference is necessary and the relevance of the questions put to the Court. The Court originally took a very liberal attitude to questions referred to it, reformulating them if they were badly drafted or if they missed the point, doing its best to establish the background from the material submitted where the national court had not adequately explained it. This helped to establish a good working relationship with national judges and encouraged them to make use of the procedure. More recently, the growing volume of cases has led the Court to take a stricter approach: it will not now answer questions which are obviously irrelevant or where the referring court has not adequately explained the facts or the national legal context.

Although the language of the Treaty might suggest otherwise, the obligation to refer, imposed on top national courts, is not an absolute one. In the famous *CILFIT* case (1982), the Court of Justice held that a top court did not have to refer (although it remained free to do so) if: (a) the question at issue had already been dealt with in previous decisions of the Court; or (b) there could be no reasonable doubt about the answer to the question (a situation sometimes described as *acte clair*). Before reaching that conclusion, the national court had to be convinced that the matter would be equally obvious to the courts of other member states and to the Court of Justice. This meant taking account of the characteristic features of Community law and the special difficulties to which its interpretation gives rise. The Court mentioned in particular the fact that the different language versions of a Community provision are equally authentic and may have to be compared in order to establish its meaning. Some lawyers believe that the *CILFIT* test is too strict and that top national courts should be given greater leeway to decide points of Community law for themselves (Anderson 1995: 170–1). They point out that those courts comprise the most highly qualified national judges and that giving them greater discretion would reduce the burden on the ECJ. Others take the view that such a move would be undesirable because it would endanger the uniform application of

---

Box 12.4 **Core ideas**

Preliminary rulings on the validity of Community acts

The EC Treaty seems to give lower national courts the same discretion regardless of whether the question raised is one of interpretation or one of validity. However, in the controversial *Foto-Frost* case (1987), the Court held that national courts had no power to declare Community acts invalid because of the danger that measures intended to apply throughout the member states would be declared invalid in some but not in others. This means that where the validity of a Community measure is seriously questioned in national court proceedings and the issue needs to be resolved in order for judgment to be given, then a reference *must* be made. This is so regardless of whether or not the national court is one whose decisions are subject to

appeal. The only exception the Court has been prepared to recognize is where the national court has been asked to grant provisional relief pending final judgment in the case. The urgency of such cases might make it impractical to wait for a preliminary ruling, so the Court has accepted that national courts may declare Community acts invalid in such circumstances provided a number of strict conditions are met. Some commentators have objected to the ruling in *Foto-Frost* on the basis that it is incompatible with the Treaty (Hartley 1996: 100), but the reasoning underlying the conclusion reached by the Court seems persuasive.

Community law, especially with the enlargement of the Union imminent. There are also doubts about whether it would make much difference to the Court's workload. The question was raised during the 2000 **intergovernmental conference** (IGC), but no amendments were made to Article 234 at Nice.

Article 234 applies in a modified form under Title IV of Part Three of the EC Treaty, a section concerned with visas, asylum, immigration, and other policies related to the free movement of persons. In cases arising under that Title, top national courts have an obligation to refer but lower national courts have no power to do so. However, the Council, the Commission, or a member state may ask the Court for a ruling on a Title IV question independently of any specific case. The object of this variant of the procedure seems to be to protect the Court from the large number of immigration and asylum cases that come before the national courts, but the effect is to make the procedure less effective as a means of securing the uniform application of the law and the protection of individual rights. At the 2000 IGC, it was suggested that the Title IV variant of the procedure should be aligned with the classic version, but the suggestion was not pursued.

Direct actions

Direct actions are proceedings which start and finish in Luxembourg. Those brought by individuals and 'legal persons', such as companies, commence in the CFI and may proceed on appeal to the Court of Justice. Those brought by member states or Community institutions are at present considered only by the Court of Justice. Since **Maastricht**, the Council has had the power to transfer such actions to the CFI as well. That power has yet to be exercised because some member states have taken the view that direct actions brought by member states or Community institutions are more likely to raise constitutional issues or affect the validity of legislation of general application, questions which ought in their view to be the exclusive preserve of the Court. However, a declaration made at Nice makes it likely that that at least some such actions will soon be transferred to the CFI. Two of the main types of direct action are **infringement proceedings** against member states and the **action for annulment**.

Under traditional international law, disputes concerning infringements of a treaty are settled among the states party to it. A novel feature of the Community system is Article 226 (formerly Article 169) of the EC Treaty, which gives the Commission, an institution independent of the member states, the power to bring before the Court any member state which it believes has failed to fulfil an obligation the Treaty imposes on it (see Chapters 9 and 22). The Commission may become aware of a possible infringement of the Treaty by a member state through its own monitoring of the application of Community law or a complaint by a private party. The Commission relies heavily on such complaints and has, in collaboration with the European Ombudsman, developed a formalized system for processing them. The Commission is not, however, bound to pursue a complaint. If it declines to do so, its decision cannot be challenged in the Court of Justice. In its *White Paper on European Governance* (2001a: 26), the European Commission undertook to draw up criteria for prioritizing suspected infringements and to codify the administrative rules on handling complaints.

If the Commission decides to pursue a possible infringement, the Treaty requires it to follow a lengthy procedure, involving not just a judicial phase but also a pre-judicial or administrative phase in which the Commission informs the state concerned of the essence of the case against it and gives it an opportunity to submit observations. If the Commission is not satisfied with the state's response, it issues a reasoned opinion laying down a deadline for compliance. If that deadline expires without the requisite steps having been taken, the Commission may then, and only then, initiate proceedings before the Court.

Where an application is made to the Court, the Commission will be required to prove that the obligation in question has not been fulfilled. As long as the Commission has complied with the procedural requirements of the Treaty, the essential question is whether, objectively speaking, the situation prevailing in the member state concerned complies with Community law. The only subjective defence open to a member state is that any failure to comply with its obligations is due to *force majeure*, that is, to some unpredictable and overwhelming catastrophe that made compliance impossible. If the Commission's application to the Court is successful, the Court will declare that the state concerned has failed to fulfil its obligations under the Treaty. The state is required by the Treaty to take the steps necessary to comply with the judgment.

The vast majority of the cases in which infringement proceedings are brought are settled before they are referred to the Court of Justice, which suggests that the threat of court proceedings is usually enough to secure compliance. However, the 1980s saw a marked increase in the number of cases brought against member states for failing to comply with previous rulings against them, a development which may have been attributable to the increased enthusiasm shown by the Commission between the late 1970s and the early 1990s for pursuing delinquent states. At Maastricht, the Court was therefore given a power to impose financial sanctions on member states which fail to comply with rulings finding them to have infringed the Treaty. The power is only triggered, however, if the Commission brings the matter back to the Court: no sanctions may be imposed in the initial proceedings under Article 226. Rather surprisingly, the Treaty does not set any limit to the amount of the sanction that may be imposed; but nor does it lay down any mechanism for dealing with states which refuse to pay up.

By the time the Maastricht Treaty was signed, the Court had held in the famous *Francovich* case, decided in 1991 under the preliminary rulings procedure, that a member state had to compensate individuals for damage caused by a breach of Community law for which it was responsible. That ruling deprived the new Treaty rule on financial penalties of much of its significance, though there remain some situations where the *Francovich* principle is unlikely to have much effect. For example, the conditions laid down by the Court before liability arises may not be met; the loss suffered by a potential claimant may be too small to justify the cost of bringing proceedings; it may be hard to prove that the breach was the cause of the claimant's loss; or it may not be desirable to wait for a willing litigant to emerge. In circumstances such as these, the Court's power to impose a financial penalty might prove useful. There is also evidence that the threat of such a

penalty can induce reluctant member states to comply with their obligations.

It would have been incompatible with the legal traditions of the six original member states (Mackenzie Stuart 1977: 11–14) and with the rule of law for the exercise, by the Community institutions, of their lawmaking powers to have escaped judicial control. Article 230 (formerly Article 173) of the EC Treaty therefore establishes a procedure known as the action for annulment under which the Court may review the legality of any acts adopted by other institutions which are intended to have legal effects. The Treaty did not originally provide for acts of the EP to be challenged. However, the Court held in *Les Verts* v *Parliament* (1986) that it would be inconsistent with the spirit of the Treaty for measures adopted by the Parliament which produced legal effects to be immune from challenge in annulment proceedings. An early beneficiary of that decision was the Council which, with the support of three member states, successfully challenged the way in which the Parliament had exercised its budgetary powers. At Maastricht, the member states amended the Treaty to reflect the decision in *Les Verts*. To succeed in an annulment action, the applicant must show that the disputed act is unlawful. The grounds on which this may be done are set out in Article 230 and are derived from French administrative law. Where one of those grounds is successfully established, the Court will declare the disputed act void. The defendant institution must then do whatever is necessary to comply with the judgment.

Various categories of applicant may being annulment proceedings. The distinction between the members of each category lies in the nature of the interest they must show in order to establish their right to bring an action. Lawyers call this 'standing' or *locus standi* and it is entirely separate from the merits of the action. It is a device that is common in national legal systems. Its purpose is to prevent the courts from being swamped and the business of government disrupted by large numbers of challenges to the validity of legislation. It can be hard to strike the right balance between these considerations and the rule of law, and the strictness of rules on standing are liable to be the subject of controversy. This is particularly true in the context of the EC Treaty, which does not require the member states, the EP, the Council, or the Commission to satisfy any rules on standing at all, but which imposes strict standing requirements on private applicants, such as individuals, interest groups, and companies. The approach of the Community Courts to the interpretation of those requirements has not been entirely consistent: the general effect of case law is to make it extremely difficult for private applicants to challenge acts other that decisions addressed to them (Arnull 1999: 40–9). Where private applicants clearly lack standing to seek the annulment of a Community act in Luxembourg, it may be possible for them to contest the validity of the act concerned in the national courts. A national court which believes that such a challenge may be well founded must refer the matter to the Court of Justice (see Box 12.4).

The case law of the Community Courts on standing has been rather slow to catch up with developments in many national systems, where corresponding rules have been progressively relaxed. The strictness of the Court contrasts strikingly with the importance it has attached to enabling individuals to assert their rights against member states. How can this be explained? Stein and Vining (1976: 222) have argued that '[t]he Community is a body at the borderline between the federal and the international and in international law the very notion of an individual having independent standing to sue before an international tribunal is little short of revolutionary'. Moreover, too many challenges to the validity of Community acts during the long period

of stagnation which ran from the mid-1960s to the early 1980s could have seriously disrupted the proper functioning of the Community. However, neither of those explanations remains convincing in 21st-century Europe. The Court has justified its continuing strictness on the basis that any reform of the system currently in force ought to be effected by way of Treaty amendment.

Key points

- The preliminary rulings procedure enables national courts to ask the Court of Justice for guidance on points of Community law which they have to decide before giving judgment.

- Direct actions are actions that begin and end in Luxembourg.

- Two of the main types of direct action are infringement proceedings and actions for annulment.

- In infringement proceedings, the Commission may bring proceedings before the Court against member states which it considers to be in breach of their obligations under the Treaty. The outcome of the proceedings will depend on whether, objectively speaking, the legal position within the state concerned is compatible with the Treaty.

- Actions for annulment enable the Community Courts to review the legality of binding Community acts.

The 'judicial activism' debate

In a modern democracy, the basic function of the courts is to apply and enforce the rules and policy choices made by a legislature composed of elected politicians. However, it is impossible to predict the full range of circumstances in which judges will be asked to apply the law, so cases will inevitably arise for which the rules laid down by the legislature do not expressly provide. There may also be cases

where the strict application of those rules would produce injustice or a result contrary to the legislature's policy objectives. Deciding such cases is a difficult task for all courts. The Court has sometimes been criticized for pursuing an agenda of its own regarding the political shape of Europe, disregarding the terms of the Treaties where they have seemed to stand in the way of its own conception of what

Europe requires. That view was first developed at length by Rasmussen (1986), who sought to show that excessive activism on the part of the Court was threatening to undermine its authority and legitimacy. Rasmussen's thesis attracted powerful dissent, but a further assault on the Court was made by Neill (1995), who argued that many of its decisions were 'logically flawed or skewed by doctrinal or idiosyncratic policy considerations'. Among the cases he singled out for comment were *Van Gend en Loos, Costa* v *ENEL, Foto-Frost, Francovich,* and *Les Verts.* The British and German governments advanced similar criticisms in the run-up to the Treaty of Amsterdam, though without any significant effect on the Treaty itself.

Much criticism of the Court for excessive activism lacks conviction because it is based on misunderstanding of the nature of the role the Court has been given, and of the issues with which it has been confronted, and a limited and unrepresentative selection of rulings. Cases such as *Faccini Dori,* which illustrate the Court's capacity for restraint, are rarely given the same degree of prominence by critics. Indeed, there are some cases which might, depending on the commentator's perspective, be presented as examples of either activism or restraint. A better description of the Court's overall approach would be radically conservative. The Court's inventiveness has been most apparent in devising mechanisms, such as direct effect, precedence, and the liability of member states in damages, which are consistent with the spirit of the Treaty and enhance its capacity to achieve its objectives. On matters of economic and social policy, however, the Court has been much more willing to defer to policy choices made by the member states, at least where they have acted in a proportionate and non-discriminatory manner (Arnull 1999: 564). A similar view was taken by the House of Lords Select Committee on the European Communities, which observed in its report on the 1996 IGC:

A strong and independent Court of Justice is an essential part of the structure of the European Union. We agree with those witnesses who stressed the important role of the Court in the consolidation of democratic structures and upholding the rule of law in the European Community. We note the criticisms of 'judicial activism' which have been levelled against the Court but these appear to be based mainly on cases where the Court has made Community law effective against defaulting Member States at the instance of individuals seeking to enforce their rights. We accept that enforceable remedies are essential to the application of Community legal obligations, with a high degree of uniformity throughout the Member States (House of Lords 1995: 65).

Key points

- In a modern democracy, the basic function of the courts is to apply and enforce the rules and policy choices made by a legislature composed of elected politicians.

- Cases will inevitably arise for which the rules laid down by the legislature do not expressly provide. There may also be cases where the strict application of those rules would produce injustice or a result contrary to the legislature's policy objectives. Deciding such cases is a difficult task for all courts.

- The Court has sometimes been criticized for pursuing an agenda of its own about the political shape of Europe, disregarding the terms of the Treaties where they have seemed to stand in the way of its own conception of what Europe requires.

- Much of such criticism lacks conviction because it is based on misunderstanding of the nature of the role the Court has been given, and of the issues with which it has been confronted, and a limited and unrepresentative selection of rulings.

Conclusion: Reforming the Union's judicial architecture

Like many national courts, the Court of Justice has had to deal with a steadily growing workload. As Table 12.1 shows, the volume of new cases brought has outpaced increases in the Court's productivity. As a result, the number of cases pending at the end of each year and the average duration of proceedings have grown significantly. Moreover, the capacity of the CFI to cope with its own workload is now giving cause for concern.

The inexorable growth in the number of new cases shows no sign of abating. The jurisdiction of the Court was widened at Amsterdam and the Union itself is on the verge of a major enlargement. New legislation, such as the regulation on the Community trade mark (Regulation 40/94), is generating extra categories of dispute which seem likely in time to impose significant additional burdens on the Courts. The commencement of the third stage of EMU is also liable to entail an increase in proceedings. To help the Community Courts cope with the demands being placed on them, the member states reached agreement at Nice on a series of provisions that seem likely to lead to significant changes in the Union's judicial architecture, which faces an almost permanent process of review and reform in the years ahead. Among the changes which can be anticipated as a result of the Treaty of Nice, the following are particularly worthy of note:

- the conferral of a limited preliminary rulings jurisdiction on the CFI, with provision for review by the Court where the unity or consistency of Community law is at issue;

Table 12.1 The workload of the Court of Justice

	1980	1990	2000
Cases brought	279	384	503
Cases completed	206	302	526
Cases pending	328	583	873
Average duration of proceedings (months and tenths of months):			
• references (in addition to the time taken in the national court)	9.0	17.4	21.6
• direct actions	18.0	25.5	23.9
• appeals	—	—	19.0

Sources: Court of Justice website; Millett (1990: 2).

- the transfer to the CFI of some direct actions brought by member states and perhaps also by Community institutions;

- the appointment of additional judges to the CFI;

- the creation of judicial panels to deal with disputes between the Community and its employees (which currently go to the CFI) and possibly other classes of action, such as cases generated by the Community trade mark regulation. Decisions of judicial panels might be subject to appeal to the CFI. In exceptional cases, the decision of the CFI might be subject to review by the Court of Justice;

- the introduction of a system for filtering appeals from the CFI to give the Court of Justice discretion in deciding whether to accept them.

It will be possible for these reforms to be made without further Treaty amendment, but the details are likely to prove controversial.

QUESTIONS

1 Describe the process followed in the Court of Justice in deciding cases. What are the strengths and weaknesses of that process?

2 Are the members of the Community Courts sufficiently protected from outside pressure to safeguard their independence?

3 What is the significance of the statement by the Court in the *Van Gend en Loos* case that 'the Community constitutes a new legal order of international law'?

4 How important has the preliminary rulings procedure been in enabling the Court to develop the legal framework within which the European Community operates?

5 What legal consequences may ensue if a member state fails to comply with its Treaty obligations?

6 What importance has the Court of Justice attached to the rights of individuals in its case law?

7 Do you agree with critics of the Court of Justice who have accused it of excessive activism?

8 Why was the CFI established? How successful has it been? What changes in its role may be anticipated?

GUIDE TO FURTHER READING

Alter, K., *Establishing the Supremacy of European Law: The Making of an International Rule of Law in Europe* (Oxford: Oxford University Press, 2001). Examines the relationship between the national courts and the Court of Justice and its contribution to the emergence of an international rule of law in Europe.

Arnull, A., *The European Union and its Court of Justice* (Oxford: Oxford University Press, 1999). A detailed analysis of the contribution of the Court to shaping the legal framework within which the EU operates.

Brown, L., and Kennedy, T., *Brown and Jacobs' The Court of Justice of the European Communities*, 5th edn (London: Sweet & Maxwell, 2000). A guide to the organization and composition of the Community Courts, their jurisdiction, and their practice and procedure.

Dehousse, R., *The European Court of Justice: The Politics of Judicial Integration* (Basingstoke: Macmillan, 1998). A non-technical examination of the political context of some of the landmark decisions of the Court.

Hartley, T., *The Foundations of European Community Law*, 4th edn (Oxford: Oxford University Press, 1998). An exhaustive analysis of the powers of the Court and the relationship between Community law and national law.

Rasmussen, H., *On Law and Policy in the European Court of Justice* (Dordrecht: Nijhoff, 1986). The first extended attempt to show that excessive activism on the part of the Court was threatening to undermine its authority and legitimacy.

WEB LINKS

http://curia.eu.int/index.htm The official website of the Community Courts.

www.jeanmonnetprogram.org/ Joint website of the European University Institute, New York University School of Law, and the Harvard Law School Jean Monnet Program, offering access to a range of materials including a useful series of working papers.

www.fd.unl.pt/je/index.htm A comprehensive source of information on European law, including the law of the member states, with links to the most important databases on European and national case law and legislation.

13 Interest groups and the European Union

Rainer Eising

READER'S GUIDE

This chapter examines the role of interest groups in the EU in the context of the broad system of **interest intermediation** that now exists at European level. It also considers the way in which the EU as a political institution influences interest group structure and activity in both European and domestic political arenas. The chapter begins with a brief overview of the relationship between the EU institutions and interest organizations, and examines the steps taken thus far to regulate that relationship. It then looks at the structure of the system, focusing in particular on two salient aspects: the difference between national and EU organizations; and the difference between business and non-business interests. Finally, the chapter addresses the **Europeanization** of interest intermediation (see also Chapter 21) to question how EU membership may have altered the structure and activities of domestic interest groups.

Introduction

The EU's institutions do not make policy in a vacuum, and the links that they have with **civil society** take many different forms. Intermediary organizations, such as interest groups, have a particularly important role to play in connecting European-level institutions to the citizens of the

EU. Indeed, the European Commission recently counted over 900 interest organizations operating in Brussels. Given the extent of this activity, the organization and function of these groups would seem worthy of analysis.

Interest groups have always been regarded as 'Janus-faced' creatures, in that they look towards both state and society. They are sometimes regarded as 'factions' that serve to undermine the general interest, as pursued by the elected representatives of the people. But interest groups are also seen as indispensable, not only because they give a voice to citizens between elections, but also because they serve as 'schools for democracy', socializing citizens as political beings, and contributing to the formation of a general will out of the specific concerns of groups. Perspectives such as these are important markers in the study of interest organization in the EU. Early on, Caporaso (1974) criticized European interest organizations for pursuing only very narrowly defined interests and thereby undermining the **legitimacy** and **accountability** of the European institutions. By contrast, other authors have asserted that interest organizations offer European civil society the potential to participate in EU policy making and institution-building (Heinelt 1998).

Before we proceed to evaluate these contradictory views on the role of interest groups, the following sections set out the broad terrain of EU **interest intermediation**. The first section highlights the institutional setting, and the second, the efforts that the EU institutions have made to regulate access by interest organizations. The third section summarizes the structure of the EU interest group system, while the fourth discusses how the EU may have affected the structure and functions of domestic interest groups, through a process which is now referred to as Europeanization.

The EU institutions and interest groups

According to **institutional theory**, political institutions, such as the EU, shape the behaviour of interest organizations. They shape the formation, the role, and the functions of interest groups as well as the strategies and tactics they use to exert influence on political decisions. Thus, although EU institutions do not *determine* political action, they are important, and for this reason this chapter begins by considering interest groups from the perspective of the EU's institutional setting. Four characteristics of the EU are particularly relevant in this context. First, the EU is a highly dynamic system; second, the EU is also a very complex system; third, the EU is a multi-level system; and fourth, the EU is a system that privileges consensus building. All of these characteristics affect how interest groups have sought to influence the European institutions. See Box 13.1.

Since the mid-1980s, the EC (and after 1993, the EU) has extended its competences far beyond market integration, to include areas such as environmental policy, justice and home affairs, and foreign and security policy. This steady accretion of functions gives some indication of the dynamism that now characterizes the European political agenda. This has had three important consequences for interest groups. First, over time, the number of groups operating at European level has steadily increased. Many of these groups were set up as a direct response to the expansion of European regulation and the growing powers of the European institutions, and, as such, were a reaction to or even anticipated EU policy initiatives. In a number of cases, the formation of European interest groups triggered responses from competing interests, which led to even more groups being established. Second, and as a consequence of this proliferation of new organizations, the interest group landscape in the EU has become much more diverse. Not only business interests, but also more diffuse social interests, now organize in the European political arena. Finally, because

Box 13.1 **Core ideas**
Lobbies and interest groups

The literature on EU interest groups rests on a body of research in the field of Comparative Politics. In this literature, non-governmental organizations (NGOs) are defined in very different ways. Lobbies, pressure groups, interest groups, and interest organizations are the terms most commonly used.

The term 'lobbyist' originates in the nineteenth century, when individuals waiting in the parliamentary lobby exerted influence on members of legislatures to pass bills on behalf of unknown customers. Lobbying was then almost exclusively regarded as a commercial activity. Later, attempts by organizations to influence public bodies were also included in this definition. Since the 1920s, the term 'pressure group' has increasingly been used in the political science literature, on the understanding that it is a familiar term needing little explanation. Its meaning comes close to that of a lobby group in that it centres on the capacity of these groups to influence—or put pressure on—Congress/Parliament or Government. The term 'interest group', its primary contender, refers to the underlying rationale of these groups and has less negative connotations. Members join groups as they share common attitudes, or interests (Truman 1972: 34). These interests include 'frames of reference for interpreting and evaluating' as well as 'attitudes toward what is needed or wanted in a given situation, observable as demands or claims upon other groups in the society' (Truman 1972: 33–9). While reserving the term 'political interest group' for those groups that place demands on public bodies, Truman often uses the term interchangeably with 'interest groups'. In several accounts, individual actors, such as large firms, are also regarded as interest groups, even though, strictly speaking, the term does not apply because they do not have members. 'Interest Organizations' refers to interest groups that are highly formalized. It highlights the fact that organizations imply continuity, they cope with complexity by means of differentiation. It also draws attention away from particular leaders and members, and towards the effects of organizational form.

interest organizations find it difficult to forecast short-term political developments in the EU and are therefore quite often uncertain about political options and stakes, particularly in the early phases of the policy process, they have no option but to devote considerable resources to monitoring EU developments.

The EU is also an extremely complex **polity**, which means that the relative importance of interest groups varies substantially across policy areas. In the first pillar of the EU, the European Community (EC) pillar (see Figure 4.2), interest groups have relatively good access to the European institutions. This is much less the case in the EU's other two pillars, which cover common foreign and security policy (CFSP) and police and judicial co-operation in criminal matters (formerly justice and home affairs). These second and third pillars operate more intergovernmentally, and, as such, involve much less input from the Commission, the European Parliament (EP), and the European Courts. This allows

member governments to prevent interest groups from gaining access to the EU policy process. For example, during the development of the EU's refugee and asylum policy in the early 1990s, Amnesty International complained that it was shut out of EU decision making to the extent that 'virtually all agreements and policy proposals ... [were] drafted behind closed doors in meetings of government officials' (van der Klaauw 1994: 279).

For most interest groups, then, the EC pillar provides the greatest potential for access to the EU institutions, not least because it comprises the vast majority of the Union's regulatory and distributive policies. And within the EC, the European Commission is the most important point of contact for interest groups. The Commission's monopoly over policy initiation in this pillar (see Chapter 9: 132) grants the Commission a crucial role in agenda setting and policy formulation. And as the EU's 'guardian of treaties', the Commission also has an important role to play in monitoring compliance with Community law by member-state and non-state (or private) actors. However, interest groups will rarely approach the Commission as a collegiate body. Rather, they tend to maintain relations with one or more Commission departments, the Directorates-General (DGs).

The EP is less important for interest groups as it does not wield as much power as either the European Commission or the EU Council, despite the much more important role it now plays in EU policy making (see Chapter 11). While the EP is likely to be more amenable to national pressures than the European Commission, its influence varies according to the issue at hand and the decision-making procedure that applies (see Chapter 1: 3–7). Within the Parliament, the heads of the Standing Committees and the *rapporteurs* responsible for particular dossiers are the most important addressees for interest group demands. And as parliamentarians are elected, they are said to be more open to 'weak' (or what are often called 'diffuse') interests, including those representing the environment, consumers, or large groups such as the unemployed and pensioners. As a consequence, some analysts regard the links forged between interest groups and Members of the European Parliament (MEPs) as 'coalitions of the weak' (Kohler-Koch 1997: 6–7).

Owing to its pivotal position, the EU Council is a highly relevant contact for interest groups. However, the Council and its administrative machinery, the Committee of Permanent Representatives (Coreper) and the Council Working Groups (see Chapter 10), are rarely lobbied directly. Rather, domestic interest groups tend to address their concerns to particular government departments, representing specific sectoral interests at national level. While the Council's policy positions evolve along national lines, in part as a consequence of pressure by domestic interests, the European Council is more removed from interest group pressure. Not only does the European Council comprise the heads of state and government, thus representing the general interest to a greater degree, but it also meets formally only once every six months, lessening its impact on the minutiae of day-to-day politics in the EU.

As the EU's judiciary, the European Court of Justice (ECJ) monitors compliance with and inter-

prets EU law. European law takes precedence over national law and grants rights to individual citizens that national courts must uphold (see Hix 1999: 108). As a consequence, the preliminary rulings procedure (see Chapter 12: 182), which offers a channel for national courts to refer questions of European law to the ECJ, allows interest groups to challenge the compatibility of domestic and EU law. This was pointed out by Jill Lovecy in her study of the liberalization of professional services in the EU. Lovecy concluded that access to the ECJ allowed individual members of the professions to challenge, in some cases successfully, restrictive national practices. Ultimately, litigation led to policy change 'by the back door' because it involved issues which both national governments and the EU had earlier refused to discuss or amend (Lovecy 1999). However, in practice, to take a case to the European Court usually demands that a body of EU law already exists. And even where this is the case, the outcome of such action is uncertain, the financial costs heavy, and the duration of the case generally lengthy, which means that this avenue is clearly not available to all citizens and interest groups, and will only be worthwhile when the stakes are felt to be especially high.

Finally, the Economic and Social Committee (ESC) is a rather distinctive institution in this context, as it was set up to channel the opinions of organized interests within the European policy process. The ESC is a tripartite body composed of individual members representing employers, workers, and other interests. Even so, it is generally considered to be of marginal importance for the representation of interests within the EU. Direct contacts between the EU institutions and interest organizations are now much more important than this institutionalized forum for interest intermediation. In this context, at least, much the same may be said of the Committee of the Regions (CoR) (though see Chapter 18: 280–2).

Policy making in the EU is not confined to the European institutions, however. Individually, the 15 member states also have an important say in decisions taken by the Union. The EU is increasingly regarded as a multi-level system (Marks and Hooghe 2001; Benz 2001; see also Chapter 8: 120–1) implying that many different public actors located at different territorial levels within the EU share political authority. As none of the EU institutions, nor any of the member states, is entirely in control of decision making, multiple points of access are open to interest organizations. Groups must take heed of political developments at both the European and national levels and need to be present at both levels (as well as in any relevant regional and local political arenas) if they hope to see their interests well represented and defended. This holds all the more, as many EU policy measures need to be transposed into national law and must be implemented at the national level. They also need to ensure that their strategies are co-ordinated across each level. But while in principle, 'interest groups at any territorial level are free to lobby government [and parliament] at any number of levels' (Constantelos 1996: 30), in reality they are far from being fully mobile. This is because they are tied to their local, regional, national, or European memberships in one form or another, and must also make sure that they use their resources as efficiently as they can. As we might expect, EU interest groups are much more involved than national groups in policy making at the EU level, while national groups dominate in the domestic political arena. The only real exceptions are very large firms that are truly mobile (see Eising 2004).

Box 13.2 presents a case study of one interest group—the British Union for the Abolition of Vivisection (BUAV)—and its activities in the late 1980s at EU level.

Owing to the complexity of the EU's political system with its emphasis on power-sharing groups, and also as a consequence of the unpredictability of the EU policy agenda, EU institutions and member states prefer to strive for consensus over political decisions taken at European level (see Katzenstein 1997). For member states, this reliance on consensual decision making guarantees some protection against being outvoted in the EU Council. However, even though it may increase the **legitimacy** of EU policy, consensual decision making may ultimately result in suboptimal policy outcomes, outcomes that satisfy no one. Decision making by consensus, rather

---

Box 13.2 **Case study**

The initiative against the testing of cosmetics on animals

At the end of the 1980s, the Commission planned to amend the EU cosmetics directive to improve product information and to implement the goals of the single market. But its draft proposals had the potential to increase animal testing for cosmetics. The British Union for the Abolition of Vivisection (BUAV) organized a coalition at the EU level against certain aspects of the proposal. The coalition initiated an EU-wide public campaign and collected more than 2.5 million signatures in support of a ban on the testing of cosmetics on animals. Lobbying at the EU level concentrated mainly in the EP and the Commission. The public campaign and a demonstration of 4,000 supporters in Brussels led to the full endorsement of these demands by the EP. In negotiations with the EP, the Commission was also prepared to accept the idea of an animal test ban, subject to certain conditions. But the 'Coalition's armoury . . . [became] depleted and it began to lose momentum' when negotiations shifted to the Council and into the member states (Fisher 1994: 236). This weakened the animal protection character of the Commission proposal. In late 1992, the Council agreed on a substantially weakened ban from 1998 onwards and rejected any further EP amendments to its position without further discussion.

However, the difficulties the BUAV had in exerting influence must be seen in light of national practices. At the national level, the BUAV was able to obtain only limited access to the British government. It 'had been unsuccessful in securing the support of the UK government on this issue and was also at loggerheads with the UK trade association' for cosmetics. The BUAV was therefore 'struck by the accessibility of the European Parliament and Commission and the openness of its officials compared to the UK' (Fisher 1994: 231–2). The EU institutions can be an important alternative channel of access for those organizations that find it difficult to access national political institutions. Moreover, the partial success of the BUAV campaign also led to a greater geographic impact than any purely national campaign would have had.

than on the basis of a majority, implies that EU institutions try to take the opinions of interest groups into account in their negotiations. They do so often for pragmatic reasons. If this were not the case, groups opposed to legislation might find it easier to build coalitions of likeminded actors and institutions against initiatives, ultimately blocking agreements. Yet, despite the norm of consensus, national groups can no longer rely on the national veto in the EU Council as a last resort, given that the use of **qualified majority voting** (QMV) has been extended dramatically since the mid-1980s (see Chapter 10: 154–7).

Key points

- Political institutions, such as the EU, influence interest group behaviour.

- The EU institutional setting (its dynamic political agenda; its complexity, its multi-level character; and its reliance on consensus) shapes patterns of interest intermediation within the EU.

- There are multiple points of access to the EU policy process, including the Commission, the Parliament, the Council, and the Court.

The regulation of interest groups in the EU

The EU is very open to interest groups, to the extent that the European institutions consider interest group involvement to be essential in the development of legitimate and appropriate EU policies. The Commission emphasized this point in its communication, 'An Open and Structured Dialogue with Interest Groups' in the early 1990s (European Commission 1992*b*: 2), with the Commission reiterating this view in a later communication on its relations with NGOs (European Commission 2000*a*), and in its 2001 White Paper on Governance (European Commission 2001*a*: 14–15). Contacts with interest groups range from informal ad hoc meetings to more formal arrangements (European Commission 2000*a*) and vary according to the practices of different parts of the Commission. Efforts at regulating EU-level interest intermediation have not sought to restrict political access, but to improve transparency and establish minimum standards. There are as yet no uniform rules on the participation of interest groups in the European policy process.

Owing to their divergent functions, the European Commission and the EP have rather different perspectives on this matter. Subject to electoral pressure and public scrutiny, the EP regards interest group influence as potentially problematic. Indeed, concern about the lack of transparency involved in interest group influence, and about the 'misbehaviour' of interest groups in the EP led to calls for their regulation (Greenwood 1997: 80–99). After a lengthy debate in 1996, the EP decided to establish a register of interest groups. After registration and on acceptance of a code of conduct, interest representatives receive a pass that eases access to the EP and is valid for a year, though it does not really grant any more rights than a normal citizen of the EU might get. Along similar lines, MEPs are obliged to indicate their paid activities and the donations they receive, clarifying any relationship they might have with groups outside the Parliament.

Unlike the EP, the Commission prefers to apply existing administrative rules to interest groups, and to operate on the basis of self-regulatory principles. Thus, the Commission has encouraged professional consultancies to develop codes of conduct that satisfy some minimum standards (European Commission 1992*b*: Appendix II), and it also put together a directory of EU-level interest groups. In contrast to the EP, the Commission did not approve of the accreditation of interest groups, as it felt that this would impede open access to EU policy makers (European Commission 2000*a*: 12). Only in its 2001 White Paper on Governance did the Commission envisage more extensive partnership arrangements and a stronger role for some groups (under certain conditions) as co-regulators (European Commission 2001*a*: 17, 21). However, thus far neither regulation by the EP nor requests for self-regulation by the Commission have had much of an impact on the practice and organization of EU-level interest intermediation.

Key points

- The EU institutions do not regulate interest group activity in any comprehensive way.

- The European Commission and the EP have introduced some initiatives in this area, but they differ in their approach.

European interest groups

There are a huge number of interest organizations operating at the level of the EU. In the second half of the 1990s, 320 firms, 131 national interest groups, 135 regional bodies, 142 public affairs firms, 160 legal firms, 46 chambers of commerce, and 14 think-tanks had set up offices in the vicinity of the EU institutions (Rucht 2000: 198). In its directory

of EU-level interest groups, which appeared in March 2000, the Secretariat-General of the European Commission listed over 900 such organizations (see Figure 13.1).

The EU institutions are important to interest groups because they influence their environment and activities, or those of their members, through

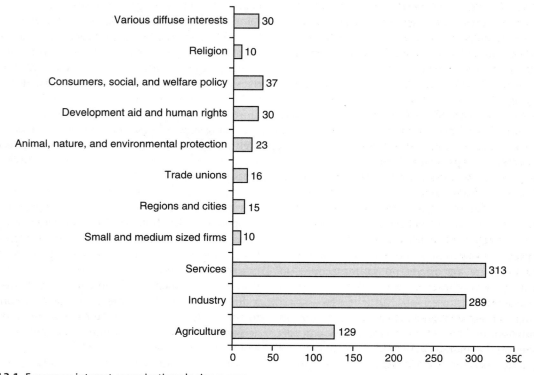

Fig. 13.1 European interest organizations by issue area

the formulation and implementation of European public policy. Conversely, interest groups are important to the EU institutions for a number of reasons. They define, aggregate, and articulate the interests of their members or their constituencies, making it easier for the European institutions to monitor social change and take on board new political concerns. Moreover, the EU institutions (and especially the Commission) rely on the special expertise of interest groups in the design of public policy. The Commission consults groups because it has only limited in-house resources and needs to draw on external sources of information and advice in order to perform its policy functions effectively. Involving interest groups in policy making is also important because the support and legitimacy of EU policy increases if the opinions of groups and their members are taken into account. In a few cases, interest groups are even allowed to formulate the policy themselves. As **social partners**, the European Trade Union Congress (ETUC), the Federation of European Industry (UNICE), and the federation representing European public-sector firms (CEEP) have been given this right in the field of EU social policy. But even where the formal role of interest organizations is less substantial, interest groups can be important implementers of European public policy. In this respect, they are sometimes considered as more democratic, more decentralized, more effective, and less bureaucratic instruments of policy implementation than public administration.

There are various ways of classifying interest groups, such as according to type, number, or the homogeneity of their members. Here, two criteria are considered in greater detail because they have particularly important implications for the EU policy process. In the first section, the differences and similarities between EU and national groups are discussed; while in the second and third sections, business and non-business interest groups are compared.

EU and national groups

It is important to distinguish national from EU-level interest groups (the latter are sometimes called 'Euro-groups), first because their organizations differ and second, because they pursue different strategies when representing their interests. EU interest groups provide expertise and arguments which they use to persuade the EU institutions of the merits of their case. National associations tend to represent their interests to national members of the EU institutions as well as to their national administrations and governments and in so doing they emphasize the *national* character of their interests whenever appropriate. Typically, EU interest groups are usually composed of national associations, rather than having a direct membership of individuals. About two-thirds of EU interest organizations are in fact federations of national interest groups, while the remainder either have a direct membership of other organizations (such as firms), or combine these two elements (Aspinwall and Greenwood 1998). An example of the latter is the European Chemical Association (CEFIC), which brings together both national associations and individual firms.

Generally, EU associations have fewer functions than their national members, and as a consequence their resources are much smaller. To different degrees, they serve to create links among their memberships, to provide and distribute information on EU activities, and to promote the interests of their members (Lindberg 1963: 98). Compared to national associations they concentrate to a greater extent on the *representation of interests* rather than on the *provision of services* for their members. This high degree of specialization can limit their capacity to steer their members' behaviour. Moreover, owing to the multinational make-up of their membership and the heterogeneity of the national settings covered by these bodies, EU groups often have real difficulty in reaching agreement internally on important policy questions. As in the EU institutions, **unanimity** rules or **qualified majority** thresholds guarantee that national interests are taken into account as groups seek to establish common positions.

Despite these differences, a fairly elaborate division of labour has evolved between the EU associations and their national counterparts. European interest groups are far more visible at the level of the EU than are national associations (Eising 2004) and have over time become important intermediaries between their national members and the EU institutions.

Business interests

At first sight, the EU interest group system looks broadly **pluralist** (see Schmitter and Streeck 1991). Both the number of groups and their huge variety suggest that a great many interests are represented in the EU institutions. Usually, no interest group enjoys a clear monopoly of representation in any one policy area. Of the 129 EU groups present in the agricultural sector, for example, many reflect particular product specializations. Some of these compete and bargain not only with groups across neighbouring policy areas, such as with environmental or consumer policy, but also with other groups within the agricultural domain. Coalitions are generally fluid and depend on shared interests. However, as is usual in advanced industrial countries, business interest organizations outnumber non-business interests (see Figure 13.1). About 82 per cent of the EU organizations listed on the Commission's database may be categorized as producer or employer interest organizations. In that, the EU does not appear to differ much from Germany where about 74 per cent of the interest groups are of an economic nature (see Sebaldt 1996) or the United States where about 76 per cent of groups represent producer or employer interests (see King and Walker 1991: 59). Box 13.3 presents some examples of business interest groups.

Business interests responded quickly to the European integration process. UNICE, the Union of Industrial and Employers' Confederations of Europe, which is the European 'peak association' of national producers' and employers' associations for private firms, was set up as early as 1958. The equivalent public-sector association, the CEEP (Centre Européen des Entreprises Publics) followed soon after, in 1961. Both of these bodies have been accorded the privileged status of a **social partner** in the EU (see Chapter 17: 274). A third body, EUROCHAMBRES, the federation of the chambers of commerce in the European Union, representing small and medium-sized enterprises (SMEs), was also founded in 1958. Eight other cross-sectoral associations also draw their membership from small and medium-sized firms. Beside these EU federations, there are a number of cross-sectoral associations that have a direct membership of firms. For example, the American

Chamber of Commerce (AmCham) represents the European Council of American Chambers of Commerce and a total of 18,000 US firms. And in 1997, the European Round Table of Industrialists was composed of around 50 executives of leading European firms. The Round Table was particularly influential in pushing for acceptance of the Single Market Programme in the mid-1980s (Cowles 1997; see also Chapter 3: 42–3).

The involvement of large firms in direct membership organizations (rather than in federations) may undermine the ability of associations to aggregate their members' interests and discipline their members' behaviour. However, the EU institutions may prefer to co-operate with these kinds of organizations as they are able to agree on common positions more easily than the EU federations. Indeed, large firms are becoming increasingly important in the interest group landscape, as is clear when we look at the restructuring of associations since the 1980s. Within UNICE, for example, large firms were able to secure top positions in the standing committees, giving them a key role in the formulation of joint positions (Cowles 1997). Moreover, in several sectors, such as automobiles, chemicals, and biotechnology, large firms, acting independently, outside the framework of interest organizations, have acquired greater influence than either the national or the EU associations. Individual lobbying by large firms is commonplace nowadays, with firms often having better access than the EU-level and national associations to both EU and domestic political institutions.

Yet, the extent to which the business community is able to pursue its interests effectively varies enormously across time and across issues. Moreover, business is far from being a unitary actor. For example, within the Single Market Programme from the late 1980s, many economic sectors such as transport, electricity and gas, and telecommunications were liberalized in the face of strong resistance from incumbent firms. Even Europe's largest utility, Electricité de France (EdF), had to accept the loss of its monopoly position on the French market, which it had done its best to defend. In the case of electricity liberalization, regional suppliers and local utilities had distinct interests deviating from those of the large utilities. In addition, large industrial energy

Box 13.3 **The facts**

Business interest groups: Some examples

The Union of Industrial and Employers' Confederations of Europe (UNICE)

UNICE was set up in 1958 to promote the common professional interests of firms in both EU decision making and the dialogue of the social partners (employers and labour). It includes 33 national member associations from 26 countries and five national associations that have observer status. UNICE claims to represent about 17 million firms in all. It has around 40 full-time members of staff. Ninety per cent of its funding is covered by membership fees.

The European Centre for Enterprises with Public Participation and of Enterprises of General Economic Interest (CEEP)

The CEEP was founded in 1961. As a cross-sectoral employer and producer association, it represents the interests of its members, mainly public-sector firms, in the EU decision-making process and also in the social dialogue. The CEEP brings together 12 national sections and one additional section for Benelux (Belgium, Luxembourg, and the Netherlands). These have as members around 280 public firms, associations, and other organizations supportive of the aims of the CEEP. It also has several associated members from four non-EU member states. It claims to represent the interests of about 15 per cent of the non-agricultural trading economy. It has a staff of less than ten members, and membership fees covering 100 per cent of its funding.

The American Chamber of Commerce, Belgium (AmCham)

Set up in 1948, AmCham represents the interests of around 1,000 American and European firms in Belgium and in the EU institutions, with the aim of improving business and investment opportunities for US firms. AmCham has a staff of six members and is financed by membership and user fees.

The European Round Table of Industrialists (ERT)

The ERT was set up in 1983 in order to contribute to an improved dialogue between industry and governments at both the national and EU levels. It is composed of 48 leaders of large firms from 18 countries, all with their headquarters in Europe, and all engaged in substantial multinational activities. Membership is personal and not corporate. However, the ERT is funded by multinational firms and has a staff of seven members.

The Association of the European Chambers of Commerce (EUROCHAMBRES)

Founded in 1958, Eurochambres represents the interests of members of the chambers of commerce and industry (small and medium-sized enterprises—SMEs) to the EU institutions. It incorporates 36 national associations of the chambers of commerce and industry, one per country, and claims to represent more than 15 million firms. It employs a staff of 20, and is largely funded by membership fees.

The European Association of Craft, Small, and Medium Sized Enterprises (UEAPME)

The UEAPME was established in 1979 to defend the interests of crafts, trades, and small and medium-sized enterprises in the EU and the candidate states. It brings together 27 national member associations from the 15 EU member states, a merger group of four associations, 26 associated members from both EU and non-EU states, and 15 European and international sectoral associations. It claims to represent seven million firms in the EU and three million in the candidate states of central and Eastern Europe. It has a staff of 15, and is entirely financed by membership fees.

Sources: European Commission Coneccs Database and the websites of the organizations discussed.

consumers across Europe endorsed liberalization because they saw it as a way of lowering their energy costs.

Yet, it is still relevant to ask whether the strong presence of the business community in the EU's political arena results from the greater variety of interests that need to be represented, or whether it has more to do with firms being better able to form interest groups and pursue their interests than is the case for more diffuse, non-economic interests. Interest group theories have predominantly focused on the latter reason, raising important questions about the democratic implications of interest group activity.

Diffuse interests

Compared to business interests, religious, social, human rights, consumer, and environmental groups remain underrepresented in the EU. Only around 18 per cent of EU-level interest organizations can be categorized as 'diffuse', reflecting the fact that these groups represent general causes or ideas or large societal groups that are not particularly (well) organized or cohesive, and cannot easily be organized. Another reason for the small number of diffuse interest groups is the relative lack of activity on the part of the EU institutions. Only intense regulatory activity has provoked the mobilization of socially orientated interest groups at the EU level. The only exceptions have been the domestic consumer organizations that formed the BEUC (Bureau Européen des Unions des Consommateurs), the European consumer association, in 1962. They did this with the support of the European Commission, as a response to market integration (Young 1998: 157–8), ultimately bringing together (by 1995) 26 member organizations from 16 countries. Box 13.4 presents some examples of diffuse interest groups.

In the early years of the European integration process, international NGOs did not generally focus their activities on the EC. Even well into the 1970s, welfare and social policy groups were conspicuously absent from Brussels (Harvey 1993: 189–90). The foundation of the European Environmental Bureau (EEB), for example, came about as a consequence of the EC's first environmental programme in 1974. Today, the EEB is the most comprehensive European environmental organization, bringing together more than 130 national associations. By the mid-1990s, some 13 European environmental associations and networks were present at the EU level (Hey and Brendle 1994: 389), a reflection of new regulatory powers in this policy area. Four of them dominate the representation of interests for this area: the EEB, the World Wide Fund for Nature, Greenpeace, and Friends of the Earth, with the others having a more specialized focus. For the vast majority of non-business interests, however, it was only in the 1980s that their numbers began to increase. They did so as a response to new European programmes. For example, the growth of anti-poverty groups in the second half of the 1980s was a direct consequence of new EU programmes in this policy area (Harvey 1993: 190).

In general, diffuse interests are characterized by their absence of a clear membership, and aside from a small number of European federations, they also tend to lack a high degree of organization. To the extent that these organizations seek to represent large groups, there is a lack of social control, and potential members have strong incentives to **free-ride** on the **collective goods** they provide. As a consequence of ideological differences, differential linkages to national member organizations, and overlapping responsibilities, organizations of this kind sometimes end up competing with each another. When this happens it can limit their effectiveness. In one example the European consumer association, BEUC, urged the European Commission to exclude the European Trade Union Committee's consumer organization (EURO-C) from its advisory committee and to have the status of consumer co-operatives (EURO-COOP) revised. BEUC justified this policy by claiming that neither of these two organizations really qualified as a consumer organization (Young 1998: 66; on migrants' associations, see Favell 1997).

The Commission and the Parliament have sought to improve the organizational capacities of diffuse interest groups so as to enhance their standing in the policy process, and have offered financial support for that purpose. These grants amount to a very small proportion of the EU budget. However, to the interest groups concerned, EU sources of funding can be of major importance (see Pollack 1997b: 581). The Commission and the EP also support the activities

Box 13.4 **The facts**

Diffuse interest groups: Some examples

The European Trade Union Confederation (ETUC)

Formed in 1973, the ETUC seeks to represent its members' interests in EU decision making and also aims to establish a Europe-wide system of industrial relations. It has a membership of 74 trade union confederations from 34 European countries, as well as 11 European industry federations. It claims to represent 60 million individual members of these confederations. The ETUC employs a staff of about 45, and according to its constitution, is mainly financed from contributions by the affiliated national confederations.

The European Consumers Organization (BEUC)

The BEUC was founded in 1962 and advocates the interests of European consumers in the EU policy process. It has a membership of 32 national consumer organizations from 22 countries and has a staff of 16. In 2001, 35 per cent of its financial means were provided by the European Commission and 65 per cent by membership fees.

The European Environmental Bureau (EEB)

The EEB was founded in 1974 to promote the protection of the environment. It is the most comprehensive of all EU environmental organizations, having 111 full member organizations, and 21 associated member organizations from 24 countries. It has a staff of 14. In the mid-1990s, funds from the European Commission amounted to 50 per cent of its financial resources.

The European Women's Lobby (EWL)

The EWL's goal is to eliminate discrimination against women and to serve as a link between the EU institutions and women's organizations. It encompasses 26 national networks or associations from the 15 EU member states and 26 European or international member organizations that operate in at least seven EU member states. It claims to represent more than 2,700 member organizations in all. It has a staff of nine, and receives around 90 per cent of its funding from the European Commission.

Sources: European Commission Coneccs Database; websites of the organizations discussed.

---

of various social groups by providing project funds within EU programmes, as in the area of women and poverty. According to a recent survey, 59 per cent of EU associations representing diffuse interests received funds from the EU (Aspinwall and Greenwood 1998). Initially, the EEB received an overwhelming proportion of its budget from such sources, and even in the 1990s it still received about 50 per cent of its financial resources from the EU (Hey and Brendle 1994). The EU consumer associations receive about 30 per cent of their basic organizational resources from the EU institutions (Young 1998: 165); and the EU institutions finance some 90 per cent of the organizational costs and programmes of the European Women's Lobby (Cullen 1999: 20). Not only does this financial support improve the organizational capacity and facilitate the staffing of these associations, but it also improves their access to relevant expertise. For example, part of the EU's financial support granted to the European Trade Union Confederation (ETUC) goes to its college, which trains unionists for EU-level activities. The EU also supports the ETUC's technical bureau which advises the ETUC on EU standardization activities (Martin and Ross 1999: 325).

However, financial support of this kind has been subject to rather *ad hoc* internal procedures and opaque criteria (see Box 13.5). Some members of social policy interest groups also fear that the support given by EU institutions is little more than a convenient way for the EU to give a human face to the Single Market. Moreover, there is a risk that interest organizations might become too dependent on the EU institutions, influencing their

Box 13.5 **Case study**

The 'red card' campaign, 1998–2000

The United Kingdom took legal action against some budget lines that supported diffuse interests, arguing that they lacked a proper legal base. The Court ruled in favour of the member states in this instance. During the internal revisions that followed this ruling, the Commission decided to freeze all budget lines lacking a legal base. This triggered the disapproval of many diffuse interest groups. In a highly visible public campaign, a large number of social, development, and human rights groups, as well as the ETUC showed the Commission the 'red card'.

In the Commission's first set of reforms, it introduced a set of guidelines for the management of grants, to establish uniform practices across its services and to provide for greater transparency. However, the funding of NGOs, which had sprung up in a piecemeal fashion, remains tied to complicated budgetary procedures in need of further revision.

political positions and activities. Financial support might allow the EU institutions to co-opt interest organizations, limiting their opposition to European initiatives. Some associations, such as Greenpeace, do not accept EU funding for that reason. Yet according to Brian Harvey, there is 'no ready evidence of attempts by the Commission to steer networks towards, or for that matter away from, particular policy positions' (Harvey 1993: 191). Rather, financial support allows 'weak' interest organizations to participate in decision making, allowing the Commission to broaden its support base and improve its expertise on the divergent positions and arguments of different groups.

The Europeanization of domestic interest groups

There is no doubt that the European integration process has provoked an increase in interest group activity at the European level. But the EU may also have important consequences for *national* interest groups. These may take a number of different forms.

First, the growing importance of EU policy may lead national interest groups to redefine their interests. In the short term, new opportunities and risks posed by EU policies may trigger a process of reassessment within domestic organizations (Eising and Jabko 2001). In the longer term, the presence of the European institutions and the importance of their policies may mean that national groups begin to look at issues from a European perspective, rather than continuing to define problems in purely national terms (Katzenstein 1997). If this were to happen, interests would become Europeanized.

Second, as a consequence of the European integration process, domestic interests will increasingly have to co-ordinate interest representation at a variety of different levels of governance. As the EU extends its remit, more and more issues of concern to interest groups are likely to involve the European institutions. As the level of negotiation shifts to the supranational level, ordinary members of national groups may feel that they are losing out. To cope with these changes, national groups may use a variety of strategies to retain control of their role in the decision-making process, for example, by making sure a consensus is reached before negotiations begin, and by confining the negotiation to the broad outline of that consensus. In sum, the Europeanization process would seem to involve a need for domestic interest groups to *adapt* to new circumstances, so as to allow them to retain some control over their involvement in the policy process. This 'need' may ultimately lead to organizational changes within the interest groups concerned.

Third, running counter to the arguments above, it is important to stress that the growing importance of the EU may not lead to changes in domestic patterns of interest intermediation, even if this is a recurrent theme in the literature on interest groups (see van Schendelen 1993: 279). For example, despite the emergence of new European policies, the majority of German, British, and French trade associations continue to lobby domestic political institutions rather than the EU institutions when seeking to represent their interests. Indeed, only a minority of national interest organizations routinely maintain contacts with both EU and national institutions (Eising 2004). It is clear then that relations with domestic institutions do not necessarily weaken because of European integration. In fact, European integration may even contribute to a strengthening of existing ties (Benz 1998: 583) in cases, for example, where there is some uncertainty over new EU legislation, prompting national actors to exchange information on the issue. Shared concerns over the impact of EU directives and regulations may lead to new or may reinforce existing domestic alliances among groups and national political institutions. In short, even if many national trade associations now take an interest in both the European and national levels of governance, and even if the changes in the institutional environment lead to some kind of adaptation, the majority of national groups still remain rooted in their domestic contexts.

Finally, it is not clear whether or how European integration changes the relative power of national governments (state actors) *vis-à-vis* interest groups (non-state actors). Moravcsik (1998) claims that national governments have gained resources because of their interface position—their roles as intermediaries and interlocutors—in the EU policy process. From this perspective, national governments can be seen as gatekeepers between the national and EU levels of decision making. Moreover, with the advent of an ever more complex multi-level system, interest

groups may well have lost a *decisive* addressee for their political demands. And finally, European integration may allow domestic institutions to gain autonomy from domestic interest groups (Grande 1994), that is, to break free from their influence. Governments may tie themselves to certain European positions as a way of rejecting unwelcome interest group demands at home.

However, several case studies have shown that easy access to the European institutions and the dependence of those institutions on interest groups have allowed certain interests to have a substantial say in the European policy process. The Single Market Programme is the best known case of this kind (Cowles 1997; see Chapter 3: 42–3). In another example, however, access to the European Court of Justice (ECJ) has allowed interest groups—and individuals in the professional services—to overturn established national rules and practices, providing them with a powerful instrument for increasing their influence over (national) state actors.

Key points

- The increase in European regulation may cause domestic interest groups to redefine or 'Europeanize' their interests.

- Interest groups may change in order to retain some control over public policy as it becomes more Europeanized.

- European integration may strengthen the relationship between domestic institutions and interest groups.

- It is unclear, however, whether European integration strengthens national governments at the expense of interest groups or vice versa.

Conclusion

European integration has left its mark on patterns of interest intermediation in the EU. A new multi-layered interest group system has emerged to reflect

the multi-level institutional set-up of the EU. While the EU is characterized by numerous points of access for interests, potentially a source of confusion, it also—because of its preference for consensual decision making—grants interest groups an important say in the European policy process. Moreover, the EU institutions actively promote the formation of European-level groups, by providing funds for weaker, more diffuse interests and supporting those involved in implementing European policy.

Compared to national groups, those operating at the EU level tend to perform a narrower set of functions, acting as information brokers, representing the interests of their affiliates, and providing linkages to other interest organizations and to the EU institutions. Some even argue that these groups have the potential to remedy the EU's **democratic deficit** (see Chapter 23), as they allow for greater political participation. However, this kind of argument has to recognize that there is a potential bias built into the system of EU interest organizations. The system is highly asymmetric, with more than four-fifths of all groups representing business interests, and only one-fifth more diffuse social interests. Lacking in organizational capacity, the latter are highly dependent on support from the European institutions. Moreover, interest groups provide for a different sort of representation than that provided by bodies such as national parliaments or subnational regional authorities. It is therefore questionable whether they offer an appropriate remedy for the problems of democracy and accountability from which the EU is currently suffering.

QUESTIONS

1   Why are there more business than non-business interests in the EU?

2   Why does the EU support interest groups financially?

3   In what way do interest organizations benefit the EU?

4   Which of the European institutions is most receptive to interest groups?

5   How does the institutional setting of the EU affect interest intermediation?

6   What are the similarities and differences between national and EU groups?

7   How might European integration affect national interest groups?

8   How have the European institutions sought to regulate European-level interest group activity?

GUIDE TO FURTHER READING

Balme, R., Chabanet, D., and Wright, V. (eds), *L'Action Collective en Europe* (Paris: Press de Science Po, 2002). This Franco-British co-production is a very comprehensive and informative compilation of articles on the theme of 'collective action'. About half the contributions are in English; the other half in French.

Greenwood, J., *Representing Interests in the European Union* (New York: St Martin's Press, 1997). This textbook provides a useful introduction to the role of interest groups in the EU, and covers a range of different types of interests from business interests to professional and territorial interests.

Imig, D., and Tarrow, S. (eds), *Contentious Europeans: Protest and Politics in an Emerging Polity* (Lanham: Rowman and Littlefield, 2001). This volume merges the literature on social movements with the literature on EU studies. Drawing on a quantitative analysis of protest events in the EU, as well as on case studies in different issue areas, the book illustrates the extent to which EU policies have been a source of political protest.

WEB LINKS

http://europa.eu.int/comm/civil_society/coneccs/index_en.htm This website is maintained by the Secretariat-General of the European Commission. It includes a list of EU-level interest organizations, and useful links to those organizations.

www.euractiv.com This internet newsletter, as well as being of general interest, provides a listing of EU-level interest organizations, structured according to categories of interest.

http://europa.eu.int/comm/governance/index_en.htm The Commission website on the governance debate, which includes contributions on political consultation, co-regulation by interest groups, and political participation.

Individual interest organizations usually also have their own websites. Here are some examples:

www.unice.org Website of the Union of Industrial and Employers' Federations.

www.beuc.org Website of the European Consumers Association.

www.eeb.org Website of the European Environmental Bureau.

www.etuc.org Website of the European Trade Union Confederation.

www.socialplatform.org Website of the Platform of European Social NGOs.

Part Four

Policies and policy making

In Part Four of *EU Politics*, a selection of European policies are thrown under the spotlight. Seven policies are covered here, chosen to demonstrate the variety and scope of both policy content and the policy process within the EU. In Chapter 14, the issue of enlargement is analysed. Enlargement is much more than (just) an EU policy, however, and this is reflected in the scope of John Glenn's chapter. In Chapter 15, Karen Smith covers the very broad topic of the EU's external relations—both its economic external relations and the more recent Common Foreign and Security Policy. Eve Fouilleux deals with the Common Agricultural Policy in Chapter 16, focusing in particular on the highly topical issue of agricultural reform. In Chapter 17, Gerda Falkner reviews the EU's social dimension, identifying the recent changes that have taken place in the way in which the EU makes policy in this area. Chapter 18 deals with the topic of 'Regional Europe'. In her chapter, Angela Bourne looks not only at the EU's regional policy, but also at broader issues and themes that affect the EU's regions. Chapter 19 covers Justice and Home affairs. Here Emek Uçarer charts the evolution of the policy from the 1970s on, and assesses the way the policy is made and how it currently operates. In Chapter 20, Amy Verdun deals with the big issue of Economic and Monetary Union, explaining how the initial idea of EMU culminated in the single currency to which (most of) the European Union has signed up.

14 EU enlargement

John K. Glenn

READER'S GUIDE

This chapter deals with the topic of enlargement, the process by which new members join the European Union (EU). From six member states in the 1950s, the European Community (EC) grew to 15 by 1995 and is likely to expand to include as many as 25 countries by 2005. This chapter begins by looking briefly at the past enlargements of the 1970s, 1980s, and 1990s, before considering the rules that now govern the EU enlargement process. The sections that follow focus more specifically on how Central and East European states, along with the southern Europeans, have sought to join the EU, and how the conditionality principle which now underpins the enlargement process has affected their efforts. The chapter also looks at some of the key problems and challenges facing EU enlargement, not least the issues of agricultural reform, migration, and international security.

Introduction

Enlargement is the process by which new countries become members of the EU. The original EC, formed by the Treaty of Rome after 1957, involved only France, West Germany, Italy, Belgium, The Netherlands, and Luxembourg. From the six original member states, the Community grew to nine in the 1970s, 12 in the 1980s, and 15 in the 1990s. The fall of the Berlin Wall and the end of Communism in Central and Eastern Europe in 1989 transformed the context of European integration by opening up the possibility of a continent-wide union stretching across Cold War boundaries. The former communist states of Central and Eastern Europe, together with Cyprus, Malta, and Turkey, were all recognized as applicants in the 1990s. Formal negotiations for membership were opened with some of these states, suggesting that the EU might in future have as many as 28 members.

For many, enlargement to include the Central and East Europeans provides a historic and moral opportunity to foster stability and security across the European continent by means of economic and political integration. Others, however, have expressed concerns about its costs and consequences for the future functioning of the EU. Each enlargement increases the complexity of interstate bargaining and makes it more difficult to reach agreement, especially in major policy initiatives. Accessions entail costs for both current members and applicants, not least as markets are gradually opened to increased competition. These issues, amongst others, are dealt with in the sections that follow.

The chapter begins, however, by reviewing the three earlier enlargements, which brought the UK, Ireland, Denmark, Greece, Spain, Portugal, Austria, Finland, and Sweden into the Union. It then identifies enlargement as a formal process of negotiation between applicant states and the EU, outlining the so-called 'classical (Community) method' of enlargement and the more recent 'Copenhagen criteria' for membership, agreed in 1993. The chapter then goes on to describe the background to the (likely) 2004 enlargement. It discusses the impact of the **conditionality** principle and some of the major challenges facing the EU in advance of this historic event, including migration and agricultural reform. International security issues affecting Turkey and Cyprus are also considered at this point. Finally, the chapter reviews and discusses possible futures for an enlarged EU.

Past enlargements

The EU has grown to its current size of 15 in three sets of enlargements (see Table 14.1):

- In the 1970s: the UK, Denmark, and Ireland became members (1973).
- In the 1980s: Greece became a member in 1981; Spain and Portugal became members in 1986.
- In the 1990s: Austria, Finland, and Sweden became members (1995).

The first round of the enlargements, sometimes called the 'Northern Enlargement', began in the 1960s, with the UK's application for membership. Controversially, the UK request was rejected twice at the instigation of the then French president, General de Gaulle, first in 1963 and then again in 1967. There were a number of reasons why the French president felt that the UK should not join the EC. First, he was concerned that the British had ulterior motives for wanting to join—that of slowing down the process of integration from within. He also feared that the UK would challenge French leadership in the EC, while at the same time allowing the USA greater influence over European policy. Only with de Gaulle's resignation in 1969 did the UK's application, along with those of Ireland and Denmark (and Norway—see below), lead to the opening of accession negotiations in June 1970, and the conclusion of those negotiations in the middle of 1971. This was not quite the end of the story, however, as although the UK, Ireland, and Denmark joined the Community on 1 January 1973, a change of government in the UK in 1975 led to the renegotiation of the Treaty of Accession and a referendum in 1975, even if in practice revisions made at this time were marginal.

In the second round of enlargements in the 1980s, membership was used as a vehicle for stabilizing the new Southern European democracies of Greece, Spain, and Portugal. At the same time, this enlargement led to rather acrimonious squabbling among existing member states fearful that enlargement to the South might damage their economic interests. As the Southern European applicants were

Table 14.1 Applications for membership in the European Union

Country	Date of application	Negotiations opened	End of negotiations/Signing of Treaty of Accession	Date of accession
Denmark	9 Aug. 1961	—	—	—
	May 1967	30 June 1970	22 Jan. 1972	1 Jan. 1973
Ireland	31 July 1961	—	—	—
	May 1967	30 June 1970	22 Jan. 1972	1 Jan. 1973
United Kingdom	9 Aug. 1961	—	—	—
	11 May 1967	30 June 1970	22 Jan. 1972	1 Jan. 1973
Norway	30 Apr. 1962	—	—	—
	May 1967	30 June 1970	22 Jan. 1972	—
	25 Nov. 1992	5 Apr. 1993	30 Mar. 1994	—
Greece	12 June 1975	27 July 1976	28 May 1979	1 Jan. 1981
Portugal	28 Mar. 1977	6 June 1978	12 June 1985	1 Jan. 1986
Spain	28 July 1977	5 Feb. 1979	12 June 1985	1 Jan. 1986
Austria	17 July 1989	1 Feb. 1993	30 Mar. 1994	1 Jan. 1995
Finland	18 Mar. 1992	1 Feb. 1993	30 Mar. 1994	1 Jan. 1995
Sweden	1 July 1991	1 Feb. 1993	30 Mar. 1994	1 Jan. 1995
Switzerland	20 May 1992	—	—	—
Bulgaria	14 Dec. 1995	15 Feb. 2000		
Cyprus	4 July 1990	31 Mar. 1998		
Czech Republic	17 Jan. 1996	31 Mar. 1998		
Estonia	27 Nov. 1995	31 Mar. 1998		
Hungary	31 Mar. 1994	31 Mar. 1998		
Latvia	27 Oct. 1995	15 Feb. 2000		
Lithuania	12 Dec. 1995	15 Feb. 2000		
Malta	16 July 1990	15 Feb. 2000		
Poland	5 Apr. 1994	31 Mar. 1998		
Romania	22 June 1995	15 Feb. 2000		
Slovak Republic	27 June 1995	15 Feb. 2000		
Slovenia	10 June 1996	31 Mar. 1998		
Turkey	14 Apr. 1987	—		

significantly poorer than the existing members of the Community, the member governments also questioned the applicants' ability to assume the obligations of membership. The conflict between the enthusiastic political rhetoric in support of the new democracies and the protracted negotiations which sought to protect economically sensitive sectors provoked bad feeling in the applicant states, where it was argued that the conditions for accession were unfair. For example, almost 85 per cent of Portuguese agricultural production was included in a ten-year transitional period, during which Community tariffs were to remain in place for Portuguese products. For the Spanish, the equivalent transition periods were longest in those sectors where Spanish exports were strongest (fruit and vegetables) and shortest in sectors where Spain was much less competitive (such as dairy and livestock). These transition periods were also accompanied by Integrated Mediterranean Programmes (IMPs) in 1984 which compensated existing members who felt threatened by competition from the new markets (at this point, the French, the Italians, and the Greeks).

This Southern enlargement occurred during a period of internal EC reform, with the initiation of the Single Market Programme launched just prior to the Spanish and Portuguese accession. But the new members had little say in the direction European integration was taking at this time. It was not until they were full members that their opinions on these constitutional questions were to matter.

The third round of enlargement in 1995, in which Austria, Sweden, and Finland became members of the newly formed EU, highlighted changing perceptions of the benefits of membership in the new post-Cold War situation of the 1990s. Increasingly, national politicians understood that the economic benefits of free trade were not necessarily the primary reason for joining the Union. Rather, applicants sought membership to be able to participate in European policy formulation, that is, to influence the rules of the game, a game they would be forced to play even if they were not full members. This did not mean that there were fewer pressures on these three applicant states, however. The pressures were simply of a different kind, reflecting the economic strength of this cohort of candidates.

The question of the neutrality of the Austrians, Finns, and Swedes was to become particularly pertinent in light of the Common Security and Foreign Policy (CSFP) established by the Maastricht Treaty in 1993. For the Austrians, there was also a specific concern related to the issue of transit by heavy vehicles once they opened up their borders. Moreover, the Nordics expressed fears that joining the EU might force them to lower their environmental standards to EU levels—to levels below what they considered to be acceptable.

All these issues were discussed as part of the negotiation process, and by 1995, the EU had been transformed into a community of 15 countries, covering almost all of Western Europe. Non-members tended to be members of the European Free Trade Association, EFTA, which was established as a competing intergovernmental community in the early 1960s. By 1995, however, only four members remained: Norway, Iceland, Switzerland, and the little principality of Liechtenstein. Norwegian governments have tried twice to join the EC/EU. On both occasions, in 1972 and in 1994, the Norwegian people voted against membership in a referendum and the government was forced to withdraw their applications. In the Swiss case, there was never any real question of membership, particularly after a referendum in 1992 rejected Swiss membership of a lesser link with the EU, known as the European Economic Area (EEA). If accepted, this would have extended the single market to Switzerland. But a re-vote dealt a blow to the aspirations of those in the elite who saw the future of Switzerland within rather than outside the EU.

Key points

- There have been three rounds of enlargement since the European Community was set up.
- In 1973, the UK, Ireland, and Denmark became members.
- In 1981 Greece joined, followed by Spain and Portugal in 1986.
- In 1995, Austria, Finland, and Sweden became members.

Who can join the EU and how?

The procedure for joining the EU, often referred to as the **accession** process, is defined in the Treaties. Article 49 of the Treaty on European Union (TEU) states that 'any European state which respects the principles set out in Article 6(1) may apply to become a member of the Union'. Article 6(1) lists these principles as 'liberty, democracy, respect for human rights and fundamental freedoms, and the rule of law'. Applying to become a member of the EU is an intergovernmental process, a matter for the governments of applicant countries and the member governments in the EU Council and European Council, acting in consultation with the European Commission and European Parliament (EP).

The accession process, which is outlined in Article O (TEU), involves several stages (see Box 14.1). Countries wishing to become members must first submit a formal application to the EU Council. The Council then requests an Opinion (also known as an '*avis*', using the equivalent French word) from the European Commission. The Opinion sets out a case for and/or against membership. If a positive Opinion is presented by the Commission and this is then adopted by the Council, an accession conference may be convened, after which negotiations can be initiated. These involve representatives of the applicant states, the Council, and the Commission, and typically concern the ability of the applicant state to take on the obligations of membership. In cases where a country is not fully able to meet these obligations within a reasonable time period, and where there is good reason, an agreement on transitional arrangements or temporary exemptions

may be made. At the end of the negotiation process, the European Parliament (EP) must give its assent to membership in a vote which requires an absolute majority of its members (see Chapter 1: 5). The agreement is then ratified in all member states, as well as in the applicant country concerned. This ratification process may include a public referendum as well as parliamentary ratification, but this varies from country to country.

In the past, enlargement was guided by a set of principles which Preston (1997) has labelled the 'classical Community method' or 'classical method' of enlargement. This pattern of enlargement made it clear that applicants must accept the obligations of membership in full with no permanent opt-outs possible; that formal accession negotiations must focus solely on the practicalities of membership; that problems created by new members would be resolved by creating new policy instruments rather than by initiating any fundamental reform; that new members join on the basis of limited incremental adaptation by the Community, with the promise of a more fundamental review only after enlargement; and, finally, that the Union prefers to negotiate with groups of states that already have close relations with each other. Most importantly, however, the classical

---

Box 14.1 **The facts**

An overview of the enlargement process

Accession is a formal process which involves countries negotiating individually with the European Commission under Article O of the TEU. It comprises the following steps:

1 Formal application: submitted to the European Council.

2 Opinion (*avis*): The Council requests an opinion from the European Commission. The Opinion is a detailed document which explains the economic and political situation in the applicant country, evaluates their ability to cope with membership, and makes a recommendation to the Council.

3 Accession Conference: With an invitation to begin negotiations, the Council convenes an accession conference with representatives of the governments of the applicant countries, the Council, and the European Commission.

4 Negotiations: Each of the 31 chapters of the *acquis communautaire* is opened, negotiated, and, upon agreement, provisionally closed.

5 Agreement: Upon the closure of all chapters, the European Commission makes a recommendation to the Council on enlargement.

6 Approval by the European Parliament: absolute majority required.

7 Ratification: by all member and applicant states' parliaments and in some cases by referendum.

method embodied the expectation that the bulk of adjustment costs should be borne by the new members, a characteristic of the process that can lead to resentment among applicant states.

Since the early 1990s, there has been a substantial development of the 'classical method'. Particularly important in shaping the enlargement process was the drafting of a list of criteria for EU membership, which have come to be known as the 'Copenhagen criteria'. These emerged at the Copenhagen European Council (summit) meeting in 1993, and have since been used to frame the accession process for the Central and Eastern European states and for those applicants in Southern Europe (Malta, Cyprus, and Turkey).

Since 1993, the principle of **conditionality** has become central to the enlargement process, especially in explaining the impact of prospective membership upon the applicant states. Conditionality implies a relationship in which one partner has leverage over another through their ability to withhold a desired benefit, in this case, EU membership. Because membership is conditional on meeting the Copenhagen criteria, applicant countries change their domestic policies and institutions to bring them into line with EU requirements.

The three conditions for membership are:

- Applicants must have fully functioning liberal democratic systems, including respect for human rights and the rule of law. This is defined not just in terms of formal institutions, but also in terms of their de facto application on the ground.

- There must be a functioning market-based economy with the capacity to withstand competitive pressure and market forces in the EU (an economic criterion).

- Applicants must be prepared to take on the obligations of membership.

The Copenhagen summit also stipulated, noting the potential impact of enlargement on the EU itself, that the Union's capacity for absorbing new members must also be a consideration within the accession process. In other words, new members must not pose any serious problems for the EU. This amounts to a de facto fourth condition for membership.

Since the first enlargements of the early 1970s, European institutions have gained greater powers and reach, so that joining the EU currently means complying with a much wider range of rules and obligations in a much broader range of issue areas than was initially the case. Yet many of the issues raised during the first three enlargements remain relevant in the post-2000 period: the question of cost and economic threats; arguments about the impact of enlargement on the security and stability of new and existing member states; practical questions of institutional reform within the EU; and, not least, whether a wider Europe necessarily implies a weakening of the European integration project.

Key points

- Enlargement is a formal process which allows non-members to begin negotiations leading ultimately in their accession.

- The classical method of enlargement places the responsibility for adjusting to European policies on the applicant states.

- The Copenhagen criteria of 1993 spell out conditions for accession.

From economic assistance to formal negotiations

The fall of Communism in Central and Eastern Europe in 1989 prompted a flood of requests to help the Central and East Europeans transform their economies and polities. In many former Communist states, the demise of the old regimes was accompanied by calls for a 'return to Europe', which found concrete expression in formal requests to join the EC (and after 1993, the new EU).

The challenges of the (largely) eastward enlargement became clearer as former Soviet-bloc countries struggled to introduce reforms. Forty years of central planning and a communist monopoly over political institutions could not be erased overnight: nor did removing them leave a 'blank slate' on which new democratic and market institutions might be constructed. Pro-democracy movements that had united against the old regimes in 1989 found it hard to transform themselves into competing political parties. In some cases, these movements quickly fell from power, judged unable to govern, while in others former communists reinvented themselves as democratic socialists or social-democrats along West European lines, even declaring European integration to be their primary political objective. Attempts to privatize state-owned companies varied across the region, ranging from the 'shock therapy' of the Polish approach, to the more gradualist voucher privatization system of the Czech Republic. Across the region as a whole, countries struggled with the corruption and cronyism that accompanied both the opportunities and the uncertainties of economic and political transformation. Lacking independent judiciaries, the Central and Eastern European countries (CEECs) sought to create strong autonomous legal institutions and to embed them in a new rule of law. Germany's experience in the former German Democratic Republic (GDR) (East Germany) highlights some of the difficulties faced in this kind of transformation. Despite impressive economic assistance, and indeed a shared language and history prior to the 1940s, Germany's eastern *Länder* continue to have a dramatically lower standard of living than West Germany.

The EC was poorly prepared for the fall of Communism. It had had only limited relationships with the CEECs before 1989. Although the development of bilateral relations had been a priority in the 1980s, these links were still in their infancy when the Cold War ended. Initial enthusiasm in the EC for rapid integration into the Community quickly gave way to differences in opinions over enlargement. While the European Commission maintained its pro-enlargement stance, member states were at times ambivalent. Germany was an active supporter of rapid enlargement, whereas some states, such as France, feared threats to their markets from cheap industrial goods and agricultural products. Recent members such as Spain also became concerned that they might lose the regional and social assistance that they received through the Structural Funds under existing agreements.

Those arguing for enlargement in the 1990s frequently declared it a historic opportunity to extend a West European zone of stability and peace continent-wide that would in turn enhance the prospects for current members. Enlargement was also a moral imperative for some, who viewed the division of Europe after the Second World War as a wrong that had to be righted. Enlargement was seen as an inevitable step, as the EU sought to extend its foreign policy role. Moreover, in economic terms, many viewed the CEECs as important potential markets for European goods.

At the same time, however, cautious voices warned against a rapid enlargement. With the collapse of Yugoslavia and the outbreak of war in the Balkans, some pointed out that enlargement could risk bringing countries under threat of civil war into the EU. Concerns were expressed about CEECs with substantial ethnic minorities, often the result of partitions after the two World Wars. Others feared the migration of East European workers seeking jobs and willing to work for low wages in the West. In economic terms, some argued that it would simply be too costly to admit East European countries before their economic institutions were capable of competing in the European market. And if the Common Agricultural Policy (CAP) and regional policy were applied to the CEECs, the funds necessary to sustain these policies would very soon bankrupt the EU.

Concerns of this kind meant that enlargement proceeded at a cautious pace in the 1990s. The first action taken by the European Community (EC) was in July 1989, when the G7 summit asked the Community to co-ordinate financial assistance to the region. In June 1989 the Community launched the PHARE programme (pronounced 'far'), which originally applied to Poland and Hungary alone. But with the fall of the soviet bloc at the end of 1989, PHARE was gradually extended to all former-communist CEECs. Subsequently a parallel programme, TACIS, was established for the former Soviet Union. But in the early 1990s, the EU was extremely reluctant to commit itself to enlargement—even in principle. It was not until summits at Copenhagen (1993) and Essen (1994) that its position changed. Even in the Europe Agreements, which created an associate status for aspiring members, the Community tried to maintain a focus on free trade and on issues such as technical assistance. But by the start of 1995, the European Council agreed that this was no longer a tenable strategy, reaffirming that the necessary steps for launching accession negotiations would take place after the Amsterdam European Council in 1997. It called on the European Commission to provide an analysis of the challenges of enlargement, which was published under the rubric of **Agenda 2000** in July of that year (see Box 14.2).

Agenda 2000 opened the door to what became the first 'wave' of candidate states, namely, Poland, Hungary, the Czech Republic, Estonia, and Slovenia, which, together with Cyprus, were set to enter the EU before the others. Negotiations began in 1998.

However, by December 1999 and the Helsinki European Council meeting, it was accepted that the other five CEECs (Bulgaria, Latvia, Lithuania, Romania, and Slovakia), together with Malta, could also start negotiations in 2000, and that there would no longer be any assumption of a first and second wave of applicant states. All candidates would subsequently be judged on the merits of their own negotiations. Turkey, it should be noted, was excluded from this line-up, a point returned to below.

Key points

- The EC was initially unprepared to respond to calls for membership from Central and Eastern Europe after the fall of Communism.

- Arguments for and against eastward enlargement have been made on both geopolitical and economic grounds.

Box 14.2 **The facts**
Agenda 2000

Agenda 2000: For a stronger and wider union is the title of the European Commission's analysis of the requirements of enlargement for both applicant countries and the EU. Published in 1997, this document reinforced the importance of the three Copenhagen criteria for membership (political, economic, and implementing the *acquis*) and elaborated the EU's two-part strategy for enlargement: accession negotiations with candidate countries and the pre-accession strategy designed to assist these countries in overcoming problems identified in negotiations.

For candidate countries, *Agenda 2000* reinforced the role of **conditionality**, stating that all new members must take on the obligations of membership as specified by the *acquis*, which they will be expected to enforce upon accession. The document relies upon the 'classical method of enlargement' whereby transition periods for troubled areas may be negotiated in the accession process. This requirement is notable in light of the fact that the current 15 members do not participate in all aspects of the EU treaties, including **Schengen** and EMU (Chapter 20).

For the EU, *Agenda 2000* noted the difficulties attached

to enlargement if new members were to join with the same rights as current members, most notably concerning subsidies for the CAP and Structural Funds for underdeveloped regions. It reaffirmed the budgetary limit of 1.27 per cent of Community GDP until 2006 and agreed the proportion devoted to Structural Funds at 0.46 per cent for that same period. Transfers to member countries were set at 4 per cent of the recipient's national GDP. Agenda 2000 made proposals for the reform of the CAP but recognized the challenges involved and the Commission's limited role in influencing this policy. It also noted that reform of EU institutions should continue in light of the need to adjust decision-making procedures within the Council and the EP.

For some, *Agenda 2000* represented a statement of the EU's negotiating position at the outset of the enlargement process. Others observed that the challenges identified for the EU's policies and institutions were valid and pressing, regardless of whether the EU enlarges to accept new members. The entire text of *Agenda 2000* can be found on the European Commission's website, given at the end of this chapter.

- Those in favour of enlargement stress the opportunities for ensuring peace in Europe and for accessing new markets, while those against enlargement express concerns about bringing instability into the EU and potential threats from cheaper goods and labour.

Conditionality and the *acquis communautaire*

In the early 1990s, the conditionality principle—associated with the Copenhagen Criteria—had been invoked as a precondition for the *initiation* of the accession process, with the EU inviting a first 'wave' of seven countries, judged to have met all three criteria, to apply for membership in 1997. After the outbreak of the war in Kosovo, the EU shifted its position to allow conditionality to be applied to the *negotiation* stage, so that in 1999, the Union was able to invite the 'second wave' countries to participate in the accession process, stating it would evaluate all applications on a case-by-case basis (see

Box 14.3). By 1999, ten out of the 13 countries that had applied for EU membership were judged to have met the first two criteria (Romania, Bulgaria, and Turkey were not). However, accession negotiations concern in large part the third criterion, which stipulates that applicants must adopt in full the *acquis communautaire*, or the rights and obligations of membership deriving from the founding treaties and subsequent legislation. The *acquis* is composed of 31 chapters, each of which focuses on a specific sector or issue area (see Box 14.4).

Given the unequal power relationship that

Box 14.3 **Case study**
EU enlargement and Slovakia

The impact of **conditionality** in the enlargement process may be seen clearly in the case of Slovakia. Part of the federal state of Czechoslovakia until 1993, Slovakia then became an independent state, with an economy that had been dependent on Cold War heavy industry, and with a substantial Hungarian minority. The re-election of Vladimir Meciar as prime minister in 1994 posed problems for Slovakia's relations with the EU. Although Meciar claimed to seek EU membership for his country, domestic political events led his government to be perceived as semi-authoritarian, with a questionable commitment to democratic principles and the rule of law. The government was indifferent to the Slovak constitutional court's ruling against its treatment of opposition parliamentarians, it harassed the independent media, and it engaged in irregularities in a referendum on the presidency. Frequent criticism of the government by European politicians provoked complaints that the EU was biased against Slovakia, as well as diplomatic overtures by Meciar to Russia.

The potential influence of the EU was made clear when the Czech Republic but not Slovakia was invited to begin

accession negotiations in 1997. The Commission wrote in its evaluation that, while Slovakia met the economic and administrative criteria for membership (that is, that the country could cope with the administrative burden of membership), it failed to meet the political criteria, with regard to the stability of its institutions, human rights and respect for minorities, and the rule of law. This confirmed to potential applicants that the political criteria really were a precondition for enlargement. Slovakia's exclusion from EU negotiations (and NATO enlargement) became the centrepiece of the domestic opposition's platform in the parliamentary elections of 1998, where Meciar was defeated by an alliance led by the Slovak Democratic Coalition (re-elected in 2002). This result was welcomed by the European Commission, which continued to exert its influence by declaring its wish for minority Hungarian parties to be included in the new government and for the new government to close its nuclear power plant in Bohunice, near the Austrian border. In 1999, Slovakia was invited to begin negotiations for membership with six other countries. By July 2002, it had closed 27 chapters of the *acquis*.

Box 14.4 **The facts**
The acquis communautaire

The *acquis communautaire* is the body of European Treaties, laws, and norms. It is composed of 31 chapters which all countries must adopt or negotiate transition periods for, prior to enlargement.

Chapter 1:   Free movement of goods
Chapter 2:   Freedom of movement for persons
Chapter 3:   Freedom to provide services
Chapter 4:   Free movement of capital
Chapter 5:   Company law
Chapter 6:   Competition policy
Chapter 7:   Agriculture
Chapter 8:   Fisheries
Chapter 9:   Transport policy
Chapter 10: Taxation
Chapter 11: Economic and Monetary Union
Chapter 12: Statistics
Chapter 13: Social policy and employment
Chapter 14: Energy
Chapter 15: Industrial policy
Chapter 16: Small and medium-sized undertakings
Chapter 17: Science and research

Chapter 19: Telecommunications and information technologies
Chapter 18: Education and training
Chapter 20: Culture and audio-visual policy
Chapter 21: Regional policy and co-ordination of structural instruments
Chapter 22: Environment
Chapter 23: Consumers and health protection
Chapter 24: Co-operation in the field of justice and home affairs
Chapter 25: Customs union
Chapter 26: External relations
Chapter 27: Common foreign and security policy
Chapter 28: Financial control
Chapter 29: Financial and budgetary provisions
Chapter 30: Institutions
Chapter 31: Other

results from the conditionality principle, it might be tempting to see enlargement as a one-way process of imitation, in which applicants simply adopt European laws and regulations. This would be an oversimplification and would obscure the varying legacies of the past which explain how and why particular countries respond to the challenges of adopting the *acquis* in the ways that they do. The post-2000 enlargement is distinctive because of the transformations occurring simultaneously within the post-Communist states, and because of the character of the new EU, after 1993. In principle, applicant countries are not allowed to opt out of parts of the treaties, although few expect them to be able to participate immediately in EMU. In practice, extended transition periods are likely to have the same effect as opt-outs. The complexities of the *acquis* have led some to argue that accession is not merely a legal process involving the approximation of legislation but a process 'changing both the legal framework in which society and the economy operate and revolutionizing the institutions of the state' (Mayhew 1998: 362).

As a consequence of conditionality, then, the EU has become the principal external 'focal point' for reform in the applicant states. Already in 1994, the Europe Agreements had called for the assimilation by CEECs of the EU's legal framework, particularly in matters of competition and intellectual property law. This pattern has been institutionalized since that time. In Hungary, for example, lawmaking bodies have been obliged to take European law into consideration in all draft bills since March 1990. An Inter-ministerial Commission in charge of co-ordinating integration-related policies was installed in April 1992, and the Hungarian Parliament set up a European Affairs Scrutiny Committee in 1994, when legal compatibility with European law was made a legal requirement.

Negotiations over the 31 chapters of the *acquis* have tended to involve the closure of uncontroversial chapters first, before turning to more difficult or sensitive chapters that would necessitate arrangements for transitional periods. The European Commission has issued periodic progress reports (the first in November 1998) which praised good performance and disciplined applicants judged not to be making satisfactory progress. Member states occasionally used the accession negotiations to pressure applicant countries to adopt particular domestic policies, as when Austria repeatedly threatened to veto the closure of the chapter on energy policy if the Czech Republic did not shut down a controversial power plant near the Austrian border. While the European Commission has repeatedly rejected this kind of approach, national politicians and activists have been less reserved. By July 2002, ten countries had provisionally closed 25 or more chapters of the *acquis*. By December 2002 it is possible that all ten countries will have closed all 31 chapters.

While the EU has exerted its influence through conditionality, it also agreed a *pre-accession strategy* designed to assist applicant countries as they prepared for membership. The strategy was adopted at the European Council meeting at Essen in December 1994. It led to the drafting of the 1995 White Paper, identifying those aspects of the Community associated with the single market that applicants had to adopt before accession. It also established a 'structured dialogue' between politicians from the candidate countries and their member state counterparts. Three major Community programmes have been used to implement the pre-accession strategy: PHARE, SAPARD, and ISPA. PHARE, as mentioned above, co-ordinates pre-accession aid generally, SAPARD targets the agricultural sector, and ISPA focuses aid on environmental and trans-

port infrastructure. Although it was accepted that substantial expenditures would be needed to close the gap between the economies of applicant and member states, the CEECs have frequently lacked the institutional infrastructure to absorb Community aid effectively, especially at the regional level. Throughout the 1990s, while the applicants complained that the level of EU assistance was far too low in light of the changes demanded of them, the EU criticized applicant countries for spending PHARE monies inappropriately, leading on a few occasions to the temporary suspension and re-evaluation of applicant country projects.

Key points

- The principal mechanism by which the EU exerts its influence on applicant countries is through the principle of conditionality by which all applicant countries must meet specific criteria to be invited to join the EU.

- All applicant countries must adopt the *acquis communautaire*, the body of laws and regulations based on the treaties that form the EU. The *acquis* consists of 31 chapters covering a wide range of economic and social policy issues.

- The EU has also initiated several programmes of economic assistance to help applicant countries prepare for membership, namely PHARE, SAPARD, and ISPA.

Issues and concerns

Although enlargement touches almost all aspects of European integration, this section identifies a number of issues of particular importance. These are agricultural reform, migration, international security, and public opinion.

Agricultural reform and the budget

One of the most fundamental problems for enlargement has been how or indeed whether the EU's

Common Agricultural Policy (CAP) might be extended to include ten or more new members (see Chapter 16: 260). Many have observed that the basic principles of the CAP—market unity, Community preference, and financial solidarity—are impossible to sustain within an enlarged EU. If the rules for allocating subsidies were applied to the CEECs, the transfers required would certainly bankrupt the Union, while existing EU members (such as Spain, Portugal, and Ireland) would lose their support. In *Agenda 2000* (see Box 14.2), the European

Commission moved to prevent this from happening by limiting the size of the EU budget (along with the proportion of the total budget devoted to Structural Funds and the amount of transfers any one country can receive). Although the issue of agricultural reform remains unresolved, the Commission proposed in 2002 that candidate countries receive 25 per cent of total agricultural subsidies, for which they would be eligible, upon becoming members. This amount would increase gradually until it is 100 per cent in 2013.

The issue remains an important one, not least because applicant countries with large agricultural sectors, and in particular Poland, have questioned why they should contribute to the EU budget on the basis of the current rules when they will not be receiving financial transfers in line with those rules. While agriculture has always been a crucial issue in the run-up to enlargements, typically resolved by the negotiation of long transition periods in sensitive sectors, this is the first time that enlargement has challenged the existence of the CAP. Of course the question of reform is not only tied to the enlargement issue (as is made clear in Chapter 16). Both internal financial constraints and international pressures have converged to force the Union to change the way agricultural subsidies are provided to European farmers.

Under the 'classical method' of enlargement, the formal burden of adjustment prior to accession fell on the applicants. Nowadays, it is generally accepted that the EU must also adapt its institutions to admit new members. The case of agricultural policy is a good example of what this means in practice. Thus while the resolution of the difficulties involved in extending the CAP (and indeed the Structural Funds—see Chapter 18) will inevitably necessitate transition periods for new members as they adapt to the constraints of EU membership, it will also involve the reform of existing EU policies and procedures.

Migration

The prospect of enlargement, particularly to Central and Eastern Europe, has raised the issue for some member states that on accession workers from the candidate countries might migrate in huge numbers to the EU to work for wages lower than those that domestic workers might accept. Responding to such fears, in 2000, the German chancellor, Gerhard Schröder, proposed that a seven-year transition period after accession should be introduced before the free movement of workers would apply to the new members. The Austrians too have expressed concerns about the potential impact of migration on their labour markets.

Not surprisingly, this proposal was not well received in the applicant states, and the issue of free movement became another bone of contention between the EU member states and the applicants during the negotiation process. This was not only a matter of economics, however, as many candidate countries made it clear that a restrictive approach towards migration could provoke domestic backlashes against joining the EU. Not only would this be uncomfortable for incumbent governments during the accession process, but it could also threaten accession itself, risking 'no' votes in the referendums that form an important element of the ratification process.

Perceptions are as important as real threats when it comes to discussing the likely impact of migration. Research on post-accession migration has tended to focus on the income gap between the applicant countries and the EU, as well as on the specific character of the CEECs' labour markets, their geographic proximity, traditions of emigration, ethnic and political problems, cultural and linguistic differences, and expectations about the future. A 2001 study by the European Commission predicted that Germany would absorb 64 per cent of all migration, and Austria an additional 10 per cent (European Commission 2001b: 8). Yet the report also suggested that fears of mass migration are unlikely to materialize. The study predicts that a maximum of 70,000 workers are likely to migrate upon enlargement and that the number will fall to half this level after ten years. Moreover, research on past enlargements found that the vast migration predicted, particularly in the cases of Spain and Portugal in the 1980s, did not happen. And strikingly, even after German unification, only 7.3 per cent of East Germans moved to West Germany.

International security

Enlargement also raises a number of critical issues with regard to international security, not least concerning the issue of EU-Russia relations. The issue of Kaliningrad, a piece of Russian territory sandwiched between Poland and Lithuania, and soon to be completely surrounded by the EU, has been the subject of recent negotiations. Talks in 2002 have revolved around the setting up of a visa corridor for residents of Kaliningrad, allowing them to pass through EU territory.

A particularly uncertain situation relates to the membership applications made by Cyprus and Turkey. Cyprus is a divided island, the North of which has been under the government of Turkish Cypriots, guaranteed by Turkey since 1974 while the South is Greek Cypriot. Since 1993, the island's application for membership has been judged by the EU to have been made on behalf of the whole island, and negotiations were initiated with the expectation that a settlement between the North and the South would soon be reached, mediated by the United Nations. For that reason, Turkish Cypriots were allowed to participate in the negotiations and are mentioned in the EU's positions papers. However, in practice the process has not been straightforward. Greece threatened to veto enlargement if Cyprus is not admitted (because of its divided status), while Turkey threatened to annex Northern Cyprus if the island joins without a resolution to the division of the island. The EU added fuel to the fire by announcing in 1999 that a political settlement would facilitate but would not be a precondition for Cyprus's accession. As of October 2002 negotiations for a settlement were continuing under the supervision of the UN.

Aside from the Cyprus question, Turkey's membership application also raises issues of international security for the EU. Turkey first applied for EU membership in 1987 and was granted applicant status in 1999 at Helsinki. Although Turkey has long been a defence partner of many European countries as a member of NATO, the Turkish application raised numerous questions for the EU regarding Turkey's suitability as a member state. Some have questioned whether Turkey should be considered European. Others have pointed to the weakness of the Turkish economy, a factor that is particularly important when we consider the size of Turkey in population terms (over 52 million). Perhaps more importantly, though, the prospect of extending the EU's borders right up to those of Islamic regimes such as Syria, Iran, and Iraq was also discussed on the grounds of international security concerns. Moreover, there remain controversial human rights issues that Turkey still has to address on the ground, particularly over the treatment of Turkey's Kurdish minority, and more generally on the conditions of prisoners—concerns raised by Amnesty International amongst others. The Turkish government initiated and repealed legislation, particularly in the summer of 2002, to respond to some of the EU's concerns (such as abolishing the death penalty), but human rights groups and many in the EU do not see Turkish membership of the EU as imminent. For that reason, as of October 2002, accession negotiations with Turkey have still not opened.

The disappointment felt in Turkey at not being included in the negotiation process led to Turkish resistance over the development of a common security/defence policy within the framework of the EU. This resistance took the form of a Turkish veto (possible as Turkey is a NATO member) of the use of NATO assets for EU actions, under the recently devised plans for a European Rapid Reaction Force.

Public opinion

Although the **democratic deficit** is usually discussed as an internal matter for the EU (see Chapter 23), it is an issue that also arises in the context of the enlargement process. Because enlargement is typically negotiated by elites that is, European and national politicians and civil servants, with little involvement, for European citizens until the end of the process, the undemocratic character of this process is one that has gained some attention. The citizens of existing EU member states and those of the applicant countries are not consulted over the decision to enlarge or accede to the EU (see Table 14.2), and there is only limited scope for societal actors to participate in the accession process during the negotiation stage. It is only once negotiations are concluded that the potential for citizen involvement increases, though in the existing member states this may only take place through parliamentary representatives when accession treaties come up for ratification. The main concern for incumbent governments is that they might lose a national referendum on enlargement after having completed all the hard work of negotiating accession, as happened twice in the Norwegian case.

Support for enlargement in the applicant countries has wavered. The discrepancy between EU rhetoric in support of democracy, on the one hand, and Union reluctance to extend certain aspects of the *acquis* to new members has generated resentments that are likely pose problems once the negotiations are concluded. Table 14.3 suggests that accession negotiations have not produced uniformly high levels of public support for EU membership within applicant countries either in the past or in

Table 14.2 Current EU member states' public opinion on enlargement, 2001 (per cent)

Questions: What is your opinion on each of the following statements? Please tell me for each proposal, whether you are for it or against it: 'The European Union should be enlarged and include new countries.'

	For	Against	Don't know
Greece	70	18	13
Ireland	59	18	24
Spain	55	17	27
Portugal	52	25	23
Italy	51	22	27
Denmark	50	40	10
Sweden	50	37	13
Finland	45	41	14
Belgium	44	39	17
Luxembourg	43	42	15
EU15	43	35	23
Netherlands	42	41	17
Germany	35	42	23
France	35	47	18
United Kingdom	35	34	31
Austria	33	49	18

Source: Eurobarometer no. 55 (Spring 2001).

Table 14.3 Public opinion in past and current enlargements (per cent)

	May 1975	Oct. 1980	Oct. 1985	Nov./ Dec. 1994	Oct. 2001
UK (Jan. 1973)*	54.2				
Ireland (Jan. 1973)*	52.2				
Denmark (Jan. 1973)*	40.5				
Greece (Jan. 1981)*		43.9			
Spain (Jan. 1986)*			67.2		
Portugal (Jan. 1986)*			60.5		
Austria (Jan. 1995)*				36.3	
Finland (Jan. 1995)*				51.2	
Sweden (Jan. 1995)*				42.6	
Bulgaria					74
Cyprus					51
Czech Republic					46
Estonia					33
Hungary					60
Latvia					33
Lithuania					41
Malta					39
Poland					51
Romania					80
Slovak Republic					58
Slovenia					41
Turkey					59

* Date of joining EC/EU given in parentheses.

Sources: Eurobarometer no. 3 (May 1975), *Eurobarometer* no. 14 (Oct. 1980), *Eurobarometer* no. 24 (Oct. 1985), *Eurobarometer* no. 42 (Nov./Dec. 1994), *Applicant Countries Eurobarometer* 2001.1 (Oct. 2001).

the current round of enlargement. Public support for joining the EU was less then 50 per cent in the immediate period after accession in Denmark and less than 50 per cent immediately prior to enlargement in Greece, Austria, and Sweden. In the current round, it is worth noting that countries that have had less difficulty meeting the requirements of membership, such as Estonia and the Czech Republic, also have the lowest levels of popular support for membership. By contrast, countries which have not progressed so far into accession negotiations, such as Romania and Bulgaria, have the highest levels of support.

Key points

- Enlargement is not a specific set of policies or institutions but concerns nearly all areas of European integration.

- Particularly contentious issues for the current enlargement include the migration of workers,

the reform of the CAP, international security, and public opinion.

- The Turkish application for membership poses particular challenges for the EU, in terms of both its claims on Northern Cyprus and matters of security.

The future of an enlarged EU

At the time of writing (late 2002), there is much speculation about the future of EU enlargement. On this basis it is possible to identify three potential scenarios for enlargement:

- Total failure owing to the opposition of existing member states.

- Piecemeal enlargement involving minimal reform of the EU institutions, resulting in the perpetuation of a 'flexible integration' model (see Chapter 24).

- Full enlargement and fundamental reform, after which the EU emerges as a coherent, streamlined actor with a reinvigorated agenda.

In practice, what ultimately happens within the enlargement process may not fall neatly into any of these three scenarios. As of late 2002 the EU is predicting that it will enlarge to ten members in mid-2004, the year of the next elections to the European Parliament (EP). But it remains unclear exactly what direction the EU will be taking by that time. Big questions, such as these, over the future of the EU are currently being addressed by the **Convention** on the future of Europe (see Chapter 4: 58–61).

With the signing of the Nice Treaty in 2001 (see Chapter 4: 57) the EU began to plan its internal reforms with the intention of preparing for the next round of enlargement. There was a general acknowledgement that European institutions that have strained to work with 15 members simply could not operate effectively with 25, and that internal reform had to cover both policies and institutional

questions. It is clear, for example, that the continued use of unanimous voting procedures in certain policy areas could lead to institutional paralysis with 25+ members. Therefore, it was agreed at Nice to extend the use of QMV into a number of new policy areas. The EU also agreed to reweight the votes within the EU Council in light of prospective new members (see Table 14.4; see also Chapter 4: 57–8). However, the Nice Treaty was unable to produce a comprehensive agreement on the reform of the EU's institutional framework, for fear that the EU's smaller and poorer countries would end up having a disproportionate influence over European policy.

Another institutional issue addressed at Nice is the future size of European institutions after enlargement. It was accepted that the expansion of the institutions would have to be limited for practical purposes. For example, if the EP were to be enlarged as it has been in the past on the basis of the population of all member states, it would already have reached over 700 members and would likely be ungovernable. Thus the Nice Treaty, after a contentious deliberation, also produced agreement on a potential distribution of seats in the EP (see Table 14.5). There was less agreement, however, on the suitability of the rotating presidency of the EU (see Chapters 10: 152–3). At the moment, the presidency is held by member states for a period of six months. In future, some of the new and smaller states may lack the resources or standing to run an efficient presidency. However, a decision on an alternative to the present system is yet to be taken.

Table 14.4 Weighting of votes in the EU Council prior to and after the Nice Treaty, 2001

	Currently	Treaty of Nice
Member countries		
Belgium	5	12
Denmark	3	7
Germany	10	29
Greece	5	12
Spain	8	27
France	10	29
Ireland	3	7
Italy	10	29
Luxembourg	2	4
Netherlands	5	13
Austria	4	10
Portugal	5	12
Finland	3	7
Sweden	4	10
United Kingdom	10	29
Sub-total	87	
Candidate countries		
Bulgaria	—	10
Cyprus	—	4
Czech Republic	—	12
Estonia	—	4
Hungary	—	12
Latvia	—	4
Lithuania	—	7
Malta	—	3
Poland	—	27
Romania	—	14
Slovakia	—	7
Slovenia	—	4
Total	—	345

Table 14.5 Seats in the European Parliament prior to and after the Nice Treaty, 2001

	Currently	After Nice Treaty
Member countries	25	22
Belgium	25	22
Denmark	16	13
Germany	99	99
Greece	25	22
Spain	64	50
France	87	72
Ireland	15	12
Italy	87	72
Luxembourg	6	6
Netherlands	30	25
Austria	21	17
Portugal	25	22
Finland	16	13
Sweden	22	18
United Kingdom	87	72
Sub-total	625	
Candidate countries		
Bulgaria	—	17
Cyprus	—	6
Czech Republic	—	20
Estonia	—	6
Hungary	—	20
Latvia	—	8
Lithuania	—	12
Malta	—	5
Poland	—	50
Romania	—	33
Slovakia	—	13
Slovenia	—	7
Total	—	732

Key points

- It remains unclear in some key areas precisely what form the Union will take when the EU enlarges.

- Enlargement has already necessitated internal EU reforms, including a reallocation of seats in the EP and a reweighting of votes in the Council, but more reform is likely in 2004.

Conclusion

Enlargement is among the most pressing concerns on the EU's agenda. While future developments will certainly overtake some of the information presented here (and readers will therefore have to update themselves on events occurring after late 2002), this chapter has raised a number of important issues and questions.

Enlargement has been considered a complex formal process with consequences for both new members and the EU itself. Over time, as the EU has changed and grown, enlargement has also become more complicated, though the process has always been contentious. In light of the concerns of current members, one might ask, why enlarge at all? Beyond the arguments for and against enlargement raised in this chapter, there are also significant costs if the EU does not enlarge. Notably, the failure to enlarge could weaken incentives for reform among applicant countries, risking instability on the European continent. Choosing not to accept new members for protective reasons could also feed scepticism about the EU among existing member states. For most, then, the question is rarely whether to enlarge, but when and how.

QUESTIONS

1 How has enlargement from six to 15 member states changed the EU?

2 Is enlargement necessary?

3 What are the biggest challenges posed by EU enlargement?

4 How did the EU respond to the demise of Communism in Central and Eastern Europe?

5 What are the arguments for and against enlargement?

6 What are the similarities and differences between past enlargements and the post-2000 enlargements?

7 What future do you predict for an enlarged EU and why?

8 What is conditionality? Why is it important?

GUIDE TO FURTHER READING

European Commission, *The Free Movement of Workers in the Context of Enlargement* (Brussels: European Commission, 2001*b*). Available at **http://europa.eu.int/com/enlargement/ docs/pdf/migration_enl.pdf**. This report provides a good overview of research on the challenges of migration for enlargement.

Mayhew, A., *Recreating Europe: The European Union's Policy towards Central and Eastern Europe* (Cambridge: Cambridge University Press, 1998). A detailed account of the EU's early responses to the fall of Communism.

Preston, C., *Enlargement and Integration in the European Union* (London: Routledge, 1997). A good overview of enlargement from a theoretical and comparative point of view.

Stark, D., and Bruszt, L., *Postsocialist Pathways: Transforming Politics and Property in East Central Europe* (Cambridge: Cambridge University Press, 1998). A valuable framework for understanding the legacy of Communism in the applicant countries, especially chapters 1 and 3.

WEB LINKS

http://europa.eu.int/comm/enlargement/index.htm The European Commission's enlargement website offers a helpful overview of the subject, including key documents such as the country reports and information on public opinion.

http:www.europarl.eu.int/enlargement/default_en.htm The European Parliament's website on enlargement offers the perspective of a wide range of EU institutions, as well as member states and applicant countries.

http://europa.eu.int/comm/dg10/epo/eb.html and **http://europa.eu.int/comm/dg10/epo/ aceb_en.html** The Eurobarometer websites for member states and applicant countries, respectively, provide useful public opinion data on attitudes towards the EU and its policies.

15 EU external relations

Karen E. Smith

READER'S GUIDE

This chapter examines how the EU conducts its external relations—its relations with non-member countries. External policies are formulated and implemented by two of the three EU **pillars**, the European Community (EC) or 'first' pillar and the Common Foreign and Security Policy (CFSP) or 'second' pillar. This chapter describes the institutions and procedures for external policy making within each of these pillars, and then explores the EU's external relations objectives. The final section analyses the opportunities for and obstacles to the conduct of EU external relations.

Introduction

For much of the European Community's life, 'external relations' meant economic relations with 'third countries' (non-members), largely conducted through the EC's Common Commercial Policy. Foreign policy, on the other hand, was co-ordinated within a separate framework, which used to be known as European Political Co-operation (EPC) and is now the Common Foreign and Security Policy (CFSP). Therefore, in the past, external policies rarely incorporated political, economic, and security objectives and instruments. However, since the establishment of European Union (EU) in 1993, external policies have become more encompassing and consistent, though the two separate policy making frameworks persist.

In recent years, the EU's external relations have developed to an astonishing extent. The European Community (EC) of the 1960s had some relations with third countries, namely former European colonies, and was beginning to assert a common stance in international trade negotiations. By contrast, the EU at the start of the twenty-first century conducts economic and political relations with virtually every country on earth, is a major player in international trade negotiations, and is currently engaged in the construction of a common security and defence policy. What accounts for this dynamism? For the most part, the answer lies with the EU's member states. For the last 30 years, they have sought to develop Europe-level mechanisms for conducting external relations. At the same time, however, they have tried to retain control over the process, jealously guarding their own autonomy in the sphere of foreign policy. This tension, between the drive to act collectively on the world stage and the desire to retain national autonomy, has shaped the institutions developed in the external relations field, as well as the outcomes produced by those institutions.

Institutions and procedures: The Community pillar

Two of the EU's most powerful external policy instruments fall under the remit of the EC or 'first' pillar of the Union: the capacity to enter into international agreements, and the provision of financial and economic assistance. There is a huge demand for agreements with the Community, the largest trading bloc in the world. Moreover, the EC is also one of the world's largest aid donors. These instruments give the Community the potential to exercise considerable influence in international affairs.

The Community can offer three basic types of agreements to third countries: trade; co-operation; and association. The first of these—trade—stems from the fact that the Community is a common market based on a customs union. Member states not only remove barriers to trade among themselves, but also establish common rules for imports into the Community (see Chapter 3). If exports to all member states are subject to the same tariffs, then individual member states cannot unilaterally negotiate changes in those tariffs. Therefore, under the Common Commercial Policy, only the Community, and not the member states, concludes trade agreements with third countries. Trade agreements usually provide a schedule for lifting trade restrictions on imports into the EC. Only two Community institutions are responsible for negotiating and concluding agreements, the Commission and the Council (see Box 15.1). The Community also plays a major role in international trade negotiations, and is a full member of the World Trade Organization (WTO). In fact, the three major powers in the WTO are clearly the European Community, the United States, and Japan.

Trade agreements are so limited in scope that they are rarely concluded nowadays. Instead, more extensive agreements are preferred, such as 'co-operation agreements'. These include measures for co-operation on economic and commercial matters, as well as for liberalizing trade. They also set up frameworks for dialogue with the third countries, which allow ministers, officials, and parliamentarians to meet regularly. Until the Maastricht Treaty entered into force in November 1993, the Community concluded two types of agreements with developing countries: co-operation agreements (as was the case with, say, India and Brazil) or association agreements (as in the case of the Lomé Agreements signed with the African, Caribbean, and Pacific (ACP) countries) from 1975 on. The **Maastricht Treaty** explicitly added development co-operation to the Community's remit, so that the Community can now negotiate development co-operation agreements with third countries. These offer EC assistance for development.

Association agreements set up a closer, more institutionalized relationship with a third country or grouping of states. In addition to trade measures, they provide for co-operation in a wide variety of sectors, and often include protocols that specify a package of EC aid and European Investment Bank loans. Association agreements can even extend the customs union (as with Turkey) or the internal market (as in the European Economic Area (EEA) with Iceland, Liechtenstein, and Norway). They also provide for meetings between ministers, officials, and parliamentarians from both sides.

Box 15.2 lists some of the countries and regional

Box 15.1 **The facts**

Decision-making procedures for international agreements

The basic procedure for negotiating and concluding an international agreement is as follows:

1   The EU Council (the General Affairs and External Relations Council) authorizes the Commission to open negotiations with a third country or international organization.

2   The Commission conducts the negotiations according to the Council's instructions and in consultation with a special committee appointed by the Council.

3   The Council concludes the agreement.

For *trade agreements*, the Council acts by qualified majority voting (QMV) and the European Parliament (EP) is not involved. For *co-operation and development co-operation agreements*, the Council acts by QMV unless the agreement covers a field for which unanimity is required to adopt internal Community policies. It concludes agreements after consulting the EP. The Parliament's assent is required for most agreements. For *association agreements*, the Council decides by unanimity. EP assent is required. The member states are free to conclude co-operation and development co-operation agreements with third countries, as long as they do not conflict with the Community's agreements, but only the Community can enter into trade agreements. If any of the above agreements include areas under the exclusive competence of the member states, such as dialogue on foreign policy matters, then ratification by the member states is also required to conclude the agreement. The Amsterdam Treaty allows the Council unanimously to authorize the country holding the presidency to negotiate agreements on CFSP or JHA matters, which would then be concluded by the Council unanimously. To suspend a Community agreement, the same procedures apply with respect to the roles of the Commission and Council. The EP is only informed of decisions to suspend agreements; it does not vote on whether or not to do so.

Box 15.2 **The facts**

EU agreements with third parties: Some examples

Trade agreements

Baltic states (1994): Estonia, Latvia, Lithuania

Co-operation agreements

Former Soviet republics (1994–): Armenia, Azerbaijan, Georgia, Kazakhstan, Kyrgyzstan, Moldova, Russia, Ukraine, Uzbekistan
Mexico (1997)
ASEAN (1980)

Association agreements

Cotonou (fomerly Lomé) Convention (2000): 77 African, Caribbean, Pacific (ACP) states
Europe Agreements (1994–): Bulgaria, Czech Republic, Estonia, Hungary, Latvia, Lithuania, Poland, Romania, Slovenia, Slovakia
Euro-Mediterranean agreements (1996–): Israel, Jordan, Morocco, Tunisia, Palestinian Authority

groupings that have concluded trade, co-operation, or association agreements with the Community. Virtually every country on earth is linked to the EU through a formal agreement, though most developed countries, including the United States, have concluded only sectoral agreements (covering trade in specific sectors).

The extent of its network of partners illustrates the influence of law on the EU's external relations. A great deal of what the EU does in international relations involves developing relations that are based on law, that is, on legal agreements (Arts 2000: 2). But power is not absent, and the Community has increasingly wielded its instruments for political purposes. The decision to conclude an agreement with a third country or a regional grouping is, in the first place, political: for example, in 1997 the Community concluded an interim association agreement with the Palestinian National Authority, clearly a political act. Second, the *kind* of agreement concluded with a country is an important political decision: association agreements signal a privileged partnership. Third, the content of agreements differs between partners. Some provide for extensive co-operation, others less so. This too reflects political considerations. But these political decisions are not necessarily taken within the CFSP or second pillar, which deals explicitly with more political issues. The Community's actions can be politicized without CFSP input (see M. Smith 1998).

Furthermore, relations with third countries are increasingly, though not always consistently, subject to **conditionality**. In other words, countries must meet political conditions, such as respect for democratic principles, before they can conclude an agreement with the Community. And all Community agreements are now to include a 'human rights clause'. This allows the Community to reduce aid, or suspend or denounce an agreement, if the third country has violated human rights or democratic principles. However, as of mid-2002, no agreement has yet been suspended or denounced on this basis, although aid to several countries (mostly in Africa) has been halted as a consequence.

The Community can also impose economic and financial sanctions on third countries, entailing the suspension of an agreement. To do so, a decision must first be taken (unanimously) within the CFSP framework; then the Community decides the legislative measures necessary to interrupt economic relations, and/or capital movements and payments. The Community has imposed sanctions on numerous occasions, often in conformity with UN Security Council decisions, as in the cases of sanctions on Haiti or Libya.

Aid to third countries and regional groupings

Although the founding treaties made no provision for the granting of assistance to third countries,

early on the Community began giving aid to developing countries, mostly the former European colonies in Africa. The Maastricht Treaty chapter on development co-operation formalized this practice. The Community also gives aid to 'countries in transition' (other European countries). The Commission manages these aid programmes, but the member states also have their own schemes. While the Commission and the member states are supposed to co-ordinate their programmes, this does not happen in practice.

The resources available to the Community for assistance to third countries have increased from a mere 0.2 per cent of the EC's budget in 1966 to 6.0 per cent in 2000. Although the Community budget is relatively small (about 1.25 per cent of EU GNP), the 2000 Community budget still provided 5.5 billion euro for external action (see Table 15.1). Outside the Community budget is the European Development Fund, for which the member states pledge funds separately. Combined, this makes the Community the fifth-largest donor of aid in the world. Nevertheless, the aid budget is

Table 15.1 Community payments for external trade action in 2000 (€m)

Pre-accession strategy (for the applicant countries)	1,696.0
Humanitarian and food aid	832.3
Co-operation with developing countries in Asia, Latin America, and southern Africa (including South Africa)	634.9
Co-operation with Mediterranean countries and the Middle East	547.9
Co-operation with Central and East European countries and the new independent states and Mongolia	779.0
Other co-operation measures	361.6
European initiative for democracy and the protection of human rights	82.5
External aspects of certain Community policies	374.3
Reserves	203.0
CFSP	30.0
Subtotal	5,541.6
European Development Fund (for the ACP countries)	2,635.0
TOTAL	**8,176.60**

Source: European Commission (2000c), *The Community Budget: The Facts in Figures* (Luxembourg: Office of the Official Publications of the European Communities).

barely enough to meet the EU's external ambitions, such as its funding promises for reconstruction in the former Yugoslavia. And there have been serious problems delivering the Community's aid, with delays notorious. To improve this record, in 2000, the Commission reorganized the way it manages aid programmes, creating a new body, EuropeAid, to that end.

Decisions to grant aid are politicized, though again not necessarily in accordance with any prior CFSP decision. And virtually all of the Community's aid is now conditional on respect for human rights and democratic principles. In addition, a small amount of aid has been targeted more specifically for the promotion of democracy and human rights in the so-called European Initiative for Democracy and Human Rights.

The Commission as the centre of attention

Because of its role in negotiating agreements and managing aid programmes, the Commission is often the 'face' of the Community best known to third countries. Almost every country on earth has a diplomatic representation to the Community, and the Commission itself has delegations in about 125 countries and to five international organizations. The Commission's delegations vary in size. Some, such as the delegation in Washington, DC, are quite large. They manage and negotiate trade and other relations with the third country. Euro-enthusiasts might consider these to be 'embassies in the making', although most member states would beg to disagree.

The Commission has reorganized its internal set-up in the external relations field on several occasions. Originally there was only one Directorate-General (Commission department) for external

Box 15.3 The facts

The European Commission under Commission President Romano Prodi, 2000–5 (external relations portfolios)

DG External Relations: Chris Patten
DG Enlargement: Gunther Verheugen
DG Development: Poul Nielsen
DG Trade: Pascal Lamy

economic relations. Now, four DGs deal specifically with aspects of external relations (see Box 15.3). Officials from all four meet regularly to co-ordinate policy. The External Relations directorate-general handles relations with a wide variety of countries, giving the Commissioner (in the 2000 Commission, Chris Patten) an especially high profile.

Key points

- Two key instruments for external policy are controlled by the European Community pillar: the capacity to enter into agreements with third countries, and the capacity to grant aid to third countries.

- These instruments can be used for political purposes: to privilege relations with key partners, and to promote certain objectives (such as respect for human rights).

- The decision-making procedures for using the Community's external policy instruments place the Commission in a central and highly visible role.

Institutions and procedures: The CFSP pillar

The CFSP pillar of the European Union was created in 1993 by the Maastricht Treaty (the Treaty on European Union), evolving out of an earlier mechanism for co-ordinating the member states' foreign policies, European Political Co-operation (EPC) (see Box 15.4). The process of foreign and security co-operation over the last 30-odd years has gradually been 'legalized', in that the rules have been clarified, codified and increasingly invested with the status of law (M. E. Smith 2001).

Through EPC, which was set up in the early 1970s, the member states hoped to speak with a louder voice in international political affairs, thus balancing their growing economic weight. But foreign policy was far too sensitive to include within the Community's remit at the time, so EPC was created as a separate framework. This meant that the Commission was only associated with EPC, that the EP played a marginal advisory role, and that the European Court of Justice (ECJ) could not review EPC decisions. EPC's goals were modest: regular consultation; co-ordination of national positions; and, where possible, common action. The foreign ministers took decisions unanimously. Occasionally they agreed a common stance, such as the 1980 Venice Declaration, in which they recognized the Palestinians' right to self-determination and declared that the Palestinian Liberation Organization (PLO) should be associated with peace negotiations. After initially refusing to bridge the EC–EPC divide, the member states gradually began to use the Community's economic resources to back up EPC decisions, as in the imposition of sanctions. But most often EPC's 'output' was limited to nothing more than a declaration.

With the end of the Cold War, the Community was increasingly expected to take on international responsibilities, such as spreading peace and security to Eastern Europe. Discussions on deepening integration, launched as a response to German unification, expanded to include the reform of EPC, which was considered inadequate for the 'new world order'. The CFSP pillar thus replaced EPC in the Maastricht Treaty.

The CFSP's institutional structure is similar to that of EPC. The European Council sets the broad guidelines and the Council of foreign ministers takes decisions to implement them. The Council's work with respect to CFSP items is prepared by a Political Committee, which in turn relies on the work of European Correspondents and CFSP working groups. The European Commission is fully associated. The EP can make recommendations, but its views do not have to be incorporated into decisions. The CFSP does not fall under the jurisdiction of the ECJ.

The CFSP's decision-making provisions were intended to improve on those of EPC. First, the Commission could propose actions, alongside the member states. This would also help to ensure consistency of action by the Community and CFSP pillars. Second, two new procedures were added. The Council can agree a Common Position or a Joint Action. The difference between them was not specified, though implicitly a Joint Action signalled that the EU was actually doing something (spending money, for example), rather than simply taking a position. Member states must ensure that their national policies conform to both types of decision. Third, **qualified majority voting** (QMV) was slipped into decision making: the Council could decide, by **unanimity**, that further decisions on a Joint Action would be taken by QMV. QMV has never actually been used, however—a sign that the member states will not easily relinquish unanimous voting over foreign policy issues.

Since the EU was to be proactive in international affairs, funding became important. EPC had no budget, so that the member states had to split the costs, if there were any. Under the Maastricht Treaty, CFSP activities can be funded through the Community budget, but the CFSP's budget is tiny compared to the Community's aid budget (see Table 15.1). The CFSP was represented externally through the presidency and the troika (the past, current, and future presidencies), just as EPC had been. There was thus still no single 'EU phone number' for third countries to call to ask what the EU's position was on international issues.

Box 15.4 **Key dates**

The evolution of a common EU foreign, security, and defence policy

March 1948: Belgium, France, Luxembourg, the Netherlands, and the UK sign the Brussels Treaty of mutual defence.

April 1949: The USA, Canada, and ten West European countries sign the North Atlantic Treaty, the basis for NATO.

May 1952: The European Defence Community (EDC) treaty is agreed by the six ECSC member states. It would have created a common European army, and permitted West Germany's rearmament. In August 1954, the French National Assembly rejects the treaty.

October 1954: The Western European Union (WEU) is created on the basis of the Brussels Treaty, and expanded to include Italy and West Germany. West Germany joins NATO. For a time the WEU serves as a framework for discussions between 'the Six' and the UK; after the UK joins the European Community, the WEU is dormant.

December 1969: At a summit in The Hague, the EC heads of state or government ask the foreign ministers to study ways to achieve progress in political (foreign policy) unification.

October 1970: The foreign ministers approve the Luxembourg Report, setting up European Political Co-operation. They will meet every six months, to co-ordinate their positions on international problems and agree common actions. They will be aided by a committee of the directors of political affairs (the Political Committee).

July 1973: The foreign ministers agree to improve EPC procedures in the Copenhagen Report. They will meet at least four times a year; the Political Committee can meet as often as necessary. European Correspondents and working groups will help prepare the Political Committee's work. The Commission can contribute its views to proceedings.

October 1981: Measures approved in the London Report include the crisis consultation mechanism: any three foreign ministers can convene an emergency EPC meeting within 48 hours. In meetings with third country representatives, the presidency can be accompanied by the preceding and succeeding presidencies (the troika). The Commission is 'fully associated with EPC'.

October 1984: The WEU is reactivated, as WEU foreign and defence ministers agree to meet regularly.

February 1986: The Single European Act (SEA) contains Title III on EPC. EPC can discuss the 'political and economic aspects of security'. EPC and the EC's external relations must be consistent. A small EPC secretariat, based in Brussels, will help the presidency.

February 1992: The Maastricht Treaty is signed, replacing EPC with the Common Foreign and Security Policy (CFSP). The Council of foreign ministers are to decide on common positions and joint actions, and qualified majority voting (QMV) can be used to implement the latter. The Commission can initiate proposals. CFSP activities can be financed by the EC budget. The EU can request the WEU to elaborate and implement decisions and actions of the Union that have defence implications.

June 1992: The Petersberg Declaration states that the WEU will engage in humanitarian and rescue tasks, peacekeeping, and crisis management tasks, including peacemaking ('Petersberg Tasks'). Three forms of WEU membership (full, associate, and observer) are created.

June and December 1992: NATO states that it will support Organization for Security and Co-operation in Europe (OSCE) and United Nations (UN) peacekeeping operations on a case-by-case basis. NATO then enforces UN Security Council resolutions on the war in Bosnia-Herzegovina.

January 1994: NATO summit agrees that NATO assets can be used by the WEU and endorses the concept of '**Combined Joint Task Forces**' (the details are approved in June 1996); US approval is needed for the use of its assets.

June 1997: The Amsterdam Treaty is signed, and contains several reforms of the CFSP pillar. QMV is to be used to implement the European Council's common strategies, and member states can abstain from decisions. A High Representative for the CFSP is created, and replaces the past presidency in the troika. The High Representative also heads a new Policy Planning and Early Warning Unit. The EU can launch the Petersberg Tasks, which are to be implemented by the WEU.

December 1998: Franco-British declaration on EU military capability at St Malo.

Box 15.4—*continued*

April 1999: NATO summit welcomes a common European policy in security and defence, and agrees to establish working arrangements with the EU. It also celebrates the accession of the Czech Republic, Hungary, and Poland the month before.

June 1999: The Cologne European Council agrees that the EU should be able to undertake the Petersberg Tasks, replacing the WEU.

December 1999: The Helsinki European Council sets the headline goal for the common European security and defence policy. By 2003, the EU should be able to deploy, within 60 days and for at least one year, military forces of up to 50,000–60,000 persons capable of the full range of Petersberg Tasks. It establishes interim committees to run it: the Political and Security Committee, the EU Military Committee, and the EU Military Staff. In December 2000, the Nice European Council formalizes the new committees.

The CFSP differs substantially from its predecessor in one respect: it covers defence. EPC had not discussed these issues at all as NATO was the organization responsible for defence (see Box 15.4). In the 1980s, some member states, concerned with the Reagan Administration's bellicosity towards the Soviet bloc, sought to develop West European co-operation in security and defence. This had to take place outside EPC, because Denmark, Greece, and neutral Ireland opposed discussing defence within this framework, largely on principled grounds. So in 1984, the other member states revived the Western European Union (WEU) as a forum in which they could discuss defence issues without a US presence. Conveniently, Denmark, Greece, and Ireland were not WEU members then, unlike the other EC member states. The WEU, formed in 1954 on the basis of a mutual defence treaty, had lain dormant for much of the Cold War. It now gradually became associated with EPC.

The end of the Cold War spurred the development of an EU defence dimension. The USA was withdrawing its troops from Western Europe, and the Europeans were expected to contribute to international peacekeeping missions. CFSP would therefore need a military dimension. But the member states were, and still are, divided over issues such as: the relationship of a European defence structure to NATO, as several do not wish to jeopardize NATO's pre-eminent role in European security; and the EU having a defence role, with several member states opposing moves to turn the EU into an alliance. But they could agree to discuss defence, and that the WEU should be the EU's defence arm. Under the

Maastricht Treaty, the Union can request the WEU 'to elaborate and implement decisions and actions of the Union which have defence implications'. This was still controversial, though. The neutrals (Ireland was joined by Austria, Finland, and Sweden in 1995) could take some comfort in the Treaty's pledge that the Union's policy 'shall not prejudice the specific character of the security and defence policy of certain Member States'. But the defence dimension, among other issues, was a step too far for Danish public opinion. After the Danes initially rejected the Maastricht Treaty in a referendum in June 1992, Denmark was granted an opt-out from the defence provisions.

There were two further problems with using the WEU as the EU's defence arm. First, at the time of the Maastricht Treaty, the WEU was not capable of implementing decisions with defence implications. The WEU Council of Ministers decided to limit its potential activity. In June 1992, in the Petersberg Declaration, they declared that the WEU would engage in humanitarian and rescue, peacekeeping, and crisis management tasks (the Petersberg Tasks), not common defence. The WEU member states pledged forces for carrying out the Petersberg Tasks, but the WEU still lacked operational resources. So in June 1996, NATO approved the concept of Combined Joint Task Forces (CJTFs). The WEU could lead a CJTF, using NATO facilities and resources. This solution proved to be far too unwieldy to be of much use in practice. Faced with the breakdown of law and order in Albania in 1997, the member states could not agree to send a WEU force. Instead, Italy assembled a 'coalition of the willing', acting under a UN mandate, to restore calm in the country.

The second problem was the differing memberships in the EU, WEU, and NATO. In an attempt to simplify matters, the WEU created several types of membership. Observers, associates, and associate partners could attend some WEU Council meetings, and participate in WEU missions. This made for a very large 'WEU family'—28 states—not the simplest of solutions.

The CFSP after Maastricht

The CFSP's record after the Maastricht Treaty entered into force in 1993 was mixed. Numerous Joint Actions and Common Positions were approved, many of which took a long-term approach to international relations. Election observers were sent to places such as Russia and South Africa, to try to ensure a smooth democratic transition; special envoys were sent to the Middle East and the Great Lakes region of Africa, to contribute to the peace processes there. Several CFSP decisions relied on Community instruments, as in the promise of a co-operation agreement with South Africa to support its transition to multiracial democracy. But there was still a feeling that the EU was not matching its economic weight with political clout. The EU was ineffective in the Bosnian war (see Box 15.5). Its most substantial contribution was to administer the divided town of Mostar, Bosnia-Herzegovina, although its success in bringing together the Muslim and Croat communities was limited. The EU's record in other crises of the mid-1990s was even less admirable. It, like the rest of the international community, stood by and watched the genocide in Rwanda, and in Albania the EU and WEU failed to take action.

This disappointment contributed to a more substantial revision of the CFSP provisions in the Amsterdam Treaty, which came into force in 1999. The decision-making machinery remained much the same, but other improvements were agreed. Unanimous voting was to become less the rule and more the exception, a necessity if CFSP was to function as the EU enlarged. The Amsterdam Treaty also provided for **constructive abstention** and the use of QMV when a Common Strategy is adopted (see Box 15.6).

In response to concerns that the EU was too reactive in the face of international crises, the member states set up a Policy Planning and Early Warning Unit within the Council Secretariat. The Policy Unit, staffed by Commission, WEU, and national officials, monitors developments of relevance to the CFSP, provides early warning of crises, and produces policy option papers. The Amsterdam Treaty also created the post of the High Representative for the CFSP to help formulate and implement policy decisions, and head the Policy Unit. The High Representative participates in a new troika, with the current and incoming presidencies, in association with the Commission. The intention was to give the CFSP more continuity in its international representation, providing that elusive 'single phone number'. But the High Representative is still only one part of the system, and really only adds a phone number to the mix. Javier Solana, a former Spanish foreign minister and NATO Secretary-General, was appointed High Representative and took up the post in October 1999. As far as the defence dimension goes, the Amsterdam Treaty did not reform substantially the Maastricht provisions. The neutral states and the UK opposed merging the EU and the WEU. Instead the Petersberg Tasks were included in the Treaty. To carry them out, the EU would have to avail itself of the WEU.

Since the Amsterdam Treaty entered into force, the CFSP's output has continued to grow. The European Council agreed three Common Strategies, on Russia (June 1999), Ukraine (December 1999), and the Mediterranean (June 2000). But they are rather bland statements of broad objectives, merely restating what the EU is already doing (Spencer 2001). In early 2000, the Council agreed with Solana's suggested improvements. Common Strategies must add value to what the EU is doing already, and should clearly set priorities. But the problem is that they provide for a long-term focus, which is worth little in rapidly changing situations. Two areas where the EU has been very active, South-Eastern Europe and the Middle East, have not been the subject of Common Strategies.

The record of the High Representative and the Policy Unit is more admired, though both suffer

Box 15.5 Case study
The EU and the war in the Former Yugoslavia

The EU's record in the wars in Croatia and Bosnia (1991–5) is dismal. Although active in the first year of the conflicts—sponsoring a peace conference, sending monitors to negotiate local ceasefires, imposing sanctions on Serbia/Montenegro—the EU did not greatly improve the prospects for peace. And in early 1992, it controversially recognized Slovenia, Croatia, and then Bosnia-Herzegovina, while Greece blocked Macedonia's recognition until after it was renamed the Former Yugoslav Republic of Macedonia (FYROM). Moreover, the member states opposed sending a WEU force to back up their diplomacy; instead they contributed to a UN peacekeeping force. From summer 1992, the EU was sidelined. It first worked *alongside* the UN to gain approval of a peace plan, without success, and then stood by as the Contact Group, composed of the USA, Russia, the UK, France, and Germany, took over the diplomacy, and NATO enforced UN resolutions. In the summer of 1995, NATO's military activity increased in Bosnia, helping to establish the conditions for a peace agreement. In the end, the USA alone mediated the Dayton peace plan, signed in Paris in December 1995, and NATO troops policed its implementation.

With peace, the EU's role grew. It was responsible for reconstruction, and built on its experiences administering the divided city of Mostar, Bosnia-Herzegovina, between 1994 and 1996. The EU also devised a strategy to strengthen regional stability. It promised trade relations, aid, and co-operation agreements, if the South-East European countries met conditions such as respect for democracy and human rights, and co-operation with their neighbours. But this did not prevent further violence. Serbia/Montenegro's leader, Slobodan Milosevic, pursued a brutal campaign to impose Belgrade's rule over Kosovo, a province of Serbia inhabited mostly by Albanian Muslims. The EU pressed Belgrade to cease offensive military actions. But after a peace conference failed in

January 1999, NATO took the military initiative, bombing Serbia until its troops withdrew from Kosovo.

Again, with peace, the EU took the lead in constructing a post-war order in south-eastern Europe, adding the Stability Pact and Stabilization and Association Agreements (SAAs) to its previous strategy, and thus bringing together diplomatic and economic instruments in a fairly consistent external policy. The Stability Pact encourages the former Yugoslav republics and Albania to co-operate with each other for the carrot of eventual EU membership. SAAs are on offer to countries meeting political and economic conditions. The EU's strategy had a better chance of success as authoritarian regimes fell: Franjo Tudjman's regime in Croatia was replaced by a pro-Western government in early 2000, and Milosevic was toppled in October 2000. The EU promised massive aid to Serbia, and moved to conclude an SAA with Croatia.

But in early 2001, inter-ethnic violence erupted in FYROM. The EU led efforts to prevent further violence and find a lasting solution to the crisis. It signed an SAA with FYROM in March 2001, a deliberate signal that the government should reach a peaceful solution to the problem. In retrospect, this carrot was offered too early, as intensive, co-ordinated diplomacy by the EU, NATO, and the USA resulted in an agreement only in August 2001. A NATO force (composed of European troops) collected weapons from ethnic Albanian rebels, while the EU pressured the FYROM government to enact a series of reforms enhancing Albanian minority rights.

As the USA concentrates on fighting terrorism, the EU's responsibility for South-Eastern Europe increases. But again a 'capabilities–expectations gap' appears: the member states have advocated a high-profile role for the EU in the region, but have been less willing to provide additional funding to support this. Whether the EU can stabilize south-eastern Europe will be a key test of its capabilities.

from a lack of financial resources and personnel. Solana has generally been perceived to be a success, contributing to the Middle East peace process and a peaceful solution to conflict in the Former Yugoslav Republic of Macedonia, and he has certainly provided a 'face' for EU foreign policy.

Towards an EU security and defence policy?

The most important development since the Amsterdam Treaty is in the security and defence dimension.

Box 15.6 **The facts**
CFSP decision-making procedures

The European Council agrees *Common Strategies*, by unanimity, in areas where the member states have interests in common. A Common Strategy sets out the EU's objectives, duration, and means to be made available to carry it out. The General Affairs and External Relations Council implements Common Strategies by agreeing *Joint Actions* and *Common Positions*; in so doing, it votes by qualified majority voting (QMV). The Council may also approve Joint Actions and Common Positions separately, not as measures implementing a Common Strategy. In this case, the Council votes by unanimity, although it may decide unanimously to implement a Joint Action by QMV. *Joint Actions* address specific situations where operational action by the EU is considered to be required. *Common Positions*

define the approach to a particular matter of geographical or thematic nature. A member state can oppose the use of QMV for reasons of important national interests (the 'national interest brake'), and QMV does not apply to decisions having military implications.

One or more member states can abstain from voting on a decision, without blocking it (the **constructive abstention** clause). But they must accept that the decision commits the Union and agree not to take action likely to conflict with it. If the member states abstaining from a decision represent more than one-third of the weighted votes, then the decision cannot be adopted. The Commission shares the right of initiative with the member states, but does not have a vote.

In 1998, the British government changed its stance on an EU defence dimension. In December 1998, the prime minister, Tony Blair, signalled the change in the St Malo initiative with France, the other major military power in Western Europe. They declared that the EU must be willing and able to respond to international crises by undertaking autonomous action, backed up by credible military forces. There are clearly differences in the British and French visions. For Britain, the EU should act when NATO does not wish to do so, whereas for France, NATO does not have such a primary role. But for the time being, the two countries can at least agree to develop the EU's military capacities (see Howorth 2001).

Surprisingly, even the neutral EU member states were willing to develop the initiative. There had been considerable dissatisfaction with the EU's role in Kosovo, where NATO was still the primary actor (see Box 15.5). The June 1999 Cologne European Council repeated the language of the St Malo declaration, and in December 1999, the Helsinki European Council set the famous 'headline goal': by 2003, the EU must be able to deploy within sixty days, and sustain for at least one year, military forces of up to 50,000–60,000 persons capable of the full range of Petersberg Tasks. In November 2000, the member states made specific commitments of personnel to attain the headline goal. In November 2001, they did the same with respect to equipment and

other resources. There are still major shortfalls, however.

To provide political guidance and strategic direction to such operations, new bodies have been set up within the Council framework, namely, a Political and Security Committee (PSC), a Military Committee, and a Military Staff. The PSC consists of ambassadors from the member states, who reside permanently in Brussels, and meet at least twice a week. It effectively replaces the Political Committee. It helps formulate and implement common EU external policies, co-ordinates CFSP working groups, and gives political direction to the development of EU military capabilities. The PSC is building strong relations with other institutions in Brussels, the Commission, High Representative, and Policy Unit. This is contributing to the 'Brusselization' of EU foreign policy, which refers to the fact that foreign policy issues are more and more discussed, and decided, in Brussels (Allen 1998). The Military Committee consists of the member states' chiefs of defence or their military representatives. It provides military advice to the PSC. The Military Staff, consisting of 135 people, provides early warning and strategic planning for the Petersberg Tasks, and is helping to identify gaps in the EU's military capabilities.

The WEU has now disappeared as an organization, and the EU-WEU-NATO triangle has effectively become a bilateral EU-NATO relationship. This raises two problems. First, the WEU was an alliance, based on a mutual defence guarantee. The future of this guarantee is unclear, as the neutral EU member states are not keen to turn the EU into an alliance. The *defence* side of the common security and defence policy thus remains undeveloped. Second, there are concerns that the EU will duplicate NATO's resources and thus compete with it. Such worries have been largely put to rest, since for the foreseeable future, the EU will need access to NATO resources to be able to carry out the Petersberg Tasks. Agreement on this had been blocked until recently, however, over the involvement of Turkey (a key NATO ally and EU applicant state) in the making of decisions to deploy an EU mission.

Key points

- The mechanisms for co-ordinating national foreign policies and agreeing common foreign policies have been in continuous evolution since 1970. The CFSP pillar replaced the earlier, informal mechanism, EPC.

- The scope of the CFSP has been extended to security and defence policy, although the Union's capacity to engage in military operations is still being developed.

- New bodies have been created within the CFSP pillar. These are based in Brussels, contributing to a shift in the locus of policy making from the national capitals to Brussels.

The Union's external relations objectives

Given the procedures identified above, what objectives do the member states seek to achieve? The EU has articulated common objectives in the Treaty and other declarations. These reflect a 'liberal internationalist' approach to international relations, encompassing a belief in the benefits of economic interdependence and democracy, and the utility of international institutions.

The objectives set out in the Treaty are somewhat vague. The common commercial policy is to contribute 'to the harmonious development of world trade, the progressive abolition of restrictions on international trade, and the lowering of customs barriers'. The Community's development policy is supposed to foster sustainable economic and social development, help integrate the developing countries into the world economy, fight poverty, and promote democracy and human rights. The CFSP's objectives are to:

- safeguard the Union's common values, interests, and independence;
- strengthen the security of the Union and its member states in all ways;

- preserve peace and strengthen international security;
- promote international co-operation; and
- develop and consolidate democracy and the rule of law, and respect for human rights.

The EU's external objectives have also been laid out in various declarations. In June 1992, the foreign ministers suggested six specific CFSP objectives:

- strengthening democracy and respect for human and minority rights;
- encouraging regional co-operation;
- contributing to the prevention and settlement of conflicts;
- contributing to more effective, international co-ordination of emergency situations;
- strengthening international co-operation in areas such as the fight against arms proliferation, terrorism, and traffic in illicit drugs; and
- promoting good government.

These objectives are also shared with the Community pillar. Regional co-operation, for example, is a long-standing Community objective. Since the 1970s, the Community has engaged in dialogues with regional groupings, specifically to this end. The EU has sponsored regional co-operation initiatives such as the Euro-Mediterranean partnership and the Pact for Stability in South-Eastern Europe. The promotion of human rights and democracy has also been an aim of Community external policy.

Recently, conflict prevention has acquired a higher profile as an EU objective (Hill 2001; Rummel 1997). The European Council meeting in Göteberg in June 2001 issued an EU Programme for the Prevention of Violent Conflicts. Certainly the EU has been actively trying to prevent outbreaks of further violence in South-Eastern Europe.

While the EU has been increasingly willing to articulate common objectives, it rarely prioritizes them. Hence the tendency for declarations, such as Common Strategies, to list numerous objectives (such as the promotion of human rights and regional co-operation) but not to indicate which are more important. This is problematic because the objectives may conflict with each other (for example, should authoritarian leaders be tolerated even if

they help combat international crime?), and it is not clear how the EU would resolve such conflicts.

Another serious problem that arises in EU external policy making is inconsistency in the pursuit of its objectives. Whereas the EU reduces aid to some third countries for human rights violations, violations in others are often ignored if it is in the political, security, or economic interests of one or more member states to continue relations uninterrupted (K. E. Smith 1998; Youngs 2001). This brings us to the fundamental question of the willingness of the member states to pursue a coherent, consistent common external policy, discussed in the next section.

Key points

- The EU's objectives reflect a liberal internationalist approach to international affairs.
- The EU has articulated shared external relations objectives, but has tended not to establish which objectives are most important and have priority.

Obstacles and opportunities

Can the EU achieve the necessary unity to achieve its various declared external policy objectives? Many observers are sceptical, and identify a fundamental obstacle—the member states themselves. The member states continue to pursue their foreign policy interests separately, or at least to ensure that any Union policy causes least damage to them (Gordon 1997/8). The Union does not come close to having exclusive jurisdiction over foreign policy. The member states may agree to act collectively, but that agreement is not mandatory nor it is always forthcoming. Even within the Community pillar, where QMV can be used, the tacit or explicit agreement of all the member states is still needed for the Union to act internationally. Agreement to lower trade barriers, for example, can be difficult to reach, as the member states hesitate to liberalize trade in

'sensitive' goods (most spectacularly, agricultural products).

The basic problem, it is argued, is that the member states do not share extensive common interests, and this 'logic of diversity' (Hoffmann 1966) tends to block agreement on creating a more supranational, foreign-policy-making machinery, as well as on common foreign policies within the current framework. Several observers even deny that common European interests can develop in the absence of a European state. If foreign policy expresses the identity and interests of a particular community, then by definition, the EU cannot formulate foreign policy because at best, the member states are linked by a weak sense of shared identity (Allen 1998).

Yet it is undeniable that the logic of diversity has not prevented the member states from continuing to develop the mechanisms for foreign policy co-operation, or from declaring that they do share common interests and objectives and desire to pursue them collectively. This does not always translate into common action, as even where there are shared interests, the member states may not agree on policy. But there are pressures for collective action, which can result in common foreign policies.

Such pressures are both external and internal. External stimuli include specific demands for EU action, and the more diffuse effects of **globalization**. The EU comes under considerable pressure to respond to the many demands on it for political dialogue, aid, trade agreements, association, membership, and so on. External demands grew with the completion of the single European market between 1987 and 1993 (which sparked fears of a 'fortress Europe') and have not diminished. Several writers have termed this 'externalization' (Schmitter 1969; Ginsberg 1999). Furthermore, the Union's economic strength can generate external expectations that it will exercise political influence. The Union is called upon to match its economic resources with a political voice. Of course, the EU may respond only partially or not at all to such external demands, but they nonetheless create pressures for collective action.

However, external demands may not always encourage common EU policies. The United States has often supported European integration, but its attitude towards the development of an independent European voice, backed up by more powerful instruments, is not always consistent. While it may push for the Europeans to share the 'burden' of ensuring security and peace, it has been less willing to share the power to determine what should be done. The EU member states have been united in resisting some American policies—such as the extraterritoriality of US sanctions on Cuba, Iran, and Libya—but their differing attitudes about transatlantic relations can also block action. Co-operation on defence policy has always developed with one eye on the US reaction.

Globalization also creates pressures on the EU to act collectively. Unilateral action is either ineffective or impossible in an interconnected world, and the member states are aware that they would be better off acting collectively. They recognize that there is a 'politics of scale': they can exercise more influence collectively than unilaterally (Ginsberg 1989, 1999). Furthermore, globalization creates opportunities for EU action: in a world in which economics is just as important as military prowess (or even more important), the EU's predominantly civilian instruments could be more influential. And finally, the new policy agenda—combating international crime, fostering human rights, and so on—is one on which the EU is better suited to act than the member states acting unilaterally. Globalization may also, however, impede collective action: the member states may be affected differently by the international system, and thus may react differently to international developments. There are cross-national ties between EU and non-EU actors, which can impede action by the EU.

There are also internal stimuli favouring EU action internationally. The member states can use the EU to pursue their own economic or security interests. They can see how the EU might 'add value' to, or supplement, their own activities. Furthermore, collective action can provide a shield. Member states can hide behind the EU, citing the exigencies of going along with their EU partners when faced with unpalatable demands from outside, or from domestic actors. Incentives for common external policies can also result from the very process of co-operation, through a process of socialization. The member states thus become more likely to perceive common interests, and more willing to make compromises in the name of collective policies (Jörgensen 1997).

EU institutions—notably the European Commission, and to a limited extent, the European Parliament—may call for EU external policy. As neo-functionalists argue (see Chapter 6), the Commission can help to articulate common European interests, suggest policy options, and encourage agreement among the member states on policies that represent more than the lowest common denominator. It has a strong initiating role in the Community pillar, but also some initiating powers in the CFSP pillar. It can thus use these powers to push for a more visible EU international role.

Now, it is obvious that the external and internal stimuli listed above do not lead to common foreign policies all of the time. But on occasion, the member states can agree on common objectives, and mobilize collective and national resources to try to achieve them. However, even with the agreement of the member states, there are two further obstacles to cohesive international action by the EU: the need for consistency, and the reaction of outside actors.

Because of the formal separation between the pillars, decisions made and actions taken in each pillar could potentially conflict with each other— the problem of consistency. The Maastricht and Amsterdam Treaties state that the Union's external activities must be consistent. In practice, the dividing line between the EC and CFSP pillars can be difficult to distinguish, although it was not always so. Until the 1980s, the member states were reticent to use Community instruments (such as economic sanctions) to back up EPC decisions. Now, comprehensive approaches, combining EC, CFSP, and JHA (justice and home affairs) instruments, are the norm, as in policies towards South-Eastern Europe and the Mediterranean. The EU's relations with third countries and regional groupings are not rigidly divided between EC and CFSP areas. The foreign ministers, in the context of the General Affairs and External Relations Council, are responsible for much of the Community's external relations and the CFSP, and the Commission is fully associated with the CFSP.

There are occasional problems. For example, there has been inter-pillar rivalry over responsibility for election monitoring and assistance. The Commission has viewed the appointment of CFSP special envoys suspiciously. And there is potential for friction between the High Representative for CFSP and the Commissioner for External Relations, if only because their high-profile institutional roles are potentially conflicting.

But interaction between the Community and CFSP pillars is improving. Solana and Patten have coordinated the EU's strategy in South-Eastern Europe, for example. The Council has agreed that before it decides on the EC budget, it should agree priorities for external action, which will reflect CFSP policies as well. The Commission and Council are putting together summary files on the whole field of relations between the Union and each of its partners, to improve the consistency of EU action.

Assuming that the member states agree and the pillars work well together, the EU may still find it difficult to influence third countries. The influence of outsiders on a country can never be overwhelming, bar outright occupation. Not even the USA always prevails—witness its lack of success in bringing peace to the Middle East. The Middle East situation has in fact prevented the EU from fulfilling the promise of the Euro-Mediterranean partnership. Still, there is often a 'capabilities–expectations gap', in that the internal and external expectations of EU influence outstrip the EU's capacity to fulfil those expectations (Hill 1993, 1998).

Key points

- The most important obstacle to common EU external policies is the member states themselves.

- There are continuous pressures for collective action, and internal demands and expectations. Nonetheless, the EU lacks the capacity to respond to these pressures fully and effectively.

- The division between the relevant pillars is becoming less noticeable, but must still be overcome if policies are to encompass a wide range of issue areas.

Conclusion

The EU is an international actor of a very particular sort: its occasional common policies, globe-spanning network of economic and political ties, and even its mere presence generate expectations that it

will undertake proactive, strategic international action, and have a genuine influence on external developments. Sometimes the EU fulfils those expectations, but too often it does not, especially in headline-grabbing crises. The EU's member states have sought to overcome these disappointments by continually reforming the mechanisms for conducting external relations.

The original mechanism for co-ordinating member state foreign policies, EPC, has evolved into CFSP, and the CFSP is now considerably more complex than its Maastricht Treaty roots. The separate Community pillar has its own procedures and institutions. There is more overlap between the pillars, however, both in terms of the way policies are conceived, but also in the content of policies, which include a mix of instruments from both EC and CFSP pillars (and increasingly the third, justice and home affairs pillar as well) (see Chapter 19).

There has been a dramatic increase in the EU's external relations 'output', but this has not always matched expectations that the EU will act decisively, consistently, and influentially in international relations. To an extent, the profusion of actors and mechanisms for conducting external relations is part of the problem, but the heart of the problem is the willingness of the member states to act collectively in international affairs. We may be witnessing a slow evolution towards more and more common policies, but the member states still have the potential to interrupt it in the name of national interests.

QUESTIONS

1   Does the success of the Union's external relations depend on the Community's policy instruments?

2   How important is the EU's 'periphery' (the rest of Europe, the Mediterranean) in the hierarchy of its external relations? Why might this be the case?

3   Are the Amsterdam Treaty provisions on CFSP an improvement on the Maastricht Treaty CFSP provisions?

4   What do you think is driving the development of the common European security and defence policy?

5   Does the EU have the capabilities to meet its external relations objectives?

6   How might the 'logic of diversity' be overcome?

7   Should all of the decision-making mechanisms and policy instruments related to external relations be brought within one single pillar?

8   How influential is the EU as an international actor?

GUIDE TO FURTHER READING

Bretherton, C., and Vogler, J., *The European Union as a Global Actor* (London: Routledge, 1999). The authors analyse the EU's 'actorness' in various policy areas, including international environmental policy and development co-operation.

Cameron, F., *The Foreign and Security Policy of the European Union* (Sheffield: Sheffield Academic Press, 1999). An introduction to the CFSP and external relations up to the June 1999 Cologne European Council.

Hill, C., and Smith, K. E. (eds), *European Foreign Policy: Key Documents* (London: Routledge, 2000). This book brings together all the key documents relevant to European foreign policy, from the 1940s to the December 1999 Helsinki European Council.

Nuttall, S., *European Political Co-operation* (Oxford: Clarendon Press, 1992), and *European Foreign Policy* (Oxford: Oxford University Press, 2000). These books are important and comprehensive histories of EPC and the Maastricht Treaty CFSP provisions, respectively.

Peterson, J., and Sjursen, H. (eds), *A Common Foreign Policy for Europe?* (London: Routledge, 1998). A valuable collection of essays analysing EU foreign policy and its operation.

Piening, C., *Global Europe: The European Union in World Affairs* (Boulder, Colo.: Lynne Rienner, 1997). This book covers the EU's extensive relations with third countries and regional groupings.

WEB LINKS

www.iue.it/EFPB The website of European Foreign Policy Bulletin online, a database of EU documents in the area of foreign policy.

http://ue.eu.int/pesc The EU Council of Ministers' CFSP website, filled with useful information on the CFSP, including CFSP declarations, annual reports, and summary files of the EU's relations with third countries.

www.europa.eu.int/comm/external_relations/index.htm The website of the European Commission's External Relations directorate-general, containing basic information on the EU's relations with numerous third countries and on EU policies in areas such as conflict prevention, or human rights promotion.

16 The Common Agricultural Policy

Eve Fouilleux

READER'S GUIDE

This chapter examines one of the first European policies—the Common Agricultural Policy (CAP). It does so by focusing on the policy's objectives, instruments, and actors. It looks at the way in which the CAP has evolved since the 1960s, and attempts to explain this evolution by asking and answering a number of important questions: why has the CAP been so problematic for European policy makers? why has it proven so resistant to change? and given the constraints identified, how has reform come about? This chapter answers these questions by focusing on the importance of the international context. It also looks at some of the challenges facing agricultural policy as the EU enlarges to include Central and Eastern European states.

Introduction

The Common Agricultural Policy (CAP) has long been of symbolic importance to the European integration process, and has been subject to calls for reform ever since the 1960s. This chapter focuses on this reform process as a way of exploring not only the character of the 'old' CAP, but the future form that this controversial policy might take. It begins with a brief introduction to the principles underpinning the CAP, principles which have largely dictated the policy instruments that have been used.

The second section presents some background on CAP reform, after which the chapter provides an explanation of why it has taken (or is taking) so long to reform this policy. The CAP reform of 1992 is the focus of the next section, after which attention turns to some of the new thinking in the agricultural policy domain— involving the integration of environmental and social concerns into the policy, and the introduction of the concept of **multifunctionality**. EU enlargement is also considered, as are more recent efforts to reform the CAP. Throughout the chapter, emphasis is placed both on the role of the international context in providing a context for reform, and on the national context, which, more often than not, acts as a constraint.

What is the CAP?

The principles and instruments of the Common Agricultural Policy were laid down in the Treaty of Rome in 1957 and subsequently at the Stresa Conference in July 1958, coming into force from 1962. Article 39 of the Treaty set out the objectives of the CAP as follows:

1 To increase agricultural productivity by promoting technical progress and by ensuring the rational development of agricultural production and the optimum utilization of the factors of production, in particular labour.

2 To ensure a fair standard of living for the agricultural community, in particular by increasing the individual earnings of persons engaged in agriculture.

3 To stabilize markets.

4 To assure the availability of supplies.

5 To ensure that supplies reach consumers at reasonable prices.

At Stresa, the question of how these objectives would be put into operation was dealt with. Three main principles were to shape the future of the Common Agricultural Policy:

• Market Unity (a single market): in other words, there should be common prices across the Community and free trade in agricultural produce amongst the EC member states;

• Community preference: that a system of tariff barriers should be put in place to protect the internal market from the instability in world markets;

• Financial solidarity: that there should be a fund set up, which would finance common expenditures in the agricultural domain.

These three principles deserve further attention. First, the initial move in establishing a European agricultural market (applying the common market principle) was the organization of Common Market Organizations (CMOs) for all agricultural products, and most notably for wheat, barley, rye, corn, rice, sugar, dairy products, bovine meat, pork, lamb, wine, and some fruits and vegetables. The common market idea was to allow free trade internally within the Community, but to erect at the same time barriers to the outside world. These CMOs usually operated on the basis of a guaranteed price. The notion of a guaranteed price is crucial to understanding how the CAP has worked. The idea was that instead of allowing the market to determine price levels, the prices farmers received for their produce (sometimes called the target price) would be fixed centrally by Community civil servants and politicians (the market or **price support** system). If the price began to fall (which would have the effect of depressing farmers' incomes), intervention agencies set up at national level would step in when the price reached a certain level (the intervention price) to buy up the surplus, thus keeping prices high. This was clearly an extremely interventionist—and indeed costly—system that was set up. It had the objective of supporting farmers' incomes and boosting agricultural production, and the more farmers produced the more money they earned.

But if the price fixed inside the EC was to be high enough to support farmers' incomes, it was imperative to prevent cheap imports from flooding the common market. Therefore, to achieve the second CAP principle, community preference, a system of border tariffs was set up for each product. Produce could generally only enter the common market if it was priced at or above a level agreed centrally— the so-called 'entry price'. Moreover, a system of 'reimbursements', similar to export subsidies, was also put in place, enabling European producers to sell their products on the world market at world prices. These subsidies covered the difference in cost between the world and the higher European prices.

Finally, so as to promote the third principle, that of financial solidarity, a common fund was set up, on the basis of Regulation 25 of 1962 (amended subsequently by Regulation 728/70), to cover the financing of the CAP. This fund is known as the European Agricultural Guidance and Guarantee Fund (EAGGF). EAGGF comprises two parts— guidance and guarantee. While the guarantee section covers costs involved with the market system, such as the costs of export refunds, the smaller guidance section is responsible for funding socio-economic (or structural) policies. The EAGGF originally represented almost all of the general budget of the European Community. However, the proportion of the budget spent on agriculture has decreased substantially since the early 1980s, falling from 65.1 per cent of the total EC budget in 1986 to 53.8 per cent in 2000.

As a policy financed collectively by the member states, the CAP has had a **redistributive** effect on the member states. The issue of who gets what, as a consequence of the funding mechanisms at the heart of the CAP, has monopolized many agricultural negotiations in the Council. To understand CAP funding, it is necessary to understand the political compromise that gave birth to the CAP. In the early 1960s Germany had a very inefficient cereal sector, but very politically powerful farmers. As a consequence, when the CAP was formed, the Germans asked for a high level of support for cereals. Though the French were more efficient in this field, and had a lower national price for cereals, they did not mind setting guaranteed prices higher under CAP, as long as they did not have to pay for them. It is for this reason that Germany has ended up as the primary contributor to the CAP since 1962, while France has always been among the main financial beneficiaries. See Box 16.1.

Key points

- The CAP was one of the first EC policies.
- There are three fundamental principles underpinning the CAP: market unity; Community preference; and financial solidarity.

Box 16.1 **Core ideas**
A marginal structural farm policy

Although the CAP was initially organized around market measures, a timid structural policy was also introduced in 1972. This introduced a socioeconomic dimension into the policy, and provided funds for such things as new technologies and equipment. In a proposal he had formulated some years earlier, the Dutch Agricultural Commissioner, Sicco Mansholt, proposed a radical revision of the CAP's market measures, together with an active structural agricultural policy at European level. This was intended to help restructure the sector. Although the plan was immediately rejected by the Council, it gave birth to an embryonic structural policy. Structural CAP measures differ from market measures not only by their objectives and instruments, but also through the funding procedures they involve. Financed by the so-called 'Guidance' section of the Agricultural Fund, EAGGF, they are allocated fixed, multi-annual budgetary 'envelopes' and are co-financed by member states. However, despite an increase in allocations since the mid-1980s, EU structural farm policy still represents a very small part of European agricultural expenditure (see Table 16.1).

Reforming the CAP

With the food shortages of the post-1945 period and the security concerns of the Cold War in mind, the aim of self-sufficiency in foodstuffs was presented as one of the major objectives of the new European Economic Community (see Table 16.1). Initially the policy was very successful, in that it very quickly met its initial political objective—self-sufficiency. But by the 1970s, over-production had become a more important political issue, with the first surpluses having appeared in the form of the famous 'butter mountains' and 'wine lakes' of this period. These problems of over-production, caused when the supply of agricultural produce outstrips demand, increased throughout the 1980s. And with an ever-increasing volume of products surplus to internal requirements being paid for at the guaranteed price, being stored at high cost, and finally being exported out of Community, with support again from the agricultural budget to compensate for lower prices on the world market, the CAP was becoming more and more costly to operate.

It is far from surprising, then, that the CAP was frequently denounced during this time for being too expensive and for taking up too many EC resources, thereby preventing the development of other potentially important political priorities. As a consequence, agricultural policy began to be a major concern for European policy makers. And the issue of CAP reform appeared on the European political agenda.

Table 16.1 Self-sufficiency rates, 1974–1993 (per cent)

	1974 EC9	1979 EC12	1983 EC12	1986 EC12	1993 EC12
Cereals	76	84	98	112	126
Wheat	105	116	127	121	141
Barley	105	113	114	120	122
Sugar	91	115	126	125	135
Bovine meat	96	97	101	102	105

Note: EC9—the then 9 EC member states; EC12—the then 12 EC member states.
Source: Eurostat, *Agricultural Statistical Yearbook*, various years. See also Ortalo-Magné with Mahé, 2001.

A variety of different policy instruments were used to implement these reforms (see Box 16.2). From the late 1970s to the end of the 1980s, the economic policy tools that were used were mainly orientated towards controlling the supply of produce, by imposing quantitative restrictions on production. These took the form of 'guaranteed ceilings' for crops in 1981, milk quotas in 1984, and a regime imposing maximum guaranteed quantities for cereals in 1987–8, generalized to other commodities in 1988–9. Despite these changes, the principle of guaranteed prices for agricultural products remained the core element of the CAP, and was not touched by the reform. The changes implemented during this first period of reform are generally understood to be marginal and incremental. As we will see in the next section, such incrementalism can be explained, on the one hand, by national political pressures, which were exported to the EC level, and on the other, by institutional factors, both of which tended towards sustaining the status quo.

Although decision makers continued to use much the same arguments for reform (the moral dimension of over-production; budgetary problems arising out of increasing agricultural costs; the need to focus on policies other than agriculture; and the implications of enlargement), a radical policy shift occurred in 1992. The original rationale for the CAP, high guaranteed prices for agricultural products, was cast aside, leading to a dramatic decrease in the level of support for farmers. This amounted to a reduction of 30 per cent for crops, namely cereals and oilseeds, and a 15 per cent decrease in levels of support for beef. The sections below examine two explanations for this policy shift, both of which originate at the international level.

To compensate for the loss of support due to the decrease of guaranteed prices, proportional, direct payments were granted to farmers on the basis of the area of land cultivated and according to historical estimates of yields on the farm and/or in the region over the reference period (an average of the past three years). The use of this mechanism ensured that the amount of support provided did not fall after the

Box 16.2 **Issues and debates**
Quotas or price cuts? Two options for the reform of the CAP

From an economic point of view, the only way of dealing with the over-production of foodstuffs (that is, when the supply of food exceeds demand) is to control the supply side. Controlling the supply of food, with the CAP guaranteeing high prices to farmers, means that there are only two options possible: production quotas or price cuts. The first option was the one chosen by policy makers during the 1980s to try to cope with CAP reform issues, whereas it is the second that has been implemented since 1992.

The quota solution aims at limiting the supply of food (the amount produced by farmers) by imposing limits on quantities produced. Since the 1970s, most agricultural economists have opposed the production quotas solution because it tends to freeze production capacity, limiting the competitive advantage of individual producers, and constructing entry barriers for the sector.

The price cut option aims to restore the role of market forces in adjusting supply and demand. On the supply side, as prices fall, farmers have less incentive to produce more food. Complementarities between agricultural sectors may affect how much food is supplied. For example, owing to the interdependencies that exist between the cereals and meat sectors, lowering the price of crops was seen as a way of boosting demand for cereals by European meat producers, so that they would have an incentive to buy European produce rather than the cheaper cereal substitutes, such as soya, which are mainly imported from outside the EU.

Most economists promote the price decrease solution because it gives regulatory powers back to the market and allows distortions between producing countries and individual farmers to be done away with. From a social perspective, it also allows farmers' revenues to be supported by the state via direct payments, but decouples those payments from the act of production.

reform was introduced. The redistributive effects of the CAP remained exactly the same after the 1992 reform as they were before. This is why many CAP specialists—economists in particular—refuse to consider the 1992 reform a major change. However, while recognizing this argument, this chapter argues that despite the modest economic and redistributive impact of the 1992 reform, its political consequences were crucial.

For various reasons, the 1992 reform was a crucial one. First, it set a new trajectory for the development of the CAP, opening the door to later reforms which would make further price cuts and compensate farmers whose income had decreased, by using direct income aids to farmers. But the 1992 reform was also important as it contributed to a transformation of the discourse on agricultural policy, ultimately fostering important changes within the CAP's policy community.

Key points

- Although the CAP was considered a political success in the early 1960s, it soon began to pose problems for policy makers.

- As the policy operated on the basis that the more farmers produce the more they get paid, agricultural surpluses (e.g. butter mountains) soon began to accumulate, as farmers became more productive.

- Early attempts to resolve these problems were incremental and marginal.

- The CAP was subject to a radical reform from 1992, which provoked a gradual dismantling of the guaranteed price system and its replacement by direct individual payments to farmers.

Why is the CAP so difficult to reform?

This section takes a step back in the CAP story, to consider why it has taken so long to reform the policy.

Agricultural decision making

The main actors in the CAP decision-making process are the European Commission and the Agricultural Council. The Commission is responsible for drafting legislation, as well as having an important managerial role within the policy, while it is the Council that takes decisions. The European Parliament (EP), which in many policy areas now shares decision-making responsibility with the Council, has only a very limited role, amounting to consultation, in agricultural policy. The only exception to this rule is where money is concerned, as the Parliament has a critical role in the EU's budgetary decision-making mechanisms (see Chapter 11: 167). The Agricultural Council meets monthly, more frequently than most of the EU Councils. One of these meetings is set aside to discuss what is called the 'price package' for the following year, at which the member states decide on such issues as the level of guaranteed prices, the quotas each member state will receive, and the criteria for calculating direct aid payments.

CAP decision making usually begins with a proposal, from the Commission, often, but not always, made on the basis of a broadly defined request from the European Council (comprising the heads of government). Once formulated, the Commission's proposal is then submitted to the EP for consultation and the Agricultural Council for decision. It is also transmitted to the Committee of Agricultural Organizations in the EC (COPA), the interest group that represents European farmers, and to other institutions as appropriate, such as the Committee of the Regions (representing regional interests), for consultation. The Agricultural Council may reject the Commission's proposal or ask for modifications. Alternatively it may begin to negotiate on the basis of what the Commission has

proposed, resulting ultimately in a decision. Within the Agricultural Council, the **unanimity** rule applies, which means that each member has a right to veto any decision. As we shall see, decision rules such as this have had important consequences for the CAP, especially regarding the pace of reform.

Brake mechanisms at the European level

This formal description of the workings of CAP decision taking only provides part of the story, however. Decision taking in this policy area is based on what might be termed an 'inflationist bargaining dynamic'. As the CAP is a redistributive policy, each member state's minister of agriculture is under pressure to bring home the maximum they can get from that part of the European budget dedicated to agriculture. As a consequence of the number of member states involved in the negotiations, the range of products involved, and the rules that govern the CAP (such as unanimity), there is an inbuilt inflationary tendency within this bargaining process. A typical example of this is in the annual 'price package' review, where each minister in the Council agrees to price increases in their neighbour's favoured products in order to get the increases that they themselves want. As a consequence, decisions that would lead to a reduction in agricultural costs, or that would change the redistributive effects of the policy, are more than likely to be rejected a priori by the Agricultural Council. This makes it very difficult for a body such as the Commission to propose reforms that cut costs (see Box 16.3).

The CAP is an excellent example of what happens when there is no real link between the EU institutions and the EU's citizens. In such circumstances it is easy for governments to use the European Commission as a scapegoat for decisions that they really do not want to take. The Commission is

Box 16.3 Issues and debates

Commission proposals on CAP reform in the 1980s

The European Commission's proposals and reflections on the CAP were rather conservative until the mid-1980s. This has been often explained as a consequence of the high degree of French influence in DG Agriculture (formerly DG VI), the Commission's agriculture department.

The situation changed radically in 1985, when Jacques Delors became Commission President. Early in his term of office he clearly expressed his support for an overarching CAP reform. Concrete proposals were put forward as early as July 1985 with the publication of the Green Paper on the future of the CAP. This pushed the idea of cuts in guaranteed farm prices, notably for crops, with this approach being presented as the most efficient way

in the long run of dealing with over-production concerns, budgetary issues, and instability in the world food market. Particularly in the cereals sector, a lower price was seen as a way of allowing cereal producers to regain market share in the animal food sector, which had been lost to American cereal substitutes in the past.

However, owing to the conservatism of the Council, it took years to translate the new reformism of the Commission into action. Even in 1987, two years after Delors came to office, the reforms proposed were still of a quantitative kind, by then out of favour with agricultural economists (see also Box 16.2).

---

restricted in what it can do when this happens, and often ends up taking the blame for a policy it would like to see reformed.

The 'stickiness' of national sectoral compromises

The Agricultural Council is a conservative body. But how might this conservatism be explained? During the 1980s, the dominant farmers' unions in each member state were completely opposed to CAP reform. Due to their ability to mobilize support in many European countries, farmers' organizations were able to exert pressure on governments to support their line on the CAP. Political influence of this kind was particularly intense in France and Germany. In both countries, farmers were important in electoral terms, as public opinion, influenced by a deep-rooted affinity for rural life, viewed farmers' interests favourably (see Box 16.4).

In the French case, the influence of farmers on agricultural policy making can be expressed using a **corporatist** policy community model (involving 'co-management' or *la cogestion*). This relies on close links between the government and the main farmers' representative organizations, the FNSEA

(*Fédération Nationale des Syndicats d'Exploitants Agricoles*) and the CNJA (*Centre National des Jeunes Agriculteurs*). Thanks to their capacity to mobilize support for their cause, and even though they were traditionally allied to right-wing political parties, these organizations were also able to impose their views on successive Socialist governments after 1981. Although the left-supporting farmers did manage to get organized during the 1980s, with the *Confédération Paysanne* established in 1987, they were still too weak to challenge the power of the right-leaning FNSEA. Consequently, over the course of the 1980s, the French position on the CAP remained very close to that of the FNSEA.

But why are French farmers opposed to CAP reform? While some commentators explain this by stating that French farmers are simply interested in protecting their economic interests, there is an additional factor to be taken into account. The conservatism of farmers' associations—and not just in France—has much to do with deep-rooted symbolic issues linked to the identity of the farming community. In the French case, for example, the FNSEA has vehemently refused (and still refuses) to replace the guaranteed price system with direct payments, even if the latter were calculated to provide a higher income for farmers than the former. Such a position can be explained by certain ethical and professional values that have been inherited by CNJA and FNSEA leaders, arising out of their early experiences in the 1950s with the Young Christian Movement, the JAC (*Jeunesse Agricole Chrétienne*). Farmers were considered to be individual entrepreneurs, actively working the land and selling the products they had grown on the food market in order to earn their living. It is for this reason that they could not tolerate the idea of living and supporting their families on the back of direct income payments, which were viewed either as salaries or, even worse, as a form of social security/welfare payment.

But a second explanation relates directly to the nature of the CAP itself. In upholding the idea that all farmers should get the same rewards, guaranteed prices symbolically feed the myth of farmer unity. This is something of a paradox, as in practice the CAP provides very different levels of support across the EU and across products. For example, the bigger you are as a farmer, the more financial support you get. In fact, guaranteed prices have always been used as a political tool by farming elites and, as such, can even be viewed as fundamental to the FNSEA's monopoly in representing French farmers. Thus, by mobilizing support to defend and promote the level of agricultural prices, particularly when the 'price-package' event takes place in Brussels, they are able to consolidate their own dominant position within the farming community.

From this perspective, quotas can be seen as a marginally more acceptable option for reform—from the farmers' point of view. Unlike the alternative option of lowering guaranteed prices, which agricultural economists have long advocated, quotas allow guaranteed prices to remain as core elements of the policy, whilst resolving—if only superficially—some of the more obvious symptoms of the CAP 'illness'. In the 1980s, the quota solution represented a compromise, allowing EC policy makers to reform whilst placating, for electoral purposes, their agricultural constituencies.

Key points

- The traditionally close relationship between governments and farmers' representatives have impeded European reform efforts.

- Because of the way in which the Agricultural Council operates, these sectoral arrangements at national level have tended to maintain the status quo and to build an inflationary bias into the policy.

- For both national and European reasons, reform progressed only incrementally during the 1980s, while the system of guaranteed prices remained in place.

The CAP reform of 1992

The direction of the CAP changed dramatically in 1992. To examine this 'U-turn', we must consider factors beyond the EU. It is to these 'international' factors that this chapter now turns.

An international learning process

World agricultural markets in the early 1980s were affected by massive instabilities. In 1982, with the aim of improving this situation, the trade ministers

of the 24 member countries of the Organization for Economic Co-operation and Development (OECD) asked the OECD Secretariat-General to undertake a review of agricultural policies implemented around the world and to analyse their effects on trade. The aim of this exercise was to seek recommendations which would lead to balanced reductions in agricultural protection, so as to better integrate agriculture into the multilateral trading system—in other words to liberalize agriculture.

Faced with the heterogeneity of agricultural

policies across the world, and never having undertaken this kind of review before, the officials in charge asked a number of academics, mainly agricultural economists, for advice. These economists provided them with both theoretical and technical tools to fulfil their mandate. Collaboration with these academic economists and the use of other analytical tools led to an economic model which enabled estimates to be made of the impact of domestic policies on world prices and trade.

These studies engendered a learning process within the international agricultural policy community, and many of the analytical tools proposed in the early 1980s are now used as routine instruments of evaluation by almost all national agriculture ministries. But beyond this, these new analytical tools have induced a profound change in the way that agricultural policy issues are defined. They were initially used to classify different national policies, ranging from the less distorting to the more distorting. Subsequently, they were seen as a way to rank policies, and to determine which of them was in most serious need of reform. They also introduced new commonsense thinking about which domestic agricultural policies should, and should not, be reformed. Most notably, it was concluded that to be less distorting, the instruments used within an agricultural policy had to be 'decoupled' from agricultural production, so that they would have no direct impact on the type and quality of commodity produced by the farmer. This conclusion spoke directly to the CAP's price support system.

The international political pressure on the CAP

Not only did the learning curve described above bring about a progressive transformation of the ideas and beliefs dominating the agricultural policy community, it also led to very concrete decisions, and ultimately to the end of the so-called 'agricultural exception' in international trade negotiations. In 1986, a new round of the GATT (the General Agreement on Tariffs and Trade) was opened at Punta del Este, Uruguay, the so-called 'Uruguay Round'. For the first time ever these negotiations included

agriculture alongside the other more conventional industrial and service sectors covered by the talks. Thus the GATT bargaining process was to be used as a means of liberalizing agricultural trade.

As is often the case in GATT Rounds, the main players were the United States and their allies, the Cairns Group, a group of 14 countries that are net exporters of agricultural produce, notably Argentina, Australia, New Zealand, Uruguay, and Thailand. This group were on the offensive from the start, arguing strongly for a radical liberalization of international agricultural markets. On the other side, the EU with Japan were in a more defensive position as countries with traditionally more protectionist agricultural regimes. The USA denounced the CAP as a system which allowed European farmers to eschew competition with the rest of the world, thereby generating trade distortions for producers in third (or non-EU) countries. They called for an end to all trade-distorting domestic subsidies and tariff barriers on agricultural produce. In waging this political war against the EU, they actively used the analytical tools and evaluations developed under the auspices of the OECD.

The Europeans were keen to avoid an outcome that was too radical, and which would have undermined the CAP as a whole. Suppressing agricultural tariff barriers without changing the price support mechanism would simply have allowed products exported at low prices by the Americans and the Cairns Group countries to flood the European market, undercutting domestic produce. Arguing that the aid the USA gave to its own farmers was much greater than the Americans admitted, the Europeans developed their own evaluation tool, known as the Global Measure of Support, and based their GATT counter-proposals on it.

When the Heysel Ministerial Conference, initially planned for the conclusion of the Round, took place in December 1990, US and EU positions were still totally at odds on the agriculture question. This led to a stalemate in the negotiations, threatening the GATT Treaty as a whole with total breakdown. To put additional pressure on the Europeans, the USA and their allies took the decision not to negotiate on any other aspect of the Round, such as on intellectual property rights, until the agricultural issue was resolved.

A radical shift in policy

The 1990 GATT crisis clearly opened a window of opportunity for European reformers. Indeed, a radical CAP reform was seen as the only way to reach an international agreement of any kind. It was at this point that the Commission decided to launch a project that it had been secretly preparing for some months. Using its right of initiative, the Commission delivered its radical CAP reform proposal to the Agricultural Council in February 1991.

In broad terms, the Commission's proposal presented an outline of a 'new' CAP, which would replace the system of agricultural price support with a system of direct support to farmers. The 'spirit' of the reform was in line with international requirements, in that it would in future provide public support through direct, 'decoupled' payments to farmers. The Commission's proposal revolved around a dramatic decrease in guaranteed prices for oilseeds and cereals, as well as an equivalent decrease for the beef sector. As this implied a serious loss of income for the farmers, the price cuts were to be compensated by individual direct payments. In addition, the Commission proposed a sliding scale of compensation for price decreases, in recognition of the fact that large producers had benefited from the CAP in the past. The biggest producers, it was felt, were strong enough to deal with competition in world markets and were therefore not compensated at all for the reduction in the level of prices. Small producers, on the other hand, who would not be able to cope with market pressures without public support, were to be fully compensated, in part on social grounds. Medium-sized farms would be only partially compensated. Other so-called 'accompanying measures' were also introduced as part of the reform package, though these remained very marginal from a budgetary point of view. They dealt mainly with agri-environmental issues, early retirement, and forestry.

The political decision to implement this radical shift in policy instruments seems to have been taken initially by Helmut Kohl and François Mitterrand, the then leaders of Germany and France. Both had been very keen to conclude the Uruguay Round.

Germany had important interests in the non-agricultural part of the negotiations, and the German industrial policy community put intense pressure on the German government to resolve the agricultural impasse. In France, the pressures came from the biggest cereal growers, who had a direct interest in the reform. Thanks to the agreed price decreases, they would be able to gain the upper hand in the European animal food market over US cereal substitutes, which had been sold in the EC at world prices (that is, with a zero border tariff) since 1967. Another important lobby was that of the aeronautical industry, so the outcome of what came to be known as the Blair House Agreement, concluding the Uruguay Round in 1993, was as much about 'Airbus' as about agriculture.

Although the political decision to reform the CAP was taken by the heads of government or state, negotiations on precisely how the reform would be implemented took place in the Agricultural Council over a period of 18 months. The deal was finally concluded on 21 May 1992. The Commission's original proposal had been largely rewritten by this stage, and for that reason the outcome of the 1992 reform was not quite as innovative as it might have been. But this agreement was still regarded in many quarters as historic (see *Financial Times*, 22 May 1992: 1–3).

Key points

- An agricultural learning process, which took place at international level, led to a profound shift in knowledge, beliefs, and ideas about agricultural policy within the international community.

- The inclusion of agriculture in the Uruguay Round of the GATT in 1986 placed an important political constraint on European governments which led to the reform of the CAP.

- The European Commission used this window of opportunity to advance its own proposals. A much altered version of these was eventually accepted in May 1992.

The changing debate on agriculture

While new ideas often run ahead of policies, sometimes new policies may induce new debates. The CAP is a good example of the way in which reform, once initiated, feeds back into discussions about the very purpose of the policy.

The emergence of the environmental issue

The environment and, more specifically, issues of **sustainable development** have found their way into the agricultural policy debate since the 1980s. The negative effects of modern farming were at the source of this new interest in agri-environmental issues. Problems identified included soil erosion in areas of intensive crop production, pollution by pesticides, water pollution caused by nitrate fertilizers in areas of intensive livestock production, and homogenization of the rural landscape. Moreover, from the 1980s, it seemed that public health problems linked to intensive farming were also multiplying, as dioxins in poultry, 'mad cow' disease (BSE), and genetically modified organisms (GMOs) hit the headlines. Environmental interest groups have intensified their activities on agricultural issues, denouncing the guaranteed price mechanism of the CAP on the basis that it provides incentives to farmers to intensify farming practices, exacerbating environmental degradation in rural areas.

This process was also backed by the decision of the 1992 reform to extend the scope of some previously existing agri-environment payments. While remaining very marginal in the CAP budget, these measures did seem to have an impact on behaviour on the ground. By taking a bottom-up, interactive approach to implementation, the measures sought to involve both farmers' representatives and non-agricultural actors, such as environmentalists, actors who had rarely been involved in these issues in the past. By importing new values and beliefs, and new ways of doing things into the agricultural policy community, the introduction of these new measures pushed traditional communities a little further in the direction of environmental consciousness. This process has not been an easy one, however, and is often resisted by farmers.

The mobilization of environmental interests became even more intense after 1992, when the support provided to farmers became more visible as a consequence of the CAP reform. Environmentalists were now able to demonstrate the link between environmental concerns and agricultural policy. Farmers who had been involved in environmentally friendly modes of farming for years without any public support, like organic farmers, also raised their voices (see Box 16.4). These actors called for the establishment of a direct link between the amount of support provided to farmers through the CAP and their environmental performance, or at least their compliance with a minimum set of environmental requirements. This is how the question of the environmental 'cross-compliance' of CAP direct payments, one of the most central issues of the current debate, was initially raised.

Social concerns: Old stakes, new items in the agricultural policy debate

Another dimension to reform, raised since the mid-1990s, relates to social justice and equity. In contrast to the environmental case, this was raised within the farming community. The calculation of compensatory direct payments made under the reformed CAP is based on historic criteria, which reproduce the redistributive effects of the old price support system. The only difference is that these criteria are now much more visible than they used to be. In other words, farmers can now see that most of the agricultural support granted in the EU is given to the biggest farmers, those that are also often the wealthiest. In the past, huge payments were even allocated to landowners like the late British Queen Mother and Prince Rainier of Monaco! In sum, with the distribution of CAP support suddenly becoming more visible as a consequence of the shift from guaranteed prices to direct payments, the old question of social justice has been raised once again.

This shift in the debate not only allowed left-wing farmers' unions, the minority in most of the member states, to gain some additional support. It also created tension and, to some extent, a shift in the balance of power within the more traditional farmers' unions. In France for example, the FNSEA is divided between those who would like to fix maximum amounts of CAP support per capita, and those who are opposed to this kind of a solution, in particular the representatives of the big cereals growers. Similar tensions have also existed within COPA in Brussels since the mid-1990s.

Key points

- By converting an opaque set of instruments (that is, guaranteed prices) into a more transparent policy (direct payments), the 1992 CAP reform has had a deep impact on the shape of the agricultural policy community in the EU.

- Agricultural policy debates have been reoriented since the early 1990s, with new items like the environment and social redistribution assuming increasing importance.

Recent reforms and new challenges

An important event that has occurred since the 1992 reform is the European Conference on Rural Development, organized by the European Commission and held in Cork, Ireland, from 7 to 9 November 1996. Reformist in the views it promoted, the conference was initially planned by the Commission as a way of building an ambitious 'integrated' approach to the countryside. The Cork Declaration, at the end of the conference, invited European policy makers to switch their public support from financing market measures to assisting rural development and agri-environmental programmes. Since that date, only slow progress has been made in pursuing this agenda, however.

Apart from minor changes in specific product regimes, such as olive oil and tobacco, the main CAP reform since 1992 was decided in March 1999 at the Berlin European Council (summit). It was included in the framework of the Commission's *Agenda 2000* preparations in advance of EU enlargement (see Chapter 14: Box 14.2). On the basis of this document, ten new regulations were adopted, with plans that they should come into force from 2000 on. The 1999 reform proposals were remarkable in that they placed a renewed emphasis on the environment and on **sustainability**, introducing the concept of '**multifunctionality**' as one of the CAP's main objectives. This new concept signals that agriculture is not just about production, but that it also incorporates the 'non-production' aspects of farming—the social, cultural, territorial, and environmental dimensions, for example.

The Berlin Agreement has continued the reform process initiated in 1992 for various products, though radical reform in the dairy and sugar sectors was postponed. New measures have led to price reductions in the form of progressive decreases of 15 per cent for cereals and dairy products, and 20 per cent on beef by 2006. These are to be partially compensated for by direct income payments to the farmers affected. As a response to calls for the decentralization of the policy, some of these direct payments take the form of 'national envelopes' (effectively national allocations) paid to the member states from the EC budget, and which each state can distribute to its farmers to target specific national and/or regional priorities.

On the environment, the new goals and the 'quality focus' mentioned at Berlin are to be achieved by three possible avenues: (i) direct payments explicitly dedicated to agri-environmental issues; (ii) making direct payments conditional upon the observance of generally applicable environmental requirements; or (iii) attaching *specific* environmental conditions to the grant of direct payments. However, this is to be implemented on a voluntary basis. Moreover, no real incentive for alternative modes of farming has been included in these plans (see Box 16.4). As regards social issues, member states are able to impose some limits on direct aids, but again this is an optional measure which, owing to national difficulties, was little implemented by the member states.

In sum, since 1992, CAP changes have mainly been rhetorical in character. If the discourses and debates changed its shape, the redistributive effects of the policy remain more or less the same. As yet, sustainability and multifunctionality objectives have not been translated into concrete policy measures. Although rural development is now presented as the 'second pillar' of the CAP (nothing to do with the three pillars of the EU), intended to enhance the multifunctionality of the agricultural policy domain, the Berlin summit allocated only 10.5 per cent of total CAP expenditure to it, as against 89.5 per cent for the support of farmers' incomes.

The CAP and future trade negotiations

CAP reform is about much more than just internal EU politics. It also has a very important international dimension. When the Uruguay Round of the GATT was concluded in 1994, the Agreement on Agriculture (AoA) settled at that time foresaw the reopening of agricultural negotiations in a matter of years. In the meantime, the GATT was converted into the World Trade Organization (WTO) in 1995. After a first failed attempt in Seattle in November 1999, a new round of negotiations, the 'Doha Development Round', was finally launched in November 2001 in Qatar, at the Fourth WTO Ministerial Conference. The mandate for these negotiations includes discussion of agriculture and services, plus a number of other issues that have been added since. The Declaration gives January 2005 as the date for completing the negotiations, with interim progress to be reviewed in 2003 at the Fifth Ministerial Conference in Mexico. Agricultural negotiations in this Round began in March 2000.

Box 16.4 **Core ideas**
Alternative ways of farming

Without public support and in opposition to 'conventional' models of agriculture, 'alternative' farmers have been proving that it is possible to farm differently. Organic farming is the best known example, but there are others. These farmers have proved that farming can be friendlier to the environment, and that farming need not contribute to intensification, pollution, and the destruction of soil and landscape, and that it can also offer better working conditions and quality of life for the farmer, with an equal or even better revenue.

Whereas this sort of farming used to be denounced as 'old fashioned' and out of line with modernity and technical progress, thanks to an opening of the agricultural debate to incorporate environmental and sustainability issues, alternative farming is gaining much more attention at both national and EU levels. These farmers are also more active politically. As an example, in April 2002 the

International Federation of Organic Agricultural Movements published a position paper on CAP reform entitled 'A Sustainable Agriculture Policy for Europe' (available at **www.ifoam.org**).

Some steps have been taken to move beyond rhetorical support for alternative modes of farming. For example, in 1991 the Agricultural Council voted to harmonize production norms for organic vegetal products. This has been operational since 1993. Alternative farming is also considered under the CAP's agri-environmental measures, with member states now authorized to support alternative models of agriculture under the EU's co-financing procedures. However, policy makers do not yet consider these models as real alternatives to the 'modernist agriculture' model, which remains based on principles of **intensification** and productivity.

As in the Uruguay Round, the agricultural negotiations are expected to reduce tariff barriers and export subsidies, and to discuss reductions in domestic agricultural support. Important in this regard is the Uruguay 'inheritance' in the form of the three 'boxes' taken from the AoA (see Box 16.5). These boxes are used to classify agricultural policy measures according to the extent to which they distort trade. Thus each country will do its utmost to be entered in the green or blue box, which will mean that they are exempt from any commitment to reduce their subsidies. In 1994, the Europeans had their post-1992 compensatory payments classified in the 'blue box'. In the current WTO Round, the fate of those in the 'blue box' is uncertain.

The positions of the four main protagonists are already well known:

- The Cairns Group will argue for a greater liberalization of agricultural trade, in line with their own domestic policies.

- The USA will also argue for greater liberalization, while continuing to support US agriculture.

- The EU will try to defend its 'European model of agricultural policy' based on an argument about 'multifunctionality'.

- Developing countries will call for specific exemptions because of their particular circumstances.

The strategy that the EU has adopted thus far involves arguing that the CAP cannot be challenged under WTO rules because it pursues non-production as well as production goals. This position was decided by the Agricultural Council in October 1999. The plan involves rejecting any cut in direct payments, on the basis that such payments enhance 'multifunctionality', which is the basis of a 'European Model of Agriculture'. This argument is one which the WTO might consider politically legitimate. However, some authors fear that the EU has become victim of its own strategy:

If the EU does not move further than the Berlin Summit, domestic support will be curtailed, while the US flexibility payments will survive untouched, and US farmers will receive hefty subsidies, deemed WTO compatible. CAP payments will be reduced but still linked to areas and headages, cross compliance will not be fully enforced and degradation of natural rural resources in areas carrying intensive crops and animal will continue (Mahè 2001: 13).

Indeed, multifunctionality has become a topical issue in domestic and international agricultural policy circles over the last decade. However,

---

Box 16.5 **The facts**

Agriculture in the WTO: A question of boxes

The Agreement on Agriculture (AoA), which allowed for the conclusion of the GATT Uruguay Round, makes a distinction between support programmes that directly stimulate production and consequently distort trade, and those that are considered to have no direct effect on production and trade. Three categories are identified along these lines.

The amber box

In the amber box are domestic measures that have a direct effect on production and that distort trade. They have to be cut.

The green box

In the green box are measures that are considered to have a minimal impact on trade, and can be freely used. To

appear in the green box, the measure must be 'decoupled from production' so that there is no linkage between the amount of payment and the production process, agricultural prices, or factors of production. The green box thus includes government services such as research, disease control, infrastructure, and food security, as well as payments made directly to farmers, such as investment aids, disaster relief, producer or resource retirement schemes, and environmental and regional assistance programmes.

The blue box

In the blue box are payments linked to programmes that limit production. These payments may not need to be reduced as long as certain conditions are met.

multifunctionality is subject to widely differing interpretations. For its detractors, the main criticism is that such a concept may be little more than a rhetorical device used to justify production and export subsidies. It is not by chance that the OECD has launched a debate to try to define this concept in a more satisfactory way (see Box 16.6). With the Uruguay Round experience in mind, the stakes were high in the negotiations within the OECD and the WTO over a common definition. With its potential use as a basis for distinguishing between permitted and prohibited types of agricultural support, the definition chosen will have a direct impact on domestic agricultural policies in the future.

Eastern enlargement and the CAP

The EU's eastern (and southern) enlargement is one of the great challenges of the next decade for the Union, with (at the time of writing) negotiations under way with ten candidate states: Cyprus, the Czech Republic, Estonia, Hungary, Poland, Slovenia, Latvia, Lithuania, Slovakia, and Malta. Agriculture and EU enlargement is a big issue and there is definitely not enough space here to discuss all aspects of this contentious matter. However, the first crucial issue is the extent to which the CAP will

be applied to the new member states, and whether these CAP instruments will have to be adapted as a consequence of enlargement. This raises the question of the economic consequences that the application of the CAP to the acceding states would have on the general structure of farming, amongst other things, particularly in the Central and East European states. Moreover, it also raises the question of how the CAP will be financed in future.

The European Commission presented its strategy for dealing with the enlargement negotiations on agriculture at the beginning of 2002. Its proposal involves offering direct payments to farmers and introducing production quotas for new member countries after they join, probably in 2004. To ease transitional problems in rural areas, and to encourage the restructuring of agricultural sectors, the Commission has also proposed complementing its financial support by means of an enhanced rural development policy. Given that the immediate introduction of 100 per cent direct payments would freeze existing structures and hamper modernization, the Commission favours a gradual introduction over a transition period of ten years, covering 25 per cent in 2004, 30 per cent in 2005, and 35 per cent in 2006, ultimately reaching 100 per cent in 2013.

For existing member states, the northern Europeans have argued that the proposal is too costly, and that there should be no direct aid to the Central and

---

Box 16.6 **Core ideas**
Multifunctionality and the OECD

Ideas about multifunctionality have been developed by the OECD since the mid-1990s. Since that time the OECD Secretariat-General has worked on a common definition of multifunctionality, notably through the building of an economic framework to evaluate 'joint-ness in production', that is, the extent to which commodity (food and fibre) and non-commodity (landscape, environment, rural development, or food security) outputs are linked.

As a member of the OECD Secretariat has argued, this research attempts to 'fill a void' in the debate, to 'help governments to develop efficient and effective policies

to internalise the external effects of agriculture and reduce the risk of conflict between domestic policies in pursuit of multi-functionality and further agricultural trade liberalisation' (Cahill 2001).

As was the case a decade earlier with the agriculture and trade issue, OECD thinking has fostered new international learning processes in the agricultural policy field. The objective of these studies is clear, but the impact on the WTO of new thinking of this kind is as yet unclear. It remains to be seen whether this will benefit or disadvantage the EU in the current round of international trade negotiations.

East Europeans in the first few years after accession. The Dutch government pointed out that no direct aid for new members was assumed in the *Agenda 2000* agreement of 1997. The Swedes argued that direct aid for the new member states would actually discourage much needed agricultural restructuring. Germany is more concerned about predictions that its net contribution to the agricultural budget would grow after enlargement. And France has also expressed concern about the cost of the Commission's strategy. As a consequence, some members have suggested that a more profound reform of the CAP needs to take place before enlargement. For their part, most of the candidate countries have reacted by saying that the Commission's proposal does not offer them enough, and that they need all of the direct aid paid from year one, not just for sectoral reasons, but to convince their publics to agree to EU membership in the first place. At the Brussels Summit on 25 October 2002, the EU heads of government finally adopted the Commission's proposal on CAP and enlargement. In order to address some national concerns, they placed their decision in a framework of financial stability from 2007 to 2013. More specifically, this meant that total annual expenditure on CAP direct payments and market-related expenditure for a Union of 25 members would not exceed the corresponding combined ceilings for 2006 (to be increased in nominal terms by 1 per cent per annum—less than the likely inflation rate).

The 2002 'Mid-term Review': a radical new shift for the CAP?

With the aim of reducing the increasing gap between discourse and practice in the CAP, and in view of forthcoming international events (EU enlargement and the next round of WTO negotiations), the European Commission issued a major new reform plan in July 2002 (European Commission 2002*b*).

The 'Mid-term Review', arguing that public expenditure for the farm sector must be better justified, and that as well as supporting farm incomes, it must do more to ensure high-quality food and animal welfare, preservation of the environment, landscapes, and cultural heritage, and to enhance social welfare and equity, proposes to reshape the CAP substantially. To achieve those goals, the Commission proposed the following changes:

1 To cut the link between production and direct payments.

2 To make those payments conditional upon compliance with environmental, food safety, animal welfare, and occupational safety standards.

3 To increase substantially EU support for rural development by adjusting direct payments, albeit exempting small farmers.

4 To introduce a new farm audit system.

5 To introduce new rural development measures to improve production quality, food safety, animal welfare, and to cover the costs of the farm audit.

In the area of market policy, the Commission proposed to complete the cereal reforms, with a final 5 per cent cut in the intervention price and a new border protection system; a decrease in the additional payment for durum wheat, accompanied by a new quality premium; a compensatory decrease in the rice intervention price; and adjustments for dried fodder, protein crops, and nuts.

To the Commission, reforming the CAP does not mean cutting off or even reducing farming support, but it does mean distributing it and allocating it more effectively. As the Agriculture Commissioner, Franz Fischler, has underlined:

We cannot expect our rural areas to prosper, our environment to be protected, our farm animals to be well looked-after, and our farmers to survive, without paying for it. In future, farmers will not be paid for overproduction, but for responding to what people want: safe food, quality production, animal welfare and a healthy environment. (Fischler 2002)

Five months after its publication, how successful has this plan been? While initially supported by the UK, Germany, and other Northern governments, the proposal is likely to be postponed until 2006, mainly due to very strong French opposition. At the time of writing, the French government is refusing to comply with the requirement to reduce its support for its larger cereal growers.

Key points

- The 1999 Berlin Agreement continued on the reform path begun in 1992, though recent reforms have had limited impact.
- While the CAP reforms were tolerated in the Uruguay Round of the GATT, CAP direct

payments may be challenged in the new WTO Round.

- European policy makers are using arguments about 'multifunctionality' to defend the CAP.
- After a big internal debate, the 15 member states decided to extend the CAP as it currently operates to the candidate states.

Conclusion: The CAP at a crossroads

Originally intended to make Western Europe self-sufficient in food, the CAP was initially equipped with 'productivist' instruments that led to an over-production of agricultural produce and serious budgetary problems for the EC/EU (see Table 16.2). In the 1980s, the first reforms tried to cope with these problems by introducing quantitative measures (such as quotas). At the beginning of the 1990s, new policy beliefs inspired the 'decoupling' of farm support from production. This provoked a radical reform of the CAP, which shifted policy instruments from market or price support to direct income support, thereby decreasing centrally planned prices, compensating for these cuts by means of direct payments to farmers.

This new path has been continued in subsequent CAP reforms, with increasing attention paid to the environmental and social dimension of the CAP. These concerns are reflected in the concept of multi-

functionality, which has been presented as the core element of a 'European model of agriculture'. Multi-functionality is also used to justify direct income support to farmers within the context of the latest round of international (WTO) trade negotiations.

The evolution of the CAP since the 1980s is an excellent illustration of the complexity of the links that exist between national, European, and international political arenas. Intersectoral deals that are not easily understood at national level become even more complicated when various governments, coalitions of interests, and European and international institutions enter the game. Caught in the crossfire between national interest and international bargains, the EU's political system is a complex, intricate, and competitive system. It is only possible to deconstruct this complexity by examining the actors involved in the policy process and the nature of the political exchanges that take place amongst them.

Table 16.2 Agricultural expenditures under the CAP (ECUs)

	1986	1991	1996	2000
EAGGF Guarantee section (market support)	22,137	32,386	39,107.7	40,466.7
% of agricultural expenditure	96.6%	93.8%	90.6%	96.6%
EAGGF Guidance section (e.g. rural development)	774	2,128	3,934.5	1,387.3
% of agricultural expenditure	3.4%	6.2%	9.1%	3.3%
Other agricultural expenses	—	—	109.8	51.5
Total EU agricultural expenses	22,911	34,514	43,152.0	41,905.5
Total EU budget	35,174	53,823	80,456.5	77,878.8

Sources: European Parliament website: 1986 and 1991 data; European Commission, Directorate-General for Agriculture: 1996 and 2000 data.

QUESTIONS

1 Why did the CAP originally aim to maintain high prices for agricultural produce?

2 What are the negative consequences of the CAP's price support mechanism?

3 How did European policy makers try to deal with the problems of over-production and increasing budgetary costs in the 1980s?

4 How did new debates about agriculture influence the 1992 reform package?

5 Why did the 1992 reform happen?

6 What are the challenges currently facing the CAP?

7 To what extent does the current round of international trade negotiations pose a threat to the CAP?

8 What is multifunctionality? What implications does it have for agricultural policy?

GUIDE TO FURTHER READING

Ackrill, R., *The Common Agricultural Policy* (Sheffield: Sheffield Academic Press, 2000). A useful contribution to the literature on agricultural policy which covers general aspects of the CAP and includes a wealth of information on agricultural reform in the EU.

Grant, W., *The Common Agricultural Policy* (Basingstoke: Macmillan, 1997). An excellent general and very accessible overview of the CAP.

Jones, A., and Clark, J., *The Modalities of European Union Governance: New Institutionalist Explanations of Agri-environmental Policy* (Oxford: Oxford University Press, 2001). An excellent study of the relationship between agricultural and environmental policy in the EU, exploring in the process many of the intricacies of the CAP.

Swinnen, J. F. M., *A Fishler Reform of the Common Agricultural Policy?* Working Document Number 173 (Brussels: Centre for European Policy Studies, 2000). A helpful guide to recent reforms.

WEB LINKS

www.defra.gov.uk The official page of the UK's Department for the Environment, Food and Rural Affairs (incorporating what was formerly the Ministry of Agriculture, Fisheries and Food).

http://europa.eu.int/comm/commissioners/fischler/index_en.htm Commissioner Franz Fischler's web page, with lots of useful information on the CAP.

http://europa.eu.int/comm/agriculture/index_en.htm The home page of the European Commission's Directorate-General for agriculture.

http://members.tripod.com/~WynGrant/WynGrantCAPpage.html Wyn Grant's CAP Page, with lots of useful information on the CAP.

17 The EU's social dimension

Gerda Falkner

READER'S GUIDE

This chapter looks at the way in which European social policy has evolved since the late 1950s. It begins by reflecting on the intergovernmental character of the policy in the early days, and on how the gradual introduction of qualified majority voting and the widening scope of the policy allowed the European institutions and European-level interest groups much more of a say in the European social dimension. The chapter also looks at the work of the European Social Fund. Focusing on newer developments, later sections chart the arrival of the open method of co-ordination, a non-regulatory approach to European policy making in this field, and the growing importance of 'social partnership', the involvement of the social partners (employers and labour representatives) in making European-level social policy. The chapter concludes by arguing that social regulation will become all the more difficult once the EU has enlarged to incorporate some or all of the Central/East European states.

Introduction

What is social policy? In a well-known definition, T. H. Marshall (1975) talked of the use of political power to supersede, supplement, or modify operations of the economic system in order to achieve results which the economic system would not achieve on its own. Such a wide definition would include, for example, **redistributive** EU actions, which provide funding through the EU's Structural

Funds (that is, the social, agricultural, **cohesion**, and regional funds) (see Chapter 18). This would go far beyond what is usually understood as European social policy and would introduce too vast an array of topics to be covered in this brief chapter. It seems therefore more useful to apply a pragmatic understanding of social policy. This involves actions which fall under the so-called 'social dimension of European integration', that is, any acts carried out under the social policy chapter of the EC Treaty; policies targeted at facilitating the freedom of movement of workers in the social realm; and last, but not least, action to harmonize the quite diverse social or labour law standards of the member states, whatever the relevant **Treaty base** may be. It should be added that most writers on EC social policy have chosen a similar approach to this.

This chapter will first outline the division of social policy competences between the EU and its member states; the interpretation of these treaty provisions in the day-to-day policy process over time; and the latest formal reforms at **Amsterdam** and **Nice**. It will then analyse the incremental development of EC/EU (see p. 271) social regulation and activities, including the European Social Fund and the so-called **open method of co-ordination**. Since patterns of decision making are quite distinctive in the social as opposed to the other fields of EU politics, this chapter will also outline how the EU-level interest groups participate therein (see also Chapter 13). The conclusion not only summarizes the results of the chapter, but also discusses the performance of European integration within its 'social dimension'.

The EEC and its member states

According to the Treaty of Rome (1957), social policy competences were to remain a largely national affair. It did not provide for the Europeanization of social policies, as too many delegations had opposed this at the negotiations leading up to the Treaty. Some governments (especially that of Germany) pleaded for a neo-liberal, free-market approach to social affairs, even in the realm of labour and social security; others opted for a limited process of **harmonization**. The French delegation, notably, argued that its comparatively high social charges and its constitutional principle of equal pay for men and women might constitute a competitive disadvantage within the newly formed European market, while Italy feared that the opening up of Community borders might prove costly for the southern part of the country, which was already economically disadvantaged. In the end, a compromise was found, but this did not include explicit EEC competences for active social policy harmonization at the European level. The dominant philosophy of the 1957 Treaty was that improvements in welfare would be provided by the economic

growth that arose as a consequence of the liberalization of the European market, and not from the regulatory and distributive form of public policy (see Barnard 2000; Leibfried and Pierson 1995).

Nevertheless, the Treaty contained a small number of concessions for the more '**interventionist**' delegations. These were the provisions on equal pay for both sexes (Article 119); the maintenance of 'existing equivalence between paid holiday schemes' (Article 120); and the establishment of a European Social Fund (Articles 123–8). Two of the three above-mentioned concessions (that is, equal pay and the Social Fund) increased in importance as the European integration process progressed. There was to be no follow-up, however, on the equivalence of paid holiday schemes.

While other provisions of the Treaty's Title III on 'social policy' included some solemn social policy provisions, they failed to empower the EEC to act. 'Underwriting this arrangement was the relative feasibility of nation-state strategies for economic development in the first decades after World War II. The common market, as it was constructed, was designed to aid and abet such national strategies, not transcend them' (Ross 1995: 360). Yet in other areas of activity the Commission was empowered to present legislative proposals to the Council, proposals that would ultimately become binding law. In the area of social policy, however, the Commission was only permitted to act by undertaking relevant studies, delivering opinions, and arranging consultations on problems arising at national level and those of concern to international organizations. In legal terms, then, Article 118 reflected a confirmation of national (as opposed to European) responsibility for social policy.

Paradoxically, the sole explicit Community competence for social policy regulation under the original EEC Treaty was not in the part of the Treaty that dealt explicitly with social policy. It belonged, rather, to Part II, on the Foundations of the Community, which contained provisions on the free movement of goods, labour, services, and capital. Articles 48 to 51 thus provided for the establishment of the freedom of movement for workers, as part of the Treaty's market-making activities. This implied the abolition of all discrimination based on the nationality of workers in the member states in the areas of employment, remuneration, and other conditions of work and employment (Article 48). In order to 'adopt such measures in the field of social security as are necessary to provide freedom of movement for workers' (Article 51), the Council was mandated to aggregate the laws of the several EEC countries, so as to establish Community-wide rights to benefits and a way of calculating the amount of those benefits for migrant workers and their dependants.

Yet although there were almost no explicit social policy competences in the original EEC Treaty, an extensive interpretation of the Treaty basis provided, in practice, some room for manoeuvre. This was possible because, where necessary or useful for market integration, intervention in the social policy field was *implicitly* allowed in the 1957 Treaty, through the so-called 'subsidiary competence' provisions. In other words, laws in the member states which 'directly affect the establishment or functioning of the common market', could be approximated by unanimous Council decision on the basis of a Commission proposal (Article 100).

Moreover, if action by the Community should prove necessary to attain, in the course of the operation of the common market, one of the objectives of the Community, and this Treaty has not provided the necessary powers, the Council shall, acting unanimously on a proposal from the Commission and after consulting the European Parliament (EP), take the appropriate measures (Article 235).

These provisions provided, from the 1970s on, a loophole for social policy harmonization at EC level. However, the unanimous Council vote necessary for this to happen constituted a high threshold for joint action. Each government could veto social measures and as a result the EEC found itself in what Scharpf (1988) has called a **joint-decision trap**.

In 1987, the Single European Act came into force as the first major Community Treaty revision (see Chapter 3: Box 3.4). As in the 1950s, an economic enterprise was at the heart of this fresh impetus in favour of European integration. But despite the member states' commitment to a Single Market Programme, the Europeanization of social policy remained controversial, for example, over how much social regulation was needed. In various so-called 'flanking' (supporting) policy areas, notably environmental and research policy, Community competence was formally extended (see Articles 130r–t and 130f–q). But this was not so for social policy: the delegations representing the EC's national governments seemed unwilling to give the Community a broader role in this field.

However, one important exception was made. Article 118a on minimum harmonization concerning health and safety of workers provided an escape route out of the **unanimity** requirement. For the first time in European social policy, it allowed directives to be agreed on the basis of a **qualified majority** of the Council members. The provisions adopted following this Article were minimum regulations only. Nevertheless, under this provision reluctant member states could be forced to align their social legislation with the majority of member states, even against their will. It should be stressed that agreement on this provision was only possible because occupational health and safety issues were closely connected to the single market.

Governments did not expect this 'technical' matter to facilitate social policy integration in the significant way that it did in the decade to follow. Extensive use of this provision was possible mainly because the wording and the definition of key terms in Article 118a were somewhat vague:

Member States shall pay particular attention to encouraging improvements, especially in the working environment, as regards the health and safety of workers, and shall set as their objective the harmonization of conditions in this area, while maintaining the improvements made. In order to help achieve the objective laid down in the first paragraph, the Council, acting by a qualified majority on a proposal from the Commission, . . . shall adopt, by means of directives, minimum requirements for gradual implementation.

This formulation made it easy to play what has since been called the 'treaty base game' (Rhodes 1995). It allowed the governments to adopt not only measures improving the working environment (for example, a directive on the maximum concentration of air-borne pollutants), but also measures which ensured the health and safety of workers by improving working conditions in a more general sense (for example, limiting working time). It was clear that this Treaty basis was frequently chosen because only this Article allowed for majority voting at the time.

Key points

- The 1957 EEC Treaty meant that social policy remained largely a national affair. The co-ordination of social security systems for migrant workers was an exception to this rule in the legislative field.

- The Single European Act introduced qualified majority voting to a limited area of social policy, though at the time governments did not realize its implications.

The treaty reforms at Maastricht, Amsterdam, and Nice

The **Intergovernmental Conference** (IGC) preceding the **Maastricht Treaty** negotiated a reform of the social policy provisions. However, under the requirement of unanimous approval by all (then) 12 member states, the social provisions could not be significantly altered because of the strong opposition from the UK government. At the end of extremely difficult negotiations which threatened existing compromises achieved within the IGC, the UK was granted an opt-out from the social policy measures agreed by the rest of the member states. In *the Protocol on Social Policy* annexed to the EC Treaty, the 11 (and after 1995, the 14—in other words all members except the UK) were authorized to use the institutions, procedures, and mechanisms of the Treaty for the purpose of implementing their 'Agreement on Social Policy' (sometimes called the 'Social Chapter').

Because of the UK opt-out (or the 'opt-in' of the other member states), the EU after Maastricht (from November 1993) had two different legal bases for the adoption of social policy measures. The EC Treaty's social provisions remained valid for all member states. As introduced in the 1986 Single European Act, they allowed for minimum harmonization as well as for **qualified majority voting (QMV)** in the area of worker health and safety provisions only. By contrast, the innovative social policy provisions of the Social Agreement, applicable to all but the UK, comprised what had been perceived during the IGC as an amendment to the social provisions of the Treaty. These constituted an extension of Community competence into a wide range of social policy issues, including working conditions; the information and consultation of workers; equality between men and women with regard to labour market opportunities and treatment at work (as opposed to only equal pay before); and the integration of persons excluded from the labour market (Article 2.1 Social Agreement). Some issues were, however, explicitly excluded from the scope of minimum harmonization under the Maastricht social policy provisions, namely: pay; the **right of association**; the right to strike; and the right to impose **lock-outs** (Article 2.6).

Additionally, QMV was extended to many more issue areas than before, including the information and consultation of workers. Unanimous decisions remained, however, for social security matters and the social protection of workers; the protection of workers whose employment contract is terminated; representation and collective defence of interests of workers and employers, including **co-determination**; conditions of employment for third-country nationals legally residing in Community territory; and financial contributions for promotion of employment and job creation (see Article 3 Social Agreement).

In contrast to the Maastricht negotiations, in the 1996–7 IGC preceding the **Amsterdam Treaty**, social policy reform was not a major issue (except for employment promotion, which can only be included in social policy if one employs a very broad notion of that area). Because of the fierce resistance to social policy reforms in the UK's Conservative government (in office until May 1997), the IGC decided to postpone the topic until the very end of the negotiation period, awaiting the result of the 1997 general election. Under the new Labour government, which came into office at this point, the UK's opt-out from the Social Agreement came to an end with the Amsterdam Treaty. Apart from this, the only significant innovation (compared to the provisions of the Social Agreement) was the new employment policy chapter (now in Articles 125–30). While excluding any harmonization of domestic laws, it provides for the co-ordination of national employment policies on the basis of annual

Table 17.1 The social policy competences of the EU

Treaty	(Additional) explicit social policy competence
Rome 1957	• free movement of workers
	• social security co-ordination
Single European Act 1986	• working environment (health and safety)
Maastricht Social Agreement 1992	• social security and protection of workers
	• protection of workers where employment contract is terminated
	• collective interest representation
	• co-determination
	• employment of third-country nationals
	• working conditions (general)
	• worker information and consultation
	• gender equality for labour force
	• integration in labour market
Amsterdam Treaty 1997	• employment policy co-ordination and funding of pilot projects and incentives for transnational co-operation in the field
	• action against discrimination (sex, race, ethnic origin, belief, disability, age, sexual orientation).
	• 'measures' fighting social exclusion
	• 'measures' assuring equal opportunities and treatment of women and men
Nice Treaty 2001	• 'measures' in other fields of Treaty Article 137

guidelines and national follow-up reports. Further-more, a new Article 13 on Community action against discrimination on the grounds of sex, race, ethnic origin, belief, disability, age, and sexual orientation was inserted.

Finally, the **Nice Treaty** of 2001 (still to be ratified at the time of writing) was not particularly innovative in terms of social policy matters. In some fields, the Council may in the future be allowed to decide unanimously upon the use of the **co-decision procedure** (see Chapter 1: 5–6) in this area. This would apply to worker protection where employment contracts were terminated; to the representation and collective defence of collective interests; and the interests of third-country nationals (non-EU nationals) (see Article 137.2). Furthermore, measures can now be adopted on all social issues, not just those concerning social exclusion and equal opportunities, as was the case after Amsterdam. Table 17.1 presents a chronological summary of social policy reforms introduced by the Treaties.

Key points

- On the basis of the Maastricht Social Protocol (Social Chapter), the UK had an opt-out that only ended after the Labour government took office in 1997.

- The Agreement on Social Policy gave the Union more competences and allowed for more majority voting.

- The Amsterdam Treaty transferred the Social Agreement's innovations into the main Treaty which is now binding for all.

- Although the recent Nice Treaty only changed a few aspects of EU social policy, it is clear that formal competences have been extended over time to a significant extent.

The development and scope of European social policy

There are a number of major subfields of social legislation, the most important of which are labour law; health and safety in the workplace; and gender equality. The following sections outline when and how they were developed. During the early years of European integration, social policy consisted almost exclusively of efforts to secure the free movement of workers and in that sense was rather non-controversial. In a number of EC regulations, national social security systems were co-ordinated with a view to improving the status of internationally mobile workers and their families (see also Chapter 25).

During the late 1960s, however, the political climate gradually became more favourable to a wider range of European social policy measures. At their 1972 Paris summit, the Community heads of state and government declared that economic expansion should not be an end in itself but should lead to improvements in more general living and working conditions. With relevant Community action in mind, they agreed a catalogue of social policy measures, that were to be elaborated by the Commission. In the resulting social action programme (that is, a list of intended legislative initiatives, covering a number of years) of 1974 ([1974] OJ C13/1), the Council expressed its intention to adopt a series of social policy measures within two years.

That the Council stated that Community social policy should furthermore be conducted under Article 235, which goes beyond purely economic considerations, was a major development. This was confirmation that governments now perceived social policy intervention as an integral part of European integration. As a consequence, the Treaty's subsidiary competence provisions were increasingly interpreted in a regulation-friendly manner in day-to-day policy making. Originally, only issues which directly restricted the single market had qualified for harmonization (or 'approximation') under Article 100.

During the 1970s, a shift occurred. Henceforth, regulation was considered legitimate if it facilitated the free movement of production factors, that is, goods, services, labour, or capital. Several of the legislative measures proposed in the 1974 Social Action Programme were adopted by the Council in the years that followed, and further Social Action Programmes followed the first (see Figure 17.1).

Figure 17.1 shows the growth in social policy directives from 1974 on. By the end of the year 2000, 51 social directives, 13 reforms of existing directives, and seven geographical extensions of directives (to the former East Germany, to new member states, and to the UK after Amsterdam) had been adopted. The total number of decisions on social directives was 71. These directives typically fall within what at the national level is called labour law, and not within the field of social security. There are three main fields: health and safety, other working conditions, and equality between women and men in the workplace.

With regard to *gender equality*, the European Court of Justice (ECJ) has been a major actor ever since it provided a broad interpretation of Article 119 on domestic measures to ensure equal pay, opening the way for action on the basis of the subsidiary competence provisions (as outlined above). Matters such as equal pay for work of equal value, the equal treatment of men and women regarding working conditions and social security, and even the issue of burden of proof in discrimination law suits were finally regulated at EU level (Hoskyns 1996; Mazey 1998).

In the field of *working conditions*, a number of directives were adopted during the late 1970s, for example on the protection of workers in cases of collective redundancy, the transfer of undertakings, or employer insolvency. Many more directives followed during the 1990s, including those on worker information, on conditions of work contracts, on the equal treatment of atypical (such as shift or part-time) workers, and on parental leave.

With regard to *health and safety at work*, regulation was based on a number of specific action programmes. Directives include the protection of workers exposed to emissions (or pollutants) and responsible for heavy loads, as well as protection against risks of chemical, physical, and biological agents at work (such as lead or asbestos). Figure 17.2 indicates the number of directives in these three subfields.

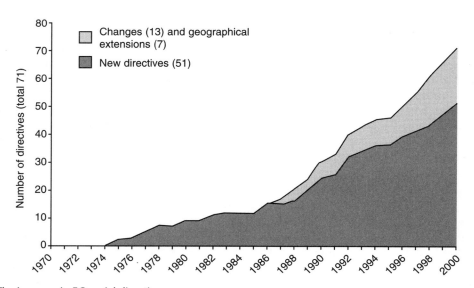

Fig. 17.1 The increase in EC social directives
Source: Author's calculations on the basis of Celex, to end 2000, 'social policy'.
Note: Thanks to Myriam Nauerz for research assistance with the figures.

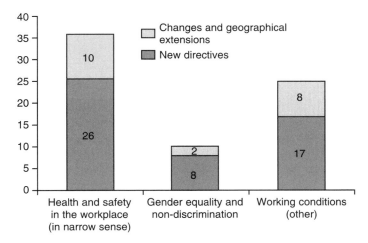

Fig. 17.2 EC social directives in three subfields
Source: Celex, to end 2000, 'social policy'.

Key points

- The development of EC social legislation has increased since the late 1950s, with the 1990s being the most active period.

- In addition to the issue of free movement of workers and equal treatment in national social security systems, the main areas of regulative European social policy are: working conditions; gender equality; and health and safety in the workplace.

The European Social Fund

EC policy is largely regulatory, and this is particularly the case in the social field. However, as this and the following section will outline, the relative importance of **regulation** has declined in recent years, as both funding opportunities and 'soft' forms of governance (see below) have increased. In the case of funding, the 1957 Treaty provided for a 'European Social Fund' (ESF). Its goal was to simplify the employment of workers, to increase their geographical and occupational mobility within the Community, and to facilitate their adaptation to change, particularly through vocational training and retraining. Initially, the ESF reimbursed member states for some of the costs involved in introducing and implementing such measures. The Fund did not have any controlling capacity, however, as the transfer of money to the member states' employment services was quasi-automatic. And in contrast to

its original objective, that of rectifying specifically Italian problems after the opening up of market borders, it tended to be the best-funded and best-organized domestic labour market administrations that received most of the money (Germany, for example). It was this anomaly in the system that prompted the first major reform of the ESF in 1971. This involved an agreement on the definition of target groups, and the co-funding of only those domestic projects considered appropriate from a Community perspective. After a number of further reforms, the ESF now co-finances projects for young people seeking employment, for the long-term unemployed, for disadvantaged groups, and for promoting gender equality in the labour market.

In addition to the Social Fund, other EU funds also seek to combat regional and social disparities (see Chapter 18). These are the European Regional

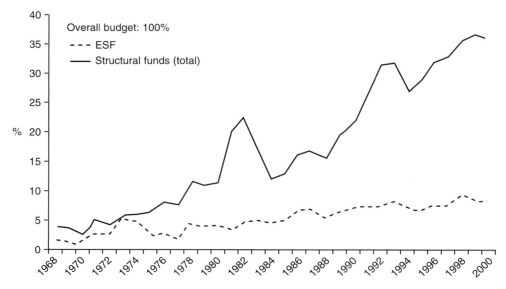

Fig. 17.3 European Social Fund and Structural Funds as percentages of total EC budget
Source: European Commission 2000c.

Development Fund, the European Agricultural Guidance and Guarantee Fund (Guarantee Section) (see Chapter 16: 248), and the Financial Instrument for Fisheries Guidance. Finally, the Cohesion Fund finances environmental projects and trans-European infrastructure networks in member states whose gross domestic product (GDP) is less than 90 per cent of the EU average. In sum, the EU's social dimension is less regulatory than is often assumed. As Figure 17.3 highlights, the funding distributed by the ESF has grown steadily, both in relative and in absolute terms.

According to data from the European Commission in 2000, the Social Fund's share of total EC spending was 1.1 per cent by 1970; 4.4 per cent by 1980; 7.3 per cent by 1990; and 8.6 per cent by 2000. The share of all Structural Funds has grown even faster—from 2.8 per cent in 1970 to 35.7 per cent in 2000 (that is €31,957 m). This increase cannot hide the fact, however, that the Guarantee Section of the Agricultural Fund is still much larger—€41,493.9 m.

Finally, the steering effect of the EU's labour market policy is much stronger than the ESF figures indicate. The latter display only the EU's part of the overall project budgets. The impact of the EU's criteria for project selection is greater than this, since national authorities also apply them, with the prospect of European co-funding in mind (in order to get national contributions back from Brussels). Moreover, the relative importance of EU funding has increased at a time of national spending cuts.

Key points

- The 1957 Treaty established a European Social Fund. Its aims are more narrow than its name might suggest since they concern employment policy alone.

- The ESF co-funds projects and programmes in the member states. It has had, since 1971, its own priorities for funding, with a certain steering effect on national policies, as national governments want a share of the EU budget to flow back into their country.

- As of 2000, the ESF expenditures have grown to almost 9 per cent of the EU budget.

New developments: The open method of co-ordination

If the legislative (or regulatory) track of EU social policy tends to have comparatively less importance at the turn of the millennium, this is not only due to a (very recent) slowdown in legislative proposals, but also because of a new (often called a 'softer') style of intervention known as 'the open method of co-ordination' (see de la Porte and Pochet 2002). Thus, the EU has a novel role as a motor and, at the same time, as a constraint on national, social, and structural reform (see Goetschy 2001).

The main features of the open method of co-ordination were developed (initially without Treaty basis) in the field of employment policy, as a follow-up to the Essen European Council of 1994. The Amsterdam Treaty's employment chapter later formalized it. Every year since, the EU has adopted employment policy guidelines. Their specification and implementation is left, however, to the national level so that the domestic situation and party political preferences can be taken into consideration. All the same, member states must present annual reports on how they have dealt with the guidelines, and why they have chosen particular strategies in their 'National Action Plans'. They have to defend their decisions at the European level in regular debates on the national employment policy, so that peer pressure comes into play and has, at least potentially, a harmonizing effect on social policies in Europe.

The open method of co-ordination has recently been extended to new fields, including pension reform, social inclusion, and education. To date, its success is hard to judge, as there is a lack of reliable data on its practical effects in the member states.

In any case, the net effect of this strategy will always be difficult to measure since there is no counterfactual basis of comparison at the researcher's disposal. It is plausible to expect that the joint policy learning (Sabatier and Jenkins-Smith 1993) and mutual adaptation (DiMaggio and Powell 1991) that results from this approach will have some beneficial effects, and that EU-level obligations, however loosely defined, will help governments to justify reforms domestically that they might otherwise not have dared to enforce for fear of electoral losses. Where national governments are not ready for policy change, however, the National Action Plans may do no more than either restate pre-existing domestic policies or perform a symbolic function (Scharpf 2002). In such cases the EU is helpless, since EU-level harmonization by means of more formal regulation (new laws) is explicitly ruled out under the open method.

Key points

- The open method of co-ordination is a new EU-level approach that is gaining in importance as an alternative to regulation.

- It is based on European guidelines, national action plans, and national reports using common indicators, and uses EU-level evaluations that feed into new policy guidelines.

- The practical effects of the open method have not been evaluated in a systematic way to date.

Social partnership at the European level

Contemporary Community social policy making is characterized by a style that some call 'Euro-corporatism' (Gorges 1996). This involves intense co-operation between public and private actors in the EU's social dimension. Corporatism is a way of making policy that includes not only public actors, but also interest groups as decisive co-actors (Streeck and Schmitter 1991; see also Chapter 13). All agree that EU social policy since Maastricht has been characterized by the entanglement of governmental negotiations in the Council and **collective bargaining** between the major economic interest group federations. As a consequence, the rather particular, closed, and stable policy network in EU social policy may be defined as a 'corporatist policy community' (Falkner 1998).

The legislative procedure in EU social policy now works as follows: when the Commission consults on any planned social policy measure, European-level employer and labour groups may inform the Commission of their wish to initiate negotiations on the matter under discussion in order to reach a collective agreement. This process brings standard EC decision making (see Chapter 1) to a standstill for nine months. If a collective agreement is signed, it can, at the joint request of the signatories, be incorporated in a 'Council decision' on the basis of a prior Commission proposal.

In recent years, bargaining on social policy issues has therefore been pursued in two quite distinctive arenas (though the two are nevertheless interdependent). The traditional pattern of social policy making is dominated by the Council and its working groups (see Chapter 10), although the adoption of a directive demands a Commission proposal and action by the European Parliament (EP), depending on the specific procedure at stake. The interests represented by politicians (and bureaucrats) involved are predominantly territorial (in the Council) and party political (in the EP). In this 'intergovernmental arena' for EU social policy, negotiations proceed according to the detailed rules about decision taking that are specified in the EC Treaty. These are complemented by informal rules which have resulted from decades of EC negotiation practice.

A second, quite different arena now surrounds negotiations between management and labour. Here, procedures are not prescribed in the Treaties. The Maastricht Social Agreement only contains provisions about 'interface situations' where the intergovernmental procedure and collective bargaining meet, notably specifying the rules on bringing to a standstill standard decision processes, or initiating Council negotiations on implementation. Since the agreement did not even specify who 'labour and management' should be, this was decided informally. Moreover, the Commission and the Council did not designate the European interest groups as responsible for carrying out the collective negotiations, even if in practice they approved the special status of the Union of Industrial and Employers' Confederations of Europe (UNICE), the European Centre of Enterprises with Public Participation (CEEP), and the European Trade Union Confederation (ETUC) as the responsible cross-sectoral **social partners**. These three groups, who wanted and received an exclusive role in 'negotiated legislation' (Dølvik 1997a) on European social policy, had already participated in a **'social dialogue'** with the Commission since the mid-1980s. When parental leave, the first issue to be discussed under the Social Agreement, was under consideration, the Commission stopped the standard legislative processes on the request of these groups and considered it appropriate to implement the agreement that resulted in a binding directive. Smaller interest groups, excluded from this process, complained about this, but the European Court rejected the legal action taken by the Union of Small and Medium-Sized Enterprises (UEAPME). Recently, both UNICE and ETUC have concluded co-operation agreements with smaller groups on the European social dialogue, while ultimately keeping their negotiation prerogatives intact.

Yet it is important to underline the point that the social partner negotiations on EC social policy issues are not entirely independent of the intergovern-

Table 17.2 Collective agreements to date

	Compulsory minimum standards	Field of application
Agreement on parental leave	• Individual right to 3 months' parental leave (distinct from maternity leave) • Leave on grounds of adoption: adjust conditions to the special circumstances • Protection against dismissal and right to return to similar job • Maintenance of acquired rights • Time off for urgent family reasons	All workers, men and women, with an employment contract or employment relationship as defined by the law, collective agreements, or practices in force in each member state
Agreement on part-time work	• Principle of non-discrimination: equal treatment with non-part-time workers	Part-time workers who have an employment contract or employment relationship as defined by the law, collective agreement, or practice in force in each member state
Agreement on fixed-term work	• Principle of non-discrimination: equal treatment with non-fixed-term workers	Fixed-term workers who have an employment contract or employment relationship as defined by the law, collective agreement, or practice in force in each member state

mental arena. There is intense contact and a large degree of interdependence amongst all relevant actors in EC social policy, that is amongst the Council, the social partners, the Commission, and, to a lesser extent, the EP. To date, three cross-sectoral collective agreements on labour law issues have been signed (Falkner 2000*a*): on parental leave (December 1995); on part-time work (June 1997); and on fixed-term work (March 1999). See Table 17.2.

A number of other negotiations failed to reach agreement, for example on the issue of temporary agency work, or were not initiated, such as on fighting sexual harassment, and on information and consultation of employees in national enterprises. A further reform of the patterns of EC social

policy making will be possible in 2004, as a consequence of discussions at the 2002–3 Constitutional **Convention**.

Key points

• Since Maastricht, EU social policy has involved a 'corporatist policy community'.

• The organized interests of labour and industry are free to agree collectively social standards that are later made binding in Council directives.

• They have done so in three cases, but have failed in others.

Conclusion

The preceding sections have indicated that European social policy has been extended and differentiated considerably, over time. Treaty bases have been revised several times to extend the range of competences. The ESF has increased its resources, and has

had a practical impact on national employment promotion projects. The number of social directives has also increased over time, with the 1990s being by far the most active decade. It should also be mentioned that the European Court of Justice (ECJ) in Luxembourg has been influential on a number of social policy issues and, as a consequence, has significantly increased the practical impact of EU social law. The equal treatment of women in the workplace and the protection of workers' interests when enterprises change hands are two important examples (Leibfried and Pierson 2000).

A full evaluation of the success of European social law is restricted by lack of knowledge about its practical effects in the member states. On the basis of the extension of EU social policy (rather than on its overall quality), four different evaluation criteria seem worth considering (Falkner 2000b). First, the closing of a number of gaps in labour law, introduced or widened by the Single Market Programme, was a major task for EU social policy (Barnard 2000: 62). According to this indicator, the EU performed much better than most experts expected during the early 1990s and all important gaps are now closed. A somewhat more far-reaching criterion for judging EU social law is the differential between Commission proposals and Council legislation. There was a huge gap during the late 1980s and early 1990s which has been almost completely filled as of 2002. Even the most controversial projects, on sexual harassment in the workplace and on employee consultation in the European Company Statute, have been adopted.

A third indicator of the scope of the EU's social dimension is action taken to prevent reductions in national social standards, potentially induced by the increased competitive pressures of the single market and Economic and Monetary Union (sometimes called **social dumping**). One possible way of preventing this from happening would have been to agree on fluctuation margins, which would have

stopped one country from gaining competitive advantages though lowering social standards. However, such proposals were only considered viable in a small number of member states, notably Belgium, France, and Germany (Busch 1988; Dispersyn et al. 1990). At the level of the Social Affairs Council there was little support. Finally, a fourth evaluation criterion might be the rather small extent to which the EU has forged a truly supranational social order.

Patterns of decision making in European social policy have also changed to a significant degree. Qualified majority voting has been introduced in Treaty reforms and has extended into day-to-day practice. Furthermore, the European-level, labour and industry groups have become key players in European social policy. They can now decide on the content of new social directives. Most recently, the style of European social policy has changed as the open method of co-ordination has become increasingly important. This means that EU social policy now employs a wider set of policy instruments, and can at the same time be active in more areas.

The forthcoming enlargement of the EU will make the adoption of common standards more difficult, as social standards will differ even more widely in an enlarged EU. This is certainly one of the main reasons for the development of this new method of influencing national social policy. Although agreement on legislation was already impossible in a number of social fields, it seems fair to conclude that, in future, common social standards will be of rather more importance. At the same time, agreement on binding standards (in particular, costly ones) will be even more difficult to achieve.

QUESTIONS

1 Why did the evolution of a 'social dimension' lag behind the market integration aspects of European integration?

2 Why is the Treaty base so important for EC social law?

3 What are the main areas of EU social law?

4 To what extent is EU social policy a regulatory policy, and how has social policy regulation developed over time?

5 How does the European Social Fund influence national policy?

6 What is the method of open co-ordination and what are its merits?

7 To what extent is EU social policy corporatist?

8 Which criteria are best used for evaluating the development of the EU's social dimension?

GUIDE TO FURTHER READING

de la Porte, C., and Pochet, P., *Building Social Europe through the Open Method of Co-ordination* Brussels/Berne/Berlin: PIE Lang, 2002). This edited book gives the most up-to-date information on the various fields of open co-ordination.

Falkner, G., *EU Social Policy in the 1990s: Towards a Corporatist Policy Community* (London: Routledge, 1998). The social dialogue between EU-level organized interests of labour and management is analysed from both the theoretical and the practical angle.

Hoskyns, C., *Integrating Gender* (London: Verso, 1996). This is still the most comprehensive book on the EU's equal treatment and gender equality policies by a political scientist.

Leibfried, S., and Pierson, P. (eds), *European Social Policy: Between Fragmentation and Integration* (Washington, DC: The Brookings Institution, 1995). This is a classic which is still a very rewarding work on EU-level social law and policy.

Scharpf, F. W., *Governing in Europe: Effective and Democratic?* (Oxford: OUP, 1999). This single-authored book puts EU social policy in the wider perspective of governance in the multi-level system.

Shaw, J. (ed.), *Social Law and Policy in an Evolving European Union* (Oxford/Portland: Hart, 2000). An excellent and recent collection of essays on EU social policy.

WEB LINKS

http://europa.eu.int/comm/employment_social/index_en.htm The home page of the European Commission's Directorate General for Employment and Social Affairs provides up-to-date information on all fields of European social law and policy.

www.eiro.eurofound.ie/ The 'European industrial relations observatory on-line' is an excellent source of information on all social dialogue issues, whether national or EU-level.

http://eiop.or.at/euroint/ 'EuroInternet' is the most comprehensive collection of information resources on the Internet relating to European integration. It contains relevant publications, institutions (both EU and national), associations, databases, people, topics, etc. A special 'subject section' is devoted to social policy.

http://eiop.or.at/erpa/ The European Research Papers Archive (ERPA) is a common access point for high-quality online working paper series (currently nine series) in the field of European integration research (including, for example, the series of the European University Institute). Hundreds of articles can be searched and the full text read, free. 'Social policy' is one of the key areas covered.

http://eiop.or.at/eiop/ 'European Integration online Papers' (EIoP) is a free, but fully reviewed, interdisciplinary E-journal on European integration issues. Since 1997, scholars from all over the world have published more than 80 articles there for over 1,300 subscribers. Social policy is covered in a number of articles.

18 Regional Europe

Angela K. Bourne

READER'S GUIDE

This chapter looks at the development, operation, and significance of the EU's regional policy and at the role of (sub-state) regions in EU politics. Regional policy aims to improve economic development in the EU's poorest regions, mainly through special financial instruments known as the Structural Funds. The policy is closely linked to the single market project, developed rapidly in the mid-1980s, and now consumes a large slice of the EU budget. 'Regional Europe' evokes the close relationship between regional activism and European integration. Regions' demands for and experience of political autonomy now includes a European dimension, manifest in the rise of an influential EU regions' lobby and the creation of the Committee of the Regions. These developments raise many fundamental questions for the EU, including whether the state in Europe is eroding from 'above' and 'below'; whether Europe is becoming a less state-centric, multi-level polity and how Europeanization affects regional autonomy and territorial relations within EU member states.

Introduction

The study of 'Regional Europe' is now a staple of EU studies. It has not always been so. If we are looking for a decisive phase that brought the spheres of regional and European governance together, both in practice and in theory, we must look to the EU's re-launch in the mid-1980s (see Chapter 3). European integration has always impinged on the life of regions, as indeed it has impinged on many aspects of member states' domestic politics. After the **Single European Act** (SEA) of 1986, and later the **Maastricht Treaty** of 1992, however, the impact of the EU on regions increased significantly. New EU powers conferred by these treaties impinged upon regional decision powers more significantly than in the past and underpinned a new interest in the defence of affected regional powers at state and EU levels. Additionally, the single market programme encouraged the EU to take regional economic development much more seriously. It prompted the inauguration of a regional policy more worthy of the name and significant increases in the 'Structural Funds', or Community funds for poorer regions. Developments such as these not only made EU policies more region-friendly, but also turned regional actors into both lobbyists and stakeholders in the EU decision process.

The emergence of a regional dimension in EU politics challenged some old ideas about the EU and gave birth to some new ones. The new, improved regional policy provided a new case for examining the dynamics of European integration more broadly. It provided an opportunity to ask questions about *why* the decision was made to expand regional policy: Was it evidence of '**spillover**'? Was it the result of **intergovernmental bargaining**? Or could the decision be explained by something else, like the popularity of new ideas about economic development? Furthermore, the presence of a new set of policy participants—regional actors—in EU

decisions invited academics to move beyond 'classical' integration theorists' concern with challenges to the state 'from above', to consider whether there was a simultaneous challenge to the state 'from below' as well. Slogans like 'Europe of the Regions' and 'multi-level governance' began to pepper book lists and articles in academic journals. These ideas have been conceptualized in a variety of different ways, but all hint at a more pressing need to conceive of the EU not as a two-level game, but as a multi-level one involving EU, state, *and* regional actors.

This chapter seeks to explore the rise and implications of this regional dimension of EU politics by looking at the abovementioned developments in more detail. It begins with discussion of the Europeanization of regional activism and the growing presence of regions in the EU's policy process. This is followed by an analysis of the origins, development, and operation of the EU's regional economic development policy. The final section considers some of the theoretical implications that these developments raise for our understanding of the nature of the EU, the process of European integration, and the impact of European unification on domestic politics within the EU member states.

Regions in EU decision making

In this chapter, 'region' is used to describe segments of divided territorial space situated immediately below the level of the state. The simplest way of identifying regions is by their formal institutions, or the presence of parliaments, executives, or administrative bodies. A region may be more or it may be less than a political space, however. For instance, a region may be a functional space, with institutions responsible for planning and the implementation of regional policies but lacking directly elected bodies. A region can also be a cultural space, especially insofar as it is inhabited by an ethnically or linguistically distinguishable group like the Basques, Catalans, Scots, Welsh, Bretons, or the Flemish.

In recent decades, the region has become a more important feature of the domestic political land-

scape in Europe. Immediately after the Second World War, there were only a handful of European states with regions exercising significant political powers, notably West Germany, Austria, and Switzerland. Since then, devolutionary reforms have begun to unravel the political centralization of many European states. New regional institutions have been set up in countries like Belgium from the 1960s, Spain, and Italy from the 1970s, and the United Kingdom since the late 1990s.

One important impact that the EU has had on this decentralizing process has been the Europeanization of regional experiences of political autonomy. European regions are affected by all sorts of EU decisions in a range of policy areas, and many now regularly take an active interest in EU decisions. In order to aid lobbying and information gathering, many regions have established regional information offices. Indeed the growth of such offices from just a couple in the mid-1980s to around 170 by 2002 (see Europe in Brussels, at **www.blbe.irisnet.be**) is an important indicator of the growing presence of regional (and local) actors in EU politics. Furthermore, many regional governments are involved in international regional associations, the number of which also bloomed from the mid-1980s. From this time, many new associations have been set up to provide a collective regional lobby and to facilitate co-operation between regions from different parts of Europe. The Assembly of European Regions is the largest of these, comprising more than 300 members from all over Europe. There are dozens of other interregional associations pursuing a vast array of objectives ranging from the development of improved transport links and economic development along the European Atlantic coast to associations encouraging the promotion and protection of minority languages.

The region has become a more important part of EU politics itself, thanks in large part to the achievements of a campaign by the regions since the Single European Act (SEA) to increase their say in EU decision making. As the process of policy deepening instigated by the SEA and Maastricht began to bite, the new regions lobby demanded recompense for the fact that the political costs of European integration were intrinsically higher for regional than for central governments. Powers transferred to the EU level in the course of the integration process came from competences allocated to both central *and* regional governments. Central governments received a form of compensation for those transferred competences, while regional governments did not. Central governments were compensated because their representatives were, until recently, the only officials able to vote in the powerful EU Council. This meant that central governments participated in decisions made in the Council, even if the policy matter in question was formally allocated to or shared with regions in domestic constitutions. Not surprisingly, regional governments demanded change to ensure that they did not 'lose' powers as a consequence of European integration, demands centred on a call for **'subsidiarity'**

and a stronger role for regions in the EU decision process.

Subsidiarity is a principle often employed in federal-type systems to regulate the distribution of competences between different levels of government in accordance with the criteria of efficiency (see also Box 5.2). In the EU, subsidiarity is encoded in Article 5 (formerly Article 3b) of the Treaty in order to limit the scope of Community action to areas where Community action is most efficient. By most accounts, subsidiarity is really only a protection for central governments against EU incursions, but it has long been an aim of regional governments to have its cover extended to lower governing tiers (Jeffrey 1997). So far, demands to extend subsidiarity to regional competences affected by the EU have met with little success but as the 2001 Laeken Declaration on the Future of the EU indicates, the issue is still on the agenda. At **Laeken** (see Chapter 4, Box 4.7), the Convention discussing the Future of the EU was asked to consider whether regions should be given 'guarantees that their spheres of competencies will not be affected [by the EU]' and highlighted the need be wary of 'encroachment upon the exclusive areas of competence of . . . regions'.

In other areas, regions' demands for a greater role in EU decision making led to changes in the EU's institutional architecture and in some cases helped to 'correct' some of the problems created by the transfer of regional powers to the EU level. The institutional changes meant that regions acquired new opportunities to participate in EU decision making via a Committee of the Regions and the EU Council.

The Committee of the Regions (CoR) was established by the Maastricht Treaty and began work in 1994 as a body of 222 representatives of EU member states' local and regional authorities. The Commission and the EU Council are obliged to consult the CoR in a range of policy areas where the EU legislates and which directly affect local and regional authorities. These include public health, education and youth, culture, employment, social matters, and the environment. It must also be consulted on economic and social cohesion matters, which includes legislation dealing with the Structural Funds.

Formally the CoR is weak. It is a purely advisory

body whose opinions can be ignored by other institutions in the legislative process. In its early years, the CoR also faced certain internal tensions that damaged its credibility, including differences between typically much weaker local governments and more powerful regional governments (Christiansen 1996: 96; McCarthy 1997: 440). It has also faced criticisms over the blandness of its opinions. Nevertheless, there is evidence to suggest that the Commission in particular, an institution that played an important role in setting up the CoR in the first place, does take its opinions seriously. Another source of strength is that some of the CoR's members are powerful and experienced politicians at home, a factor that adds political weight to CoR opinions (Loughlin 1997: 160).

Despite ambivalence over the CoR's effectiveness as a tool for factoring regional views into EU decision making, the very creation of such a body in the EU was a significant breakthrough. It recognized regional authorities as legitimate participants in EU decision making and represented an important departure from the hitherto prevalent idea that only central governments ought to represent their state in the EU. Furthermore, there is added value for regional and local authorities insofar as it provides a venue for networking, exchanging information and expertise, and facilitating co-operation on specific issues (McCarthy 1997: 449). For the government of the Basque Autonomous Community in Spain, for example, such advantages justify an active involvement (see Box 18.1). Its representative has usually been a member of two or three (of a total of seven) CoR Commissions (or sub-committees). Furthermore, between 1994 and 1998, the Basque representative has presented 69 amendments to CoR opinions, 80 per cent of which were accepted (Basque Government 1998).

Box 18.1 **Case study**
The Basque Country's European policy

The Basque government is the executive institution of the Basque Autonomous Community, one of the 17 regional entities established in Spain in the late 1970s. The Basque Nationalist Party (*El Partido Nacionalist Vasco* or PNV) has always been dominant in the Basque government. It is a moderate, Christian democratic, Basque nationalist party with a long tradition of supporting European unity. Its official policy pursues the creation of a 'Europe of Peoples', a position very similar to the regional-federalist model of a 'Europe of the Regions'. From its position at the helm of the Basque government's European policy machinery, the PNV has been able to pursue the Basque nationalist agenda abroad by presenting itself as a foreign policy player or by pursuing policies popular in the Basque Country that have not had Spanish central government support. Not surprisingly, this tactic has often caused tensions between Basque and Spanish central governments.

However, like other Spanish Autonomous Communities and indeed, many other regional governments in the EU, the Basque government pursues many other interests at the EU level. The Basque government has paid close attention to each major round of Structural Fund reform and in the most recent *Agenda 2000* round unsuccessfully battled against the odds to get part of its territory declared an 'Objective 1' area (see Box 18.3). The Basque government also has an interest in the progress of EU decisions in many other fields, including agriculture, fishing, transport, and competition policy, and it routinely lobbies EU decision makers—at both national and supranational levels—to try to influence EU laws. The Basque government also has a strong interest in the development of a more powerful institutionalized role for regions in EU decision making and has often contributed to Europe-wide regional campaigns pursuing this aim.

In some respects, the Basque and other Autonomous Communities in Spain have paid a high price for EU membership. When Spain joined the EU in 1986 and with the ratification of the Single European Act (SEA) and the Maastricht Treaty, many important Autonomous Community powers were transferred to the EU. Unlike the EU's federal states, the Spanish Autonomous Communities are still not allowed to share their central government's negotiating privileges in the EU Council. Basque and other Autonomous Communities only have access to EU decision forums via an array of rather weak channels, including one CoR representative each, official delegation offices in Brussels, and membership of Europe-wide regional associations.

Another amendment agreed at Maastricht (Article 203, formerly Article 146) opened up the possibility that regional ministers could represent their state—in some cases with voice and vote—in the EU Council and its working groups. The details, however, were left to each individual state to decide. The consequence is that not all EU regions are allowed access to the Council. So far, only the German and Austrian *Länder*, Belgian Communities and Regions, and representatives from Welsh and Scottish regional institutions have participated. There is mounting pressure in Spain for this privilege to be extended to the Spanish Autonomous Communities.

Importantly, the treaty changes did not allow regional ministers to participate as representatives of their own regions' interests. Regional ministers, like central government ministers, represent and must vote for their state as a whole. Interestingly, one of the suggestions made to the Convention on the Future of the EU is that states be allowed to split their vote in the Council and in so doing allow regional and central government representatives in member state delegations to vote differently on a single piece of EU legislation. But until such changes are agreed, if at all, the importance of regional participation in the Council will be the opportunities it provides for regional ministers to steer negotiations in a direction that may correspond to regional interests more generally and to provide insider information and contacts that regions can use to their advantage in both domestic and EU decision processes.

Key points

- Since the mid-1980s, regional governments' experience of political autonomy has acquired a significant European dimension. Many regional governments have offices in Brussels, participate in international regional associations, and regularly lobby EU decision-makers.

- European integration can be very costly for regions. The EU's institutional arrangements tend to disempower regional governments relative to central governments.

- Since the Maastricht Treaty, important institutional changes have helped 'correct' this problem, but have not yet fully solved it. The CoR and provisions allowing regional governments to participate in the EU Council are two key reforms improving opportunities for regional influence in the EU.

The origins, development, and implementation of EU regional policy

Regional Europe evokes more than just a new role for regions in the EU. Reforms in the mid-1980s and early 1990s also bolstered EU activity aimed at improving regional economic conditions, though some aspects of these reforms had implications for the role of regions in the EU and must, therefore, be considered part of the broader theme discussed in the last section of this chapter. The incentives that became attached to regional lobbying, arising out vast increases in structural funding (see Figure 18.1) and new 'partnership' rules encouraging regional participation in Structural Fund implementation, for example, are a vital part of the story about the Europeanization of regions. However, the dynamism of EU regional policy development after the SEA also touches on broader issues to do with the dynamics of integration more generally, including the relevance of **'spillover'**, **intergovernmental bargaining**, and other influences on policy choices. This last set of isues is the general theme of the analysis in this section, analysis which begins with a discussion of the pre-SEA origins of the policy, the SEA and Maastricht Treaty reforms, and the EU's distinctive regime for regional policy implementation.

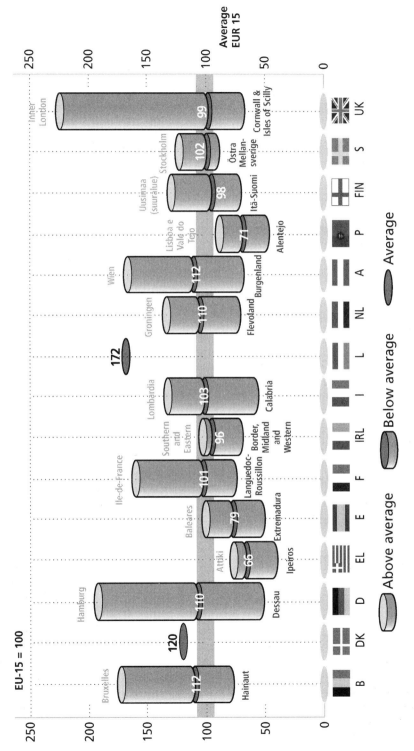

Fig. 18.1 Regional disparities between the member states in per capita GDP, 1997 (purchasing power standards)

Note: The regions indicated (NUTS 2) are those where per capita GDP is respectively the lowest and the highest in each country.

A necessary preliminary, however, is a brief introduction to the aims and objectives of regional policy in advanced industrial economies.

What is EU regional policy and why is it necessary?

Regional policy aims to reduce regional economic disparities. In other words, it aims to ameliorate conditions within regions that have lower economic growth, employment, or per capital income levels than other regions. There are some very significant economic disparities between EU regions. Regions such as Ipeiros in Greece and Alentejo in Portugal have per capita GDP levels below 50 per cent of the EU average and even the richer regions of these states have GDP per capita figures below the EU average. This contrasts with GDP per capita figures in Inner London and in Hamburg (Germany), regions where GDP per capita reaches around or over 200 per cent of the EU average (see Figure 18.1).

EU member states already have their own regional policies. Why, then, do they also need a supranational policy? In the first place, the integration of markets tends to exacerbate regional economic disparities. Economic integration does not affect all regions in the same way. It generally favours regions geographically at the centre of the single market. In the EU, for instance, these central regions have the advantage of being closer to the main population centres and thus large numbers of consumers and workers (Armstrong and Taylor 2000: 309). It appears likely that deepening economic integration, as undertaken in the single market programme and EMU, further exacerbates regional economic disparities between the centre and the periphery. At the same time, the process of creating a single market has obliged member states to give up some important policy instruments that could be used to improve regional economic disparities at home. For example, those states taking part in economic and monetary union (EMU) can no longer manipulate their exchange rates to assist poorer regions (George 1996: 231) and there are limits placed, in the context of EU competition policy, on the amount of subsidies member governments can spend on their regions.

Presented in this manner, the justification for creating an EU-level regional policy appears to lend weight to the neo-functionalist 'spillover' thesis (see Chapter 6). **Functional 'spillover'** describes the process whereby integration in some sectors leads to pressures for integration in others, a process that sets in motion an incremental movement towards closer union. Applied to the case of EU regional policy, it could be argued that the problems that market integration and monetary union create—that is, the marginalization of peripheral regions and the removal of regional policy instruments—makes EU regional policy more necessary. But there is also a case for the argument that the rationale behind EU regional policy is largely political and that factors other than spillover account for its development. As the following section will show in more detail, there is evidence that the exigencies of intergovernmental bargaining have been the crucial factors. And in an indication of the complexity of EU policy development, the ambitions of supranational actors like the Commission and changing policy-making fashions also appear to have played some part in the reform process.

The origins and development of EU regional policy

The Treaty of Rome provided the seeds of a European regional policy. In the Treaty's Preamble, member states noted their desire to 'ensure their harmonious development by reducing differences existing between the various regions and the backwardness of the less-favoured regions'. However, it was not until 1975 that the Community established the European Regional Development Fund (ERDF), the Community's first policy instrument specifically dedicated to the problem of unequal development between EU regions. With the creation of this fund, the first of a series of phases in the development of EU regional policy commenced. The creation of the ERDF was to be followed in the second phase (1985–97) by reforms creating a more substantial regional policy and in the third and current phase (1997–present) by further major reforms to meet the challenge of enlargement.

The first moves to create the ERDF were made by the Commission, which produced the first legislative proposal for a Community regional policy in 1969. While the Commission's proposal originally found little support from most member states, other key decisions taken at that time soon helped produce a new coalition favourable to the creation of an ERDF (George 1996: 231–2). At the 1969 summit in The Hague, member states decided to pursue EMU and to open accession negotiations with the UK, Ireland, Denmark, and Norway. The entry of the UK and Ireland in particular—both of which had regional problems more serious than most member states (with the notable exception of Italy)—increased the number of potential beneficiaries of a regional fund. Furthermore, their insistence that an ERDF was a necessary condition for their participation in EMU went a long way towards winning over the previously reluctant **net contributors** to such a fund, especially West Germany (George 1996: 233). The fact that the final decision to set up the fund was eventually made at the 1972 and 1974 Paris summits, rather than on the basis of the Commission's proposal, indicated that the regional policy ball was firmly in the member governments' court. So, too, was the merely symbolic figure of around 5 per cent of the Community budget that they allocated to the fund. There was no real likelihood that such a small figure could significantly reduce regional disparities.

The Single European Act laid the basis for a genuine EU regional policy. A new 'social and economic cohesion' title (Title XVII, Articles 158–62, formerly Title XIV, Articles 130a–e) was inserted into the Treaty of Rome entrenching a commitment to reduce regional economic disparities and the 'backwardness' of the Community's 'least favoured regions'. The three financial instruments, from then on collectively denominated as the 'Structural Funds', were to be the principal mechanism for achieving these objectives (see Box 18.2). Another crucial change following from the SEA was the first in a series of massive increases in the money allocated to structural funding in the Community budget. In 1988, member states sanctioned the Delors I financial perspective and doubled their structural fund commitments for 1989–93. Later, in the 1992 Delors II package, they doubled it again for the 1993–9 period. These represented increases from around 5 per cent of the Community budget in 1975 to just under 40 per cent by 1999.

More changes were just around the corner. At Maastricht, member states also established a new and generously resourced financial instrument known as the Cohesion Fund. The Cohesion Fund was set up to assist those states—*not* the regions within them—that were expected to find it difficult to meet the **convergence criteria** for EMU. The Cohesion Fund would provide financial contributions to projects in the field of environment and

---

Box 18.2 **The facts**
EU funds for regional development

The Structural Funds

European Regional Development Fund (ERDF): finances infrastructure, job-creating investments, local development projects, and aid for small firms.

European Social Fund (ESF): promotes the return of the unemployed and disadvantaged groups to the workforce, mainly by financing training and systems of recruitment aid.

'Guidance' Section of the European Agricultural Guidance and Guarantee Fund: finances rural development measures and aid for farmers, mainly in regions lagging in develop-

ment. The 'Guarantee' Section of this Fund also supports rural development under the CAP in all other areas of the Union.

Financial Instrument for Fisheries Guidance: helps adapt and modernize the fishing industry.

The Cohesion Fund

Set up in 1993, this fund provides assistance to the four poorest EU member states—Greece, Portugal, Italy, and Spain—to finance major projects in the field of environment and transport. The Cohesion Fund amounts to €18 bn. for the current budget period (to 2006).

transport networks for those states whose GDP per capita was less than 90 per cent of the EU average (Spain, Portugal, Greece, and Ireland). The Cohesion Fund was allocated €15 bn. for 1993–9 and €18 bn. for 2000–6.

These policy changes were an integral part of the re-launch of the Community in the mid-1980s. They were intimately linked to the desire to complete the common market and later to support EMU, while combating some of the likely problems these steps would bring, namely the marginalization of peripheral regions and the abolition of key domestic regional policy tools. But as in the 1970s, enlargement and policy deepening were once again triggers for change. In the 1980s, Community membership expanded to include Greece (1981) and Portugal and Spain (1986). As Figure 18.1 indicates, each of these states has a far lower total GDP per capita level than all other member states (except Ireland) and each includes regions with extremely low levels of GDP per capita. Like the previous enlargement bringing in the UK and Ireland, this increased the coalition of states pushing for a more generous regional policy fund. And once again, this coalition of potential net recipients made regional funding a condition of their participation and consent to this second attempt at EMU (George 1996: 237). In other words, EU regional funds served as a 'side payment', or as a kind of 'compensation', used by richer EU member states to 'buy' the consent of poorer ones in order to facilitate bargains over other non-regional policy-related issues (Allen 2000: 245). After a decade of expansion, however, the challenge of enlargement meant member states would have to rethink their common regional policy once again.

The influx of membership applications from the Central and Eastern European (CEE) states brought with it a case for regional policy reforms. The CEE states emerged from the Communist era with a series of structural problems and, collectively, were a great deal worse off economically than existing member states. Together, the ten CEEs which have applied to the EU have an average GDP per capita of around one-third that of existing member states and around one-half the GDP per capita of EU's poorest states— Spain, Portugal, Greece, and Ireland (Baun 1999: 271). Similarly, major structural differences exist.

For example, more than 22 per cent of the CEE work-force is employed in agriculture compared to around 5 per cent in the existing member states.

These differences have very important implications for many EU policies and especially for the budgetary aspects of the Community structural and agricultural policies (see Chapters 14 and 16: 262). Virtually all CEE applicant states would be eligible for the highest structural funding contributions and under existing rules many would qualify for similarly high CAP subsidies (Armstrong and Taylor 2000: 315). Given that, together, structural and agricultural spending consume most of the EU budget, significant budgetary increases would be needed to meet such demands. At the same time, enlargement is likely to bring further challenges for existing EU regions. Research published by the Commission suggests that enlargement will be much more beneficial for regions in the UK, France, and especially those in Germany than for poorer peripheral regions of the EU, including those in Southern Europe (European Commission 1996). Member states had good reason to support the structural adjustment of future member states, but the economic disparities and new problems facing regions in existing member states meant a new balance had to be struck between the demands of enlargement and persisting regional problems.

After the Treaty of Amsterdam negotiations, in July 1997, the Commission presented its comprehensive *Agenda 2000* document, which included, among other things, proposals to reform EU regional policy to make way for enlargement (European Commission 1997; see also Box 14.2). In it, the Commission argued that economic and social cohesion should remain one of the basic functions of EU action. However, taking note of the critical mood in many member states when faced with the prospect of an expansion of the EC Budget, the Commission recommended that structural and cohesion spending should be stabilized. Negotiations leading up to the deal eventually made at the Berlin European Council in March 1999 revived old cleavages between **net contributors**—now including Germany, the Netherlands, Austria, and Sweden—and the **net recipients**, enthusiastically led by Spain (Laffan and Shackleton 2000: 231–6). In the end a deal was struck and structural funds were allocated €258 bn. (at 1999 prices) between 2000 and 2006: €213 bn. for needy regions within existing member states; €45 bn. for CEE applicant states before and after accession; and €18 bn. for the Cohesion Fund. The growth and decline of structural funding between 1988 and 2006 is shown in Figure 18.2.

The implementation of EU regional policy

This section is about how the Community manages its regional policy and more specifically the operation of the Structural Funds. Reforms after the Single European Act (SEA) of 1986 established the basic systems and ground rules for the implementation of EU regional policy that continue to be used today. Reforms took place in three rounds. The first were set out in a series of 1988 Regulations; the second in Regulations which came into force in 1993; and the third, since *Agenda 2000*, were implemented in 1999. There are five main principles governing the Structural Funds: co-ordination, concentration, programming, additionality and partnership.

1   Originally, *co-ordination* involved the integration of all the Structural Funds into a single framework centred on the achievement of six key objectives. Reforms since *Agenda 2000* reduced these to three (see Box 18.3). The 1988 reforms also set aside a small amount of the Structural Fund budget for Community Initiatives. Compared to other structural fund spending, which involves a great deal of input from member states, Community Initiatives are predominantly governed by the Commission. There are now four Community Initiatives, consuming 5.35 per cent of the Structural Funds and directed towards cross-border co-operation; sustainable development in cities; rural development; and labour market equality.

2   The *concentration* principle requires that Structural Fund spending go to those regions in the greatest need. In practice, this has meant that Objective 1 regions, defined as the EU's least developed areas, have consistently received about two-thirds of all Structural Funds. Unsurprisingly, the concentration of Structural Funds on Objective 1 regions has prompted many regional bodies, including the Basque government (Box 18.1) and the Welsh National Assembly (Box 18.4), to clamour for the ignominious title of 'backward' or 'underdeveloped' EU region.

3   *Programming* requires that structural fund expenditure is not just distributed on an *ad hoc*, project-by-project basis. Funds are distributed in

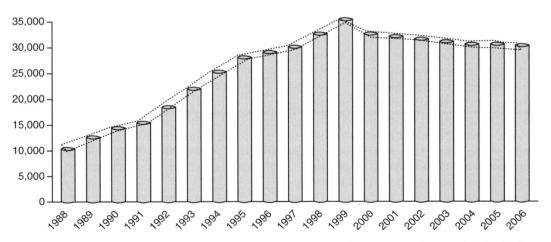

Fig. 18.2 Annual resources of the Structural Funds and the Cohesion Fund, 1988–2006 (€m., at 1999 prices)
Source: European Commission, Interegio website (**www.inforegion.cec.eu.int**).

Box 18.3 **The facts**
Structural Fund objectives

The 1988 Structural Fund reforms established six objectives under which regions might obtain funds.

Three of these were limited in their geographical scope to disadvantaged regions. These were:

- Objective 1: development and structural adjustment of least-developed regions.
- Objective 2: conversion of regions facing industrial decline.
- Objective 5b: development of rural areas.

The remaining priorities were focused on the whole EU:

- Objective 3: combating long-term unemployment.
- Objective 4: combating youth unemployment.
- Objective 5a: adjustment of agricultural structures.

When Sweden and Finland joined the EU in 1995, a new objective was added:

- Objective 6: help low-population density regions.

The *Agenda 2000* round of Structural Fund reforms cut the number of objectives from seven to three:

- The new Objective 1 remained unchanged in its focus on the regions whose development is lagging behind, although it did come to incorporate the aims of the old Objective 6.
- The new Objective 2 brought together the old Objectives 2 (industrial decline) and 5b (rural development) and became broader in scope, aiming 'to support the economic and social conversion of areas facing structural difficulties'.
- The new Objective 3, a horizontal objective focusing on all of the EU and not just disadvantaged regions, brought together the social aims of the old Objectives 3 and 4 to focus on 'supporting the adaptation and modernization of policies and systems of education, training and employment'.

Box 18.4 **Case study**
West Wales and the Valleys: 'Objective 1' funding

After an intensive campaign by Welsh authorities, West Wales and the Valleys became an Objective 1 region for 2000–6. Acquiring this status meant this part of Wales officially became one of the poorest and least-developed areas of the EU. But this ignominious title came with a healthy reward of €1,853.4 m over the six-year period. The money is going towards projects designed, among other things, to increase the competitiveness of the region by improving economic conditions for small and medium-sized enterprizes and the use of new technologies. Additionally, funding will be spent on combating social exclusion and helping the unemployed by increasing their access to business opportunities, education, and training. Further support is targeted towards rural development needs, the sustainable use of natural resources, and infrastructure development, including transportation.

accordance with pre-planned, multi-annual programmes, bringing together a range of projects designed to improve economic conditions in individual regions. Initially, in the 1988 Structural Fund regulations, programming was a way for the Commission to exercise some control over the way member states spent their allocations. However in subsequent reforms, reductions in the Commission's influence over the content

of programmes was one way in which member states 'clawed back' control from member state governments in this policy area (Allen 2000: 255).

4 The *additionality* principle requires that structural fund spending must not substitute for member states' regional policy expenditure, but that it should complement, or be 'additional' to that expenditure.

Implementing additionality has been one of the hardest principles to put into operation. From the outset, as Joanne Scott, observed, 'member state governments have tended to regard ERDF commitments as a welcome but unexpected windfall' which could be used as a 'reimbursement' of their own regional aid expenditure' (1995: 17). The Commission, has, nevertheless, doggedly pursued additionality and has even used its powers to withhold Structural Fund payments when there was a strong case that additionality had been violated (John 1996).

5   The 1988 Structural Fund Regulations entrenched the *partnership* principle into the Community's regional policy regime. Partnership required that in addition to the central governments, the regions and the Commission should have a role in the preparation of programmes and in the assessment and monitoring of those programmes as they are put into practice. Partnership was a crucial innovation, important insofar as it illustrated the influence of supranational policy actors and the impact of new ideas on the EU's institutional design. Partnership reflects new ideas, championed by the Commission, about the best way to achieve regional policy objectives. Previously, EU regional policy had predominantly been the responsibility of member states' governments. The new method focused on developing regions' endogenous economic potential but also establishing new decentralized decision procedures, bringing together public and private actors from multiple levels of government (Kohler-Koch 1996; Tömmel 1998). The Commission initially met some resistance from member governments, but it eventually saw the institutionalization of its new approach in the 1988 regional policy implementing system. When it was introduced, partnership excited a great deal of academic interest. It brought together actors from multiple levels of government into new transnational policy networks and in so doing seemed to empower both regional and EU-level institutions (Marks 1992). Since the 1988 reforms, however, there have been important changes significantly diluting the potential of partnership as a source of regional influence. In the 1993 round of Structural Fund reforms, 'partnership' was extended to include 'economic and social partners' and after 1999 it was extended again to include 'any other relevant competent body', such as environmental and social equality groups. Moreover, at the planning or programming stages, procedures were 'streamlined' and 'simplified', changes that effectively meant the exclusion of partners, and central government domination of the process (Allen 2000: 254).

Key points

- EU regional policy developments may be divided into three main phases: an early phase inaugurated by the creation of the ERDF; an expansive phase corresponding to the SEA and Maastricht Treaty reforms; and a final phase characterized by the pressures of enlargement.

- Part of the explanation for EU regional policy lies in functional imperatives captured by the metaphor of functional spillover. Justifications include the negative effects of market integration on peripheral regions and the fact that European integration restricts the range of policy instruments that member states can use to combat such differences.

- There are also political explanations for regional policy expansion. Progressive enlargements helped build a coalition of potential net contributors and policy deepening provided an opportunity for them to link demands for funds to issues like EMU.

- While intergovernmental bargains were crucial in budgetary issues, Commission influence was more prevalent in matters of institutional design such as in the development of partnership.

Regions and European integration: Theoretical issues

The emergence of a regions' lobby in the EU, the strong presence of a European dimension in regional politics, and subsequent EU regional policy reforms—especially partnership—raise some important theoretical issues. The most important of these concerns whether regional activism and European integration have altered the role and contemporary relevance of the state in Europe. They also have a bearing on theories about the nature of the EU. This section explores these issues by analysing recurring themes in the literature on regionalism and European integration. The first is the idea that the EU is becoming a 'Europe of the Regions'.

This is a high-profile—but poorly substantiated—idea. The basic thrust of the proposal is that a politically unified federal Europe could, or more correctly should, be established whose integral units are regions (not existing states) identified principally in terms of ethnocultural and linguistic features. As a political programme, this regional-federalist project remains influential especially among some European minority nationalist parties (see, for example, Box 18.1). However as an analytical concept most analysts reject the Europe of the Regions model as a description of current circumstances. Problems with the model include the lack of sufficient regional consciousness across Europe, significant differences in regional institutional forms, and the absence of an adequate European-level bureaucratic machine (Sharpe 1993: 3; Marks and Hooghe 1996: 73).

The second major theme is whether the state's political authority and capacity to act are being simultaneously eroded from 'above' and 'below'. The best-known theory addressing this question is Multi-level governance (MLG), developed principally by Gary Marks and Liesbet Hooghe (Marks 1992; Hooghe 1996; Marks, Hooghe, and Blank 1996; see also Chapter 8: 120–1). The main argument of MLG is that the role of the state has changed because 'the state no longer monopolizes European-level policy-making'. Marks and Hooghe accept the inter-

governmental argument that central governments remain the most important players in EU politics. But alongside this assumption they bring in the **neofunctionalist** idea that EU supranational institutions like the Commission, the ECJ, and the EP have independent influence in policy making (see Chapter 6: 84). Importantly, they also argue that regional actors may have a role in EU-level decision making that does not always involve the mediation of central governments. These fundamental changes in the role of the state suggest the emergence of MLG, or a new multi-level EU polity, where regions and EU supranational institutions become important actors alongside central state institutions (see Chapter 8: 120).

There are several key features of this posited multi-level polity. It is a polity (i) where regional, state, and supranational actors share control over many activities that take place in their respective territories; (ii) where states are one among a variety of actors contesting decisions that are made at a variety of levels; and (iii) where there are transnational linkages between actors located in and representing different-level political arenas (Marks, Hooghe, and Blank 1996: 346–7). Marks, Hooghe, and Blank argue that although this multi-level polity is not yet fully defined, its features are discernible. Importantly, it is in the area of EU regional policy, and precisely at those stages of the policy process governed by partnership, that multi-level governance is most clearly visible.

Multi-level polity approaches are not without their critics. There is some empirical evidence of regional-EU institutional alliances, particularly between regions and the European Commission's regional policy directorate-general, which has at times given support to regions on issues opposed by their central governments (John 1996). But the significance of this evidence is contested. Patrick Le Gales and Christian Lequesne, for example, argue that optimism about regions becoming more important players in EU politics has not materialized and that regions, therefore, remain minor actors in European governance (1998: 8). Others criticize a tendency to confuse regional participation or involvement in EU decisions with an ability to influence them, a tendency that they argue shows significant weaknesses in the descriptive accuracy and explanatory power of such approaches (Kohler-Koch 1996: 375). Other critics take the argument a step further, suggesting that central governments have significant 'gate-keeping' abilities that allow them to block actions by EU institutions, in support of the regions where actions may significantly affect the interests of the central government or state as a whole (Anderson 1990; Bache 1999*a*).

This gate-keeping argument is a central element of an alternative, intergovernmental theory for understanding the impact of regionalism and European integration on the role of the state (see Chapter 7). From the intergovernmental perspective, EU decision making is basically seen as a process dominated by central government bargains. Supra-national institutions are seen as agents or servants of member states rather than autonomous political actors. It follows from this argument that European integration will have no effect on the political authority of central governments because regions will not be able to form alliances with EU actors in a way that allows them significantly to affect EU decisions. From this perspective, as Mark Pollack argues, regional and EU authorities are merely actors in an 'intergovernmental play' (Pollack 1995: 362).

Central governments dominate the EU's decision-making apparatus and this allows them to 'establish the institutional context within which both the Commission and regional governments act'. Any role that regions may have in EU decision making takes place when regions' views are subsumed into the negotiating position that their state's central government defends in EU decision arenas (Moravcsik 1993: 483–5).

Key points

- The close relationship between regional activism, especially in the field of EU regional policy, raises important theoretical issues about the contemporary role of the state and the nature of the EU.

- The Multi-level Governance (MLG) model reconceptualizes the EU as a polity where decision-making authority is shared between actors from multiple levels of government, including regional governments.

- In contrast, intergovernmentalists argue that member states still act as gate-keepers capable of blocking decisions where key interests are at stake. This is one of the most important counter-arguments against MLG. From this view, the only real chance regions have of influence is via central government support.

Conclusion

This chapter explored 'Regional Europe' from three viewpoints. It described the Europeanization of regional activism and the growing presence of regions in EU policy making. It examined the origins, development, and implementation of the EU's regional economic development policy. The chapter also analysed some of the theoretical implications of these developments.

A number of conclusions can be drawn from this discussion. The first is that Regional Europe

emerged as a much more important topic in analysis of European integration from the mid-1980s. It was at this time that the number and strength of European regions began to grow and when the transfer of regional powers to the EU began to intensify. It was also at this time that important EU regional policy reforms took place. These focused attention on the 'region' in a much more direct manner. Academics responded by inventing new or resurrecting old vocabulary to describe these changes. That is why it was in the 1980s and 1990s that concepts like Europe of the Regions and MLG hit the limelight.

A second, more fundamental, conclusion is that analysis of Regional Europe provides ample material with which to examine a whole range of theories and ideas about the EU. The explosion of regional information offices in Brussels shows just how much European politics and policy making penetrates politics and policy making within EU member states (see Chapter 21). The negative impact that transfers of powers to EU-level institutions can have on regional autonomy within member states is an illustration of this very close relationship between domestic and European levels of governance. The Europeanization of regional activism and the formation of Europe-wide regional associations show how economic integration can also bolster political integration. And the growing presence of regions in EU decision making forces us to rethink our understanding of statehood based on the idea of bounded territorial spaces with impermeable borders.

The development of EU regional policy provides a case study in which contrasting theories of European integration may be examined. In some ways, regional policy development seems to provide a very clear example of functional spillover. The possible negative effects of the single market and monetary union projects created pressures to develop an EU-level regional policy that might alleviate these effects. But at the same time, the centrality of government-to-government negotiations and the way major regional policy decisions were linked to other issues with little regard for the economic logic of policy expansion casts doubt on the significance of **spillover** as a dynamic of European integration. Moving to the level of policy implementation, and particularly the innovation of partnership and Structural Fund rules giving the Commission important powers, the tide may have turned yet again. In these developments those associated with multi-level governance (MLG) have sought to resuscitate neo-functionalist ideas about the autonomy of EU institutions and the limits to control by member states' governments. Although this approach has not been unchallenged, and intergovernmentalists put forward some good counter-arguments, it is hard to deny that MLG helps capture something of an important new reality in EU policy making. It also lends support to the idea that EU policy making must be disaggregated and that history-making decisions such as those that relate to budget allocations might operate differently from low-politics decision making like Structural Fund implementation (Peterson and Bomberg 1999). If nothing else, the Europeanization of regionalism and the recent evolution of EU regional policy developments did force many to rethink or at least defend once more some old ideas about European integration and the nature of the EU.

QUESTIONS

1   Does the EU need a regional policy?

2   Why have enlargement and EMU been such important triggers in EU regional policy development?

3   Why has the implementation of the 'additionality' principle been so controversial?

4   What is the significance of the EU regional policy's 'partnership' principle?

5   What problems does enlargement pose for EU regional policy?

6   To what extent is Europe becoming a 'Europe of the Regions'?

7   Does European integration present more costs than opportunities for EU regions?

8   Does the neo-functionalist spillover thesis of European integration explain the development of EU regional policy?

GUIDE TO FURTHER READING

Bache, I., *The Politics of European Union Regional Policy: Multi-level Governance or Flexible Gatekeeping* (Sheffield: Sheffield Academic Press, 1999). This book provides an up-to-date and theoretically informed account of EU regional policy development.

Hooghe, L. (ed.), *Cohesion Policy and European Integration: Building Multi-level governance* (Oxford: Oxford University Press, 1996). Through a series of country-by-country case studies, this book applies the ideas of MLG in the area of EU regional policy.

Keating, M., *New Regionalism in Western Europe* (Cheltenham: Edward Elgar, 2000). The book provides an up-to-date analysis of European regionalism by one of the most authoritative authors on this topic.

Marks, G., Hooghe, L., and Blank, K., 'European Integration from the 1980s: State-Centric v. Multi-level Governance', *Journal of Common Market Studies*, vol. 34, no. 3 (1996): 341–78. This article provides an excellent overview of the debate between multi-level governance and intergovernmentalism on the issue of the changing role of the state in EU politics.

Scott, J., *Development Dilemmas in the European Community* (Buckingham: Open University Press, 1995). This book provides another good analysis of the origins and development of EU regional policy.

WEB LINKS

www.are-regions-europe.org/ The Assembly of European Regions (AER) is a political organization bringing together around 300 European regions. The website contains information on AER activities, a comprehensive database on constitutional, political, and socio-economic characteristics of its members, and an extensive list of other region-orientated weblinks.

www.cor.eu.int/ The Committee of the Regions (CoR) is a consultative organ of the EU composed of 222 representatives of regional and local bodies. The website contains up-to-date information on CoR activities and research resources like CoR opinions and declarations.

www.inforegio.cec.eu.int/ Inforegio is a European Commission regional policy directorate-general website specifically on EU funds. It contains detailed but accessible information on the operation of EU regional policy, country-by-country profiles of fund spending and programmes, as well as access to in-depth analysis, reports, and relevant official documents.

19 Justice and Home Affairs

Emek M. Uçarer

READER'S GUIDE

This chapter looks at one of the most recent European policies, that of Justice and Home Affairs (JHA). JHA comprises policy areas such as immigration and asylum, and policy and judicial co-operation, some elements of which comprise the EU's third pillar (the other two being the EC pillar and the Common Foreign and Security Policy pillar). The chapter focuses first on the early years of co-operation in this policy area, including the **Schengen** Agreement, then reviews the procedural steps taken first by the Maastricht Treaty (1993) and then at Amsterdam (1999). The second half of the chapter concentrates on policy and policy output, again looking at steps taken at Maastricht and Amsterdam, but also more recently in the landmark Tampere European Council meeting. It argues that although steps have already been taken to Europeanize JHA policy, it still remains based on intergovernmental co-operation. Moreover, given the inherent tensions in the policy, numerous challenges remain to be resolved over coming decades.

Introduction

Justice and Home Affairs (JHA) co-operation has undergone a remarkable ascent—from humble beginnings to a full-fledged and vibrant EU policy. Co-operation in this policy field seeks to engage EU member states in efforts at European-level policy making in the fields of immigration, asylum, police, and judicial co-operation, and is one of the newest competencies of the EU. Because of the sensitive nature of the issues involved, co-operation has been slow and difficult. However, it has nonetheless resulted in a body of policies that apply across the EU's internal and external borders, and which have locked previously inward-looking national authorities into a multilateral process. This has involved significant political compomise, which has led to the introduction of a complicated mix of communitarized and intergovernmental institutional procedures peculiar to this field. The EU is now well on its way to developing a complex immigration and asylum regime, and is also making some progress on police and judicial co-operation. Particularly after the conclusion of the **Amsterdam** Treaty, the EUs capacity to reach collective and binding decisions in the JHA field has improved considerably. This has both created momentum towards further co-operation and increased concerns about

the creation of a '**Fortress Europe**' into which access is increasingly restricted.

The chapter begins by looking at the origins of the EU's policy on JHA. It then considers the impact of the Schengen Agreement and the single market on JHA matters. Sections on Maastricht and Amsterdam review the procedural steps taken to enhance decision making in the 1990s. Of particular note here are the implications of the creation of the three-pillar structure of the EU at Maastricht, with the 'third pillar' created as the JHA element (and then the shift of some JHA policies into the first pillar at Amsterdam). After considering the procedural dimension of JHA, the chapter then turns to consider the policy output itself, focusing on its four elements—immigration, asylum, police co-operation, and judicial co-operation. Finally, it concludes by emphasizing the challenges that JHA policy in the EU still faces.

Preludes to co-operation

If, in the late 1960s, government ministers responsible for home affairs and justice had been told that they would soon need to consult with fellow EC/EU ministers while formulating policies regarding immigration, asylum, judicial, and police matters, they would no doubt have found that a very unlikely, and undesirable, prospect. Yet, during the last two decades of the twentieth century, issues falling within the mandate of interior and justice ministries have increasingly become of collective EU concern, provoking efforts to deal with them at the European, rather than exclusively at the national level. Beginning in the mid-1970s and gathering steam in the 1980s, immigration, asylum, police, and judicial co-operation increasingly appeared on the collective political agenda. This led to the creation of new, overlapping forums within which these issues could be discussed.

There were two broad sets of catalysts behind this development. The first related to the consequences of increased cross-border movements into and among the EC member states. After the Second World War, Western Europe soon became an area of

immigration. Cross-border movements increased, straining border patrols, and causing delays at points of entry. With the rise in cross-border movements came growing concerns about transnational crime, which could proliferate by taking advantage of weak border controls and the lack of effective communication among European national law enforcement agencies. The second catalyst concerned the revitalization of the European integration agenda after the signing of the Single European Act (SEA) in 1986, and the commitment of the single market programme to the completion of the common market (see Chapter 3). The removal of internal EU border controls had been written into the 1957 Rome Treaty, even though this had not been fully realized by the early 1980s. With this goal back on the agenda, attention turned to the need to create external Community borders and to develop common and coherent rules regarding access. Early efforts targeted three groups: citizens of the EC/EU (whose freedom of movement with the Community was to be secured); long-term EU residents of third countries (non-EU citizens who had relocated to the

Box 19.1 **Core ideas**

Catalysts for early co-operation in Justice and Home Affairs matters

Catalysts linked to immigration

- Increase in cross-border movements between West European countries.

- Increase in labour and family reunification migration into West European countries.

- Increase in applications for asylum.

- Concerns about cross-border organized crime.

Catalysts linked to the European integration project

- Undesirable impact on economic activities of delays at borders.

- Desire to complete the single market by gradually removing controls at the Union's internal borders.

- Recognition of the need to develop common measures to apply to external borders before doing away with controls at the internal borders.

EU and who held residence and work permits); and third-country nationals (TCNs), including labour migrants and refugees seeking to enter the collective territory of the EC/EU (see Box 19.1).

There were several early attempts to bring JHA matters within the ambit of European policy making. Perhaps the earliest of these were launched by the Council of Europe (CoE), a regional international organization, distinct from the European Community (EC), which was created in 1949 and whose membership comprised both Eastern and West European countries. Judicial matters were quite often raised at CoE meetings, leading to binding treaties that would subsequently be incorporated into EU law. The CoE regularly brought together officials from member states, and served to accustom member states to co-operation in this area. But while the work pursued in the CoE was in many respects path-breaking, the drawbacks of consultative policy making of this kind also became clear. Because of the need to reconcile a wide variety of divergent interests and opinions, policy output was meagre and slow and the instruments adopted frequently reflected little more than the lowest common denominator.

With the shortcomings of the CoE in mind, members of the EC tried to set up an ad hoc institutional framework in the mid-1970s to facilitate decision making. This led to the creation of the 'Trevi Group' at the Rome European Council of 1975. It was initially set up as an informal assembly to deal with issues of cross-border terrorism by encouraging closer co-operation among EC law enforcement

authorities. Trevi (named after the Trevi Fountain in Rome and the group's first chairman whose name was Fonteijn, or fountain) was really more of a loose network than an institution, with the results of its consultations non-binding. It had no secretariat, and it met (at ministerial level) only intermittently. Most of its work, however, was conducted in working groups composed of bureaucrats and officers, and dealt with questions of shared intelligence and security, and policing. It fostered further co-operation on organized international crime, including drug and arms trafficking.

Despite the absence of binding policy output and its weak institutional characteristics Trevi was important as it showed that member states were willing to discuss these issues at the European level. Moreover, it led to the establishment of several other groups, such as the Judicial Co-operation Group, the Customs Mutual Assistance Group, and the Ad Hoc Groups on Immigration and Organized Crime. These groups spanned the four policy clusters that were gradually becoming Europeanized: immigration policy, asylum policy, police co-operation, and judicial co-operation. (See Box 19.2).

Key points

- Co-operation in the field of Justice and Home Affairs (JHA) was not foreseen in the Treaty of Rome.

Box 19.2 **The facts**
Early multilateral forums and networks

Trevi	1975	Combating terrorism, international crime, and drug trafficking
The EPC Group	1970	Promoting EC/EU co-operation on justice matters
CAHAR	1978	Council of Europe committee that deals with asylum matters
Informal consultations	1985	Informal information exchange on asylum, refugee, and immigration matters
Group of Co-ordinators	1988	Created in an effort to co-ordinate the work of the various forums in existence
Ad Hoc Group on Immigration (AHIG)	1986	Discussing and making co-ordinated policy proposals on JHA issues

- The Council of Europe (not an EC institution) was the main forum for the discussion of JHA issues, but it worked slowly and its output was meagre.

- The Trevi Group was set up in 1975 as a loose network within which terrorism might be discussed at European level. It led to the setting up of similar groups in related areas.

The Schengen experiment

Aside from the Council of Europe (CoE) and the many new groupings such as Trevi, perhaps the most ambitious project of these early years was what became known as **Schengen**. In 1985, a number of EC member states decided to lift border controls between them. This was formalized in the Schengen Agreement (1985) and later the Schengen Implementation Convention of 1990. Belgium, the Netherlands, Luxembourg, Germany, France, and Italy thus created a new structure which would impinge on their police forces and customs authorities. They also created the Schengen Information System, an innovative, shared database that stored important information (such as criminal records and asylum applications) and which was accessible by national law enforcement authorities.

Schengen's primary objective was to develop policies that would apply to the Community's external borders, with the aim of making it easier to remove the EC's internal borders. This was a very ambitious goal, and some member states, namely the United Kingdom, Ireland, and Denmark, remained extremely sceptical about the kind of co-operation

that would undermine the sovereign right of member states to control their own borders. Given this opposition, Schengen was a compromise, and despite the fact that only some of the member states were involved, it became a model for the EC (and later the Union) as a whole.

Within the Schengen framework significant progress was made in each of the four emergent areas of co-operation. With respect to asylum, Schengen instituted a new system for determining the state responsible for reviewing asylum claims in individual cases. Signatory states agreed to assign responsibility to one state in order to put a stop to multiple asylum applications (by the same person at the same time, or sequentially, in various member states). With this system in place, member states hoped to reduce the administrative costs of processing duplicate asylum claims. Schengen also provided the groundwork for an EU visa policy by negotiating a common list of countries, whose citizens would need an entry visa. Up until this point, each of the Schengen states maintained their own list. Furthermore, member states agreed to issue uniform

Box 19.3 **Case study**
What is Schengen?

Named after the small Luxembourg border town where a subset of EU member states resolved to lift border controls, the Schengen system was hailed as a path-breaking initiative which aimed to provide for ease of travel between its member states. In 1985, France, Germany, Belgium, the Netherlands, and Luxembourg signed the first Schengen Agreement. They were later joined by eight other countries, bringing the total number of participating states to 15. The Schengen accords sought to remove controls on persons—including third-country nationals—at their internal borders while allowing member states to reintroduce them only in limited circumstances. In order to do so, member states agreed to develop common entry policies for their collective territory; issue common entry visas to entrants; designate a responsible state for reviewing asylum claims; and jointly combat transnational crime. At the time of writing the Schengen members are Austria, Belgium, Denmark, Finland, France, Germany, Greece, Iceland, Italy, Luxembourg, the Netherlands, Norway, Portugal, Spain, and Sweden. Two of these countries (Norway and Iceland) are not members of the EU. Two EU countries (the UK and Ireland) are not part of the Schengen system, though they have recently chosen to opt in on an issue-by-issue basis.

Schengen visas that would allow entry into all of the Schengen states.

Under the heading of judicial co-operation, there was a more modest start which involved attempts to remove obstacles preventing extradition between member states. Finally, the Schengen Implementation Convention also foresaw co-operation on law enforcement matters, particularly those involving drug trafficking. Once the Implementation Convention was in place, a group of liaison officers were given responsibility for creating lines of communication, fostering consultation and information exchange between the member states' police forces. New co-operative arrangements within Schengen, such as these, established routine consultation among parts of national civil services that had previously been unconnected and, though initial policy output was limited, opened the door to the possibility of further co-operation. However, it should be noted that since most of this work fell outside the framework of the EC decision-making structure, it was conducted away from the scrutiny of the general public or their elected representatives. See Box 19.3 for a summary of the Schengen system.

Key points

- The 1985 Schengen Agreement was a commitment by a subset of EC member states to remove controls at their internal borders.

- Steps were taken by the Schengen members to agree on common rules on their external borders with regard to visa policy, for example.

- For those countries involved, Schengen allowed national civil servants in these fields to become accustomed to European-level co-operation.

Maastricht and the 'third pillar'

If the 1970s and early 1980s saw increasing, if sporadic, consultation between some West European states on immigration, asylum, judicial, and police matters, the early 1990s represented an intensification of these efforts and a shift in the locus of decision making towards the European institutions.

However, this would involve the consolidation of existing groupings as well as the creation of a new institutional framework within which JHA matters could be discussed. This proved to be difficult to achieve.

With the coming into force of the Treaty on European Union (TEU or **Maastricht Treaty**) in 1993, JHA was brought under the auspices of the EU, forming the 'third pillar' of the Union. The Treaty identified nine areas of 'common interest': asylum policy; rules applicable to the crossing of the Union's external borders; immigration policy and the handling of third-country nationals (TCNs); combating drug addiction and drug trafficking; tackling international fraud; judicial co-operation in civil matters and in criminal matters; customs co-operation; police co-operation to combat and prevent terrorism; and police co-operation in tackling international organized crime.

The Treaty also created a new and relatively coherent institutional home for the plethora of groups that had been set up in earlier decades, and created a decision-making framework within which negotiations could occur. However, this new JHA pillar was the product of a rather awkward interstate compromise. In the run-up to Maastricht, a majority of the member states had been in favour of bringing JHA matters into the Union. However, they remained divided over the form that this should take. Some argued that JHA should be handled within the EC (in what became the 'first' or EC pillar), as a supranational policy. Others were uncomfortable with handing control over to the European institutions in such sensitive a field and preferred to keep JHA as a largely intergovernmental dialogue. The challenge at the time was to find a compromise that all member states could support.

Title VI of the Maastricht Treaty reflected the institutional consequences of this political compomise. In creating a **third pillar** of the European Union (see Chapter 4: Figure 4.1), the Treaty established an intergovernmental negotiating sphere which marginalized the Community institutions—particularly the European Commission—from the JHA decision-making process. This third pillar set-up diverged significantly from standard decision making in the EC (see Chapter 1: 4). For one thing, JHA co-operation was placed within a five-tier negotiation framework (see Figure 19.1). In the **first pillar** (or the EC pillar), by contrast, there were only three levels. Not surprisingly, this meant that the JHA framework was particularly cumbersome. Adding two new levels, as member states soon found out, slowed down the policy process dramatically.

The key decision-taking body was to be the JHA Council. By contrast, the European Commission was given a rather marginal role. Its usual function as the initiator of European legislation (see Chapter 9) was constrained by that fact that there was to be a shared right of initiative in JHA, so that the Commission was designated as only one of 16 possible points of origin for JHA policies (the other 15 being the member states themselves) (Uçarer 2001*a*). The role of the European Parliament (EP) did not extend beyond consultation, a situation that led to accusations that JHA exacerbated the Union's **democratic deficit** (see Chapter 23). Moreover, the European Court of Justice (ECJ), the body that might have enhanced the accountability and judicial oversight of policy, was excluded from JHA matters.

Although bringing JHA into the EU was an important step, the critics of the 'third pillar' far outnumbered those who lauded the outcome agreed at Maastricht. Two sets of inter-related criticisms followed the implementation of the Treaty. The first referred to the lack of policy progress in the initial post-Maastricht period. Indeed, what little was accomplished after 1993 seemed to relate to policies that had already been in progress before Maastricht. The policy-making push that had been expected had not materialized. It seemed that while some of this apparent inertia was due to a lingering reluctance by member states to yield to the Union on JHA matters, it was also regarded as a consequence of a much larger set of problems that were institutional in nature.

The problem was that the post-Maastricht institutional arrangements were ill equipped to handle the projected or indeed the existing workload falling under JHA. The decision-making framework was cumbersome, with the often non-binding policy instruments necessitating long drawn-out (and potentially inconclusive) negotiations. All decisions in the third pillar had to be arrived at unanimously in the JHA Council, and this often meant deadlock.

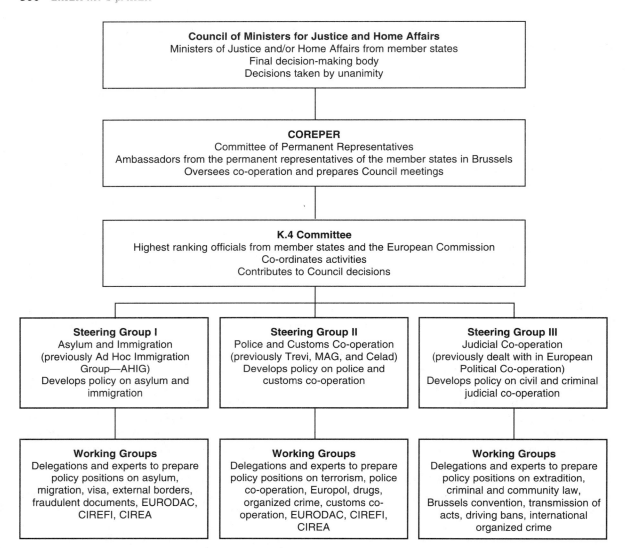

Council of Ministers for Justice and Home Affairs
Ministers of Justice and/or Home Affairs from member states
Final decision-making body
Decisions taken by unanimity

COREPER
Committee of Permanent Representatives
Ambassadors from the permanent representatives of the member states in Brussels
Oversees co-operation and prepares Council meetings

K.4 Committee
Highest ranking officials from member states and the European Commission
Co-ordinates activities
Contributes to Council decisions

Steering Group I
Asylum and Immigration
(previously Ad Hoc Immigration
Group—AHIG)
Develops policy on asylum and
immigration

Steering Group II
Police and Customs Co-operation
(previously Trevi, MAG, and Celad)
Develops policy on police and
customs co-operation

Steering Group III
Judicial Co-operation
(previously dealt with in European
Political Co-operation)
Develops policy on civil and criminal
judicial co-operation

Working Groups
Delegations and experts to prepare
policy positions on asylum,
migration, visa, external borders,
fraudulent documents, EURODAC,
CIREFI, CIREA

Working Groups
Delegations and experts to prepare
policy positions on terrorism, police
co-operation, Europol, drugs,
organized crime, customs co-
operation, EURODAC, CIREFI,
CIREA

Working Groups
Delegations and experts to prepare
policy positions on extradition,
criminal and community law,
Brussels convention, transmission of
acts, driving bans, international
organized crime

Fig. 19.1 Decision making in the third pillar after Maastricht
Source: Adapted from Uçarer 1999.

And when unanimity was reached, the result was often a lowest common denominator compromise that pleased few. Even if a policy position were adopted, its implementation was left up to the member states. Moreover, the negotiations continued to be secretive and the EP remained marginalized. This was particularly problematic at a time when the Union was trying very hard to improve its image *vis-à-vis* its citizens.

Key points

- The Maastricht Treaty (Treaty on European Union or TEU) which came into effect in 1993 created a 'third pillar' for Justice and Home Affairs.

- The institutional framework put in place was intergovernmental and cumbersome and was subject to much criticism in the mid-1990s.

The Amsterdam Treaty and JHA

The criticisms that followed Maastricht led to the reform of JHA co-operation in changes introduced by the Amsterdam Treaty in 1999. In the run-up to Amsterdam, the suggestions for improving the efficacy of the policy included enhanced roles for the Commission, Parliament, and Court; the elimination of the unanimity rule; and the incorporation of the Schengen system into the EU. As with Maastricht, there was a fierce political debate over these issues.

The challenge facing those drafting the Amsterdam Treaty was to make the Union 'more relevant to its citizens and more responsive to their concerns' by creating 'an area of freedom, security and justice (AFSJ)' (Council of the European Union 1996). The idea was that within such an area, barriers to the free movement of people across borders should be minimized, but without jeopardizing the safety and security and the human rights of EU citizens. The Treaty, representing yet another compromise, led to three important changes. First, parts of the Maastricht third pillar were transferred to the first (or EC) pillar. In other words, certain third pillar issues were **communitarized**. Second, the institutional framework for issues that remained within the third pillar was streamlined; and third, the Schengen framework was incorporated into the Union's *acquis*, now falling under rather than outside the EU proper.

New first pillar issues under Amsterdam

The insertion of Title IV into the Treaty was the most significant development at Amsterdam with respect to JHA matters. This brought a number of third pillar issues into the first or EC pillar for the first time. These provisions called for the Council to adopt policies (within five years after the entry into force of the treaty, by 1 May 2004) which would ensure the free movement of persons within the Union, while at the same time putting in place security measures with respect to immigration, asylum, and external border controls. These measures, articulated in Articles 61–4, involve the development of:

- standards and procedures for carrying out checks at the external borders of the Union;
- rules on entry visas for third-country citizens;
- measures to apply to the travel of third-country nationals (TCNs) within the Union;
- measures on asylum; and
- measures to prevent and combat crime.

Also included, though not earmarked for completion in the first five years after Amsterdam, were the adoption of:

- minimum standards for the reception of asylum seekers, the qualification of third-country nationals (TCNs) as refugees, and the granting and withdrawing of refugee status;
- a system to ensure a burden-sharing mechanism for EU recipients of displaced persons;
- common policies for issuing long-term visas and residence permits;
- common policies to combat illegal immigration and residence; and
- joint measures to define the rights of legally resident TCNs to relocate within the EU.

Article 67 specified new decision-making rules. For the first five years after the entry into force of the Amsterdam Treaty, a transition period would be in place. Thus, **unanimity** was to be required in the JHA Council following consultations with the EP. The Council would act on a proposal from the Commission or a member state, the latter retaining their shared right of initiative. In other words, the Maastricht decision rules were to remain in place. After five years, however, the Commission would gain an exclusive right of initiative. And while the Parliament's access to the decision-making procedure would still be limited to consultation in most cases, an automatic shift to the **co-decision**

procedure, which would give the EP much more of a say, was foreseen in the area of uniform visa rules and the procedures for issuing visas. The European Court of Justice (ECJ) also received a mandate for the first time, allowing it to interpret Title IV and to undertake preliminary rulings in policy areas falling within the first pillar, in response to requests by national courts (see Chapter 12). The new and complicated rules introduced at Amsterdam led some observers to question whether the third pillar issues had really been shifted in the first pillar, or whether Amsterdam had allowed third pillar procedures to creep surreptitiously into the first. Indeed, the new Amsterdam architecture turned out to be a formidable maze created through masterful 'legal engineering' for political ends, opaque for even seasoned experts (European Parliament 1997).

The left-over third pillar: Co-operation in criminal matters

The reforms at Amsterdam left criminal matters in the third pillar. Issues that were to be dealt with here under the amended Title VI included combating crime, terrorism, trafficking in persons and offences against children, illicit drugs and arms trafficking, corruption, and fraud (European Union 1997). The treaty envisioned closer co-operation between police forces, customs and judicial authorities, and with Europol (see below), with an eye to the approximation of the criminal justice systems of the member states as necessary. Progress was to be made by developing and adopting common positions defining the Union's policy on a particular question, and by taking framework decisions and intergovernmentally negotiated and legally binding conventions.

The new Title VI retained the intergovernmental framework created at Maastricht. However, the Commission obtained a shared right of initiative in this area for the first time (this had not been the case at Maastricht), an improvement over its pre-Amsterdam position nonetheless. The Parliament gained the right to be consulted, but that was all. The Treaty constrained the ECJ in a similar fashion

in that it recognized the jurisdiction of the Court to issue preliminary rulings (that is, to comment on relevant cases before domestic courts) on the instruments adopted under Title VI, but importantly it made this dependent on the assent of the member states. While the Commission, Parliament, and Court were to continue to struggle to play an active role in the third pillar, the Council retained its dominant decision-making function, and unanimity remained the decision rule used in third pillar legislation. Table 19.1 summarizes the institutional development of JHA from its early origins to its post-Amsterdam state.

Absorbing Schengen

After much debate, **Schengen** was incorporated into the EU by means of a protocol appended to the Amsterdam Treaty. The Protocol provided for the closer co-operation of the Schengen 13 (that is, the EU15 minus Ireland and the United Kingdom) within the EU framework. With the changes made at Amsterdam and the incorporation of Schengen, co-operation on JHA matters became even more complicated than before, creating various overlapping groupings that co-operated in various ways. There were those EU members that agreed to be bound by the Amsterdam changes (EU12); Denmark, which chose to opt out, and the other two that would remain outside unless they chose to opt in (the UK and Ireland). Moreover, there were actually 15 signatories to the Schengen agreement (the Schengen 15), of which 13 were EU members and two were not (Iceland and Norway). The two members of the EU that remained outside the Schengen system, the UK and Ireland, decided to take part in some elements of Schengen, including police and judicial co-operation. In essence, the incorporation of Schengen into the EU *acquis* did not result in the simplification hoped for, but rather maintained, if not augmented, the convoluted system that had been put in place in the early 1990s. Not surprisingly, some now regard JHA as the ultimate example of a **multi-speed** or **à la carte** Europe (see Chapter 24 for a full discussion).

Table 19.1 Justice and Home Affairs co-operation: From Trevi to Tampere

	Pre-Maastricht JHA	Post-Maastricht third pillar	Post-Amsterdam first pillar (Communitarized areas of former third pillar) Immigration, Asylum, Police and Judicial Co-operation in Civil Matters Title IV TEC, Articles 61–9		Post-Amsterdam third pillar (Non-Communitarized areas of former third pillar) Police and Judicial co-operation in criminal matters Title VI TEU Articles 29–42
		Title VI TEU Article K	1999–2004	Post-2004	
European Parliament	No role	Limited role restricted to consultation	Consultation	Co-decision	Consultation
European Court of Justice	No jurisdiction	No jurisdiction	Referral for an obligatory first ruling for national courts of final instance	Preliminary rulings on the validity and interpretation of framework decisions and decisions, on the interpretation of conventions established under Title VI, and on the validity and interpretation of the measures implementing them.	
Council	No direct role	Dominant actor	Dominant actor but Commission and Parliament increasingly empowered	Shared power position in decision making	Dominant actor
Commission	Consultative. Occasional observer status at intergovernmental meetings	Shared right of initiative for the Commission and member states except judicial and police co-operation matters in which there is no right of initiative	Commission has shared right of initiative (member states have encouraged the Commission to assume an exclusive right for asylum issues)	Commission has exclusive right of initiative	Shared right of initiative (previously not possible)
Decision-making mechanisms	Intergovernmental negotiations	Unanimity rule on all issues	Council acts unanimously on proposals from Commission and member states *for the first five years.*	Council will act unanimously on proposals from the Commission	Council acts unanimously on proposals from Commission and member states
	Non-binding decisions in the form of resolutions		UK, Ireland, and Denmark not bound unless they choose to opt in	A move towards QMV (with no need for national ratification of this decision) possible following a unanimous decision of the Council	
	Binding decisions in the form of treaties			UK, Ireland, and Denmark retain opt-in	

Note: This covers asylum policy, crossing of the external borders of the Union, immigration policy and the handling of third-country nationals, combating drug addiction and trafficking, tackling international fraud, judicial co-operation in civil and criminal matters, customs co-operation, and police co-operation to combat and prevent terrorism and organized international crime.
Source: Adapted and expanded from Uçarer 2001*a*.

Key points

- The Amsterdam Treaty sought to address the shortcomings of the third pillar by bringing immigration and asylum as well as judicial and police co-operation in civil matters into the first pillar.

- The third pillar, co-operation in criminal matters (police and judicial co-operation) remained intergovernmental.

- Schengen was brought within the Treaty, but this did not imply any process of simplification given the overlapping memberships involved in this Agreement.

Policy output: Baby steps to bold agendas

A great deal has changed in policy terms since the humble beginnings of JHA co-operation. There have been several spurts of policy, building on the early pre-Maastricht efforts, but gathering steam after Maastricht and Amsterdam. More recently, in addition to making progress on the four main dossiers (immigration, asylum, police co-operation, and judicial co-operation), the EU has acknowledged the importance of the external dimension of JHA, and has embarked on attempts to export its emergent policies beyond the Union.

Post-Maastricht developments in policy

After Maastricht, member states first focused their attention on the rules that would apply to third-country nationals (TCNs) coming into the Union territory, reaching a consensus on various restrictive measures for entry. The Council formulated common rules in this area for employment and educational purposes, and recommended common rules for the expulsion of TCNs. They also suggested a common format for 'bilateral readmission agreements' (which would allow for the return of TCNs to their home state) between member states of the Union and third countries. In 1997, an extradition convention was concluded among the EU member states. Agreement was also reached on the format of a uniform visa as well as on a list of countries whose nationals required a visa to enter EU territory. These agreements sought to develop comparable procedural steps for the entry, sojourn (stay), and

expulsion of TCNs. However, many argued that the policy pursued after Maastricht was relatively unambitious, given the context in which it was being made, that of the expeditious elimination of border controls within the Union.

In the field of asylum the policy was also disappointing for some. The most notable development was the conclusion of the 1990 Dublin Convention—an instrument of binding regional international law—which designated one member state to be responsible for the handling of each asylum claim. Member states also agreed to adhere to non-binding common criteria when judging the merits of an asylum claim. The politically significant London Resolutions introduced the concepts of safe countries of origin and transit into the EU, rejecting applications lodged by the nationals of countries deemed safe or by those who had passed through safe countries en route to Union territory. Refugee rights activists frowned upon these policies as they deemed them excessively restrictive, and argued that such rules could potentially weaken refugee protection. Subsequent JHA Councils adopted resolutions on the definition of a refugee, minimum guarantees for asylum procedures, and a common format to help determine which was the responsible state for reviewing an asylum claim. The Council also adopted a resolution on burden sharing, which sought to commit member states to assist other member states with the temporary admission and residence of displaced persons in situations of mass influx. During this period, work also began on the EURODAC fingerprinting system, which would allow member states to keep track of asylum seekers, as well as on the negotiation of a common framework for the reception of individuals seeking temporary protection status in Union territory.

It was not only in the fields of immigration and asylum that progress was made post-Maastricht. The Maastricht Treaty also took earlier efforts to co-operate in customs, public safety, and cross-border matters further by embarking on the ambitious agenda to create a European Police Office (Europol), a project that was initiated by Germany in 1991. The plan was to set up a European Central Criminal Office by the end of 1993. This would serve to enhance police co-operation and information exchange in combating terrorism and the illicit trafficking of drugs and human beings. Europol was formally created by the 1995 Cannes European Council and became operational on 1 October 1998. Based in The Hague in the Netherlands, it employs around 200 people. Two new bodies—the Centre for Information, Discussion, and Exchange on the Crossing of Frontiers and Immigration (CIREFI) and the Centre for Information, Discussion and Exchange on Asylum (CIREA)—were approved in 1994 to facilitate co-operation between practitioners in the field. Ministers of the member states also signed an agreement in 1993 to create a European Drugs Unit (EDU) to assist in criminal investigations. Through the EDU, the Union sought to enlist the help of countries that the EU considered to be suppliers contributing to the drugs problem, particularly in the Caribbean and in Latin America. The Union also strengthened its ties with the United States which itself had declared a war on drugs.

Despite progress made in JHA dossiers over this period, policy still reflected unresolved differences in the member states' positions. Europol symbolized these differences as it was essentially a compromise which excluded the Europol Convention from the European Court's mandate and restricted it to being little more than a forum for information exchange (Monar 1997).

Amsterdam, Tampere, and beyond

Following the signing of the Amsterdam Treaty and its relatively rapid entry into force in 1999, progress in JHA co-operation accelerated substantially. The then Commission President, Jacques Santer, suggested organizing a special European Council summit dedicated exclusively to JHA. The objective of this summit was to take stock of developments to date, evaluate the impact of Amsterdam, and discuss the future direction of JHA co-operation. It was convened in Tampere, Finland in October 1999. At Tampere, the member states restated their commitment to develop an Area of Freedom, Security, and Justice (AFSJ) and outlined the policy steps that they would be prepared to take towards this end. Included in the 'Tampere milestones' were a commitment to human rights, basic institutions, and the rule of law; the creation of a common market complete with freedom of movement; the development of common rules for and the fair treatment of third-country nationals (TCNs), which were to include rules for dealing with racism and xenophobia, the convergence of judicial systems, and the fostering of transparency and democratic control. Among the more far-reaching goals were the attainment of better controls on and management of migration and the deterring of trafficking in human beings. Tampere thus signalled a new phase in JHA, and led to the launching of numerous new initiatives. Importantly, the member states asked the Commission to keep track of and report on the progress made in all of the relevant dossiers.

On matters of immigration and asylum, Tampere advocated a 'comprehensive approach', strongly pushed by the Commission which, since its 1994 Communication, had been arguing that a 'root causes' approach should be adopted in developing policies to respond to increasing migratory pressures into the Union. This comprehensive approach was to be closely linked to the combating of poverty and the removal of the political and economic conditions that compel individuals to leave their homes in the first place. An initial attempt at developing this kind of approach was made with the creation of the High Level Working Group on Asylum and Immigration (HLWG) (van Selm 2002). Approved in 1998, the HLWG began its work by undertaking several country-specific studies. By the time Tampere was convened in 1999, the HLWG had prepared six Action Plans (on Albania/Kosovo, Afghanistan, Iraq, Morocco, Somalia, and Sri Lanka), presenting five of them at Tampere to the European Council. In these studies, the HLWG suggested the framing of JHA policies *vis-à-vis* third countries, by developing links to and utilizing the tools of foreign policy, development co-operation, and economic relations, rather than thinking of JHA purely as an internal EU matter. Thus, the Action Plans called for intensified co-operation between countries of origin and transit to address the causes of flight, to empower countries in the neighbouring region to offer adequate protection to those in flight, and to speed up the removal of illegal immigrants from Union territory.

At Tampere, EU member states committed themselves to creating a common European asylum system that would include specific rules to determine which EU state would be responsible for reviewing an asylum claim, common standards for reviewing claims, common minimum conditions for the reception of asylum seekers as they await the outcome of their applications, and approximate rules for refugee recognition. Even though the Commission's monopoly on policy proposals was still several years away, the Tampere European Council called upon the Commission to act as the co-ordinator of policy proposals dealing with asylum. With this new charge, the Commission soon introduced numerous proposals relating to asylum.

After Tampere work in the asylum field included proposals to ensure similar and comparable reception conditions for refugees in the member countries, a common set of minimum standards for the review of asylum claims, as well as common family reunification schemes for refugees. Furthermore, the Union approved the creation of the European Refugee Fund, designed to aid EU recipient states during massive refugee influxes, such as those recently experienced during the fallout from Bosnia and Kosovo. By this point, the Dublin Convention had taken effect, and the EURODAC fingerprinting system was now functioning. The creation of the common European asylum system seemed well on the way.

In matters of judicial and police co-operation, still third pillar matters, the ambition to create a European Judicial Area (EJA), championed by Elizabeth Guigou (a former MEP and the French minister of justice at the time) occupied a prominent place at Tampere. The proposed EJA was to involve the mutual recognition of judicial decisions, cross-border information exchange for prosecutions, as

well as minimum standards for civil procedural law. With respect to criminal matters, the Council was required to expedite the ratification of the EU Conventions on extradition. Co-operation on criminal matters was prioritized and the collective attention of the EU was focused on the fights against organized transnational crime, trafficking in human beings, and terrorism. Europol was named as the lead agency in these efforts. Tampere also called for the creation of a European Police Chiefs Operational Task Force to facilitate the exchange of best practice and information on criminal trends and practices.

Tampere created a new body—'Eurojust'. This was to be composed of national prosecutors, magistrates, and police officers and would aid national prosecuting authorities in their criminal investigations of organized crime. Furthermore, a European Police College (which would also admit officers from the candidate countries) was also planned. This would train senior law enforcement officials and establish a network of national police colleges. Tampere also established priorities for the development of measures to approximate the judicial and police practices in the member states, with particular regard to money laundering, corruption, Euro counterfeiting, drug trafficking, trafficking in human beings, the exploitation of women, the sexual exploitation of children, and high tech and environmental crime. To these ends, the Tampere European Council urged the timely implementation of the Money Laundering Directive, which developed common standards to apply to the freezing of assets suspected of being linked to organized crime, and extended Europol's mandate to include money laundering.

Tampere not only focused attention on JHA matters, but also established benchmarks and set deadlines for the accomplishment of its goals. In the months following Tampere, several of the initiatives foreseen in the presidency conclusions, published at the end of the summit, came into being. The drafting of an EU Charter of Fundamental Rights was completed by December 2000, and progress was also made in the mutual recognition of judicial decisions. The Commission developed a framework decision, under the new Title VI, on combating terrorism, which was adopted on 13 June 2002.

Debate on the numerous items on the agenda after

Tampere proved to be protracted and frustrating. The European Council meeting held in Laeken in December 2001, set up to review progress on the Tampere programme, could not ensure timely achievement of the Tampere goals, because it was unable to produce a timetable for agreements on the outstanding proposals. Blame for the delays was variously attributed. While the member states (operating through the Council) blamed the Commission for the delays, critics noted that the Council itself was in no particular hurry to press forward with the adoption of these measures. Nevertheless, these was some progress in 2002 on immigration and asylum, through the adoption of a comprehensive plan to combat illegal immigration and to regulate the management of external borders. During this year, the Commission tabled new and revised initiatives relating to asylum procedures, on reception conditions for asylum seekers, on the definition and status of refugees, and on a First Pillar instrument to replace the Dublin Convention. However, the Presidency Conclusions issued at the end of the

European Council meeting in Seville in June 2002 called emphatically for a 'speeding up' of work, suggesting continued frustration with the progress made since Tampere.

Key points

- Since the inclusion of JHA in the EU's mandate, significant policy progress has been made in the fields of immigration, asylum, police, and judicial co-operation, even though policy output has fallen short of initial expectations.

- Policy making has centred on developing common rules for travel within and entry into the Union, harmonizing policies offering protection to asylum seekers and refugees, creating better information exchange and co-operation between law enforcement officials, and developing mutual recognition of judicial decisions within the EU.

Extending JHA co-operation outwards

During the initial phases of JHA co-operation, the immediate goal was to lift barriers to the free movement of persons within the EU. As the 1990s progressed, the planned enlargement of the Union projected the collective territory outwards, making it necessary to discuss JHA matters with the Union's *future* borders in mind. As noted above, members states began, early on, to involve certain third countries in some of their initiatives, attempting to solidify EU border controls by recruiting other countries to tighten their own border controls (Lavenex and Uçarer 2002). This involved entering into collective agreements with countries of origin and transit. These attempts to recruit neighbouring countries to adopt close variations of the EU's emergent border management regime were particularly pronounced in Central and Eastern Europe (CEE), the Maghreb, and the Mediterranean basin—because of the proximity of these areas to the EU.

EU policies began to radiate out to neighbouring countries, particularly those applying for membership, in a variety of ways. The Schengen countries collectively signed agreements with Poland, Hungary, and the Czech Republic, in which the latter countries agreed to readmit individuals returned from EU territory. Most CEE countries were declared safe countries of origin and transit, which meant that they had to accept asylum seekers who had travelled through their territory to get to the EU. At the 1993 Copenhagen European Council, future membership was made conditional upon rapid incorporation of the EU's JHA *acquis* (which, after Amsterdam, also included the Schengen *acquis*). And the accession partnerships concluded with applicant countries included an aid component, some of which was tied to the improvement of border controls. The EU assumed an advisory role for policy making in CEE countries with the aim of helping them develop policies in line with those of the EU (Grabbe 2000), and applicant countries began to adopt JHA policies that the EU had earlier agreed.

The EU expects similar adjustments of countries that are not part of the enlargement process. These expectations are situated in the broader setting of the Union's external relations (see Chapter 15), and, more specifically, have become part of its aid and trade policies. Thus, North African, non-enlargement Mediterranean, and African, Caribbean, and Pacific countries are steered towards adopting some of the Union's deflective immigration and asylum policies. The aim of this approach is to ease migratory pressures into the Union by including sending and transit countries in the screening process. To these ends, the EU is in the process of negotiating readmission agreements (at the time of writing) with Morocco, Sri Lanka, Russia, Pakistan, Hong Kong, Macao, and Ukraine, while working on obtaining a mandate to start negotiations with Albania, Algeria, China, and Turkey. The EU has signed a readmission agreement concluded with Hong Kong on 27 November 2002, which is the first

of its kind between the EU and a third country. Yet the EU's efforts to extend its strict border controls outwards by assisting (and in some cases demanding) the adoption of stricter border control measures elsewhere involves an irony. While the EU attempts to liberalize the freedom of movement within its territory, it does so by applying potentially illiberal policies at its borders and by advocating such policies in its relations with third countries (Uçarer 2001b). See Box 19.4.

Key points

- JHA co-operation has developed a significant external dimension, particularly *vis-à-vis* the Union's neighbours.

- The enlargement of the Union not only pushes its borders (and therefore the Area of Freedom, Security and Justice (AFSJ)) eastward, but also commits applicant countries to adopt JHA rules before their accession.

- JHA policy output also has an impact on countries that are not part of the enlargement process.

Conclusion

JHA co-operation has come a long way since its obscure beginnings in the 1970s. It currently occupies a prominent and permanent position in EU governance. During the 1980s and 1990s, the locus of co-operation cautiously shifted from national capitals to Brussels. The European Commission now has a more active role in JHA, facilitated by the creation within it of a new JHA Directorate-General, as well as by the appointment of a new and dynamic Commissioner in 1999. The Parliament and the Court have also improved their status since Amsterdam and remain hopeful about the prospects for further institutional gains in the future. However, the Council remains the key actor, and decision making is still hamstrung by the unanimity rule. Matters discussed within the JHA framework continue to strain the sovereign

sensibilities of the EU's member states, and the policy remains intrinsically intergovernmental. However, few believe that the Union can achieve its common market goals without making significant progress in JHA. As the fallout in the USA of the events of 11 September 2001 clearly demonstrates, the tackling of transborder issues so typical of the JHA dossier demands co-ordination and co-operation beyond the state.

JHA is a young field compared to the other more established competences of the EU. Its birth pains, as well as the continuing difficulties it faces, are comparable to the state of affairs in, say, the common agricultural policy or environmental policy some decades ago. But there are also a number of important, and sometimes conflicting challenges specific to JHA co-operation. In order to lift internal border

Box 19.4 **Case study**
Fighting terrorism in the European Union

JHA co-operation owes its genesis partly to the efforts of the Trevi Group, whose main goal was to establish cross-border co-operation in the fight against organized crime and terrorism. These matters were subsequently incorporated into the Union under Title VI of the Maastricht Treaty and revised by the Amsterdam Treaty. EU members authorized the creation of Europol to facilitate the tracking down and prosecution of transborder criminals and established jointly accessible databases to enhance police co-operation. After Tampere, efforts to articulate common policies to combat terrorism resulted in the drafting of the Commission's proposal for a Council Framework Decision on Combating Terrorism. Noting that terrorism 'constitutes one of the most serious threats to democracy, to the free exercise of human rights and to economic and social development', the Commission began its work in late 1999 to develop an instrument that would outline the Union's position. The instrument was to address not only terrorist acts directed against member states and the Union itself, but also international terrorism. The Commission noted that, at the present time, only six member states had legal instruments that covered terrorism, resulting in a need to develop converging policies.

Following the 11 September 2001 attacks on the twin towers of the World Trade Center in New York and the Pentagon in Washington, DC, JHA ministers were called to an Extraordinary EU Council on Justice and Home Affairs, held on 21 September 2001. At this and the following meeting on 19 October of the European Council, EU politicians expressed their solidarity with the USA and confirmed their support for the military operations launched in Afghanistan. While many of the items on the agenda for this meeting were instruments that were long under discussion, the events in the USA gave impetus to the EU's efforts to move speedily towards adopting anti-terrorist policies. In the draft text, terrorism was defined as 'offenses intentionally committed by an individual or a group against one or more countries, their institutions or people, with the aim of intimidating them and seriously altering or destroying the political, economic, or social structures of a country' (European Commission 2001c). At its meeting on 19 October, the Council expressed its intention to 'fast track' the Framework Decisions on Terrorism and the European Arrest Warrant and reported progress on the Union's Action Plan against terrorism. It committed the Union to adopting a common definition of terrorist offences, a common decision on the freezing of assets with links to suspected terrorists, and establishing the European Arrest Warrant which is designed to replace the protracted extradition procedures between EU member states with an automatic transfer of suspected persons from one EU country to another. It urged better co-ordination between Europol, Eurojust, intelligence units, police corps, and judicial authorities and announced work on a list of terrorist organizations that would be jointly drawn up by the end of 2001. It called for increased vigilance with regard to possible biological and chemical attacks, even though such attacks had never previously occurred in the EU. Finally, linking the fight against terrorism to effective border controls, the Council insisted on the intensification of efforts to combat falsified and forged travel documents and visas (European Council 2001). The framework decision on combating terrorism and the framework decision for the European Arrest Warrant (which included a list of 32 Euro-crimes) were adopted in June 2002.

While the urgent attention directed towards anti-terrorist measures is certainly warranted, the EU's efforts in this field have already attracted criticism from civil liberties and migrants' rights advocates. Organizations such as *Statewatch* criticized the definition of terrorism as far too broad and possibly even applicable to protests and urban violence (Statewatch 2001: see also the Statewatch website, listed in Web Links). Migrants' rights activists cautioned against a possible backlash against migrants of Arab descent and argued against fastening the Union's outer doors even more firmly. Refugee rights activists were concerned about the blanket support for military action (which would result in massive forced displacement) and questioned whether the EU would stand ready to extend temporary protection to fleeing Afghans if needed. Criticism aside, the events of 11 September seem to have brought JHA co-operation full circle to its Trevi origins. It is certain that this dossier will remain very lively in the near future and is likely to result in the conclusion of new treaties and the ratification of those that have been completed. It remains to be seen whether progress will be regarded as satisfactory or whether member states will clamour (individually or collectively) for the communitarization of the terrorism dossier.

controls on people moving within the EU, the Union must articulate and implement policies to manage its *external* borders. These policies should foster the freedom of movement of EU citizens and third-country nationals (TCNs) within the EU. They should also spell out common rules on the entry of TCNs into the Union. To demonstrate its commitment to basic human rights and democratic principles, the EU must protect TCNs against arbitrary actions, uphold their civil liberties, and deter acts of violence against them. To maintain the rule of law, the EU must press forward with judicial and police co-operation, while ensuring the privacy and civil liberties of those living in the EU. To live up to its international obligations, the EU must keep its policies in line with its pre-existing treaty obligations, particularly in the field of refugee protection. To protect its legitimacy and instil confidence in the public, the EU must take pains to address issues of transparency and democratic deficit. And finally, it must undertake these endeavours without raising the spectre of an impenetrable 'Fortress Europe', which some argue already exists. The challenges facing the policy remain substantial.

QUESTIONS

1 What were the catalysts that led to the Europeanization of JHA policy?

2 Fostering co-operation in JHA matters has not been a straightforward process. What have been the impediments to effective co-operation in this field?

3 The issues dealt with in JHA can also be addressed through unilateral decisions by individual countries, or by bilateral agreements concluded with interested parties. Why, then, is there such an effort to develop multilateral and collective responses in this field?

4 What are some of the lingering shortcomings of post-Amsterdam JHA co-operation?

5 How might the EU improve transparency and close the democratic deficit in JHA?

6 What are the negative consequences of closer co-operation in JHA matters?

7 How is the EU extending the impact of its JHA policies beyond its borders?

8 To what extent was the European Council meeting held at Tampere a watershed in the evolution of JHA policy?

GUIDE TO FURTHER READING

Bieber, R., and Monar, J. (eds), *Justice and Home Affairs in the European Union: The Development of the Third Pillar* (Brussels: European Interuniversity Press, 1995). Covers the third pillar after Maastricht, focusing on the institutional framework and on early policy developments, particularly in the fields of immigration and asylum.

Den Boer, M., and Wallace, W., 'Justice and Home Affairs: Integration through Incrementalism?', in H. Wallace and W. Wallace (eds), *Policy-making in the European Union*, 4th edn (Oxford: Oxford University Press, 2000). A very helpful textbook treatment of JHA to supplement the present chapter.

Geddes, A., *Immigration and European Integration: Towards Fortress Europe?* (Manchester: Manchester University Press, 2000). One of the first single-authored studies of the EU's immigration regime. Very accessible and well informed.

Monar, J., 'The Dynamics of Justice and Home Affairs: Laboratories, Driving Factors and Costs', *Journal of Common Market Studies*. vol. 39, no. 4 (2001): 747–64. A useful article which seeks to explain the rapid development of JHA policy, by looking at early 'laboratories' (such as the Trevi Group) and at driving factors (such as challenges to internal security). It also point to the costs of this rapid evolution, in terms of the democratic deficit and other problems with the policy.

—— and Morgan, R. (eds), *The Third Pillar of the European Union: Co-operation in the Fields of Justice and Home Affairs* (Brussels: European Interuniversity Press, 1994). A volume of chapters, particularly focused on the early institutional and legal developments in the field of JHA, and which reflects the early optimism of writing in the area at that time.

Uçarer, E., 'Co-operation on Justice and Home Affairs Matters', in L. Cram, D. Dinan, and N. Nugent (eds), *Developments in the European Union* (New York: St. Martin's Press, 1999): 247–65. Another straightforward and accessible introduction to the topic of JHA by the author of the present chapter.

WEB LINKS

http://europa.eu.int/comm/dgs/justice_home/

http://ue.eu.int/jai/

www.europarl.eu.int/topics/ The EU's documents are the best source of information on JHA matters. In line with its efforts to foster transparency in this field, the Commission, Council, and Parliament have all created websites which present policy initiatives.

www.statewatch.org Statewatch website. This provides a more critical approach to the JHA policy of the EU than you will find on the EU websites.

www.migpolgroup.com Migration Policy Group website, including the monthly *Migration News Sheet*.

http://migration.ucdavis.edu/mn/index.html) Migration Dialogue of the University of California at Davis, which publishes the monthly, *Migration News*.

20 Economic and Monetary Union

Amy Verdun

READER'S GUIDE

This chapter provides an introduction to Economic and Monetary Union (EMU) and discusses what it is all about.[1] It describes the key components of EMU and what happens when countries join. It argues that EMU was not an overnight event but rather one that was carefully prepared, and based on collaboration and learning over a period of two decades. The chapter provides a historical background to the process. It discusses both the period from 1969 to 1991—the year in which the European Council agreed to EMU— and the period after 1991 in which EMU was actually being prepared. The 1990s were witness to multiple difficulties which posed challenges to the project prior to the launch of euro banknotes and coins in 2002. Besides discussing the day-to-day events we also look behind the scenes to examine why EMU happened. Various economic and political theoretical explanations of why EMU was created are reviewed. Furthermore the chapter reviews criticisms of the EMU project. The chapter discusses why a majority of the population in some EU countries is against EMU and it examines the criticisms of EMU's institutional design. Finally the chapter looks to the future, and discusses what we can expect in the years to come.

Introduction

The introduction of euro banknotes and coins on 1 January 2002 was a major happening. From one day to the next more than 300 million people in 12 European Union (EU) member states converted from their national currencies to the euro. All EU member states except Denmark, Sweden, and the United Kingdom (UK) participated. It was without doubt the biggest logistical operation in contemporary Europe during peace time. It also signalled the start of a new era in the history of the EU. The majority of European citizens are now confronted daily with a concrete symbol of European integration. What can be more prominent than sharing a common currency?

Although it may seem obvious and logical to have a single currency in light of progress in European integration, the preparations for the introduction of the euro were by no means easy; nor were they uncontested. In order to appreciate this historic moment, we need to look behind the big eye-catching event of 1 January 2002 and examine the path that led to the euro.

Economic and Monetary Union (EMU) has been an integral part of the European integration process since the early 1970s, but it did not always find the necessary support. Once it was back on the agenda in the late 1980s and the 1990s, supporters wanted to make sure that it was done properly. Member states agreed that there should be sufficient economic and monetary convergence prior to starting EMU. They also agreed that there must be criteria that each country had to meet before it could join. At the same time, there were member states that initially did not want to join EMU. Even today there are those that are highly sceptical about the whole EMU project.

What is EMU?

Having an economic and monetary union is not unique to the EU. Various countries have joined forces in similar ways at certain points in history. For example, the Romans had a single currency which was used throughout their entire empire. Belgium, France, Italy, Switzerland, and others were part of a Latin Monetary Union (LMU) from 1865 to 1927. They minted francs that were of equal value across their union. In 1872, the Danes, Norwegians, and Swedes launched a single currency: the Scandinavian Krona. The Scandinavian Monetary Union lasted until the outbreak of the First World War in 1914. The Belgium and Luxembourg Economic Union (BLEU) included a successful monetary union after 1922 which was only formally ended with the start of EMU. However, although the nineteenth-century European monetary unions were significant, the scale and scope of EMU in the EU is without doubt the most spectacular and ambitious such union in recent history.

The component parts of EMU

EMU as we know it in the EU refers to a union in which participating countries have agreed to a single monetary policy, a single monetary authority, a single currency, and co-ordinated **macro-economic policies**.

Let us clarify these features. First of all, what is monetary policy? Central banks pursue monetary policy. They aim to influence the money supply and credit conditions. **Central banks** set a key **interest rate** (often termed a policy rate), which through its influence over other interest rates is capable of changing the financial climate in a way conducive to the control of **inflation**. But what does it mean to have a single monetary policy, and no longer a national monetary policy? It means that any participating country no longer pursues monetary policy at the national level. Instead of having the national central bank (in some cases in collaboration with a ministry of finance and sometimes also assisted by a ministry of economics) determine the monetary policy, this policy is now formulated at the European level by a single monetary authority: the **European Central Bank** (ECB). In December 1991, at the **Maastricht** summit, the heads of state and government of the European Community (EC) member states agreed to create this new European institution to deal with the single monetary policy in EMU. The formal name of the new institution is the **European System of Central Banks** (ESCB). Besides the ECB, the ESCB consists of the already existing national central banks. Under EMU the latter are just 'branches' of the new ECB. The ECB is responsible for formulation of the monetary policy for the participating countries—the **Eurozone**. In EMU the ECB pursues monetary policy for all EMU countries. It is responsible for the new single currency, sets interest rates, and monitors the **money supply**.

EMU of course is famous for having introduced a single currency—the euro—in the EU. Nevertheless, as was mentioned above, strictly speaking EMU could have been introduced without having a single currency. There were two alternatives. Participating countries could have kept their national currencies, but just agreed to fix their exchange rates irrevocably, or they could have introduced a common currency in parallel to the national currencies already circulating in the member states. In fact, the British government made such a proposal in 1990— it was called the 'hard ecu proposal'. But that plan was not adopted. While a parallel currency is introduced alongside existing national currencies, a single currency *replaces* them. The European heads of state and government preferred to have a single currency rather than fixed exchange rates or a parallel currency. A single currency would be beneficial economically, as it would reduce the transaction costs that banks charge when currencies are exchanged. But, more importantly, it was considered to be politically more attractive, as it would signal a full commitment to EMU.

Finally, in order to have a successful policy mix between fiscal and monetary policies EMU envisaged the co-ordination of macroeconomic policies. This implies that member states need to pursue adjacent policies in such a way that they do not undermine the aims of EMU. For example, when EMU was re-conceptualized in the late 1980s and early 1990s, it was felt that the single currency should be a low-inflation currency. Also, member states' governments should not have excessive debts and deficits. Thus, it was decided that there should be rules on **public debts** and **budgetary deficits**. Furthermore it was agreed that monetary financing of the debts and deficits would not be permitted. This meant that countries could no longer use the printing press to print more money without that being backed up by economic fundamentals. Some countries had done so in the past, thereby enabling governments gradually to reduce their public debts but at the expense of increased inflation. Under EMU this behaviour would not be acceptable. Co-ordination of macroeconomic policies can include much more than is currently envisaged. In fact, if one looks at the acronym, EMU, one sees a union with two components: 'economic' and 'monetary'.

The term 'Economic' and 'Monetary' Union is a little awkward. In fact, most commentators in daily newspapers erroneously refer to the acronym EMU as 'European' Monetary Union. This is not very surprising as the most prominent feature of EMU is indeed the 'monetary' component. The reason EMU is called '*Economic and* Monetary Union' can be traced back to the discussions in the late 1960s and early 1970s. Policy makers at the time were not sure how best to create EMU. To have **fixed exchange rates**—and ultimately a single currency—required some co-ordination of macroeconomic policies. But some countries—Belgium, Luxembourg, and France—thought that one could fix the exchange rate, and that the necessary co-operation of the adjacent macroeconomic policies would naturally start to occur. The proponents of this strategy towards EMU became known as the 'Monetarists'.[2] The then Federal Republic of Germany and the Netherlands on the other hand held the opposite position. In their view, macroeconomic policies needed to be co-ordinated *before* one fixed exchange rates or introduced a single currency. The proponents of this strategy towards EMU became known as the 'Economists'. This debate is referred to as the debate between the 'Monetarists and the Economists'.

The question of how to reach EMU had already been discussed in some detail by the economic thinkers of the 1960s such as Bela Balassa and Jan Tinbergen. According to these and other authors, economic integration may be subdivided into a number of stages (see also Chapter 3: 29).

The least far-reaching form of integration is a *Free Trade Area* (*FTA*). In an FTA, participating members remove barriers to trade amongst themselves but maintain the right to levy tariffs on third countries. The next stage of integration is a *Customs Union* (CU). In addition to the free trade amongst members, a CU sets common external tariffs on goods and services from third countries. Third, a *Common Market* (CM) is characterized by the free movement of goods, services, labour, and capital among the participating states and common rules, tariffs (for example), *vis-à-vis* third countries. An *Economic Union* implies not only a CM but also a high degree of co-ordination of the most important areas of economic policy, market regulation, as well as macroeconomic and monetary policies and income redistribution policies. A *Monetary Union* contains a CM but also further integration in the area of currency co-operation.[3] It has either irrevocably fixed exchange rates and full **convertibility** of currencies, or a common or single currency circulating within the monetary union. It also requires integration of macroeconomic and budgetary policies. An *Economic and Monetary Union* (EMU) combines the features of the economic union and the monetary union. This combination is what EC leaders had in mind when they discussed EMU in 1969 and again in 1988. A *Full Economic Union* (FEU) implies the complete unification of the economies of participating member states and common policies for most economic matters. A *Full Political Union* (FPU) is the term used when, in addition to the FEU, political governance and policy making has moved to the **supranational** level. Effectively political unification occurs when the final stage of integration has taken place and a new **confederation** or **federation** has been created (see Chapter 5: 67–70).

The eventual institutional design of EMU in the 1980s and 1990s was an asymmetric one (Verdun 2000: 14). It featured a relatively well-developed monetary union, but a much less developed economic union. In the sphere of monetary policy a complete transfer of policy making to a new European supranational institution was envisaged, whereas in the area of economic policy making, decisions remained to be made by the national governments. One observes here the difference between **positive integration** and **negative integration**. Positive integration refers to the creation of common rules, norms, and policies. Negative integration is all about taking away obstacles, eliminating rules and procedures that are an obstruction to integration.[4] Regarding EMU we find that in the area of monetary policy a new institution and a common policy are created. By contrast, in the area of economic union one observes mainly negative integration: the completion of the single market (that is, removing barriers to trade), and accepting only numerical ceilings on budgetary policies—which should have the effect of co-ordinating policies. Neither a common institution nor a common policy was created in this area of policy making. As we shall see in the next section, the reason for this asymmetry was that in the area of monetary policy a convergence of policy making had occurred, whereas in the area of economic policy there was still a great deal of divergence.

Key points

- Before the introduction of EMU there were other monetary unions, such as the Latin Monetary Union and the Scandinavian Monetary Union.

- EMU consists of a single monetary policy, a single monetary authority, a single currency, and co-ordinated macroeconomic policies.

- There were differences in opinion as to how to obtain EMU. The debate was between the 'Monetarists' and the 'Economists'.

- There are various stages of integration from a free trade area to a full political union.

From The Hague to Maastricht (1969–1991)

At the 1969 summit in The Hague, the heads of state and government decided to explore a possible path to EMU. A group of experts, headed by Pierre Werner, the prime minister of Luxembourg, was asked to draft a possible blueprint. The subsequent Werner Plan (1970) provided a path to EMU. It consisted of a timetable for reaching EMU in three stages by 1980. On the institutional side two supranational bodies were to be created: 'a Community System for the Central Banks' and a 'Centre of Decision for Economic Policy'. The former would pursue monetary policies whereas the latter would co-ordinate macroeconomic policies (including some tax policies). Though the Council accepted in broad terms the EMU proposals as set out in the Werner Plan, EMU did not take off in the subsequent years.

There were two reasons why the process of creating an EMU in the 1970s stalled. First, there were substantial differences among the member states about how to get to EMU (the difference of opinion between the 'Monetarists' and the 'Economists'). Second, the international economic and monetary situation rapidly changed in the early 1970s, making for a totally different climate for co-operation. During the post-Second World War era the so-called **Bretton Woods** system had made possible stable exchange rates in Western Europe. This came to an end in August 1971. West European countries responded by setting up their own exchange rate mechanism, the so-called '**snake**'. During the 1970s the 'snake' functioned with moderate success. Not all member states were part of it. Some member states currencies dropped out, whereas the currencies of several non-members participated in it.

Developments leading to the relaunch of EMU in the late 1980s

In 1979 an **exchange rate mechanism** (ERM) was developed as part of the **European Monetary System** (EMS). All European Community (EC) member states participated in the EMS, though not all were immediately part of its most important feature, the ERM—a system of fixed but adjustable exchange rates. For example, the UK was not part of the ERM throughout the entire 1980s but its currency was part of the **European Currency Unit** (ECU)—the unit of account at the heart of the EMS. In 1991 the British pound did finally join the ERM, however. Other countries, such as Italy, participated in the ERM from the outset but were initially given more leeway. Throughout the 1980s the Italian lira was permitted to fluctuate more than other currencies within the ERM. The rules stipulated that most currencies could not fluctuate more than ±2.25 per cent from an agreed **parity**, whereas the bandwidth for those that needed more leeway was set at ±6 per cent from the parity. If a currency threatened to move outside the agreed band, central banks would intervene by buying or selling currencies in order to keep the currency from leaving the band. If an imbalance was persistent the so-called EC Monetary Committee would decide whether or not to adjust the parities. The Monetary Committee had been created by the Treaty of Rome and at the start of EMU was renamed Economic and Financial Committee. It is an informal advisory body that discusses monetary policy and exchange rate matters. It consists of two officials from each member state (one representative from the ministry of finance, and one representing the national central bank).

The ERM needed some time to become successful. The first four years (1979–83) were learning years. This period was characterized by numerous parity adjustments and exchange rates fluctuations. Between 1983 and 1987 the participating currencies became more stable, and between 1987 and 1992 the ERM witnessed no realignments. It had become an important 'symbol' of successful European integration.

As a result of the exchange rate co-operation of the 1980s, the German currency, the Deutschmark or D-mark, became the 'anchor currency'. Because it had been such a **strong currency** monetary authorities in ERM countries took German monetary policies as their point of reference. Most EC central banks followed the decisions of the German central bank (the Bundesbank) quite closely. By doing so, these countries imported some of the Bundesbank's and the D-mark's reputation. As the 1980s came to a close another form of co-operation had manifested itself once again: Franco-German co-operation. These countries collaborated on matters such as economic and monetary integration before they were formally discussed in EC meetings. The political leaders of both countries favoured the idea of EMU and were prepared to pave the way for its creation. The three stages of EMU are summarized in Box 20.1.

During the 1980s a few other important developments took place that eventually helped relaunch the EMU process. In the mid-1980s the **Single European Act** (SEA) facilitated the completion of the single (internal) market and it mentioned the need to relaunch EMU. Furthermore the Council agreed to the **liberalization of capital markets** by 1 July 1990. EMU was given new life at the Hanover Council meeting in 1988. The Council asked Jacques Delors to head a committee that would to study how to obtain EMU. The committee was composed of central bank presidents, another EC commissioner, and a few experts. The Delors Committee produced its report in April 1989. Shortly thereafter, the report was accepted as a basis for the creation of EMU. Like the earlier Werner Report the Delors Report proposed developing EMU in three stages. It also envisaged the

need for a European System of Central Banks. In contrast to the Werner Report, it did not find it necessary to set up a similar supranational institution in the economic sphere. But the end aim was the same: full freedom of goods, services, capital, and labour, and if possible and if the political will was there, the introduction of a single currency. To discuss how EMU would be incorporated in the Treaty of Rome an **intergovernmental conference (IGC)** was held. This started in Rome in December 1990 and closed in Maastricht in December 1991 (see Chapter 4: 48). Strictly speaking there were two IGCs, one on EMU and another on political union. One of the decisions taken during the IGC negotiations was that, in order to safeguard a successful EMU with low inflation and a stable currency, countries would have to meet certain criteria, which were dubbed 'convergence criteria'.

The **convergence criteria** (see Box 20.2) referred to good performance in the area of inflation rates, interest rates, and exchange rates. Moreover participating countries should not have excessive budgetary deficits or public debts. Finally, the national central bank needed to be made independent of political influence, and national monetary authorities could no longer use the printing press (monetary financing) to deal with public debts and budgetary deficits. It is important to note that right from the outset there were 'escape clauses' built into

Box 20.1 **The facts**
Three stages to Economic and Monetary Union

First stage	1 July 1990 to 31 Dec. 1993	• Free movement of capital between member states
		• Closer co-ordination of economic policies
		• Closer co-operation between central banks
Second stage	1 Jan. 1994 to 31 Dec. 1998	• Convergence of the economic and monetary policies of the member states (to ensure stability of prices and sound public finances)
		• Creation of the European Monetary Institute
Third stage	From 1 Jan. 1999	• Establishment of a European Central Bank
		• Fixed exchange rates
		• Introduction of a single currency

Box 20.2 **The facts**

The Maastricht convergence criteria

Convergence criteria

- Budget deficits should be no more than 3 per cent of Gross Domestic Product (GDP).

- Accumulated public debt should be no more than 60 per cent of GDP.

- Exchange rates should have stayed within the normal margins set by the exchange rate mechanism for at least the previous two years.

- Inflation should not exceed by more than 1½ points the average of the three best performers.

- Long-term interest rates should be no more than 2 points above the average of the lowest three.

Source: Consolidated Version of the Treaty Establishing the European Community, Article 121 and Protocols.

Debt and deficit escape clauses

- Regarding the deficit and debt criteria the Treaty stipulated that the reference value had to be met or else the debt and deficit needed to have 'declined substantially and continuously and reached a level that comes close to the reference value', or that the situation was only 'exceptional and temporary' and 'stayed close to the reference value'.

- Regarding the debt the Treaty stated that an exception was acceptable if 'the ratio is sufficiently diminishing and approaching the reference value at a satisfactory pace'.

Source: Consolidated Version of the Treaty Establishing the European Community, Article 104.

---

the wording incorporated in the Maastricht Treaty. It was generally thought that the rules would be applied generously for the debt criterion, as it was understood that some countries, such as Belgium and Italy, would never be able to meet the **reference value** in less than a decade. As for the budgetary criteria, they *had* to be met.

It has been suggested that the creation of EMU was assisted by the coincidence that the autumn of 1989 also witnessed the end of Communist regimes in Central and Eastern Europe and in 1990 the fall of the Berlin Wall. The observant reader will have noted, however, that the Delors Report had already been completed by April 1989, and therefore preceded these turbulent political developments. Nevertheless, the political determination of the German chancellor, Helmut Kohl, to secure EMU was connected to his eagerness to move ahead quickly with German reunification. In any event, the IGCs were completed in December 1991 in Maastricht with a summit meeting that agreed to revise the Treaty of Rome, and accept a new Treaty on European Union. It was signed on 7 February 1992,

and eventually came into force on 1 November 1993 after the national parliaments of all of the then 12 member states had ratified it (see **ratification**). As we shall see below, not all member states' parliaments and citizens were immediately very happy with the new Treaty.

Key points

- In the 1970s EMU stalled because of differences in opinion among the member states and because of changing international circumstances.

- Various developments—such as the 'snake', the EMS, and the SEA—contributed to the relaunch of EMU in the late 1980s.

- The Delors Report offered a blueprint for EMU.

- The Treaty changes necessary for acceptance and implementation of EMU were negotiated in an IGC which was completed in Maastricht in 1991.

- To participate in EMU, member states needed to meet the 'convergence criteria'.

From treaty to reality (1992–2002)

This section examines how the EMU project almost died before being brought back to life by a combination of time, bureaucratic perseverance, political support of the elites, and institutional **path dependence**.

Ratification problems

Though signed in 1992 by the heads of state and government, the Maastricht Treaty still had to be ratified by the parliaments of all the then 12 EC member states before it could enter into force. This ratification process turned out to be very tricky. Only months after the Treaty was signed, on 2 June 1992, Danish citizens voted against the Treaty in a referendum. Even though its outcome was very close (50.7 per cent against versus 49.3 per cent in favour), the Treaty was rejected.[5]

In a reaction to the Danish referendum, the French president, François Mitterrand, decided also to hold a referendum in France on the acceptability of the Treaty. It was held on 20 September 1992. Even though the French were in principle supporters of the European integration process, during the summer, opinion polls showed that the French were not so supportive of EMU and signalled that a majority might vote against the Treaty. The result was heavy speculation in the financial markets. The ERM that had been doing well from 1987 through the first part of 1992 now came under heavy pressure. Currencies such as the British pound (which had just recently joined), the Italian lira, the Spanish peseta, as well as the French and Belgian francs came under attack. The turbulence in the foreign exchange markets led to the British pound and the Italian lira falling out of the ERM in September 1992 days before the French referendum. The referendum result was a *'petit oui'* ('little yes'): 51.05 per cent in favour and 48.95 per cent against accepting the Treaty on European Union. Some have since argued that this was a vote against Mitterrand rather than against the Treaty. But even though the outcome was 'positive' it did not convince the markets or the general public. The damage had been done.

The 1992–1993 ERM crisis

The next 12 months were extremely difficult for exchange rate co-operation. The crisis reached a new climax in the summer of 1993. This time the Monetary Committee decided that it could no longer maintain the rules set up in the original 1979 agreement, according to which the system had operated more or less successfully during the 14 years of its existence. Financial markets could make 'one-way bets' that central banks could not counter by intervening in the currency markets. At the same time the EC leaders and the Monetary Committee were confronted with the agreement in the Maastricht Treaty that stated that in order to qualify for EMU member states would needed to have participated successfully in the narrow band of the ERM (i.e. the ±2.25 per cent band). Thus abandoning the ERM altogether was no option. The solution was a beautiful compromise. The so-called narrow bands were stretched from ±2.25 per cent to ±15 per cent (with the exception of the Dutch-German exchange rate which was to stay within the original band). It is of interest to note that after that decision was made, member states usually succeeded in staying within the original band. The compromise enabled central banks to avoid having to counter heavy market speculation at all times. At the same time the Maastricht Treaty stipulations were respected. EMU remained on track.

Meanwhile the UK parliament, the most eurosceptical of them all, had to approve the Maastricht Treaty. It had secured opt-outs on the **Social Chapter** (see Chapter 17: 267), and one on EMU. However, the UK parliament was still not sure that it was in favour of accepting the Treaty. It took until the summer of 1993 to think it over and discuss it in heated parliamentary debates. In the wake of the collapse of the ERM the Conservative government decided to accept the Maastricht Treaty, proclaiming that EMU was clearly not likely to happen in any case.

The ERM crises showed that the ERM could not be relied on to secure stable exchange rates in the EU. It indicated that the status quo could not be maintained in the long run. It was important either to move forward and commit to EMU or to accept that exchange rate stability could not be secured in the EU and drop the whole idea. The latter would pose problems for the internal market. Exchange rate fluctuations can cause arbitrary changes in relative competitiveness. In other words, firms may end up struggling to compete or going out of business through no fault of their own. When that happens domestic actors often demand protective measures. However, within the context of the internal market, protective measures would undermine its underlying principles. Thus, though the ERM crises could in the first instance be interpreted as a blow to the EMU project, its longer-term effects were to heighten awareness that EMU was needed to secure the success of the internal market.

The stability and growth pact and the convergence criteria

In the mid-1990s the German finance minister, Theo Waigel, suggested that there should be arrangements for EMU beyond the convergence criteria. He wanted to formulate rules that countries had to obey once in EMU. These rules took the form of the Stability and Growth Pact (SGP). The SGP was put in place to ensure that no single member state, once a member of EMU, could free-ride on the system, for example by incurring high debts and deficits. Under the SGP, member states that violate the rules to keep their public debt and budgetary deficit low can be penalized and may have to pay a fine. Yet the SGP was not without its critics. In fact, many have argued that the criteria are totally artificial and will be impossible to implement. Romano Prodi, president of the European Commission, even went so far as to call it 'stupid'. It caused a major controversy, indicating how delicate the whole subject has become. Nevertheless, observers have noted that the SGP probably works as a deterrent, and offers a

political symbol important for countries, such as Germany, that were worried about the likely behaviour of high debt countries (such as Belgium and in particular Italy) once they became members of EMU. It is, however, ironic that Germany has since been one of the countries to have problems meeting the rules and objectives of the SGP. See Box 20.3.

At the start of the 1990s it seemed that many countries could easily meet the convergence criteria. However, as time went on, it became clear that even the largest country (and in the monetary sense the most important country) Germany, would be unable to do so. At one point only Luxembourg, a country with less than half a million inhabitants, met the criteria. Thus, throughout the 1990s it was unclear what politicians would do with this lack of adequate performance.

Location of the ECB and who should be its president

Two other big issues that emerged over the course of the 1990s were the question of where the new European Central Bank (ECB) should be located, and who should be its first president. Both issues are examples of the political nature of the European integration process. Hosting an EU institution is desirable to any member state. At the same time all realize that these institutions have to be spread out evenly. But the case of the location of the ECB was particularly political as the ECB would be replacing the de facto monetary leader, the German central bank—the Bundesbank. After considerable political discussion, it was decided that the new ECB should be in Frankfurt, which also hosts the Bundesbank. The reasoning was that it would give the right signals to the financial markets: that the new institution would be as good as the Bundesbank in safeguarding low inflation.

The issue of who would be its first president attracted more political heat. As with location, all member states are usually keen to put forward a candidate of their own. But here, more than in the case of the location, it was not clear why one candidate rather than another would be chosen. In

Box 20.3 **The facts**
The Stability and Growth Pact

The Stability and Growth Pact aims to ensure that the member states continue their budgetary discipline efforts after the introduction of the euro.

Dates

The Stability and Growth Pact was a European Council resolution (adopted at Amsterdam on 17 June 1997) and two Council Regulations of 7 July 1997

Annually since 1 March 1999

Decisions

- The surveillance of budgetary positions and co-ordination of economic policies
- Implementing the excessive deficit procedure

- Member states have undertaken to pursue the objective of a balanced or nearly balanced budget and to present the Council and the Commission with a stability programme
- States not taking part in the third stage of EMU are required to submit a convergence programme

The Stability and Growth Pact enables the Council to penalize any participating member state which fails to take appropriate measures to end an excessive deficit. Initially, the penalty would take the form of a non-interest-bearing deposit with the Community, but it could be converted into a fine if the excessive deficit is not corrected within two years.

Source: **http://europa.eu.int/scadplus/leg/en/cig/g4000s.htm35s9a**.

---

the end Dr Willem Duisenberg, the former president of the Dutch central bank, became the consensus candidate. As the Dutch and German monetary authorities had been the most successful in the 1980s, it was felt that Duisenberg was an excellent candidate. However, after he had informally been approved by all member states, the French had second thoughts. They wanted to promote their own candidate, Jean-Claude Trichet. Once they realized that the other member states did not want to abandon the consensus candidate, they suggested that Duisenberg and Trichet share the eight-year term and each serve four years. In the end it seemed that some kind of compromise had been made, which envisaged that Duisenberg would step down before the full eight years were up, in light of his age (he would be past 65 years of age after the first four years of his term). Many observers thought this political compromise damaged the credibility of the 'independent' ECB.

What to name the new currency and what it should look like

Another anecdote that illustrates the highly political nature of the EMU process relates to the naming of the single currency. As we saw above, since 1979, a calculation unit had existed in the EMS called the European Currency Unit (ECU). The ECU was a unit of account based on a basket of currencies of the EC member states participating in the EMS. The relative weight of each national currency depended in part on the economic size of the country it represented and that currency's performance *vis-à-vis* other currencies. Hence, the ECU was an established monetary unit. Therefore, the Maastricht Treaty talked about the ECU as the single currency. However, over the course of the 1990s the Germans had second thoughts. They felt strongly that ECU was not a good name for a currency that still had to prove itself. As it was strongly desirable that the new single currency would be as strong as the German currency, the D-mark, the Germans stressed that the new currency should not be named after a currency that had been depreciating over time. (The ECU had been depreciating because it was a weighted average of all EMS currencies. Given that the D-mark was the strongest, and the ECU a weighted average, the ECU had been depreciating *vis-à-vis* the D-mark.) Thus a whole debate started about what then to call it.

Various proposals and suggestions were discussed. Some Germans suggested the name 'mark' to signal the new currency's strength and stability. The French proposed a continuation of the name 'ecu' (making reference to the fact that there had existed in medieval times a coin called the *écu* which was used in France and England). Belgium, France, and Luxembourg at another point suggested christening the new single currency the 'franc', the name of the unit that had been used in the nineteenth-century Latin Monetary Union. It was also the name of each of their currencies. Another suggestion was the 'Europa' after the Greek goddess who gave her name to the continent. And many other names were proposed. At some point the idea emerged that each country should keep its national name but insert the prefix 'euro'. Thus, the Spanish would call the new currency the euro-peseta, the Portuguese the euro-escudo, the Austrians the euro-schilling, and so on. But that was considered too confusing. Eventually, during the Madrid summit of December 1995 the name of the currency was decided upon: 'the euro'. This decision was not made on the basis of anyone's strongly felt enthusiasm for that name, but rather due to the lack of opposition. The decision was a compromise solution. The name 'euro' did not offend anyone nor did it suggest favouring any one country (or group of countries) over another, though everyone agreed that it was possibly the most boring name of all of those proposed.

The design of the euro banknotes and coins contains another interesting story. A contest was held to determine the design of the euro banknotes, which was open to designers from all EU member states, who could submit their proposals anonymously. The winner was Robert Kalina of the Austrian central bank, whose designs are inspired by the theme 'ages and styles of Europe' and depict major European buildings. It was decided that one side of the euro coin should be uniform, whereas the other side should contain national symbols. It was up to the individual states to decide what should be on the other side. Some countries felt the need to maintain the 'Queen's head' (for example the Netherlands). Others put important national symbols on their coins, such as the Italians who have Botticelli's painting 'The birth of Venus' on their ten cent coin.

Who should join the eurozone?

Eventually the 1998 deadline approached by which time the European Council had to decide which countries were ready to join EMU. During the 1990s the European Monetary Institute, set up in 1994 (and the forerunner of the ECB), had already designated some countries as being ready to join EMU. Many observers were surprised to discover the countries so designated. Not only Ireland, but also Denmark, the Netherlands, Spain, Portugal, and Austria were amongst the first group of countries to have fulfilled the convergence criteria. By contrast, France and Germany, traditionally the lead countries on EMU, were *not* part of this first group that were earmarked ahead of time to be ready.

France and Germany were having difficulties meeting the criteria: they had problems in particular with the debt and deficit criteria. It is not fair to say, however, that they were doing very much worse than the other countries. Rather the text of the Treaty stipulated that countries needed to meet the convergence criteria or should be moving continuously and steadily in the right direction. Both France and Germany had performed well on these criteria in the early 1990s. In fact, when the criteria were determined they either met or almost met them, but moved away from them as the 1990s progressed. In Germany poor performance was a consequence of German reunification. In the case of France the weaker performance of the 1990s was a lack of economic restructuring. Other countries, by contrast, had been doing less well in the early 1990s and eventually progressed rapidly in the right direction. Thus, ironically, it looked as though EMU might happen with a group of countries that traditionally had been considered second-tier countries, while the participation of France and Germany—traditionally the leaders of the European integration process—was not yet formally approved. Reports in the media in 1997 and 1998 even suggested that France and Germany were 'cooking the books', and there was talk of 'creative accounting'. Yet everyone realized that EMU would be unthinkable without France and Germany. Finally, in May 1998, the European Council decided that 11 countries would participate in EMU from 1 January 1999—the day when exchange rates would be irrevocably fixed between the participating member states. However, Greece was not yet ready, and Denmark, Sweden, and the UK did not want to join at that point. On 19 June 2000, the EU Council assessed that Greece fulfilled the requirements of the Treaty and, thus, approved its accession to the euro area as a twelfth member as of 1 January 2001.

With the forthcoming fifth enlargement in which Central and Eastern European countries (CEECs) will be joining the European Union, new members will once again have to fulfil the convergence criteria before they can enter EMU. It is thought that these countries will need some time before they can become members. Yet, once in the EU they will have the right to join EMU whenever they meet the criteria. On the other hand, they will not be obliged to join before they are ready.

Key points

- The period following the signing of the Maastricht Treaty posed challenges to the EMU project. The challenges included:
  - difficulties with the ratification of the Treaty;
  - the ERM crises;
  - difficulties meeting the convergence criteria;
  - politicking over the location and presidency of the ECB; and
  - disagreement over the choice of name for the new single currency.

Explaining EMU

Let us now turn to a few explanations of why EMU happened, examining explanations from economics and political science.

Explaining EMU from an economics perspective

In the field of economics, discussions of EMU place the main emphasis on the question of whether it would make economic sense to create an EMU in the EU. There are two schools of thought. The first school argues that EU member states should only move forward to the next stage of integration (that is, from a common market to an economic and monetary union) if they constitute a so-called **optimum currency area** (OCA).

According to OCA theory, countries should adopt a single currency only when they are sufficiently integrated economically, when they have mechanisms in place that can deal with **transfer payments** if one part of the country is affected by an economic downturn, and when they no longer need the exchange rate instrument to make those adjustments. Most analysts claim that the EU is *not* an OCA, though a few think that a small number of its countries come close to being one. OCA theory states that if countries do not fulfil the conditions of constituting an OCA they should not give up the exchange rate instrument but use it to make adjustments as the economic situation dictates. Those analysts argue that the EU should not have moved to monetary union. Others who have also observed that the EU does indeed constitute an OCA are less critical of this situation. They use a broader definition of an OCA claiming that the original OCA theory is too rigid. They point out that according to the original definition none of the current federations (such as Canada, Germany, the United States) would constitute an OCA. Hence, they argue that there is no problem in the EU introducing a single currency just as has happened in any other monetary union or federal state. In their view it does not 'cost' too much to give up the exchange rate instrument.

Another school focuses on central banks and the importance of credibility. It argues that over the past two decades the EU has witnessed long periods of collaboration in central banking. From this perspective, central banks can only be effective if financial markets have confidence in their policies. In the case of the ERM, participating countries had to keep their exchange rates stable. In order to do that, they focused on the monetary policy of the strongest currency, the D-mark. Hence, individual central banks followed the policies of the leader (in the case of ERM countries this was the Bundesbank), and hence in practice had no opportunity to pursue alternative policies. The most credible way to secure monetary policies is to commit to them firmly in a Treaty. That is in fact what happened with the Maastricht Treaty. A regime was set up that envisaged full central bank independence, and gave the ECB a clear and single mandate, namely to maintain price stability.

Explaining EMU from a political science perspective

In the political science literature, explanations have followed the so-called European integration theories (see Chapters 5–8). It is noteworthy that scholars from opposing schools of thought have more or less convincingly argued that EMU can be explained using different theoretical approaches. For reasons of simplicity we shall focus on the two best-known opposing schools in order to capture a larger set of arguments.

A *neo-functionalist* explanation claims that EMU can be best explained by considering it to be the result of spillover and incremental policy making (see Chapter 6). The liberalization of capital in the EC, the completion of the single market, and the success of the ERM necessitated further collaboration in the area of monetary integration. To maximize the benefits of these three developments, EMU was needed. Furthermore, significant monetary policy convergence had occurred, arising out of collaboration within the framework of the ERM and the tracking of German policies by other member states. Hence, EMU could be seen as a natural step forward. Moreover, it is argued that supranational actors were instrumental in creating EMU—which is another characteristic of the neo-functionalist explanation of European integration. The supranational actors involved were not only the Commission president and the services of the European Commission (in particular the Directorate-General for Economic and Financial Affairs), but also various EC committees—such as the Monetary Committee. Each of these supranational actors and institutions proved to be influential.

An intergovernmentalist explanation argues that EMU can best be understood by examining the interests and bargaining behaviour of the largest member states (see Chapter 7). This approach sees the European Council meetings as crucial for decisions such as the creation of EMU. Thus, by examining the interests of the largest member states, one is able to see why EMU happened. From this point of view EMU was in the interests of France, Germany, and the UK, and this made it acceptable. France was in favour of EMU because it was a way to contain German **hegemony**. Germany, in turn, was able to secure a monetary policy regime that was sufficiently close to its domestic regime. Some argue that Germany was in favour of EMU in the early 1990s because it wanted to signal its full commitment to the European integration project, having just completed German unification. The UK was not so much in favour of EMU, but was aware that EMU was likely to happen. Thus, the UK aimed to take part in the process and to be involved in the agenda setting and the determination of the process. It has also been argued that EMU served the economic interests of business communities within these countries, which subsequently led governments to be more supportive of the project.

Although some authors have argued that the above-mentioned approaches are mutually exclusive, and that one is 'more correct' than the other, both approaches have something to offer. It may be, then, that only when they are taken together is one able to appreciate fully why EMU happened.

Key points

- There are numerous economics and political science explanations as to why EMU might occur.

- Two economics explanations include the theory of the Optimum Currency Area (OCA) and the importance of credibility and central banks.

- The two political science explanations discussed are derived from integration theories: neo-functionalism and intergovernmentalism

Criticisms of EMU

This section discusses various criticisms of EMU. These are quite diverse, ranging from popular opposition to the whole project to elite criticism of its institutional design.

Countries opposing EMU

Denmark and Sweden are very proud of their own political, social, and economic achievements and doubt that joining EMU will benefit their respective countries. Their populations have been relatively sceptical about the EU more generally, and many have seen EMU as yet another example of unnecessary or undesirable European integration. In a referendum in 2000 the Danish population voted against joining EMU. Thus Denmark decided to stay outside the Eurozone. The Swedish government did not hold a referendum, yet has decided to do the same. In recent opinion polls, however, there appears to be more support for EMU. Therefore, it is not unthinkable that these countries may join EMU in the years to come.

The case of the UK reflects an even more euro-sceptic population. A large segment of the population of the UK has had doubts about European integration ever since the UK first joined the EC in 1973. The UK has been slow in adjusting its opinion. Some British citizens seem deeply suspicious about policy making in continental Europe and fear they will have to make too many changes if they follow the lead of the 'Europeans'. Another argument often heard in the UK is that citizens are unconvinced that there is any real need to create a single currency.

Given that there is no strong economic rationale for it, they remain unconvinced that it is necessary at all. The benefits of the euro have been calculated to be around 1 per cent of GDP.

The main benefits of EMU are the elimination of transaction costs (costs related to the exchange of money), a strong monetary policy, the fact that a single currency further strengthens the single (or 'internal') market, and the dynamic effects that come about as a result of clarity about prices once they are all denominated in the same currency. Yet these benefits are not guaranteed. It is possible for example that monetary policy pursued by the ECB may not benefit all countries equally. Some have argued that the case of the UK is different from all others because the UK's business cycle and the financial structure of business are not fully in line with those of continental Europe (and are closer to those of the USA). Hence, they argue that a common monetary policy might do more harm than good. Others state that the City of London is a special feature of the UK economy and this places the UK in a unique position.

However, it is not fully clear whether these issues really make very much difference. In recent years, the UK business cycle has become much more closely aligned with that of continental Europe as a result of the larger share of total trade going to the EU. Thus, regardless of the importance of these concerns originally, they do now carry less weight. But more than whether the UK is ready economically, the core question is whether it is ready politically. In his first election campaign, the Labour leader Tony Blair rejected the idea that the UK might join EMU during his first term of office. However, after he entered his second term he kept the door open for possible entry. Blair announced that a referendum would be held on EMU, and it was agreed that the UK might join if it met five 'economic tests'. Although at the time of writing these issues are still unresolved and the source of heated debate, it is generally expected that the UK will join EMU at some point in the not so distant future.

Germany's opposition to the euro is more subtle as it is related to German identity. Given Germany's chequered history, the Germans took considerable pride in the success of their national currency and in West Germany's economic performance since 1945. Many German citizens found it difficult to accept giving up the successful D-mark for a completely new and untested currency. Though particularly important in Germany, this concern also plays a role in the three aforementioned countries—Denmark, Sweden, and the UK. Elsewhere in the EU citizens have generally been supportive of the introduction of the euro. The populations of some countries are wholeheartedly enthusiastic (such as Italy) or have a two-thirds majority in favour (Belgium, Ireland, and Spain, for example), whereas others have been more subdued though still see a majority supporting the single currency (as in Austria, Germany, and France).

Criticism of the institutional design of EMU

Aside from popular opposition to the introduction of the euro, EMU has been criticized for its poor institutional design. The scholarly literature, in particular, has picked up on this issue. It argues, for instance, that the extreme independence of the ECB may lead to problems of **legitimacy** and **accountability**. The argument is developed in three steps. First, the ECB is more independent than any other central bank in the world. Its independence and its primary mandate (to secure price stability—in effect, low inflation) are firmly anchored in the Treaty on European Union.[6] The Treaty also stipulates that no one is allowed to give instructions to the ECB; nor should it seek instructions from any-

one. Second, it is close to impossible to change the ECB mandate. A change to the ECB statutes requires a Treaty change which needs the unanimity of the heads of state and government of all EU member states as well as ratification by all EU national parliaments (and possibly referendums too). Third, there are very few checks and balances in place to ensure that the policies pursued are those that the member states want—except for the one clear one, namely to secure price stability (low inflation). And even on that issue there is not too much control. The ECB president gives quarterly reports to the European Parliament (EP), but the EP cannot give instructions to the ECB. Thus, one merely has to trust that the ECB will pursue policies in accordance with its mandate and that the policy outcome will benefit the EU as a whole. Fourth, no supranational institution can pursue flanking policies that may correct imbalances occurring as a result of the policies pursued by the ECB. Let us clarify this issue a little further.

Compared to mature federations the institutional design of EMU is incomplete. On the one hand there is a strong ECB that decides monetary policy for the entire Eurozone. Yet, there is no equivalent economic institution that sets economic policies for that same area. Thus, budgetary and fiscal policies remain to be pursued by the governments of national states. Though countries such as France argued strongly in favour of creating such an 'economic government' (*gouvernement économique*), the choice was made not to go down that route. What would be the advantages and disadvantages of having a European 'economic government'? The advantages would be that policies could then be pursued to correct imbalances that result from a strict monetary policy (one that focuses on combating inflation). An example may serve to clarify this.

Let us imagine a situation in which the ECB is pursuing restrictive monetary policies (that is, that set its interest rate fairly high so that the supply of money in the economy is restricted). The result is that the average inflation rate in the whole Eurozone stays at 2 per cent or below. Let us also assume that there is divergence in growth throughout the Eurozone. For example, in Ireland the economy is growing at 8 per cent, whereas there is a **recession** in Germany. Hence a good monetary policy for Ireland might be an even more restrictive monetary policy (higher interest rates), whereas in Germany the economy would have benefited from a more relaxed monetary policy (lower interest rates). The situation described here is much the same as the ones that occur within individual member states. For example, the UK has had moments where the North of England or Scotland would have benefited from lower interest rates, whilst the Greater London area was booming and hence needed higher interest rates. What happens within a single country is that in those situations a number of so-called automatic stabilizers come into effect. For example, if there is higher unemployment in the depressed areas more funding will go to those areas in the form of un-employment benefit. Also, the government can decide to use other policies to make necessary correc-tions. It can decide to adjust taxes so that tax breaks benefit the depressed areas. It could also spend more money in those areas: make investments in infra-structure and so on. Coming back to our example, if the Eurozone was governed by an economic

government, that body would examine what it would need to do to alleviate the negative effects of the monetary policy for the entire Eurozone and make necessary adjustments. It would be able to smooth out any imbalances.

The disadvantage of an economic government is that such a body would only make sense if a majority of the citizens of the Eurozone felt comfortable with an economic government at the EU level. If it did not have that support, then a decision by such a body would seem illegitimate. The current situation in Europe is that most citizens feel most comfortable with their national government. Thus even though there may be good economic and political reasons to flank a monetary institution with an economic government, if there is insufficient support for it the time is not right to create such a body. Maybe in the future it will seem more necessary, if an EMU *without* an economic government becomes too costly an experiment for particular sectors, regions, or countries. Figure 20.1 illustrates support by EU citizens for the euro from 1993 to 2001.

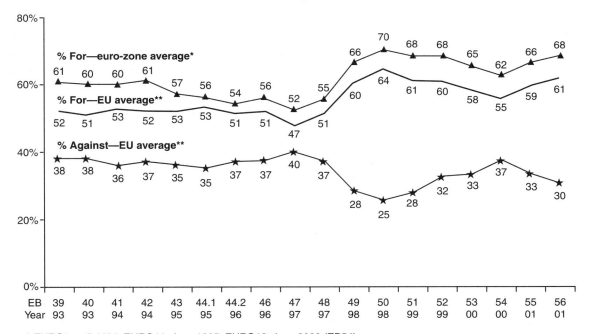

* EURO9 until 1994; EURO11 since 1995; EURO12 since 2000 (EB54)
** EU12 until 1994; EU15 since 1995
Percentage 'don't know' not shown

Fig. 20.1 Support for the single currency, 1993–2001 (EU12 and EU15)
Source: European Commission, *Standard Eurobarometer* no. 56, p. 59, Fig. 5.1.

Key points

- In some countries a majority of the population is against joining EMU (Denmark, Sweden, the UK, and to a lesser extent Germany).

- There has been criticism of the institutional design of EMU.

Conclusion

Euro banknotes and coins were introduced overnight, but it has taken more than 30 years to create Economic and Monetary Union (EMU). It was a slow and long process that ultimately led to the creation of a single monetary policy, a new European Central Bank (ECB), and rules on budgetary policies and public debt. Behind the fanfare and festivities of the introduction of the new currency lay a lengthy and gradual process of learning about economic and monetary co-operation. Not only was it necessary for countries to meet the immediate criteria, the so-called convergence criteria, but it was also crucial that member states had practised maintaining stable exchange rates during the 1970s and 1980s, and that they had agreed on common goals for EMU.

We have seen that there were both economic and political motivations underlying the plan to move to EMU. Though one can make a case for a purely economic rationale for EMU, its ultimate creation cannot be understood without an appreciation of the political dimension. EMU is seen as a new step in European integration. It signals the capability of EU member states to take firm action together. It also places the EU more clearly on the international map. Yet, a number of issues remain unresolved. The discussion of an asymmetrical EMU indicated how fragile the balance is between 'economic' and 'monetary' union. It is not unthinkable that in the future further integration might be needed in the area of 'economic union', or indeed that steps might be necessary towards further political unification, if only to redistribute more evenly the costs and benefits of EMU. At the same time, we have seen that European integration is a gradual process that if pushed ahead too quickly may lack legitimacy.

What will the future of the EU look like with EMU in place? The euro is a currency that has been introduced into a Eurozone which contains more than 300 million citizens. As such, the euro may become a leading world currency—one that may eventually rival the US dollar. For example, it may become a leading international trade currency used in, for example, the purchase of oil. The strength of this currency may well give the EU a stronger position in world politics, if only because it might offer an alternative to the US dollar. As such the euro contributes to the symbolism of European integration. It offers a concrete token indicating the rapid and far-reaching process of integration taking place in the EU.

As for the regional use of the euro, its initial successful launch on 1 January 2002 suggests that politicians and citizens can be pleased with the result. The euro is legal tender in the 12 member states of the Eurozone. It is not unthinkable that some of the EU member states still outside the Eurozone may want to join in the not so distant future (such as Denmark, Sweden, and the UK), thereby adding more credibility and strength to the euro. Furthermore, the new EU member countries in Central and Eastern Europe may also join in the years to come, once they have met the convergence criteria. Yet, not all monetary unions in the past have lasted. EMU will only survive if it continues to be supported by citizens and the national and European politicians. Leaders will have to keep listening to the needs of their citizens. If they are able to do this satisfactorily, the euro may well have a very promising future.

QUESTIONS

1 Why was the term 'economic' and 'monetary' union used? What, in this regard, is an 'asymmetrical EMU'?

2 What was the argument between the 'Economists' and the 'Monetarists'?

3 Name and describe the various stages of economic integration from a Free Trade Area to Full Political Unification.

4 Describe the path to EMU from The Hague to Maastricht.

5 What are the convergence criteria, and why were they invented?

6 There are two opposing political science theories explaining why EMU happened. What are they? Do you agree that they are opposing theories or do you think that are they complementary?

7 What are the main criticisms of EMU?

8 Discuss how the creation of EMU was both an economic and a politically driven process.

GUIDE TO FURTHER READING

De Grauwe, P., *The Economics of Monetary Integration* (Oxford: Oxford University Press, 1992). A popular introductory textbook on monetary integration, which focuses on the economic theory of monetary union, and evaluates the costs and benefits of monetary integration.

Dyson, K., *Elusive Union: The Process of Economic and Monetary Union in Europe* (London: Longman, 1994). This book considers the move to monetary union in Europe from a political perspective, dealing with both historical and theoretical questions in the process.

—— and Featherstone, K., *The Road to Maastricht: Negotiating Economic and Monetary Union* (Oxford: Oxford University Press, 1999). A very influential volume which looks at the steps leading to the agreement on EMU at Maastricht, based on hundreds of interviews with key informants.

Gros, D., and Thygesen, N., *European Monetary Integration. From the European Monetary System to Economic and Monetary Union*, 2nd edn (Harlow, Essex/New York: Longman, 1998). This textbook sets out the economics of EMU. It is considered by many to be the 'economics' guidebook to understanding the EMU process.

Tsoukalis, L., *The Politics and Economics of European Monetary Integration* (London: George Allen & Unwin, 1977). A seminal book on the history of the EMU.

Verdun, A., *European Responses to Globalization and Financial Market Integration: Perceptions of Economic and Monetary Union in Britain, France and Germany* (Basingstoke: Palgrave-Macmillan; New York: St Martin's Press, 2000, paperback 2002). A volume on EMU, based on original research, covering the policy from the perspective of the member states, and which considers how actors use EMU to serve or frustrate their interests.

—— (ed.), *The Euro: European Integration Theory and Economic and Monetary Union* (Lanham, Md.: Rowman and Littlefield, 2002). An edited book which focuses on EMU as part of a wider process of European integration. The book looks at various theoretical approaches applied to monetary integration, and reviews the origins and development of progress towards the introduction of the euro.

WEB LINKS

www.ecb.int The European Central Bank's website.

www.europa.eu.int/pol/EMU/index_en.htm The EU's own EMU website.

http://europa.eu.int/euro/html/home5.html?lang=5 The EU's website on the euro.

http://europa.eu.int/comm/economy_finance/euro_en.htm The European Commission's website on EMU.

ENDNOTES

1 The author wishes to thank Michael Artis, Patrick Crowley, and Michelle Cini for useful comments on earlier drafts of this chapter. Research assistance by Lloy Wylie, and the financial support of the Social Sciences and Humanities Research Council (Canada) (SSHRC) (grant no. 410–1999–0081) are also gratefully acknowledged.

2 This early 1970s term 'monetarist' should not be confused with the 'monetarist' views of the economist, Milton Friedman. Due to the confusion in use of the term monetarism some recent writers have changed these original labels and prefer to use different labels: the 'Economists' are in favour of a 'coronation approach', whereas the 'Monetarists' favoured a 'locomotive approach'.

3 This is not *always* the case. The Scandinavian Monetary Union did not contain a Customs Union.

4 The words 'positive' and 'negative' *do not* have a normative implication, i.e. positive is *not* meant as 'good' and negative as 'bad'.

5 The UK had already during the IGCs secured an opt-out on EMU and on the so-called social chapter (see Chapters 4 and 17). To accommodate the Danish concern the Danes too were given an opt-out on EMU. When they held another referendum on 18 May 1993 the result was a majority of 56.7 per cent in favour and 43.3 per cent against.

6 Note that the Treaty does stipulate that it should also aim at the overall economic prosperity of the EU (Article 2).

Part Five

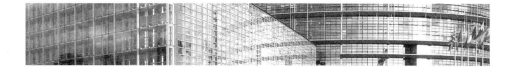

Issues and debates

In the fifth and final part of *EU Politics*, five themes or issues have been selected, covering some of the key debates reflected in the academic literature on the European Union. In Chapter 21 Johan Olsen reviews the literature on Europeanization, and addresses, more specifically, how the EU has impacted upon domestic political arenas. In Chapter 22, Michelle Cini deals with the issue of policy implementation. The issue is an important one as the EU's role in implementation has been much criticized in recent years, contributing to accusations of fraud made against the European institutions and their agents. In Chapter 23, Dimitris Chryssochoou tackles the thorny question of the EU's democratic deficit. He not only defines this concept, but also situates it in a broader context of EU democracy, raising important questions about our expectations of the European integration process and the future of the EU polity. In Chapter 24, Kerstin Junge introduces the concept of 'differentiation' (or flexibility) whereby not all member states participate in European policies at the same pace or to the same extent. This feature of the EU landscape is likely to become even more important as the EU enlarges. And in the final chapter, Chapter 25, Antje Wiener provides a fascinating overview of the origins and substance of European citizenship, asking what this 'institution' means for the 'Europolity' and how it might further develop in future.

21 Europeanization

Johan P. Olsen

READER'S GUIDE

The widespread use of the term 'Europeanization' is a relatively recent phenomenon. A close look at what the term implies points to a number of different conceptions of 'Europeanization'. This chapter questions the usefulness of the concept of Europeanization in analysing EU politics. It unpacks the various ways in which the term has been used, identifying five discrete definitions, referring to: (i) the territorial expansion of Europe's (or the EU's) borders (enlargement); (ii) a process of European-level institutionalization; (iii) the export of European institutions (rules, structures, norms, for example) to the wider world; (iv) the strengthening of the European integration 'project' or the 'European Construction' as a political ambition; and (v) the domestic impact of European-level institutions. It considers the kinds of mechanisms of change involved in these different definitions of Europeanization, and draws some conclusions about how these processes might influence future research on the European polity.

Introduction

Since the 1980s, a wealth of studies have appeared on the subject of **Europeanization**. This chapter serves a number of different functions with regard to this phenomenon. It explores what Europeanization is, and considers some of the mechanisms of change that might allow Europeanization to occur. It also unpacks the concept of Europeanization on the grounds that conceptual clarity is an important precursor to understanding the transformations currently taking place on the European continent.[1]

The chapter begins by acknowledging that Europeanization has become an extremely fashionable term in the social science literature on Europe. The first section questions whether it is also a useful term. For example, if Europeanization has many different dimensions, surely its application can only serve to confuse rather than to clarify change processes at work. Reserving judgement on this question, the chapter is divided into five sections, each of which deals with one discrete definition of Europeanization. The first section deals with Europeanization as the territorial expansion of Europe's (or the EU's) borders. The second section sees Europeanization as a synonym for European-level institutionalization. The third section defines Europeanization more broadly as the export of European institutions to the rest of the world. The fourth section associates Europeanization with the strengthening of the European integration project as a political objective. The fifth section deals with Europeanization as shorthand for the domestic impact of European-level institutions. This latter idea has begun to spawn a vast range of empirical literature, some of which will be touched on in this concluding part of the chapter.

Europeanization: A fashionable term, but is it useful?

'Europeanization' is a fashionable but contested concept. It is used in different ways to describe a variety of phenomena and processes of change. As yet, there is no common definition. Because Europeanization has no precise or stable meaning, it has been argued that the term is too unwieldy to be used as an organizing concept (Kassim 2000: 238). Yet it may be premature to abandon the term, as most studies of Europeanization are of recent origin and there have as yet been few systematic attempts to map and compare its different uses. Efforts to account for the dynamics of 'Europeanization' are scarce and the evidence is uneven and often contested. Rather than reject the term outright, therefore, the following sections attempt to create a little more order in a disorderly field of research. The challenge addressed here is not only to identify what Europeanization is, but also to explore the ways in which (or indeed whether) the term might be useful for understanding the dynamics of the evolving European polity.

A first step towards understanding Europeanization involves the separation of the different phenomena referred to by the term. The aim here is to identify precisely what it is that is changing when we talk of Europeanization. There are five possible uses:

- Europeanization as changes in external territorial boundaries (such as in the case of enlargement).
- Europeanization as the development of institutions of governance at the European level (European-level institutionalization).
- Europeanization as the export of European forms of political organization and governance beyond Europe.
- Europeanization as a political project in support of the construction of a unified and politically strong Europe.
- Europeanization as the penetration of European-level institutions into national and subnational systems of governance.

These five categories of Europeanization will be considered in more depth below. Even at this point, however, given the wide variation in usage that this list implies, one might assume 'Europeanization' to be a rather disappointing term, one that ought to be abandoned. To what extent might it be of use in understanding the ongoing transformation of the

Box 21.1 Core ideas
Two dimensions of institutional change

This chapter is interested in how existing institutional arrangements impact on two key dimensions of institutional change (March and Olsen 1995). The *first* is changes in political organization: the development of an organizational and financial capacity for common action and governance through processes of reorganization and redirecting of resources. The *second* is changes in structures of meaning and peoples' minds. That is, focus is on the development and redefinition of political ideas—common visions and purposes, codes of meaning, causal beliefs, and worldviews—that give direction and meaning to common capabilities and capacities.

European political order? In any case, is it helpful to subsume a variety of phenomena and **change mechanisms** under one term? Or are we in danger of misunderstanding the process and nature of Europeanization because we misuse the term (Wallace 1999: 2)?

It is argued below that research into processes of Europeanization need not be hampered by competing definitions, as long as their meaning, the phenomena identified above, the simplifying assumptions behind the definitions, the models of change, and the theoretical challenges involved, are all clarified. However, even where this is done, Europeanization may turn out to be less useful as an explanatory concept than as an attention-directing device and as a point of departure for further research.

It is clear that Europeanization involves a change or transformation of some sort. But what are the mechanisms involved in such changes? Various models exist to help us explain these. They point to the fact that change may be a result of *rule following* and the application of standard operating procedures to appropriate situations, or to *argumentation* and *persuasion*. Alternatively, it may be a consequence of *choice—problem-solving* as well as *conflict*

resolution, diffusion, or *socialization*. Finally, change may also be produced by adaptation through processes of *learning* or *competitive selection*.

In the real world, most of the time, complex mixes of processes will apply simultaneously. While one process or mechanism may fit a particular phenomenon or situation better than the others, there is no reason to expect a one-to-one relationship between a phenomenon and a process or mechanism of change. This will also be true of Europeanization. However, one of the aims of this chapter is to explore how change might occur in each of the five categories of Europeanization. Therefore, for each of the five, one or two relevant processes are suggested (see Box 21.1).

Key points

- Europeanization has no precise or stable definition, which raises the question—is it a useful concept?

- It is possible to identify at least five different ways in which the term 'Europeanization' is used in the social science literature on Europe.

The changing boundaries of 'Europe'

The first category of Europeanization is *Europeanization as changes in external territorial boundaries.* This presupposes that Europe is a geographical concept, and that external boundary can be delimited

and defined (Jönsson, Tägil, and Törnqvist 2000: 7). European transformations are not limited to the EU and its member states—nor indeed to Western Europe, for that matter. It should not be forgotten that cross-border relations in Europe have been and continue to be managed through a wide variety of transnational regimes and institutions, beyond the EU (Wallace 2000*a*). But even though there are many different examples of institution building at the European level, the EU has been extremely successful in institutionalizing a system of governance that includes a large, and increasing, part of the continent. There can be no doubt that the EU is currently the core political project in Europe and the example most often analysed in the literature on Europeanization.

For the EU enlargement has been a recurrent process. Union membership has turned out to be an appealing prospect for most European states and the list of applicant countries remains long. How, then, can we account for the dynamics of expansion? More specifically, why have existing member states been so prepared to welcome new members (see, for example, Schimmelfennig 2001)?

Assuming that Europeanization of this kind involves a process of *rule following*, change may be seen as quasi-mechanical, that is, as following from the routine application of stable criteria for entry and of standard operating procedures to pre-specified situations. In other words, if an applicant country meets the membership criteria (see Chapter 14: 216) it is admitted. If not, the door is closed. However, in less automatic situations the underlying process may be one of *argument and persuasion* on the part of the applicants. Where this applies, actors are more likely to appeal to a shared collective identity in order to evoke common standards of truth and morals. As beliefs change, so too does the likelihood of enlargement taking place.

It is not clear, however, why rule following applies in some cases and argument and persuasion in others. The EU entry criteria may ostensibly be liberal democratic, implying that the Union will admit countries that adhere to some universal and impartial criteria in their domestic and international conduct (Schimmelfennig 2001). Criteria may also be institution specific and related to the principles on which an institution is founded, as is clear in the Copenhagen Declaration of 1993 (see Chapter 14: 216). Alternatively they may take the form of a moral imperative based on a general sense of 'kinship-based' duty, which has to do with belonging to a specific political community (Sjursen 2001). This is illustrated when actors argue that Europe has a historic opportunity to 'reunify Europe' after decades of artificial separation (Notre Europe 2001). Furthermore, interpretations of obligations may also be history specific. For example, Sedelmeier argues that, during the Cold War, EU policy makers constructed for themselves a specific role, which implied a responsibility towards the Central and Eastern European countries (the CEECs). Such commitments were unevenly distributed across policy makers, yet once the Cold War ended, they had an important impact on the enlargement process (Sedelmeier 2001).

It is commonplace to observe that the EU agreed to enlarge before they calculated the consequences. In other words, there was no guarantee that the benefits accruing to each member state would outweigh the costs involved. Enlargement cannot therefore be seen purely as the result of a strategic or **rational choice**, a cost–benefit analysis on the part of states. However, it is also commonplace to observe that participants in the enlargement process are indeed concerned with costs and benefits, and that they bargain in defence of self-interest and economic and security gains. If that is the case, what, then, are the mechanisms through which identities and norms have an impact? More specifically, do actors use identities and norms genuinely or instrumentally? Here it is important to understand the relations and possible tension between a **logic of appropriateness** and norm-driven behaviour, on the one hand, and a **logic of calculation** on the other (March and Olsen 1989). Schimmelfennig (2001) argues his case primarily within a logic of self-interested (rational) calculation rather than a **logic of appropriateness**. Yet the enlargement process is surely characterized by the strategic use of norm-based arguments and appeals to democratic identities and values. Member states have been entrapped rhetorically, which means that they have no choice but to support enlargement if they want to retain their reputations as Community members. Therefore, we might say that strategic behaviour is constrained by the constitutive ideas of the Community and actors' prior identification with the Union. Sedelmeier (2001: 184) is more open to whether identities and norms are used genuinely or instrumentally. Sjursen

(2001), too, emphasizes the *genuine* role of internalized norms. In this context, norms constitute the identity of actors, as well as regulating their behaviour. From this perspective, decisions are made as actors reason together and assess the moral validity of each others' arguments (Sjursen 2001).

Many of the EU's own documents portray enlargement as consistent with liberal-democratic principles and EU values, as well as being in the interests of existing members and applicant countries (European Commission 2001*b*). Yet for scholars aspiring to theorize Europeanization, this kind of harmony cannot be taken for granted. There is no doubt that actors often follow rules. Yet, they are also often aware of the consequences of rule-driven behaviour; and may not be willing to accept those consequences. In some situations one's identity may be dominant and provide clear normative imperatives. In other situations there may be many competing identities, giving vague guidelines for action. Therefore, interests and understandings of means and ends may be either clear or obscure. One possibility is that a clear logic of action

will dominate a less clear logic. Another alternative is that learning over time will produce rules and norm-driven action, while highly unfavourable consequences will make existing rules suspect and activate a **logic of calculation** (March and Olsen 1998). A third possibility is that different logics are relevant for different issues. For example, enlargement may be decided through the application of basic norms, while the distribution of the costs of enlargement may be decided through self-interested calculation and bargaining.

Key points

- Europeanization can apply to the extension of the territorial reach of 'Europe'. An example of this is EU enlargement.

- There is evidence of various change processes at work in this case, with some evidence of rule following and of argument and persuasion characterizing the enlargement process.

Developing European-level institutions

The second category of Europeanization sees the term as a sort of synonym for institution building and institution development at the European level. Thus, many scholars portray Europeanization as the the institutionalization, at European level, of a distinct system of governance with common institutions, and the authority to make, implement, and enforce Europe-wide binding policies. This view is illustrated by Risse, Cowles, and Caporaso who define Europeanization as:

the emergence and development at the European level of distinct structures of governance, that is, of political, legal, and social institutions associated with the problem solving that formalizes interactions among the actors, and of policy networks specializing in the creation of authoritative European rules (Risse, Cowles, and Caporaso 2001: 3).

Europeanization here includes both the strengthening of an organizational capacity for collective action and the development of common ideas, like new norms and collective understandings of citizenship and membership (Checkel 2001*a*: 180). A possible frame for understanding the dynamics and outcomes of European-level institutional development is *purposeful choice*. Within this rationalist frame, which is used in particular by intergovernmentalists (see Chapter 7), a group of actors have a choice among alternative forms of organization and governance. They have normative criteria that make it possible to discriminate between available alternatives and their outcomes, and they choose the one that, according to its inherent properties or expected effects, is deemed to be most valuable. Institutional developments, then, are seen as reflecting the will, power, and understanding of identifiable actors. The research challenge is, then, to identify those actors, as well as the motivations and forces that determine their choices.

In a *problem-solving* mode objectives are shared and institutional change is the outcome of voluntary agreements among relevant actors. The challenge for institutional architects is to discover or design forms of organization and governance that make all participants come out better than they could do when acting on their own. For instance, the EU is assumed to be involved in a continuous search for 'the right formula for building lasting and stable institutions' in order to improve the functionality, legitimacy, and credibility of the institutions of governance (Patten 2001). From this perspective, the participants first have to agree common objectives and substantive political programmes. They then have to develop institutional arrangements as organizational tools for their policies.

In a *conflict resolution* mode, by contrast, change reflects the interests and beliefs of the most powerful actors, as they bargain, build coalitions, and make threats or promises based on their political, military, or economic power. There is an explicit focus here on competing conceptions of European unity and forms of political organization and governance. Likewise, there is a focus on power, that is, on how Europeanization reflects and modifies the ways in which political power is constituted, legitimated, exercised, controlled, and redistributed. Like other political orders, the emerging European order has to cope with tensions between unity and integration and disunity and disintegration (March and Olsen 1998). So even though EU officials emphasize norms of consensus and voluntary co-operation and argue that 'power politics have lost their influence' (Prodi 2001: 3), this perspective assumes a need to understand the power relations and cleavages shaping Europe.

While there is some agreement that the Union is 'an extraordinary achievement in modern world politics' (Moravcsik 1998: 1), there is less consensus when it comes to the nature of the Union, and the causes of its development. For instance, the importance of explicit intervention and choice in the development of European-level institutions has been contested. Intergovernmentalists emphasize institutional choices made by the governments of (the major) member states (Moravcsik 1998). A competing view is that systems of **supranational governance** have their roots in the Europe-wide transactions, group formation, and networks of transnational society, while governments primarily play a reactive role (Stone Sweet and Sandholtz 1998). An institutional approach, with an emphasis on 'historical inefficiency', focuses on how willed change is influenced and constrained by existing institutional arrangements (March and Olsen 1989, for example). From this perspective it is expected that the significance and nature of deliberate choice depends on existing institutional configurations and that the importance of purposeful choice will change as the degree of institutionalization at the European level changes.

One possible source of improved understanding of the scope of purposeful institutional choice in contemporary Europe is to compare in a systematic way different European institution-building efforts, such as the EU, EFTA, NATO, the Nordic Council, and the Council of Europe. Another option is to compare attempts at institution building within the EU. The EU has been characterized as a 'non-state' and a 'non-nation' (Schmitter 2000) and as 'a relatively incoherent polity in institutional terms' (Caporaso and Stone Sweet 2001: 228). The Union's capacity and legitimacy for institution building has varied across institutional spheres, in areas such as competition policy, monetary affairs, external and internal security, and culture, for example, and the ongoing development from (primarily) market building to polity building creates a need to attend to the different dynamics of various institutional spheres and policy sectors.

Studies of state and nation building in Europe (Rokkan 1999) suggest four dimensions that are relevant both for comparing institutional spheres within the EU and for comparing the Union with other European institution-building efforts:

- *Regulatory institutions*: which build a unified administrative and military apparatus for the control of a population, a territory, and its external borders, including the ability to extract resources for common tasks.

- *Socializing institutions*: which develop, through education and **socialization**, a territorial identity and a cultural community with a sense of belonging, emotional attachment, and shared codes of meaning.

- *Democratic institutions*: which create democratic citizenship, representative institutions, equal rights of political participation, legitimized opposition, organized parties, and forums for public debate and popular enlightenment.

- *Welfare institutions*: which develop social and economic citizenship and rights, and a community that accepts collective responsibility for securing more equal life chances for its citizens through public service, the reallocation of resources, and the regulation of the use of private resources.

Comparison of the different dynamics of institutional spheres and policy sectors is particularly important when institution building is seen to involve changes in action capabilities and in identities, codes of meaning, and normative criteria, giving direction to capabilities. Like other political systems, the EU makes efforts to justify its institutions, to develop a sense of belonging, and to create emotional identification with the system among citizens. Thus aspirations of governance include not only changes in behavioural regulation, opportunity, and incentive structures, but also the moulding of individuals and changes in mentality, causal and moral beliefs, and ways of thinking.

For example, EU institutions, including the Council, have taken an interest in the democratic and European dimensions of education, hoping to make young people more conscious of European ideas and of being European (Beukel 2001: 131). Member states, however, have been reluctant to give the Union authority to shape the institutional framework for education and socialization. Control over educational institutions—including changes in universities (Dineen 1992) and in national history writing (Geyer 1989)—is a sensitive issue precisely because it is closely linked to national and subnational identities. An implication is that students of European institutional dynamics, for theoretical as well as practical reasons, need to supplement their interest in decision-making and decision-implementing institutions with an increased interest in the dynamics of educational and socializing institutions at the European level.

Key points

- Europeanization can refer to the process of institutionalization and polity building that is taking place at European level.

- The change mechanisms involved are likely to work through processes of education and socialization.

Exporting European-level institutions

Inward-looking definitions of Europeanization are a twentieth-century phenomenon (Mjøset 1997). Historically, Europeanization has been understood as the spread of forms of life and production, habits of drinking and eating, religion, language, and political principles, institutions, and identities beyond the European continent. The global extension of the territorial state system is just one outstanding example of how European models of **polity** and society have spread throughout the globe, making European developments key to understanding the rest of the world (Geyer 1989: 339).

A basic frame for understanding these *diffusion* processes is borrowed from epidemiology. Thus when studying the spread of a form of political organization and governance through a territory and a population, questions to address include: What is the pattern of diffusion? How fast, how far, and to whom does it (first) spread? Does it stick, or fade away and disappear? And what are the political processes involved? An institutional perspective suggests that diffusion will be affected by the interaction of outside impulses, internal institutional traditions, and historical experiences. Diffusion processes are unlikely to produce a perfect cloning of the prescriptions offered, however, as what is diffused is likely to be transformed during the diffusion process.

In practice, the spread of European models of organization and governance has often involved colonization, coercion, and imposition. Consequently, European institutions and principles have meant the penetration and destruction of traditions and institutions in other continents. They have disrupted and undermined the coherence of established polities and societies and created political counter-mobilization and confrontations. However, diffusion has also taken the form of imitation and voluntaristic borrowing. Those affected have copied European arrangements because of their perceived uses and legitimacy.

Because the major European states have lost their world **hegemony**, hierarchical command and coercion is now less likely to be the most important process for spreading European institutions and principles outside Europe. Diffusion patterns are more likely to depend on exposure to and the attractiveness of European forms of governance. The issue then becomes: among the many, competing ideas about exemplary or appropriate political organization and governance available at the global scene, how distinctive and attractive are the European options?

There is scant empirical documentation of external diffusion processes over the last few decades. Indeed, the **new institutionalism** in sociology tends to deny that there are in fact distinct European models of organization and governance (Meyer 2001: 238). The focus, then, is on the diffusion of *global* prescriptions—templates and standards of universal rationality and validity—spread through a global system of cultural communication (see, for example, Powell and DiMaggio 1991).

The attractiveness of European prescriptions and normative standards has also been questioned. For instance, Garton Ash argues that the UK looks primarily to the United States for inspiration. There is a fascination with American solutions and 'idealized America trumps idealized Europe' (Garton Ash 2001: 12). The attraction of American enterprise, innovation, and flexibility is hardly limited to the UK, however. Yet there is also increasing attention being paid to questions of European identity and to the civilizational differences between Europe and the United States. This is illustrated by debates over federalism, the desire to combine better economic efficiency with social justice and responsibility over issues such as the use of the death penalty, resistance to treating language and culture as commodities, new conceptions of security, and environmental issues. Europe currently finds itself in a new period of experimentation and innovation, with new forms of organization and governance in the making. These new forms and processes of change may serve to inspire efforts at regional integration in other parts of the world (Telò 2001).

European states are increasingly making attempts to assert themselves on the international stage—particularly through the EU. For instance, one dimension of the development of a Common Foreign and Security Policy (CFSP) relates to the status and role of the EU in the international system (see Chapter 15). Aspirations include turning the Union into an influential actor in the development of a new international order through the World Trade Organization, NATO, and the United Nations, as well as in bilateral negotiations. The goal is to make the Union's political power better reflect its economic power.

The power aspect is also observed when the 'European Union' is identified closely with 'Europe', and when the focus is on the diffusion of institutions, standards, and identities within the European continent. In recent enlargement negotiations with the CEECs, phrases like 'catching up' with the West, the conditionality of aid, and the need to accept EU standards and norms in order to become member states, indicate status and power differentials. Yet, it has also been observed that leaders in the former communist states are improving their ability to differentiate between those aspects of European integration that are useful for their own political purposes and those that are not. Imitation often has a political logic distinct from faddish mimicry (Jacoby 2001: 173, 190).

While coercion is not the main process of change, therefore, the diffusion of forms of political organization and governance is likely to reflect more than just the attractiveness of European templates. Diffusion processes involve issues of power and status. They also take place within a framework of resources and capabilities, incentives and sanctions. Resources can be used to give voice to ideas and practices, to make them more visible and more attractive. Forms of governance supported by the resourceful are *ceteris paribus* more likely to spread. Therefore, we have to look at how resources may be mobilized to promote European forms of governance in other parts of the world, as well as at the resources available for non-Europeans to resist unattractive options.

In sum, students of Europeanization—as the diffusion of European forms of organization and governance beyond the region—have to understand the distinctiveness, attractiveness, and legitimacy of European models, as well as the resources backing their diffusion. The shifting long-term European export-import balance of forms of organization and governance is one possible indicator of whether Europe is becoming a more or less important entity in its interaction with non-Europe.

Key points

- Europeanization may be a process by which European institutions are spread around the world.

- Understanding the spread of European institutions in a non-coercive fashion means looking at the distinctiveness, attractiveness, and legitimacy of European models, and at the resources backing their diffusion.

The political unification of Europe

The fourth conception defines Europeanization as a political exercise to turn Europe into a stronger and more coherent political entity. This implies a process by which sovereign states would be unified into a single system of governance. Coherent structural arrangements would provide a strong basis for concerted action both internally and externally. The development of a 'European public sphere' would contribute to common understandings of what legitimate political organization and governance is, and shared feelings of belonging. Internal borders would be weakened or removed and external borders strengthened. And there would be discrimination between members (citizens) and non-members (non-citizens). In sum, from this perspective, Europeanization implies a process whereby a fragmented European state system becomes unified, as the boundaries of political space are extended beyond individual member states. Europeanization in the sense of (strong) political unification is an aspiration, then, which is present in some reform programmes (see, for example, Habermas 1998).

As yet, there are few agreed-upon indicators of Europeanization—as political unification. A strong Europe does not simply equate with maximizing territory, the building of a new political centre, the adaptation of national and subnational systems of governance, and the export of European solutions. First, the institutionalization of political borders, authority, power, and responsibility is a delicate balancing act. While EU enlargement will increase the Union's territory, population, and resources, it will also make it more diverse and place tougher demands on the Union's institutions. Second, a stronger centre and a single hierarchical control and command system may, under some circumstances, make it possible for the EU to act in a more coherent way and play a more significant role in global developments. Yet, strong pressures to adapt may also generate new levels of protest and resistance from those who disagree with common policies. Third, the vigorous adaptation of domestic systems without an adequate respect for local autonomy, diversity, and the protection of minorities may provoke conflict and obstruction. And finally, while the export of European solutions may indicate success, this may also depend on *imports* from other parts of the world. Such a complex balancing act is unlikely to involve a single process of change.

The processes of institutional change discussed so far, namely rule application, argument and persuasion, choice, adaptation through experiential learning or competitive selection and diffusion, are seen as complementary rather than mutually exclusive. In varying combinations they are likely to be helpful in understanding contemporary ecologies of co-evolving institutions. This complexity may also explain why students of European change have often observed that the dynamics of transformation take the form of *mutual adaptation among co-evolving institutions* at different levels and sectors of governance.

On the one hand, change is not unilateral. Global, European, national, and subnational processes interact in complex ways. Typically, there is no single dominant and deterministic causal relation. Causal chains are often indirect, long, and complex. Effects are difficult to identify and disentangle, and interactive processes of feedback, mutual influence, and adaptation produce interpenetration across levels of governance and among institutions. On the other hand, the observed complexity is often bracketed. For example, Risse, Cowles, and Caporaso (2001: 12) write: 'Although the causality between Europeanization and domestic structure runs in both directions, we have chosen to emphasize the downward causation from Europeanization to domestic structure'. The dilemma is obvious. A focus on uni-causal relations, and the language and logic of fixed **dependent** and **independent variables**, can become a strait-jacket preventing an adequate theoretical and empirical analysis of European dynamics of change. However, no coherent empirical research programme is possible if everything is seen as endogenous and in flux.

Current European developments may illustrate a basic property of human beings—that they are capable of producing more complex behaviour and institutions than they are capable of understanding (Lave and March 1975: 6). A world where many actors are adapting to each other simultaneously, and therefore changing the context in which other actors are adapting, is a world that is difficult to predict, understand, and control. It is difficult both to infer proper lessons on the basis of experience and to know what action to take as a consequence (Axelrod and Cohen 1999: 8).

Political leaders facing a situation where institutions evolve and unfold through an unguided process, with weak elements of shared understanding and control, may place their trust in processes of natural selection—competitive markets, for instance. Where this is the case, the task of prospective leaders is to establish simple rules of fair competition and to harness complexity by protecting variation, exploration, and innovation. A complementary position may be to try to make institutional change a more guided process, by improving elements of shared understanding and co-ordination and by reducing complexity. Examples of this might involve institutional actors monitoring each other, exchanging information, introducing arrangements for consultation before decisions are made, developing shared statistics and accounts, making explicit efforts to reduce incompatibilities and redundancies, and setting up networks of contact and interaction, joint projects, and common rules and institutions.

Europeanization as unification makes it necessary to rethink research strategies. In simple models of institutional change, action is often assumed to be a response to a fixed environment. As argued by March (1981), the assumption is convenient, but it is also often inconsistent with institutional realities. Assuming that institutions create their environments in part—that they are part of an ecology of interaction, control, co-operation, and competition, with organized units responding to each other—complicates the model-building task considerably.

One research strategy is to design research projects that aim at specifying which conditions for each process are likely to be most significant for understanding European transformations. Another research strategy—and an even more challenging one—is to focus on how institutional transformation may be understood as an ecology of mutual adaptation. Empirically, the latter research strategy means studying how non-European, European-level, national, and subnational institutions and actors all change at the same time and in association with one another, as they try to find a place within the complex multi-layered and multi-centred system that is the EU.

Key points

- Europeanization can be a political project, which aims to deepen the integration of the European continent.

- This conception of Europeanization leads us to study change as a process of mutual adaptation of co-evolving institutions.

The domestic impact of European-level institutions

The fifth conception of Europeanization focuses on changes to domestic institutions of governance and politics. This is understood as a consequence of the development of European-level institutions, identities, and policies. European-level developments, then, are treated as the explanatory factors, and changes in the domestic systems of governance as the **dependent variable**. The task is one of accounting for variations in European impacts and explaining the varying responses and robustness of domestic institutions against pressures from the European level. The bulk of the empirical literature concerns the effects of the EU on the member states. Most often these studies focus on impacts on domestic policies and behaviour. Yet, there are also studies which deal with changes in domestic structures and practices, in resources, and in the legitimation of collective understandings and codes of meaning. Through what processes and mechanisms, then, do European-level developments penetrate the domestic level to produce change? See Box 21.2.

Two basic frames for analysing Europeanization as an adaptive processes are experiential learning and competitive selection. In *experiential learning*, institutions change on the basis of their experience with and interpretations of likely responses to alternative forms of domestic organization and governance. For example, actors may be indifferent to the domestic institution in question or they may actively promote specific institutional forms; they

may be extremely prescriptive, or allow considerable discretion and local autonomy. In all cases perceived successes are more likely to be repeated and developed, whereas unsuccessful efforts are more likely to be avoided. In this frame, we need to understand which experiences actors are exposed to, how and why they interpret and assess what has happened, and the degree to which they are able to store, retrieve, and act upon such information.

In models of *competitive selection*, environmental imperatives drive the change process. In such models, it is important to understand mechanisms of variation, selection, and retention. Institutions and actors are fixed and their survival and growth rates depend on their performance, their comparative advantages, and how well they 'match' the changing environment. Only the most efficient institutions survive. The others disappear.

What, then, are the factors that influence patterns of adaptation? Which European-level institutions and actors matter? Why do some states and institutions undergo more profound change than others? What determines the responses, adaptability, and robustness of domestic institutions, including their ability to ignore, buffer, redefine, or exploit external European-level pressures?

We should not expect processes of experiential learning and competitive selection always to be perfect, making adaptation automatic, continuous, and precise. Adaptation is often taking place in a world not easily understood or controlled. The rate

Box 21.2 **Case study**

The European Union, the Greek state, and open markets

In an article published by Kevin Featherstone in 1998, entitled ' "Europeanization" and the Centre Periphery: the Case of Greece in the 1990s', the author highlights the impact of EU membership on the Greek political economy. He identifies six basic themes:

- A monetary and fiscal straitjacket: the acceptance of the terms of entry into EMU acts as a major constraint on domestic policy choices—indeed, it largely defines the agenda—and it closely affects the nature of the discourse between the major policy actors.

- A penetrated state administration: EU integration in a wider sense has penetrated deeply into the practices of the state administration itself; has entailed a very substantial financial dependence of the state on EU aid schemes, such that the latter are crucial to all new large-scale infrastructure projects; and has encouraged a form of administrative decentralization.

- Power to the market: the context of EU policy often involves a shift of power away from the Greek state to market forces, both domestic and international, as deregulation opens up a home market based on heavy-handed protection and control.

- Imported policy philosophies: in EU negotiations, successive Greek governments have been generally

placed in a weak bargaining position and have had only a marginal impact on a number of important collective EU agreements: they are thus more the 'import agents' of new measures than the key authors of them.

- Core executive dominance: where influence or discretion is available to the Greek government in connection with EU policies, the nature of EU policy making is such that it tends to advantage small circles of actors, creating a 'democratic deficit' in EU policies at home as well as at the EU level.

- Fragmentation effect: the domestic response to the impact of the EU can be differentiated between groups which are more positive (and 'Europeanized') and those which are more resistant: this is particularly apparent at the elite level, within and beyond the state institutions; EU policies also privilege certain types of actor—notably the technocratic—relative to those upholding the interests of the 'party-state'.

Source: Featherstone 1998: 26–7.

---

of adaptation may be inconsistent with the rate of change in the environment to which the institution is adapting, and there may be no single optimal institutional response to such changes (March 1981). The most standard institutional response to novelty is to find a routine in the existing repertoire of routines that can be used to cope (March and Olsen 1989: 34). Thus, external changes are often interpreted and responded to through existing institutional frameworks, which include existing causal and normative beliefs about legitimate institutions and the appropriate distribution, exercise, and control of power.

Differentiated responses and patterns of adaptation, as well as institutional robustness, can be expected in political settings like the EU. This is because European institution building and policy

making are unevenly developed across institutional spheres and policy areas. This means that the adaptive pressures on states and institutions vary considerably. For instance, Jacobson has suggested some potential impacts that the EU and other supra-, inter-, and transnational institutions, regimes, and organizations might have. These are more likely to have an impact where their legal foundation is more precise; when they are based on (hard) law rather than **soft law**; when the affected parties (constituent units) have been involved in developing the arrangement; the greater the independence of their secretariat; where the secretariat is single headed rather than multiple headed; and the greater the financial autonomy of the institution or regime (Jacobson 2001: 20).

Differentiated responses are also likely as the

(West) European political order is characterized by long, strong, and varied institutional histories, with different trajectories of state and nation building, resources, and capabilities (Rokkan 1999). However, while some domestic actors are proud of their historic achievements and do their best to protect them, others are eager to get beyond 'the burdens of the past'. As a result, while extensive penetration of domestic institutions by the EU is taking place in some spheres, there are also many examples of protected spaces, stubborn resistance, and non-penetration (Wallace 1999: 3). One implication of this is that it becomes important to pay attention to how institutional spheres are affected differently and how they attend to, interpret, and respond to European developments in non-synchronized ways (see Box 21.3).

Despite the existence of a considerable number of empirical studies, there is limited agreement about the degree to which Europeanization (as the development of institutions at the European level) creates Europeanization in the sense of changing domestic institutions. For instance, a veteran student of European integration asks: 'Why is it that we are so ill-equipped to make compelling generalizations about how the European arena, as constituted by the European Union (EU), impacts on the member states in terms of the politics of the countries? . . . Why are our efforts to compare countries' experiences of EU membership so feeble?' (Wallace 1999: 1). On the one hand, European-level arrangements have been seen as strengthening the territorial state and

the state-based order and to create *more* national government rather than *less* (Milward 1992). On the other hand, they have been accused of negatively affecting the substantive problem-solving capacity of the state, and of reducing the role of democratic politics in society (Scharpf 1999). Furthermore, they have been seen as transforming, rather than strengthening or weakening, the territorial state or the state system (Kohler-Koch and Eising 1999).

On the basis of the empirical evidence, there has been a significant and persistent shift of domestic attention, resources, and personnel to European-level institutions and their decision-making cycles. There also seems to be some convergence in patterns of attention, behaviour, and policy. Yet, a main finding (although with many nuances) is that there has been no revolutionary change in any of the national systems and certainly no significant convergence towards a common institutional model, homogenizing the domestic structures of the European states. In other words, no new harmonized or unified model of dealing with Union matters has emerged. The conclusion must be that EU arrangements are compatible with the maintenance of distinct national institutional arrangements and may even reconfirm and restore established national structures and practices. In sum, structural diversity persists among the core domestic structures of governance, despite increasing contact and competition between national models. Established national patterns are resistant but also flexible enough to cope with changes at the European level.

Box 21.3 **Case study**
Political contention in a Europeanizing polity

Doug Imig and Sidney Tarrow's work on political contention has examined the way in which the EU presents new opportunities and constraints for domestic social actors. Actors not only are able to engage in domestic forms of contentious action (protest), but can be linked in cross-border actions with others like themselves from across Europe. However, they argue that there remain substantial barriers to this kind of transnational action. Most individuals continue to have difficulty seeing the connection between their own grievances and the EU, and there are (transaction) costs involved in organizing collective action across national boundaries. Most citizens therefore tend to use 'tried and true routines of collective action' at national level.

Source: Imig and Tarrow 2001.

While European developments have been presented as an important reason for administrative reforms (Raadschelders and Toonen 1992: 16), and as creating a need for improved domestic co-ordination (Kassim 2000: 236), governments and administrative systems have adapted differently to European pressures on their own terms. That is, adaptation has reflected institutional resources and traditions, the pre-existing balance of domestic institutional structures, and also 'the broader matrices of values which define the nature of appropriate political forms in the case of each national polity' (Harmsen 1999: 81). Likewise, a study of ten smaller West European states—both member and non-member states—concluded that adaptations to the EU were influenced by existing institutional arrangements and traditions (Hanf and Soetendorp 1998).

Europeanization as domestic impacts is not limited to structural and policy changes, however. European values and policy paradigms are also to some (varying) degree internalized at the domestic level, shaping discourses and identities (Checkel 2001b). For example, the Europeanization of foreign policy has produced shared norms and rules that are gradually accumulated (Sjursen 2001: 199–200). Likewise, common concepts of appropriate fiscal behaviour, taxing, and 'sound' money and finance have developed at the elite level (Radaelli 1997).

Simultaneously, among ordinary citizens, national identities are reaffirmed. There has been a revival in nationalism and ethnic-based identities that may represent a major source of potential resistance to Europeanization (Schlesinger 1993). While there are relatively few studies of how Europeanization contributes to moulding public opinion and changing the role and significance of civil society in such processes (Venturelli 1993), new boundaries of solidarity have been drawn within and among organized interests (Dølvik 1997b). Even churches and spiritual associations have come under pressure to adapt their structures and state-church relations to the changing European context. They have been asked to 'help to interpret and give meaning to the process of European unification' and their responses have been affected by different privileges and national arrangements

(Jansen 2000: 103, 105). Likewise, there have been a limited number of studies of the adaptation of domestic politics, including changes in political cleavages, voting behaviour, elections, political parties, and party systems. The conclusions of such studies seem to support rather than contradict studies of governmental and administrative systems (see, for example, Goetz and Hix 2001).

In sum, European-level developments do not dictate specific forms of institutional adaptation but leave considerable discretion to domestic actors and institutions. There are significant impacts, yet the actual ability of the European level to penetrate domestic institutions is not perfect, universal, or constant. Adaptation reflects variations in European pressure as well as domestic motivations and abilities to adapt. European signals are interpreted and modified through domestic traditions, institutions, identities, and resources in ways that limit the degree of convergence and homogenization.

As students of European dynamics are beginning to understand better the conditions for interactions between European and domestic factors, more nuance in the conclusions can be expected. So far, however, institutional learning across national borders is limited (Kassim 2000: 242). Moreover, Goetz concludes that, as it stands, this particular literature on Europeanization 'casts some doubt over the explanatory power of "European integration" as major force driving domestic executive change' (Goetz 2001: 220). He finds no straightforward connection between adaptive pressure and adaptive reactions and he prescribes caution in treating European integration as a major independent source of change. Rather, European-level changes are just one among several drivers of domestic change (Goetz 2001: 214–15, 227).

By way of an example, it is clear that developments favouring independent central banks (Cowles and Risse 2001: 232–3) or a shared concept of 'appropriate fiscal behavior' (Sbragia 2001: 80) are not solely European phenomena. Transnational professionals such as economists spread predominant ideas globally and the high intensity of competitive selection in the telecommunications sector is to a considerable extent a result of strong global pressure (Schneider 2001: 78). Even changes in educational policy have been understood in terms of (economic) factors outside the range of the EU (Beukel 2001: 139). Thus, while there have been interesting attempts to separate the effects of Europeanization from those of globalization (Verdier and Breen 2001), a major challenge, that of tracing changes at the domestic level back to European-level institutions, policies, or events, remains. In practice it proved to be difficult to isolate European effects (Radaelli 1997: 572; 2000; Bulmer and Burch 2001: 76) and to disentangle the impact of European arrangements from global, national, and subnational sources of change.

Key points

- A fifth understanding of Europeanization involves the domestic impact of European-level institutions.

- It is difficult to generalize about the domestic impact of European-level institutions. While it is generally agreed that EU institutions change domestic politics, the ways in which they are changed vary across nations, institutions, and policy areas. Both learning and competitive selection are less than perfect as adaptive

Conclusion

This chapter began by asking two questions: first, 'What is Europeanization?' and second, 'What are the mechanisms of change that drive Europeanization?' It addressed these questions by identifying five definitions of Europeanization. The first referred to the territorial expansion of the EU's borders (enlargement); the second to a process of European-level institutionalization. The third definition referred to the export of European institutions beyond Europe; while the fourth concerned the integration process as a political project. Finally, the fifth definition of Europeanization referred to the domestic impact of European-level institutions. However, while conceptual clarity is of great importance (Radaelli 2000), the challenge here is not primarily one of inventing definitions. The challenge, rather, is to model the dynamics of change in

ways that make the simplifying assumptions behind various definitions explicit. The chapter suggests, therefore, that the way ahead in this respect lies in *integrating* perspectives on institutional dynamics, rather than choosing among them. In other words, there is no single **grand theory** of 'Europeanization' to help us understand how institutions co-evolve through processes of mutual adaptation. Nor is there a single set of simplifying assumptions about change, institutions, and actors that will capture the complexity of European transformations. Yet, there does exist a limited repertoire of **middle-range** models of institutional change that may he helpful for capturing European dynamics. Exploring the characteristics of each model is a beginning. Understanding their interaction is a much more difficult, long-term challenge.

QUESTIONS

1 What is Europeanization?

2 Is Europeanization a useful concept in explaining the transformation of the European polity?

3 In what ways is Europeanization related to the enlargement of the EU? Answer with reference EITHER to the impact of the EU on economic and political reform in Central and Eastern Europe OR with reference to the idea of Europeanization as a process which extends the territorial reach of 'Europe'.

4   How relevant is it to talk of Europeanization as involving the spread of European rules and norms beyond Europe?

5   Is Europeanization a political project?

6   Can Europeanization be a synonym for the European integration process?

7   How has the EU impacted upon national administrations in the EU's member states?

8   What effect has the EU had on domestic policy? Answer with reference to EITHER foreign policy or EMU.

GUIDE TO FURTHER READING

Cowles, M. G., Caporaso, J. A., and Risse, T. (eds), *Transforming Europe: Europeanization and Domestic Change* (Ithaca, NY: Cornell University Press, 2001). An edited book on Europeanization which covers both general issues and more specific case studies concerning the impact of the EU on domestic politics.

Dyson, K., 'EMU as Europeanization: Convergence, diversity and contingency', *Journal of Common Market Studies*, vol. 38, no. 4 (2000): 645–66. An article which looks empirically at EMU as a process of Europeanization.

Goetz, K. H., and Hix, S. (eds), *Europeanized Politics. European Integration and National Political Systems* (London: Frank Cass, 2001). An edited book which brings together a number of papers on Europeanization arising out of a workshop on the topic. It covers a range of both theoretical and empirical issues.

Page, E. C., and Wouters, L., 'The Europeanization of national bureaucracies?', in J. Pierre (ed.), *Bureaucracy in the Modern State* (Aldershot: Edward Elgar, 1995). A chapter which points to the way in which national civil services have changed as a consequence of Europeanization.

Radaelli, C. M., 'Whither Europeanization? Concept Stretching and Substantive Change', **http://eiop.or.at/eiop/texte/2000-008.htm** . This paper looks at Europeanization from a theoretical perspective, and seeks to review the existing literature on this topic.

WEB LINKS

www.arena.uio.no Website of ARENA (Advanced Research on the Europeanization of the Nation State). Includes many very relevant research papers on the subject of Europeanization.

www.qub.ac.uk/ies/ The Institute for European Studies at The Queen's University, Belfast has an online paper series on Europeanization.

ENDNOTE

1. This chapter draws on Olsen (2002), an article published in the *Journal of Common Market Studies*, which expands on the arguments made in this chapter. Warm thanks to Ulf I. Sverdrup for his co-operation during the first part of this project and to Michelle Cini. I am also thankful for constructive comments from Svein S. Andersen, Peggy S. Brønn, Simon Bulmer, James Caporaso, Jeffrey T. Checkel, Dag Harald Claes, Jon Erik Dølvik, Morten Egeberg, Beate Kohler-Koch, Ragnar Lie, James G. March, Claudio Radaelli, Helene Sjursen, Trygve Ugland, Helen Wallace, and Wolfgang Wessels.

22 Implementation

Michelle Cini

READER'S GUIDE

This chapter focuses attention on the **implementation** stage of the European policy process, that is, on policy implementation. In this chapter policy implementation refers to the 'putting into effect' of European laws and policies. First, three different forms of policy implementation are identified. The first and most common is **indirect implementation**. This is where national governments assume all or most of the responsibility for putting European Union policy into effect. The second form of policy implementation is **direct implementation**. In this case, responsibility for European policy implementation rests with the European Commission. This is a somewhat rarer phenomenon. Finally, the chapter also touches on European-level rule making—a less conventional use of the term 'policy implementation'. In this context, implementation refers to the Commission's **executive** role in 'filling in the gaps' of European legislation which has already been agreed by the EU Council and (usually) the European Parliament. For various reasons, however, **compliance** with European law remains incomplete, and it has been argued that the EU, as a consequence, suffers from an 'implementation deficit', a deficit that may even rival that of the **democratic deficit** in its importance for the **legitimacy** of the EU.

Introduction

Policy implementation refers to the putting into effect of legislation, decisions, or policies formulated and agreed by the EU's policy-making institutions—the Commission, Parliament, and Council. From this perspective, one might imagine policy implementation as a discrete stage in the policy process, which occurs after European legislation has been approved. While this is certainly one way of understanding what implementation is all about, it is now more common to see policy implementation as an integral part of the European policy-making process. Implicit in this latter conceptualization is the idea that, in practice, policy may be *made* at the implementation stage as well as during the formal legislative process.

For a long time, the study of policy implementation was an aspect of European integration that political scientists largely ignored. This situation has been changing, however, and for good reason. Since the 1970s, implementation studies have been able to shed a great deal of light on political systems: the potential for such studies to assist in explaining and, indeed, improving the way in which EU does business has become clear. The importance of implementation is beyond doubt. 'The capacity to implement policy is a central defining feature of any political system, and if in the future the EU is to be a functioning government then implementation becomes a crucial question' (Peters 2000: 203). The success of any policy clearly depends very much upon its implementation. Thus implementation not only is important, but may be crucial for the effectiveness of EU policy and, for perceptions of EU effectiveness more generally. And this is likely to make an important contribution to the overall **legitimacy** of the EU.

The chapter begins by identifying three different conceptions of implementation. The first is indirect implementation. This form of implementation rests on the co-operation of the European institutions and actors within the member states: it is what most commentators mean when they talk of the implementation of European law and policy. The second conception is less common, but still important. This is direct implementation. Direct implementation takes place in the small number of cases where the European Commission alone is responsible for implementing European law. Finally, in a much looser understanding of implementation, the chapter also focuses on the Commission's executive role as a rule maker. After clarifying the distinction between these three types of implementation, the chapter questions how theories of implementation might shed light on the EU's implementation process. Some of these theories account for what is identified in the EU as an 'implementation deficit', the subject of the following section. Finally, the chapter tries to account for the increased interest in European policy implementation over the course of the 1990s. Although implementation in the second and third pillars is also very important, this chapter's emphasis is largely on the first, EC, pillar.

Three conceptions of implementation

In this chapter, three conceptions of policy implementation are identified. The first is **indirect implementation**, the second **direct implementation**, and the third, **executive rule making**. The first two of these are the more conventional understandings of the term implementation. In each, implementation implies a process of policy management, whether by the Commission or by national/local authorities and agencies. In the third case, implementation refers to the agreement of implementing rules by the Commission, rules that are necessary for putting into operation legislation

agreed by the EU Council and (usually) the European Parliament (EP).

Indirect implementation

It is almost conventional wisdom that while European legislation is made by the European institutions, it is not implemented at European level. Rather, national and subnational governments, administrations, and their agencies, whether alone or in co-operation with the European Commission, are responsible for this aspect of the EU policy process. Thus, although the European Commission oversees the enforcement of EU law, its implementation functions are, in all but exceptional cases, restricted to monitoring, co-ordination, laying down ground-rules, carrying out investigations, and in certain cases giving rulings (Nugent 1999: 123). 'Street-level' implementation is, by contrast, dealt with at national level or below—that is, in domestic political arenas. Where policies are implemented through (multi-annual) programmes, the language used may be that of 'programme management' rather than policy implementation, but in practice it amounts to much the same thing (Levy 2000) (see Box 22.1).

This division of responsibilities between the EU and its member states was intentional. It was felt by those drafting the original treaties in the 1950s that it would be both inappropriate and, indeed, unworkable for the Community to involve itself in all aspects of the policy process. Thus, even though the Commission has an important role in the implementation process in several respects (see Chapter 9), its main function is to ensure that member state actors do not pursue their own agendas at the expense of a more generally defined *European* interest.

Moreover, handing over greater responsibility for policy implementation to the European institutions would be inappropriate, given that the European integration process was expected to be as much about co-operation between levels of government, as it was about top-down control. On a more practical note, such a step might also be unworkable, since the EU would not have the resources to do the job effectively. This latter point is particularly salient for policies that have budgetary implications, such as regional policy or research policy, where national and subnational governments are expected to foot much of the bill. In such cases, the European Commission 'is relieved of many "conventional" administrative duties and in many policy areas does

---

Box 22.1 **Core ideas**
Three forms of project management

Drawing on the work of Strasser (1992), Levy (2000*a*) identifies three ways in which European project management is organized within the EU.

Direct management

In the case of direct management, all parts of the budget are managed solely by the Commission. In the field of research policy, the Commission is responsible for operational management in only limited areas, such as the Joint Research Centre at Ispra, Italy, which is under direct Commission control

Decentralized management

In decentralized management, implementation is delegated to national or local agencies. Supervision is carried out through regulations or directives specific to the programme area or functions concerned. Implementing agencies have discretion over how to implement the objectives set out in the legislation. The Commission operates at a supervisory level only. This sort of approach occurs in the collection of EU revenues (where there are directives); and in the CAP (regulations). Outside the EU,

development aid programmes are also managed in this way.

Shared management

In cases of shared management, programmes are jointly funded by the EU and by others (particularly national governments, but also universities). Shared management operates in a similar way to decentralized management. The Structural Funds are managed in this way (1988/1993), with the Commission supporting between 25 and 75 per cent of the programme. The regulatory framework is less detailed and prescriptive than for the CAP, and emphasis is placed on delegation to member state agencies, regulatory monitoring, and review and evaluation by both the Commission and the partner agencies. Generally, programme/project management is handled by a programme management committee, locally, with a nominated Commission official to link local implementation to Brussels.

not have to concern itself unduly with complex and detailed questions of service provision' (Peters 2000: 195).

Yet, attempting to generalize about indirect implementation is something of a challenge. Just as there is no one policy style within the EU (Mazey and Richardson 1993), neither is there only one model of implementation. As a consequence, implementation studies tend to focus on policy case studies. Studies of this sort seek to explain how specific policies are implemented. There is generally agreement that European policy implementation takes place in a 'multi-level system' (Levy 2000: 5). And much of the debate about indirect policy implementation, as we shall see below, acknowledges that this can be problematic when it comes to putting European policies into effect.

To understand how indirect implementation operates, it is first necessary to explain the policy instruments that the EU has at its disposal, as these have a bearing on the issue. There are three such types of legal instrument: decisions, regulations, and directives. *Decisions* are addressed to particular individual legal actors, such as companies or a state or a group of states. They are not generally applicable across the Union. By contrast, *regulations* are **directly effective** under Article 249 (formerly Article 189) of the Treaty on European Union, and apply to all member states (see Chapter 12: 183). Regulations tend to include a lot of detail. They spell out not only the end goal of the legislation, but also the means by which those goals must be achieved, and thus leave little room for manoeuvre by national and subnational bodies charged with their implementation. Importantly for our purposes, 'Regulations do not have to be incorporated into national law through national legal instruments, but it is still usually the responsibility of national administrative authorities to ensure that they are applied' (George and Bache 2001: 226). A third legal instrument, the *directive*, is now the most common policy tool at the EU's disposal. Directives allow national and subnational governments a substantial degree of flexibility when it comes to implementing European legislation. They usually state a time limit for implementation and a very specific goal to be reached, but give member states discretion over the procedures and instruments that are to be used in achieving that

end. Thus, while directives respond to the reality of an EU characterized by institutional and cultural diversity, they also add complexity to an already challenging implementation process, providing, for example, 'a window of opportunity for national governments to "erode" the original objectives of EU policies' (Dimitrakopoulos and Richardson 2001: 337).

The indirect implementation of European directives is really a two-step process. The first step is largely legal (and is often referred to as the legal or formal implementation stage), whereas the second involves a more administrative or practical process. The first step necessitates the **incorporation** or **transposition** of the European directive into national legislation. In other words, in order to be put into effect on the ground, a directive usually has first to be integrated into the body of domestic law. This normally involves the enactment or revision of national legal instruments, ultimately leading to a situation where EU law has the same status as national acts. As with any national law-making process, this process takes time. Transposition is not always straightforward. It may involve, for example, a complex reworking of existing national legislation, such as the repeal of domestic laws where they clash with new European legislation (as EU law takes precedence over national law if there is such a clash). Moreover, transposition may mean the involvement of national parliaments in the approval of these changes, parliaments that had little if any input into the drafting of the legislation in the first place and which may oppose the legislation or wish to embarrass the government supporting it.

Ultimately it is the national government that must take responsibility for implementation. After all, the Treaty is clear when it states that 'Member States shall take all appropriate measures . . . to ensure fulfilment of the obligations arising out of this Treaty or resulting from action taken by institutions of the Community' (Article 10, EC Treaty). If at all possible, governments try to exclude parliamentary involvement (Dimitrakopoulos and Richardson 2001: 342), but this too may defer problems to a later date. Indeed, 'The Commission is particularly wary of transposition by administrative circulars in Member States, which may be altered at will, rather than by primary or secondary legislation' (Butt Philip 2000: 271).

Practical implementation is 'ground' or 'street-level' implementation, involving the direct application of the legislation (rather than simply its translation into domestic law). This is what most people understand by the word 'implementation', and it is the second step in the indirect implementation process. In most cases, national governments are not directly responsible for this type of implementation, but delegate this function to subnational authorities and other executive agencies, such as those dealing with health and safety, environmental regulation, and customs. Good co-ordination between government departments and implementing authorities and agencies is essential at this stage. See Figure 22.1 for an illustration of how directives and regulations affect implementation.

Direct implementation

Although the norm may be for implementation responsibilities to be shared between the Commission and member states, or to lie in the hands of the national governments alone, there are a small number of policies for which the Commission's role is much more substantial. These tend to be regulatory policies identified as 'common policies'. They includes the administration of the EU's humanitarian aid programme, the common fisheries policy, and assistance to the states of Central and Eastern Europe.

But perhaps the most high profile of all the policies directly implemented by the Commission is the EU's competition regime. Under the broad label of competition policy fall the EU's policies on restrictive practices, monopolies, and mergers, as well as its control of nationally granted state aid (subsidy policy). Excluding the latter, competition policy has a direct impact on the conduct of firms within the EU, and indeed outside it. This is because one of the primary aims of EU competition policy is to prevent firms from constructing new barriers to trade (by dividing up markets or fixing prices, for example), in response to the removal of governmental or regulatory barriers as a consequence of single market legislation.

Within the EU's competition regime, direct implementation means that, with the relevant treaty provisions and broad-ranging regulations agreed by national governments in the Council, the Commission is subsequently left to take formal decisions that have a direct impact on what firms can or cannot do. An example of this is in merger policy, where a Commission decision could prevent a large merger from taking place. This is an implementing decision, as it implements the rules set out by the Council. Yet it is also a decision whose political significance will not go unnoticed. Clearly, through

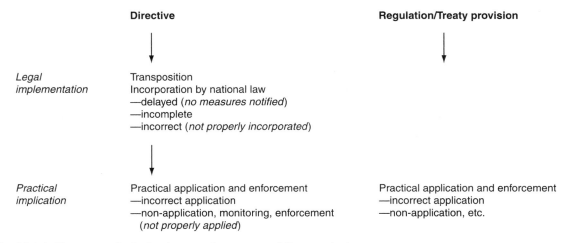

Fig. 22.1 Infringements in the implementation process of Community law
Source: Börzel 2001: 5.

the cumulative effects of decisions taken, and, moreover, as a consequence of the judgments of the European Court where decisions are appealed against, the EU's policy on competition is likely to evolve—and without the input of either national governments or the EP. It is for this reason that direct implementation is of great political importance. But it must also be recognized that it creates an enormous workload for the Commission. For that reason, the Commission has been keen, in recent years, to offload some of its enforcement responsibilities in competition matters to national competition agencies and to domestic courts, handing back aspects of its implementation role to the member states, while retaining overall control of the policy direction (see Cini and McGowan 1997).

Rule making and comitology

To some, rule making and implementation are entirely separate processes. However, it is possible to see this executive function of the Commission as a form of implementation. To explain why this is the case, it is necessary to summarize this dimension of the Commission's work. Rule making refers to the taking of administrative decisions and regulations, which enable European legislation to be put into operation. In other words, these rules fill in the incomplete gaps in the legislation that has already been approved by the EU Council and (usually) the EP. A distinction that is made between policy law and administrative law is helpful in explaining this function. Thus, while the EP and the Council make policy law, the Commission later fills in the gaps in that law via administrative law, that is, via executive rule making.

Rule making at European level has arisen as a consequence of the **delegation** of certain powers from the EU's legislative bodies, the Council and Parliament, to the Commission, so as to allow the latter to take legally binding 'technical' or 'administrative' decisions. While the Council was originally considered the primary executive body for the EC, the heavy workload it faced led it to share that function with the European Commission. However, the Council (or rather the member governments)

were keen not to lose control over this aspect of policy making. As a result, the Council has established committees which, though usually chaired by the Commission, are composed of national representatives whose job it is to vet administrative laws/rules proposed by the Commission. These are particularly prevalent in the field of agricultural policy. The system as a whole came to be known as **comitology**. There are three types of comitology committee: advisory committees, which make recommendations to the Commission; management committees, which allow the Commission to decide, unless the committee opposes the measures on the basis of a qualified majority of its members; and regulatory committees, which allow the Commission to decide, but only if the Council approves the measure by a qualified majority. These committees had proliferated by the mid-1980s in many areas of policy besides agriculture. And even after attempts to codify them at the end of the 1980s, decisions over which committee and procedure should be used, the secrecy of their operation, and the lack of involvement by the EP, remain contentious issues (see Hix 1999: 41–5).

In a sense, Commission rule making and comitology prove the point implied in the Introduction to this chapter—that there is no clear-cut dividing line between policy making and policy implementation. In other words, one way of understanding rule making is to see it as both a legislative and an implementing function simultaneously performed by the Commission and the comitology committees. It is legislation in the sense that law is being made, but implementation in that the function of that legislation is to implement policy law. Of course, implementation in this sense is very different from implementation in the conventional sense of the word. Yet, although the process is far removed from the street-level actors who put policies into effect in a practical way, it is possible to argue that it is implementation all the same.

Key points

- There are three conceptions of European policy implementation: indirect implementation; direct implementation; and executive rule making by the Commission.

- Indirect implementation is the responsibility of national governments and their agents, though it is sometimes shared with the European Commission. It can be divided into two stages: legal and practical implementation.

- Direct implementation is, with some exceptions, the sole responsibility of the European Commission.

- Executive rule making by the Commission involves filling in the gaps in EU legislation.

Theories of implementation

Since the 1970s, theories of implementation have sought to conceptualize the way in which law and policy are put into effect. But to what extent are theories of implementation useful in explaining the European case? To answer that question, it is helpful to explain the distinction between 'top-down' and 'bottom-up' perspectives on policy implementation. In the 'top-down' perspective, the emphasis is placed on the control that is wielded by the centre—in this case the European Commission and the European Court of Justice (ECJ). The general idea behind this approach is that law should drive policy—in other words, that implementation should be guided by the intentions of those who drafted the legislation—though the emphasis is often placed not only on 'control', but also on '**accountability**', and the role that leaders play within the policy process.

The seminal study associated with this approach is Pressman and Wildavsky's work on an economic development programme adopted in Washington, DC and implemented in Oakland, California (Pressman and Wildavsky 1984). Their conclusions on the project reflected a rather pessimistic view of implementation. The authors explained the failures of implementation in this case in terms of the number of 'clearance and decision points' through which the programme had to pass before being translated into action. In other words, Pressman and Wildavsky identified the large number of separate decisions that were necessary for the policy to be put into effect, and the wide range of actors involved in that process, as huge hurdles to be overcome if the policy was to be implemented in the way the drafters

had intended. They argued that, as a consequence of these multiple actors and decisions, success in implementing policy was likely to be very difficult from the outset. Applied to the EU case, this approach is associated with arguments that the member states, and actors within them, are to blame for implementation failures; or rather that the various levels of government and the many actors involved in EU policy explain why implementation in the EU is particularly challenging.

In the second approach, which adopts the more fashionable 'bottom-up' perspective, implementation is not so much a question of control, as one of negotiation and bargaining between those drafting the legislation and those putting it into effect on the ground. The assumption in this second case is that lower-level actors, that is, those that are responsible for implementing policy on the ground, are as important as those who originally drafted the law. Thus, it is necessary to identify the way in which 'street-level' officials (Lipsky 1980: 29) and networks of actors cumulatively take decisions that shape policy outcomes in an EU context. This approach is associated with studies that argue that it is not that implementation failures within the EU are caused by problems within the member states, but that when policies are unsuccessful the EU institutions themselves must take much of the blame for failing to negotiate effectively. Thus, bottom-up studies show that policies are 'ineffective not because they are poorly implemented but because they are poorly conceived' (Jordan 1999: 72). Both top-down and bottom-up perspectives are mirrored in accounts of the EU's implementation deficit.

Key points

- There are two main theoretical/conceptual approaches to the study of implementation.
- The top-down approach to policy implementation emphasizes control, accountability, and leadership.
- The bottom-up approach to policy

implementation stresses negotiation and the establishment of networks.

- While top-down approaches focus on the implementation problems faced by member states and their agents, bottom-up approaches to implementation highlight the problems within the EU institutions at the policy-making stage.

The implementation deficit: Causes and constraints

Since the 1980s, frequent reference has been made to the EU's **implementation deficit**. An implementation deficit is said to arise as a consequence of problems in translating a 'stated policy' into an 'operational policy' (Peters 2000: 192). It might also be defined as the gap between policy goals and policy outcomes (Jordan 1999: 69), or more specifically as the 'shortfall between the goals embodied in particular directives and their practical effects in member states' (Jordan 1999: 72). To repeat a point made early in this chapter, policy implementation, or the lack of it, is important, as the success of EU policy rests with its impact on the ground; and policy success is a potent source of **legitimacy** for the EU. Moreover, non-implementation will undermine the single market's **level playing-field** principle, if it means that policies are put into effect in different ways in different parts of the Union. This would lead to a situation in which unfair competitive advantages are gained by non-implementing states at the expense of those complying with EU law. See Box 22.2.

However, the implementation deficit is not merely a consequence of non-implementation. An even more pervasive challenge to the effectiveness of EU policy comes from what might be called incomplete or partial implementation. This is where governments and the agencies to which they delegate implementing powers diverge from the letter or the principle of the law. In transposing European legislation into domestic law, provisions may be omitted or reworded, and the intentions of

the drafters changed. For example, in the mid-1990s, the Commission reported that there were serious problems with the implementation of directives on rights of residence for people who were not in employment (students, retired people), arising out of late or incorrect implementation. The Commission tried to pursue these cases by initiating infringement proceedings against the states concerned. However, it was also recognized that besides the need to ensure strict compliance with Community law, the problem might also be solved through a consolidation and rationalization of the existing legislation, so that the rules were improved and simplified, enabling citizens to understand them more easily.

But, as we have seen above, this is a by no means unusual characteristic of implementation. Why then should we be surprised to find an implementation deficit? To address this question, it is necessary to reflect further on the distinction made in the section above between top-down and bottom-up perspectives on implementation. Clearly, some of the fundamental assumptions about the EU's implementation deficit arise out of what is now considered a rather old-fashioned view of implementation: that it is all about control by policy makers. Identifying where the barriers to effective implementation lie, from this perspective, means focusing on what goes on within the EU's member states. Yet, there is an alternative conceptualization of the implementation deficit, one that seeks to identify the weaknesses in the EU's own policy process. This second approach,

Box 22.2 **Case study**

Non-implementation: Press releases

A Press release from the European Commission's Northern Ireland Office in March 2002, included the following short reports:

Air quality and emissions: Commission moves against the United Kingdom over non-implementation of EU laws

The European Commission has decided to take legal action against several Member States for failing to implement, or inadequately implement [sic.], EU laws on air quality and air emissions. These Member States have been referred to the European Court of Justice for failing to implement Directives into national law and notify the Commission of implementation. France, Germany, the United Kingdom, Italy and Spain in relation to a Directive on consumer access to full economy and CO2 emissions data; Italy and the United Kingdom concerning an amendment to the Fuel Standards Directive. The United Kingdom has received a Reasoned Opinion (second written warning) for

failing to adopt the necessary legislation to transpose the Volatile Organic Compounds (VOC) Directive.

Radiation: The Commission takes the United Kingdom to Court for non-transposition of EU laws

The European Commission has decided to take several EU countries, including the United Kingdom, to the European Court under the Euratom (European Atomic Energy Community) Treaty. This constitutes failure to adopt and communicate to the Commission transposing measures for Council Directives on Basic Safety Standards and on Medical Exposures, both of which aim to provide protection from ionising radiation. The Commission has also decided to refer Ireland to the Court for non-transposition of the Directive on Medical Exposures.

Source: EU Weekly, published by The European Commission Representation in the United Kingdom (Belfast: Northern Ireland Press Office, 20 March 2002).

Box 22.3 **Core ideas**

Implementation failure in European environment policy

Of all EU policy areas, it seems that environment policy implementation is best analysed by the academic litera-ture. There is a wealth of studies on this topic. Many of these focus on the failure of implementation up until the 1980s. Jordan (1999: 74) identifies four reasons for what he calls a 'conspiracy of silence':

1   Political symbolism: environmental policy was judged on the amount of legislation produced rather than on its effectiveness.

2   The extent of European integration: directives were

originally considered as a declaration of intent (rather than a hard obligation).

3   Bureaucratic politics: the Commission was concerned early on to enhance its own position and leave implementation to member states. DG XI was weak—there was little scrutiny of environmental proposals.

4   Institutional power relations: the Commission was responsible for enforcement, but the member states were responsible for implementation. This put the Commission in a weak position.

by contrast, draws on bottom-up understand-ings of implementation as part of a negotiated policy process. In the rest of this section, we focus on these two different approaches in order to

uncover some of the barriers to the effective imple-mentation of European policy. Box 22.3 looks at implementation faiture in one EU policy case—the environment.

The causes of the implementation deficit: A top-down perspective

From a top-down perspective, responsibility for implementation failures lie unequivocally at the feet of the member states. After all, as national governments and administrations are responsible for the implementation of European law and policy, who else is there to blame? But this does not necessarily mean that implementation problems arise intentionally. It is possible to identify four sets of reasons that account for the failure of implementation always to meet the expectations of policy makers—and only one of these implies an intention to do so on the part of those doing the implementing.

First, the EU's implementation deficit may be an inherent consequence of the structure or organization of the EU. Within the EU, responsibility for implementation is shared both vertically (Commission and Court, governments and bureaucracies, regional and local authorities and autonomous agencies), and horizontally (across the 15 member states). Therefore, the success of implementation rests with the potential for co-operation and co-ordination within and across the Union. As Peters has said, 'the multi-tiered and loosely coupled system is hardly an enviable implementation structure for Government attempting to impose its policies and its will over a territory' (Peters 2000: 191). While the potential difficulties might appear on the surface to be more problematic for federal states than for unitary states where authority is centralized, trends towards the decentralization of public policy since the 1980s have made it harder for all states to 'control' street-level implementation. This is because much largers numbers of actors tend to be involved in policy implementation nowadays. If this is a problem for national governments, it is an even greater problem for the Commission. Metcalfe (1992) is aware of this when he argues that the Commission increasingly needs to act as a manager of networks when it oversees the implementation process at national level.

A second set of factors similarly focuses on structural and institutional characteristics within the EU, but is more specific to individual member states.

Thus, there may be practical reasons why some states find it difficult to implement European legislation. With the EU intentionally choosing to use regulatory instruments (legislation) to pursue policy ends, this means that the costs of legislating are shifted on to national and local authorities, or indeed on to private actors, at the implementation stage. Inadequate financial resources may be a major barrier to effective implementation, but so too are other resource-related problems, such as the lack of adequately trained staff or inadequate infrastructure. This problem was recognized by the EU in the Cohesion Fund, which provides monies for the poorest of the EU's members, to allow them to resolve problems of this kind.

Third, it is possible to identify a discrete category of cultural factors that have been identified as a source of poor implementation at national and sub-national level. Cultural factors may be important in shaping the way in which European legislation is received at national level. For example, common law cultures, which rest on custom and precedence (representing the law of the courts based on past decisions), and Napoleonic cultures, which are 'all-embracing, systematic and coherent' (Stevens 2001: 33) and based on codes and statutes (written law), are likely to react to European legislation in different ways from the more legalistic cultures of Germany and Austria (Peters 2000: 200). Moreover, political, as well as legal, cultures are likely to be important. Whereas some states are imbued with a culture of compliance others have cultures in which law breaking is much less of a taboo. It should be noted, however, that distinctions of this sort can be overstated, and may rely more on stereotype than on hard evidence. As George and Bache (2001: 227) point out, countries that have traditionally had a reputation as being more reluctant Europeans, such as the UK and Denmark, tend to have less of an implementation deficit than those that have traditionally been more supportive of European integration. And 'some of the member states that are most ready to sign up to integrative measures are the least willing to implement' (George and Bache 2001: 227). However, as implementation rates vary across policy areas, it is not always easy to make generalizations country-by-country. And as Börzel (2000) has pointed out, claims that the implementation deficit is a particularly Southern European problem are not sustainable on the basis of hard evidence.

Finally, however, it would be naive to claim that implementation failures arise only by accident, as a consequence of institutional and cultural factors. Clearly, there are more intentional barriers to implementation. These take a number of different forms and occur for different reasons. For example, one reason why implementation failures arise is as a consequence of fraud (see Box 22.4). Another reason is that national or local elites may wish to sabotage the legislation for some reason (Peters 2000: 193), and this they may do in a number of ways, such as through an excessive attention to procedure, which ends up wrecking the original intentional of the legislation. In controlling the speed or extent of implementation, governments and their officials are able to control the impact of European regulation in a way that they cannot do at the policy formulation stage (Jordan 1999: 71). As Dimitrakopoulos and Richardson (2001: 337) have put it, 'The implementation process presents opportunities to re-fight battles lost in the policy formulation stage'. To justify such behaviour—should they need any justification—national governments may claim that they have more legitimacy than the Commission and that they therefore have the right not to implement legislation should they so desire.

However, more often than not, governments prefer to challenge accusations of non-implementation.

After all, governments rarely like to be found to be breaking laws to which they have signed up—unless there is substantial public support for doing so. An absence of public support or parliamentary approval may cause problems for governments, particularly if opposition to a particular policy or piece of legislation is picked up by the national or local media. It is important to remember, however, that poor implementation may arise out of unresolved differences of opinion over substance, and that procedural factors are often only part of the story. However, at a societal level, resistance to implementation is likely to arise from issues such as the costs involved, or the impact on local employment. The influence of economic interests and the activism and organization of non-governmental actors, and the extent to which they are able to mobilize opposition to European legislation, will clearly affect the ease with which that legislation is implemented (see Box 22.5).

Causes of and constraints on the implementation deficit: A bottom-up perspective

While the EU's institutions have had substantial successes in getting legislation agreed at European level, their involvement in implementation is much less impressive. As Jordan says, 'when it comes to putting the *acquis communautaire* into effect at

---

Box 22.4 **Case study**
Fraud in the European Union

The EU's annual budget is £98.6 bn. (2002). It has been estimated that fraud accounts for between 5 and 10 per cent of the budget. Most of this occurs within the member states, and it is the national governments' responsibility to investigate and prosecute those involved. The link between fraud and implementation may not be intuitive, but, as this chapter recounts, the fact that the actors and institutions implementing the policy have been divorced from the actors and institutions making the policy has made it hard for the Commission to perform

its enforcement function (that of 'legal watchdog'). Accusations that managerial weaknesses are partly to blame are convincing. In short, the implementation deficit, and the sources of it, create a policy environment which provides incentives to defraud. This is particularly the case in the Common Agricultural Policy (CAP), which is the source of a great deal of fraudulent activity according to recent reports published by the European Court of Auditors.

Box 22.5 **Case study**
The ban on UK beef exports

A ban on the export of beef from the UK to other EU member states was imposed in 1994 to protect animals from the spread of BSE (Bovine Spongiform Encephalopathy). On 16 March 1998, a Commission decision set out arrangements for the lifting of this emergency measure, and the ban was formally removed on 1 August 1999 (once again by a decision of the Commission on the basis of advice from the 'Scientific Steering Committee' (SSC)). However, on 8 October 1999, the French government submitted documentation which stated reasons for its failure to implement this decision. The SSC took the view that there was no new scientific information which justified the French position, though there was substantial public support in France for the continuation of the ban. The European Commission decided to pursue

infraction proceedings against the French government for non-implementation of the decision of 1 August 1999. However, it was not until 2 October 2002 that the French government agreed to lift the ban. This came just before the imposition of fines on France by the European Court for failing to abide by its earlier ruling that it had to open up its market to UK beef. One might question the motivation of the French government in persisting with the ban, and then lifting it. For example, to what extent was it motivated by public health concerns, by public opinion, or by farmers keen to keep the competition out? And to what extent was the decision to lift the ban really taken on the basis of 'hard' scientific evidence provided to the French government?

Source: The European Commission Representation in the UK, *Background briefings*, 20 March 2002; *Guardian* website (**www.guardian.co.uk**), 3 October 2002.

---

national level, the Commission is on a steep upward slope, possessing neither the political resources nor the legal competence to delve substantially into national affairs' (1999: 70). But it is not only the structure and diversity of the Union that provide the source of the EU's implementation deficit, it is also the involvement of the EU institutions in and their approach to the legislative process.

The complexity of European legislative processes provides the key to understanding this issue. Complexity (as Pressman and Wildavsky 1984 pointed out) may lead to poor legislation, making the effective and consistent implementation of that legislation demanding, if not impossible (Peters 2000: 190). For a start, as it may be particularly difficult for the Commission to get agreement on legislation, it will not be in its interest to spell out potential problems that could make this exercise even more difficult than it would otherwise be (Jordan 1999: 71). When this is coupled with a lack of adequate information on the part of the Commission, and implementation/monitoring mechanisms that are limited, the scope for engaging in a negotiated form of implementation may seem extremely unlikely. Even if attitudes are changing, institutions, much

slower to change, still tend to favour more of a top-down approach to implementation.

Thus, criticisms of the EU institutions and their role in the implementation deficit do not translate automatically into support for a bottom-up approach to implementation. Rather, such criticisms are more likely to stress the inadequacy of the Commission's control mechanisms. The role of the Commission in policy **enforcement** is one area of difficulty. Indeed, although this is a huge responsibility, the resources the Commission has at its disposal to perform this task are few, particularly given that it is supposed to oversee thousands of individual pieces of legislation across the 15 member states. For much of the time, the Commission relies on complaints made by national governments and by interest groups. For example, in September 2002, the newspaper *European Voice* (19 September 2002: 6) reported that animal welfare activists were claiming that the 1995 EU Directive which deals with the transportation of animals, and which states that animals in a standard lorry may only be transported for eight hours, was being systematically flouted. They therefore called on the Commission to take legal action against the member states concerned.

Moreover, the Commission has been notoriously bad at performing its implementation function. Its skills have traditionally lain in policy formulation rather than policy implementation. The Commission's poor performance has been exacerbated as a consequence of the increasing policy responsibilities entrusted to the Commission by the EU's member states, the limited experience of officials in newer policy areas (Peters 2000: 194), and its weak powers of inspection. As Butt Philip (2000: 272) says, the Commission 'does not normally have the means to check outside those areas of responsibility that are under its direct control'. This has been something that the Commission began to address as part of its post-2000 reform, and is a crucial factor, given that, as Peters has pointed out, failure to enforce laws may threaten the very existence of the EU in a way it does not with, say, the United States or France. Yet, inherent design faults may be inevitable in EU policy as a consequence of tensions between supranationalism and intergovernmentalism in the Council (Dimitrakopoulos and Richardson 2001: 340). In other words, as Scharpf (1988) has argued, it is the multi-level character of the EU that makes it vulnerable to 'joint decision-making traps' (see Chapter 7: 102), which drag policies down to a lowest common denominator of state preferences.

What evidence for an implementation deficit?

Without questioning whether there is in fact an implementation deficit, it may be premature to focus on the barriers to effective implementation—whether at national or EU level. At this point, it might come as a surprise to discover that there are some commentators who suggest that policy implementation within the EU is no worse than that at national level (see, for example, Börzel 2001). Indeed, if our expectations are tied too closely to some sort of ideal of perfect implementation (Hood 1976) then we are likely to be dissatisfied, as perfection of this sort does not exist in the real world. Even so, this does not mean that we should resign ourselves to believing that effective implementation is unattainable (Peters 2000: 191). But we must

recognize that implementation will always be problematic as long as it takes place in a liberal democratic political context, one in which policy outcomes are open, at least to some extent, to public scrutiny, and where policy implementation is undertaken through a variety of institutions and by a host of different actors, both elected and appointed. Moreover, it is possible that 'Implementation deficits will be difficult to eradicate completely because they serve to maintain the delicate "balance" between governmental and supranational elements in the EU' (Jordan 1999: 69). This is a rather subtle notion, which suggests that the implementation deficit serves as a device that is used to counter trends towards or away from supranationalism at the policy-making stage of the European policy process.

Yet, if we accept the implication of Peters' argument, that is, that the Commission does still have a responsibility for trying to ensure that legislation agreed by Parliament and Council is put into effect on the ground, then it is clear that there is a need for information on implementation rates to be collated. This is far from an easy task, not least because the Commission is largely reliant on the very member states that are in breach of EU legislation to provide the relevant figures. Where it publishes data of this sort, these relate mainly to the transposition stage of the process, rather than to practical implementation on the ground, which is much harder to scrutinize.

The data on practical implementation are largely rather ad hoc and anecdotal, and arise out of specific studies of individual directives. For example, Butt Philip (2000: 237) has tried to identify the legislation that is the least well implemented in the EU. He mentions, in the field of the environment, the 'Birds' Directive, the Environmental Impact Assessment Directive, and the Water Quality Directive. But poor implementation is also found in other policy areas, such as public procurement, technical standards, and the working hours of lorry drivers. Inevitably, assessments of this sort tend to be qualitative rather than quantitative, making it difficult to counter some of the myths that circulate about 'good states' and 'bad states'. As a consequence we are left with a rather patchy impression of the implementation deficit.

Key points

- The EU is said to be characterized by an implementation deficit, though opinions differ as to its importance.
- Some of the sources of the implementation deficit are said to occur within the member states.

- Other sources can be attributed to the EU institutions and the way in which policy is made.
- The Commission collates information on implementation rates in order to help it assess where transposition is incomplete.

Implementation comes of age

EU implementation studies have been few and far between in the EU politics literature. Levy (2000*b*: 2) suggests that this has much to do with the fact that academic concerns have reflected practitioner interests, and that this is a difficult area to research, given that 'it is diverse, dispersed and imperfect by nature'. Since the end of the 1980s, however, there has been a burgeoning academic and practitioner interest in the implementation of European legislation, to the extent that there has even been a politicization of the issue of implementation.

This growing interest in implementation was in part driven by the single market programme of the late 1980s and early 1990s. Here the logic was that competition amongst firms and states within the EU should be both free and fair (see Chapter 3). In order to be fair, European legislation had to be implemented consistently across all member states, so that a 'level playing-field' might be created for Europe's business community. The European institutions have had a major role to play in this project. Not only has the EP pushed questions of implementation to the top of the agenda, but also the European Court of Justice (ECJ) has forced the issue by blurring the distinction between regulations and directives (Macrory 1992) and by adding to case law in this area.

The proliferation of European legislation, as a consequence of the single market programme, was also important in driving this agenda. As the legislative or policy-*making* responsibilities of the EU expanded after the mid-1980s to cover almost all policy areas, there began a shift in attention away from legislation and towards the *effect* of legislation, that is, from policy outputs to policy outcomes. As a consequence, the challenge of improving implementation led to a statement of commitment within the Treaty on European Union (TEU), as drafted at Maastricht in December 1991. It said that 'each Member State should fully and accurately transpose into national law the Community directives addressed to it within the deadlines laid down' to ensure that EU law is 'applied with the same effectiveness and rigour [as] . . . national law' (see Article 226, formerly Article 169). While this is not a particularly controversial statement to have included in the new Treaty, it was an explicit acknowledgement that implementation could not be taken for granted. It also embodies a somewhat top-down conception of implementation.

Although the focus on the single market is important, it is impossible to ignore a more general sea-change in EU thinking that began to emerge out of post-Maastricht concerns about popular apathy and growing opposition to European integration. This sort of thinking is linked closely to concerns about the **legitimacy** of the Union, and how the EU might be made more legitimate in the eyes of European citizens. Although legitimacy may well involve a process of democratization (see Chapter 23), it also rests on the effectiveness of policy output—that is, on the difference (or perhaps more accurately, the perception of the difference) that the EU can make to the lives of ordinary people. It is in this sense that the importance of implementation for the future of Europe is already understood.

Key points

- There has been increasing attention to implementation issues since the end of the 1980s.

- Interest began with the single market programme, but has been intensified as a consequence of post-**Maastricht** concerns with improving the quality and effectiveness of European law and policy.

Conclusion

This chapter has outlined the way in which the EU is involved in the implementation of its legislation and policies. It has distinguished between indirect and direct implementation, and has broadened out the concept to include the Commission's executive rule making functions. In drawing on the theoretical literatures, a distinction was made between top-down and bottom-up perspectives as a way of structuring an understanding of the implementation deficit. However, it was also suggested that implementation failures may be no worse than those at national level, and that the extent of the implementation deficit ought not to be exaggerated.

But even if striving for *perfect* implementation is bound to end in failure, some of the problems associated with *imperfect* implementation do still have to be addressed. As Peters (2000: 194) has suggested, the Commission needs to balance the requirement for uniformity and legality against the requirement for flexibility and political sensitivity, so as not to offend less committed Europeans. But

just how much variation should be permitted? Is it enough to adhere to the spirit of law, rather than to its letter? Moreover, is a convergence of implementation structures likely to occur? Peters (2000: 204) has noted the possibility of two different types of convergence: structural convergence, which relates to changes in the organization of public management; and individual convergence, which involves the socialization (or Europeanization) of civil servants dealing with EU matters. It is perhaps as a consequence of individual convergence that structures may change and become more homogeneous in the future. This is likely to happen if even more emphasis is placed on the 'bottom-up' conception of policy implementation. There is some evidence of this happening already—at least in certain European policy areas, such as environmental policy. Greater attention paid to how the EU makes policy, together with the European Commission's involvement, if only as a facilitator or 'manager of networks', at the implementation stage, may pay dividends in the future.

QUESTIONS

1   In which three ways is European policy implemented?

2   What is the difference between indirect and direct implementation?

3   What is the difference between transposition and practical implementation?

4   In what way is Commission rule making a form of implementation?

5   Why did the comitology system emerge?

6   What is the difference between the enforcement of European policy and its implementation?

7 Does the top-down theory of implementation provide a better explanation of European implementation than the bottom-up theory?

8 What is the EU's implementation deficit?

GUIDE TO FURTHER READING

Dimitrakopoulos, D., and Richardson, J., 'Implementing EU Public Policy', in J. Richardson (ed.), *European Union. Power and Policymaking*, 2nd edn (London: Routledge, 2001). A very useful chapter on EU implementation, which, amongst other questions, considers why implementation in the EU is 'imperfect'.

Jordan, A., 'The implementation of EU environmental policy: a policy problem without a political solution?', *Environment and Planning C: Government and Policy*, vol. 17, no. 11 (1999): 69–90. An excellent article which looks at implementation at the 'sharp end' in the field of EU environmental policy, and particularly at the implementation deficit in this policy area.

Levy, R., *Implementing European Union Public Policy* (Cheltenham: Edward Elgar, 2000). A wealth of detail on programme management in EU policies, focusing on a number of policy case studies (Agriculture, Structural Actions, Research and Development, and Co-operation and Development and the European Development Fund).

Peters, B. G., 'The Commission and Implementation in the EU: Is there an Implementation Deficit and Why?', in N. Nugent (ed.), *At the Heart of the Union: Studies of the European Commission*, 2nd edn (Basingstoke: Palgrave, 2000). A fascinating chapter which looks generally at the issue of the EU's implementation deficit, but also raises broader questions about the character of the EU implementation process.

WEB LINKS

http://europa.eu.ing/comm/secretariat_general/sgb/droit_com/index_en.htm Recent decisions and data on infringements of European law from the Commission website.

http://europa.eu.int/comm/internal_market/eu/update/score Information on the implementation of internal market legislation from the Commission website.

http://europa.eu.int/comm/environmental/impel The web page of the EU network for the implementation and enforcement of environmental law.

23 EU democracy and the democratic deficit

Dimitris N. Chryssochoou

READER'S GUIDE

This chapter examines the European Union (EU) from a democratic standpoint. The chapter introduces the idea of the **democratic deficit**, and explores how one might understand this much-used concept. It differentiates between divergent proposals for rectifying the democratic deficit by distinguishing between institutional and socio-psychological perspectives on this issue. While an *institutional* perspective on democracy-building focuses attention on power sharing both at the European level and nationally, a *socio-psychological* perspective on the democratic deficit addresses the absence of a European **demos**, a politically organized community of citizens. Although these two perspectives imply different strategies for democratic reform, the issue is further complicated by the fact that there is no consensus over the future of the EU polity. The chapter emphasizes this important point by identifying four models of democracy—the parliamentary, **consociational**, **federal**, and the **confederal**—and asks which of these best reflects the existing characteristics of the EU, and which is likely to be the most appropriate model for European democratic governance in the future. It answers that while the confederal and consociational models best reflect the EU of today, these are not models to which the Union should aspire if it wishes to democratize itself. Finally, the chapter considers whether recent institutional reforms of the EU have begun to address its democratic deficit.

Introduction

What is the **democratic deficit**? Although this term is used in a variety of contexts, its EU application is the focus of this chapter. Here, the democratic deficit points to a negative side-effect of the European integration process—the growing dissonance between the essential requirements of modern democratic government and the actual conditions upon which the political management of EU affairs is based. To be more specific than that is to pre-empt the discussion below, which stresses the contested nature of the democratic deficit (though see Box 23.1 for a few more definitions). In other words, not only does the debate revolve around how to resolve the democratic deficit, but it also concerns the nature of the problem. Indeed, as we shall see, the two are inextricably linked.

The chapter begins by explaining what the democratic deficit is. To help in this process the first section distinguishes between institutional and socio-psychological perspectives. Whereas *institutional* perspectives on the democratic deficit focus attention on power-sharing and on institutional reform as a solution to the perceived problems of EU democracy, *socio-psychological* perspectives are much more concerned with questions of European identity and with the absence of a European **demos** (the absence of a civic-minded body of citizens). As the democratic deficit debate raises fundamental questions about the future form of the EU, the chapter then considers four models of democratic governance—the parliamentary, consociational, federal, and confederal models. Each of these models is judged not only as a possible future for the EU, but also in light of what it can tell us about today's EU.

To explore these questions further, the chapter examines recent institutional reforms and considers whether the treaty revisions at Amsterdam and Nice have helped to democratize the Union. The chapter's conclusions are unequivocal. The Amsterdam and Nice Treaties have failed to enhance the democratic properties of the EU in any fundamental way. For the moment, the EU therefore continues to remain closer to an intergovernmentally co-ordinated system of democracies than it does to a democratic system in its own right.

Box 23.1 **Core ideas**
Some definitions of the democratic deficit

'The idea behind the notion of a "democratic deficit" is that decisions in the EU are in some ways insufficiently representative of, or accountable to, the nations and people of Europe' (Lord 2001: 165).

'It has become a received wisdom that the EU suffers from a "democratic deficit". It suffers from deficiencies in representation, representativeness, accountability and support. The problem is not merely that of the establishment of an additional layer of governance, further removed from the peoples of Europe. It is also that this process contributes to the transformation of the Member States, so that each Member State can no longer claim to be the source of its own legitimacy' (Eriksen and Fossum 2002: 401).

'The limited ability of Europeans to influence the work of the major EU institutions is a problem that has become so entrenched as to merit its own label: the democratic deficit' (McCormick 1999: 147).

The democratic deficit is 'the combination of two phenomena: (a) the transfer of powers from the Member States to the European Community; and (b) the exercise of those powers at the Community level by institutions other than the European Parliament, even though, before the transfer, the national parliaments held power to pass laws in the areas concerned' (European Parliament 1988: 10–11, quoted J. Smith 1999: 13).

Understanding the 'democratic deficit'

When the European integration process began in the late 1950s no one gave much thought to its democratic credentials. For decades since, the European Community (EC) has rested on what has been identified as a 'permissive consensus', the tacit agreement of the citizens of its member states. The legitimacy of the EC came from elsewhere—from the peace and prosperity that European integration would bring to Western Europe—rather than from its democratic characteristics (Newman 2001: 358). (See Box 23.2 on democracy.) But since the early 1990s and the **ratification crisis** which followed the signing of the **Maastricht Treaty** in 1992, this permissive consensus is said to have broken down. In its place have arisen new discourses which offer conflicting solutions to the problem of democratizing the Union. The argument goes something like this: in a period when transnational pressures are challenging both intra- and interstate relations, it may no longer be enough to confine democracy to within the territorial boundaries of the traditional nation state. Indeed, if democracy

Box 23.2 **Core ideas**
What is democracy?

Democracy is a method of organizing public life that allows the concerns and interests of citizens to be articulated within government. Democracy's defining properties are its institutional controls, the peaceful resolution of conflicts in society, meaningful legislative representation, as well as civic inclusion, and political participation. Important in understanding democracy is the concept of the demos. The demos is, in short, the collective citizen body. It also represents the idea of a political community of shared values and identities. One possible model of democracy involves the demos participating in the making of decisions that affect its members (Arblaster 1987: 105).

There are various ways of understanding democracy. It may be defined as an institutional arrangement for arriving at publicly binding decisions, with the legitimacy of those decisions resting on competitive elections. This suggests that the institutions of democracy are ends in themselves. Alternatively, democracy may be viewed as a means of realizing the common good through the electoral process. Here, institutions are merely means to much deeper ends. Democracy may also be defined in terms of active civic involvement in the affairs of the polity (democracy in input) or by focusing more on policy outputs and policy performance (democracy in output) (Scharpf 1999).

Whatever the definitional approach, democracy comprises a mixture of an ideal, on the one hand, and a procedural arrangement, on the other. It involves principles, norms, and values that are shared amongst citizens, and which provide the institutional means through which ideals are embodied in political institutions and through which the demos of a political community engages actively to arrive at publicly binding decisions. This implies that the concentration of political authority in unaccountable hands is incompatible with the democratic process.

But which set of institutions or institutional mechanisms can best ensure the transformation of democratic norms into policy structures? For many of its students, democracy implies a particular type of interaction of state and society, or government and the demos. Thus for democracy to exist, it is imperative that state actors (or policy makers) are answerable to society. The need for governments to be responsible in this way rests on the understanding that government must give an account of itself to the demos, usually by answering questions in the legislature. In Western liberal-democratic political systems, controls over government are usually enshrined in a Constitution, to be exercised in a number of ways—through parliamentary control, in court rulings, via discussions in the media, through pressure from interest groups and social movements, or by individual citizens themselves.

within states is to be sustained, it will need to deal with the implications of new forms of governance beyond the national state, as in the case of the EU.

This understanding raises new questions for political theorists and policy analysts, such as how it might be possible to hold EU decision makers to account to citizens who belong to different political systems. Questions of this kind reflect concerns about the effect of European integration on democracy in Europe, concerns that have grown as the EU has evolved away from being merely a diplomatic forum for interstate bargaining and towards a fully fledged **polity** or political system. This has led to scholarly interest in the idea that the EU might one day transform itself into a transnational political system based on democratic functions. While there is some measure of agreement that the EU system is not democratic, there is no consensus on how the EU might become so, with many different proposals for reform circulating. One of the reasons for this lack of agreement on reform is that there are two quite different (though in some forms compatible) understandings of what the democratic deficit is.

The first focuses on its institutional characteristics. From this perspective, the democratic deficit is an institutional phenomenon in that the problem of EU democracy is tied to the flawed inter-institutional relationships that characterize the Union. As a consequence, proposals for reform often speak of the EU's 'institutional imbalance', and of the need to enhance the accountability and representative nature of EU policy makers. The second understanding of the democratic deficit, by contrast, focuses on socio-psychological factors, arguing that the democratic deficit occurs because there is no European **demos**. As a consequence, this second perspective is more interested in European identity and the extent to which there is a feeling of community amongst European citizens across the different member states. Acknowledging that the absence of a demos is a barrier to the creation of a democratic EU, proposals for reform tend to suggest how a European civic body might be created. The subsections that follow look in more detail at these two perspectives on the democratic deficit.

The democratic deficit: An institutional perspective

The orthodox view of the EU's 'democratic deficit' is that the transfer of legislative powers from national parliaments to the EU institutions has not been matched by an equivalent degree of democratic accountability and legislative input on the part of the European Parliament (EP), the only directly elected institution at EU level. This has been the dominant view of the democratic deficit since the first EP elections of 1979, and one which has become more convincing since the **Single European Act** extended the scope of EU competences and the use of **qualified majority voting (QMV)** in the Council (see Chapter 3: Box 3.4). Although greater majority rule in the EU Council has been seen as good for decision making *efficiency*, not least because it speeds up the adoption of European legislation, it has exacerbated the already marginal role that national parliaments enjoy within the European integration process. This is because there is no guarantee that the scrutiny of national parliaments will matter when national governments may be outvoted in the Council.

The orthodox view also brings together two forms of institutional 'democratic deficit'. The first refers to the 'de-parliamentarization' of national political systems and the growing influence of the **executive** (Chryssochoou, Tsinisizelis, Stavridis, and Infantis 1998). The second focuses more directly on the transfer of decision-making authority from the national (or indeed subnational) to the supranational level. Implicit in this reading of the democratic deficit is that the shift from national to European level (the European democratic deficit) has, *at the same time*, benefited executive decision makers, that is governments and bureaucrats, at the expense of parliamentarians. This weakens the link between the electorate and de facto legislators. Shifting control of the European integration/policy process from national governments (ministers in the EU Council and heads of state or government in the European Council), from the national civil servants who support them and, indeed, from the unelected European institutions, seems to provide an obvious solution to the democratic deficit. Therefore, perhaps the most familiar argument is that a loss of control by national parliaments must be compensated by a process of parliamentarization at the European level. In other words, the EP must be given more powers if it is to perform the functions of a 'real' parliament. This usually implies a move towards a **bi-cameral** system at the European level—of direct and popular representation within the EP and indirect, territorial representation within the EU Council.

This has been the general approach of the EP to the democratic deficit since well before the treaty reforms of the 1980s. Since the 1970s, the Parliament has been successful in enhancing its own legislative role, albeit incrementally. The arguments supporting this kind of approach seemed all the more convincing after members of the EP were directly elected from 1979. In the reforms of the 1980s and 1990s, then, the Parliament was able to convince national governments of the need to increase its decision-making role, by introducing new procedures—first **co-operation**, in 1986, and then **co-decision** (see Chapter 1) at Maastricht—in order to compensate for the loss of national parliamentary control that resulted from the extension of majority voting in the Council. In addition the Parliament gained new powers of scrutiny over the appointment of the president of the Commission and the College of Commissioners.

Yet the Parliament, and others who argue for an extension of the parliamentary system to the EU, recognize that the EP's gains have not entirely compensated for losses at national level, and that the European integration process remains very much controlled by national and European-level executives (supported by the European and domestic courts). As a consequence, proposals to extend further the EP's involvement both in the legislative process and in scrutinizing the executive have been made—for example in the form of an extension of the co-decision procedure, so that all provisions falling under co-decision also operate on the basis of a qualified majority in the Council; and by extending the EP's involvement in the appointment of the Commission, possibly by allowing MEPs to choose the president of the Commission from a short-list put forward by the European Council.

But not everyone sees the logic in extending the powers of the EP in this way. For example, there is growing support for increasing the involvement of national parliaments (rather than just the EP) in the European policy process. National deputies or parliamentarians already have an important role to play in scrutinizing European legislation, though in practice they are often unable to perform that function very effectively. Parliaments have shown concern over this in the past and have proposed a number of ways of improving the situation. For example, the UK Parliament in the mid-1990s campaigned to ensure that it was given sufficient time to consider European legislation *before* the Council took its decision. By contrast, the Danish Parliament has always had strong institutional controls over its executive when dealing with European affairs. These not only allow a parliamentary committee time to scrutinize draft legislation, but also give it control over the government's negotiating position within the Council. The Danish case is the exception, however.

Since Nice (2001), there has been renewed interest in giving national parliaments more of a formal role in the EU's legislative process. One suggestion is that national parliaments should have a say over whether legislation at European level has been made on the basis of the **subsidiarity** principle. In other words, they should decide whether decisions are being taken at the most appropriate level of government. Others have sought to reinstate national parliamentary assizes, though possibly in a more formal way by adding a second chamber to the EP (see Box 23.3), even if critics note that a similar experiment was attempted in 1990 with little success.

The political agenda of those who favour a greater role for national parliaments sometimes stretches to support for the de facto renationalization of European policies. For this group, arguments about the EU's democratic deficit may mask a more general hostility to the EU project as a whole. Alternatively, it may assume that the EU is incapable of democratic reform of the kind necessary. For those who hold this view, the only viable solution to the EU's democratic deficit is for the EU institutions to play much less of a role in domestic politics and for the EU to become more **intergovernmental** than it currently is.

While European integration is said to privilege executives at the expense of directly elected

Box 23.3 **Issues and debates**
A second parliamentary chamber for Europe

The following paragraphs are drawn from the UK Parliament's Select Committee on European Union (Seventh Report), 2001.

PART 1: INTRODUCTION

1 Why would the European Union need another parliamentary chamber? We have decided to produce this Report on this question at this time [2001] for several reasons. First the Prime Minister has made a significant proposal for the creation of a new parliamentary body (which he referred to as a 'second chamber of the European Parliament') to be composed of members of national parliaments with primary functions of overseeing the operation of the principles of subsidiarity; and of scrutinising the European Union's Common Foreign and Security Policy.

2 Secondly, the case for such an additional chamber has been made in various forms and over a number of years by many other distinguished individuals and organisations on a number of grounds. These include concern that the European Union suffers from 'a democratic deficit', arising from the perceived distance between ordinary citizens and the EU institutions; and a concern that national parliaments should be encouraged to play a more active part in debating the European agenda and in scrutinising proposals from Brussels.

3 There is also pressure from those who see a collective role for national parliaments in scrutinising the operation of the principles of subsidiarity; from those who are concerned that inter-governmental co-operation in the areas of Foreign and Defence Policy and Justice and Home Affairs (the second and third pillars of the Treaty of the European Union [*sic.*]) are insufficiently subject to democratic scrutiny; and from those who wish the institutions of the European Union to develop not only a directly elected parliamentary chamber (the European Parliament) but also a balancing chamber of Member States.

4 While the emphasis is generally on the functions that such a second chamber could perform in scrutinising subsidiarity and second and third pillar issues, the fact that there are a variety of different forms of second chamber proposed, and that the argument is still coalescing, are further reasons why we considered that this inquiry would be timely.

5 A final reason for exploring this issue now is that preparations are about to begin for the next Inter-Governmental Conference (IGC) scheduled for 2004. The IGC will look at the role of national parliaments and it will be no surprise that proposals for a second chamber, and an analysis of the reasons for such proposals, are bound to feature highly in the preparations for the IGC.

Source: **www.parliament.the-stationery-office.co.uk/pa/ld200102/ldselect/ldeucom/48/4.**

legislatures, arguments about the democratic deficit often revolve more broadly around the powers of those European institutions that are not (directly) elected, and the extent to which these institutions are (un)accountable to elected bodies. Thus, the criticism is not just that parliaments do not have sufficient powers, but that non-elected bodies possess too many.

In this vein, many in the past have attacked the European Commission for being the archetypal undemocratic institution. After all, the Commission is composed of a college of 20 commissioners *appointed* by national governments. And as an administrative body, the Commission is deemed a civil service with policy-making (if not formal legislative) powers (see Chapter 9). There are various possible perspectives on such criticisms, whether they are justified or not. Perhaps the most relevant has been that this issue is really about **accountability** and institutional autonomy. In other words, the question to be addressed is the extent to which the Commission, as an executive body, is answerable to European citizens; or to put it another way, the degree to which the Commission has been able to break free from the control of national governments and parliaments, to act independently, thereby directly influencing policy and integrative outcomes in a manner not originally intended. While there was an extension to the scrutiny role that the EP has over the Commission in the treaty revisions of the 1980s and 1990s, the Commission does retain a degree of discretion over how it performs its initiative function—at least in much of the first, EC, pillar of the Union. Whether this is undemocratic or not is disputed, however.

It is not only the Commission that is subject to criticism of this kind. The European Courts have also been attacked for having a teleological pro-integrationist bias. While the Courts have an obligation to interpret the treaties, and have also been instrumental in pushing out the boundaries of European law, there is once again little agreement on the extent to which the Court really plays an autonomous role in the EU integration and policy process. But as is clear from Chapter 12 (p. 189), the role played by the Court may be 'inventive', but it is also very much in line with the spirit of the Treaties that it was set up to interpret.

Although the Commission is often considered as the EU's executive, the Council of the EU also performs executive (alongside its legislative) functions. This makes the Council a rather unusual body. While the Council has been happy to extend the Parliament's scrutiny over the Commission, it has been less keen to allow much oversight of its own internal workings. One reason such criticism is deemed credible is that the Council is an extremely secretive and arcane body, whose legislative decisions are taken behind closed doors.

Underpinning arguments that the non-parliamentary European institutions need to be more open and accountable is a more general point—that the EC/EU has traditionally been an extremely technocratic body, which has valued expertise (and effectiveness) much more than representation (and democracy). Since the early 1990s, the democracy debate within the EU has been extended, so that even where it remains institutionally orientated, it has become inextricably linked with issues of public participation in the EU policy process. Thus,

democratizing the EU is not just about rejigging the institutional balance of the Union to give this or that institution more of a policy role. It is not solely reliant on the representative role of parliaments. It is also about bringing the EU closer to ordinary people, ensuring that the European integration process is no longer simply an elite process, distant or even irrelevant for the vast majority of European citizens. There are various dimensions to these arguments. One of these relates to the representation of regions and localities in the EU. Regions, in particular, have been losers in the European integration process. This is because they have lost competencies without any gain in involvement in the European policy process. This was the argument advanced at the time of the Maastricht Treaty, and which led to the setting up of the Committee of the Regions (CoR). The importance of involving the CoR, a body representing local governments and regional authorities at EU level, in the making of EU legislation is often emphasized as an institutional solution to subnational representation, though few would imagine that the CoR would be able to resolve this issue on its own (see Chapter 18: 280–12).

Other perspectives tie the democratic deficit debate to issues of transparency and simplification (Dinan 2000: 133). Here, democracy is said to be facilitated through greater institutional openness, with examples including the availability of Council minutes, or enhanced public consultation by the Commission in advance of formal legislative proposals (see Box 23.4). But even with what appeared to be good intentions in the early 1990s, there has been a spate of legal cases condemning the EU's tendency towards secrecy, as in the case brought by the *Guardian* newspaper in the mid-1990s. On a related issue, there is an argument that the EU will be more democratic if it is not only more open, but better understood. The criticism here is that the EU has become more and more complex and difficult for the ordinary citizen to understand. While there have been attempts to simplify certain aspects of EU business, by cutting down the number of legislative proposals and reworking the treaty, this is still very much work-in-progress.

To conclude this section, then, an institutional perspective raises a number of different solutions

Box 23.4 **Issues and debates**
'No freedom of information in the EU'

The principle of freedom of information is in the first Article of the current code of access to EU documents. Citizens have the right to request any document, subject only to very specific and narrow exceptions, held by an EU institution. The current code has been in place since 1993 and its operation has been greatly improved by challenges in the Court of First Instance and to the European Ombudsman. These initiatives backed by six member states—Denmark, Finland, Sweden and often the Netherlands and the UK and sometimes Ireland—have led to significant improvements. The other nine member states, led by Germany and France, have consistently opposed more openness. The commitment made in Amsterdam in June 1997 was intended to 'enshrine' the citizen's right of access to EU documents. It was meant to build on the existing code and practice and turn it into a true freedom of information law. This would have meant opening up to public view—subject to specific and narrow exceptions—thousands of documents influencing policy-making not on agendas of Council meetings, Commission interdepartmental consultations, reports on implementing policies and correspondence between institutions and third parties and much more. However none of these advances are on the agendas of the three institutions—the Council, European Commission and the European Parliament—charged with agreeing the new code under the co-decision procedure by 1 May [2001].

Instead the Amsterdam commitment is being used to turn the clock back. All the draft proposals from the three institutions want to introduce a 'space to think' for officials (public servants) and to remove the principle of the right to ask for any document held. The current draft common position of the Council would permanently exclude from public access: a) 'space to think' documents: discussion documents, opinions of departments, preparatory documents, documents in preparation, texts which express personal opinions reflecting views as part or preliminary consultations, deliberations within the institutions (reports and correspondence); b) Documents covered by 'third party' vetoes including those from: non-EU states (eg: USA), international organisations and agencies (like NATO or G8); and c) the following will be subject to special procedures: All 'Top Secret', 'Secret' and 'Confidential' documents concerning foreign policy, military policy, non-military crisis management (including policing, border controls, trade and aid) and any document referring to them. The status of 'third parties', with the

right to veto access to documents, is also to be given under the Council draft to EU member states. The 15 EU member states are the Council of the European Union. If a member state submits a document on EU policymaking with a view to changing or influencing it then it should clearly be in the public domain.

The idea that a member state (a government) has the same rights of 'authorship' as a playwright or a songwriter is sheer nonsense. Government documents and EU documents are public documents submitted in the name of the people, they are not the product of individual endeavour. The Council draft also wants to introduce what has been long feared: a veto by the Brussels-based institutions over access to EU documents requested by citizens under national laws on freedom of information. The exclusion from public access to 'space to think' documents will also exclude 'space to act' documents concerning the implementation of policies once adopted. It should be inconceivable in a democracy that governments, whether national or European, should seek to be so unaccountable, so removed from public scrutiny but that is what is being proposed. And where does civil society, the 'fourth party' to the discussions, come into the equation? The answer is that it does not. The Commission never published a discussion paper to elicit views and reactions from civil society. The Council has been discussing its draft position behind closed doors (leaked drafts of the Council's common position are on the statewatch website (**www.statewatch.org**/news). The incoming Swedish Presidency inherited a draft common position from the French with which it disagrees. Faced with an impossible timetable and the positions of all three institutions being quite different on fundamental issues, it has been decided to hold a series of three 'trilogue' meetings in order to reach a 'compromise'. Of course, these meetings too are being held in secret, behind closed doors, with the objective of producing a deal by the end of February leaving just time to complete the formalities by 1 May. So much for openness!

The new code raises wider issues than simply access to documents or freedom of information, issues that concern the democratic future of the EU. When Statewatch applied for a document setting out far-reaching changes to the 1993 code of public access to EU documents in July (the now infamous 'Solana Decision') the Council said its release 'could fuel public discussion on the subject'. It is hard to think of a more undemocratic argument. Access

Box 23.4—*continued*

to documents is fundamental to a healthy, critical and thriving democracy. It enables civil society to understand, analyse and participate in a discussion. People have a right to know all the views considered and rejected and all the influences brought to bear on policymaking. They have a right to see these documents as they are produced or received—not after a new policy is adopted, but before. Access to documents does indeed 'fuel public discussion' and so it should. The resolution of this issue will be a defining moment for the EU. The argument is really very simple: In a democratic system, citizens have a right to know how and why decisions are made. Without freedom of information, access to documents, there is no accountability and without accountability there is no democracy. As long as I can remember there has been a 'democratic deficit' in the EU and there still is even as the EU prepares for enlargement. The 'democratic deficit' is not just about the powers

of parliaments—national or European—it is much deeper than that. It is about changing the democratic culture into a culture of openness, of an informed public and responsible and accountable institutions. Many suspected that the 'dinosaurs' (to use the European Ombudsman's phrase) would come out of hiding. Officials and vested interests would try and use the commitment in Article 255 of the Amsterdam Treaty not to 'enshrine' the right of public access but to limit and shackle it—to end up with not a code of access for citizens but 'A Regulation for the Protection of the Efficient Workings of the Institutions'. Unless there is a dramatic turnaround in the next few weeks this is exactly what we will get and democracy will be the poorer. We will have a new code of access to documents that is worse than the present one and we will not have freedom of information.

Source: Article by Tony Bunyan, Statewatch editor, in *European Voice*, 8 February 2001, **www.statewatch.org**.

to the democratic deficit. The common strand is that these solutions are institutional in character, reflecting the understanding that the democratic deficit itself is an institutional problem, demanding institutional solutions. As we shall see below, not all commentators agree with this claim.

The democratic deficit: A socio-psychological perspective

The problem with institutional approaches to the democratic deficit is that they leave the equally important socio-psychological dimension of this phenomenon unexplored. A socio-psychological perspective shifts the emphasis from the question of 'Who governs and how?' to the more demanding question of 'Who is governed?', thereby focusing more on the treatment of the disease (the disease being the democratic deficit) than on its symptoms. The starting point, then, is that without a European demos there can be no European democracy, and that at the heart of the EU's democratic deficit lies the absence of 'civic we-ness'—that

is, a sense of common identity amongst Europeans (Chryssochoou 2000).

This perspective on the democratic deficit builds on the wider assumption that democracy, in the form of representative and responsible government, presupposes a popular infrastructure upon which certain basic properties, such as adherence to and acceptance of majority rule, apply in any given political community. A transnational demos can be defined as a composite citizen body, whose members share an active interest in the democratic governance of the larger polity and who can identify with the central institutions of governance. In other words, it is the demos itself that endows the EU with **legitimacy**. It also follows that the transformation of the EU 'from democracies to democracy' (from the plural to the singular) requires the positive feelings of the constituent publics to be stronger than any divisive issues that may arise as European integration proceeds. As Cohen put it, 'there can be no larger part unless the larger part and the smaller parts are indeed parts of one whole' (Cohen 1971: 46).

The more the EU relies on democratic principles and procedures, the more important it is for citizens to have feelings of belonging to an 'inclusive' transnational polity. In this context, the emergence of a European civic identity out of the many democratic traditions that currently exist in the EU is imperative, not only for the viability of European democracy, but also if the democratic integrity of the constituent populations is to be respected, and for cultural variation and multiple identity holding to be fostered. For a European demos to exist, its members must recognize their collective existence. Merely being granted common citizenship rights, as was the case in the Maastricht Treaty, is far from adequate. This is not a question of institutional or policy change, but of changes in the way that Europeans think about themselves and the way in which they view the communities to which they belong.

As the polity of the EU cannot be detached from its constituent identities, transnational demos formation does not imply a melting-pot type of society in which pre-existing identities are assimilated into a new supranational identity. The idea is not to create one European identity which suppresses all other territorial identities. Rather, transnational demos formation projects an image of a pluralist polity, within which the civic demos emerges as the unchallenged unit of transnational authority and the ultimate focus of political purpose. 'Many people, one demos', rather than 'many demoi, one people', epitomizes this. Put differently, this implies 'a many turned into one without ceasing to be many'. A European demos can, therefore, be said to exist when the constituent publics see themselves as part of a democratic whole, and are given the institutional means to mark their impact in European governance, even though they retain their regional and national identities. It is possible, as a consequence, to identify the following as necessary for European civic demos formation: the democratic self-consciousness of the collective citizen body; adherence to shared democratic values; public awareness of the transnational political process; and a desire to shape democratically the future of a plurality of interrelated peoples, without, however, endangering the very essence of that plurality, its diversity.

Key points

- There are two main perspectives applied to the study of the democratic deficit—the institutional and the socio-psychological.

- An institutional perspective emphasizes the need for democratic power sharing, which might give the European Parliament (EP) or national parliaments more of a role in the European policy process, or make other institutions more accountable to elected bodies.

- A socio-psychological perspective stresses the absence of a European demos and identifies what it would take to construct a community of Europeans as a prerequisite for the democratization of the EU.

Models of European democracy

Resolving the democratic deficit is no easy task as it would require some form of agreement about the sort of model of democratic governance to which the EU should adhere. Up to now, the EC (more recently the EU) has evolved incrementally, and despite the reform projects of the 1980s and 1990s, there has been no consensus on the future shape of the EU. At the time of writing, the European **Convention** is discussing these issues with a view to agreeing in 2004 a European Constitution, or Constitutional Treaty (which by necessity would imply a particular model of European governance). This section looks at four possible models that could be used to guide the democratization of the Union—the parliamentary, the consociational, the federal, and the confederal models.

The parliamentary model

The parliamentary model emphasizes the role of the elected assembly as legislator. Crucial within this model is the parliament's role within a representative and often **majoritarian** system of government, one that allows executives to govern as long as they have the confidence of a majority of the members of the assembly. The model draws our attention to a number of features that relate to the EU and most notably: the use of **qualified majority voting** (QMV) in EU decision making; the role of the EP in law making; and the role of national parliaments in the monitoring of legislation. But despite having certain parliamentary characteristics, the EU is not a parliamentary system, as it is not based on the **separation of powers** between executive and legislative institutions. Neither is there a clear division of competences among different levels of governance (European, national, subnational).

There are important implications for the legitimacy of the EU should a European parliamentary system be established, as this implies that majority rule would be extended to all European policy areas. The parliamentary model presupposes some form of social unity, which allows the minority to identify with the central institutions. Given the fragmented nature of the European citizenry, there would seem to be no such social unity of this kind within the EU at the present time. For the moment, majority voting still applies to areas of EU action that are not prone to intense conflict, that is, in areas where the member governments want to see collective progress rather than to hold on to their national prerogatives (Taylor 1996: 85–8). Major policy initiatives and decisions on constitutional reform take place through the formal revision of the treaties in the European Council, and this continues to be agreed on the basis of **unanimity** (with each state holding a potential veto) (see Chapter 10: 151). Where majority decisions *are* at issue, they are more often than not subject to a lowest common denominator approach, with the informal norm of consensus usually overriding the idea of a decision at any cost. Indeed, no single state is prepared to be outvoted on a regular basis in the EU Council. Taylor summarizes the above discussion well: 'Majority voting merely cloaked the continuing need to obtain the assent of all states . . . In a system of sovereign states, it could not be otherwise' (Taylor 1996: 86).

On the other hand, supporters of the parliamentary model stress the importance of democratically monitoring European legislation through the institutional checks and balances offered by deliberative plenary sessions and specialized parliamentary committees. The advantage of a parliamentary model applied to the EU is that it would allow elected representatives more of a substantial role in the European policy process. Given that the EU needs to engage to a greater degree with its own citizens, a parliamentary system might allow this to happen.

The confederal model

Confederation involves the merging of distinct politically organized states into some form of union, without losing either their national identity or their individual sovereignty. The confederal model emphasizes the intergovernmental properties of the EU, highlighting its treaty-based nature. This model suggests that democracy in the EU is better served by establishing a democratic society of European states, rather than by forging a new polity and EU democracy. The confederal model sees European integration as a predominantly interstate affair, and favours the diffusion of authoritative decision-making power to the segments (or member states), rather than to the regional centre (the EU level). The end-product of integration takes the form of a:

treaty-constituted body politic, [where the] condition of the last say rests with the partners to it, rather than with an independent political entity operating at a level beyond the traditional state. . . . [Being] far more directly a contractual creature than the normal state . . . [the European confederation is not] . . . the constituted unity of one *people* or *nation*, but a unity constituted by *states* (Forsyth 1981: 15–16).

Thus, confederation takes the form of a 'halfway house' between 'normal' interstate and 'normal' intrastate (or domestic) relations, with the constituent units reserving the right to revert to democratic self-rule. What this implies is that integration 'falls short of a complete fusion or incorporation in which one or all the members lose their identity as states'

(Forsyth 1981: 1). The main characteristic of a con-federation as 'a system of governments' is that it provides states with a variety of opportunities, enabling them to achieve mutually advantageous co-operation without resigning their individual sovereignty to a single common government, either in the form of a federally constituted authority or in the shape of a new regional state. This form of governance is achieved by focusing primarily on intergovernmental relationships as a means of managing co-operation and with it the process of monitoring agreements.

Accordingly, the idea of power sharing at the EU level, which involves the management of certain policies over which there is a form of joint sover-eignty, provides an alternative to the creation of a new political centre 'beyond the nation state'. Although the confederal model incorporates a wide range of institutional possibilities, including for example power-sharing arrangements among dif-ferent actors, the larger political entity ultimately rests upon the separate constitutional orders of the member states which, by virtue of their sovereign nature, continue to act as 'masters of the treaties'. The fact that formal treaty revisions require the unanimous consent of the member governments alone makes this point all the more resonant, as does the understanding that it is the member states and not a self-conscious and politically active trans-national demos that legitimizes the larger political unit. In this model, as a consequence, resolving the democratic deficit might involve a renationalization of policies, to allow for the greater involvement of national parliaments. It would not imply the democratization of the European institutions nor any attempt to create a European, transnational demos.

The federal model

The federal model foresees the creation of a 'union of *people* in a body politic', as opposed to merely a 'union of *states* in a body politic' (see also Chapter 5). This task recognizes that individuals who come under the federal compact must be moved by such strong 'we-feelings' that it propels them not only to use but also to support federal policy

outcomes. Students of democracy hold the view that federalism, by implying a diffusion of political power, moderates conflicts and offers a greater opportunity for 'political schooling', a condition for socializing minorities into a civic culture. From this view stems the importance of institutional arrange-ments that allow each state to be represented in the federal polity, without disturbing the overall effectiveness of the system or indeed challenging its political legitimacy. Federalism aims to establish a co-operative democratic ethos in relations between the centre and the subunits. It seeks to reconcile the parallel demands for greater political union (although not necessarily unity) of the whole, at the same time as ensuring adequate constitutional guarantees for the autonomy of the parts, in order to establish unity without uniformity and diversity without anarchy. Thus an understanding of federation emerges as a living, pluralist order that builds itself from the ground upwards. In such a model, the question of democratic representation becomes a crucial balancing factor, which also allows territorial and non-territorial claims to find expression.

When this model is applied to the EU, a frequent criticism is that it places too much emphasis on the idea of a central constitutional settlement and, by extension, the need for a clear (and somewhat static) demarcation of competences between higher- (EU) and lower-level (national, subnational) authorities. In so doing, it ignores the inherently dynamic nature of European integration and the complexity of competence allocation (or 'who does what?') within the EU. The making of a European political federation also presupposes the creation of a new sovereignty at the higher level and the establishment of a **bi-cameral** system in which the EP is given the power to initiate and co-decide legislation with the Council. However, the democratic properties normally associated with federal polities, where a composite civic demos forms the 'constituting authority' of the federation—in other words, where the federal model is composed of one 'people'—seems absent from this EU version of federalism. In the absence of an 'inclusive' European demos, it is difficult to imagine the qualitative transformation of the EU from a confederal to a federal-type organization and, hence, from a collective system of shared management to a polity constituted by a unity of the people.

The consociational model

Consociationalism is a model of governance which has been used in territories inhabited by more than one community or societal group. In particular, it seeks to forge a community of territorial entities in order to provide an institutional defence against the abuse of minority rights. It has four main features: a grand coalition of elites; proportionality; segmental autonomy; and mutual vetoes. A *grand coalition*, or a 'cartel of elites' (Dahrendorf 1967: 267), is an institutional setting—a council for example—within which decisions are taken and bargains are struck among the groups of elites. *Proportionality* implies that all societal forces or communities are represented within the government, in a way that reflects their size. *Segmental autonomy* means that each elite has control over its own particular territory, in areas that do not impinge on other elites within the consociation. Finally the existence of *mutual vetoes* means that for important decisions unanimous approval of all elites is required. No community can be outvoted, which means that the majority is unable to dominate the minority. These features of the consociational model can all be found within the present-day EU.

The consociational model is particularly relevant to the case of the EU as it emphasizes the consensual nature of EU decision making. It does so by focusing on the way in which the governing elites of the member states seek to reach mutually acceptable compromises. Consociational governance is related to the politics of accommodation and consensus building employed behind the closed doors of the EU Council and the European Council, resulting in carefully negotiated package deals among the elites. With the absence of a single European demos, the argument goes, **majoritarian** patterns of politics (as in the parliamentary model above) would imply serious exclusionary practices harmful to Europe's minorities. Thus consociationalism avoids excluding minority interests by institutionalizing new ways of reaching mutually acceptable compromises.

There is ample evidence to suggest that the EU already possesses certain features of a consociational democracy. *Grand coalitions* are found in the sectoral EU Councils as well as in the European Council (see Chapter 10). *Proportionality* appears in the idea that states are assigned different votes in the Council according to their size and/or population, and in that all the member states are represented in the central decision-making institutions. *Segmental autonomy* exists in the way that EU member states retain their distinctive features as separate constitutional entities so that they remain responsible for dealing with issues that are exclusive to their jurisdiction. And finally, *mutual vetoes* allow EU states to block decisions of which they strongly disapprove, especially where their vital national interests are at stake. With the extension of majority voting since the end of the 1980s, the veto is no longer the norm in EU decision making. However, as already noted, constitutional-type decisions remain subject to the unanimity principle, while elsewhere consensual decision making is the norm.

According to the consociational model, the EU represents a compound polity whose distinct culturally defined and political organized units are bound in a consensual form of union. The aim of this union is to further certain common ends without sacrificing collective national identities or resigning individual sovereignty to a higher authority. Central to the workings of this European consociation is the practice of political co-determination, that is, the common management of separate sovereignties through means and objectives that have been agreed in advance. The result is a system of considerable interconnectedness co-existing with high levels of autonomy. In this consociation, the dominant elites resist the strengthening of horizontal links among their respective publics, preferring instead to promote vertical integration so as to retain ultimate control within their own subcultures and, therefore, to increase their power base domestically. This also allows national political elites to exercise managerial control over European integration, while deciding on the bases of acceptable behaviour within the larger system.

The advantage of this particular model is that it allows for a less rigid understanding of statehood and national self-determination than is found in the other models reviewed in this section. In brief, national and collective systems of governance are bound together in a symbiotic relationship. The EU takes the form of a composite political system that accommodates divergent expectations in joint decisions. As for democracy, in this model it is not so much an end in itself as an institutional device used to arrive at mutually acceptable compromises among sovereign states. In this sense, consociational democracy is inherently elitist. For this reason, while consociationalism might reflect many of the characteristics of the EU, it may not be the most appropriate model if our aim is that of enhancing EU democracy.

Which model to resolve the democratic deficit?

So what conclusions might we draw from these four models of democratic governance? First, the EU is clearly a hybrid of all four models, in that elements of all four are currently reflected in the organization and operation of the Union. Second, the models that reflect the Union's character most closely are the confederal and consociational models. As the confederal model assumes that democracy will be located at the national and not the European level, from this perspective, the democratic deficit could only be resolved by a shift in an intergovernmental direction. Moreover, the inherently elitist character of the consociational model, reflecting key charac-

teristics of the EU, also seems to preclude any possibility of democratization transnationally. If we are seeking solutions to the democratic deficit at the European level, it would appear then that neither the confederal nor the consociational model provides an answer to the Union's problems. Rather, European-level democratization will be much more feasible if the EU were to adopt a parliamentary and/or a federal approach. The section that follows asks whether recent treaty reforms demonstrate evidence of the beginnings of such a shift.

Key points

- There are at least four models of democratic governance that resonate with the EU.
- Although the EU has certain parliamentary characteristics, it does not exactly fit the parliamentary model.
- The confederal model resembles the EU system substantially.
- The absence of a demos would seem to preclude the application of a federal model at this time.
- There are some substantial similarities between the consociational model and the EU.
- While the confederal and consociational models best fit the EU as it is today, these models do not provide an avenue for democratizing the EU.

Democracy and treaty reform

As the **Amsterdam Treaty** (1997) was largely an attempt to rectify the deficiencies of the **Maastricht Treaty**, signed in 1992, this would seem to provide a fitting start for an assessment of democratic reform in the EU. Although Maastricht preserved many of the confederal features of the EU system, it also introduced principles such as **co-decision, subsidiarity**, and **proportionality**, which are much more federal in character, or have at least a federalizing

potential. According to Taylor, however, what this treaty revision brought about was a 'symbiotic consociation' (Taylor 1996), the decisional outcomes of which are informed by an informal culture of consensus building at the highest political level. In other words, Taylor is arguing that Maastricht made the EU more consociational in nature, and not more federal. This end-result of the Maastricht process was that the EU and the member states became increasingly locked together in a mutually reinforcing relationship that left much to be desired from a democratic standpoint. That the issue of democracy was to occupy a more prominent position in the negotiations that led to the signing of the Amsterdam Treaty on 2 October 1997 was a reflection of increasing public concern about this aspect of the European integration process. Thus a widespread consensus emerged during the Amsterdam negotiations—that the EU had to find ways of developing closer links with its citizens. However, this consensus did not leave much of a mark on the Treaty itself.

Hailed by some as a 'reasonable step', but criticized by others as 'lacking ambition', the Amsterdam Treaty consolidated state competences by preserving the EU's three-pillar structure (see Chapter 4). According to Devuyst, '[r]ather than focusing on pre-emptive institutional spillover in preparation for enlargement, the Amsterdam negotiation was characterized by a "maintaining national control trend" ' (Devuyst 1998: 615).

One of the most important questions to be addressed at Amsterdam concerned the institutional structure that would permit the future enlargement of the Union to take place. In the end, the agreement, which to many eyes was unsatisfactory, was that after the first enlargement the big states would lose their second commissioner, provided that they were compensated through a reweighting of votes in the Council. This decision points to an accommodationist-type arrangement between smaller and larger states, although it was agreed that a final decision would only be taken at least a year before EU membership exceeds 20.

Although the Amsterdam Treaty increased the role of the EP by extending the scope of the **co-decision procedure** and by simplifying the **conciliation** process, the reform did not address more fundamental issues of parliamentary involvement in EU decision making. For example, the Treaty failed to agree that co-decision would always be used with QMV in the Council, and it did not extend the EP's involvement in third-pillar issues (police and judicial co-operation) to cover the financial implications of such policies. It also failed to alter the EP's role in treaty reform where it remained marginalized.

As for transparency, although the Amsterdam Treaty established a conditional right of public access to official EU documents and a simplification of legislative procedures, this was coupled by an institutionalization of other practices, such as exceptions, reservations, safeguards, protocols, and declarations, which further complicated matters. However, the formalization of transparency rules, that is, their *de jure* incorporation into the Treaty, did allow the European Court of Justice (ECJ) to monitor their implementation more effectively.

The largest deficiency of the Amsterdam process, however, was that it prioritized specific policy issues over broader questions relating to the EU's future. On the basis of the (largely incomplete) outcome of the Amsterdam process, it would seem that the treaty revision reflected a preference by member states for a managerialist type of reform that would improve the *effectiveness* of policy output rather than its democratic character. Those who had hoped that the Amsterdam process would forge a new democratic European polity had no grounds for celebration, as political pragmatism won the day. Indeed, it is not overstating the case to argue that Amsterdam was characterized by a profound lack of vision about the future of the EU, offering instead a series of marginal changes. In this sense, it failed to produce a common democratic vision for the Union.

Similarly, the Treaty of Nice, signed in 2001, provides a good example of the limits of EU polity building. As the *Guardian* put it: 'At every stage of the prolonged negotiation, raw national interest has overshadowed the broader vision'. For example, the 'declaratory' **Charter of Fundamental Rights**, signed at Nice, but not incorporated into the Treaty, seemed a missed opportunity for European democracy. The institutionalization of fundamental rights within the EU is likely to have strengthened the credibility of member states' commitments to protect the rights of persons residing within their territory, while empowering the ECJ to ensure that principles underpinning the Charter were respected. It is also likely to have advanced the fight against various forms of discrimination within the EU, placing the citizen at the heart of the EU's activities by further strengthening common citizenship rights, and contributing to the preservation and further development of shared values, while at the same time respecting and protecting the diversity of constituent cultures, traditions, and identities.

The Nice Treaty was intended to deal with what were called the 'Amsterdam leftovers', those issues that remained unresolved in the last round of treaty reforms. As a consequence, some might argue that Nice was lacking in ambition and vision even before the summit began. After four days of marathon talks in December 2000, an agreement was finally reached that the larger states would retain their second commissioner until 2005, while each member state would nominate one commissioner until the EU expands to 27 members. It was also agreed that the four largest states would each have 29 instead of 10 votes in the Council, which meant that three large states and a small one could now form a blocking minority, while the small and medium-sized members would each have between three and 13 votes (which meant that while the larger states' votes have increased threefold, those of the smaller states have only doubled). The threshold of seats in the EP was raised to 732 and QMV was extended to a number of relatively non-controversial areas. Finally, the states agreed to yet another round of constitutional reforms in 2004, covering questions of competence allocation, the status of the Charter of Fundamental Rights, the simplification of the treaties, and the future role of national parliaments.

What conclusion can we draw from the Nice process as regards the state of the EU today? And what are the implications of the Treaty of Nice for the EU polity and for its transformation into a democratic system? Three points deserve our attention. First, although the EU has sought to create large-scale civil society, the development of a shared civic identity among its constituent publics has not yet materialized. Nice did nothing to change this situation. Second, the EU is still characterized by its diversity and, moreover, by a lack of agreement on where European integration will end. It seems caught between federalist aspirations (see Chapter 5) and a modified type of state-centrism (see Chapter 7). Despite the increase in substantive policy competences, the EU has not become a federal political system, and remains a **consensual** form of governance, albeit one that has achieved a level of integration comparable to many federal political systems. Third, by acknowledging how important it is that member states retain ultimate control over formal treaty changes, the Nice reforms have revealed the limits of democratization in the EU. Once again the EP is excluded from this process, and national parliaments only get a say at the end of the process, at the **ratification** stage. Moreover, in failing to strengthen common citizenship rights (see Chapter 25) and to decouple the legitimacy of the EU from the performance of its policies, Nice, like Amsterdam, has been a missed opportunity for EU democracy.

Key points

- The Amsterdam Treaty was little more than a manageralist reform which aimed to increase policy effectiveness, but has little effect on the democratic deficit.

- After Nice, there is still no evidence of the emergence of a large-scale civic identity in Europe. The democratic deficit remains unresolved.

Conclusion

The discussion of EU democracy and the **democratic deficit** in this chapter is underpinned by a belief that it is increasingly important for the EU to address issues of democratic governance and to ensure that its decisions are informed by public discourse. The chapter began by distinguishing between two perspectives on the democratic deficit—institutional and socio-psychological. It went on to consider the relevance to the EU of four models of democratic governance. While it is argued in this chapter that the EU is closer to the confederal and consociational models of democracy than to the other models reviewed, and that recent treaty reforms seem to have made the EU even more so, this is judged to be far from an ideal end-state for the Union, as it is likely to hinder the development of a European demos by favouring a system of elite government based on consensus. As the EU was founded and is still based on an international treaty, the transition to a model of governance which allows European citizens to play a role, whether directly or indirectly, in the shape and content of the European integration and European policy process, is likely to be neither easy nor linear. This is because the EU will continue to be confronted with the reality of its multiple states and peoples (demoi), as well as by the fact that the present institutional structure of the EU favours pragmatic and accommodationist reform rather than a more fundamental transformation. Nevertheless, the search for democracy will remain one of the principal challenges that the EU will face in the years to come.

QUESTIONS

1 What is the democratic deficit?

2 Why is democracy important for the EU?

3 How might one rectify the EU's democratic deficit (from an institutionalist perspective)?

4 'To democratize the EU, one must increase the powers of the European Parliament.' Discuss.

5 What does a socio-psychological perspective on the democratic deficit contribute to our understanding of this phenomenon?

6 Is a European demos necessary for European democracy?

7 Which model of European governance is most likely to democratize the EU?

8 To what extent have the treaties of Amsterdam and Nice enhanced the democracy of the EU?

GUIDE TO FURTHER READING

Abromeit, H., *Democracy in Europe: Legitimizing Politics in a Non-State Polity* (Oxford: Berghahn Books, 1996). This book makes an important contribution to the theoretical debate about governance beyond the state and suggests the need for a more flexible system to supplement the European decision-making process to increase the accountability of policy.

Beetham, D., and Lord, C., *Legitimacy in the European Union* (London: Addison Wesley Longman, 1996). Provides a synthesis and an original perspective on the issue of political legitimacy.

Chryssochoou, D., *Democracy in the European Union* (London: I. B. Taurus, 2000). A rich analysis of the relationship between democracy and European integration, offering alternative approaches to understanding the democratic deficit.

Eriksen, E. O., and Fossum, J. E. (eds), *Democracy in the European Union* (London: Routledge, 2000). This book takes a theoretical approach to understanding democracy in the EU, assessing the prospects for EU-level democracy and arguing that the way in which we understand democracy impacts on how we understand the democratic deficit.

Lord, C., *Democracy in the European Union* (Sheffield: Sheffield Academic Press, 1998). An excellent assessment of the EU's democratic deficit and the problems associated with the construction of a transnational democracy.

Newman, M., *Democracy, Sovereignty and the European Union* (London: Hurst, 1996). A critical view of democracy and sovereignty issues in the EU, presenting a strong case for a democratic Europe.

WEB LINKS

www.statewatch.org The website of the non-governmental organization, Statewatch.

http://europa.eu.int.comm/public_opinion/Eurobarometer The EU's Eurobarometer website, which brings together surveys of public opinion on European issues.

http://european-convention.eu.int The website of the European Convention.

http://conventionwatch.iue.it Website hosted by the European University Institute in Florence on the European Convention.

24 Differentiated integration

Kerstin Junge

READER'S GUIDE

Differentiated integration (or '**differentiation**') is a general concept which refers to methods of European integration that do not require all member states to participate in every integration project, or which allow member countries to implement European policies at their own pace. This chapter explores the issue of differentiated integration by discussing three main questions. First, against the background of an apparent growth in the popularity of differentiated integration, the chapter asks why EU policy makers came to embrace this idea in the 1990s. The second question addresses the main methods of differentiation, analysing how these might be distinguished from each other, and suggesting their potential impact on the political structure of the EU. The chapter concludes by considering the main benefits and problems arising from differentiation and how, or whether, these might be resolved in the future.

Introduction

Differentiated integration (or '**differentiation**') is used in this chapter as a collective term that covers all methods of European Union (EU) integration that do not require member states to participate in every integration project, or which allow member countries to implement European policies at their own pace. It is related to the concepts of '**flexibility**' and '**enhanced co-operation**' (known in the Amsterdam Treaty and sometimes elsewhere as '**closer co-operation**'), which have also been used in the European context. Differentiated integration has become extremely fashionable within the EU, not least because of the challenges posed by the prospect of enlargement to Central and Eastern Europe. The idea that *all* EU member states must apply *all* EU rules, uniformly and simultaneously, seems increasingly untenable as the EU increases in size. However, differentiated integration is not an entirely new phenomenon, as we shall see below.

The chapter begins by looking at the traditional characteristics of European integration, and argues that while uniformity has been the norm, there are precedents for differentiation. Yet the differentiated integration of the 1990s and after is distinctive in that it sets itself up as a possible alternative to the earlier '**Community method**'. In the second section,

three types of differentiation are identified: multi-speed, à la carte, and concentric circles. It is claimed that the introduction of 'enhanced' co-operation' in the Nice Treaty reflects an à la carte approach. The third section of the chapter points to some of the potential problems caused by differentiation. It argues that ultimately this new approach to European integration might propel the EU forwards, rather than leading to its disintegration, as some have claimed.

Differentiation, uniformity, and the future of European integration

In the 1990s, the idea of making the European integration process more flexible became increasingly popular with practitioners involved in European policy making. Indeed, all of the Treaty amendments concluded in the 1990s include arrangements for the differentiation of (certain) EU policies. Thus, the 1992 Treaty on European Union (the **Maastricht Treaty**) allowed, for the first time, the non-participation of some member states in policies that form part of the European Community, most notably in the fields of monetary union (EMU), defence, and social policy (see also Chapters 20: 322–3; 15: 238–40; and 17: 267–8 respectively). While, at the time of their adoption, such measures were regarded as unique exemptions, subsequent treaty revisions introduced clauses into European law that were designed to allow for a more systematic differentiation of the European integration process. In particular, the 1997 Treaty of **Amsterdam** incorporated provisions on what was called 'closer co-operation'. This instrument allows a sub-group of member states to integrate or 'deepen' a number of policies in the first (EC) and third (justice and home affairs—JHA) pillars of the EU framework (see Chapter 1: Box 1.5; and Figures 4.1 and 4.2), without involving all 15 national governments. The provision was modified in the Nice Treaty which, among other things, extended the scope of the instrument to the second pillar, that is, to foreign

policy matters (see Chapter 15) while modifying some of the conditions for its use.

A tradition of uniformity?

Arrangements introducing a more flexible integration process signal a departure from the traditional method of deepening the EU-uniform integration. This demanded that all countries must agree on new integration initiatives and implement all new policies at the same time. This paradigm of uniformity originated in the early political and economic motives for European integration, as well as in the fact that law was to be the chosen instrument to accomplish them. After the end of the Second World War, France, West Germany, Italy, Belgium, the Netherlands, and Luxembourg sought to pool their sovereignty in order to prevent future wars and accelerate their economic recovery. These objectives were clearly stated in the Preamble of the 1957 Treaty of Rome, in which the six founder members of the European Economic Community (EEC) declared that they intended to 'lay the foundations of an *ever closer union among the peoples of Europe*' and to 'ensure the economic and social progress of their countries *by common action* to eliminate the barriers which divide Europe' (emphases added). These common political and economic objectives demanded the participation of all six member states in the policies set out in the Treaty. There was also a legal requirement for uniform integration, however. As Martenczuk (2000) points out, law is the instrument used to realize the objectives of the integration process. If the EU is to be deepened towards an 'ever closer union', European law must apply and be enforced in a uniform manner across the Union, in the interests of consistency. It is against this backdrop that the European Court of Justice (ECJ), in its case law, has continuously emphasized the importance of interpreting and applying Community law in a uniform way (see Chapter 12: 182–6).

The political and economic motives underlying the origins of the EEC, as well as the use of law as the instrument with which to achieve them, are thus responsible for making uniformity the dominant **paradigm** of European integration. However, these requirements do not mean that the European integration process has always advanced in a uniform manner. In fact, there are a multitude of examples of variation in the application of European law. For instance, new member states are usually granted transition periods when they join the EC/EU, permitting them to transpose certain parts of the *acquis communautaire* (the existing body of EU law and norms) into the domestic arena gradually, albeit within a pre-determined period of time. Moreover, within EU law, there are now a number of provisions that allow member states to adopt more far-reaching rules than those agreed at European level—another form of variation. In addition to these differences in the time and level of implementation, there are also examples of subgroups of member states co-operating on specific issues outside the framework of the EU. For instance, in 1985, West Germany, France, and the Benelux countries established what came to be known as **Schengen** co-operation, for the purpose of facilitating passport-free travel across national borders. The remaining EU member states joined only gradually (and even now not all countries participate fully) (see Chapter 19: 297–8). European defence co-operation provides another example: in 1992, France, Germany, Belgium, and Spain set up the **Eurocorps**, creating a multinational army brigade. In a certain sense, then, the idea of a uniform EU has always been more myth than reality (Wallace and Wallace 1995).

Despite these considerable variations, proposals for making the integration process more flexible or differentiated have tended to attract considerable scepticism, so that a more systematic use of methods of differentiation was rejected in the past. This is because differentiated integration differs substantially from variations traditionally permitted in EU law in a number important respects. In early examples, the flexibility employed was strictly limited in scope. Rather than being used in an extensive manner across a wide range of policies, it took place on an ad hoc basis and in a controlled way. Deviations from uniform integration were usually regarded as unique exemptions to the paradigm of uniformity. They concerned a very limited number of policies and a restricted timeframe. This type of flexibility thus offered a sense of security that the more systematic method of differentiation would not provide, making it more acceptable to European policy makers. However, from the mid-1990s, member states began viewing differentiation in a more benign light. The inclusion and extension of 'closer' or 'enhanced co-operation' in the Treaties of Amsterdam and Nice signalled a change of thinking. The reasons for this development may be found in the external pressures on the EU that emerged after the end of the Cold War.

Differentiation in the 1990s

In anticipation of the difficulties likely to be faced by the EU in combining the tasks of **deepening** and **widening**, member states in the 1990s prepared to depart from the long-established tradition of advancing European integration in a uniform manner. This change was fed, first and foremost, by an unprecedented pressure on the Union to enlarge, following the collapse of Communism in Central and Eastern Europe (see Chapter 14).

Enlargement on such a scale is likely to be detrimental to the further uniform deepening of the EU. Taking in as many as 12 new countries will greatly increase the political and economic heterogeneity of the Union. Member states' preferences for integration and the ability of new states to participate in new projects are likely to vary because of the different historical experiences, geopolitical interests, and socio-economic structures that they will bring to the Union. An agreement by most or all countries on a transfer of decision-making competence to the EU, a further development of existing policy, or the granting of new powers to the supranational EU institutions, may thus become very difficult if not, in many instances, impossible. The accession of the Central and East European countries (CEECs) will be particularly problematic, as they are relatively weak economically. As a result, they are unlikely to be willing or even able to participate in all developments in areas such as social or environmental policy. Thus, if the EU is to continue to work towards the fulfilment of the integration agenda initiated at Maastricht after the next enlargements, uniform integration may no longer be *possible*.

Moreover, maintaining uniform integration after the next enlargement may no longer be *desirable*. In a Union that extends from the Atlantic to the Bosphorus, and from the Mediterranean to the North Pole, the requirements for regulation will differ enormously. This could make centralized decision making in Brussels obsolete, as legislation may fail to address adequately the divergent needs of EU member states. Moreover, the present method of EU decision making may become redundant if, because of the need to decentralize, centralized decision making results in regulations that are so watered down and weak that they are in fact meaningless (see Box 24.1).

Key points

- Uniformity evolved as the dominant method of integration because the original six member states had similar ideas about the objectives of European integration and because law was the main instrument of integration.

- There have always been variations in the time-frame within which, and the degree to which, European law was applied in the member states. However, such variations were ad hoc, unsystematic, and limited.

- The prospect of enlargement has led existing member states to think more seriously about employing methods of differentiation within the EU framework.

Methods of differentiation

Differentiated integration is a rather ambiguous term. Since the 1970s, a wide variety of concepts along similar lines have been developed, including: graduated integration; core Europe; flexible integration; and variable geometry. Metaphors like 'flying geese', 'ships in convoy', or 'Olympic rings' have also been used to explain the various kind of differentiation either proposed or implemented. Understanding the terminology of differentiated integration is made more difficult as authors often use the same terms to describe different types of differentiation. In the 1990s a growing number of authors, pioneered by Stubb (1996), attempted to categorize these ideas into groups and thus clarify the language of differentiated integration. However, a standard terminology has still not evolved.

Even so, it may be helpful to provide a brief outline of the main methods of differentiation. Three distinct approaches may be identified: **multispeed** Europe; Europe **à la carte**; and a Europe of '**concentric circles**'.

The idea of a *multispeed Europe* is the least radical method of differentiation because it maintains the basic principles that have traditionally underpinned the European integration process. Thus, proponents of a multispeed Europe assume that member states are able to define the common goals of integration and that these goals are accepted and then implemented by all countries. However, they acknowledge that 'objective', that is, economic, differences between member states may make it impossible to achieve these goals at the same time.

Box 24.1 **The facts**
The provisions on enhanced co-operation in the Nice Treaty

The Treaty provisions on 'enhanced co-operation' are divided into general (enabling) clauses and clauses specific to each **pillar** of the EU.

General clauses

Title VII 'Provisions on Enhanced Co-operation' of the Treaty on European Union (TEU) contains some general conditions for the use of the instrument in the EU framework. They are sometimes referred to as 'enabling clauses' because they give a general permission to interested member states to create 'enhanced co-operation' within the framework of the Treaties.

According to Article 43, member states may establish closer co-operation between themselves and may, to this end, make use of the EU institutions, procedures, and mechanisms if the co-operation: is aimed at furthering the objectives of the Union and the Community, at advancing the integration process, and at protecting and serving their interests; respects the Treaties, the single institutional framework, and the *acquis communautaire*; concerns Union or Community policies but not those that fall within the exclusive competence of the Community; does not undermine the internal market or economic and social cohesion; does not constitute a barrier to or discrimination in trade between the member states and does not distort competition between them; involves a minimum of eight member states; respects the competences, rights, and obligations of non-participating member states; does not affect the Schengen protocol; and is open to all member states.

According to Article 43a, enhanced co-operation may only be used as a last resort. Article 43b requires that enhanced co-operation is open to all member states as long as they comply with the conditions for participation; both Commission and participating member states shall encourage as many EU countries as possible to take part.

According to Article 44(1), all member states take part in the deliberations on enhanced co-operation, but only the participating member states adopt the provisions.

Specific clauses

In addition to these general provisions, there are specific clauses for each EU pillar. They mostly concern decision-making procedures.

In the first pillar (the EC pillar), EU institutions have more influence over the establishment of an example of enhanced co-operation. According to the new Article 11, the Commission has the right to propose enhanced co-operation after interested member states have requested it to do so. Authorization for enhanced co-operation is given by the Council by a qualified majority on a proposal from the Commission and after consulting the EP. When enhanced co-operation is to be established in an area where the **co-decision** procedure applies, the assent of the EP is required. A member state may also request that the matter be referred to the European Council for discussion. After the matter has been raised before the European Council, decision making proceeds as outlined above.

The Treaty of Nice also introduces new clauses on 'enhanced co-operation' in the second (Common Foreign and Security Policy) pillar. According to Articles 27a–e, enhanced co-operation may be used for joint actions or common positions, but not in matters having military or defence implications. Interested member states address a request to the European Council to authorize the co-operation. The Commission 'shall give its opinion particularly on whether the enhanced co-operation proposed is consistent with Union policies' (Article 27c). Otherwise, the Commission and the EP must only be informed about developments.

In the third (justice and home affairs) pillar, also, member states wanting to establish enhanced co-operation may ask the Commission to submit a proposal. However, in contrast to the first pillar, if the Commission refuses to submit a proposal, the interested member states may develop a proposal themselves and submit it to the Council for authorization. Authorization is given by a qualified majority and after consulting the EP. Again, a member state may request that the matter be referred to the European Council.

While all member states will eventually have to apply the agreed policy objective, multispeed integration allows countries to do so in their own time. Economically advanced countries may thus forge ahead, while member states unable to follow because of 'objective' difficulties are permitted to progress according to their abilities. The aim of multispeed integration is therefore to achieve not permanently but merely *temporarily* different degrees of integration. In contrast to transition periods or **derogations**, commonly used for the implementation of EU directives or to facilitate the accession of new member states, multispeed integration does not involve fixed timetables for implementation. The different degrees of implementation are maintained for an indefinite period of time. However, in order to prevent a permanent separation of the faster from the slower member states, the 'laggards' are supported in the process of catching up. Multispeed Europe thus maintains the legal and institutional structure of the EU as well as the objective of an ever closer union among all member states. Yet, it adapts the method of achieving this goal in response to the increasing (economic) heterogeneity of the Union.

The second method of differentiation, *Europe à la carte*, is the most radical method. In terms of underlying assumptions, method, and outcome it is everything that multispeed integration is not. Europe à la carte allows member states to 'pick and choose' their European policies. While the current paradigm of uniform integration, and for that matter multispeed Europe, is based on the assumption that member states will find a common denominator that will allow them to progress together, proponents of an à la carte Europe regard the increasing social, political, and economic heterogeneity of the EU as an insurmountable obstacle to the creation of an ever closer union. Moreover, this method acknowledges the growing reluctance of certain member states to transfer sovereignty to the EU level. Proponents of à la carte integration argue that each member state should be allowed to decide which policies it wishes to participate in. In the most radical variant of all, Europe à la carte opens up all EU policies to 'picking and choosing'. Most à la carte proposals, however, require a common base of policies in which all countries must participate if they want to become an EU member state. This common base is usually the single market, but also includes some flanking (supporting) policies. Independent of the extent to which 'picking and choosing' is allowed, however, à la carte integration will produce numerous partnerships of varying membership and potentially different degrees of supranationality. Unlike multispeed Europe, Europe

à la carte thus allows for different degrees and forms of integration on a permanent basis, and gives up on the idea of uniform progression towards a supranational, and possibly even an eventual federal political system. While a unified supranational system is not excluded as end-goal of the integration process, and the different 'partnerships' are presumed to be open to those not initially involved, it is assumed that the predominance of national interests within this model will move the EU in the direction of a purely intergovernmental organization.

The final distinct method of differentiation is a Europe of *concentric circles*. This model differs in its scope from the previous two methods. While multispeed Europe and Europe à la carte focus exclusively on the EU, the concentric circles method tends to look at the European continent as a whole. It divides Europe into several concentric circles, so that around the smallest central layer several other layers are arranged. These circles increase in size the further away they are from the centre. Conversely, the intensity of supranational integration increases from the largest inner (or bottom) layer to the outer (or top) one. A member of a smaller circle is also a member of the wider circles. Membership in one circle is not permanent, however, and 'upward mobility' (or maybe we should say 'inward mobility') is possible as soon as the necessary economic conditions are fulfilled, or when the political will for further integration is found. In contrast to the Europe à la carte approach, it will not be possible, using this method, to decide to deepen only one single policy. Rather, the different layers are made up of a whole set of policies: the more highly integrated a circle is, the more the policies within it are communitarized or Europeanized. The decision by a country to move towards or away from the centre of the circle implies an acceptance of all the policies in that chosen circle. Thus, the concentric circles method does not make single policies available for picking and choosing but limits the choice to different types of international organization or institutional arrangements. The geometric result of this method of differentiation resembles a wedding cake, looked upon from above, or perhaps the ripple effect of a stone thrown into water.

Multispeed integration, à la carte integration, and

concentric circles thus vary greatly in terms of their method of differentiation and possible end-product. In brief, multispeed Europe differentiates by time, à la carte integration by policy area, and concentric circles by space (Stubb 1996). The three methods also differ in terms of their outcome. As multispeed integration merely differentiates by time, it eventually produces a higher degree of integration for every member state. Europe à la carte, by contrast, results in permanently different degrees of integration, as member states participate in different policies. The concentric circles method, finally, creates a deeper form of integration across a wide range of issues for some member states, and lower levels or integration for others, as it groups member states into circles depending on their ability and willingness to progress. As a result of their different potential impacts on the future shape of the EU, the three methods of differentiation have attracted different degrees of scepticism and support from the member states. While multispeed integration tends to be regarded as largely unproblematic, à la carte integration was for a long time rejected as a model for European integration. It is here that the recent shift of opinion is most obvious, as the provisions on 'closer co-operation' (now 'enhanced co-operation') inserted into the Treaties since Amsterdam strongly resemble the kind of functional differentiation that à la carte integration implies (see Box 24.1). Table 24.1 presents one typology of the three methods.

Table 24.1 Causes and visions: Alex Warleigh's typology

Model	Main cause of differentiation	Vision of integration
Multispeed	Inability to implement policy (short term)	Policy regimes with different members: laggards commit to catch up over time
Concentric circles	Inability to implement policy (long term)	Various tiers of member states around a hard core
A la carte	Choice not to participate in certain policies	Policy regimes with different memberships over the long term

Source: Warleigh 2002: 10.

Key points

- Three main types of differentiated integration have evolved: multispeed integration; à la carte integration; and concentric circles.

- The three methods differ in the kind of differentiation employed: 'multispeed' uses time as the main variable of differentiation; 'à la carte' integration differentiates by policy area; and 'concentric circles' differentiates by space.

- The 'enhanced co-operation' provisions included in the Amsterdam Treaty, and the revised 'enhanced co-operation' provisions agreed at Nice, resemble 'à la carte' integration.

Differentiation and the future of Europe

In allowing for the temporal or functional differentiation of EU policies, it is possible to resolve two of the fundamental challenges posed by the next round of enlargement. Multispeed integration would prevent the integration process from stagnating, an outcome that might result otherwise from the inability of some member states to participate immediately in costly policies (for instance environmental or social policies). These countries would be able to opt out of the more ambitious EU ventures until their socio-economic situation had improved. Therefore, multispeed integration would enable obstacles to future integrative projects based on socio-economic differences between EU countries to be addressed within the EU.

A la carte integration also allows the deepening of the EU to continue, despite the political objections of certain member states. It permits states that are willing to integrate to leave unenthusiastic countries behind and ensures that the latter do not hold back the integration process. This method of differentiation addresses the political obstacles to the future development of the EU. Moreover, à la carte integration also speaks to the perception that uniform integration is no longer desirable in a Union of 25 or more members. By permitting the creation of functional circles, à la carte integration allows groups of member states with similar problems to find solutions that are most appropriate for them. To a limited extent this kind of co-operation may already be found in today's Europe. There is, for instance, co-operation on the protection of the North Sea by those countries bordering on it. A similar arrangement exists for the protection of the Danube. An extension of this kind of functional co-operation would allow the creation of similar co-operation on a much wider range of issues. The functional differentiation of the European integration process thus opens up the possibility of creating solutions that are more tailored to the increasingly diverging needs of the member states. Used in this way, à la carte integration may even be a supplement to the **subsidiarity** principle (requiring decisions to be taken at the most appropriate level of governance—not necessarily the European level), introduced in the Maastricht Treaty.

Finally, the 'concentric circles' idea addresses both the economic and political problems posed by enlargement. It offers the possibility of delaying enlargement until the economies of the accession candidates have improved, while attending to the political needs of applicants by offering a more structured relationship. Within the EU, the concentric circles model allows weaker and unwilling member states to remain on the outside, thereby permitting 'core countries' to pursue a comprehensive deepening.

Problems of differentiation

Although differentiation has some obvious benefits, academics and EU policy makers have tended to oppose its extensive use. The idea of à la carte integration is particularly controversial. Scepticism towards differentiation stems from the fact that the concept challenges some of the fundamental principles on which the European integration pro-

ject, up to now, has been based, As a result, it risks creating serious political problems in the future. Of the various principles that have come to underpin the European integration process (Devuyst 1999), differentiated integration challenges, above all, the following: (i) the gradual process towards 'ever closer union'; (ii) the principle of solidarity amongst EU member states; (iii) non-hegemonic (consensual) decision making; and (iv) 'democratic' decision making.

First, traditionally, the European integration process has advanced by means of a gradual transfer of power to the EU level, resulting in an 'ever closer union' of all member states. Differentiated integration puts an end to this paradigm. A la carte integration and the concentric circles model allow for permanent differences in the degree of integration in which member states are involved. Thus, rather than moving member states towards 'an ever closer union', these two methods of differentiation risk fragmenting the EU. If member states are allowed to 'pick and choose' from a wide variety of EU policies or 'circles', and the EU continues to enlarge, the probability is that not all member states will participate in all EU policies. As a consequence, the EU is likely to break up into subsystems, each with a different membership, and each forming permanently different configurations of 'Europe'. While these disintegrating tendencies would obviously be most pronounced in the case of à la carte integration, the implementation of multispeed integration could also produce similar outcomes. Although the method of temporal differentiation implied by the multispeed model, foresees all member states eventually catching up with the 'leaders', a number of factors might obstruct this dynamic. For instance, a change of government in a derogating member state could change that state's policy preferences. Changes in the economic situation might also result in a defection from previously agreed policies. Finally, the realization that policies opted into by a few do not really work or are expensive to operate may, quite sensibly perhaps, prevent a derogating country from making an effort to catch up.

Differentiation also challenges the principle of solidarity which is said to operate amongst member states. But what is meant by solidarity here? As Devuyst (1999: 112) explains:

Schuman insisted that Europe had to 'be built by practical actions whose first result will be to create a *de facto* solidarity.' An extensive differentiation of the integration process threatens this principle. . . . the risks are greatest if *à la carte* integration and concentric circles is extended. . . . However, temporal differentiation might have the same effect if the faster (and thus richer) member states decide against transfer payments to their poorer partners in order to avoid the double financial burden of implementing the new policies and helping the poorer countries catch up. In all three instances the result of a loss of solidarity could thus be a two-class Community in which the poor and unwilling member states are left behind permanently while the remaining ones create ever more sophisticated integration projects. A two-class Community, however, will intensify the problems of decision-making and democratic legitimacy that risk being created by the use of differentiated integration in general.

Differentiated integration also risks putting an end to the principle of non-hegemonic decision making, that is, the premise that the bigger member states should not be able to dominate the decision-making process and thus impose their preferences on the smaller members. Differentiated integration threatens this principle in two ways. A la carte integration and the 'concentric circles' approach pose a direct threat to non-hegemonic decision making. In both cases, a member state's abstention will result from a desire not to participate in further policy integration. It is therefore logical that those states should not be involved in setting up the co-operation, as this might dilute the provisions, rendering them less effective or even useless. These two methods of differentiation therefore assume that subgroups of member states will continue to deepen EU policies unilaterally, without granting a say over this new co-operation to non-participants. What this means is that if the initially unwilling member states do decide to participate, they must comply with provisions into which they have had no input. In such cases, Europe à la carte and 'concentric circles' permit the initially willing member states to dictate the provisions that might ultimately apply to the rest of the Union.

In addition to this potential for hegemonic decision making, there are two more indirect processes that might encourage the dominance of some member states in EU decision making over differentiated policies. First, a failure to participate (fully) in an EU policy may raise doubts about a country's commitment to European integration. As a result, that country might be taken less seriously in deliberations on policies in which it does participate, and it may not be able to advance its interest as effectively as it otherwise might. Second, member states that do not participate (fully) in a policy may also lose the desire to take the initiative in neighbouring policies. If this happens, it will forfeit its 'first-mover' advantage on new legislation that could derive, for example, from basing a new proposal on existing national legislation. These two processes are independent of the method of differentiation used: they can apply to both functional and temporal differentiation, as in both cases some member states would not participate fully in new policy initiatives.

Ultimately, however, a shift towards 'hegemonic decision making' also causes problems for the democratic legitimacy of decisions adopted. If the more integration-minded member states are able to set the tone of policy content, countries joining late will have no choice but to comply with provisions adopted by others. Those governments cannot, therefore, be held accountable for the differentiated policy. This problem of democratic legitimacy could be exacerbated by the fact that supranational institutions may be less likely to play a key role in initiating and developing differentiated policy, as this will probably fall in an area over which member states will want to retain complete control, thus intensifying further the EU's **democratic deficit** (see Chapter 23).

Finally, an extensive use of differentiated integration is also likely to create problems of transparency. EU member states may end up belonging to different functional circles inside and outside the EU and, as a consequence, may be implementing a range of different policies at different speeds. These different levels of participation in the European integration process may lead to varying degrees of participation in EU decision making. Thus, the composition of the EU Council will vary depending on the differentiated policy discussed and the mode of differentiation used. This means that it would be even harder than it is now for non-specialists to make sense of the EU's already complicated policy process. It also means that it will probably be more difficult to develop a sense of 'European identity' amongst the peoples of Europe, however that is defined, an issue that some consider an increasingly necessary prerequisite for further integration.

A more extensive use of the different methods of differentiation thus risks creating serious problems for the EU. In challenging the four principles discussed above—an 'ever closer union' characterized by solidarity and non-hegemonic and democratic decision making—differentiation shakes the foundations of past integrative successes. It risks creating political tensions amongst member states that might prevent progress even in areas where there is, in fact, a common interest. Moreover, public support for integration might diminish even further as a consequence, and this, in its turn, might make governments more reluctant to embark on new integration projects. Ultimately, the EU might end up as little more than a glorified free trade area. Box 24.2 presents one view on flexibility and diversity.

Neither inevitable nor insurmountable

For the reasons identified above, differentiated integration, with the Europe à la carte model most problematic, attracts strong criticism. This, however, creates a dilemma: a greater differentiation of the European integration process seems inevitable after the next round of enlargement. Yet, more flexibility within the EU may result in exactly the situation it set out to address, that is, the disintegration of the Union. Does this mean that we should refrain from differentiated integration altogether? While the problems outlined above are severe enough to warrant some serious thought, differentiation should not be discarded out of hand, since many of the problems outlined above are neither inevitable nor insurmountable.

While much of the criticism levelled at differentiated integration is based on the assumption that it is used in an unrestricted fashion, in practice this is unlikely to happen. The provisions on 'enhanced co-operation' in the Nice Treaty impose a far-reaching set of conditions on their application. In practice, a scenario in which all EU policies are

differentiated is extremely difficult to envisage. This in itself reduces the degree of fragmentation and opacity that is likely to be created. However, limits imposed on the application of differentiation open up the possibility that an entirely different set of dynamics might apply. For instance, much of the criticism of à la carte integration is static. It implies that once a policy is differentiated it will stay that way. While such a scenario cannot be excluded, it is possible that more dynamic developments might arise out of an initial decision to create a differentiated policy. Functional differentiation may in fact *raise* the level of integration for all EU member states. A differentiated policy (or a new 'circle') might exert a 'magnetic attraction' (Dahrendorf 1979) on non-participants, encouraging them to join earlier than initially expected. For instance, non-participating member states may see abstention as politically or economically harmful to their interests. Thus, they may fear becoming victims of hegemonic decision making or suspect that their economies will suffer from staying out. These developments could encourage non-participants to change their attitude to joining, or might encourage them to catch up more quickly than they had initially planned. Thus the differentiation of an EU policy might even lead to a faster process of integration than would have been possible had all member states been forced to reach an agreement from the start. In this case, differentiation might be little more than a rather laborious way of taking majority decisions on further integration. Some of the 'disadvantages' of differentiation, such as the dangers associated with creating two classes of EU membership, may even contribute to a 'positive' integration dynamic. This would also mean that the dangers arising from a lack of transparency would be considerably reduced.

This dynamic does not address the issue of hegemonic decision making by the more pro-integration member states, however. Indeed, it may even intensify the problem, as it suggests that an eventual 'Communitarization' of the differentiated policy is likely. The problem could be minimized in two ways. First, future laggards and 'outs' could become involved in the creation of a differentiated policy, to ensure that their interests are safeguarded. This has been practised with some success during the EMU negotiations, with both countries

Box 24.2 **Core ideas**
Enhanced co-operation in the Nice Treaty: An analysis

Enhanced co-operation, or flexibility, . . . acknowledges the fact of diversity among the Member States, and its emergence is even more closely linked to the diversity expected to result from the prospective enlargement. A general flexibility regime was inaugurated at Amsterdam (and adapted at Nice) with the avowed purpose of coping with an enlarged membership that risked making it difficult, even under qualified majority voting, for the Union as a whole to pursue deeper and perhaps more adventurous integration.

But flexibility's relation to enlargement also needs to be examined more closely. At its core, enhanced co-operation is designed to protect the interests of the Member States that seek to use the Community system to achieve deeper or more far-reaching integration, not the Member States who are unable and/or unwilling to participate in that deeper or more far-reaching integration. Of course, the system does not leave reluctant or unqualified States wholly unprotected. At least until the Treaty of Nice is ratified, any State may block an exercise in closer co-operation by a subset of other States. But this is protection from enhanced co-operation, not protection through enhanced co-operation. The other guarantees that flexibility offers to

reluctant or unqualified States may be reduced to broad assurances to the effect that those States (a) will not be bound by the decisions taken by enhanced co-operation, (b) will not be prevented from joining the bandwagon as soon as they are willing and able to do so, and (c) will not discover that enhanced co-operation has upset the existing acquis communautaire.

These are impressive guarantees, but by definition they do not address the challenge of adapting the deliberative process to the realities of enlargement. The real challenge lies in finding legislative solutions at the Community level that entail the political participation of all Member States and that bind all Member States, even while permitting differential solutions or otherwise responding to the diversity of circumstances and needs among the how-ever-many-are-then number of Member States. Indeed, the current flexibility regime sweeps this whole problem 'under the rug' by asserting, summarily, that enhanced co-operation may not be pursued except as a 'last resort,' presumably meaning unless and until the ordinary legislative channels in which all the Member States participate have been exhausted.

Source: Bermann 2001.

with an opt-out, Britain and Denmark, and those that derogated, Greece and Sweden, participating fully in the negotiations leading to the formulation of the EMU provisions. However, granting prospective non-participants a say over the differentiated provisions is not without risk. Being unable or unwilling to participate from the start, they may insist on expensive transfer provisions, thus making the undertaking too expensive, or they may try to dilute the provisions, making the project less effective. Second, then, there may be another way of making decision taking in the run-up to the establishment of a differentiated policy less hegemonic, if the (supranational) European institutions are allowed to become involved in setting up this kind of differentiated policy. If they play the role of 'honest brokers', this might ensure that the

chosen solutions correspond with Union interests as well as national ones (see Box 24.3).

Key points

- Differentiated integration challenges some of the fundamental principles that underpin the European integration process.

- Differentiated integration may lead to the fragmentation and ultimately the disintegration of the Union.

- However, the differentiation of a policy could lead quickly to the participation of all member states, if the costs involved in staying out are perceived to outweigh those resulting from membership.

Box 24.3 **Issues and debates**
Some thoughts on the future of differentiation

The post-Nice process offers an opportunity for reform in which **flexibility** could play a major part. The elaboration of flexibility to date has been confused and excessively cautious, and illustrates the fact that seeking to marry it with the **Community Method** is a task with small prospects of success. Bolder and more imaginative thinking is thus necessary. In all likelihood, the new IGC [intergovernmental conference] in 2004 will not produce anything closely resembling a 'final solution' to the problems of EU governance. However, as an officially sanctioned means of making the Union function more effectively, this process and the eventual summit which will be its culmula-

tion must address these deficiencies squarely. They must also address the fact that the different member states have often fundamentally different views about what the solutions to these problems can, or should, be. Flexibility is an asset which cannot be ignored in such a situation: it is surely no coincidence that the RRF [rapid reaction force], which will allow the Union to play a more constructive part in the security governance of the continent, has been established as a result, and as a new form, of flexibility. As the EU assumes a more important role in world affairs while facing greater internal diversity, it is likely to require such solutions with increasing frequency.

Source: Warleigh 2002: 97.

Conclusion

This chapter discusses three issues: the reasons for the popularity of differentiated integration in the 1990s; the main methods of differentiation; and the benefits and problems of a more flexible integration process. It has been argued that the intensification of debate on differentiated integration in the 1990s was triggered by the prospect of a greatly enlarged Union. The prospect of an EU of 25 or more member states encouraged policy makers to think more creatively about how the European integration process might be advanced. Integrating the EU in a uniform manner will become increasingly difficult after enlargement, as the policy preferences and the economic needs of member states diverge. The 'enhanced co-operation' provisions must be seen in this context: they offer the possibility that willing and able member states might continue to deepen the EU after the accession of the candidate countries.

The inclusion of rules on differentiated integration in the Treaties marks the beginning of an à la carte EU allowing member states to 'pick and choose' the integration projects they want. Of the three methods of differentiation discussed in this chapter, à la carte

integration is the most radical, as it could lead ultimately to a disintegration of the EU as we know it today. Multispeed integration would seem to be less problematic, as it foresees different levels of integration, but only on a temporary basis. Concentric circles is somewhat in the middle, creating various 'classes' of EU membership but at the same time offering the possibility of maintaining current organizational arrangements.

While the three methods of differentiation might help to alleviate political or economic obstacles to further integration after the next round of enlargement, they also create new problems. Differentiation challenges some of the fundamental principles underpinning the integration process and risks undermining what has been achieved thus far. While the theory might suggest that these problems are particularly likely in the case of à la carte integration, even the use of temporal differentiation and concentric circles could be risky.

However, while the effects of differentiation are a source of concern to policy-makers, they may even enhance the level of integration in the EU. The involvement of some member states might encourage others to follow suit, especially if non-participation is perceived to entail some form of political or economic disadvantage. Ultimately, the success of applying methods of differentiation in the EU depends on a careful balancing of risks and advantages. If this is achieved, differentiated integration could become an essential instrument to ensure the continuation of a 'forward dynamic' within the European integration process.

QUESTIONS

1   Why was European integration traditionally based on the principle of uniformity?

2   How does enlargement challenge the paradigm of uniform integration?

3   How might differentiation resolve some of the problems associated with the enlargement of the EU?

4   What are the three main methods of differentiated integration and how do they differ from each other?

5   What problems are involved in introducing differentiation into the EU?

6   Is 'enhanced co-operation' as incorporated in the Nice Treaty a useful instrument for addressing the challenges facing the EU?

7   What effects might a greater use of differentiated integration have on the EU?

8   Is differentiation desirable?

GUIDE TO FURTHER READING

De Búrca, G., and Scott, J. (eds), *Constitutional Change in the EU. From Uniformity to Flexibility?* (Oxford: Hart, 2000). This is a comprehensive examination of the issue of flexibility. The authors assess the possibilities for applying differentiated integration in general, and 'enhanced co-operation' in particular, in selected EU policies and discuss the possible consequences of more differentiation for the (emerging) EU constitution.

Dewatripont, M., et al., *Flexible Integration*, Monitoring European Integration 6 (London: Centre for Economic Policy Research, 1995). This book develops a new concept of differentiated integration, flexible integration, but also discusses some of the problems associated with a more extensive use of differentiation.

Tuytschaever, F., *Differentiation in European Union Law* (Oxford: Hart, 1999). A discussion of differentiated integration from a legal perspective. The book categorizes some of the concepts of differentiated integration and gives examples of differentiation in EU law and policy.

Wallace, H., *Europe: The Challenge of Diversity*, Royal Institute of International Affairs: Chatham House Papers 29 (London: Routledge & Kegan Paul, 1985). This book analyses the origins of diversity in the EU and its implications for the future development of the EU, and explains the main strategies of differentiation developed to address these problems.

Warleigh, A., *Flexible Integration. Which Model for the European Union* (Sheffield: Sheffield Academic Press, 2002). This book examines why 'flexibility' has become such an important feature of the EU. It develops a typology to explain the models through which this concept might be understood. The author argues that there is ample scope for flexibility to make a positive contribution to the European integration process.

WEB LINKS

http://europa.eu.int/futurum/index en.htm The EU website on the Future of Europe debate, which includes comments on the possible further development of enhanced co-operation.

http://europa.eu.int/scadplus/leg/en/lvb/928000.htm The EU website which covers the Amsterdam Treaty provisions on closer co-operation.

http://europa.eu.int/comm/nice treaty/index en.htm The European Commission's website on the Nice Treaty (including its provisions on enhanced co-operation).

25 Citizenship

Antje Wiener

READER'S GUIDE

This chapter is about **Citizenship** of the Union,[1] which it identifies not only as a new legal **institution**, but also as a new social practice. Institution in this context refers to rules and norms; practice refers to social interaction in the process of establishing the meaning of this institution. It points to the new rights that EU citizens enjoy over and above their *national* citizenship rights and obligations. As well as looking at the formal definition of citizenship (that is: who qualifies as a citizen; what the political, civil, social, and cultural rights of citizens are; and which obligations are involved), the chapter also considers citizenship in the context of the EU's political system (the 'Europolity').

Introduction

Citizenship is about rights, access, and belonging to a particular community. As a legal **institution** (that is, a system of rules and norms) based within the constitution of a state, citizenship defines who has a right to belong inside and who does not qualify (see Figure 25.1). While citizenship always entails universally defined rights and obligations of membership, each community's definition and interpretation of citizenship differs according to its particular historical trajectory, that is, according to the social practices that define the meaning of citizenship

within and for that particular **polity**. The politics and policy that contribute to that particular meaning of citizenship are defined as **citizenship practice**, whereas the meaning endowed in citizenship is defined as the **citizenship ideal**. From citizenship *practice*, different rights, terms of access to participation, and identities emerge. The question for EU Citizenship is thus whether we can identify rights, terms of access to participation, and identity that are specific to *European* citizens.

This chapter begins by establishing the facts of

Union Citizenship. It considers what Union Citizenship means in formal terms: that is, its legal definition, and the political rights it confers. The chapter also examines the role of citizenship in the history of modern state building; and the meaning we attach to the concept of citizenship. The chapter then moves on to offer a brief introduction to the history of Citizenship in more general terms, and in the next section reviews the emergence of Citizenship of the Union from this perspective. This section accounts for the dynamics and the context in which Union Citizenship was created, and explores the relevant legal texts, policy proposals, and documents that were produced in the process. It asks how this citizenship took shape to acquire substance and how it adds to national citizenship. The final section offers an assessment of the possible impact of Union

Citizenship on the day-to-day practice of individuals (residents, citizens, and visitors) on the courts and in EU politics, and questions how it may affect our understanding of citizenship in general. It is argued that Union Citizenship represents an innovative step towards changing the concept of citizenship as we know it within the contexts of modern nation states.

Three questions will need to be elaborated more fully by future research in this area. First, the potential political impact of Union Citizenship will need to be explored. Second, the role of Union Citizenship in the EU enlargement process deserves further attention. And, finally, the implications of citizenship as an organizing principle in the international system needs to be considered, given that Union Citizenship contributes to the fragmentation of citizenship rights in an entirely novel way.

Citizenship of the Union

Dealing with citizenship is a multidisciplinary endeavour. Legal scholars, political scientists, sociologists, historians, and philosophers all engage in the debate. Though coming at the topic from a political science perspective, this chapter will therefore cast light on different views and interpretations of this new citizenship. While there are now increasing efforts to engage in interdisciplinary work on citizenship, it is helpful to distinguish between the distinctive and leading questions that lie at the heart of the respective work of lawyers, on the one hand, and political scientists, on the other. Lawyers are, for example, especially interested in how particular legal conditions paved the way for the expansion of Community law. Typically, they ask the following questions:

• When, why, and how were citizens directly linked to the 'Europolity' as subjects of the law?

• When was citizenship first mentioned in a court ruling?

• What did that ruling mean, and did it have implications on later rulings and legislation?

• What form did the new Treaty provisions take?

• How do these rulings contribute to the legalization of the Europolity; and what was their impact on changes in national law?

In turn, political scientists are interested in the politics and policy which brought this citizenship on to the political agenda, which contributed to its **constitutionalization** in the 1993 Maastricht Treaty, and which follow on from it. Their questions are the following:

• What triggered the institutionalization of citizenship at the supranational level?

• Which actors and political interests led to the inclusion citizenship in the Treaty?

• What forms did the relevant agenda setting, bargaining, and process take?

• What are the political implications of this citizenship for the EU, for the member states, and for the accession countries?

• What political innovations, with regard to the direction and quality of European integration, are likely to follow?

• What type of *institutional* adaptation can be observed in current and future member states?

Citizenship of the Union was established by the **Maastricht Treaty** in 1991 (Article 8, EC Treaty). Since its ratification in November 1993, citizens of the EU have enjoyed a number of rights that are directly conveyed by and enforceable through the Union. They include the right of residence and the right to free movement; the right to vote and stand as a candidate at municipal elections in the member state of residence; the right to vote and stand as a candidate in elections to the European Parliament (EP) in the member state of residence; diplomatic protection while in third countries: and the right to petition the EP. Achieving the status of Citizen of the Union is the exclusive right of 'every person holding the nationality of a Member State' (Article 8, EC Treaty).

After the Treaty revisions in the 1997 **Amsterdam Treaty**, the content of the Citizenship Article was slightly revised and renumbered (see Box 25.1). More importantly, a clarification of the relationship between national and Union Citizenship was added at Amsterdam. Thus, while the Maastricht Treaty stipulates that: 'Citizenship of the Union is hereby established. Every person holding the nationality of a Member State shall be a citizen of the Union. Citizens of the Union shall enjoy the rights conferred by this Treaty and shall be subject to the duties imposed thereby' (Article 8, EC Treaty), the Amsterdam Treaty adds a distinctive line on the complementarity of European and national citizenship. It states that 'Citizenship of the Union is hereby established. Every person holding the nationality of a Member State shall be a citizen of the Union. *Citizenship of the Union shall complement and not replace national citizenship*' (Article 17, EC Treaty). As Shaw (2000: 373) points out:

[T]he reference to the nationalities of the Member States is important. It states clearly the limited nature of EU citizenship. It links back directly to one of the framework 'constitutional' provisions of the TEU itself, Article 6(3) TEU: 'The Union shall respect the national identities of its Member States, whose systems of government are founded on the principles of democracy'.

Further to these provisions, there are a number of other articles in the Treaties that relate either directly or indirectly to the citizens of the EU (see Box 25.2).

Box 25.1 **The facts**
Citizenship of the Union

Citizenship of the Union means the following for all citizens of the Union:

• the right to move freely and to reside on the territory of the member states (Article 18 of the EC Treaty);

• the right to vote and to *stand as a candidate in elections to the European Parliament* (EP) and in *municipal elections* in the member state in which he or she resides, under the same conditions as nationals of that state (Article 19 of the EC Treaty);

• the right, in the territory of a third country in which a national is not represented, to *protection by the diplomatic* or consular authorities of another member state, on the same conditions as the nationals of that state (Article 20 of the EC Treaty);

• the right to petition the EP (Article 21 of the EC Treaty) and the right to apply to the **ombudsman** (Article 21 of the EC Treaty) in order to bring to his or her attention any cases of poor administration by the Community institutions and bodies, with the exception of legal bodies.

It also means, following the entry into force of the Amsterdam Treaty in 1999:

• the right to apply to the European institutions in one of the official languages and to receive a reply in that language (Article 22 of the EC Treaty);

• the right to have access to EP, Council, and Commission documents under certain conditions (Article 255 of the EC Treaty).

The last three rights also apply to natural or legal persons, such as companies, that have their residence or headquarters in one of the member states of the EU.

Source:
http://europa.eu.int/scadplus/leg/en/lvb/l23001.htm.

Box 25.2 **The facts**
Citizens' rights elsewhere in the Treaties

- Article 1 TEU (ever closer Union, decision taking close to citizens)

- Article 2 TEU (identity on international level, *acquis communautaire*)

- Article 6(1) TEU (principles of freedom, democracy, human rights, basic freedoms, rule of law)

- Article 6(2) TEU (fundamental rights, European Convention on Human Rights (ECHR), member state constitutions)

- Article 6(3) TEU (national identity of member states)

- Article 12 TEC (no discrimination on grounds of nationality)

- Article 14 TEC (creating a market without internal frontiers)

- Article 39 TEC (free movement of workers)

- Article 141 TEC (equal pay for men and women)

The inclusion of Citizenship of the Union in the Maastricht Treaty triggered a wide range of reactions from lawyers and social scientists, as well as from political actors and other social forces. Amongst others, non-governmental organizations (NGOs) debated what this citizenship meant. While all these responses took a critical line on the new citizenship, maintaining that it had left substantial gaps, especially when compared to the more familiar national citizenship rights and duties, it is possible to distinguish two discrete approaches. Lawyers tended to discuss Union Citizenship from the perspective of what it *was*, whereas NGOs, lobby groups, and philosophers discussed what it *should become* or *ought to be*. The formal legal components of European citizenship were often compared to the experience of citizenship in national states, or to the needs of those affected by it, that is, citizens and residents of the EU. Alternatively, it was viewed as a concept of modern political philosophy.

To understand and deal with Union Citizenship, therefore, means identifying the perspectives and interests of those who address this concept. Thus, some stress the limitations of Union Citizenship, comparing its legal trajectory and potential to national citizenship. They conclude that Union Citizenship is comparatively 'thin', in that it has less to offer than national citizenship rights. Others assess Union Citizenship as a social concept that develops over time. This reflects a view of citizenship as 'thick' and 'under construction'. It could, for example, be extended to include 'place-orientated'

citizenship rights, so that third-country nationals (TCNs) who are long-term residents in the EU might obtain Union Citizenship. According to Meehan (1993), these two different—thin and thick—approaches to citizenship can be distinguished as *minimalist* and *dynamic* approaches. Whereas the minimalists pursue a formal approach focusing on the evaluation of legal rights in the EU, the dynamic approach has been endorsed by social scientists keen to consider new policy options and opportunities and to discuss ways of rethinking citizenship.

As an evolving concept, 'European' citizenship has now been part of European integration for three decades. However, awareness of this citizenship has had a much shorter lifespan. The big debates were only sparked relatively recently by its constitutionalization within the Maastricht Treaty. Before then, and since the late 1960s, European citizenship was largely hidden from academic and public view, with a few notable exceptions (such as Meehan 1993; Evans 1984; Magiera 1991; and Closa 1992).

This first supranational citizenship has wider implications for our understanding of the changing nature of citizenship, both as a concept in the social sciences and as a legal **institution**. The key to understanding just how innovative this new citizenship is reflects the fact that it was put *on a par* with national citizenship. In other words, Citizenship of the Union creates an additional citizenship for the nationals of EU member states. At the same time, however, residents of the EU who do not hold a member state passport, for example Turkish residents in Germany, or Moroccan residents in France, are distinguished from EU citizens and labelled as third-country nationals (TCNs) (see Chapter 19). Thus, while one group gained new rights, another was explicitly excluded—the political consequences of which this chapter will return to later.

Key points

- Lawyers and political scientists both study Union Citizenship, though the questions they pose may differ.

- Union Citizenship was introduced in 1991 by the Maastricht Treaty, which came into force in 1993.

- Understanding Union Citizenship means identifying the interests and perspectives of those who address the concept.

- There are two main understandings of Union Citizenship—a 'thick' and a 'thin' version.

A brief history of citizenship

This section looks at the constitutive and historical elements of citizenship in order to explore what citizenship is, and how its meaning has evolved over time.

The constitutive elements of citizenship

In the broadest sense, the role of citizenship in a constitutional context can be defined as follows: citizenship establishes institutionalized links between citizens and their political community. The rules and norms which regulate the practice of citizenship include principles of justice, formal political and legal procedures, norms, and values. All contribute to establishing the procedures of political participation and day-to-day practices of citizen participation within a particular politically defined community. Nationality entails the entitlement to belong to that community (see Figure 25.1).

The *community* has the right and indeed the obligation to represent community interests *vis-à-vis* other communities and the citizens as well. This relationship then links two types of entities, the individual citizen on the one side, and the representative of a sovereign community (Queen/estate/ nation state, or in generic terms, a **polity**) on the other. This relationship represents the basic pattern

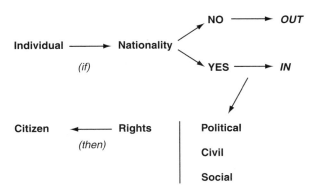

Fig. 25.1 Modern citizenship
Source: Wiener 1997.

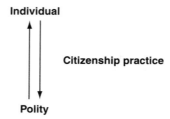

Fig. 25.2 The constitutive elements of citizenship
Source: Wiener 1998: 22.

of citizenship. To study citizenship, then, three elements need to be considered: the individual, the polity, and the relationship between the two. These elements are called the three *constitutive elements* of citizenship (see Figure 25.2).

The relationship between citizens and the polity has, for a long time, been intrinsically linked to modern state building: that is, the way that individuals saw themselves as linked to the central institutions of political authority, together with the struggles over citizenship rights, tended to support the emergence of a particular type of state, political institutions, and constitutional framework. Indeed, it is possible to state that citizenship, or the discourse surrounding it, defines the 'borders of order' (Kratochwil 1994). It sets the rules of who belongs to a community and who does not. While there are exceptions to this, such as dual citizenship (Koslowski 1998; Joppke 1998), by and large, citizenship is an exclusive concept. It is about entitlements and duties for a chosen few, with a view to binding and grounding them within one particular community. As such, it forms the core of the politically organized modern community.

However, citizenship is not restricted to *top-down* institution building. Historical studies have demonstrated that political struggles over the expansion of citizenship rights have contributed to the formation of new communities. For example, the British sociologist, T. H. Marshall, observed that in the UK, civil, political, and social rights developed over the course of two centuries. His studies suggest an incremental extension of rights from *civil rights*, that is, the right to liberty of the person, freedom of speech, thought, and faith, to own property, to conclude valid contracts, to *political rights*, the right to participate in the exercise of political power,

and ultimately *social rights*, that is, the right to basic social welfare and security, to share in social heritage and live the life of a civilized being (Marshall 1950: 10–11; see also Figure 25.3). *Bottom-up* mobilization is another important factor in the emergence of citizenship (Tilly 1975; Bendix 1964; Jenson 1992; Turner 1990).

In sum, talking about citizenship invariably involves a notion of '**stateness**' (Barbalet 1988; Brubaker 1989; Turner 1990; Hobe 1993). Since citizenship of the Union was introduced in the constitutional framework of the EU, which is not a state, this citizenship challenges assumptions about the link between citizenship and stateness. Apart from being a new supranational institution, as a new transnational practice it also calls into question the role of national citizenship. Yet, as Curtin points out, 'the unique *sui generis* nature of the Community, its true world-historical significance [is constituted by its character] as a cohesive legal unit which confers rights on individuals' (Curtin 1993: 67; Shaw 2001: 381).

The historical elements of citizenship

The development of modern citizenship has involved the gradual expansion of citizenship rights through the political interaction of nationals (including both the governors and the governed) within a polity. It is characterized along two dimensions which are central to the construction of borders—both political borders between states, and sociocultural boundaries between classes and other sociocultural groups. The first dimension concerns *rights*, including the right to free movement, the political right to vote, and the social right of access to education and the distribution of welfare. The second dimension is about *identity*, that is, belonging to a particular national community. Both dimensions are linked to the establishment of modern states and the fixing of their territorial borders.

In political philosophy, these dimensions are represented by liberal and republican approaches to citizenship. The liberal assumption is that citizenship is about individual rights *vis-à-vis* the state and other citizens. These rights are universally derived and locally established. For example, they are often written down in a constitution or in legal statutes. In the republican approach, by contrast, citizenship is about the process of governing and being governed. This places a stronger focus on political participation within a community, a practice which ultimately contributes to the establishment of a particular identity which, in turn, makes communities distinguishable from each other.

Historical studies of citizenship reveal the key role of three historical elements of citizenship. The first element is *rights* which establish how the individual is legally related to the polity. *Access*, as the second element of citizenship, concerns the conditions for practising the relationship between citizen and community. This is best understood as access to political participation. Conditions of access are set by regulatory policies, such as social policy and visa policy. They are crucial determinants of whether individuals are fit to participate politically. Access therefore hinges on sociocultural, economic, and political mechanisms of inclusion and exclusion: that is, while rights may have been stipulated, access may be denied because the means to *use* citizenship rights, such as education, communication, transportation, have not been sufficiently established.

The third historical element encompasses two modes of *belonging* to a community. One is identity based and evolves through social practices within a community. The other is based on the legal stipulation of nationality and hinges upon legal linkages to an entity. These are currently based either on the law of soil (*ius solis*) or of blood (*ius sanguinis*), or, as in the EU, on the nationality of one of the member states. Potentially, every person residing within a particular area has the opportunity to participate in the creation of collective identities, which may evolve through, for example, participation in the work place, in cultural matters, or in other areas of social life. Residence is therefore a key requirement for participation. This importance of sociocultural practices notwithstanding, it is the legal status— nationality 'yes' or 'no' (see Figure 25.1)—that confirms whether an individual is considered as a citizen who has the potential to achieve full membership rights within a community. As T. H. Marshall (1950: 28) writes:

[T]here is no universal principle that determines what those rights and duties shall be, but societies in which citizenship is a developing institution create an image of an ideal citizenship against which achievement can be measured and towards which aspiration can be directed. The urge forward along the path thus plotted is an urge towards a fuller measure of equality, an enrichment of the stuff of which the status is made and an increase in the number of those on whom the status is bestowed.

There is, therefore, an important distinction to be made between nationality as a status that defines a citizen's legal belonging to a polity, on the one hand, and citizenship in the meaning of full membership of a community, on the other. Full membership means that citizens enjoy the rights and opportunities of full participation within a community. In reality, however, full membership has always remained exclusive. For example, women have been excluded from suffrage (the vote), and are still excluded from military service in many countries (see also Jenson and Papillon 2000: 2). Therefore, in order to investigate the degree of membership that citizens enjoy within a particular community, it is necessary to consider the three historical elements of citizenship.

To understand the meaning of citizenship, then— that is, how universal citizenship rights are realized within a particular community at a particular time—the interplay between citizenship, in terms of both practice and theory, is useful. From this perspective it is possible to identify how citizenship is continuously contested and reconstructed over time. It offers a methodology for examining historical differences based on the three historical elements of *rights*, *access*, and *belonging* (see Figure 25.3).

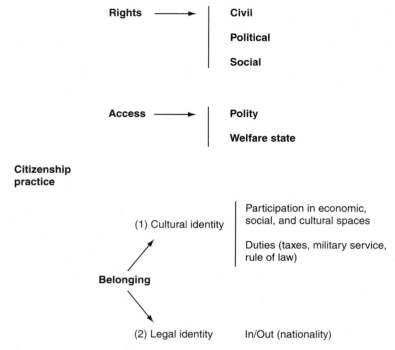

Fig. 25.3 The historical elements of citizenship
Source: Wiener 1998: 26.

Belonging is not restricted to the legal status of citizenship. It is also about borders, as citizens derive certain rights and opportunities of access based on their belonging to a bounded sphere. More specifically this feeling of belonging depends on an earlier process of 'drawing boundaries' around the terrains designed for those citizens who belong.

In sum, a sociohistorical perspective sheds light on relational aspects of citizenship. It highlights the tension between the universal assumption of the equality of all citizens, and the reality of persisting inequality. It allows us to see citizenship practice as a way of dealing with this tension and of accommodating diversity. Importantly, perceptions of ideal citizenship are rooted in society. They evolve over time in relation to **citizenship practice**. If we are to understand the meaning of citizenship within a particular context, that is, if we are, in Marshall's words, looking for the source of the **citizenship ideal**, we need to focus our attention more on source practices.

Two insights about the role of citizenship in the formation of political communities may be gleaned from history. First, citizenship is a product of an ongoing process which involves debates about the terms of citizenship and struggles for access to participation. This process contributes to the creation of shared values and norms, forging feelings of belonging to specific groups or communities. Second, the three key types of modern citizenship rights have been shaped and established over two centuries. Importantly, Marshall's study points to the often-overlooked fact that citizenship rights are rarely introduced all at once; nor does their institutionalization mean that all citizens will benefit from them in an equal and fair way. Indeed, modern citizenship rights were bundled together only relatively recently in modern welfare states in the second half of the twentieth century. It follows that citizenship consists of different elements which might be bundled into one set at some times and stay fragmented at different levels and with different implications for the involved citizens at other times.

Indeed, they had been fragmented for about two hundred years, before they were bundled in the post-1945 period. Since the 1980s, there has been evidence of renewed fragmentation, however. Therefore, social scientists might legitimately ask whether the current period of fragmentation will lead to another phase of 'bundled' citizenship. And if so, what, if not the nation state, will be the new reference point for citizenship?

The perception of citizenship as an evolving institution provides a helpful point of departure for understanding the changing conditions of citizenship in the EU. If, as Marshall suggests, citizenship ideals are formed within societies, it follows that blurred geographical boundaries and pooled sovereignties challenge that nationally constructed type of bundled citizenship. In turn, the lack of what we might call an updated citizenship ideal, reflecting the new transnational context of citizenship practice, poses a threat to the organizing capacity of citizenship. This threat is well reflected in the debate over the '**democratic deficit**' in the EU, which is based on the lack of a shared identity (*ethnos*) and the absence of a 'European' political community (*demos*) (see Chapter 23).

Key points

- The constitutive elements of citizenship are the individual, the polity, and the relationship between the two, i.e. citizenship practice.

- Citizenship has generally involved the notion of 'stateness'. Citizenship of the Union, therefore, challenges conventional understandings of citizenship (as the EU is not a state).

- There are three historic elements of citizenship: rights, access, and belonging.

The evolving institutions and practice of European citizenship

The literature on citizenship tells at least two stories about the emergence of European citizenship, each following a distinctive trajectory. The first story takes a legal perspective, focusing on the expansion of rights, based on freedom of movement, as pushed by the case law of the European Court of Justice (ECJ). The second story is based on a series of discussions and deliberations among policy makers and politicians about the EU as a political entity. A distinction is made here between the term 'Union Citizenship', which is used when indicating exclusive reference to the formal rules and norms entrenched in the EC Treaty (Articles 7 to 22) and the wider concept (in other Articles and provisions elsewhere in the Treaty as well as the socio-culturally constructed meanings of citizenship) which will be referred to by the term 'European citizenship'.

Evolving legal institutions and practice

The legal perspective on Union Citizenship focuses on the gradual enhancing of citizens' rights from 'market citizenship' towards 'political citizenship', through legal integration. In other words, cases brought to the ECJ by EU citizens are the main empirical material for lawyers. Legal scholars are also interested in how citizenship rights and citizens, as the subjects of law, figure within the emerging trans- and supranational legal order. For example, they are interested in how legal practice and new institutions impact on the strict distinction between national or constitutional law, on the one hand, and international law, on the other; and the implications for the practice of national law within each member state of the EU.

International law, European law, and the national legal contexts of the 15-plus current member states, all have an impact on perceptions of the role and meaning of Union Citizenship. For example, each member state has to adapt its legal procedures and legislation in line with new European directives. Is it, for example, legitimate to speak of a particular European citizenship law in the making? The direct link between citizens and the EU seems to suggest such an interpretation. There are doubts, however, as to whether or not the substance of Union Citizenship is comparable to 'nationality' or 'national citizenship'. Are there possibilities of further developing this institution legally? What are the likely legal practices involved? Which rules guide this process? And which institution has the competence to define the rules?

To answer these questions, lawyers recall the evolution of European citizenship, which began in the 1950s with the introduction of **'market citizenship'** (Kadelbach 2002: 2; Marias 1994: 1). They point to the fact that it was in the late 1950s that European integration began to push beyond the narrow confines of a freedom of movement principle that was originally related exclusively to the market. They show that what were originally conceived of as the rights of *'market* citizens', were gradually expanded. As Kostakopoulou states, for example, 'workers are not seen as mere factors of economic production, but as human beings' (2001: 40). Subsequent rulings on labour and social rights also followed this line. For example, as early as 1958, two regulations on the social security of migrant workers were passed in the Council, one of which characterized the right to freedom of movement as a *fundamental right of workers* to improve their standard of living, which must be exercised in 'freedom and dignity'.

Overall it is important to understand that the process of **negative integration**, that is, the removal of obstacles to free trade across internal borders within the Community, guided the first steps towards the construction of a European citizenship. It set the framework for **positive integration** which focused on more explicit policy steps towards creating European citizenship that were developed from the 1970s onwards. The market-based logic suggests that the

Treaties already entailed an 'incipient form of European citizenship' in 1958, if only for certain groups, such as workers, professionals, service providers, and their families (Plender 1978; Kostakopoulou 2001: 41). The **four freedoms** (see Chapter 3: 30), among them the freedom of movement, are not generally seen as contributing in any strict legal sense to Union Citizenship. Yet, as Shaw notes, 'it is out of the field of free movement that the concept of citizenship in the EU context largely emerged' (2000: 377).

In sum, the case law of the ECJ laid the early foundation of a 'rights-based' approach to freedom of movement. That 'market citizens' were moving across borders and residing in member states other than that of their own nationality raised all sorts of practical issues, including social insurance, fundamental rights, non-discrimination on the grounds of nationality, and so forth. Two larger issues had an impact on the evolving concept of European citizenship (O'Leary 1996), namely the protection of social rights, and the question of political inequality. The first was largely dealt with by the case law of the ECJ; the second was taken up by political actors such as the EU institutions and interest groups. This chapter first recalls the first issue and then turns to the second issue in the following section.

A notable case was *Martinez Sala* v *Freistaat Bayern*.[2] The *Martinez Sala* case is important as it offers an account of the link between legal practice and the evolving concept of Union Citizenship. In this case an unemployed Spanish citizen had moved as a 'market citizen' to Germany and had been living there since 1964. However, while she had not had a residence permit since 1984, she put in a request for family (child-raising) allowance in 1993. Her application was rejected on the ground that she did not have German nationality, a residence entitlement, or a residence permit. The key question put to the Court was whether, as an unemployed person, Ms Martinez Sala had the right to freedom of movement and residence according to Article 18 EC and whether she could put her case forward as a Union citizen. Martinez Sala finally won her case. The ECJ ruled that:

for the purposes of recognition of the right of residence, a residence permit could only have declaratory and probative force. Consequently for a member state to require a national of another member state who wished to receive a benefit such as the allowance at issue in the main proceedings to produce a document which was constitutive of the right to the benefit and which was issued by its own authorities, when its own nationals were not required to produce any such document, amounted to unequal treatment which, in the absence of any justification, constituted discrimination prohibited by art 6 of the EC Treaty. It followed that Community law precluded a member state from requiring nationals of other member states authorized to reside in its territory to produce a formal residence permit issued by the national authorities in order to receive a child-raising allowance, when the member state's own nationals were only required to be permanently or ordinarily resident in that member state (ECJ 1998).

The legal reasoning in the judgment makes explicit reference to Martinez Sala's right to non-discrimination on the grounds of nationality (as in Article 12, EC Treaty). However, it does not make the case on the basis of Union citizenship.

Other important cases that demonstrate the fragmented quality of citizens' rights in the EU, that is, cases that involve demands that are not necessarily or exclusively based on the citizenship clauses in the Treaty but which are situated elsewhere in the Treaties (see Box 25.2), include the application of the right to equal pay for men and women (Article 141, EC Treaty), a right that generated from French labour law. This stipulates that 'Each member state shall . . . ensure and subsequently maintain the application of the principle that men and women should receive equal pay for equal work'. The expanded Equal Treatment Directive (76/207/EEC) included access to employment, vocational training and promotion, and working conditions. A good example of the application of this European right was the *Tanja Kreil* case.

In this case, a German woman complained about her exclusion from the German military exclusively on the grounds of sex (Case C–285/98 *Tanja Kreil* v *Bundesrepublik*). Kreil sued the German armed forces, claiming that the rejection of her application on grounds based solely on her sex was contrary to European law. She stated that Article 12a of the Basic Law of the Federal Republic of Germany 'constitutes direct discrimination' (C–285/98, Judgment, 11 January 2000: No. 11). The ECJ ruled in her favour (Wobbe 2002: 15–16). Case law thus offers important information about how Union Citizenship affects the lives of citizens, and the development of legal and political institutions and procedures, both in the member states and at EU level. The second issue of political inequality was taken up by political actors, triggering deeper questions about equality and citizenship, as the following section shows.

Evolving political institutions and practice

From the early 1970s policy making on Union Citizenship unfolded on the basis of two policy packages including the objectives of: 'special rights' for Community citizens; and a 'passport union'. These policy objectives were adopted in the Final Communiqué of the 1974 Paris Summit. Both touch on crucial aspects of modern citizenship, such as borders and how to cross them (passport union), and citizens' right to vote and stand for elections (special rights). These have been central to the debates about citizenship, European identity, and political union that have been evolving since the early 1970s and received a strong push after the Maastricht IGC. This section demonstrates that the step-by-step development and application of these two policy packages provides an insight into how citizenship was eventually included in the Maastricht Treaty twenty years later. It also suggests that over time Union Citizenship acquired a specific meaning, forging a European citizenship ideal which was both fragmented and transnational. It is important to note, however, that those who identified the goals and policy objectives of citizenship practice in the early 1970s had not envisaged this outcome. The story of European citizenship practice (see Box 25.3) thus reveals a case of institution building which had unintended consequences (North 1990; Pierson 1995; Wiener 2001).

In the early 1970s EC politicians and practitioners expressed their desire to enhance the 'European' presence on the global stage. To that end, it was suggested that the Community should work towards a stronger European identity. The adoption of the 1976 Council Decision implementing direct universal suffrage, the first European elections in 1979, and the adoption of a Council Resolution on the

Box 25.3 **Core ideas**

The kick-off for 'European citizenship'

'I have at times compared Europe with Tarzan. It has a relatively advanced morphology but its speech is still fairly scanty.'

Etienne Davignon (1972)
in *Agence Europe*, (1973: 7)

'Who speaks for Europe?'

Henry Kissinger (1973),
quoted in Dinan (1994: 85)

creation of a single European passport in 1981, were crucial first steps. Besides these institutional changes, the citizenship discourse had also been expanded to incorporate the idea of 'Europeanness', introduced in a document on 'European Identity' in 1973. Thus, from early on, citizenship practice was linked to the project of building a European Union, based on the project of creating a stronger sense of identity in the European Community.

In the 1980s, the bold political 'kick-off' for citizenship practice that had occurred during the previous decade was slowed down. Economic uncertainty, widespread concerns over ungovernability in the member states, an increasing fear of **Eurosclerosis**, unsolved budgetary problems, and a general feeling of pessimism, all led to a stronger focus on market making or *economic* integration. Instead of the aspirations of positive integration (building the European Union, creating citizenship), negative integration (removing obstacles within the free market) was prioritized, with the freedom of movement of workers as a key condition for economic flexibility. In other words, it was not access to the polity (the political right to vote) but access to participation in a socio-economic sense, that became the major concern of citizenship practice during this period. The call of the then president of the European Commission, Jacques Delors, for a 'Europe without frontiers by 1992' guided this effort. Thus, aside from abolishing internal Community borders, the related Single Market Programme included new strategies for the creation of

a European identity. As a European Commission White Paper explained:

Recognition as a 'Community centre of excellence' for establishments giving additional training or conducting very advanced research in specialized areas would help towards *the increased mobility of students and research scientists* within the Community. The European Council should express its support for these types of activity, which *will promote the European identity* in the eyes of the economic and social decision-makers of the future of the Community (European Commission 1985).

This involved the extension of access to the market on a group-by-group basis. For example, a new mobility policy targeted groups such as young people, teachers, and students. Among these programmes were the European Community Action Scheme for the Mobility of University Students (ERASMUS), and the Young Workers' Exchange Scheme (YES). The European Parliament (EP) stressed the importance of programmes such as these in the building of an ever closer union, when it observed that '[c]ooperation among the Member States of the Community in the field of education and culture is inherent to the process of the construction of Europe, and reflects the spirit of the Treaties, since there is no doubt that it promotes closer relations between peoples' (Laffan 1996).

Three new directives established the right of residence for workers and their families and for students. Two types of 'special rights' were also negotiated. First, a series of social rights, including health care, the right to establishment, an old-age pension, and the recognition of diplomas, were defined with the **Social Charter**. These rights were the economic and social conditions that would prevent **social dumping**. Importantly, for the development of 'European' citizenship, crossing borders to work in another member state meant that so-called 'foreigners' (in this case, Community citizens working in a member state of which they were not nationals) and nationals shared day-to-day economic life, yet remained divided when it came to their political rights. Second, this situation evoked awareness of a '**democratic deficit**' in the EC. For example, the Commission identified that the impact of economic integration at times implied a loss of political status. Citizens who moved across internal community borders faced a loss of access to political participation. To overcome this dilemma the Commission proposed the establishment of voting rights for 'foreigners' in municipal elections. This proposal for a Council directive was drafted with a view to closing the gap between foreigners and nationals. Bringing the political right to vote back on to the policy agenda was largely facilitated by the possibility of 'dusting off' a previously created informal resource of the *acquis*, namely equal political rights for European citizens.

Demands for greater access to participation, both in political and socio-economic terms, were renewed in the 1990s. With the Maastricht Treaty and the end of the Cold War, the political project of building the Union was back on the political agenda. Critical perspectives on European identity as part of citizenship practice were brought to the fore. '[F]rom the outset, the Community had considered itself as synonymous with "Europe." With the Cold War over, [the question became] could the Community foster a sense of pan-European solidarity and genuinely pan-European integration?' (Dinan 1994: 158). These questions challenged the discourse on 'European' identity which had been so crucial for the emergence of citizenship practice in the early 1970s. At that time, 'European' identity had meant West Europeans only. Now, the end of the Cold War cast a new light on the term, emphasizing that some Europeans had been left out all along. Also significant for citizenship practice was the instability of the **Paris–Bonn axis**, which had proved a solid foundation for European integration thus far, as the German chancellor, Helmut Kohl, pushed for fast German unification while the French president, François Mitterrand, was 'torn between an instinctive antipathy toward German unification . . . and an equally instinctive affinity for European integration' (Dinan 1994: 163). One way of addressing this tension was to forge a link between German unification and European integration. This solution contributed to a renewed emphasis on political integration. It created an opportunity for those actors interested in establishing a European citizenship. In particular, a number of Spanish proposals pushed the process of citizenship practice in the period immediately before the Maastricht IGCs (see Box 25.4).

Box 25.4 **Core ideas**
The Spanish proposals on citizenship

The Spanish contribution to the 1990 IGC proposed a 'concept of Community citizenship [which] was different from the notion of the Europe of citizens that had been introduced at the Fontainebleau summit' in that it would include political, economic, and social citizenship rights.

Source: European Commission 1990: 1–4.

Until that point two types of policy resource had been mobilized by citizenship practice since the early 1970s. First, citizenship was to grant rights that were specific to the EC as a polity and as a social space. Second, the visible sign of Union Citizenship, when travelling outside the Community, was to be the uniform burgundy-coloured passport. Both of these resources were formalized at Maastricht in Article 8 (EC Treaty).

To summarize, while the end of the Cold War in 1989 and the renewed emphasis on political integration in Europe had created an opportunity to establish political citizenship rights, the larger history of citizenship practice since the 1970s reveals that the meaning of Union Citizenship is not derived from the sum of the member states' national citizenship rights and practices; nor can its substance be deduced from the concept of modern citizenship. Instead, citizenship of the Union was constructed anew, albeit with its own characteristic features. The 1990s saw the institutionalization of political and legal citizenship rights. Although the historical element of belonging had been addressed in the previous two periods, now the focus was set on establishing legal ties. Not only were these important for redefining the link between citizens and the Community, they also raised questions about the political content of nationality. (See Box 25.5). This third period of the developing practice of European citizenship also meant a shift away from 'modern' citizenship by making nationality of an EU member state the precondition for Union Citizenship.

The constitutionalization of 'thin' citizenship

Box 25.5 Issues and debates
European Parliament demands for Union Citizenship

Along the lines of the Spanish proposals, which had called for a concept of Community citizenship (see Box 25.4), the European Parliament demanded that Union Citizenship be included in the Maastricht Treaty as a separate title comprising the central aspects of 'social rights including a substantial widening of the proposals contained in the Social Charter; equal rights between men and women; the political right to vote and stand for election in local and EP elections at one's place of residence, as well as the political right to full political participation at one's place of residence; and the civil right to free movement and residence in all Member States'. Importantly, the Report repeatedly emphasized the need to rethink citizenship as it could no longer be reduced to the 'traditional dichotomy between citizen and foreigner or to the exclusive relationship between the state and the citizens as individuals' (European Parliament 1991).

Source: Bindi Report I.

meant in practice an institutionalized fragmentation of citizenship. In other words, some rights of European citizens were identified by the Citizenship Articles (Articles 17–22, EC Treaty), whereas others were outlined elsewhere in the Treaties (see Box 25.2). As the Commission states in its Third Report on Union Citizenship:

under the terms of Article 17(2) of the EC Treaty, *citizens of the Union are to enjoy the rights conferred by this treaty and are to be subject of the duties imposed thereby.* The rights that feature in Part Two of the Treaty, under the heading Citizenship of the Union, thus form the core of the rights conferred by citizenship, but are not an exhaustive list. The EC Treaty confers on citizens of the Union other rights which appear elsewhere in the Treaties, such as protection from all forms of discrimination on grounds of nationality (Article 12). It is therefore legitimate for this Third Report on Citizenship of the Union to go beyond the specific rights featuring in the second part of the EC Treaty and to examine subjects that have an obvious connection with citizenship of the Union, such as the fight against all forms of discrimination and, more generally, the protection of fundamental rights in the Union (European Commission 2001d: 6).

A fourth period in the history of citizenship practice demonstrated a growing mobilization around and a rising confusion over the consequences of this fragmentation. The EP organized hearings in Brussels during which non-governmental organizations (NGOs) could express their demands to the IGC. While NGOs were not formally entitled to participate in the IGC process, and had no formal channels for participation, these hearings nevertheless offered space for discussion. Post-Maastricht a new debate unfolded over the gap between politically included and excluded residents, that is, between citizens who had legal ties with the Union, and TCNs, individuals who had no legal ties but are likely to have developed feelings of belonging nonetheless. This debate was pushed by interest groups and by the EP. (See Box 25.5.)

In the debate over TCNs it is important to recall that once the Berlin Wall came down, the EC had to face a new challenge in the area of border politics; namely visa and asylum policy, which involves the question of East–West migration (see Chapter 19). One idea that was promoted as a way of solving this potential political problem was the establishment of 'place-oriented citizenship' (Wiener 1996). This entered the EP debate (see the Outrive and Imbeni Reports) and has led to pressure from social movements to change citizenship legislation in the Treaty. For example, instead of granting citizenship of the Union to 'Every person holding the nationality of a Member State' (Article 8 (1)), as was the case after Maastricht, a number of advocacy groups such as the European Citizen Action Service (ECAS) or the ARNE Group (the Antiracist Network for Equality in Europe) requested citizenship for '[e]very person holding the nationality of a Member State *and every person residing within the territory of the European Union*' (ARNE 1995). However, the Amsterdam Treaty did not reflect these demands. On the contrary, the nationality component of citizenship was re-inforced, within revised Articles 6(3) TEU and 17 TEC which state that the national identities of the member states must be respected. The potential flexibility of the citizenship article (Article 8e EC Treaty) was thus left unexplored. Yet while the formal institutional aspects of Union Citizenship thus largely remained as they were, the informal aspects of 'European' citizenship witnessed further reform in the post-Amsterdam period, so that the European institutions began to work more with national representations, national parliaments, and NGOs on citizens' demands, in order to react to growing disaffection with the European integration process. 'Citizens First' and its successor programme, 'Dialogues with Citizens and Business', campaigns initiated by the EP and introduced to the member states by the Commission to bring Europe closer to its citizens, are examples of this change of emphasis.

Key points

- The case law of the ECJ allowed rights which originally applied to market citizens to be expanded.

- Union citizenship involves both past experiences with national citizenship in each member state and present experience with European citizenship practice.

- Four periods of European citizenship practice are identifiable in the history of European integration. While the first period stressed a unified European identity based on 'special rights' for European citizens, the fourth period has produced different types of identities. Instead of special rights for one particular type of European citizen, groups of citizens, for example workers or students, now enjoy specialized rights.

Challenges for the future

Despite formal institutional changes in the Treaty and in the constitutions of the EU member states, Union citizenship remains contested, that is, citizens are not really sure what this new citizenship actually means for them. As the European Commission correctly states in its *Second Report on Citizenship of the Union*:

The introduction of citizenship of the Union has raised citizens' expectations as to the rights they expect to see conferred and enforced. Citizens are entitled to be aware of these rights and to have them honoured in practice by the Member States. Otherwise citizens will regard EU citizenship as a vague and distant concept (European Commission 2001*d*: 26).

Lawyers and political scientists differ in their assessments of what this citizenship means, as it now stands, and regarding its future potential.

As both a new supranational institution and as a transnational practice, this new citizenship has repercussions for the relationship between citizens and 'their' community. This occurs along three core dimensions: first, the *identity* of citizens (who belongs where and why?); second, the type and range of *rights* citizens can evoke (which rights can be evoked within which institution and on what level?); and third, the channels of *access* to participation in the wider political and social community of 'European' citizens (who is allowed to participate, on what grounds and where?). It goes without saying that these three dimensions have wider implications for the type of community the EU might become. Elaborating on them provides some insights into the character of the EU. See Box 25.6.

From Aristotle's dictum 'the citizen is the state' (Koslowski 2001), to more recent observations about how the negotiation of citizens' rights have contributed to the building of the modern state (Marshall 1950; Tilly 1975), the most significant aspect of citizenship has been how it has been defined *vis-à-vis* the state. Its political function seemed clear, namely that 'in Western, liberal

Box 25.6 Core ideas

The polis *and the citizen*

the constitution of a polis involves in itself some sort of association, and its members must initially be associated in a common place of residence. To be fellow-citizens is to be sharers in one state, and to have one state is also to have one place of residence. (There must therefore always be sharing in a common neighbourhood.) (Aristotle 1981: 39–40).

democracies public authority requires legitimation through one principal source: The citizens of the polity' (Weiler 1996: 6). Thus, much of the literature suggests that the explanatory potential of citizenship lies in the contribution it makes to the forging of a central authority in modern communities.

But Europeanization and globalization present significant challenges to modern state-citizenship relations. Thus, as is evident from the European context, 'the processes which created and sustained sovereign territorial states in this region are being reversed' (Linklater 1996: 77). While the merger of *demos* and *ethnos* contributed to construct the vision of overlapping political and national borders within 'imagined communities' (Anderson 1991), the fragmentation of identities and the diffusion of state sovereignty in the EU raise serious questions about the stability of this image. After all, once individuals began to enjoy different types of rights in a new world that reflected flexibility and mobility, it became increasingly difficult to define citizenship practice as based solely on nationality. Meehan captured this fragmented aspect of European citizenship noting that it is:

neither national nor cosmopolitan but . . . multiple in the sense that the identities, rights and obligations associated . . . with citizenship, are expressed through an increasingly com-

plex configuration of common Community institutions, states, national and transnational voluntary associations, regions and alliances of regions (Meehan 1993: 1).

Questions which remain to be further explored as citizenship develops, and as European integration proceeds, are whether and how this fragmented concept of citizenship, the specialized identities, and the pluralist institutional setting which arise as a consequence of citizenship practice will have an impact on the future of the polity. In other words, what is the role of citizenship (and citizens) in the ongoing constitutional debate about the future of Europe? Furthermore, the introduction of citizenship within the Treaty has a number of implications in the member states as well as for the candidate countries. For example, member states are responsible for reforming electoral laws and procedures in line with EU legislation. Furthermore, according to the transition rules agreed as part of the current round of enlargement, the freedom of movement of workers will remain restricted, if only for a limited period. As a consequence, new Union citizens may feel that they are being unfairly treated, a situation that could create some conflict in the Union. Here it will be interesting to observe whether the new Union citizens of the candidate countries will turn for support to the ECJ, demanding full and equal citizenship rights.

Key points

- The difference in the meaning of national and Union citizenship remains to be explained to European citizens.

- While access to Union Citizenship is based on nationality of a member state, European citizenship practice has been constitutive for our understanding of citizenship as a fragmented concept.

Conclusion

This chapter has explored the definition and meaning of the concept of Union Citizenship from legal and political perspectives. It identified the rights conferred an each citizen of the EU by the concept of Union Citizenship, and discussed the legal and political meaning of this new supranational form of citizenship. The chapter also considered the implications of Union Citizenship for European integration. By comparing the citizenship of the Union to citizenship as a universal concept, as well as a concept that lies at the core of modern state formation, the chapter also pointed to the ways in which this new citizenship differs in meaning and reach from earlier 'modern' understandings. As a universal concept, citizenship allocates fundamental rights and identities to individuals within a particular community. As a historical concept, citizenship sets the conditions for individuals to achieve full membership of a bounded political community, based on rights, access, and belonging. However, as the EU is not a state as such, Union citizenship challenges conventional understandings of citizenship and draws attention to the way in which citizenship has become an increasingly fragmented concept, not only in Europe but also throughout the world.

QUESTIONS

1 What is citizenship?

2 What is the relationship between a community's citizenship ideal and citizenship practice?

3 How do lawyers and political scientists differ in their approach to Union Citizenship?

4 To what extent was the issue of European citizenship raised prior to the Maastricht Treaty?

5 In what way did the Maastricht and Amsterdam Treaties constitutionalize Union Citizenship?

6 What are the constitutive elements of citizenship? And what are the historic elements of citizenship?

7 Why do academics believe that European citizenship is becoming increasingly fragmented?

8 What are the major challenges facing Union Citizenship?

GUIDE TO FURTHER READING

Kostakopoulou, D., *Citizenship, Identity and Immigration in the European Union* (Manchester: Manchester University Press, 2001). A helpful study which emphasises the theorizing of citizenship in a post-national and post-statist context, and considers possible alternative institutional designs. Works with theoretical approaches to citizenship, identity, and migration, respectively.

Marshall, T. H., *Citizenship and Social Class* (Cambridge: Cambridge University Press, 1950). Deals with the prospect for social equality in post-war Britain and what has thus far been achieved. Offers a historical approach to institutional change and the construction of a citizenship ideal, pointing out the evolution of civic, political, and social citizenship rights in Britain in the nineteenth and twentieth centuries.

Meehan, E., *Citizenship and the European Community* (London: Sage, 1993). This is one of the first books dealing with the topic of European citizenship in a comprehensive way. It considers the link between civil, political, and social citizenship.

O'Leary, S., *The Evolving Concept of Community Citizenship* (London: Kluwer, 1996). This book considers the concept of Community or Union citizenship. It focuses on the importance of member state nationality for issues concerning free movement of persons and also views Union citizenship from the perspective of the principle of equal treatment.

La Torre, M. (ed.), *European Citizenship– an Institutional Challenge* (The Hague: Kluwer, 1998). An edited book which covers a broad range of aspects of European citizenship.

Wiener, A., *'European' Citizenship Practice– Building Institutions of a Non-State* (Oxford: Westview, 1998). This book focuses on the constitutive role of citizenship practice for polity-formation. It develops the concept of citizenship practice as the process of policy making and/or politics that contributes to institutionalize the terms of citizenship. It draws both on a comparative-historical literature and on institutionalist theories of European integration.

WEB LINKS

http://europa.eu.int/abc/cit3_en.htm EU web page on European citizenship, with links to legal documents and practical information.

www.citizen.org.uk/speak_out.html The website of the Institute for Citizenship, which includes some material on European citizenship.

www.ecas.org The website of the European Citizen Action Service (ECAS), a non-governmental organization which focuses on information for European citizens.

ENDNOTES

1. For helpful comments on earlier versions of this chapter I thank Jo Shaw and, in particular, Stefan Kadelbach.

2. 1998. *Maria Martinez Sala* v *Freistaat Bayern*, NL 98/3/10 Rs. C–85/96 (ECJ). See **www.sbg.ac.at/oim/docs/98_3/98_3_10.htm**.

Glossary

Accountability the requirement for representatives to answer to the represented on how they have performed their duties and powers, and for those representatives to act upon criticisms made of them and accept responsibility for failure, incompetence, or deceit.

Acquis communautaire the *acquis* is the Community patrimony, the body of common rights and obligations which bind the member states together. It includes the content of the Treaties, legislation, international agreements, and other measures such as norms and conventions.

Action for annulment a court case which might lead to the rejection of a law.

Adenauer, Konrad (1876–1967). First Chancellor of the Federal Republic of Germany after the end of the Second World War. He held office for 14 years, and was responsible for overseeing the reconstruction of West Germany in the 1950s, particularly in the context of European integration—of which he was a key supporter.

Agenda 2000 an influential action programme adopted by the Commission on 15 July 1987, which set out the reforms needed for the EU to enlarge.

Agenda setting the process by which an issue or problem emerges on to the political scene and is framed for subsequent debate.

A la carte a non-uniform method of integration which allows member states to select policies as if from a menu.

Amsterdam (Treaty of) signed in October 1997, and in force from 1 May 1999, the Treaty amended certain provisions of the Treaty on European Union and the European Community Treaties.

Assent a legislative procedure in which the Council must first obtain the European Parliament's assent before certain important decisions can be taken. It applies to decisions about the accession of new members to the European Union.

Authority the right or capacity (or both) to have proposals, prescriptions, or instructions accepted without recourse to persuasion, bargaining, or force; more simply, the power or right to control, judge, or prohibit the actions of others.

Barriers to trade protectionist technical and fiscal rules, and physical constraints that carve up or prevent the creation of the internal market.

Benelux short for 'Belgium, Netherlands, and Luxembourg'. The term originally related to the 1944 Customs Union between these three countries, and is said to have been coined by the Brussels correspondent of *The Economist* in 1947.

Bi-cameral involving two chambers. Usually refers to parliaments divided into an upper and a lower house.

Bretton Woods agreement signed by 44 countries in July 1944 to support an international monetary system of stable exchange rates. The aim of the Agreement was to make national currencies convertible on current account, to encourage multilateral world trade, and to avoid disruptive devaluations and financial crashes.

Budgetary deficits governmental shortfalls of current revenue over current expenditure.

Central banks bankers to the government and to commercial banks. They manage public debt, control the money supply, and regulate the monetary and credit system.

Change mechanisms processes through which change takes place. Examples include 'rule-following', 'learning', and 'argument and persuasion'.

Charter of Fundamental Rights signed at the Nice European Council meeting in December 2000, the Charter of Fundamental Rights sets out fundamental rights associated with EU membership. It is not a legally binding document, but is expected to be incorporated into the Treaties at some point in the future.

Citizenship the condition or status of a citizen as a member of a community, which is usually determined by law. It entails certain rights and obligations.

Citizenship ideal the meaning endowed in a particular concept of citizenship.

Citizenship practice the politics and policy that contribute to a particular meaning of citizenship; how citizenship as a concept is operationalized in the political sphere.

Civil society an intermediate realm between the state and the individual or family; or a particular type of political society rooted in principles of citizenship.

Closer co-operation established by the Amsterdam Treaty, it introduces instruments which allow groups of states that wish to integrate further than provided for in the Treaties to do so. It was renamed 'enhanced co-operation' at Nice.

Co-decision procedure a complicated three-stage decision-making procedure that involves both the EU Council and the European Parliament in making European legislation, thereby enhancing the role of the Parliament in the legislative process. It was introduced in the Treaty on European Union at Maastricht (Article 251, formerly Article 189b) and simplified in the subsequent Amsterdam Treaty.

Co-determination employee participation in the decision making of firms, through, for example, works councils.

Cohesion a principle that favours the reduction of regional and social disparities across the European Union.

Collective bargain an agreement negotiated by trade unions and employers or their associations on incomes or the working conditions of employees.

Collective goods goods that cannot be excluded from those who have not paid for them (such as 'clean air').

Collegiality a principle which implies that decisions taken by one are the collective responsibility of all.

Comitology refers to the network or procedures of committees designed to oversee the agreement of implementing measures taken by the EU's executive bodies.

Common external tariff a central element of any customs union. A set of common tariffs, agreed by all members, imposed on goods coming into the Union from outside its borders.

Common market an economic agreement that extends co-operation beyond a customs union, to provide for the free movement of goods, services, capital, and labour.

Communitarized Communitarization is the process by which responsibility for a policy is moved from Pillars 2 or 3 to Pillar 1, the EC pillar. It implies the increased involvement of the supranational European institutions in European decision making.

Community method the use of the 'established' process of EC decision making, which involves a Commission legislative initiative being agreed by the Council, and now usually the European Parliament. It also implies that the

Court of Justice (ECJ) will have jurisdiction over any decision taken.

Compliance the act of complying or acquiescing to the law.

Concentric circles a concept which envisages a Europe structured out of subsets of states which have achieved different levels of integration.

Conciliation process the third stage of the co-decision procedure, at which point an equal number of representatives of the Parliament and Council get together to try to work out an agreement acceptable to all.

Conditionality the principle that applicant states must meet certain conditions before they can become members of the European Union.

Confederal see **Confederation**.

Confederation a political model which involves a loose grouping of states, characterized by the centre having fewer powers than the states or regions.

Consensual type of decision making that involves the agreement of all, even where this is not formally a requirement.

Consociational(ism) a political model which brings together distinct communities in shared decision making, while protecting the interests of minorities.

Constitutionalization the formalization of the rules of the game, which in a European Union context might involve a process whereby the Treaties become over time—*de jure* or just de facto—a Constitution.

'Constitutive' tradition an understanding of the world which problematizes the relationship between theory and reality, which are deemed to be tied closely one to the other.

Constructive abstention allows member states to abstain in the EU Council on Common Foreign and Security Policy decisions, without blocking a unanimous agreement.

Constructivism or 'social constructivism'. A theoretical approach that claims that politics is affected as much by ideas as by power. It argues that the fundamental structures of political life are social rather than material.

Consultation the original EC decision-making procedure, which gave the Commission the exclusive right of initiative and the Council the ability to take decisions, but which allowed the Parliament only a consultative role in the legislative process.

Convention (on the Future of Europe) a body set up in 2002 to debate alternative models and visions of the European Union, and to prepare a draft Constitution which could be used as the basis of discussion in the intergovernmental conference of 2004.

Convergence criteria the rules that member states had to meet before they could join Economic and Monetary Union in 1999.

Convertibility where one currency is freely exchangeable into other currencies.

Co-operation usually implies government-to-government relations (with little supranational involvement).

Co-operation procedure a legislative procedure introduced in the Single European Act (Article 252, formerly Article 198c), which allows the European Parliament a second reading of draft legislation. Since Amsterdam, it is now very little used, as most policies originally falling under this procedure now come under the **co-decision procedure**.

Core Europe or 'hard core': a small group of countries able and willing to enter into **closer co-operation** with one another.

Corporatist corporatism is a model of policy making that links producer interests to the state, and where interest organizations are incorporated into the system. Corporatism (as opposed to neo-corporatism) is often associated with (Italian) fascism of the 1930s and 1940s.

Customs union an economic association of states based on an agreement to eliminate tariffs and other obstacles to trade, and which also includes a common trade policy *vis-à-vis* third countries, usually by establishing a common external tariff on goods imported into the union.

Davignon Report a document issued by EC foreign ministers in 1970, outlining how the Community might develop its own foreign policy, and setting out some initial steps to that end.

Decision a legislative act, directed at one particular actor or group of actors, or state, rather than being generally applicable.

Deepening the integration dynamic; a term usually describing an intensification of integration processes and structures.

de Gaulle, Charles President of France from 1959 to 1969. Responsible for keeping the UK out of the EC in the

1960s, and for the 'empty chair policy' which is said to have ushered in a more intergovernmental European integration process after 1966.

Delegated legislation legislation usually made by executive bodies on behalf of legislatures. It often involves the making of administrative rules, and the filling in of gaps in existing legislation.

Delegation an act which allows a legitimate political institution to hand powers over to a body which then acts on its behalf.

Democratic deficit the loss of democracy caused by the transfer of powers to the European institutions and to member state executives arising out of European integration. It implies that representative institutions (parliaments) lose out in this process.

Demos the people of a nation as a political unit; a politically defined public community.

Dependent variable the object of study; the phenomenon one is trying to explain.

Derogations temporary exceptions to legislation.

Differentiated integration see **Differentiation**.

Differentiation the idea that sub-sets of member states might engage in European integration projects that do not involve all existing members; contrasts with the notion of the EU as a uniform exercise in integration.

Direct actions cases brought directly before the European Courts.

Direct implementation the putting into effect of European legislation by the European institutions (rather than by national governments).

Directives legislative instruments that specify the aims to be achieved, but which generally leave the question of how to achieve those ends up to national governments or their agents.

Directly effective having a quality which allows provisions of Community law to be enforced in national courts, and which impose obligations on those against whom they are enforced.

Dirigiste see **Interventionist**.

Enforcement the process of ensuring that (Community) rules are implemented. It may involve taking action in the European Courts.

Enhanced co-operation see **Closer co-operation**.

Enlargement the expansion of the European Union to include new member states.

Epistemology theory of knowledge, which accounts for the way in which knowledge about the world is acquired.

Ethnos a shared identity; an imaginary community of descent and affiliation; somewhere between 'tribe' and 'nation'.

Eurocorps a multinational military force of 50,000 set up in 1995 to promote co-operation across the EU's armed forces. Involves France, Germany, Spain, Belgium, and Luxembourg.

European Central Bank (ECB) established in Frankfurt in 1999, the ECB is responsible for the single monetary policy of the 'Eurozone'.

European Coal and Steel Community (ECSC) established by six states in April 1951 by the Treaty of Paris, the ECSC allowed for the pooling of authority over coal and steel industries. As it was based on a 50-year treaty, the ECSC ceased to exist on 23 July 2002.

European Currency Unit (ECU) the unit of account under the European Monetary System, composed of a 'basket of currencies'. It was replaced by the 'euro'.

European Monetary System (EMS) a regulated exchange rate system established in the EC in 1979 after a failed attempt to set up an Economic and Monetary Union earlier in the decade. The EMS aimed to promote monetary co-operation and exchange rate stability.

European Political Co-operation (EPC) foreign policy co-operation prior to Maastricht, set up after 1970 and formalized by the Single European Act.

European System of Central Banks (ECSB) the national central banks together with the European Central Bank.

Europeanization defined in various ways (see Chapter 22). For example, it may refer either to the process of European integration itself, or may be used as a shorthand for the 'Europeanization of domestic institutions, politics and identities'.

Eurosclerosis a word used to characterize the period of EC history between 1966 and the early 1980s, when the process of integration appeared to be slowing down, and when the common market objective within the Treaty of Rome was not persued.

Eurozone the economic area which covers the 12 countries that have so far joined the EU's single currency.

Exchange Rate Mechanism (ERM) the main element of the European Monetary System—a mechanism that aimed to create a zone of monetary stability within Western Europe.

Executive(s) branch of government, responsible for implementing laws taken by parliament; the administration.

Executive rule-making the making of administrative law, which usually involves decision taking by civil servants. In the EU, this will often mean regulation by the Commission (albeit overseen by committees of member state representatives).

Federal see **Federalism**.

Federalist promoting federal ideas or ideology.

Federalism an ideological position that suggests that everyone can be satisfied by combining national and regional/territorial interests in a complex web of checks and balances between a central government and a multiplicity of regional governments. In a European Union context it tends to imply an ideological approach that advocates the creation of a federal state in Europe.

Federation a way of organizing a political system that involves the constitutionally defined sharing of functions between a federal centre and the states. A federation will usually have a bicameral parliament, a constitutional court, and a written Constitution.

First pillar The European Union is divided into three pillars. The first pillar is the European Community pillar. Most European policies fall under this part of the Union.

Fixed exchange rates exchange rates tied together (with no fluctuations possible) having the same effect as a single currency, but allowing states to keep their own currencies.

Flexibility see **Differentiation**.

Fortress Europe the image of a European single market, liberalized internally, but protectionist *vis-à-vis* the outside world.

Fouchet Plan a plan proposed in 1961 and pushed by the French government, which would have led to the creation of a European intergovernmental defence organization, but which was rejected by the EC's member states.

Four freedoms a central pillar of the single market programme of 1985 was the promotion of the free movement of goods, services, labour, and capital—the 'four freedoms'.

Framework decisions decisions that sketch the broad outline of a policy, and which usually rely on further legislation before implementation is possible.

Franco–German axis see **Paris–Bonn axis.**

Free-ride To reap the benefits of a collective agreement without having participated in efforts to forge the agreement or to implement it. See also **Collective goods;** a free-rider is someone who benefits from collective activity without participating in it.

Functional 'spillover' the knock-on effect of integration in one sector, which is said by neo-functionalists to provoke pressures for integration in neighbouring sectors.

Globalization a contested concept, which usually refers to the growing economic independence of state and non-state actors worldwide. Often associated with increased capital mobility and the spread of neo-liberal ideas, for example. It implies that market authority is enhanced at the cost of formal political authority.

Grand theory a theory that tries to explain the entirety of a political process, such as European integration.

Harmonization the act of setting common European standards from which states are unable to deviate (either upwards or downwards).

Hegemony power, control, or influence exercised by a leading state over other states.

Implementation carrying out or putting into effect adopted policies, whether legally or practically.

Incorporation see **Transposition.**

Independent variable one discrete factor contributing to an explanation of some phenomenon (to a dependent variable).

Indirect implementation the putting into effect of European legislation, which involves action by national governments or their agents.

Inflation a progressive increase in the general level of prices brought about by expansion in demand or in the money supply.

Infringement proceedings the act of initiating a procedure for breach of European law, which may result in a court case.

Institution an institution is a network of principles, rules, norms, and procedures. It is sometimes more narrowly

used in a European Union context as a synonym for 'organization', as when one talks of the 'European institutions'.

Institutional theory theory that sees an important role for structures (such as rules and norms) in political life, rather than simply focusing on the interactions of individuals and groups.

Integration a general concept, which implies the act of combining parts to make a unified whole—a dynamic process of change. European integration is usually associated with the intensely institutionalized form of co-operation found in Western Europe after 1951.

Intensification a method of farming that aims to use land more and more efficiently by increasing productivity, but which may have negative long-term consequences for the environment.

Interdependence a condition in which the actions of one state impact upon others.

Interest intermediation the process of translating interests into policy, through the medium of interest organizations.

Interest rate the rate of return on savings, or the rate paid on borrowings.

Intergovernmental bargaining the bargaining that takes place between governments, particularly in the EU Council or European Council; and which usually excludes supranational actors.

Intergovernmental Conference (IGC) structured negotiations among the EU's member states, which usually leads to a treaty revision.

Intergovernmental co-operation co-operation that involves sovereign states, and which occurs on a government-to-government basis, rather than through the extensive involvement of supranational actors.

Intergovernmentalism a theory of European integration which privileges the role of states.

Intervening variables factors that may influence a particular phenomenon, but which do so by filtering or altering the effects of '**independent variables**'.

Interventionist interventionism is where governments involve themselves in the regulation of markets, by means of government policy, rather than leaving markets to regulate themselves.

Joint-decision trap the idea promoted by Fritz Scharpf in 1988 that while it might be increasingly difficult in future for further integration to take place, it will also be impossible for states to go back on agreements already made. By this means states are 'trapped' within the European integration process.

Keynesian a position held which supports J. M. Keynes' economic theory, and which has as its starting point the assumption that state finances should be used to counteract cyclical economic downturns. The argument implies that governments should focus on issues of employment and economic growth, rather on variables such as inflation.

Laeken European Council (summit) meeting which took place on 14–15 December 2001. At Laeken, governments decided to hold a Convention which would debate the Future of Europe.

Laissez-faire an economic position which argues that the state (governments) should play only a minimal regulatory role in economic affairs, with decisions left mainly to the market.

League of Nations an international organization set up in 1922 which had as its rationale the maintenance of peace in Europe.

Legal basis see **Treaty bases**.

Legitimacy the idea that a regime's procedures for making and enforcing laws are acceptable to all its subjects; the right to rule.

Level playing-field an expression that implies that member states should be subject to the same rules, and should expect the same successes from their participation in the European integration process.

Liberal Intergovernmentalism Andrew Moravcsik's update on classical intergovernmentalism (see Chapter 7).

Liberalization of capital markets the removal of exchange controls by states, allowing capital to flow freely across state borders.

Lock-out a situation where employers lock employees out of their place of work as a consequence of a labour dispute.

Logic of appropriateness assumes that actors do not take decisions on the basis of rational choice, but are constrained by social and cultural 'scripts' which shape their conduct.

Logic of calculation assumes that actors are rational beings. See **Rationalist**.

Maastricht (Treaty) see **Treaty on European Union**.

Macro-economic policies economic policies that deal with aggregates such as national income and investment in the economy.

Majoritarian application of majority rule. The principle that the majority should be allowed to govern the minority.

Market citizenship the concept introduced to the European Community in the 1950s whereby citizens of member states become endowed with certain rights as workers within the EC.

Market integration the breaking down of barriers to trade among the EU's member states, plus any regulation necessary to ensure the smooth running of the single market. It does not involve an explicitly political dimension.

Middle-range theories theories that aim to explain only part of a political process and that do not have totalizing ambitions.

Money supply the stock of liquid assets in an economy that can be freely exchanged for goods and services.

Monnet, Jean (1888–1979). One of the founders of the European integration project. The driving force behind the 1950 Schuman Plan which led to the establishment of the European Coal and Steel Community, Monnet became the first head of the ECSC's High Authority. He continued to play an active role in European integration throughout his life, though often behind the scenes.

Monnet method see **Community method**.

Multifunctionality the notion in agricultural policy that policy can be used to serve a range of functions, including environmental protection and rural development.

Multi-level governance an approach to the study of EU politics that emphasizes the interaction of the many different actors at the European, national, and regional/local levels of governance, who influence European policy outcomes.

Multispeed (Europe) a method of differentiated integration whereby common objectives are pursued by a group of member states, able and willing to advance further that others in the integration process.

Mutual recognition the principle that an economic product sold in one member state should not be prohibited from sale anywhere in the EU. This was upheld in the famous *Cassis de Dijon* case (1979). Exceptions can be made in cases of public health and safety, however.

Negative integration a form of European integration which involves the removal of barriers between the member states.

Neo-corporatist neo-corporatism is a model of policy making that links producer interests to the state, and where interest organizations are incorporated into the system. The neo- prefix was added in the 1970s to distinguish this from corporatism in the past—particularly in the fascist era.

Neo-functionalism a theory of European integration that views integration as an incremental process, involving the spillover of integration in one sector to others, ultimately leading to some kind of political community.

Neo-functionalist see **Neo-functionalism**.

Neo-liberalism an economic school, which advocates the reduction of state influence in the market, the liberalization of the economy, the privatization of state-owned firms, and tight control of money supply, and supports a general trend towards deregulation.

Neo-realism an International Relations theory, associated with the work of Kenneth Waltz, which claims that the international state system is anarchic, and as such that state uncertainty is a given. States will want to maintain their independence, and survival will be their primary objective, but they may, all the same, engage in cooperative European integration ventures if this serves their ends.

Net contributors those countries that get less out of the EU budget than they contribute.

Net recipients those countries that get more out of the EU budget than they contribute.

New institutionalism a conceptual approach to the study of politics, which restates the importance of institutional factors in political life. It takes a number of very different forms, from rational institutionalism and historical institutionalism to sociological institutionalism.

Nice Treaty treaty revision agreed at Nice in December 2000, signed in February 2001, and ratified in 2002. It introduced a number of institutional reforms that paved the way for the enlargement of the Union in 2004 or after.

Non-state actors usually any actor that is not a national government. Often refers to transnational actors, such as interest groups (rather than to international organizations).

Non-tariff barriers see **Barriers to trade**.

Ombudsman an official who investigates citizens' complaints against the state or its servants.

Ontology relates to the nature of being; an underlying conception of the world; that which is being presupposed by a theory.

'Open method of co-ordination' an approach to EU policy making that is an alternative to regulation, and which involves more informal means of encouraging compliance.

Optimum currency area (OCA) a theoretical notion that implies that monetary union will only work effectively when the states participating are economically very similar.

Package deals policy issues tied together into one package of legislation, so as to facilitate agreement. The European Commission has used this strategy in the past.

Parachutage the act of appointing someone to a top job, usually from outside the organization.

Paradigm a model or pattern.

Paris–Bonn axis the relationship between France and Germany, which is often said to lie at the heart of the European integration process.

Parsimony a parsimonious theory is one that provides an extremely simplified depiction of reality.

Path dependence the idea that decisions taken in the past limit the scope of decisions in the present (and future).

Pillar one of three parts of the European Union, which since its inception at Maastricht has been divided into Pillar 1 (the EC pillar), Pillar 2 (Common Foreign and Security Policy), and Pillar 3 (formerly Justice and Home Affairs, now Police and Judicial Co-operation in Criminal Matters).

Pluralist pluralism is a general approach that implies that organized groups play an important role in the political process.

Policy entrepreneurs policy actors who are able to set or manipulate the political 'marketplace'.

Polity a politically organized society.

Positive integration a form of integration that involves the construction of policies and/or institutions.

Positive-sum outcomes outcomes that constitute more than the sum of their parts. Often talked of in EU terms as an 'upgrading of the common interest'.

Power the ability to control outcomes. The capacity for A to force B to do something in A's interest.

Preliminary rulings acts of the European Court, which arise as responses to questions of European law posed in domestic courts.

Price support the system of agricultural support that involves keeping food prices higher than the market price so as to give farmers a higher and more stable income.

Proportionality a principle that implies that the means should not exceed the ends—applies to decision making and to the legislative process.

Public debts the amount of money owed by the state.

Qualified majority voting (QMV) system of voting in the EU Council, which attributes a number of votes to each member state (very roughly related to their size). A majority of these votes (currently 71 per cent) is needed for legislation to be agreed in the Council, implying that some states will be outvoted, but will have to apply the legislation all the same.

Ratification formal approval. In the EU context, it implies approval of treaty revisions by national parliaments and sometimes also by popular referendum.

Ratification crisis (1992) the crisis provoked by the Danish 'no vote' in their 1992 referendum on the Maastricht Treaty.

Rational choice see **Rationalist**.

Rationalist theories that are rationalist assume that individuals (or states) are able to make rank orderings of their preferences and to choose the best available preference.

Realism a rationalist theory of International Relations, which sees power as the main driving force behind human action, and states as the key actors in international affairs.

Realist see **Realism**.

Recession a temporary depression in economic activity or prosperity.

Redistributive policy that transfers wealth from one group to another.

Reference value a baseline. A measure from which an assessment of economic progress can be made.

Regime principles, norms, rules, and decision-making procedures around which actors' expectations occur. An international regime is usually considered to take the form of an international organization. It is a concept associated with **neo-realism**.

Regulation the act of making rules or legislation in order to provoke certain policy outcomes.

Regulations one of the legislative instruments used by the EU. Regulations are directly effective, spelling out not just the aims of legislation, but what must be done and how.

Representation the principle by which delegates are chosen to act for a particular constituency (group of electors).

Right of association the democratic right of people to form groups such as trade unions.

Schengen an agreement to create a border-free European Community. It was originally outside the EC, but was incorporated into it at Amsterdam.

Schuman Plan signed on 9 May 1950, it led to the setting up of the European Coal and Steel Community.

Second pillar The part of the European Union that deals with Common Foreign and Security Policy and for which there are discrete decision-making procedures.

Sectoral integration a description of or strategy for integration which involves an incremental sector-by-sector approach. See also **Spillover**.

Separation of powers a condition of democratic political systems where the executive, legislature, and judiciary are separate, and provide checks and balances which serve to prevent abuses of power.

Single European Act (SEA) the first of the large-scale Treaty revisions, signed in 1986. It came into force in 1987, and served as a 'vehicle' for the single market programme.

Single market the idea of having one unified internal EU market, free of (national) barriers to trade. While the idea was included in the Treaty of Rome, the single market is usually associated with the revitalization of the Community from the mid-1980s.

'Snake' a system that aimed to stabilize exchange rates within the European Community in the 1970s.

Social Chapter agreed at Maastricht, the Social Chapter establishes minimum social conditions within the

European Union. Until Amsterdam, the Chapter was annexed to the Treaty, as the UK Conservative government had decided not to sign up to it.

Social Charter a declaration on social conditions and standards, signed by all member states except the UK in 1989 and which ultimately fed into the **Social Chapter** signed at Maastricht.

Social dialogue joint consultation procedure involving social partners at European Union level, to discuss and negotiate agreements where relevant.

Social dumping the undercutting of social standards in order to improve competitiveness.

Social partner(s) refers to labour (the unions) and capital (employers) acting together. The two sides of industry.

Socialization the process by which an individual's norms and beliefs alter, as a consequence of interaction with others.

Soft law documents that are not formally or legally binding but which may still produce political effects.

Sovereignty a condition in which states are not subject to any higher authority; supreme, unrestricted power (of a state).

Spillover a mechanism identified by neo-functionalist theorists who claimed that sectoral integration in one area would have knock-on effects in others, and would 'spill over', thereby increasing the scope of European integration.

Spinelli, Altiero an important federalist thinker and politician (1907–86), responsible for the influential Ventotene Manifesto of 1944 (distributed clandestinely at this time), and for the European Parliament's Draft Treaty on European Union (1984), which helped to shape the European political agenda of the late 1980s.

State-centrism a conceptual approach to understanding European integration which gives primacy to the role of state actors within the process.

Statehood the condition of being a state. See **Stateness**.

Stateness the quality of being a state, that is, a legal territorial entity with a stable population and a government.

Strong currency a situation arising out of the relative levels of exchange rates whereby the value of national money is increased. This has the effect of lowering the price of imports (making imported goods cheaper), but also of increasing the price of exports, making exports less competitive in international markets.

Subsidiarity the principle that tries to ensure that decisions are taken as close as possible to the citizen.

Supranational that which is above the national level. It may refer to institutions, policies, or a particular 'type' of co-operation and or integration.

Supranational governance a theory of European integration proposed by Wayne Sandholtz and Alec Stone Sweet which draws on neo-functionalism, and provides an alternative approach to Moravcsik's Liberal Intergovernmentalism.

Sustainability or 'sustainable development'. The ability to meet the needs of the present without compromising the needs of future generations.

Third pillar that part of the European Union that deals with police and judicial co-operation in criminal matters. From Maastricht to Amsterdam it was called Justice and Home Affairs.

Transfer payments payments that are not made in return for any contribution to current output. Usually refers to agricultural subsidies.

Transparency a term used in the EU to refer to the extent of openness within the European Union institutions.

Transposition the translation of European law (Directives) into domestic law.

Treaty base the provision of the Treaty which underpins a particular piece of European legislation.

Treaty base game the act of selecting the treaty base underpinning a piece of legislation for political ends.

Treaty of Rome Signed in 1957, the Rome Treaty formally established the European Economic Community (EEC) and EURATOM, the European Atomic Energy Community.

Treaty on European Union Treaty agreed at Maastricht in the Netherlands in December 1991, signed February 1992, and came into effect 1 November 1993.

Unanimity a method of voting whereby all member states in the Council must be in agreement before a proposal can be adopted (and which permits all member states to veto decisions).

Variable geometry an image of the European Union which foresees the breakdown of a unified form of co-operation, and the introduction of a 'pick and choose' approach to further integration.

Western European Union a collaborative defence agreement and extension of the 1948 Treaty of Brussels, signed in 1955. It was designed to allow for the re-armament of West Germany. It was revitalized in the 1980s, and subsequently served as a bridge between NATO and the European Union. Its functions have lately been subsumed within the European Union.

Widening generally refers to the enlargement of the European Union, but may also be used to denote the increasing scope of Community or Union competences.

Zero-sum game a game played (by states) in which the victory of one group implies the loss of another.

Zollverein a customs union between German states in the eighteenth century. The economic basis for German unification under Bismarck in the nineteenth century.

References

Agence Europe (1973), AE No. 713, 5 January, p. 7 (reporting on interview with Etienne Davignon in *Libre Belgique*, 28 December 1972.

Allen, D. (1998), ' "Who Speaks for Europe?" The Search for an Effective and Coherent External Policy', in J. Peterson and H. Sjursen, *A Common Foreign Policy for Europe?* (London: Routledge).

—— (2000), 'Cohesion and the Structural Funds: Transfers and Trade-Offs', in H. Wallace and W. Wallace (eds), *Policy-making in the European Union* (Oxford: Oxford University Press).

Alter, K. (2001), *Establishing the Supremacy of European Law: The Making of an International Rule of Law in Europe* (Oxford: Oxford University Press).

Amin, A., and Tomaney, J. (1995), *Behind the Myth of European Union: Prospects for Cohesion* (London: Routledge).

Anderson, B. (1991), *Imagined Communities* (London: Verso).

Anderson, D. (1995), *References to the European Court* (London: Sweet & Maxwell).

Anderson, J. (1990), 'Skeptical Reflections on a Europe of the Regions: Britain, Germany and the ERDF', *Journal of Public Policy*, vol. 10, no. 4: 417–47.

Arblaster, A. (1987), *Democracy* (Minneapolis: University of Minnesota Press).

Armstrong, H., and Taylor, J. (2000), *Regional Economics and Policy*, 3rd edn (Oxford: Blackwell).

Armstrong, K., and Bulmer, S. (1998), *The Governance of the Single European Market* (Manchester: Manchester University Press).

ARNE (1995), *Modifications to the Maastricht Treaty in Sight of the 1996 Inter-Governmental Conference* (Rome: unpublished document).

Arnull, A. (1999), *The European Union and its Court of Justice* (Oxford: Oxford University Press).

—— (2002), 'The rule of law in the European Union', in A. Arnull and D. Wincott (eds), *Accountability and Legitimacy in the European Union* (Oxford: Oxford University Press).

Aron, R., and Lerner, D. (eds) (1957), *France Defeats EDC* (New York: Praeger).

Arter, D. (1993), *The Politics of European Integration in the Twentieth Century* (Aldershot: Dartmouth).

Arts, K. (2000), *Integrating Human Rights into Development Cooperation: The Case of the Lomé Convention* (The Hague: Kluwer Law International).

Aspinwall, M., and Greenwood, J. (1998), 'Conceptualizing collective action in the European Union: an introduction', in J. Greenwood and M. Aspinwall (eds), *Collective Action in the European Union. Interests and the New Politics of Associability* (London: Routledge).

——, and Schneider, G. (2001), 'Institutionalist Research on the European Union: mapping the field', in G. Schneider and M. Aspinwall (eds), *The Rules of Integration: Institutionalist Approaches to the Study of Europe* (Manchester: Manchester University Press).

Axelrod, R., and Cohen, M. D. (1999), *Harnessing Complexity. Organizational Implications of a Scientific Frontier* (New York: Free Press).

Bache, I. (1999a), 'The Extended Gate-keeper: Central Government and the Implementation of EC Regional Policy in the UK', *Journal of European Public Policy*, vol. 6, no. 1: 28–45.

—— (1999b), *The Politics of European Union Regional Policy: Multi-level governance or Flexible Gatekeeping* (Sheffield: Sheffield Academic Press).

Barbalet, J. M. (1988), *Emotion, Social Theory and Social Structure* (Cambridge: Cambridge University Press).

Barber, L. (1995), 'The Men Who Run Europe', *Financial Times*, 11–12 March, Section 2, 1–2.

Barnard, C. (2000), 'Regulating Competitive Federalism in the European Union? The Case of EC Social Policy', in J. Shaw (ed.), *Social Law and Policy in an Evolving European Union* (Oxford: Hart).

Basque Government, Secretariat-General of External Affairs (1998), *Participación y Labor del Gobierno Vasco en el Comité de las Regiones* (Basque Country: Vitoria-Gasteiz).

Baun, M. (1999), 'Enlargement', in L. Cram, D. Dinan, and N. Nugent (eds), *Developments in the European Union* (Basingstoke: Macmillan).

Baylis, J., and Smith, S. (eds) (2001), *The Globalization of World Politics: an Introduction to International Relations* (Oxford: Oxford University Press).

Bendix, R. (1964), *Nation Building and Citizenship* (New York: John Wiley).

Benz, A. (1998), 'Politikverflechtung ohne Politikverflechtungsfalle—Koordination und Strukturdynamik im europäischen Mehrebenensystem', *Politische Vierteljahresschrift*, vol. 39, no. 4: 558–89.

—— (2001), 'From association of local governments to "Regional Governance" in urban regions', *German Journal of Urban Studies*, vol. 40, no. 2.

Berger, S., and Dore, R. (1996), *National Diversity and Global Capitalism* (Ithaca, NY: Cornell University Press).

Bergman, T., and Raunio, T. (2001), 'Parliaments and Policy-making in the European Union', in J. Richardson (ed.), *European Union: Power and Policy-making*, 2nd edn (London: Routledge).

Bermann, G. A. (2001), 'Law in a Enlarged European Union', *EUSA Review*, vol. 14, no. 3: 4–6.

Bertrand, R. (1956) 'The European Common Market Proposal', *International Organization*, vol. 10, no. 4: 559–74.

Beukel, E. (2001), 'Educational policy: Institutionalization and multi-level governance', in S. S. Andersen and K. A. Eliassen (eds), *Making Policy in Europe* (London: Sage).

Bieber, R., and Monar, J. (eds) (1995), *Justice and Home Affairs in the European Union: The Development of the Third Pillar* (Brussels, European Interuniversity Press).

Bindi Report I (European Parliament) (1991). PE 150.034/fin., 23 May.

Blondel, J., Sinnott, R., and Svensson, P. (1998), *People and Parliament in the European Union: Participation, Democracy, and Legitimacy* (Oxford: Clarendon Press).

Börzel, T. A. (2000), 'Why there is no Southern problem. On environmental leaders and laggards in the EU', *Journal of European Public Policy*, vol. 7, no. 1: 141–62.

—— (2001), 'Non-Compliance in the European Union. Pathology or Statistical Artifact?', EUI Working Paper RSC No. 2001/28 (Florence: European University Institute).

—— (2002), 'Member State responses to Europeanization', *Journal of Common Market Studies*, vol. 40, no. 2: 195–214.

—— and Risse, T. (2000), 'When Europe hits home: Europeanization and Domestic Change', *European Integration Online Papers*, 27, 29 November.

Breslin, S., Hughes, C., Phillips, N., and Rosamond, B. (eds) (2002), *New Regionalisms in the Global Political Economy: Theories and Cases* (London: Routledge).

Breyer, S. G. (1982), *Regulation and its Reform* (Cambridge, Mass.: Harvard University Press).

Brubaker, R. (1989), 'The Manichean Myth: rethinking the distinction between "civic" and "ethnic" nationalism', in H. Kriesi et al. (eds), *Movements in Western Europe: a comparative analysis* (Minneapolis: University of Minnesota Press).

Bulmer, S. (1983), 'Domestic Politics and European Community Policy-Making', *Journal of Common Market Studies*, vol. 21, no. 4: 349–63.

—— and Burch, M. (2001), 'The "Europeanization" of central government', in G. Schneider and M. Aspinwall (eds), *The Rules of Integration. Institutionalist Approaches to the Study of Europe*: 73–96 (Manchester: Manchester University Press).

Burgess, M. (1989), *Federalism and European Union: Political Ideas, Influences and Strategies in the European Community, 1972–1987* (London: Routledge).

—— (1995), *The British Tradition of Federalism* (London: Cassell).

—— (2000), *Federalism and European Union: The Building of Europe, 1950–2000* (London: Routledge).

Burley, A. M., and Mattli, W. (1993), 'Europe Before the Court: A Political Theory of Legal Integration', *International Organization*, vol. 47: 41–76.

Busch, K. (1988), *The Corridor Model—a concept for further development of an EU Social Policy* (Brussels: European Trade Union Institute).

Butt Philip, A. (2000), 'Implementation', in D. Dinan (ed.), *Encyclopedia of the European Union* (Basingstoke: Macmillan).

Cahill, C. (2001), 'The multifunctionality of agriculture: what does it mean?, *Euro choices*, Spring: 36–40.

Cameron, D. (1992) 'The 1992 initiative: causes and consequences', in A. Sbragia (ed.), *Europolitics—Institutions and Policy-making in the 'New' European Community* (Washington, DC: Brookings Institution).

Caporaso, J. A. (1974), *Structure and Function of European Integration* (Pacific Palisades, Cal.: Goodyear Publishing Company).

—— and Stone Sweet, A. (2001), 'Conclusion: Institutional logics of European integration', in A. Stone Sweet, W. Sandholtz, and N. Fliegstein (eds), *The Institutionalization of Europe*: 221–36 (Oxford: Oxford University Press).

Carney, F. S. (1964), *The Politics of Johannes Althusius* (London: Eyre and Spottiswoode).

Checkel, J. T. (2001a), 'The Europeanization of citizenship?', in M. G. Cowles, J. A. Caporaso, and T. Risse (eds), *Transforming Europe: Europeanization and Domestic Change*: 180–97 (Ithaca, NY: Cornell University Press).

—— (2001b), 'Why comply? Social learning and European identity change', *International Organization*, vol. 55, no. 3: 553–88.

—— (2001c), 'A Constructivist Research Programme in EU Studies', *European Union Politics*, vol. 2, no. 2: 219–26.

—— (2001d), 'Social Construction and Integration', in T. Christiansen, K. E. Jørgensen, and A. Wiener (eds), *The Social Construction of Europe* (London, Sage).

Christiansen, T. (1996), 'Second Thoughts on Europe's "Third Level": The European Union's Committee of the Regions', *Publius—The Journal of Federalism*, vol. 26, no. 1: 93–116.

—— Jørgensen, K. E., and Wiener, A. (2001a), 'Constructivism and European Studies', in T. Christiansen, K. E. Jørgensen, and A. Wiener (eds), *The Social Construction of Europe* (London: Sage).

—— —— —— (eds) (2001b), *The Social Construction of Europe* (London: Sage).

Chryssochoou, D. (2000), *Democracy in the European Union* (London: Taurus).

—— Tsinisizelis, J., Stavridis, S., and Infantis, K. (1998), *Theory and Reform in the European Union* (Manchester: Manchester University Press).

Church, C. H. (1996), *European Integration Theory in the 1990s*, European Dossier Series (London: University of North London).

Cini, M. (1996), *The European Commission: Leadership, Organisation and Culture in the EU Administration* (Manchester: Manchester University Press).

—— and McGowan, L. (1997), *Competition Policy in the European Union* (Basingstoke: Macmillan).

Clark, A. (1993), *Diaries* (London: Weidenfeld & Nicolson).

Closa, C. (1992), 'The Concept of Citizenship in the Treaty of European Union', *Common Market Law Review*, vol. 29: 1137–69.

Coen, D. (1998), 'The European business interest and the nation state: Large-firm lobbying in the European Union and member states', *Journal of Public Policy*, vol. 18, no. 1: 75–100.

Cohen, B. J. (1971), *The Future of Sterling as an International Currency* (London: Macmillan).

Constantelos, J. (1996), 'Multi-level lobbying in the European Union: A paired sectoral comparison across the French-Italian border', *Regional and Federal Studies*, vol. 6, no. 3: 28–55.

Coombes, D. (1970), *Politics and Bureaucracy in the European Community. A Portrait of the Commission of the E.E.C.* (London: George Allen & Unwin).

Corbett, R. (1996), 'Governance and Institutional Developments', *Journal of Common Market Studies*, vol. 34: 29–42.

—— (1998), *The European Parliament's Role in Closer EU Integration* (London: Macmillan).

—— (1999), 'The European Parliament and the Idea of European Representative Government', in J. Pinder (ed.), *Foundations of Democracy in the European Union: From the Genesis of Parliamentary Democracy to the European Parliament* (London: Macmillan).

—— Jacobs, F., and Shackleton, M. (1995), *The European Parliament*, 3rd edn (London: Cartermill).

Cosgrove Twitchett, C. (1981) *Harmonisation in the EEC* (London: Macmiilan).

Council of the European Union (1996), *The European Union Today and Tomorrow, Adapting the European Union for the Benefit of Its Peoples and Preparing It for the Future: A General Outline for a Draft Revision of the Treaties* (Brussels: Council).

Cowles, M. G. (1995), 'Seizing the Agenda for the New Europe: the ERT and EC 1992', *Journal of Common Market Studies*, vol. 33, no. 4: 501–26.

—— (1997), 'Organizing industrial coalitions: A challenge for the future?', in H. Wallace and A. R. Young (eds), *Participation and Policy-Making in the European Union* (Oxford: Clarendon Press).

—— and Risse, T. (2001), 'Transforming Europe: Conclusions', in M. G. Cowles, J. A. Caporaso, and T. Risse (eds), *Transforming Europe: Europeanization and Domestic Change* (Ithaca, NY: Cornell University Press).

Craig, P. P., and De Burca, G. (2002), *EU Law*, 3rd edn (Oxford: Oxford University Press).

Cram, L. (1993), 'Calling the Tune without Paying the Piper', *Policy and Politics*, vol. 21: 135–46.

—— (2001), 'Integration Theory and the Study of the European Policy Process: towards a Synthesis of Approaches', in J. Richardson (ed.), *European Union. Power and Policy Making* (London: Routledge).

Crombez, C. (2001), 'The Treaty of Amsterdam and the co-decision procedure', in G. Schneider and M. Aspinwall (eds), *The Rules of Integration: Institutionalist Approaches to the Study of Europe* (Manchester: Manchester University Press).

Cullen, P. P. (1999), 'Pan-European non-governmental organizations: European Union sponsored mobilization and activism for social rights', Paper presented to the 6th Biennial Conference of the European Communities Studies Association, Pittsburgh, 2–5 June.

Curtin, D. (1993), 'The Constitutional Structure of the Union: a Europe of bits and pieces', *Common Market Law Review*, vol. 30, no. 1: 17–69.

Dahrendorf, R. (1967), *Society and Democracy in Germany* (London: Weidenfeld & Nicolson).

—— (1979), *A Third Europe?* (Florence: European University Institute).

Dashwood, A. (1983), 'Hastening Slowly the Community's path towards Harmonisation', in H. Wallace et al., *Policy-Making in the European Community*, 2nd edn (Chichester: John Wiley).

Davis, S. R. (1978), *The Federal Principle: A Journey Through Time in Quest of a Meaning* (London: University of California Press, Ltd).

Dedman, M. (1996), *The Origins and Development of the European Union 1945–95* (London: Routledge).

de la Porte, C., and Pochet, P. (2002), *Building Social Europe through the Open Method of Co-ordination* (Brussels/Berne/Berlin: PIE Lang).

de Villiers, B. (1995), *Bundestreue: The Soul of an Intergovernmental Partnership* (Johannesburg: Occasional Papers, Konrad Adenauer Stiftung, March).

de Witte, B. (1998), 'The Pillar Structure and the Nature of the European Union: Greek Temple or French Gothic Cathedral?', in T. Heukels et al. (eds), *The European Union after Amsterdam: A Legal Analysis* (The Hague: Kluwer Law International).

Den Boer, M., and Wallace, W. (2000), 'Justice and Home Affairs: Integration through Incrementalism?', in H. Wallace and W. Wallace (eds), *Policy-making in the European Union*, 4th edn (Oxford: Oxford University Press).

Devuyst, Y. (1998), 'Treaty reform in the European Union: the Amsterdam process', *Journal of European Public Policy*, vol. 5, no. 4: 615–31.

—— (1999), 'The Community method after Amsterdam', *Journal of Common Market Studies*, vol. 37, no. 1: 109–20.

Diebold, W. (1959), *The Schuman Plan* (New York: Praeger).

DiMaggio, P., and Powell, W. (1991), 'The Iron Cage Revisited: Institutional Isomorphism and Collective Rationality in Organizational Fields', in W. Powell and P. DiMaggio (eds), *The New Institutionalism in Organizational Analysis* (Chicago: University of Chicago Press).

Dimitrakopoulos, D., and Richardson, J. (2001), 'Implementing EU Public Policy', in J. Richardson (ed.), *European Union. Power and Policy-making*, 2nd edn (London: Routledge).

Dinan, D. (1994), *Ever Closer Union? An Introduction to the European Community* (Boulder, Colo.: Lynne Rienner).

—— (2000), *Encyclopedia of the European Union* (Basingstoke: Macmillan).

Dineen, D. A. (1992), 'Europeanization of Irish universities', *Higher Education*, vol. 24: 391–411.

Dispersyn, M., van der Vorst, P., et al. (1990), 'La construction d'un serpent social européen', *Revue Belge de Sécurité Sociale*, vol. 12.

Dølvik, J. E. (1997a), *ETUC and Europeanisation of Trade Unionism in the 1990s* (Oslo: University of Oslo).

—— (1997b), *Redrawing Boundaries of Solidarity? ETUC, social dialogue and the Europeanization of trade unions in the 1990s.* Oslo: ARENA Report no. 5/97.

Dowding, K. (2000), 'Institutionalist Research on the European Union: A Critical Review', *European Union Politics*, vol. 1, no. 1: 125–44.

Duchene, F. (1994), *Jean Monnet: the First Statesman of Interdependence* (London: W. W. Norton & Co.).

Duff, A. (1994), 'Building a Parliamentary Europe', *Government and Opposition*, vol. 29: 147–65.

Dyson, K. (2000), 'EMU as Europeanization: Convergence, diversity and contingency', *Journal of Common Market Studies*, vol. 38, no. 4: 645–66.

Edwards, G., and Spence, D. (1997) (eds), *The European Commission*, 2nd edn (London: Cartermill).

Egan, M. (2001), *Constructing a European Market: Standards, Regulation, and Governance* (Oxford: Oxford University Press).

Egeberg, M. (1996), 'Organization and Nationality in the European Commission Services', *Public Administration*, vol. 74, no. 4: 721–35.

—— (1999), 'Transcending Intergovernmentalism? Identity and Role Perceptions of National Officials in EU Decision-Making', *Journal of European Public Policy*, vol. 6, no. 3: 456–74.

Eising, R. (2004), 'Multi-level governance and business interests in the European Union', *Governance*, vol. 17, no. 2: forthcoming.

—— (forthcoming 2003), 'The Europeanization of interest groups and of interest intermediation', in K. Dyson and K. H. Goetz (eds), *Germany in Europe: A 'Europeanized' Germany?* (Oxford: Oxford University Press).

—— and Jabko, M. (2001), 'Moving Targets. National Interests and Electricity Liberalization in the European Union', *Comparative Political Studies*, vol. 34, no. 7: 742–67.

Elazar, D. J. (1987), *Exploring Federalism* (Tuscaloosa, Ala.: University of Alabama Press).

—— (1989), 'Federal-Type Solutions and European Integration', in C. L. Brown-John (ed.), *Federal-Type Solutions and European Integration* (Lanham, Md.: University Press of America).

Eriksen, E. O., and Fossum, J. E. (2000) (eds), *Democracy in the European Union* (London: Routledge).

—— —— (2002), 'Democracy through strong publics in the European Union', *Journal of Common Market Studies*, vol. 40, no. 3: 401–24.

European Commission (1985), *White Paper: Completing the Internal Market*, COM (85) 130 final (Brussels: European Commission).

European Commission (1990), *Spanish Proposals on European Citizenship*, SG(90) D/06601 (Brussels: European Commission).

European Commission (1992a), *The Internal Market After 1992: Meeting the Challenge* (The Sutherland Report), SEC(92) 2044, October (Brussels: European Commission).

European Commission (1992b), *An Open and Structured Dialogue between the Commission and Special Interest Groups*, SEC(92) 2272 final, Brussels, 2 December.

European Commission (1995), *White Paper on the Preparation of the Associated Countries of Central and Eastern Europe for Integration into the Internal Market of the Union*, COM (95) 163 final (Brussels: European Commission).

European Commission (1996), *First Cohesion Report*, **http://europa.eu.int/comm/regional_policy/sources/docoffic/official/reports/repco_en.htm**

European Commission (1997), *Agenda 2000* COM (97) 2000, 15 July (Brussels: European Commission).

European Commission (2000a), *The Commission and Non-Governmental Organisations: Building a Stronger Partnership. A Commission Discussion Paper* (Brussels: European Commission).

European Commission (2000b), *Reforming the Commission.* Consultative Document, Communication from Mr Kinnock in agreement with the President and Ms Schreyer, CG3(2000) 1/17, 18 January (Brussels: European Commission).

European Commission (2000c), *The Community Budget: the Facts in Figures* (Luxembourg: Office of Official Publications).

European Commission (2001a), *European Governance: A White Paper*, COM (2001) 428, 25 July (Brussels: European Commission).

European Commission (2001b), *Making a Success of Enlargement. Strategy Paper and Report of the European Commission on the Progress towards Accession by each of the*

Candidate Countries. **http://europa.eu.int/comm/ enlargement/report2001/strategy_en.pdf**

European Commission (2001*c*), *Proposal for a Council Framework Decision on Combating Terrorism*, COM (2001) 521 final (Brussels: European Commission).

European Commission (2001*d*), *Third Report on Citizenship of the Union*, COM (01) 506 final, September, (Brussels: European Commission).

European Commission (2002*a*), *A Project for the European Union* COM (2002) 247 final, 22 May (Brussels: European Commission).

European Commission (2002*b*), *Mid-term Review of the Common Agricultural Policy* COM (2002) 394 final (Brussels: European Commission).

European Council (2001), *Declaration by the Heads of State or Government of the European Union and the President of the Commission: Follow-up to the September 11 Attacks and the Fight against Terrorism*, SN 4296/2/01 Rev. 2. Gent.

European Parliament (1988), *Toussaint Report*, PE 111.236/fin. 1, February: 10–11.

European Parliament (1997), *Note on the European Parliament's Priorities for the IGC and the New Amsterdam Treaty: Report and Initial Evaluation of the Results*, available at **www.europarl.eu.int/topics/treaty/report/part1_en. htm**

European Parliament, Directorate General for Research (1988), Action Taken Series, 3/11: 103.

European Union (1997), 'Treaty on European Union', *Official Journal of the European Communities*, C340: 145–72.

Evans, A. C. (1984), 'European Citizenship: a novel concept in EEC law', *American Journal of Comparative Law*, vol. 32, no. 4: 679–715.

Falkner, G. (1998), *EU Social Policy in the 1990s: Towards a Corporatist Policy Community* (London: Routledge).

—— (1999), 'European social policy: towards multi-level and multi-actor governance', in B. Kohler-Koch and R. Eising (eds.), *The Transformation of Governance in the European Union* (London: Routledge).

—— (2000*a*), 'The Council or the social partners? EC social policy between diplomacy and collective bargaining', *Journal of European Public Policy*, vol. 7, no. 5: 705–24.

—— (2000*b*), 'EG-Sozialpolitik nach Verflechtungsfalle und Entscheidungslücke: Bewertungsmaßstäbe und Entwicklungstrends', *Politische Vierteljahresschrift*, vol. 41, no. 2: 279–301.

Favell, A. (1997), 'Citizenship and immigration: pathologies of a progressive philosophy', *New Community*, vol. 23, no. 2: 173–95.

Featherstone, K. (1998), ' "Europeanization" and the Centre Periphery: the Case of Greece in the 1990s', *South European Society and Politics*, vol. 3, no. 1: 23–39.

Fischler, F. (2002), Statement delivered in the Press Room, European Commission, 10 July.

Fisher, C. (1994), 'The lobby to stop testing cosmetics on animals', in R. H. Pedler and M. P. C. M. Van Schendelen (eds), *Lobbying the European Union. Companies, Trade Associations and Issue Groups* (Aldershot: Dartmouth).

Forster, A. (1998), 'Britain and the Negotiation of the Maastricht Treaty: a Critique of Liberal Intergovernmentalism', *Journal of Common Market Studies*, vol. 36, no. 2: 347–68.

Forsyth, M. (1981), *Unions of States: the Theory and Practice of Confederation* (Leicester: Leicester University Press).

Franklin, M. (2001), 'How structural factors cause turnout variation at European Parliament elections', *European Union Politics*, vol. 2, no. 3: 309–28.

Fursdon, E. (1980), *The European Defence Community* (Basingstoke: Macmillan).

Galloway, D. (1999), 'Keynote Article: Agenda 2000— Packaging the Deal', in *The European Union: Annual Reviews* (Oxford: Blackwell).

Garrett, G. (1992), 'International Cooperation and Institutional Choice: The European Community's Internal Market', *International Organization*, vol. 46, no. 2: 533–560.

—— and Tsebelis, G. (1996), 'An Institutionalist Critique of Intergovernmentalism', *International Organization*, vol. 50: 269–99.

Garton Ash, T. (2001), 'Is Britain European?', *International Affairs*, vol. 77, no. 1: 1–13.

Geddes, A. (2000*a*), 'Lobbying for Migrant Inclusion in the European Union: New Opportunities for Transnational Advocacy?', *Journal of European Public Policy*, vol. 7, no. 4: 632–49.

—— (2000*b*), *Immigration and European Integration: Towards Fortress Europe?* (Manchester: Manchester University Press).

George, S. (1996), *Politics and Policy in the European Union* (Oxford: Oxford University Press).

—— and Bache, I. (2001), *Politics in the European Union* (Oxford: Oxford University Press).

Geyer, M. (1989), 'Historical fictions of autonomy and the Europeanization of national history', *Central European History*, vol. 22, no. 3–4: 316–42.

Ginsberg, R. (1989), *The Foreign Policy Actions of the European Community* (Boulder, Colo.: Lynne Rienner).

—— (1999), 'Conceptualizing the EU as an International Actor: Narrowing the Theoretical Capability-Expectations Gap', *Journal of Common Market Studies*, vol. 37, no. 3: 429–54.

Goetschy, J. (2001), 'The European Employment Strategy from Amsterdam to Stockholm: Has it Reached its Cruising Speed Yet?', *Industrial Relations Journal*, vol. 35, no. 4: 401–18

Goetz, K. H. (2001), 'European integration and national executives: A cause in search of an effect', in K. H. Goetz and S. Hix (eds) *Europeanised Politics. European Integration and National Political Systems*: 211–31 (London: Frank Cass).

Goetz, K. H., and Hix, S. (eds) (2001), *Europeanised Politics? European Integration and National Political Systems* (London: Frank Class).

—— and Peterson, J. (2001), 'No One is in Control: The EU's Impossibly Busy Foreign Ministers', *European Foreign Affairs Review*, vol. 6, no. 1: 53–74.

Gordon, P. (1997/8), 'Europe's Uncommon Foreign Policy', *International Security*, vol. 22, no. 3: 74–100.

Gorges, M. J. (1996), *Euro-Corporatism? Interest Intermediation in the European Community* (Lanham/New York/London: University Press of America).

Gormley, L. (ed.) (1998), *Introduction to the Law of the EEC*, (3rd edn) (London: Kluwer Law).

Grabbe, H. (2000), 'The Sharp Edges of Europe: Extending Schengen Eastwards', *International Affairs*, vol. 76, no. 3: 519–36.

Grande, E. (1994), *Vom Nationalstaat zur europäischen Politikverflechtung. Expansion und Transformation moderner Staatlichkeit—untersucht am Beispiel der Forschungs- und Technologiepolitik* (University of Constance: Habilitationsschrift).

Greenwood, J. (1997), *Representing Interests in the European Union* (New York: St. Martin's Press).

—— and Webster, R. (2000), 'Are EU Business Associations Governable?', *European Integration Online Papers*, vol. 4, no. 3.

Grieco, J. M. (1995), 'The Maastricht Treaty, Economic and Monetary Union and the Neo-Realist Research Programme', *Review of International Studies*, vol. 21, no. 1: 21–40.

—— (1996), 'State Interests and International Rule Trajectories: A Neorealist Interpretation of the Maastricht Treaty and European Economic and Monetary Union', *Security Studies*, vol. 5, no. 2: 176–222.

Guay, T. R. (1996), 'Integration and Europe's defence industry: A "reactive spillover" approach', *Political Studies Journal*, vol. 24, no. 3: 404–16.

Haas, E. B. (1958), *The Uniting of Europe: Political, Social and Economic Forces, 1950–1957* (Stanford, Cal.: Stanford University Press).

—— (1963), 'International integration—the European and the universal process', in E. B. Haas et al., *Limits and Problems of European Integration* (The Hague: Martinus Nijhoff).

—— (1964), *Beyond the Nation-State—Functionalism and International Organization* (Stanford, Cal.: Stanford University Press).

—— (1971), 'The Study of Regional Integration: Reflections on the Joy and Anguish of Pretheorizing', in L. N. Lindberg and A. Scheingold (eds), *Regional Integration—Theories and Research* (Harvard: Harvard University Press).

—— (1975), *The Obsolescence of Regional of Integration Theory*. Research Studies 25 (Berkeley, Cal.: Institute of International Studies).

—— (1976), 'Turbulent fields and the theory of regional integration', *International Organization*, vol. 30, no. 2: 173–212.

—— (2001), 'Does Constructivism subsume Neo-functionalism?', in T. Christiansen, K. E. Jørgensen, and A. Wiener (eds), *The Social Construction of Europe* (London: Sage).

—— and Schmitter, P. C. (1964), 'Economic and Differential Patterns of Political Integration: Projections About Unity in Latin America', *International Organization*, vol. 18, no. 3: 705–38.

Habermas, J. (1998), 'Does Europe need a constitution? Response to Dieter Grimm', in J. Habermas, *The Inclusion of the Other. Studies in Political Theory* (eds C. Cronin and P. De Greiff) (Cambridge, Mass.: MIT Press).

Hall, P. (1986), *Governing the Economy: The Politics of State Intervention in Britain and France* (Cambridge: Polity Press).

—— and Soskice, D. (2001), *Varieties of Capitalism* (Oxford: Oxford University Press).

—— and Taylor, R. (1996), 'Political Science and the Three New Institutionalisms', *Political Studies*, vol. 44, no. 5: 936–57.

Hanf, K., and Soetendorp, B. (1998), 'Small states and the Europeanization of public policy', in K. Hanf and B. Soetendorp (eds), *Adapting to European Integration. Small States and the European Union* (London: Longman).

Harmsen, R. (1999), 'The Europeanization of National Administrations: A Comparative Study of France and the Netherlands', *Governance*, vol. 12, no. 1: 81–113.

Harrison, R. J. (1974), *Europe in Question* (London: George Allen & Unwin).

Hartley, T. (1996), 'The European Court, Judicial Objectivity and the Constitution of the European Union', *Law Quarterly Review*, vol. 112: 95–109.

Hayes-Renshaw, F. (2001), 'The Council of Ministers', in J. Peterson and M. Shackleton (eds), *The Institutions of the European Union* (Oxford: Oxford University Press).

—— and Wallace, H. (1997), *The Council of Ministers* (New York: St. Martin's Press).

Heinelt, H. (1998), 'Zivilgesellschaftliche Perspektiven einer democratischen Transformation de Europäischen Union', *Zeitschrift für Internationale Beziehungen*, vol. 5, no. 1: 79–107.

Héritier, A. (1996), 'The Accommodation of Diversity in European Policy-Making and its Outcomes: Regulatory Policy as Patchwork', *Journal of European Public Policy*, vol. 3, no. 2: 149–67.

—— et al. (1994), *Die Veränderung von Staatlichkeit in Europa. Ein regulativer Wettbewerb: Deutschland, Großbritannien und Frankreich in der Europäischen Union* (Opladen: Leske and Budrich).

Hey, C., and Brendle, U. (1994), *Umweltverbände und EG: Strategien, politische Kulturen und Organisationsformen* (Opladen: Westdeutscher Verlag).

Hill, C. (1993), 'The Capability-Expectations Gap, or Conceptualising Europe's Foreign Policy', *Journal of Common Market Studies*, vol. 31, no. 3: 305–28.

—— (1998), 'Closing the Capability-Expectations Gap', in J. Peterson and H. Sjursen, *A Common Foreign Policy for Europe?* (London: Routledge).

—— (2001), 'The EU's Capacity for Conflict Prevention', *European Foreign Affairs Review*, vol. 6, no. 3: 315–33.

Hirst, P., and Thompson, G. (1996), *Globalization in Question: the International Economy and the Possibilities of Governance* (Cambridge: Polity Press).

Hix, S. (1994), 'The Study of the European Union: the Challenge to Comparative Politics', *West European Politics*, vol. 17, no. 1: 1–30.

—— (1999), *The Political System of the European Union* (Basingstoke: Macmillan).

—— (2002a), 'Constitutional Agenda-Setting Through Discretion in Rule Interpretation: Why the European Parliament Won at Amsterdam', *British Journal of Political Science*, vol. 32, no. 2: 259–80.

—— (2002b), 'Parliamentary Behaviour with Two Principals: Preferences, Parties and Voting in the European Parliament', *American Journal of Political Science*, vol. 46, no. 3: 688–98.

—— and Lord, C. (1997), *Political Parties and the European Union* (London: Macmillan).

Hobe, S. (1993), 'Die Unionsbürgerschaft nach dem Vertrag von Maastricht. Auf dem Weg zum Europäischen Bundesstaat?', *Der Staat*: 245–68.

Hoffmann, S. (1966), 'Obstinate or Obsolete? The Fate of the Nation-State and the Case of Western Europe', *Daedalus*, vol. 95, no. 3: 862–915.

—— (1995), 'Introduction', in S. Hoffmann (ed.), *The European Sisyphus. Essays on Europe 1964–94* (Oxford: Westview).

Hogan, M. J. (1987), *The Marshall Plan* (Cambridge: Cambridge University Press).

Hood, C. C. (1976), *The Limits of Administration* (London: Wiley).

Hooghe, L. (1999), 'Supranational activists or intergovernmental agents?', *Comparative Political Studies*, vol. 32, no. 4: 435–63.

—— (2001), 'Top Commission official on capitalism: an institutionalist understanding of preferences', in G. Schneider and M. Aspinwall (eds), *The Rules of Integration: Institutionalist Approaches to the Study of Europe* (Manchester: Manchester University Press).

—— (2002), *The European Commission and the Integration of Europe. Images of Governance* (Cambridge: Cambridge University Press).

—— (ed.) (1996), *Cohesion Policy and European Integration: Building Multi-level governance* (Oxford: Oxford University Press).

—— and Marks, G. (1997), 'The Making of a Polity: The Struggle Over European Integration', *European Integration online Papers* (EIoP), vol. 1, no. 4. At **http://eiop.or.at/ eiop/texte/1997–004a.htm**

—— —— (2001), *Multi-Level Governance and European Integration* (Boulder, Colo.: Rowman and Littlefield).

Hoskyns, C. (1996), *Integrating Gender* (London: Verso).

House of Lords (1995), *1996 Inter-Governmental Conference*, Select Committee on the European Communities, Session 1994–95, 21st Report, HL Paper 105 (London: HMSO).

Howorth, J. (2001), 'European Defence and the Changing Politics of the EU: Hanging Together or Hanging Separately?', *Journal of Common Market Studies*, vol. 39, no. 4: 765–89.

Hueglin, T. O. (1999), *Early Modern Concepts for a Late Modern World: Althusius on Community and Federalism* (Waterloo, Ont.: Wilfrid Laurier University Press).

Hurrell, A., and Menon, A. (1996), 'Politics Like Any Other? Comparative Politics, International Relations and the Study of the EU', *West European Politics*, vol. 19, no. 2: 386–402.

Imbeni Report (European Parliament) (1993), *Citizenship of the EU (rapporteur, R. Imbeni)*, PE 206.762, A3-0437/93.

Imig, D., and Tarrow, S. (2001), 'Political Contention in a Europeanising Polity', in K. H. Goetz and S. Hix (eds), *Europeanised Politics? European Integration and National Political Systems* (London: Frank Cass).

Jachtenfuchs, M. (1997), 'Conceptualizing European Governance', in K. E. Jørgensen (ed.), *Reflective Approaches to European Governance* (Basingstoke: Macmillan).

—— (2001), 'The Governance Approach to European Integration', *Journal of Common Market Studies*, vol. 39, no. 2: 245–64.

Jacobson, H. K. (2001), 'Doing collaborative research in international legal topics: An autobiographical account', *International Studies Review*, vol. 3, no. 1: 15–23.

Jacoby, W. (2001), 'Tutors and pupils: International organizations, Central European elites, and Western models', *Governance*, vol. 14, no. 2: 169–200.

Jansen, T. (2000), 'Europe and religions: the dialogue between the European Commission and Churches or religious communities', *Social Compass*, vol. 47, no. 1: 103–12.

Jeffrey, C. (1997), 'Farewell the Third Level? The German Länder and the European Policy Process', *Regional and Federal Studies*, vol. 6, no. 2: 56–75.

Jensen, C. S. (2000), 'Neofunctionalist Theories and the Development of European Social and Labour Market Policy', *Journal of Common Market Studies*, vol. 38, no. 1: 71–92.

Jenson, J. (1992), 'Citizenship and Equity. Variations Across Time and Space', in J. Hiebert (ed.), *Political Ethics: A Canadian Perspective*, in *Research Studies on the Royal Commission on Electoral Reform and Party Financing*, vol. 12 (Toronto: Dundurn Press).

—— and Papillon, M. (2000), *The Changing Boundaries of Citizenship. A Review and a Research Agenda* (Montreal and Toronto). At **www.cprn.com/family/files/cbcr_e.pdf**

Jørgensen, K. E. (1997), 'PoCo: The Diplomatic Republic of Europe', in K.E. Jørgensen (ed.), *Reflective Approaches to European Governance* (Basingstoke: Macmillan).

Joerges, C. (1991), 'Markt ohne Staat?—Die Wirtschaftsverfassung der Gemeinschaft und die regulative Politik', in R. Wildenmann (ed.), *Staatswerdung Europas? Optionen für eine Europäische Union* (Baden-Baden: Nomos).

John, P. (1996), 'Centralisation, Decentralisation and the European Union: The Dynamics of Triadic Relationships', *Public Administration*, vol. 74: 293–313.

Jönsson, C., Tägil, S., and Törnqvist, G. (2000), *Organizing European Space* (London: Sage).

Jordan, A. (1999), 'The Implementation of EU Environment Policy: a Policy Problem without a Political Solution', *Environment and Planning C: Government and Policy*, vol. 17, no. 1: 69–90.

Jörgensen, K. E., and Rosamond, B. (2002), 'Europe: Regional Laboratory for a Global Polity?', in M. Ougaard and R. Higgott (eds), *Towards a Global Polity* (London: Routledge).

Kadelbach, S. (2002), 'Europäisches Bürgerrecht', in A. V. Bogdandy (ed.), *Europäisches Verfassungsrecht. Theoretische und dogmatische Grundzüge* (Berlin: Springer).

Kaelble, H. (1989), *A Social History of Western Europe 1880–1980* (Dublin: Gill and Macmillan).

Kassim, H. (1994), 'Policy Networks and European Union Policy Making: A Sceptical View', *West European Politics*, vol. 17, no. 4: 12–27.

—— (2000), 'Conclusion', in H. Kassim, B. G. Peters, and V. Wright (eds), *The National Co-ordination of EU Policy* (Oxford: Oxford University Press).

Katzenstein, P. (1996), 'Introduction', in P. Katzenstein (ed.), *The Culture of National Security: Norms and Identity in World Politics* (Ithaca, NY: Cornell University Press).

—— (1997), 'United Germany in an Integrating Europe', in P. J. Katzenstein (ed.), *Tamed Power. Germany in Europe*, (Ithaca, NY: Cornell University Press).

—— Keohane, R. O. and Krasner, S. D. (1998), 'International Organization and the Study of World Politics', *International Organization*, vol. 52, no. 4: 463–85.

Keohane, R. O. (1988), 'International Institutions: Two Approaches', *International Studies Quarterly*, vol. 32, no. 4: 379–396.

—— (1989), *International Institutions and State Power: Essays in International Relations Theory* (Boulder, Colo.: Westview).

—— and Nye, J. (1975), 'International Interdependence and Integration', in F. Greenstein and N. Polsby (eds), *Handbook of Political Science* (Andover, Mass.: Addison-Wesley).

—— —— (1976), *Power and Interdependence: World Politics in Transition* (Boston: Little Brown).

—— and Hoffmann, S. (eds) (1991), *The New European Community: Decision Making and Institutional Change* (Boulder, Colo: Westview).

King, D. C., and Walker, J. L. (1991), 'The Origins and Maintenance of Groups', in J. L. Walker, *Mobilizing Interest Groups in America. Patrons, Professions, and Social Movements* (Ann Arbor, Mich.: University of Michigan Press).

King, P. (1982), *Federalism and Federation* (London: Croom Helm).

Kohler-Koch, B. (1996), 'Catching up with Change: The Transformation of Governance in the European Union', *Journal of European Public Policy*, vol. 3, no. 3: 359–80.

—— (1997), 'Organized Interests in the EC and the European Parliament', *European Integration Online Papers*, vol. 1, no. 9.

—— and Eising, R. (eds) (1999), *The Transformation of Governance in the European Union* (London: Routledge).

Koslowski, R. (2001), 'Dual Nationality as a New International Norm? Demise of the Demographic Boundary Maintenance Regime and its Ramifications for World Politics', in M. Albert, D. Jacobson, and Y. Lapid (eds), *Identities, Borders, Orders: New Directions in IR Theory* (Minneapolis: University of Minnesota Press).

Kostakopoulou, D. (2001), *Citizenship, Identity and Immigration in the European Union* (Manchester: Manchester University Press).

Kostakopoulou, T. (2000), 'The "Protective Union": Change and Continuity in Migration Law and Policy in Post-Amsterdam Europe', *Journal of Common Market Studies*, vol. 38, no. 3: 497–518.

Kratochwil, F. (1994), 'Citizenship: The Border of Order', *Alternatives*, vol. 19: 485–506.

Kreppel, A. (1999), 'What Affects the European Parliament's Legislative Influence? An Analysis of the Success of EP Amendments', *Journal of Common Market Studies*, vol. 37: 521–37.

—— and Tsebelis, G. (1999), 'Coalition Formation in the European Parliament', *Comparative Political Studies*, vol. 8: 933–66.

Laffan, B. (1996), 'The Politics of Identity and Political Order in Europe', *Journal of Common Market Studies*, vol. 34, no. 1: 97.

—— and Shackleton, M. (2000), 'The Budget: Who Gets What, When and How', in H. Wallace and W. Wallace (eds), *Policy-making in the European Union* (Oxford: Oxford University Press).

Lasswell, H. D. (1950), *Politics: Who Gets What, When, How* (New York: Peter Smith).

Laurent, P. H. (1970), 'Paul-Henri Spaak and the Diplomatic Origins of the Common Market, 1955–56', *Political Science Quarterly*, vol. 3: 373–96.

Lave, C. A., and March, J. G. (1975), *An Introduction to Models in the Social Sciences* (New York: Harper and Row).

Lavenex, S. (2001), 'The Europeanization of Refugee Policy: Normative Challenges and Institutional Legacies', *Journal of Common Market Studies*, vol. 39, no. 5: 825–50.

—— and Uçarer, E. M. (2002), 'The Emergent EU Migration Regime and Its External Impact', in E. M. Uçarer (ed.), *Migration and the Externalities of European Integration* (Lanham, Md.: Lexington Books).

Le Galés, P., and Lequesne, C. (eds) (1998), *Regions in Europe* (London: Routledge).

Leibfried, S., and Pierson, P. (1995), 'Semisovereign Welfare States: Social Policy in a Multitiered Europe', in S. Leibfried and P. Pierson (eds), *European Social Policy: Between Fragmentation and Integration* (Washington, DC: Brookings Institution).

—— —— (2000), 'Social Policy. Left to Court and Markets?', in H. Wallace and W. Wallace (eds.), *Policy-making in the European Union. The New European Union Series* (Oxford: Oxford University Press).

Leinen, J., and Méndez de Vigo, I. (2001), 'Report on the Laeken European Council and the Future of the Union', *European Parliament Report*, A5–0368/2001, Brussels, 23 October.

Lenaerts, K. (1993), 'Regulating the regulatory process: "delegation of powers" in the European Community', *European Law Review*, vol. 18, no. 1: 23–49.

Levy, R. (2000*a*), 'Managing the Managers: the Commission's Role in the Implementation of Spending Programmes', in N. Nugent (ed.), *At the Heart of the Union: Studies of the European Commission*, 2nd edn (Basingstoke: Palgrave).

—— (2000*b*), *Implementing European Union Public Policy* (Cheltenham: Edward Elgar).

Lindberg, L. N. (1963), *The Political Dynamics of European Economic Integration* (Stanford, Cal.: Stanford University Press).

—— (1971), 'Political integration as a multidimensional phenomenon requiring multivariate measurement', in L. Lindberg and S. Scheingold (eds), *Regional Integration—Theory and Research* (Cambridge, Mass: Harward University Press).

—— and Scheingold, S. A. (1970), *Europe's Would-Be Polity—Patterns of Change in the European Community* (New Jersey: Prentice-Hall).

—— —— (eds) (1971), *Regional Integration—Theory and Research* (Cambridge, Mass.: Harvard University Press).

Lindblom, C. (1977), *Politics and Markets* (New York: Basic Books).

Linklater, A. (1996), 'Citizenship and Sovereignty in the Post-Westphalian State', *European Journal of International Relations*, vol. 2, no. 1: 77–103.

Lipsky, M. (1980), *Street-level bureaucracy: dilemmas of the individual in public services* (New York: Russell Sage Foundation).

Lord, C. (1998), *Democracy in the European Union* (Sheffield: Sheffield Academic Press).

—— (2001), 'Democracy and Democratization in the European Union', in S. Bromley (ed.), *Governing the European Union* (London: Sage).

Loughlin, J. (1996), ' "Europe of the Regions" and the Federalisation of Europe', *Publius: The Journal of Federalism*, vol. 24, no. 4: 141–62.

—— (1997), 'Representing Regions in Europe: The Committee of the Regions', *Regional and Federal Studies*, vol. 6, no. 2: 147–65.

Lovecy, J. (1999), 'Governance Transformation in the Professional Services Sector: a case of market integration "by the back door"?', in B. Kohler-Koch and R. Eising (eds), *The Transformation of Governance in the European Union* (London: Routledge).

Mackenzie Stuart, Lord (1977), *The European Communities and the Rule of Law* (London: Stevens).

Macrory, R. (1992), 'The enforcement of Community laws—some critical issues', *Common Market Law Review*, vol. 29, no. 2: 347–69.

Magiera, S. (1991), 'A Citizens' Europe: Personal, Political, and Cultural Rights', in D. Held and C. Pollitt (eds), *New Forms of Democracy* (London: Sage).

Mahè, L.-P. (2001), 'Can the European Model be negotiable in the WTO?', *Eurochoices*, Spring.

Mair, P. (2000), 'The Limited Impact of Europe on National Party Systems', *West European Politics*, vol. 23: 27–51.

Majone, G. (1994), 'The Rise of the Regulatory State in Europe', *West European Politics*, vol. 17, no. 3: 77–101.

—— (1995), *The Development of Social Regulation in the European Community: Policy Externalities, Transaction Costs, Motivational Factors* (Florence: EUI Working Paper).

—— (1996), *Regulating Europe* (London: Routledge).

March, J. G. (1981), 'Footnotes to organizational change', *Administrative Science Quarterly*, vol. 26: 563–77.

—— and Olsen, J. P. (1989), *Rediscovering Institutions* (New York: Free Press).

—— —— (1995), *Democratic Governance* (New York: Free Press).

—— —— (1998), 'The institutional dynamics of international political orders', *International Organization*, vol. 52, no. 4: 943–69.

Marenin, O. (ed.) (1996), *Policing Change, Changing Police: International Perspectives* (New York: Garland Publishing).

Marias, E. (1994), 'From Market Citizen to Union Citizen', in E. Marias (ed.), *European Citizenship* (Maastricht: EIPA).

Marks, G. (1992), 'Structural Policy in the European Community', in A. Sbragia (ed.), *Europolitics—Institutions and Policy-making in the 'New' European Community* (Washington, DC: Brookings Institution).

Marks, G., and Hooghe, L. (1996), ' "Europe with the Regions": Channels of Regional Representation in the European Union', *Publius: The Journal of Federalism*, vol. 26, no. 1: 73–92.

—— —— (2001), *Multi-level governance and European integration* (Lanham, Md.: Rowman & Littlefield).

—— —— and Blank, K. (1996), 'European Integration from the 1980s: State-Centric v. Multilevel Governance', *Journal of Common Market Studies*, vol. 34, no. 5: 341–78.

—— Nielsen, F., Ray, L., and Salk, J. (1996), 'Competencies, Cracks and Conflicts: Regional Mobilization in the European Union', in G. Marks, F. W. Scharpf, P. C. Schmitter, and W. Streeck, *Governance in the European Union* (London: Sage).

Marshall, T. H. (1950), *Citizenship and Social Class* (Cambridge: Cambridge University Press).

—— (1975), *Social Policy* (London: Hutchinson).

Martenczuk, B. (2000), 'Die differenzierte Integration und die föderale Struktur der Europäischen Union', *Europarecht*, vol. 35, no. 3: 351–64.

Martin, A., and, Ross, G. (1999), 'In the line of fire: The Europeanization of labor representation', in A. Martin and G. Ross (eds), *Brave New World of European Labor* (Oxford: Barghatin).

Mayhew, A. (1998), *Recreating Europe: The European Union's Policy towards Central and Eastern Europe* (Cambridge: Cambridge University Press).

Mazey, S. (1998), 'The European Union and women's rights: from the Europeanisation of national agendas to the nationalisation of a European agenda?', in D. Hine and H. Kassim (eds), *Beyond the Market: The EU and National Social Policy* (London: Routledge).

—— (2001), 'European integration: unfinished journey or journey without end?', in J. Richardson (ed.), *European Union: Power and Policy-Making*, 2nd edn (London: Routledge).

—— and Richardson, J. (eds) (1993), *Lobbying in the European Community* (Oxford: Oxford University Press).

McCarthy, R. (1997), 'The Committee of the Regions: An Advisory Body's Tortuous Path to Influence', *Journal of European Public Policy*, vol. 4, no. 3: 439–54.

McLean, I. (ed.), (1996), *The Concise Oxford Dictionary of Politics* (Oxford: Oxford University Press).

McCormick, J. (1999), *Understanding the European Union* (Basingstoke: Macmillan).

—— (2002), *Understanding the European Union*, 2nd edn (Basingstoke: Palgrave).

McKay, D. (1996), *Rush to Union* (Oxford: Oxford University Press).

—— (2001), *Designing Europe: Comparative Lessons from the Federal Experience* (Oxford: Oxford University Press).

Meehan, E. (1993), *Citizenship and the European Community* (London: Sage).

Messerlin, P. (2001), *Measuring the Costs of Protection in Europe* (Washington: IIE).

Metcalfe, L. (1992), 'After 1992: Can the Commission manage Europe?', *Australian Journal of Public Administration*, vol. 51, no. 1: 117–30.

—— (1996), 'Building capacities for integration: the future role of the Commission', *Eipascope*, vol. 2: 2–8.

Meyer, J. W. (1996), 'Otherhood: Promulgation and transmission of ideas in the modern organizational environment', in B. Czarniawska and G. Sevón (eds), *Translating Organizational Change* (Berlin: de Gruyter).

—— (2001), 'The European Union and the globalization of culture', in S. S. Andersen (ed.), *Institutional Approaches to the European Union*, Proceedings of an ARENA Workshop: 227–45. (Oslo: ARENA Report No 3/2001.)

Millett, T. (1990), *The Court of First Instance of the European Communities* (London: Butterworths).

Milward, A. S. (1984), *The Reconstruction of Western Europe, 1945–51* (London: Methuen).

—— (1992), *The European Rescue of the Nation-State* (London: Routledge).

—— (1999), *The European Rescue of the Nation-State*, 2nd edn (London: Routledge).

Mjøset, L. (1997), 'Les significations historiques de l'européanisation', *L'Année de la régulation*, vol. 1: 85–127.

Monar, J. (1997), 'European Union—Justice and Home Affairs: A Balance Sheet and an Agenda for Reform', in A. Pijpers, (ed.), *The Politics of European Treaty Reform: The 1996 Intergovernmental Conference and Beyond* (London: Pinter).

—— (2001), 'The Dynamics of Justice and Home Affairs: Laboratories, Driving Factors and Costs', *Journal of Common Market Studies*, vol. 39, no. 4: 747–64.

—— and Morgan, R. (eds) (1994), *The Third Pillar of the European Union: Co-operation in the Fields of Justice and Home Affairs* (Brussels: European Interuniversity Press).

Monnet, J. (1978), *Memoirs* (New York: Doubleday).

Moravcsik, A. (1991), 'Negotiating the Single European Act: National Interests and Conventional Statecraft in the European Community', *International Organization*, vol. 45: 19–56.

—— (1993), 'Preferences and Power in the European Community: A Liberal Intergovernmentalist Approach', *Journal of Common Market Studies*, vol. 34, no. 4: 473–524.

—— (1998), *The Choice for Europe. Social Purpose and State Power from Messina to Maastricht* (London: UCL Press).

—— (2001), 'A Constructivist Research Programme for EU Studies', *European Union Politics*, vol. 2, no. 2: 226–49.

Morgenthau, H. (1985), *Politics Among Nations: The Struggle for Power and Peace*, 6th edn (New York: Knopf).

Moser, P. (1996), 'The European Parliament as a Conditional Agenda Setter: What are the Conditions? A Critique of Tsebelis (1994)', *American Political Science Review*, vol. 90: 834–8.

—— (1997), 'The benefits of the conciliation procedure to the European Parliament: Comment to George Tsebelis', *Aussenwirtschaft*, vol. 52, nos 1–2: 57–62.

Neill, P. (1995), *The European Court of Justice: A Case Study in Judicial Activism* (London: European Policy Forum).

Neunreither, K. (2000), 'Political Representation in the European Union: A Common Whole, Various Wholes, or Just a Hole?', in K. Neunreither and A. Weiner (eds), *European Integration After Amsterdam: Institutional Dynamics and Prospects for Democracy* (Oxford: Oxford University Press).

Newman, (1996), *Democracy, Sovereignty and the European Union* (London: Hurst).

—— (2001), 'Democracy and Accountability in the EU', in J. Richardson (ed.), *European Union. Power and Policy Making* (London: Routledge).

Nicholson, F., and East, R. (1987), *From the Six to the Twelve: The Enlargement of the European Communities* (London: Longman).

Niedermayer, O., and Sinnott, R. (1995), 'Democratic Legitimacy and the European Parliament', in O. Niedermayer and Sinnott, R. (eds), *Public Opinion and Institutionalized Governance: Beliefs in Government*, vol. 2 (Oxford: Oxford University Press).

Noll, G. (2000), *Negotiating Asylum: The EU Acquis, Extraterritorial Protection and the Common Market of Deflection* (The Hague: Kluwer Law International).

North, D. (1990), *Institutions, Institutional change and Economic Performance* (Cambridge: Cambridge University Press).

Notre Europe (2001), 'A wake-up call for Europe', at **www.notre-europe.asso.fr/appel-en.htm**

Nugent, N. (1999), *The Government and Politics of the European Union* (Basingstoke: Macmillan).

Nugent, N. (2000a), *The European Commission* (Basingstoke: Palgrave).

—— (ed.) (2000b), *At the Heart of the Union: Studies of the European Commission*, 2nd edn (Basingstoke: Palgrave).

Nye, J. S. (1971), 'Comparing Common Markets: A Revised Neo-Functionalist Model', in L. N. Lindberg and S. A. Scheingold (eds), *Regional Integration—Theory and Research* (Harvard, Mass.: Harvard University Press).

O'Leary, S. (1996), *The Evolving Concept of Community Citizenship* (The Hague: Kluwer Law International).

O'Neill, M. (1996), *The Politics of European Integration. A Reader* (London: Routledge).

Olsen, J. P. (2002), 'The Many Faces of Europeanization', *Journal of Common Market Studies*, vol. 40, no. 5: 921–52.

Ortalo-Magné, F., with L.-P. Mahè (2001), *Politique Agricole. Un Modele Européan?* (Paris: Presses de Sciences Po).

Outrive Report (European Parliament) (1992), *The entry into force of the Schengen agreements (rapporteur, L. van Dutrive)*, A3–0288/92, adopted 6 June.

Packenham, R. (1970), 'Legislatures and Political Development', in A. Kornberg and L. Musolf (eds), *Legislatures in Developmental Perspective* (Durham, NC: Duke University Press).

Page, E. C. (1997), *People Who Run Europe* (Oxford: Clarendon Press).

Patten, C. (2001), 'Sovereignty, democracy and constitutions—finding the right formula', 2001 Schuman Lecture, Australian National University, Canberra, 19 April.

Pearce, J., and Sutton, J. (1983), *Protection and Industrial Policy in Europe* (London: Routledge).

Pelkmans, J. (1987), 'The New Approach to Technical Harmonization and Standardization', *Journal of Common Market Studies*, vol. 25: 249–69.

—— (1997), *European Integration, Methods and Economic Analysis* (London: Longman).

—— and Winters, A. (1988), *Europe's Domestic Market* (London: Royal Institute of International Affairs).

Pentland, C. (1973), *International Theory and European Integration* (New York: Free Press).

Peters, B. G. (2000), 'The Commission and Implementation in the EU: Is there an Implementation Deficit and Why?', in N. Nugent (ed.), *At the Heart of the Union: Studies of the European Commission*, 2nd edn (Basingstoke: Palgrave).

Peterson, J. (1995), 'Decision Making in the European Union: towards a Framework for Analysis', *Journal of European Public Policy*, vol. 2, no. 1: 69–93.

—— (1995a), 'Policy Networks and European Union Policy Making: a reply to Kassim', *West European Politics*, vol. 18, no. 2: 387–407.

—— and Bomberg, E. (1999), *Decision-Making in the European Union* (Basingstoke: Macmillan).

—— and Bomberg, E. (2000), 'The EU after the 1990s: Explaining Continuity and Change', in M. G. Cowles and M. Smith (eds), *The State of the European Union, vol. 5: Risks, Reforms, Resistance, and Revival* (Oxford: Oxford University Press).

Pierre, J. (ed.) (2001), *Debating Governance: Authority, Steering, and Democracy* (Oxford: Oxford University Press).

Pierson, P. (1996), 'The Path to European Integration: A Historical Institutionalist Perspective', *Comparative Politics*, vol. 29, no. 2: 123–163.

—— (1998), 'The Path to European Integration: A Historical Institutionalist Analysis', in W. Sandholtz and A. Stone Sweet (eds), *European Integration and Supranational Governance* (Oxford: Oxford University Press).

Pinder, J. (ed.) (1998), *Altiero Spinelli and the British Federalists* (London: The Federal Trust).

Plender, R. (1978), 'Direct elections and the Constitutional Order of the UK', in G. Dogos-Docovich (ed.), *The European Parliament* (Athens: The Greek Parliament).

Poidevin, R., and Spierenburg, D. (1994), *The History of the High Authority of the European Coal and Steel Community* (London: Wiedenfeld & Nicolson).

Pollack, M. (1995), 'Regional Actors in an Intergovernmental Play: The Making and Implementation of EC Structural Funds', in S. Mazey and C. Rhodes (eds), *State of the European Union, vol. 3, Building a European Polity* (Boulder, Colo.: Lynne Rienner, and London: Longman).

—— (1997*a*), 'Delegation, Agency and Agenda Setting in the European Community', *International Organization*, vol. 51, no. 1: 99–134.

—— (1997*b*), 'Representing Diffuse Interests in the European Union', *Journal of European Public Policy*, vol. 4, no. 4: 572–90.

Powell, W. W., and DiMaggio, P. J. (1991), *The New Institutionalism in Organizational Analysis* (Chicago: University of Chicago Press).

Pressman, J. L., and Wildavsky, A. (1984), *Implementation: how great expectations in Washington D.C. are dashed in Oakland*, 3rd edn (London: University of California Press).

Preston, C. (1997), *Enlargement and Integration in the European Union* (London: Routledge).

Prodi, R. (2001), 'For a strong Europe, with a grand design and the means of action', Speech at Institut d'Etudes Politiques, Paris, 29 May. At **http://europa.eu.int/comm/commissioners/prodi/paris-en.htm**

Puchala, D. J. (1971), *International Politics Today* (New York: Dodd Mead).

—— (1999), 'Institutionalism, intergovernmentalism and European integration: A review article', *Journal of Common Market Studies*, vol. 37, no. 2: 317–31.

Putnam, R. (1988), 'Diplomacy and Domestic Politics: the Logic of Two-Level Games', *International Organization*, vol. 42, no. 3: 427–60.

Raadschelders, J. C. N., and Toonen, T. A. J., (1992), 'Public sector reform in Western Europe: A comparative view' (Leiden: Leiden University, Department of Public Administration: unpublished manuscript).

Radaelli, C. (1997), 'How does Europeanization produce domestic policy change. Corporate tax policy in Italy and the United Kingdom', *Comparative Political Studies*, vol. 30, no. 5: 553–75.

—— (1998), *Governing European Regulation: The Challenges Ahead*, RSC Policy Paper No. 98/3 (Florence: European University Institute).

—— (2000), 'Whither Europeanization? Concept stretching and substantive change', European Integration Online Paper 4(8). At **http://eiop.or.at/eiop/texte/2000–008a.htm**

Rasmussen, H. (1986), *On Law and Policy in the European Court of Justice* (Dordrecht: Nijhoff).

Raunio, T. (1997), *The European Perspective: Transnational Party Groups in the 1989–1994 European Parliament* (London: Ashgate).

Rhodes, M. (1995), 'A Regulatory Conundrum: Industrial Relations and the "Social Dimension" ', in S. Leibfried, and P. Pierson (eds), *Fragmented Social Policy: The European Union's Social Dimension in Comparative Perspective* (Washington, DC: Brookings Institution).

—— and van Apeldoorn, B. (1998), 'Capital Unbound? The Transformation of European Corporate Governance', *Journal of European Public Policy*, vol. 5, no. 3: 407–28.

Richardson, J. (2001), 'Policy-making in the EU: interests, ideas and garbage cases of primaeval soup', in J. Richardson (ed.), *European Union. Power and Policy-making* (London: Routledge).

Riley, P. (1973), 'Rousseau as a Theorist of National and International Federalism', *Publius: The Journal of Federalism*, vol. 3, no. 1: 5–18.

—— (1976), 'Three Seventeenth Century Theorists of Federalism: Althusius, Hugo and Leibniz', *Publius: The Journal of Federalism*, vol. 6, no. 3: 7–42.

—— (1979), 'Federalism in Kant's Political Philosophy', *Publius: The Journal of Federalism*, vol. 9, no. 4: 43–64.

Risse, T., Cowles, M. G., and Caporaso, J. (2001), 'Europeanization and domestic change: Introduction', in M. G. Cowles, J. A. Caporaso, and T. Risse (eds), *Transforming Europe: Europeanization and Domestic Change* (Ithaca, NY: Cornell University Press).

Risse-Kappen, T. (1996), 'Exploring the nature of the beast: International Relations Theory and Comparative Policy Analysis Meet the European Union', *Journal of Common Market Studies*, vol. 34, no. 1: 54–81.

Rittberger, B. (2000), 'Impatient Legislators and New Issue Dimensions: a Critique of Garrett and Tsebelis' "Standard Version" of Legislative Politics', *Journal of European Public Policy*, vol. 7: 554–75.

Rokkan, S. (1999) (ed. P. Flora with S. Kuhnle and D. Urwin), *State Formation, Nation-Building, and Mass Politics in Europe. The theory of Stein Rokkan* (Oxford: Oxford University Press).

Rosamond, B. (2000), *Theories of European Integration* (Basingstoke: Palgrave).

Rosenau, J. N., and Durfee, M. (1995), *Thinking Theory Thoroughly: Coherent Approaches in an Incoherent World* (Boulder, Colo.: Westview).

Ross, G. (1995), 'Assessing the Delors Era and Social Policy', in S. Leibfried and Pierson, P. (eds), *European Social Policy: Between Fragmentation and Integration* (Washington DC: Brookings Institution).

Rucht, D. (2000), 'Zur Europäisierung politischer Mobilisierung', *Berliner Journal für Soziologie*, vol. 2: 185–202.

Ruggie, J. G. (1998), *Constructing the World Polity: Essays on International Institutionalization* (London: Routledge).

Rummel, R. (1997), 'The CFSP's Conflict Prevention Policy', in Holland, M. *Common Foreign and Security Policy: The Record and Reforms* (London: Pinter).

Sabatier, P. A., and Jenkins-Smith, H. C. (eds) (1993), *Policy Change and Learning: An Advocacy Coalition Approach* (Boulder, Colo.: Westview Press).

Sandholtz, W. (1998), 'The Emergence of a Supranational Telecommunications Regime', in W. Sandholtz and A. Stone Sweet (eds), *European Integration and Supranational Governance* (Oxford: Oxford University Press).

—— and Zysman, J. (1989), '1992: Recasting the European Bargain', *World Politics*, vol. 42: 95–128.

—— and Stone Sweet, A. (eds) (1998), *European Integration and Supranational Governance* (Oxford: Oxford University Press).

Sbragia, A. M. (1992), 'Thinking about the European Future: the uses of Comparison', in A. M. Sbragia (ed.), *Europolitics—Institutions and Policy-making in the 'New' European Community* (Washington, DC: Brookings Institution).

—— (2001), 'Italy pays for Europe: Political leadership, political choice, and institutional adaptation', in M. G. Cowles, J. A. Caporaso, and T. Risse (eds), *Transforming Europe: Europeanization and Domestic Change* (Ithaca, NY: Cornell University Press).

—— (ed.) (1992), *Europolitics—Institutions and Policy-making in the 'New' European Community* (Washington, DC: Brookings Institution).

Schaefer, G. F., Egeberg, M., Korez, S., and Trondal, J. (2000), 'The Experience of Member States Officials in EU Committees: A Report on Initial Findings of an Empirical Study', *Eipascope*, vol. 3: 29–35.

Scharpf, F. W. (1988), 'The joint-decision trap—lessons from German Federalism and European Integration', *Public Administration*, vol. 66: 239–78.

—— (1999), *Governing in Europe* (Oxford: Oxford University Press).

—— (2002), 'The European Social Model: Coping with the Challenges of Diversity', *Journal of Common Market Studies*, vol. 40, no. 4: 645–70.

Schimmelfennig, F. (2001), 'The community trap: Liberal norms, rhetorical action, and the Eastern enlargement of the European Union', *International Organization*, vol. 55, no. 1: 47–80.

Schlesinger, P. R. (1993), 'Wishful thinking. Cultural Politics, Media and Collective Identities in Europe', *Journal of Communication*, vol. 43, no. 2: 6–17.

Schmidt, V. A. (1999), 'National Patterns of Governance Under Siege', in B. Kohler-Koch and R. Eising (eds), *The Transformation of Governance in the European Union* (London: Routledge).

Schmitter, P. C. (1969), 'Three Neofunctional Hypotheses about International Integration', *International Organization*, vol. 23, no. 1: 161–6.

—— (1974), 'Still the Century of Corporatism?', *Review of Politics*, vol. 36, no. 1: 85–131.

—— (1996), 'Imagining the Future of the Euro-Polity with the help of New Concepts', in G. Marks, F. W. Scharpf, P. C. Schmitter, and W. Streeck, *Governance in the European Union* (London: Sage).

—— (2000), *How to Democratize the European Union . . . And Why Bother* (Boston: Rowman and Littlefield).

—— and Streek, W. (1991), 'From national corporation to transnational pluralism: organized interests in the Single European Market', *Politics and Society*, vol. 19: 133–64.

Schneider, G., and Aspinwall, M. (2001), *The Rules of Integration: Institutionalist Approaches to the Study of Europe* (Manchester: Manchester University Press).

Schneider, V. (2001), 'Institutional reform in telecommunications: The European Union in transnational policy diffusion', in M. G. Cowles, J. A. Caporaso, and T. Risse (eds), *Transforming Europe: Europeanization and Domestic Change*: 60–78 (Ithaca, NY: Cornell University Press).

Schreiber, K. (1991), 'The New Approach to Technical Harmonisation and Standards', in L. Hurwitz and C. Lesquesne (eds), *The State of the European Community: Politics, Institutions and Debates in the Transition Debates* (Boulder, Colo.: Lynne Reinner).

Scott, J. (1995), *Development Dilemmas in the European Community* (Buckingham: Open University Press).

Scott, W. R. (1992), *Organizations. Rational, Natural, and Open Systems*, 3rd edn (Englewood Cliffs, NJ: Prentice-Hall).

Scully, R. (1997*a*), 'The European Parliament and the Co-Decision Procedure: A Reassessment', *Journal of Legislative Studies*, vol. 3: 58–73.

—— (1997*b*), 'The European Parliament and Co-Decision: a Rejoinder to Tsebelis and Garrett', *Journal of Legislative Studies*, vol. 3: 93–103.

—— (2000), 'Democracy, Legitimacy and the European Parliament', in M. G. Cowles and M. Smith (eds), *The State of the European Union, vol. 5: Risk, Reform, Resistance, and Revival* (Oxford: Oxford University Press).

—— (2003 forthcoming), *Becoming Europeans? Attitudes, Roles and Socialisation in the European Parliament* (London: Palgrave).

Sebaldt, M. (1996), *Organisierter Pluralismus. Kräftefeld, Selbstverständnis und politische Arbeit deutscher Interessengruppen* (Opladen: Westdeutscher Verlag).

Sedelmeier, U. (2001), 'Eastern enlargement: Risk, rationality, and role-compliance', in M. G. Cowles and M. Smith (eds), *The State of the European Union, vol. 5: Risk. Reform, Resistance, and Revival*: 164–85 (Oxford: Oxford University Press).

Shackleton, M. (2000), 'The Politics of Co-decision', *Journal of Common Market Studies*, vol. 38: 325–42.

Shapiro, M. (1992), 'The European Court of Justice', in A. Sbragia (ed.), *Europolitics—Institutions and Policy-making in the 'New' European Community* (Washington, DC: Brookings Institution).

Sharpe, L. (ed.) (1993), *The Rise of Meso Government in Europe* (London: Sage).

Shaw, J. (2000), *Law of the European Union*, 3rd edn (Basingstoke: Palgrave Law Masters).

—— (2001), 'Process, Responsibility and Inclusion in EU Constitutionalism: a contribution to the debate', Constitutionalism Webpapers (CoNWeb), no. 4.

Simonian, H. (1985), *The Privileged Partnership* (Oxford: Clarendon Press).

Sjursen, H. (2001), 'Why expand? Questions of justification of the EU's enlargement policy', Oslo: ARENA Working Paper 2001, No. 6.

Slaughter, A.-M., Stone, A., and Weiler, J. (1998), *The European Court and National Courts: Doctrine and Jurisprudence* (Oxford: Hart).

Smith, J. (1999), *Europe's Elected Parliament* (Sheffield: Sheffield Academic Press).

Smith, K. E. (1998), 'The Use of Political Conditionality in the EU's Relations with Third Countries: How Effective?', *European Foreign Affairs Review*, vol. 3, no. 2: 253–74.

Smith, M. (1998), 'Does the Flag Follow Trade?: "Politicisation" and the Emergence of a European Foreign Policy', in J. Peterson and H. Sjursen, *A Common Foreign Policy for Europe?* (London: Routledge).

—— (2001), 'The EU as an International Actor', in J. Richardson (ed.), *European Union: Power and Policy-Making*, 2nd edn (London: Routledge).

Smith, M. E. (2001), 'Diplomacy by Decree: The Legalization of EU Foreign Policy', *Journal of Common Market Studies*, vol. 39, no. 1: 79–104.

Smith, S. (2001), 'Reflectivist and constructivist approaches to international theory', in J. Baylis and S. Smith (eds), *The Globalization of World Politics: An Introduction to International Relations*, 2nd edn (Oxford: Oxford University Press).

Soysal, Y. N. (1996), 'Changing Citizenship in Europe', in D. Cesarain and M. Fulbrook (eds), *Citizenship, Nationality and Migration in Europe* (London: Routledge).

Spaak, P.-H. (The Intergovernmental Committee on European Integration) (1956), *The Brussels Report on the General Common Market* (Spaak Report) (Brussels: Intergovernmental Committee).

Spencer, C. (2001), 'The EU and Common Strategies: The Revealing Case of the Mediterranean', *European Foreign Affairs Review*, vol. 6, no. 2: 31–51.

Statewatch (2001), *The 'Conclusions' of the Special Justice and Home Affairs Council on 20 September 2001 and Their Implications for Civil Liberties*, available at **www.statewatch.org/observatory2.htm** (accessed 20 October 2001).

Stein, E., and Vining, G. (1976), 'Citizen Access to Judicial Review of Administrative Action in a Transnational and Federal Context', *American Journal of International Law*, vol. 70: 219–41.

Stevens, A. (with H. Stevens) (2001), *Brussels Bureaucrats? The Administration of the European Union* (Basingstoke: Palgrave).

Stirk, P. M., and Willis, D. (eds.) (1991), *Shaping Postwar Europe* (London: Pinter).

Stone Sweet, A., and Brunell, T. L. (1998), 'Constructing a Supranational Constitution: Dispute resolution and governance in the European Community', *American Political Science Review*, vol. 92, no. 1: 63–81.

—— and Caporaso, J. (1998), 'From Free Trade to Supranational Polity: The European Court and Integration', in W. Sandholtz and A. Stone Sweet (eds), *European Integration and Supranational Governance* (Oxford: Oxford University Press).

—— and Sandholtz, W. (1998), 'Integration, Supranational Governance, and the Institutionalization of the European Polity', in W. Sandholtz and A. Stone Sweet (eds), *European Integration and Supranational Governance*: (Oxford: Oxford University Press).

Strasses, D. (1992), *The Finances of Europe*, 7th edn (Luxembourg: Office of Official Publications).

Streeck, W., and Schmitter, P. C. (1991), 'From National Corporatism to Transnational Pluralism: Organized Interests in the Single European Market', *Politics and Society*, vol. 19, no. 2: 133–65.

Stubb, A. C.-G. (1996), 'A Categorisation of Differentiated Integration', *Journal of Common Market Studies*, vol. 34, no. 2: 283–95.

Sun, J. M., and Pelkmans, J. (1995) 'Regulatory Competition in the Single Market', *Journal of Common Market Studies*, vol. 33, no. 1: 67–89.

Taylor, P. (1975), 'The Politics of the European Communities: the Confederal Phase', *World Politics*, April: 335–60.

—— (1990), 'Regionalism and Functionalism reconsidered', in P. Taylor and A. J. R. Groom (eds), *Frameworks for International Co-operation* (London: Pinter).

—— (1993), *International Organization in the Modern World— The Regional and the Global Process* (New York: Pinter).

—— (1996), *The European Union in the 1990s* (Oxford: Oxford University Press).

Telò, M. (ed.) (2001), *European Union and New Regionalism. Regional Actors and Global Governance in a Post-Hegemonic Era* (Aldershot: Ashgate).

Tichy, G. (1998), 'Macro-Economic Employment Policies— Employment Problems from Lack of Policy Co-ordination within the EU', in B. Marin, D. Meulders, and D. Snower (eds), *Innovative Employment Initiatives* (Aldershot: Ashgate).

Tilly, C. (ed.) (1975), *The Formation of National States in Western Europe* (Princeton: Princeton University Press).

Tömmel, I. (1998), 'Transformation of Governance: The

European Commission's Strategy for creating a "Europe of the Regions" ', *Regional and Federal Studies*, vol. 8, no. 2: 52–80.

Tranholm-Mikkelsen, J. (1991), 'Neo-functionalism: Obstinate or Obsolete? A Reappraisal in the Light of the New Dynamism of the EC', *Millennium: Journal of International Studies*, vol. 20: 1–22.

Truman, D. (1972), *The Governmental Process. Political Interests and Public Opinion* (New York: Alfred A. Knopf).

Tsebelis, G. (1994), 'The Power of the European Parliament as a Conditional Agenda Setter', *American Political Science Review*, vol. 88, no. 1: 128–42.

—— and Garrett, G. (1997), 'Agenda Setting, Vetoes and the European Union's Co-decision Procedure', *Journal of Legislative Studies*, vol. 3: 74–92.

—— Jensen, C. B., Kalandrakis, A., and Kreppel, A. (2001), 'Legislative Procedures in the European Union: An Empirical Analysis', *British Journal of Political Science*, vol. 31: 573–99.

Tsoukalis, L. (1997), *The New European Community* (Oxford: Oxford University Press).

Turner, B. (1990), 'Outline of a Theory of Citizenship', *Sociology*, vol. 24, no. 2: 189–217.

Uçarer, E. (1999), 'Co-operation on Justice and Home Affairs Matters', in L. Cram, D. Dinan, and N. Nugent (eds), *Developments in the European Union* (New York: St. Martin's Press).

—— (2001*a*), 'From the Sidelines to Center Stage: Sidekick No More? The European Commission in Justice and Home Affairs', *European Integration online Papers* (EIoP), vol. 5, no. 5. At **http://eiop.or.at/eiop/texte/2001–005a.htm**

—— (2001*b*), 'Managing Asylum and European Integration: Expanding Spheres of Exclusion?', *International Studies Perspectives*, vol. 2, no. 3: 291–307.

Urwin, D. W. (1995), *The Community of Europe* (London: Longman).

—— (1997), A *Political History of Western Europe since 1945* (London: Longman).

van der Eijk, C., and Franklin, M. (eds) (1996), *Choosing Europe? The European Electorate and National Politics in the Face of Union* (Ann Arbor, Mich.: University of Michigan Press).

van der Klaauw, J. (1994), 'Amnesty Lobbies for Refugees', in R. H. Pedler and M. P. C. M. van Schendelen (eds), *Lobbying the European Union. Companies, Trade Associations and Issue Groups* (Aldershot: Dartmouth).

van Schendelen, M. P. C. M. (1993), 'Conclusion: From National State Power to Spontaneous Lobbying', in M. P. C. M. van Schendelen (ed.), *National Public and Private EC Lobbying* (Aldershot: Dartmouth).

van Selm, J. (2002), 'Immigration and Asylum or Foreign Policy: The EU's Approach to Migrants and Their Countries of Origin', in E. M. Uçarer (ed.), *Migration and the Externalities of European Integration* (Lanham, Md.: Lexington Books).

van Waarden, F. (1992), 'Dimensions and types of policy networks', *European Journal of Political Research*, vol. 21, no. 1: 29–52.

Venturelli, S. S. (1993), 'The imagined transnational public sphere in the European Community's broadcast philosophy: Implications for democracy', *European Journal of Communication*, vol. 8: 491–518.

Verdier, D., and Breen, R. (2001), 'Europeanization and globalization: Politics against Markets in the European Union', *Comparative Politics Studies*, vol. 34, no. 3: 227–62.

Verdier, A. (2000), *European Responses to Globalization and Financial Market Integration: Perceptions of Economic and Monetary Union in Britain, France and Germany* (Basingstoke: Palgrave Macmillan; New York: St Martin's Press).

von der Groeben, H. (1985), *The European Community: The Formative Years* (Luxembourg: Official Publication of the European Communities).

Wallace, H. (1996), 'The Institutions of the EU: Experience and Experiments', in H. Wallace and W. Wallace (eds), *Policy-making in the European Union*, 3rd edn (Oxford: Oxford University Press).

—— (1999), 'The domestication of Europe: Contrasting experiences of EU membership and non-membership' (Leiden: University of Leiden, Department of Political Science: Sixth Daalder Lecture).

—— (2000*a*), 'Europeanisation and globalisation: Complementary or contradictory trends?', *New Political Economy*, vol. 5, no. 3: 369–82.

—— (2000*b*), 'The Institutional Setting: Five Variations on a Theme', in H. Wallace and W. Wallace (eds), *Policy making in the European Union*, 4th edn (Oxford: Oxford University Press).

—— and Hayes-Renshaw, F. (1995), 'Executive Power in the European Union: The Functions and Limits of the Council of Ministers', *Journal of European Public Policy*, vol. 2, no. 4: 559–82.

—— and Wallace, W. (1995), *Flying together in a larger and more diverse European Union*, Working Documents, W87 (The Hague: Netherlands Scientific Council for Government Policy).

—— and Young, A. (2000), 'The Single Market', in H. Wallace and W. Wallace (eds), *Policy-making in the European Union*, 4th edn (Oxford: Oxford University Press).

Wallace, W. (1982), 'Europe as a Confederation: the Community and the Nation State', *Journal of Common Market Studies*, vol. 21, no. 1: 57–68.

Waltz, K. (1979), *Theory of International Politics* (New York: McGraw Hill).

Warleigh, A. (2002), *Flexible Integration. Which Model for the European Union?* (Sheffield: Sheffield Academic Press).

Warren, M. E. (2001), *Democracy and Association* (Princeton, N.J.: Princeton University Press).

Watts, R. L. (1999), *Comparing Federal Systems*, 2nd edn (Montreal: McGill-Queen's University Press).

Weiler, J. H. H. (1996), 'European Citizenship and Human Rights', in J. A. Winter, D. M. Curtin, A. E. Kellermann, and B. de Witte (eds), *Reforming the Treaty on European Union—The Legal Debate* (The Hague: Kluwer Law International).

Wendt, A. (1999), *Social Theory of International Politics* (Cambridge: Cambridge University Press).

Wessels, W. (1997), 'Ever Closer Fusion? A Dynamic Macropolitical View on Integration Processes', *Journal of Common Market Studies*, vol. 35, no. 2: 267–99.

—— and Rometsch, D. (1996), 'Conclusion: European Union and National Institutions', in D. Rometsch and W. Wessels (eds), *The European Union and Member States: Towards Institutional Fusion?* (Manchester and New York: Manchester University Press).

Westlake, M. (1995), *The Council of the European Union* (London: Cartermill).

—— (1998), 'The European Parliament's Emerging Powers of Appointment', *Journal of Common Market Studies*, vol. 36: 431–44.

Whitaker, R. (2001), 'Party Control in a Committee-Based Legislature? The case of the European Parliament', *Journal of Legislative Studies*, vol. 7, no. 4: 63–88.

Wiener, A. (1996), 'Rethinking Citizenship: The Quest for Place-oriented Participation in the EU', *Oxford International Review*, vol. 7, no. 3: 44–51.

—— (1997), 'Making Sense of the New Geography of Citizenship—Fragmented Citizenship in the European Union', *Theory and Society*, vol. 26, no. 4: 529–60.

—— (1998), *'European' Citizenship Practice—Building Institutions of a Non-State* (Oxford: Westview).

—— (2001), 'Zur Verfassungspolitik jenseits des Staates: Die Vermittlung von Bedeutung am Beispiel der Unionsbürgerschaft', *Zeitschrift für Internationale Beziehungen*, vol. 8, no. 1: 73–104.

Wincott, D. (1994), 'Human Rights, Democratization and the Role of the Court of Justice', *Democratization*, vol. 1: 251–71.

—— (1995), 'Institutional Interaction and European Integration: Towards an Everyday Critique of Liberal Intergovernmentalism', *Journal of Common Market Studies*, vol. 33, no. 4: 597–609.

Wobbe, T. (2003), 'From Protecting to Promoting: Evolving EU Sex Equality Norms in an Organizational Field', *European Law Journal*, vol. 9, no. 1 (forthcoming).

Young, A. R. (1998), 'European Consumer Groups: Multiple Levels of Governance and Multiple Logics of Collective Action', in J. Greenwood and M. Aspinwall (eds), *Collective Action in the European Union. Interests and the New Politics of Associability* (London: Routledge).

Youngs, R. (2001), 'European Union Democracy Promotion Policies: Ten Years On', *European Foreign Affairs Review*, vol. 6, no. 3: 355–73.

Zysman, J. (1994), 'How Institutions Create Historically-Rooted Trajectories of Growth', *Industrial and Corporate Change*, vol. 3, no. 1: 243–83.

Index